The
Continental
Congress

by Edmund Cody Burnett

Y · INC ·

CONTENTS

Contents

PREFACE

The birthday of the United States of America has been officially fixed at the adoption of the Declaration of Independence, July 4, 1776, while the attainment of the nation's majority is placed, though not quite with the same precision and finality, at the adoption of the Constitution of 1787. These events, however, do but mark decisive stages in the nation's infancy and youth. Neither the Declaration nor the Constitution possesses quite that primal creative character commonly ascribed to them. The birth of the nation was, by an immutable law of nature, preceded by a period of gestation, and there are many reasons for the conclusion that, not until long after the inauguration of the government under the Constitution, were the United States of America possessed of a genuine national spirit. There were, to be sure, national beginnings, indeed a multitude of them, many elements astir, many forces in motion, but not until these had come together in harmonious growth and unity could it be truly said that a nation had come into being.

This growth, this process of development, is best revealed, indeed in its fullness is only discoverable, in the life of that body known as the Continental Congress. Beginning as a consultative assembly of the several colonies, the medium through which they voiced their common grievances and common desires, the Congress presently became the active head in the promotion of that movement whereby those several dependent political entities were drawn into cooperation for the attainment of their common aims. Gradually, in the course of these endeavors, the common purpose became transformed, the colonies individually and collectively severed their former bonds of dependence, and thereupon set about, albeit clumsily at times, ineffectively always, the endeavor to weld their disparate governments into an efficient national unity.

It is this growth of national beginnings, rooted, indeed in great part germinated, in the Continental Congress, with which this narrative is particularly concerned. The aim of the volume, then, is to relate the life-story of that Congress, from its inception in 1774 to the moment when it feebly passed the torch to its successor in March, 1789, and to relate it in such a manner as will afford a clear and comprehensive understanding of its life and labors, and more particularly of the part which it had in laying the foundations of our national structure.

Although the Continental Congress has its place in any history of the American Revolution, hitherto it has usually constituted but a part of a group picture, seldom if ever being made the central figure in that group. Probably the nearest approach that has been made to such a presentation of the Congress, inadequate in many respects though that presentation be, is in the several prefaces to the author's collection in eight volumes of the *Letters of Members of the Continental Congress.*

In addition this author has from time to time published studies of particular phases of the subject, such as the following: "The Committee of the States, 1784" (American Historical Association, *Annual Report,* 1913); "The Name 'United States of America'" (*American Historical Review,* October, 1925); "The Continental Congress and Agricultural Supplies" (*Agricultural History,* July, 1928); "Perquisites of the President of the Continental Congress" (*American Historical Review,* October, 1929); "Who was the First President of the United States?" (Carnegie Institution, 1932; reprinted in *Carnegie Magazine,* June, 1932); "Washington and Committees at Headquarters" (American Historical Association, *Annual Report,* 1932); "Our Union of States in the Making" (*World Affairs,* September, 1935; reprinted, Carnegie Institution, 1935); "Southern Statesmen and the Confederation" (*North Carolina Historical Review,* October, 1937); "The 'More Perfect Union': the Continental Congress Seeks a Formula" (*Catholic Historical Review,* April, 1938); "The Catholic Signers of the Constitution" (in *The Constitution of the United States: Addresses in commemoration of the Sesquicentennial of the Signing, 17 September, 1787;* Washington, 1938).

Noteworthy among recent studies by others are: Jennings B. Sanders, *The Presidency of the Continental Congress,* 1774-1789 (Chicago, 1930); the same author, *Evolution of the Executive Departments of the Continental Congress,* 1774-1789 (University of North Carolina Press, 1935); and John J. Meng, Historical Introduction to *Despatches and Instructions of Conrad Alexandre Gérard, 1778-1780* (Johns Hopkins Press, 1939). Two books of significance, dealing with special phases of the subject have appeared since this volume was written. They are: Merrill Jensen, *The Articles of Confederation: An Interpretation of the Social-Constitutional History of the American Revolution, 1774-1781* (University of Wisconsin Press, 1940), and Bernhard Knollenberg, *Washington and the Revolution: A Reappraisal* (The Macmillan Company, 1940).

All these are but separate and partial aspects of the picture. It is as the central figure of the Revolutionary scene, for such it actually was, that this volume purposes to depict the Continental Congress. In no sense is it the purpose to relate the history of the American Revolution as a whole. Military activities, for instance, are only incidentally brought into the picture. There are likewise other aspects of the life of that assembly, other forces that impinged upon it, to which not the remotest allusion is made in these pages; many and many the deeds done in that body that are not here chronicled. Indeed if even the half of them were told, it would require many books to hold them.

It is the purpose rather to present the more significant phases of the drama called the American Revolution as they were enacted on the central stage which was the Continental Congress. For it was on that stage that the many strands of plan and purpose were drawn together, and it was there that these strands were woven into a consistent fabric. It was thither that, as from time to time the scenes shifted, came messengers and messages from the widely scattered fields of activities—political, economic, military— to inform and to animate. It was on that stage that most of the great actors in the drama played their stellar parts, and across those boards that many of the lesser actors ofttimes strode or strutted.

Of the parts there played, whether great or small, it is hoped that enough has been told to make definite the meaning, the movement, and the tone of the drama. Or, to put it otherwise, it is hoped that the principal activities of the Congress, whether it be the things done, the things only meditated or debated, or the things busily left undone, have been set forth with suffi- icent circumstance to make clear not only whereunto the Congress had been called but in what manner and to what degree it fulfilled its mission.

The name Continental Congress, be it understood, was at no time the official designation of the body so called. Officially it was simply "The Congress", until the adoption of the Articles of the Confederation, then it became "The United States in Congress Assembled". But there were so many provincial congresses in that day that some distinctive title was neces- sary for the congress of all the colonies. For a time the title most often used was "The General Congress", but, as "the Continent" came to be the popular and even the semi-official designation for the colonies as a unit, the Continental Congress came to be the accepted name for their common assembly.

Many historians have drawn a distinction between the Continental Con- gress and the Congress of the Confederation, applying the first name to the period before the adoption of the Articles of Confederation, the latter to the subsequent period. This latter appellation is valid enough in point of fact, but the limitation of the name Continental Congress to the earlier period is not in accord with the usage of the time. Inasmuch as there was no essential change in the fundamental character of the Congress from 1774 to 1789, the present writer has chosen to follow the popular usage in applying the name Continental Congress to the entire period.

As originally planned this book was to include a chapter bearing some such title as "The Continental Congress, Architect and Builder", which would endeavor to point out circumstantially the contributions that the old Congress made to our governmental structure, a thesis which, in the opinion of this author, has not hitherto been adequately developed. So striking was the contrast, in point of efficiency, between the old government and the new that it became a commonplace assumption, accepted almost as a truism, that the sole contribution of the Continental Congress was a negative one, the lesson of failure heaped upon failure.

Not a little of this conception of the old Congress is true, particularly in those years after the war had been fought and won, years when the states chiefly busied themselves with their own concerns, to the almost total disregard of their common and larger interests. Congress did in those years ofttimes flounder futilely in the mire, but it was a slough not so much of its own making as it was one into which it had been thrust by its constituent states, now become almost wholly self-centred and wrapped in the deceptive mantle of supposed self-sufficiency. It came about therefore that Congress was often pointed at contemptuously as only the mockery of a government, and that too by the very men who had most contributed to making it a mockery.

It was not alone in its failures, however, not alone in its instructive teaching of how not to carry on the business of a nation, valuable as were these lessons of trial and error, that the Continental Congress made its chief contributions to the building of the nation. This same Congress, which has been charged, even down to our own day, with embracing shadows, chasing will-o'-the-wisps, puttering with futilities, was, despite its lack of power to conduct national affairs with national mastery, in all this time building out of its experience a body of constructive legislation and compacting a fund of principles and practises which in time were transmitted to its successor to form an essential part of the new and more adequate system of government. It was, in fact, in the Continental Congress that were developed and formulated many of those fundamental principles of government that have become our national heritage. Indeed it is not too much to say that a great part of the materials built into the structure of the Constitution itself were wrought in the forge of the Continental Congress. Only with a full comprehension of what the Continental Congress did or sought to do can the Federal Convention and the Constitution that it framed be adequately understood.

Nor is this all. There came a time, the long struggle for independence won and peace consummated at last, when many men throughout the length and breadth of the continent were prone to turn their eyes from the broader national scene and fix their gaze upon their own states. It was the independence of the individual state rather than the independence of the states in union that most stirred their gratification and their pride. It was the future of their own state that chiefly animated their hopes and their endeavors. A goodly number of such men were not the least averse to dispensing altogether with that Congress to which, through the long and arduous years of the contest, they had looked as their leader and guide; they were even content that the union they had striven to build at the cost of so much toil and sweat and blood should dissolve and be no more.

Some of them, but not all. Other men there were, and not all of them of the Congress, who

      . . . . . . dipt into the future, far as human eye could see,
Saw the Vision of the world, and all the wonder that would be;

and in their vision beheld a great nation rising on these shores—if perchance it were not crushed in its infancy by the men of shorter vision but of longer arm. To these men of farther vision the vanishing of the Congress, the dissolution of the union, foreboded the perishing of all hopes for a greater and a brighter America. Why snuff out the one light that shone in the darkness? Though the fire had grown feeble, it must at all hazards be kept burning. The union must not be permitted to perish, and the Congress must be preserved as the symbol of that union, preserved unto that better day when a more perfect union might be enabled to take its place. Amid this confusion of voices it was the call of these men of vision and of faith to which Congress at length hearkened, even though not without some faltering. It was their faith in the ultimate growth of the infant nation into virile strength that the Congress was in time brought to embrace, and that faith should be accounted unto it for righteousness worthy of its meed.

The threads of this thesis are indeed to be found running through this narrative, yet to trace them with adequate particularity and to segregate them would require more than a single chapter of limited length. Besides, such a study, it was realized, was somewhat apart from the scope and character of this book as a whole, a book designed primarily to throw upon the screen the living and moving Congress as it went about its multitudinous tasks of gathering together the inchoate materials of thirteen colonial dependencies and fashioning them into one nation. Accordingly the study of the Continental Congress as architect and builder has been reserved for a future offering.

In this narrative and interpretative pursuit of the Continental Congress the author has chosen a mode of treatment that is for the most part chronological rather than topical, for the reason that, in his opinion, such a method will better enable the reader to obtain a view of the actual manner in which Congress performed its tasks, will better afford him a comprehension of the problems as from day to day they bore down upon Congress, will upon the whole give him a clearer conception of that assembly throughout the long reaches of its strivings, as from the cradle to the grave it grew and plodded and at last went into decline. That certain of its endeavors and achievements will not stand forth with that degree of distinctness that a topical treatment would have effected, is freely acknowledged.

The author has likewise chosen to make liberal use of the precise language —words, phrases, extracts of letters and remarks—of those who took part in the contest and have left us some expression of their views. How better than by consorting thus intimately with those who bore the burden, fought the fight, and with stalwart and steadfast faith pressed ever forward toward the goal may one sense their thoughts, their feelings, their fears, their hopes, their triumphs? How else than by hearkening to the utterances of those who were themselves of the blood-stream of those events, utterances fresh from

the scenes of action, even hot, it may be, from the furnace of political strife?
Whether laden with wisdom or weighted down with prejudice and passion,
the words of the actors themselves, far better than any second-hand trans-
formation of them, enable us to see and seeing to perceive the moving drama
of the American Revolution. That the quotations given are no more than
"samplings" of sentiments and conclusions, hardly needs to be pointed out.

Inevitably some addict to modern historiography, if perchance any such
should venture in amongst these pages, will inquire, why no footnotes?
To which the author will be tempted to blurt out the reply, why should
there be? Is it not reasonable to indulge the hope that any student of the
Revolution will be able to find his way through the narrative without feeling
the impulsion to pause and consult some source or other? For such, however, as require the stimulating cocktail of footnotes or bibliography, let
this suffice: the basic source of the narrative is the *Letters of Members* previously mentioned. Necessarily many of the facts and not a few of the
quotations are drawn directly from the *Journals* of Congress. A third source
of which considerable use has been made is the *Writings* of George Washington. As for the preliminary chapter on the causes of the Revolution,
that chapter professes to be no more than a compact of accessible and
acceptable authorities on that phase of American history.

To all wayfaring readers, those who refrain from arrogating to themselves the quality of historian, if any such shall be drawn within the orbit
of this narrative, the author sends greetings and voices the hope that, one
and all, they will be duly appreciative of the care that has been taken to
clear their path of every obstacle, such as foot-notes, against which they
might stub an unoffending toe. Most, if not all, of the needful dates are
to be found in the lines of the text, usually in parentheses, over which a
practised eye may easily glide.

Notwithstanding these modest disclaimers, the author deems it incumbent upon him to toss one small sop to that Cerberus who would fend
unwary students of history from stumbling into some pathless morass.
Toward the close of Chapter XXV mention is made of new light thrown
upon the accession of Maryland to the Confederation. For that new light
let the reader consult the following: St. George L. Sioussat, "The Chevalier
de La Luzerne and the Ratification of the Articles of Confederation, 1780-
1781" (in *Pennsylvania Magazine of History and Biography,* October,
1936); Mother Kathryn Sullivan, *Maryland and France, 1774-1789* (University of Pennsylvania Press, 1936); and William Emmett O'Donnell,
*The Chevalier de La Luzerne, French Minister to the United States, 1779-
1784* (Bruges, 1938).

In recounting the life-story of the old Congress the author indulges
himself in the conviction that he has sought to tell a true story, untainted
by predilections, and with as little bias as is possible for one who through
a good many years has seemed to himself to be dwelling on terms of intimacy

with the men who stride, majestically or stumblingly, across these pages. He has sought not to magnify their virtues or to minimize their faults, but to depict them in their weaknesses as well as in their strength, in their follies no less than in their wisdom.

Naturally and necessarily he has told the story from the American point of view, yet he is not conscious of having unduly twisted the British lion's tail. In truth, the idea that the Revolution was not the one-sided affair customarily set forth in our early school texts, was firmly implanted in the author's youthful mind by his father, who, notwithstanding his own grandfather had met his death at the hands of Tories in the Revolution, and notwithstanding the universal prevalence, in his time and place, of a definitely anti-British attitude, appears to have viewed the Revolution with as great a degree of objectivity as any historian of the present day and time. Accordingly the author seems to himself to have approached his study of the American Revolution with an open mind.

In the planning of this volume and in some of the tentative steps toward its preparation the author was privileged to consult that wisest and best of counsellors in all matters pertaining to American history, the late Dr. J. Franklin Jameson. To discuss with Dr. Jameson historical problems and projects was at all times an inspiration and one that deepened and broadened with the years. No American has ever given himself more unstintedly or more unselfishly to what he himself often spoke of as the cause of history than did Dr. Jameson; and this writer counts it one of the benedictions of his life that for a goodly span of years it was his rare privilege to live and work in close intimacy with that masterful mind and most engaging spirit. It is one of his most poignant regrets that he could not have had the benefit of Dr. Jameson's wise and fertile counsel throughout the preparation of this volume.

In further recording his obligations for aid and comfort, the author desires first of all to express his wholehearted appreciation of the generous assistance given by the Carnegie Institution of Washington through a grant which made the writing of this book possible; and no less an acknowledgment is due and freely extended to Dr. John C. Merriam, late president of the Institution, for his manifest personal interest in the undertaking and for his gracious encouragement to the author. Furthermore, the liberal cooperation of the Institution in the publication of the book magnifies the obligation and enhances the author's appreciation.

A like sense of obligation and appreciation is extended to Dr. Waldo G. Leland, long-time fellow-laborer in the common cause, for advice and admonition, graciously bestowed, throughout the progress of the work. Dr. Leland read the whole of the book in its first complete draft, and, from the rich stores of his knowledge and skill, shared freely with the author his convictions respecting the content, the scope, the form, the structure, and the style of the book.

Dr. Leo Francis Stock is another comrade-at-arms in the cause of history to whom the author is greatly indebted for unstinted counsel and admonition at all stages of the undertaking, counsel drawn from the greater deeps of his knowledge and experience in matters pertaining to the promulgation of the truth as it is in history.

Professor Samuel F. Bemis, who has manifested an especially active interest in this project from its inception, has not only been unfailing in his personal encouragement but has at all times shared to the fullest measure his scholarly advice and counsel.

Professor Max Farrand has lent a friendly hand by furnishing from the reservoir of his historical studies a comparative examination of the Franklin and the Dickinson plans of confederation, for which the author extends his cordial thanks.

Mrs. William Henry Harrison of the Carnegie Institution read the whole of the manuscript with an expertly critical eye and has earned the author's unbounded gratitude for divesting the text of many of its infelicities of phrase and style. Such infelicities as remain must be charged to the account of the author as deeds meet for repentance.

Mr. David M. Matteson likewise read the manuscript in its entirety, and, from the vantage point of his intimate knowledge of the period, endeavored to fend the author against historical inaccuracies. It is cause for genuine rejoicing that the volume is enabled to fare forth with an index prepared by Mr. Matteson's especially competent hand.

To one other member of the administrative staff of the Carnegie Institution the author owes a debt of thanks. Colonel Theodore H. Dillon, as Director of the Office of Publications, not only faithfully and well promoted the publication of the book, but at all times manifested an eager interest in its content. He likewise read the book in manuscript and contributed helpful comment.

In reading the proofs the author has had the benefit of the scholarly mind and practised eye of his niece, Miss Frances Gass.

The author can not forbear to record here his sense of gratification over the pleasing format of the book and to extend to the publishers, The Macmillan Company, his cordial thanks for their painstaking care in its production. To the editorial department in particular he would make his bow of delighted acknowledgments. Three ladies of that department, namely, Miss Lois Dwight Cole, Associate Editor, Miss Susan S. Prink, and Miss Mary S. Thompson, have served in their respective spheres as his guides, furnishing not consent alone, but likewise advice and counsel, without which he could not but have stumbled. They have graciously piloted him through the mazes of publication, along paths of pleasantness and through delectable groves. To these the choicest orchids in his garden.

Washington, July, 1941.   EDMUND CODY BURNETT.

CHAPTER I

THE GATHERING STORM
CAUSES OF THE REVOLUTION

The causes of the War of Independence have been related innumerable times and have been discussed from every angle; ofttimes indeed without due discrimination amongst the remoter causes, the silent propelling forces, and those more immediate incitements that served rather as provocations. Once upon a time it was customary to enumerate and to name those causes with precision and finality. Nowadays, when we look more closely into that period of storm and stress and strife, we are not so certain of either their numbers or their names; and we become all the more uncertain when we discover that the chief actors in the affair were themselves not always in agreement with regard to the objects of their protests or the objectives of their endeavors.

Of one thing, however, we do become fairly well convinced: that what were once set forth so confidently as the causes were far from being the most significant of the motive forces that produced the American Revolution. The slogans and the aphorisms, coined from the crude ore of moving events, hammered out in the hot furnace of popular emotion, were immensely useful in organizing resistance; but the tough fiber of that resistance was not digged from any shallow pit; it was a matured growth from the soil of American life. The real American Revolution, that is, the revolution in the American mind in its conception of what ought to be the relation between the colonies and the mother country, had in great measure come about before ever the struggle for independence was begun. In short, the colonies had reached that stage in their development when they felt that they no longer had need of a doting parent—and they resented subjection to a domineering one.

What is more, this natural development had been promoted by the course of events and without conscious purpose on the part of either the mother country or the colonies. In the first place, the colonies had in great part been peopled by the more individualistic spirits, people who were prone to go their own ways and to resent any interference with those ways. In the second place, the home government had been content, through the long years of slow colonial growth, to leave the colonies largely to their own devices. To be sure, there had been annoying trade restrictions, royal vetoes, and the like; but the colonists had usually found easy ways of circumventing those obstacles, so that they were not often seriously discommoded thereby. In the third place, the two divisions of the British stock, those who had migrated and those who had remained at home, separated as they were by a wide ocean, subject to differing influences, internal and external, had developed divergent ideas of life, political, social, economic. There was needed therefore only some sharp turn of events, some compelling occurrence, to bring these differences into the forefront of consciousness; only some act of provocation on the part of the home government, some excessive manifestation of the protective or controlling hand, to arouse in the colonies the spirit of protest. And the spirit of protest once aroused, unless promptly quieted by a reasonable compliance with its demands, would inevitably develop into a spirit of revolt. It came about that provocations aplenty were offered, that protests were not heeded, or not heeded in time, and revolt was the consequence.

The first such provocation of which it is needful to take note was the employment, in 1761, of so-called "writs of assistance", that is, general search warrants authorizing officers of the law to enter the house of any person, without naming him, suspected of complicity in smuggling. This not only interfered with a lucrative business of colonial traders, it ran counter to colonial ideas of personal liberty, for was it not fundamental in English law that a man's house was his castle? In Boston, James Otis, the advocate general of Massachusetts, became so wrought-up over the use of writs of assistance that he resigned his office in order to plead the cause of the opposition; and he made so impassioned a speech against their use that, though he lost his case, he received universal applause. Otis denounced the use of writs of assistance as in violation of the spirit of the English constitution, thus setting up the doctrine of a fundamental law as superior to a mere legislative enactment. The whole affair was little more than a flurry, yet, in the light of after events, it was interpreted as having pointed to the parting of the ways. "Then and there", declaimed John Adams years afterward, "the child independence was born." Adam's idea may not have been so far wrong, even if his figure of speech does seem to have been somewhat out of line. At all events, repugnance to general warrants as dangerous to personal liberty came to permeate the American mind to such a degree that a prohibition of them was afterward inserted in nearly all the state constitutions and also in the Federal Constitution.

The noise of this affair was scarcely heard beyond the confines of Massachusetts; but some two years later another peal of thunder, celebrated in history as "the Parson's Cause", reverberated down in Virginia. The flurry there was over the question whether the clergy should be paid so many pounds of tobacco or a money commutation of lesser value. Again the law was clear enough, but a complicated situation had arisen in consequence of a royal veto, after a long delay, of an act of the Virginia assembly. Then up rose one Patrick Henry, to proclaim the doctrine that all government rests upon an original compact between people and rulers and that when the compact is broken by one party, government becomes dissolved. To give point to the doctrine in this particular case, Henry maintained that, in disallowing the Virginia act, the king had degenerated into a tyrant and had forfeited all right to the obedience of his subjects. There was nothing particularly new in the doctrine of government founded on compact, or, for that matter, in its corollary, the right of revolution. The idea had long been floating down the stream of political thinking and gathering bulk and content all the while, but Henry had been bold enough to make a direct application of the idea of revolution to the American situation. He had given an additional agitation to the American political whirlpool.

The thunders of Otis and Henry were, to be sure, violent enough, but theirs was the violence of voices and words, nothing more. There was as yet no more than the suggestion of revolt; no actual defiance of authority, no bashing of heads, no destruction of property. These appropriate manifestations would, however, appear in due course, unless perchance wisdom should thrust in a diverting hand. For the colonial sense of loyalty to the home government was weakening, their sense of the right of self-determination was gaining strength. Moreover, an event of momentous consequences was about to furnish a powerful impetus to the colonial feeling of self-sufficiency, while at the same time it would start a series of provocations that would propel them toward self-direction.

The long struggle between Great Britain and France, brought to a close in 1763, had ended in the destruction of French power in America, and by virtue of that fact had freed the colonies in great measure from their sense of dependence upon Great Britain for protection. The Indians might still give trouble, but the colonies were disposed to think that they could handle the Indian problem without assistance. Such was the aspect of the situation as viewed through colonial eyes, but the statesmen of Great Britain were beginning to peer at America from a very different angle. Great Britain's victory in the contest had virtually transformed that power from a small island kingdom into a world empire. Such an empire offered possibilities, responsibilities, and of course serious problems of management. In attacking the problem of administering the empire British statesmen would naturally think of the empire as a unit and therefore might not give sufficient consideration to existing differences between different parts of the empire; not at least until these differences of interest and differences of political ideas should be forced upon their attention. For another thing, the wars had been costly, and it was altogether natural that British statesmen should come to the conclusion that the colonies ought to bear a greater proportion of the cost of their own defense than they had hitherto done.

Even before the war had ended the British minister, George Grenville, had been mulling over the problem, had formed his plan, and, as soon as the peace had been signed, he set about putting his plan into effect. It was deemed needful to keep a small body of troops stationed in America, chiefly for the purpose of defending the colonies against the Indians, a task to which he believed the colonies unequal, and he thought it only right that the colonies should bear a part of the cost. His plan was twofold: he would enforce the navigation laws and make them earn a revenue, which for long they had not been doing, and he would inaugurate a scheme of internal taxes.

The first part of the Grenville plan would certainly play havoc with the extensive smuggling trade. Moreover, although the new Sugar Act of 1764, which was a part of the project, carried lower duties than the old Sugar Act of 1733, it carried also a prohibition against trade with the French and Dutch West Indies. If, therefore, its new machinery of enforcement should be effectively applied, it would administer a death-blow to the important trade of the northern and middle colonies with those islands.

As a result of all these things, protests and remonstrances flew thick and fast. Among them was one emanating from Boston, which deserves to be remembered, because it assailed the laying of any taxes "without our having a legal representation where they are laid", claiming for the colonies the same rights as "our fellow-subjects who are natives of Britain", and, further, beseeching a united protest by all the colonies. The doctrines enunciated in the Boston remonstrance would, in one form or another, soon be filling every mouth; but as for stirring the colonies to a united protest, that would have to wait until more of them had felt the pinch. The withers of the southern colonies were as yet unwrung.

They had not long to wait, however, for something that seemed to menace all alike. The ministry had proposed a stamp tax, but first they wished to learn what the attitude of the colonies would be toward the measure. Would they prefer that the tax take some other form? If so, what would they propose? The colonies had no hesitancy in voicing their objection to the stamp tax—any tax, in fact; but they had no other plan to offer, unless it be that of requisitions upon the colonies. This was a suggestion of Benjamin Franklin, but even Franklin doubted whether the colonies could agree upon their respective quotas. It is worth bearing in mind that when the colonies came to organize their union, they adopted this very system of requisitions, unsatisfactory though it was, and long refused even to mention such a thing as taxes. The confident ministry accordingly put through Parliament (March, 1765) an act requiring stamps to be affixed to all legal documents, and to a variety of other documents as well. Protests followed as a matter of course, nevertheless it was the general opinion that the act would be enforced without serious difficulty. It was something of a surprise there-fore when it was discovered that thereby a big lump of fat had been thrown into the fire, with the result that there was soon much sizzling.

The remonstrances that sprang up here, there, and everywhere, took on numerous forms and hues; but in one respect there was general agreement: the colonies were not represented in the British Parliament, therefore they were being taxed without their own consent; and this was in violation of a time-honored principle of the English constitution. The British contention was that the colonies were virtually represented in Parliament, on the theory that a member of Parliament represented the whole realm and not merely the constituency that elected him. Here, then, were two conflicts: a conflict between two interpretations of the meaning of representation, and a conflict of ideas respecting the nature of the British empire. The reflecting Britisher (and some reflecting colonials as well) took the view that the unity of the empire depended upon a power in Parliament to bind all its parts. On the other hand, a good many of the colonists espoused the idea that the colonies were united to England only under the person of the sovereign, and that the authority of Parliament did not run in the colonies. The fallaciousness of this argument was, however, soon recognized, and, from first taking refuge in the tent of the monarch, the colonists presently drew off and began to hurl their missiles mainly at the king. The chief trouble was that both sides had befuddled themselves with theories, to the disregard of rational facts and clarifying common sense.

The contest between befuddlements might well have subsided into a peaceful argument and the argument into an agreement not to agree, and so have come to a conclusion, with both parties content to drop their weapons, had it not come about that Patrick Henry, in his best manner, dropped a live coal into an open powder keg. Henry had once before made a small experiment with coals and powder and probably had a very good idea of what the result would be. In the Virginia House of Burgesses, Henry moved a set of resolutions urging resistance to the Stamp Act and supported his resolutions with such fiery eloquence that they were adopted, although by a small majority. The burden of Henry's plea was that Virginians had from the beginning possessed all the rights of Englishmen, that "in the article of taxes and internal police" they had enjoyed the right of being governed by their own assembly, that this right had been acknowledged by the British government, and had never been forfeited. Furthermore, he maintained that the general assembly had the exclusive right to lay taxes and imposts upon the inhabitants of the colony, and that every attempt to vest any other person or persons with such power was "illegal, unconstitutional, and unjust, and has a manifest tendency to destroy British as well as American liberty." In fact he went the length of declaring that any one who held otherwise was an enemy to the colony.

Having tossed his live coal in the direction of the powder magazine, Henry was content, strange to tell, to gather up his saddle bags, bridle his horse (so lame that it had to be led), and trudge back into the Virginia hills. Meanwhile some members of the House of Burgesses who had been powerfully wrought upon by Henry's eloquence and had voted for his resolutions cooled off during the night, so that next morning they joined in having the more objectionable of the resolutions rescinded. But what booted this belated rescinding? The whole batch of them had already gone flying into the other colonies, setting fire to the tinder with which every one of them was liberally strewn. Thereupon violence ceased to be confined to voices and words. Far and wide the wild men of the colonies gathered their mobs to destroy the stamps, cow the stamp collectors into resigning or hiding, and to do sundry other kinds of devilment.

Came the first of November, when the Stamp Act was to go into force, and scarcely a stamp could be found, to say nothing of the sudden scarcity of the duly appointed stamp collectors. In the interval, however, a more pacific course of action had been initiated in that unpacific colony of Massachusetts. It chanced that on the very day that Patrick Henry, in the Virginia House of Burgesses, was violently denouncing the act and seeking to incite resistance, the Massachusetts assembly (the "General Court") gathered in session and at once set on foot a plan to assemble a congress of representatives of all the colonies to take the serious situation into consideration and propose a plan of procedure. The resulting Congress, known as the Stamp Act Congress, which met in New York on October 7, included representatives, twenty-seven in all, from nine of the thirteen colonies, Massachusetts to Maryland inclusive, and remote South Carolina. Of the four that failed to send representatives, New Hampshire gave assurance of being "ready to join in any address" that might be agreed upon by the congress, while the gov-

ernors of the other three, Virginia, North Carolina, and Georgia, declined to call the assemblies together for the purpose. From Georgia,
however, did come an unofficial promise of cooperation.

The Stamp Act Congress was, upon the whole, a body of moderates,
and, despite the howlings of the mob, they chose, as became their characters, to propose moderate measures. The congress was in session
eighteen days, formulated a declaration of rights, drew up a petition to
the king and memorials to the House of Lords and House of Commons.
Although the addresses to the king and Parliament were restrained in
tone, they were at the same time firm in their assertion of colonial
rights and of the unconstitutionality of the Stamp Act. It is in their
"Declaration of Rights and Grievances", however, that the case against
the Stamp Act is set forth with the greatest cogency, albeit with con-
ciseness.

The declaration begins with an acknowledgment that the colonists
owe the same allegiance to the crown and "all due subordination" to
Parliament as those born within the realm, but significantly adds that
they are entitled to "all the inherent rights and privileges" as natural-
born subjects. Then comes the meat of the declaration; that one of the
"undoubted rights of Englishmen", one that is "inseparably essential
to the freedom of a people", is "that no taxes should be imposed on
them, but with their own consent, given personally, or by their representatives". As a disclaimer to the thesis that the colonies were "virtually" represented in Parliament, the declaration simply asserts that
"these colonies are not, and from their local circumstances, cannot be
represented in the house of commons in Great Britain", and that therefore their only representatives are the respective colonial legislatures,
which alone can constitutionally impose taxes on them. Combating the
provision of the Stamp Act that cases arising under it should be tried
in the admiralty courts, the congress asserted that "trial by jury is the
inherent and invaluable right of every British subject in these colonies."
Lastly, the congress made its "humble application to both houses of
parliament" to procure the repeal of the Stamp Act, and likewise of
"other late acts for the restriction of the American commerce". The several addresses, pitched to somewhat different keys, elaborate upon all
these points.

The Stamp Act Congress stands out as a beacon light on the highroad leading to the union of the American colonies and their ultimate independence. Had not the movement toward union been turned aside for a time, that congress might well have marked the actual beginning of the American nation. Although not quite all the colonies were represented in it, it did very nearly attain the status of a continental congress; it served in several respects as a model for the First Continental Congress, so-called; and, what is perhaps of greater importance, though not itself counseling resistance, and though its voice of moderation was unable to quell the turbulence round about, it set forth the essential principles on which the colonies were destined to take their stand in their resistance to the encroaching power of the British government.

While the pronouncements of the Stamp Act Congress were generally approved in America, they were not otherwise of especial influence on the immediate situation. Within a week of its adjournment came the day for the act to go into effect, but not an official would dare try to enforce it. Followed a war of pamphlets and arguments on both sides of the Atlantic, and finally, in January, 1766, a memorable debate in Parliament, in which some British statesmen virtually took the American point of view, namely, that, although Parliament might regulate colonial trade in the interest of the empire, it could not impose on the colonies an internal tax. Meanwhile, a new ministry came into power and, convinced that discretion was better than stubborn valor, while at the same time not uninfluenced by petitions from English merchants who found their trade suffering in consequence of the situation in America, obtained the repeal of the Stamp Act. Side by side with the repeal, however, was passed a "Declaratory Act," which maintained the right of Parliament "to bind the colonies and people of America . . . in all cases whatsoever". Thereupon the colonies let out a great rejoicing, as having been victorious in their contention. What booted it how strenuously Parliament asserted the right, so long as it made no effort to enforce it?

Alas! for all these high hopes, trouble unexpectedly made a return visit. The reverberations of the exultant shouts over the repeal of the Stamp Act had scarcely died away, the protestations of undying love for the mother country were still echoing throughout the land, when

there occurred another change of personnel in the ministry, whereby
Charles Townshend became chancellor of the exchequer and therefore
for the moment the dominating personality of the government, so far
as America was concerned. Imbued with the idea of imperial control
as set forth in the Declaratory Act, he would do just that, but he would
do it by indirection. It was only internal taxes, was it, to which the
colonies objected? They had acknowledged, had they not, the right of
Parliament to levy external taxes? Very well; he would try some external taxes on them. He would levy imposts on a variety of articles, a
carefully chosen list, one of which was tea. (It is not essential to remember the others, but to remember tea is inescapable. No American
ever thinks of the Revolution without remembering tea.)

The proceeds of these taxes would be used particularly for the payment of governors and judges, thus making them independent of the
colonial assemblies; and, for the better enforcement of the measure, it
was deemed needful to implement it with other measures, such as
legalizing writs of assistance and providing for the trial of revenue cases
in the admiralty courts, that is, courts without juries. On top of all
these measures came a renewed effort to enforce the billeting act, with
the result that New York in particular put up a stout resistance. Thereupon the assembly of that colony was suspended until it should yield
compliance. There was a similar protest in Massachusetts, but there the
incident was limited to a controversy between the governor and the
assembly. Altogether the colonies had set down before them a rather
unsavory kettle of fish, and in consequence there was once again a rain
of protests, addresses, and denunciations of the acts. Now, however, the
colonies began to shift their ground and to declaim against any tax by
Parliament, whether internal or external.

Moreover, resistance to the Townshend acts took particularly the
form of non-importation agreements. Agreements of the sort had been
used in opposition to the Stamp Act, but they now began to assume a
more determined aspect and more formidable proportions. One of the
first such was put forward in Massachusetts in October, 1767, and it was
followed shortly afterward by a circular letter to the other colonies beseeching united action. The Massachusetts authorities deemed it the
part of wisdom to disclaim any thought of independence, yet on the

other side of the water it was made to appear that independence was precisely what they did aim at. Thereupon the Massachusetts assembly was peremptorily called upon to rescind the circular letter, and the assemblies of the other colonies were threatened with dissolution in the event that they took sides with their sister colony in the issue. As might have been foreseen by statesmen unafflicted with political cataract, the Massachusetts assembly did not rescind the circular letter, and the other colonial assemblies did take their stand beside her. Virginia in particular sent out a circular letter of her own, calling upon the colonies to unite in petitioning for a redress of grievances. In short, the ministry found itself confronted with what looked to them like sedition among the colonies, and sedition it doubtless was. There ensued accordingly, on the one part, dissolutions of assemblies galore; on the other, bold denunciations of the government. There were arguments restrained and arguments violent, and occasionally acts that were not arguments at all. In Boston, for instance, a ship of the merchant-prince, John Hancock, was seized by the authorities for violations of the customs (the authorities appear to have had a good case), whereupon there was a riot that frightened the customs officers out of their wits.

Such doings were bound to stir the wrath of the British ministers and induce them to take measures for the preservation of governmental dignity and authority. One measure was to send troops into Boston; another was to dig up an ancient law whereby any American accused of treason might be taken to England for trial. This was worse than adding insult to injury; it was adding injury to insult. The mere threat of using such a law raised gorge that had not hitherto been stirred. Theretofore the quarrel had revolved mainly around questions that involved property rights; but here was a threat to the dearest of personal rights. This time it was Virginia that took the lead. In May, 1769, the Virginia House of Burgesses adopted a series of resolutions, first of all condemning the Townshend acts as violative of colonial rights, then denouncing this new-old treason law as "highly derogatory of the rights of British subjects". The resolves were by order of the assembly sent to the other colonies, which for the most part took similar action. As punishment for its rash action the governor of Virginia dissolved the assembly, but the burgesses straightway gathered in a private house and adopted a non-importation agreement that became a model for the whole continent.

Associations, as these covenants were generally called, speedily sprang up all over the country; and their enforcement, which was generally in the hands of local committees, was not always in a manner that was either peaceful or gentle. They did, however, prove effectual for the main purpose for which they were instituted: they put such pressure upon the British merchants that the latter finally besought the repeal of the acts; and again, as in the case of the Stamp Act, the government swapped valor for discretion. Ostensibly the repeal was in part justified on the ground that the duties had been laid "contrary to the true principles of commerce"; but once again the ministry chose to keep its grip on the doctrine of the supremacy of Parliament, and to that end left the tax on tea unrepealed. That, to be sure, was annoying to the colonists, yet so long as no tea was actually imported they could swallow down their spittle and not worry over much.

Unfortunately for a return to the even tenor of colonial ways and a renewal of the old-time professions of devotion to the mother land, at almost the moment when the Townshend acts were being repealed, another little volcano erupted in the town of Boston. This was the so-called "Boston Massacre". To call it a massacre is a gross misuse of words, for it was nothing more than a small clash between the populace and the soldiers stationed in Boston, wherein five people were killed and six wounded. The affair was initiated, so it appears, by resentful and wrathful citizenry with a barrage of epithets so provocative in their nature and their tone that soldierly discipline was undone; some guns were fired, some citizens fell dead or wounded. It could scarcely be expected that a spirit of amity would straightway hover over the scene, and it fitted the Bostonian mood to magnify the incident into a massacre and set apart the anniversary of this eventful March 5, 1770, as a day for lamentation—and oratory. The "Boston Massacre" has thus been made to stand out as one of the important events leading to the Revolution, the first spilling of blood—if revolutions must be marked by spilled blood. What is of greater significance is the fact that the presence of the soldiers was resented as an act of military dictatorship and in defiance of the constitutional rights of the colonies. After the "massacre" the demand for the removal of the troops was made with such insistence that Lieutenant Governor Hutchinson reluctantly yielded. One direct result of the experience of Boston was an intensification of the fear of a standing army, and that fear, throughout the contest for independence, was responsible for much of the weakness of the American defense.

Despite this and a multitude of lesser incitements, the spirit of calm timidly returned to hover over the colonies for a time. Credit (or debit) for disturbing the calm has often been laid at the door of Samuel Adams; and that he had much to do with keeping the fires of resistance from dying out is not to be doubted. Adams was never averse to making use for his own purposes of any inflammable tinder; and in good time a woolgathered ministry would furnish him and his likes with a copious supply. In the meantime, however, he was devoting himself mainly to the task of making ready for the contest which, to his mind, was bound to come. Fanatically zealous for the constitutional liberties of the colonies, his ultimate goal, according to much good evidence, was the independence of America; and he began the work of organization by knitting together the towns of his own Massachusetts through committees of correspondence. In due time this same device (committees of correspondence) would be the chief instrumentalities by which the several colonies would be brought into cooperation. It was Virginia, however, that took the first important step toward this larger organization; and, oddly enough, it was a small affair in Rhode Island that served to set Virginia agog.

The burning of the *Gaspee* in Narragansett Bay is often pointed to as one of the patriotic acts which helped to bring on the Revolution. May be so. (In truth that affair was long held in such reverent esteem that the room in which the *Gaspee* plot was hatched was piously preserved, although it was in time snugly surrounded by a new-built house. Even to this day, so it would seem, Rhode Islanders turn their memories more fondly upon the burning of the bad ship *Gaspee* than upon the part they did not take in launching the "Good Ship Constitution".) The *Gaspee* was engaged in the revenue service, and its captain, as he plied his vessel up and down Narragansett Bay, had made himself notorious and obnoxious for his arbitrary methods and occasional insolence, to say nothing of his interference with the smuggling business. Whether it was that the captain had been too arbitrary or too successful, on the night of June 9, 1772, the *Gaspee* was brought to the end of its career, when it was boarded by a troop of armed men and put to the torch. Rhode Islanders might applaud the deed and acclaim the doers, yet no individual of those who took part in the affair ever offered himself for public accolade. A commission was indeed set to work to ferret out the perpetrators, but in the end the committee was compelled to acknowledge that not one of them could be found.

And what had Virginia to do with an incident in faraway Narragansett Bay? Nothing in particular; but much in general. For while Samuel Adams, Joseph Warren, *et al.,* were marshalling and training their forces in Massachusetts and keeping an eagle eye on the horizon for the appearance of opportunity, down in Virginia a group of like spirits, which included Thomas Jefferson, Patrick Henry, Richard Henry Lee, and a few others—men characterized by Jefferson as possessed of that "forwardness and zeal which the times required"—had taken high perches from which they could watch the rise and ebb of the political tides. For some time the watch had been dull and dreary, when suddenly the *Gaspee* affair drew their attention, and more especially the authorization to the investigating commission to send offenders to England for trial. The watchful Virginia group, startled by such a proposal, at once offered in the assembly a carefully drawn set of resolutions authorizing the appointment of a committee to investigate the creation of this "court of inquiry" and to request of the other colonies that like committees of correspondence be appointed on their part (March 12, 1773). The resolutions were unanimously adopted, the committee appointed, and, although the governor dissolved the assembly therefor, the resolutions and the committee's circular letter were transmitted to the other colonies. All the New England colonies promptly complied, as did also South Carolina. Richard Henry Lee, one of those responsible for the resolutions, characterized the measure "as leading to that union, and perfect understanding of each other, on which the political salvation of America so eminently depends" (April 4, 1773). Commenting upon the movement, the *New Hampshire Gazette* ventured this significant utterance:

The Union of the Colonies which is now taking place is big with the most important Advantages to this Continent. . . . The United Americans may bid Defiance to all their open as well as secret foes; therefore let it be the Study of all to make the Union of the Colonies firm and perpetual, as it will be the great Basis for Liberty and every public Blessing in America.

A good beginning had at least been made toward creating the necessary machinery for effectively promoting concerted action among the colonies, and, given an appropriate impulse, the machinery would speedily be set in motion.

Even at that moment the British ministry was about to furnish the needed impulse. The immediate objective was to help the East India Company out of a financial hole, and to do that some of the wise men of London conceived the bright idea of permitting the company to ship tea directly to America without paying the customary duty to the home government. Moreover, the plan would enable Americans to drink tea at far less cost than would be possible for Englishmen, and that privilege, reflected the planners gleefully, would induce them to forget that little tax on tea to which they had so strenuously objected. Accordingly, in the autumn of 1773, some small cargoes of tea were consigned to Boston, New York, Philadelphia, and Charleston. Annapolis also won a corner in the tea picture, with the burning of the *Peggy Stewart,* but that was later (October, 1774).

To the sublimely confident promotors of the plan it was no small shock that at none of these ports was the tea permitted to get into the market. In Charleston it was allowed to land but was chucked into a cellar, where it remained until 1776. In New York and Philadelphia the vessels were not allowed to discharge their cargoes of tea, but compelled to return them to England. In Boston there was great pother between the port authorities, on the one hand, who insisted that the tea should be landed before the vessels could be cleared for the return voyage, and sundry citizens, in mass-meeting assembled, on the other, who as stoutly insisted it should not. It began to appear that the authorities might win the contest, for it was their plan that, at the expiration of the period required by law, the tea would be seized and stored. The sundry citizens were at the end of their argument, but not, as soon appeared, at the end of their tether. In the evening of December 16 some fifty or sixty men disguised as Indians boarded the vessels and emptied the tea into the waters of Boston harbor.

As a matter of course, the British authorities, when they learned of these outrageous doings, were exceeding wroth. Indeed some of the best friends of the colonies denounced the act as criminal, and even Franklin himself declared that it called for reparation. King George, for his part, was determined that Massachusetts should be punished, and his purpose was warmly seconded by the prime minister, Lord North. As for Parliament, there would be no difficulty whatever in putting through any measures that the ministry might decide upon. In those days Parliament seldom failed to hearken to its master's voice. There were indeed a few who were for conciliatory measures, another few who even counseled that the colonies be allowed to depart in peace; but Burke and Chatham, advocates of conciliation though they were, drew back from any step leading to the break-up of the empire.

Accordingly a series of repressive measures were enacted, measures which the colonists soon began to denounce as the "intolerable acts". Most obnoxious of them, and destined to be the most potent in stirring the colonies to united resistance, was that which closed the port of Boston until such time as the destroyed tea should be paid for. Another, known as the "Regulating Act", practically set aside the form of government that had existed in Massachusetts under the charter, and established in its stead an autocratic system that left to the people little more than the election of members of the assembly. A third act, anticipating possible riots and probable difficulties in obtaining fair trials for persons involved in quelling such riots, provided that such persons, with their witnesses, might be sent to some other colony or to England for trial. A fourth act, called the "Quartering Act", and designed to implement the enforcement of the others, provided for the lodgment of the soldiers amongst the inhabitants where the troops might be required.

A fifth act, against which the colonists loudly declaimed, seems to have had no relation to the repressive acts, either in its origin or in its purposes; but, inasmuch as it was passed about the same time, the colonists generally interpreted it as intended for their punishment. This was the Quebec Act, which extended the Province of Quebec to include the French settlements of the Illinois country, subsequently to become the Northwest Territory, and made provisions for a more effectual government of the region. Instead of being repressive in intent, its aim was rather a liberalization of the government by allowing the French inhabitants to have their own judicial procedure and freedom of worship. As for any purpose to cut off the colonies from westward expansion, that does not appear to have entered into the minds of the statesmen who conceived the measure. What they were mainly concerned with was a needed betterment of administration. From the very first, however, since the act fell upon the country along with the acts known to be repressive in purpose and oppressive in nature, the colonists were suspicious of it, and suspicion speedily deepened into conviction, a conviction that found abundant and vehement modes of expression, notably in the Declaration of Independence. Notwithstanding this erroneous interpretation, the Quebec Act played its part in uniting the colonies and adding strength to their resistance.

The act for closing the port of Boston, since known to fame as the Boston Port Bill, entered that devoted port on the 10th of May, 1774, and made itself known to the inhabitants round about. The day of doom was set for the first of June. The Bostonians straightway inquired of the other colonies whether they would consider Boston as suffering for the common cause, suggesting at the same time that the colonies unite in an agreement to stop importations and exportations from and to Great Britain. Some of the colonies had not even waited for Boston's call for help, but had immediately offered their sympathies and pledged their assistance. From a town meeting in Providence, Rhode Island, and from the committees of correspondence in Philadelphia and New York came proposals (May 21, 23) of a general congress of all the colonies for the purpose of bringing about united action in the emergency, whilst the Virginians took such definite steps as put that colony in the forefront of the movement. First of all, immediately upon learning of the Boston Port Bill, the House of Burgesses, on the initiation of Thomas Jefferson, adopted (May 24) a resolution setting apart June 1 (the day the bill was to go into effect) as "a day of fasting, humiliation, and prayer; devoutly to implore the divine interposition, for averting the heavy calamity which threatens destruction to our civil rights, and the evils of civil war; to give us one heart and one mind firmly to op-

pose, by all just and proper means, every injury to American rights".
Nor did they fail to beseech that "the minds of his majesty and his
Parliament may be inspired from above with wisdom, and justice".

Such obstreperous conduct on the part of the assembly was bound to
rouse the ire of the governor, who declared the resolution to be "conceived in such terms as reflect highly upon his Majesty and the Parliament of Great Britain", and thereupon dissolved the assembly. As once
before, however, the burgesses were not to be balked by a dissolution.
On May 27 they reassembled unofficially, formed themselves into an
association, indited a ringing denunciation of the Boston Port Act as
"a most dangerous attempt to destroy the constitutional liberty and
rights of all North America", declared that an attack upon one colony
was an attack upon all, and recommended a general congress of deputies from all the colonies, to meet annually, to deliberate on such
measures as "the united interests of America may from time to time
require". Hard upon the heels of this action came expresses from Boston, Philadelphia, and Annapolis, all voicing their resentment against
the oppressive act and recommending to their southern brethren united
action for appropriate measures. Thereupon those burgesses, twenty-
five in number, who were still in Williamsburg, the colonial seat of
government, again came together and sent out a call for a "convention"
of deputies from Virginia counties to meet on the first of August.

Encouraged by the responses from the other colonies, the Massachusetts House of Representatives, on June 17, resolved "that a meeting
of Committees, from the several Colonies on this Continent is highly
expedient and necessary, to consult upon the present state of the Colonies", appointed five delegates, and suggested Philadelphia as the
place and September 1st as the time for the meeting. The General Assembly of Rhode Island had already (on June 15), in anticipation of the
meeting, appointed her delegates. Similarly in anticipation, the Connecticut House of Representatives had (on June 3) provided for the
appointment of delegates by the committee of correspondence, and
that committee made the appointments on July 13. Within the next
few weeks all the other colonies except Georgia had, by one process or
another, chosen their delegates to the congress.

In Pennsylvania the election (July 22) was by the regularly constituted legislature. In the remaining colonies the elections were accomplished, directly or indirectly, by revolutionary bodies. In Maryland, New Hampshire, New Jersey, Delaware, and North Carolina, it was by provincial congresses (although not in every instance then so designated) called primarily for the purpose. In Maryland, for instance (June 22-25), it was by a "Meeting of the Committees appointed by the several Counties". In New Hampshire (July 21) the electing body is designated as "a meeting of the deputies appointed by the several towns". In New Jersey (July 23) it was a convention of "Committees appointed by the several Counties". In Delaware (August 1) the electing body is characterized as a meeting of "Representatives of the freemen . . . chosen and appointed for that among other purposes, by the freeholders and freemen" of the three counties. In North Carolina (August 25) it was "at a general meeting of the deputies of the Inhabitants". In South Carolina the actual election (July 6-8) was "at a general meeting of the inhabitants" at Charleston, but the choice was ratified (August 2) by the Commons House of Assembly. In Virginia (August 1) the election was by that revolutionary body the "convention", called together by a group of the Burgesses.

New York was such a squirming mass of contending factions that no unity in the colony had as yet been effected. In the city, "By duly certifyed polls, taken by proper persons, in seven wards", five delegates were chosen (July 28), and these were afterward approved by "Committees of several districts" in the county of Westchester, by like committees in the county of Dutchess, by "the Inhabitants of Palatine District, Tryon County", by "a Vote of the Inhabitants of the precincts of Pokeepsich", and by "a Vote of the Inhabitants of the City and County of Albany". The counties of Suffolk, Orange, and Kings, each chose its own delegate or delegates. It is significant of the confusion in the colony that, according to Joseph Galloway of Pennsylvania, the election in Kings County was accomplished by two men, Simon Boerum and one other, who constituted themselves a committee for the county and unanimously elected Boerum a delegate to the congress!

The summoning of the congress had been engineered chiefly by the radical element, with only here and there the intervention of a moderating hand; nevertheless, even as the wild men raged, and some not so wild imagined vain things, the men chosen for the momentous task of charting the course that America should pursue were, more largely than might have been expected, men of wisdom and understanding. As for the country at large, it was on tiptoe to learn what counsel the congress would offer, what its manner and what the tone of its voice as it sought to speak for that combined group of political entities presently to be designated in common speech as "the Continent". Then, when the delegates of the several colonies set out on their eventful journey to Philadelphia, the eagerness to know what manner of men they were was immensely heightened.

CHAPTER II

THE COMMON CAUSE
THE COLONIES TAKE COUNSEL WITH ONE ANOTHER

"The Continent", now about to gather itself a congress, was in fact little more than a slender strip along the Atlantic seaboard; yet, for the dozen of small political communities, the problems involved in the gathering were not simple and the labor was not light. Heavier they were by far than now devolve upon their heirs and assigns, fourfold in number and far-flung across the width of a continent in fact. Whether it be from New Hampshire and Massachusetts at one extreme or South Carolina at the other, the journey to Philadelphia was slow, dreary, and toilsome. For most of the delegates to the congress it must be on horseback, with bulging saddlebags, or by lumbering stagecoach. The South Carolinians did indeed find transportation by wind and water more feasible, still not as swift as the winds.

Of the journeyings of the delegates from the southward not a great deal is known. The southerners may not have been less conscious of posterity than their New England compatriots, but they seem never to have contracted to the same degree the habit of communing with posterity through the medium of a diary. Of the journey of the Massachusetts delegates, however, we have a circumstantial account, recorded by that indefatigable diarist, John Adams—the journal of a veritable triumphal procession from Boston, down through Connecticut, New York, New Jersey, and on into Philadelphia.

"The Committee for the Congress", as Adams characterizes the Massachusetts delegation, set out from Boston on the 10th of August, and so leisurely was their journey that they did not arrive in Philadelphia until the 29th. They were bent on surveying the political landscape as they journeyed, therefore they lingered and tarried wherever the lingering and the tarrying offered them good mental and spiritual grazing. For one thing, they would take a measure of the depth and breadth of

23

the sympathies with Boston, of the genuineness of those offers to make the cause of Boston their own. For another thing, they would have a look in advance at as many as possible of the men whom the colonies to the south of them had chosen for the great conclave, would discover what manner of men they would encounter in Philadelphia and what their views. They would have opportunities also to meet and to measure other men, men not destined to appear in the coming congress, but important figures in their own colonies. This eagerness to probe, to pry, to discover was not of course all on the part of the Massachusetts delegates; they, in turn, would be objects of interest, subjects for careful inspection.

In Hartford they encountered Silas Deane, one of the Connecticut delegates. Deane was to stand forth as one of the impressive figures in the congress, but destined to become a pathetic one before the contest had ended. "The Congress", declared Deane magniloquently, "is the grandest and most important assembly ever held in America, . . . *all* of America is intrusted to it and depends upon it." His enthusiasm however swept him over far, when he declaimed, "The resolutions of the congress shall be the laws of the Medes and the Persians." In New Haven they met and had converse with another of Connecticut's delegates, that "solid, sensible man", Roger Sherman, who then and there proved his right to the characterization by boldly offering the opinion that Massachusetts might well "have rescinded that part of their Circular Letter where they allow Parliament to be the supreme Legislature over the Colonies in any case".

Ten days of this leisurely browsing brought them to New York City, where the hobnobbing continued on an even more extensive scale. Isaac Low, one of New York's delegates-elect, would loudly profess attachment to the cause of liberty, but (so it was whispered) there were those who doubted his sincerity. (Many another man, during the succeeding months, would be pursued by interrogation points.) John Alsop, another delegate, was reputed to be "of a good heart", but "unequal to the trust in point of abilities." Adams thought him "a soft, sweet man". (Too soft and too sweet, no doubt, for such parlous times, Alsop went along cheerfully until they came to that parting of the ways called the Declaration of Independence; then he refused to follow the procession farther.) In contrast, Philip Livingston was "a downright, straight forward man", "a great, rough, rapid mortal", who "blusters away" in such a manner that "there is no holding any conversation with him". Evidently Livingston wished to do some of the talking himself. He did taunt Adams with a reminder that Massachusetts had once indulged in a bit of Quaker-hanging. More than that, he opened his mouth and shockingly prophesied: "If England should turn us adrift, we should instantly go to civil wars among ourselves, to determine which colony should govern all the rest." Of James Duane, with whom Adams would soon be engaged in a tough wrestling match on the floor of Congress, the first impressions were that he had "a sly, surveying eye, a little squint eyed ... very sensible, I think, and very artful". Of John Jay, also to become one of the leading antagonists of the Adams program, the Bostonian learned little except that he was a bright young lawyer and a good speaker. All this round of "breakfasting, dining, drinking coffee, etc., about the city" was "very disagreeable on some accounts", still it had its uses.

Ambling on down through New Jersey they came to Princeton, where they met the president of the college, the Reverend Doctor Witherspoon, drank a glass of wine with him at his house, afterward shared a dish of coffee with him at their lodgings. Between the wine and the coffee Adams became convinced that Doctor Witherspoon was "as high a son of liberty as any man in America". The next day being Sunday, Adams also took the doctor's measure as a preacher: "Heard Dr. Witherspoon all day", he recorded. While Witherspoon would not be in the congress now gathering, he was destined to become, at a vital moment, a member of the subsequent congress and to prove his right to the title, "high son of liberty". Meanwhile, as he had taken an important part in the New Jersey proceedings, he could furnish the Massachusetts delegate much enlightenment respecting the state of mind in New Jersey in general, and more particularly of the state and the quality of mind of one of the New Jersey delegates, namely, William Livingston, whom he characterized as "very sincere and very able in the public cause, but a bad speaker, though a good writer". From a young lawyer named Jonathan Dickinson Sergeant, himself also destined to become a member of the so-called "Second Congress", they learned much respecting the delegates-elect of other states, particularly those of

New York, Pennsylvania, and Virginia. Of two of their delegates, said Sergeant, the Virginians speak in raptures. Patrick Henry and Richard Henry Lee were the Demosthenes and Cicero of America. No doubt a feast of oratory would be spread when the congress assembled; but Adams, impatient for action, was to become "fed-up" on oratory.

On to Philadelphia. If for a time all eyes had been turned toward Boston, now all were focused on Philadelphia, about to become the dazzling center of the somewhat dazed American world. And Philadelphia was all primed to do its part nobly and effectively. For one thing, it would give these men of the other colonies the time of their lives. It would extend to them such a joyous welcome and spread before them such lavish entertainments that the memories thereof would be cherished to the closing days of their lives. For another thing, if the eastern delegates had been eager to take the measures of those of the other colonies, certainly the statesmen of Pennsylvania would be no less eager to discover what manner of men the New Englanders were, and more especially those two Bostonian fire-eaters, Samuel and John Adams. To begin the zestful welcome a goodly number of the notables of the city, together with a few of the recently arrived delegates from other colonies, journeyed out beyond the city limits to greet the cavalcade of eastern delegates, even as weary and sore they jogged along on this last lap of their pilgrimage, and to escort them into the city, where the welcome would be redoubled and entertainments multiplied. At the city tavern other notables, along with "a multitude" of the less notable, awaited them, "dirty, dusty, and fatigued" though they were, to engage them in conversation, then to offer them a supper, "as elegant as ever was laid on a table".

This was Monday, August 29, and, though the Congress was scheduled to assemble on the following Thursday, another Monday would come before there would be delegates enough to organize and get down to business. Perhaps it was just as well. The week could be profitably occupied in spying out the land and one another; for others than James Duane had eager ears, if not also sly, surveying eyes. And how better could all this be done than at sumptuous tables? Philadelphia could and did provide the sumptuous tables. Breakfasts, dinners, suppers, followed one another in unbroken procession; and even betwixt times groups might gather to drink punch and eat dried smoked sprats. There were "mighty feasts", "sinful feasts", every imaginable thing to eat, every desirable thing to drink. And if now and then some of the delegates became "very high" (it is open to question whether Adams uses the expression with a political or a bibulous connotation), it is not of record that any of them at any time became *very low*. Adams avers that for his part, unaccustomed though he was, he met the tests with a fair degree of success.

Strange to tell, however, the Pennsylvania delegates for the most part seem to have made themselves conspicuous by their absence from these tables, as they likewise for the most part failed to take conspicuous parts in the later contest. The chief exception was Thomas Mifflin, who practically kept open house for the visiting delegates—"a grand, spacious, and elegant house", Adams records. What was more, Quaker though he was, Mifflin proved himself militant enough to satisfy the Massachusetts men. Another Philadelphian who assiduously cultivated the men of the east was John Dickinson, author of the famous "Letters of a Pennsylvania Farmer". To make his first call on the Bostonians he drove from his country seat "in his coach with four beautiful horses". He hoped to make a good impression, and he did. "Mr. Dickinson", Adams confided to his Diary, "is a very modest man, and very ingenious as well as very agreeable; he has an excellent heart, and the cause of his country lies near it." Though not yet a delegate to the Congress he soon would be, and in due time he and Adams would find themselves crossing political swords and clashing sharp tongues. Fortunately Adams did not afterward turn back the pages of his Diary to erase the record of his first impressions. Rather, he dug deep into his vocabulary for other labels.

It was on the second morning of their sojourn in Philadelphia that Adams and his brethren "had much conversation" with a man named Charles Thomson, reputed to be "the Sam Adams of Philadelphia, the life of the cause of liberty, they say". They say! Could it be possible that the man who was the life of the cause of liberty in Philadelphia had remained wholly unknown to the men who had been playing similar parts in Boston, that "cradle of liberty"? Certainly the lusty cries of the Boston infant had been heard in Philadelphia. But this is only one of the many revelations of the profound ignorance of one another that prevailed amongst the colonies. No wonder that in such soil jealousies and suspicions should take root and grow. Anyway, all the delegates would soon know this Charles Thomson, for he was about to become the secretary of Congress, to remain the wedded spouse of that body until the demise of the Congress did them part.

Among the first to extend the welcoming hand to the Massachusetts delegation was Thomas McKean, essentially of the Philadelphia group, although actually a delegate from the "Three Lower Counties", already in business for themselves and presently to constitute themselves the state of Delaware. There seemed to be no reason why Adams should not be satisfied with McKean and McKean with Adams. But it was another delegate from the Three Lower Counties that actually set John Adams to gurgling. "Caesar Rodney", Adams wrote, "is the oddest looking man in the world; he is tall, thin and slender as a reed, pale; his face is not bigger than a large apple, yet there is sense and fire, spirit, wit, and humor in his countenance." Rodney himself was meanwhile measuring his associates in the Congress. "All the seven delegates appointed for Virginia are here", he wrote, "and more sensible fine fellows you'd never wish to see, in short it is the greatest assembly (in proportion to the number) that ever was collected in America." The Bostonians, he went on to say, had been condemned by many for their violence, but, compared to those from Virginia, South Carolina, and Rhode Island, they were moderate men.

Of the southern delegates Adams was less sure than was Rodney, but in characteristic manner he proceeded to measure them and to label them. Henry Middleton of South Carolina he found to be "silent and reserved"—evidently inclined to keep his own counsel. Of the two brothers Rutledge, the appearance of the elder, John, was "not very promising". "There is no keenness in his eye, no depth in his countenance; nothing of the profound, sagacious, brilliant, or sparkling." Later, when he found Rutledge and himself more in unison, he conceived a better opinion of him. Edward Rutledge was "high enough" (meaning evidently his political views); likewise he was "sprightly", "but not deep", "good natured though conceited". But the South Carolinian soon got on the New Englander's nerves. "Young Ned Rutledge", Adams later wrote, "is a perfect Bob-o-Lincoln—a swallow, a sparrow, a peacock; excessively vain, excessively weak, and excessively variable and unsteady; jejune, inane, and puerile." (Can it be that John Adams had exhausted his vocabulary?) Thomas Lynch is characterized as "a solid, firm, judicious man", with whom they were all "vastly pleased". At a dinner, "Mr. Lynch gave us a sentiment: 'The brave Dantzickers, who declare they will be free in the face of the greatest monarch in Europe'." (Roll away a hundred and sixty-five years, and lo! Poland would again be undergoing dismemberment; but Danzig will have reversed the picture.) Silas Deane amplified in several particulars the portrait of Lynch, who, declared Deane, "carries with him more force in his very appearance than most powdered folks in their conversation. He wears his hair strait, his clothes in the plainest order, and is highly esteemed." Perhaps the best known of all the South Carolinians was the fiery Christopher Gadsden, of whom Deane wrote: "Mr. Gadsden leaves all New England Sons of Liberty far behind, for he is for taking up his firelock and marching direct to Boston." Indeed Gadsden had affirmed that, "were his wife and children all in Boston, and they were to perish by the sword, it would not alter his sentiment or proceeding for American Liberty". (Gadsden seems to have been unduly rash, even for times so raw.)

Inasmuch as Virginia had been most forward in support of Massachusetts, Adams was especially eager to meet the Virginia delegates, four of whom, Peyton Randolph, Benjamin Harrison, Richard Henry Lee, and Richard Bland, arrived in the afternoon of September 2. A little converse with them, and Adams declared, "These gentlemen from Virginia appear to be the most spirited and consistent of any. Harrison said he would have come on foot rather than not come. Bland said he would have gone, upon this occasion, if it had been to Jericho." After a breakfast-table talk with Lee next morning, Adams set Lee down as "a masterly man". Physically, Randolph was "a large, well looking man", Lee "a tall, spare man", Bland "a learned, bookish man". Silas Deane drew a better portrait of Randolph: "Of an affable, open, and majestic deportment, large in size, though not out of proportion, he commands respect and esteem by his very aspect." It was Deane who described Harrison as "an uncommonly large man . . . rather rough in his dress and speech"; but it was Adams who later characterized him as "an indolent, luxurious, heavy gentleman, of no use in Congress or committee, but a great embarrassment to both". This, however, was when enthusiasms had cooled and the wires of purposes had become crossed. As the other Virginia delegates, Edmund Pendleton, Patrick Henry, and George Washington, did not arrive until Sunday, they failed to get their portraits hung in the Adams gallery at this time. It was Deane again, who a few days later supplied sketches of them. Pendleton was "of easy and cheerful countenance, polite in address, and elegant if not eloquent in style and elocution". Henry was "the compleatest speaker" he had ever heard. (Congress had then had some "samples" of the celebrated Virginian's oratory.) Colonel Washington was a tall man, of a "hard" countenance, "yet with a very young look, and an easy, soldier like air and gesture . . . speaks very modestly and in determined style and accent". What particularly placed him high in the estimation of the New Englanders was the speech he was said to have made in the House of Burgesses, when he offered to raise and arm and lead one thousand men himself at his own expense for the defense of the country.

Came Saturday night, and all the delegates who had arrived gathered for one grand feast of reason and flow of soul. "We drank sentiments till eleven o'clock", says Adams, and among the toasts were: "Union of the Colonies"; "Unanimity to the Congress"; "Union of Britain and the Colonies on a Constitutional Foundation". The toasts were in fact prayers, and well might they pray, for their aims would be long in the attainment and not without many a hard wrestle.

Others than John Adams had no doubt been busy the while plying their political thermometers and stethoscopes, but Adams beyond all others has left charts of his tests and diagnoses. Fortunately one who was for the moment the chief of the rival school of political medicos has left some record of his probes and prognoses. Joseph Galloway, speaker of the Pennsylvania House of Representatives and delegate in Congress for that colony, was as eager as any man to discover what the Congress was like to do, and none more anxious to steer its course away from the vortexes of extreme measures. At the close of that busy week of dinings and winings and diplomatic maneuverings Galloway made a report of progress to Governor William Franklin of New Jersey, a man of like opinions and purposes. He had been endeavoring, he wrote, "to find out the Temper of the Delegates" and, after sounding them as best he could, he was of opinion that they would "behave with Temper and Moderation".

The Boston commissioners were "warm" (no one could have expected them to be cool), although "in their Behaviour and Conversation very modest, yet not so much so as not to throw out Hints, which, like Straws and Feathers, tell us from which Point of the Compass the Wind comes." One man he had found with views that marched side by side with his own (in so far as he had explained himself)—John Rutledge of South Carolina, who, beyond all others, had weighed the arguments pro and con and was keenly aware of the consequences that would flow from rash measures. To a number of the delegates Galloway had intimated his own idea of the moderate and tentative course that the Congress should adopt, such a course as could not, in his opinion, "fail to give Strength to our Cause, and, if not immediately, in the End bring the Government to attend to Reason and redress our Aggrievances".

John Adams would no doubt have been delighted to know that Galloway, of all men, had deemed him modest in his behavior and conversation. Midway the sitting of Congress he confided to William Tudor: "We have had numberless prejudices to remove here. We have been obliged to act with great delicacy and caution. We have been obliged to keep ourselves out of sight, and to feel pulses, and to sound the depths; to insinuate our sentiments, designs, and desires, by means of other persons, sometimes of one province, and sometimes of another." For the feeling of pulses, the sounding of depths, the insinuations of designs had not ceased with the preliminary week of amenities; skirmishing continued through the session, notwithstanding the frequent frontal attacks and the stanch defenses.

By Sunday, September 4, the majority of the delegates destined to the Congress had arrived, with only a few stragglers to make their belated appearance. The stage was set; the drama about to begin. Taking the Congress as a whole, it was a notable body of men; with a few exceptions, probably the pick of the colonies. Nine of them, namely, Eliphalet

Dyer of Connecticut, Philip Livingston of New York, Thomas McKean and Caesar Rodney of Delaware, John Dickinson and John Morton of Pennsylvania, and Thomas Lynch, Christopher Gadsden, and John Rutledge of South Carolina, had been members of the Stamp Act Congress of 1765, constituting in fact one-third of that body. One of them, Stephen Hopkins of Rhode Island, had been a member of the Albany Congress of 1754. Of the fifty-six men who, first and last, attended the Congress of 1774, most of them would reappear in the succeeding Congress. On the other hand, many of them, as the years went by and the political winds shifted their courses, would be compelled to yield their places to others. A few indeed would of their own will and purpose slip away, to commune no more with the men on revolution bent.

CHAPTER III

THE FIRST CONGRESS

DECLARATION OF RIGHTS, THE ASSOCIATION

From the beginning it was clear enough that the Congress would be divided into two main groups, conservatives, aiming at patching up the quarrel, and radicals, determined upon resistance. In the forefront of the conservative forces were Galloway of Pennsylvania and Duane and Jay of New York, whilst strenuously pressing for "vigorous measures" were the Massachusetts and Virginia delegations, each group with its allies. One of the first tests of strength came before ever their organization had been effected, and was over the apparently innocuous question where Congress should hold its sessions.

The question arose as of course when the delegates first drew together informally at the City Tavern. Galloway, as speaker of the Pennsylvania assembly, offered the use of the State House, the carpenters their own hall, the one a provincial chamber, the other a private house. Duane contended that acceptance of the speaker's offer was "a piece of respect" due to him; but the fact that the Galloway party preferred the State House was a good reason why the other party should not. The choice of Carpenter's Hall, they argued, would be "highly agreeable to the mechanics and citizens in general". Good politics. Travel might be slow, but minds were quick and keen. They would take a view of each; but first, to Carpenter's Hall. From the City Tavern to Carpenter's Hall therefore they proceeded, on foot. "The general cry was that this was a good room." For one thing, there was an "excellent library"; for another, there was "a long entry where gentlemen may walk". The library would be useful, and there would no doubt come times when gentlemen would do well to take a walk. A little walking sometimes served to cool mental heats, to promote calmer reflection. The vote, although not quite unanimous, was to stay. (Gallo-

way afterward asserted that the question had already been "privately
settled by an Interest made out of Doors".)

Proceeding then to organization, the choice of a chairman, Peyton
Randolph, speaker of the Virginia House of Burgesses, was accomplished with complete unanimity; but when it came to the election of
a secretary the two parties again found themselves at odds. The Galloway party wished to choose a member of the Congress, and they appear
to have picked on Silas Deane of Connecticut. The froward faction,
on the other hand, nominated Charles Thomson, leader of the radical
movement in Pennsylvania, and elected him. (That matter also, Galloway declared, had been fixed out of doors.) Galloway, to whom Thomson was as rank poison, had in fact maneuvered the election of delegates in Pennsylvania so as to eliminate Thomson and was therefore
greatly chagrined that his purpose to keep Thomson out of Congress
had been defeated. The majority for Thomson as secretary was, however, so large that opposition was withdrawn, and his election also was
recorded as unanimous. (No need for straws and feathers to determine
the direction of that wind.)

Between the election of the chairman and the election of the secretary came two other decisions, not even officially recorded (James
Duane does, however, record them), namely, that the body should be
called "The Congress", and the chairman should be styled "The President". Thus originated the two principal titles in our present governmental organization. The Congress provided for by the Constitution of
1787 is in a real sense the successor of the Congress of 1774; on the
other hand, the President of the United States is scarcely in any sense
the successor of the presidents of the old Congress. The presidents of
Congress were almost solely presiding officers, possessing scarcely a
shred of executive or administrative functions; whereas the President
of the United States is almost solely an executive officer, with no presiding duties at all. Barring a likeness in social and diplomatic pre-
cedence, the two offices are identical only in the possession of the same
title.

The reading of the credentials of the several delegations was a reminder, if any were needed, that the purpose of the Congress was not
revolution, however much some delegates may have had such an ob-

jective in the back of their heads; rather, it was the redress of grievances, the restoration of harmony with Great Britain. Massachusetts, for
instance, the raging center of the disturbance, instructed her delegates

to consult upon the present state of the Colonies, and the miseries to which
they are and must be reduced by the operation of certain acts of parliament
respecting America, and to deliberate and determine upon wise and proper
measures, to be by them recommended to all the Colonies, for the recovery
and establishment of their just rights and liberties, civil and religious, and
the restoration of union and harmony between Great Britain and the Colonies, most ardently desired by all good men.

The New Hampshire delegates were instructed

to devise, consult, and adopt measures, as may have the most likely tendency
to extricate the Colonies from their present difficulties; to secure and perpetuate their rights, liberties, and privileges, and to restore that peace, harmony, and mutual confidence which once happily subsisted between the
parent country and her Colonies.

Rhode Island likewise aimed at "proper measures to establish the
rights and liberties of the Colonies, upon a just and solid foundation".
Connecticut merely specified as the objective "proper measures for advancing the best good of the Colonies". The New York and New Jersey delegates came without specific instructions.

The credentials of the Pennsylvania delegates pointed out that the
purpose of the Congress was

to consult together upon the unhappy State of the Colonies, and to form
and adopt a plan for the purpose of obtaining redress of American grievances, ascertaining American rights upon the most solid and constitutional
principles, and for establishing that Union and harmony between Great
Britain and the Colonies, which is indispensably necessary to the welfare
and happiness of both.

"The Three Counties, Newcastle, Kent, and Sussex, on Delaware"
went to a greater length than did any of the other colonies in specifying
the measures of the British government that were deemed to be obnoxious, then authorized her delegates, in consultation with the deputies from the other colonies, "to determine upon all such prudent and

lawful measures, as may be judged most expedient for the Colonies immediately and unitedly to adopt, in order to obtain relief for an oppressed people, and the redress of our general grievances." Maryland's instructions, coherent enough, but without fervor or flourish, were "to effect one general plan of conduct, operating on the commercial connexion of the colonies with the mother country, for the relief of Boston, and preservation of American liberty."

The Virginia convention expressed as its opinion

that it will be highly conducive to the security and happiness of the British Empire, that a general congress of deputies from all the Colonies, assemble as quickly as the nature of their situations will admit, to consider of the most proper and effectual manner of so operating on the commercial connexion of the colonies with the Mother Country, as to procure redress for the much injured province of Massachusetts-Bay, to secure British America from the ravage and ruin of arbitrary taxes, and speedily as possible to procure the return of that harmony and Union, so beneficial to the whole Empire, and so ardently desired by all British America.

The North Carolina credentials (presented September 14) expressed approval of the proposed congress

to deliberate upon the present state of British America, and to take such measures, as they may deem prudent, to effect the purpose of describing with certainty the rights of Americans, repairing the breaches made in those rights, and for guarding them for the future from any such violations done under the sanction of public Authority.

South Carolina, like Delaware, cited the several "grievances under which America labors", "which acts and bills in the precedent and consequences affect the whole Continent of America", and empowered her delegates "to concert, agree to, and effectually to prosecute such legal measures, as . . . shall be most likely to obtain a repeal of the said acts, and a redress of those grievances".

In perfecting the organization of the Congress it was essential at the outset to determine the method of voting, "whether it should be by Colonies, or by the poll, or by Interests". In the Stamp Act Congress the vote had been by colonies, but Patrick Henry insisted that the practice of that Congress should not be accepted as a precedent. The congress now gathered, said Henry, was really the first general congress convened on the continent, but he was of opinion that "we should have occasion for more general congresses", therefore a precedent ought to be established now, by the formation of "such a System as would give each Colony a Just Weight in our deliberations". "It would be a great injustice", he argued, "if a little Colony should have the same weight in the councils of America as a great one." For his part he would be content if the relative weights should be determined on the basis of populations, although, he took pains to say, he would not include slaves in the count. In the course of his remarks upon this subject Henry launched into an eloquent dissertation upon the thesis that, by the oppression of Parliament, "Government is dissolved. . . . We are in a state of nature, sir." Swept on by his enthusiasm he exclaimed, "The distinctions between Virginians, Pennsylvanians, New Yorkers, and New Englanders, are no more. I am not a Virginian, but an American."

Detached from its context Henry's declamation sounds like a proposal to wipe out all colonial boundaries and start out anew; yet every one in that assembly knew well enough that the Virginian was only contending that his colony should have a voice in the determinations of Congress in accordance with its relative importance. Nevertheless he started thoughts that went beyond the simple question at issue. John Jay, for instance—no rampant revolutionist he, the rather a cautious and wise counsellor, mindful of the instructions by which the delegates were bound, and anxious to check impetuous decisions—declined to follow the Virginian in his headlong plunge to the conclusion that all government was at an end and wild, crude nature had taken its place. It was not for this Congress, he maintained, to set about framing an American system of government. Not yet. Spoke he: "The measure of arbitrary power is not full, and I think it must run over, before we undertake to frame a new constitution." The task rather was to endeavor "to correct the faults in an old one". "Arbitrary power not run over!" some of his hearers must have snorted. "What then do you call this mess into which we have been plunged?" Henry's colleague, Benjamin Harrison, chimed in with a warning that "if such a disrespect should be put upon his countrymen" as not to allow Virginia any greater weight in the determinations than one of the smallest colonies, he was "very apprehensive . . . we should never see them at another convention".

Others, among them Lynch of South Carolina, would have the relative weights determined by a combination of numbers and property. To all the arguments, whether for numbers or property or the two combined, the smaller colonies had one short, crisp reply: "We come if necessary to make a Sacrifice of our all, and the weakest Colony by such a Sacrifice would suffer as much as the greatest." It was John Rutledge of South Carolina who offered the timely reminder that, after all, Congress was only a body of representatives, ambassadors, as it were, gathered for consultation and counsel. Said he: "We have no legal authority; and obedience to our determinations will only follow the reasonableness, the apparent utility and necessity of the measures we adopt. . . . Our constituents are bound only in honor to observe our determinations." The discussion was brought to a conclusion by the general acknowledgement that the means for determining the relative weights of the colonies were not immediately available, even if such a criterion for voting should be resolved upon; therefore it was agreed that each colony should have one vote. But to make sure that the decision should not be drawn into a precedent by any future congress, it was resolved to make an entry in the Journal to that effect. The entry was duly made; but precedent nevertheless it did in fact become.

The debate over the method of voting had unquestionably waxed warm, and there were no doubt a good many exhibitions of temper. Thought Thomas Cushing of Massachusetts, it might be conducive to harmony if Congress had a season of prayer every morning before entering upon the daily grind, and he accordingly made a motion to that end. But no, declared some of the members; that will never do. Commingled sects, as we are—Episcopalians, Congregationalists, Presbyterians, Quakers, Anabaptists—"we could not join in the same act of worship". Whereupon up rose Samuel Adams—a man of piety he (notwithstanding his addiction to devious political ways)—to declare that he was "no bigot"; he "could hear a prayer from a gentleman of piety and virtue, who was at the same time a friend to his country"; therefore he moved that the Reverend Mr. Duché, an Episcopal clergyman, be requested to open Congress tomorrow morning with prayers.

The motion was seconded, carried, and the invitation extended accordingly. Adams himself acknowledged that his pious purpose was not uninfluenced by a political motive. "Many of our warmest friends", he confided, "are members of the Church of England."

But for an intervening event, it is quite probable that the hour of devotions that Wednesday morning, September 7, would have left little record other than a brief entry in the Journal or some incidental allusion such as that of the unemotional Duane. It came about however that, before adjournment on the 6th, Congress had been thrown into a fever of excitement by a confused account of a bombardment of Boston, wherein, shouted the rumor, six of the inhabitants had been killed. "This City is in the utmost confusion", Silas Deane wrote to his wife that night; "all the bells toll muffled, and the most unfeigned marks of sorrow appear in every countenance." Next morning came what appeared to be a confirmation of the report, and Deane again took up his pen to write: "All is confusion . . . every tongue pronounces revenge. The bells toll muffled, and the people run as in a case of extremity, they know not where nor why." "War! war! war! was the cry", wrote John Adams, "and it was pronounced in a tone which would have done honor to the oratory of a Briton or a Roman."

It was in such an atmosphere of tenseness that the Rev. Mr. Duché arose that September morning to open Congress with prayer. Turning to the psalter for the seventh day of the month, which included the thirty-fifth psalm, he read:

Plead my cause, O Lord, with them that strive with me; fight against them that fight against me. Take hold of shield and buckler, and stand up for mine help. Draw out also the spear, and stop the way against them that persecute me: say unto my soul, I am thy salvation. Let them be confounded and put to shame that seek after my soul: let them be turned back and brought to confusion that devise my hurt. Let them be as chaff before the wind: and let the angel of the Lord chase them. Let their way be dark and slippery: and let the angel of the Lord persecute them. For without cause have they hid for me their net in a pit, which without cause they have digged for my soul. Let destruction come upon him at unawares; and let his net that he hath hid catch himself: into that very destruction let him fall. And my soul shall be joyful in the Lord; it shall rejoice in his salvation.

. . . They rewarded me evil for good to the spoiling of my soul. . . . I behaved myself as though he had been my friend or brother; I bowed down heavily, as one that mourneth for his mother. . . . With hypocritical mockers in feasts, they gnashed upon me with their teeth. Lord, how long wilt thou look on? rescue my soul from their destructions. . . . For they speak not peace; but they devise deceitful matters against them that are quiet in the land. . . . Stir up thyself, and awake to my judgment, even unto my cause, my God and my Lord. . . .

Still more he read; and as he read, "I never", declared John Adams, "saw a greater effect upon an audience. It seemed as if Heaven had ordained that psalm to be read on that morning. After this Mr. Duché, unexpectedly to everybody, struck out into an extemporary prayer . . . a prayer . . . as pertinent, as affectionate, as sublime, as devout, as I ever heard offered up to Heaven. He filled every bosom present." It was a prayer, wrote Silas Deane, "worth riding one hundred miles to hear". He "prayed without book about ten minutes so pertinently, with such fervency, purity and sublimity of style and sentiment, and with such an apparent sensibility of the scenes and business before us, that even Quakers shed tears". Declared Samuel Ward, it was "one of the most sublime, catholic, well-adapted prayers I ever heard". "A most excellent extemporary prayer", wrote Samuel Adams with customary restraint, rejoicing inwardly the while over the happy outcome of his little maneuver. And he could not but have been deeply gratified, when a little later he learned, as doubtless he did, what Joseph Reed had whispered to John Adams, that Congress was never "more guilty of a more masterly stroke of policy" than when they put up the Rev. Mr. Duché to read prayers.

The story of the bombardment of Boston proved to have been false; for all that had happened was that General Gage had taken away the provincial powder from the magazine at Cambridge, and *"no blood had been spilled"*; nevertheless it had served to lift Congress to new heights of perfervid zeal for the defense of American rights. It "made us completely miserable for two days", John Adams wrote to his wife. "If it had proved true, you would have heard the thunder of an American Congress." Meanwhile the Rev. Mr. Duché basked in a blaze of glory, his praise on every lip. Another day, and if he heard half the hard, the harsh, the ungracious things then said about him, his ears would have burned with a different kind of fire.

It was in this tense mood, amid this quickening of enthusiasms, that Congress attacked the important task that lay before it. Two committees were appointed; the one, to prepare a statement of the rights of the colonies, the infringements of those rights, and the most proper means of obtaining a restoration of them; the other, to report upon the several statutes that affected the trade and manufactures of the colonies. To the first committee were assigned two members from each colony; to the second, one member from each. As only eleven colonies were then represented, these committees consisted of twenty-two and eleven members, respectively; but upon the appearance on September 14 of the North Carolina members, William Hooper and Joseph Hewes, both were assigned to the first committee, and Hooper also to the second. On September 17, as a concession to the three most populous colonies, Massachusetts, Virginia, and Pennsylvania, each of them was given an additional member on the large committee.

While these committees were actively engaged in their respective tasks, Congress assembled only occasionally. In pursuit of its objectives, the large committee created (September 9) a sub-committee to draw up a statement of rights, and another (September 14) to prepare a statement respecting the infringements. On September 17 the committee to examine the statutes made its report, which was referred to the committee on rights. The latter committee presently offered two reports, one on rights (September 22), another on infringements (September 24). Of what went on in these committees little is definitely known, except that, on September 8, James Duane addressed the committee on rights on the subject before them, later offered a series of propositions, while Samuel Ward recorded, under September 9: "The Committee met, agreed to found our rights upon the laws of nature, the principles of the English Constitution, and charters and compacts."

Years afterward John Adams, drawing upon his recollections, summarized the chief perplexities thus:

The two points which labored most were: 1. Whether we should recur to the law of nature, as well as to the British constitution, and our American charters and grants. . . . 2. The other great question was, what authority we should concede to Parliament; whether we should deny the authority of Parliament in all cases; whether we should allow any authority to it in our internal affairs; or whether we should allow it to regulate the trade of the empire with or without any restrictions.

It was while this controversy was raging that, with some degree of finesse credited to Samuel Adams, a small bomb, loaded with political explosives, was touched off in the assembled Congress. This was a concoction of revolutionary resolves brought down from Suffolk County, Massachusetts (the county of Boston), and laid before Congress September 17. Similar resolves from Middlesex County had been laid before Congress, September 14, and, according to Samuel Adams, were "read by the several members of this Body with high Applause". More particularly John Adams wrote: "The spirit, the firmness, the prudence of our province are vastly applauded, and we are universally acknowledged, the saviours and defenders of American liberty." (He could not refrain from adding, "A Tory here is the most despicable animal in the creation. Spiders, toads, snakes are their only proper emblems.")

It was the "Suffolk Resolves", however, that stirred Congress to action. Although predicated upon General Gage's movements to fortify the town of Boston, these resolves of the Suffolk Convention were a ringing indictment of the late acts of Parliament respecting the colonies, particularly those affecting Massachusetts, and declared that "no obedience is due from this province to either or any part of the acts", recommended to collectors of public moneys "not to make any payment thereof to the provincial county treasurer until the civil government of the province is placed upon a constitutional foundation", proposed a severance of trade relations with Great Britain, and further recommended that a provincial congress be called "to consult such measures as may be adopted, and vigorously executed by the whole people". Meanwhile, so the convention declared, despite "the many insults and oppressions" which they had experienced at the hands of the British government, they were "determined to act merely upon the defensive, so long as such conduct may be vindicated by reason and the principles of self-preservation, but no longer". Indeed the bold conventioners of the county of Suffolk indicated that any attempt to enforce the obnoxious measures would be resisted with what might they possessed. At the same time they were not neglectful of a becoming stroke of diplomacy. "Confiding in the wisdom and integrity of the continental Congress", they were disposed to "pay all due respect and submission" to such measures as the Congress should recommend "for the restoration and establishment of our just rights, civil and religious, and for renewing that harmony and union between Great-Britain and the colonies, so earnestly wished for by all good men".

The shrewd conventioners did not go amiss in their calculations. Congress bent a listful ear to their pleadings and straightway

Resolved unan, That this assembly deeply feels the sufferings of their countrymen in the Massachusetts-Bay . . . that they most thoroughly approve the wisdom and fortitude, with which opposition to these wicked ministerial measures has hitherto been conducted, and they earnestly recommend to their brethren, a perseverance in the same firm and temperate conduct as expressed in the resolutions determined upon . . . trusting that the effects of the united efforts of North America in their behalf, will carry such conviction to the British nation, of the unwise, unjust, and ruinous policy of the present administration, as quickly to introduce better men and wiser measures.

And that this their decision might be known of all men, good or bad, the Congress ordered their resolution, together with the Suffolk Resolves, to be printed. In a further resolution it was recommended that the colonies continue their contributions "for supplying the necessities, and alleviating the distresses of our brethren at Boston".

That night, before he laid him down to sleep, John Adams unbosomed himself to his Diary thus: "This was one of the happiest days of my life. In Congress we had generous, noble sentiments, and manly eloquence. This day convinced me that America will support the Massachusetts or perish with her." And the next day he wrote to his wife:

The esteem, the affection, the admiration for the people of Boston and the Massachusetts which were expressed yesterday, and the fixed determination that they should be supported, were enough to melt a heart of stone. I saw tears gush into the eyes of the old grave pacific Quakers of Pennsylvania.

"The spirited and patriotick Resolves of your County of Suffolk", Samuel Adams wrote to Charles Chauncy two days later, ". . . were read with great applause", and he assured his correspondent that the resolutions passed by Congress gave but a faint idea of the spirit of that assembly. Indeed he was ready to promise "that America will make a point of supporting Boston to the utmost".

With the results thus far Adams seems to have been well satisfied, and he was doubtless more so when, five days later (September 22), Congress espoused another request of the Suffolk convention by recommending a suspension of commercial intercourse with Great Britain, "until the sense of Congress, on the means to be taken for the preservation of the liberties of America, is made public". Adams must, however, have reflected upon his assurance that Congress would support Boston "to the utmost"; for on September 25 he addressed to James Warren a note of caution respecting the matter of resistance. Congress had not come to final resolutions, he stated, therefore it became them "to be deliberate"—but "they have great dependence upon your tried patience and fortitude". As to the proposal to call a provincial congress, he very much questioned "whether they will ever be prevailed on to think it necessary for you to set up another form of government". It was of the greatest importance, he added, not only that American opposition be united, but that it should "be conducted so as to concur with the opposition of our friends in England". And Samuel Adams knew, none better, how to watch the hands of the political clock.

John Adams likewise, though more prone than his colleague and namesake to impatience, spoke his word of caution to his compatriots in Boston (he was writing to Joseph Palmer). As he interpreted the general opinion in Congress, it was deemed practicable for Massachusetts "to live wholly without a Legislature and Courts of Justice as long as will be necessary to obtain Relief". In short, their answer was, "Stand still, bear with Patience, if you come to a Rupture with the Troops all is lost." It would certainly involve the whole continent in a war. In fact, the ministry would rejoice at such an excuse for pushing hostilities against us. "Resuming the first Charter, Absolute Indepen-[den]cy, etc.", Adams ventured to remark, "are Ideas which Startle People here." (To be sure, the Massachusetts leaders had solemnly asseverated that they were not aiming at independence; but even so, was that any reason why the word should not be used between bosom friends concealed behind the shrubbery?) Ventured Adams a little later: "We have a delicate course to steer."

In all this while the parties of the second part felt that they also had a delicate course to steer, and there was accordingly much maneuvering and not a little dallying. In Philadelphia the round of dinners and banquets went merrily on.

Friday [September 16] we had a grand entertainment at the State House [Silas Deane wrote to his wife] . . . plenty of every thing eatable and drinkable, and no scarcity of good humor and diversion. . . . You will begin to suspect we do nothing else, but I assure you it is hard work. We meet at nine and sit until three, by which time we are unable to do anything but eat and drink the rest of the day.

"My time", wrote John Adams (September 14), "is totally filled from the moment I get out of bed until I return to it. Visits, ceremonies, company, business, newspapers, pamphlets, etc., etc., etc." From nine to three "most earnestly engaged in debates upon the most abstruse mysteries of state", at four a dinner "with some of the nobles of Pennsylvania", where they would "feast upon ten thousand delicacies, and sit drinking Madeira, Claret, and Burgundy, till six or seven, and then go home fatigued to death. . . . Yet I hold it out surprisingly." At one dinner they sat down to "Turtle, and every other thing, flummery, jellies, sweetmeats of twenty sorts, trifles, whipped sillabubs, floating islands, fools, etc., and then a dessert of fruits, raisins, almonds, pears, peaches. Wines most excellent and admirable. I drank Madeira at a great rate, and found no inconvenience in it." At all events, he was able to get to his lodgings and write it all down. A month of this, and he sighed, "I shall be killed with kindness in this place."

Ten days more of it, and his patience was exhausted, his nerves worn to a frazzle. "I am wearied to death with the life I lead", he groaned. "The business of Congress is tedious beyond expression. This assembly is like no other that ever existed. Every man in it . . . must show his oratory, his criticism, and his political abilities." Every question was discussed "with a moderation, an acuteness, a minuteness equal to that of Queen Elizabeth's privy council". He supposed that upon a motion that three and two make five, "we should be entertained with logic and rhetoric, law, history, politics, and mathematics." The consequence was that business was "drawn and spun out to an immeasurable length". At another time he wrote: "Tedious indeed is our business—slow as snails. . . . Fifty gentlemen meeting together, all strangers, are not acquainted with each other's language, ideas, views, designs. They are therefore jealous of each other—fearful, timid, skittish." Such in fact was the diversity of religions, educations, manners, interests, he declared, that it would seem "almost impossible to unite in any one plan of conduct". Adams was by no means, however, the only one who was impatient at the tedious delay. From the opposite camp also came grumbling. "There is very little in all this bustle", wrote George Read of Delaware. "We are wide of our business."

Not yet able to agree on what were their rights or what the infringements upon them, Congress turned aside, September 24, from the consideration of those questions to devote a period of deliberation to "the means most proper to be pursued for a restoration of our rights". Already the nature of the means to be adopted had been indicated in the general approval of the Suffolk Resolves, particularly in the non-intercourse resolution of September 22. Followed two or three days of debate, partly over the questions whether the means should include a non-exportation and a non-consumption, as well as a non-importation measure; but more especially whether these measures should be put into effect immediately or on the first of November or the first of December. In the course of the debate tobacco and wheat, rice and indigo, tar, pitch, and turpentine, flax seed and lumber, fish and oil, sugar and molasses, coffee, wine, and even tea, wrestled and tussled all over the lot. On September 27, Congress got so far as to resolve (and that unanimously) in favor of non-importation and non-consumption and to fix the date at December 1st. When it came, however, to the question of non-exportation, the contest became fierce. Many believed that a scheme of non-exportation would be ruinous, especially to the southern colonies, whose markets were almost wholly in Europe. Rice, in particular, entered the lists against all comers, demanding to be made an exception. It lost in the first bout, but later returned to the combat and won. On the 30th of September it was resolved that, from September 10, 1775, the exportation of every commodity whatsoever to Great Britain, Ireland, and the West Indies ought to cease unless the grievances of America had been redressed before that time. The adoption of this resolve did not entirely end the struggle, but it completed roughly the foundation on which would be laid what came to be called the Association.

Meanwhile, two days before, Congress had been set by the ears by the sudden stirring of a question of another kind. This was nothing less than "A Plan of a proposed Union between Great Britain and the Colonies", thrust upon Congress by Joseph Galloway. On the face of things there seemed to be the best of reasons for proposing some plan of union at this time. Had not statesmen here, there, and everywhere been proclaiming from the housetops that a threat against one colony was a threat against all? Had they not preached fervently and without ceasing the gospel of the "common cause" and pressed upon one and all the need for united effort amongst the colonies? Did not the very instructions that most of the delegates to Congress brought with them ring with assertions that the one great purpose of the Congress was a restoration of union and harmony between Great Britain and the colonies, "most ardently desired by all good men"? To that sentiment Galloway himself heartily subscribed, none more ardently. But were all those who piously professed such a desire and such an aim sincere? Were all of them good men? Galloway had his doubts on both scores.

There was Samuel Adams, for instance, a man who was "equal to most men in popular intrigue" and "most decisive and indefatigable in the pursuit of his objects". Aided and abetted by his colleagues, Adams had kept "continual expresses" going back and forth between Philadelphia and Boston, managing at one and the same time the faction in Congress and the factions in New England. Were they laboring so earnestly in behalf of a restoration of union and harmony? Not at all. On the contrary, their unceasing intrigues had a very different objective. They were busily stirring up sedition and aiming at a complete severance of the colonies from the mother country. Those "inflammatory resolves of the county of Suffolk", for instance, fomented by none other than this indefatigable and intriguing Samuel Adams, contained a complete declaration of war against Great Britain; while the several non-intercourse propositions that followed definitely tended in the same direction—"to inflame rather than reconcile—to produce war instead of peace between the two countries".

For his part, far from approving the ministerial policy or derogating from colonial rights, Galloway stanchly advocated asserting and safeguarding those rights; only he would have it done under the ægis of the British empire. It was therefore for the purpose of preserving that empire that he had offered his plan of union. But to save the colonies to the empire it was necessary to save the colonies to themselves. Accordingly he argued cogently that the welfare of the colonies depended upon the preservation of the union with Great Britain, and he besought Congress "candidly and thoroughly" to examine the real merits of the dispute with the mother country and to "take such ground as shall firmly unite us under one system of polity, and make us one people".

Accordingly, in introducing his plan, Galloway first of all endeavored to point out to Congress "the true line of their duty", by "tracing the rights of the Colonies to their origin, and fixing them on the most solid principles; and thence shewing the necessity of an union with the Mother State, for the recovery of them". Said he: "I am as much a friend of liberty as exists; and no man shall go further in point of fortune, or in point of blood, than the man who now addresses you." The gist of his argument was that "there must be one supreme legislative head in every civil society, whose authority must extend to the regulation and final decision of every matter susceptible of human direction", that "every member of the society . . . must be subordinate to its supreme will, signified in its laws", that, without this supremacy and subordination, "no society ever did or could exist".

From their first settlement, Galloway continued, Parliamentary jurisdiction had been constantly exercised over the colonies, which had always professed allegiance to the British government and claimed its protection (and protection and allegiance were reciprocal duties); and, if the authority of the parent state should be weakened or annulled, "the seeds of discord are plentifully sowed in the constitution of the colonies" such as could probably "only be settled by an appeal to the sword". The colonies were, in fact, only "so many inferior societies, destitute of any supreme direction or decision whatever; in short, "in respect to each other, in a perfect state of nature". He was free to confess that the exercise of Parliamentary authority was "not perfectly constitutional in respect to the colonies", in that "neither the land nor the people of America hold the least participation in the legislative authority of the State", a participation that was "the great principle upon which the freedom of the British Government is established and secured"; and it was his wish to see that right extended in some form, not only to America, but to all the British dominions, otherwise he feared "that profound and excellent fabrick of civil polity will, ere long, crumble to pieces".

The essence of Galloway's plan of union, which is similar in some respects to the plan proposed at Albany in 1754, is set forth in the first paragraph: "a British and American legislature, for regulating the administration of the general affairs of America", each colony to "retain its present constitution, and powers of regulating and governing its own internal police, in all cases whatsoever". In its simplest terms the plan provided that the government should be administered by a President-General, to be appointed by the king and to hold office during the king's pleasure, together with a Grand Council to be chosen once in three years by the assemblies of the several colonies, to meet once a year or oftener, as occasion might require, and to exercise all the rights, liberties, and privileges exercised by the House of Commons; but the assent of the President-General was requisite to all acts of the Grand Council. Further, it was provided that the President-General and the Grand Council should constitute "an inferior and distinct branch of the British legislature, united and incorporated with it" for the general purposes affecting the colonies, and that such general regulations might originate either in the Parliament of Great Britain or in the Grand Council, although the assent of both should be requisite to their validity.

It was not proposed, Galloway later stated, "as a perfect plan", nor one altogether in accord with his judgment; it would "admit of some very material additions", but he had purposely omitted whatever might obstruct that "accommodation" at which he aimed. In Congress the plan had the definite approval of Jay and Duane of New York and Edward Rutledge of South Carolina and had sufficient support other-

wise to obtain a vote for its future consideration. Subsequently, however, the critics of any plan that seemed designed to bind the colonies
more closely to Great Britain were able to muster a majority, and they
went so far as to expunge the whole matter from the record (October
22). By this time, in fact, what Galloway called "the violent party" had
gained such complete control of Congress that the moderates could be
pushed aside with but small consideration.

Although objections of a sort were offered to the plan, the real
objections do not stand out very clearly. It was contended, for instance,
that "the Delegates did not come with authority to consent to a political
union between the two countries"; to which it was replied that "they
had such authority or none". In any event, the proponents of the plan
insisted, "the Congress ought, in justice to their country, to digest and
form one, and recommend it to their respective Assemblies, by whom
it would be presented with more constitutional propriety than by any
other body of men". A second objection was that "it deprived the
Colony Legislatures of a part of their rights". (In the long struggle that
was to ensue over the consummation of a union this reluctance to part
with "rights" would be one of the most formidable obstacles.) The
answer now offered was that the plan, far from diminishing the rights
of any colony legislature, actually extended them, "by giving to each
a new jurisdiction to decide upon regulations which relate to the
general affairs of the colonies". In concluding his advocacy of the plan
Galloway appealed to Congress: "If we do not approve of a representation in Parliament, let us ask for a participation in the freedom and
power of the English constitution in some other mode of incorporation."

Congress might now scorn Galloway's doctrine of the necessity of
"one supreme legislative head", but before it had progressed very far
in its contest it would find itself in the predicament of trying to defend
and to further the common cause without the requisite power and
authority, and then it would take refuge behind that same principle—
the necessity of "a supreme controlling power".

Having now pretty effectually squelched all efforts toward conciliation and having decided upon the principal means to be adopted to
obtain a restoration of colonial rights, Congress next appointed a committee "to bring in a plan for carrying into effect the non-importation,

non-consumption, and non-exportation resolved on". At this juncture (October 1) the pacificators succeeded nevertheless in prevailing upon Congress to send a "loyal address" to his majesty; and a few days later (October 12) it was decided that it would be a good stroke of policy to send an address also to the people of Great Britain. Many of the people in the homeland, some of them in high authority, were sympathetic with the colonies in their contentions, and might do much to sweeten the temper of the ministry. Still later (October 21) Congress concluded that it would be wise to lay their case before those North American colonies that were not represented in the Congress—Quebec, St. John's in Nova Scotia, Georgia, and East and West Florida—particularly Quebec. These addresses were all prepared with great care and subjected to close scrutiny in Congress. That they were admirably drawn no less an authority than the Earl of Chatham gave testimony.

It was of course the petition to the king that gave Congress the greatest concern, and a carefully picked committee was assigned to the task of preparing it—Richard Henry Lee, John Adams, Thomas Johnson, Patrick Henry, and John Rutledge. The committee, for its part, chose the oratorical Mr. Henry to draft it. Apparently, however, Henry's pen did not prove itself the peer of his tongue and his voice, for his proposed address was so unsatisfactory Congress demanded that it be rewritten and added John Dickinson to the committee for the purpose (October 21). Dickinson, who had taken his seat in Congress only a few days before, had made a reputation as the wielder of a facile and a powerful pen; and Congress was not disappointed in the result. The petition as drawn by Dickinson was approved October 25.

With the first draft of the address to the people of England, Congress was more deeply disappointed than it had been even with that to the king. It was another instance of an orator having failed with his pen, for the drafting of that address had been entrusted to Richard Henry Lee. The story of that address comes to us from Jefferson, as related to him by Benjamin Harrison and Edmund Pendleton. When Lee's production was read, "every countenance fell and a dead silence ensued for many minutes." The consideration of the address was postponed until the following day (October 19). Probably William Livingston and John Jay, the other members of the committee, were not surprised at what had taken place, for Jay also had prepared an address, and at Livingston's suggestion it was read. As told to Jefferson and retold by him, "there was but one sentiment of admiration."

While Congress was mulling over these addresses, consideration was being given betwixt times to other matters, which, if not weightier, were at least more to the point of their immediate purpose. A statement of colonial rights having been postponed until the means for recovering them had been determined upon, it now behooved Congress to decide, if it could, what in particular were those rights they had so stoutly resolved to maintain. To be sure, they had, in that first tussle with the problem, scrubbed it all over the threshing floor, until the threshers themselves were all but worn to a frazzle; but they must needs thresh it over again. So once again the two main questions were raised and debated: should they plant their main batteries of defense on the law of nature, and what authority, if any, should be allowed to Parliament in the regulation of their trade? Duane, Galloway, and their group had no very large idea of the law of nature as a defensive position, whereas John Adams and others of the philosophically minded members had a notion that, although some of the suggested positions might not be impregnable, the law of nature was one post they could defend against all the cohorts of the enemy.

Duane, for his part, had labored earnestly with the problem and had presented to the committee on rights a carefully reasoned statement of the case, as he conceived it, taking pains to preface his propositions with the general statement that "A firm Union between the Parent State and her Colonies ought to be the great object of this Congress." (This, be it remembered, was before Galloway had offered his plan of union, which Duane heartily espoused.) "It is this alone", he asserted, "which can ensure the permanent Stability of the british empire and the mutual Happiness of its respective Members." Therefore, he contended, "the Prerogatives of the Crown, the interest of Great Britain, and the Rights of the Colonies ought each to have their proper Influence" in any resolves that might be adopted, whereas the proceedings of Congress ought to be "tempered not only with a Regard to Justice but a desire of Reconciliation". Touching the supremacy of the crown he maintained that the same allegiance was due the king from the colonies as from his subjects within the realm of England. The rights of the colonies, Duane submitted, were derived from three sources: "1. From the Common Law of England and such ancient Statutes applicable to our local Circumstances, as existed at the time of our Colonization, which are fundamentals in our Constitution. 2. From our respective Charters confirming these Rights. 3. From our several Codes of provincial Laws." Those acts of trade that had been submitted to and recognized for more than a century "ought to be considered in the Light of an ancient Compact between the parent State and the Colonies". From the spirit of this compact, he went on to say, and because of the expediency of a controlling power over the general commerce of the empire, as well as for the protection the colonies had always derived from the mother country, the authority of Parliament in matters of trade "ought not to be questioned", provided that authority is "exercised bona fide for the Purposes of securing the Advantages of the Commerce of the whole Empire to Great Britain, with a Just Regard to the Interests of its respective Members".

A good deal of Duane's reasoning and phraseology was presently embodied in the so-called "Declaration of Rights", which, by the 14th of October, had been whipped into a shape sufficiently satisfactory to obtain a vote of approval. One sentence of especial significance (cited below) seemed to catch everybody's fancy, with the result that it was incorporated in the Declaration with only a few verbal changes. Taken as a whole, this Declaration, which includes a review of the measures of the British government which the colonies deemed to be obnoxious, is an admirable statement, in the form of ten resolutions, of the fundamental rights on which the colonies laid hold as indubitably theirs—rights derived from "the immutable laws of nature, the principles of the English constitution, and the several charters or compacts".

In view of the fact that "the violent party" was now in the ascendancy in Congress, it is little short of remarkable that the Declaration of Rights is so restrained in tone. Enumerating the rights of the colonists, the Declaration sets forth that they are entitled to life, liberty, and property, that these rights had never been ceded to any sovereign power whatever, and that neither these nor any other of the "rights, liberties, and immunities of free and natural born subjects, within the realm of

England" had been forfeited by emigration. Next is posited what is termed "the foundation of English liberty, and of all free government", namely, "a right in the people to participate in their legislative council". This was an old bone of contention, and it was deftly disposed of thus: inasmuch as the colonies can not, "from their local and other circumstances", be represented in the British Parliament, "they are entitled to a free and exclusive power of legislation in their several provincial legislatures . . . subject only to the negative of their sovereign, in such manner as has been heretofore used and accustomed". Then follows the carefully phrased proviso, taken over almost verbatim from the proposition earlier laid down by Duane:

But from the necessity of the case, and a regard to the mutual interest of both countries, we cheerfully consent to the operation of such acts of the British parliament, as are bona fide, restrained to the regulation of our external commerce, for the purpose of securing the commercial advantages of the whole empire to the mother country, and the commercial benefits of its respective members; excluding every idea of taxation, internal or external, for raising a revenue on the subjects in America, without their consent.

Among the other rights specified were that the colonies were entitled to the common law of England, "and more especially to the great and inestimable privilege of being tried by their peers of the vicinage", the right of assembly and petition, and lastly the right to be free of a standing army in times of peace, unless by "the consent of the legislature of that colony, in which such army is kept". The tenth resolution is, in effect, a criticism of a principal feature of the Galloway plan of union. Good government and conformity to the English constitution rendered it indispensably necessary "that the constituent branches of the legislature be independent of each other; that, therefore, the exercise of legislative power in the several colonies, by a council appointed, during pleasure, by the crown, is unconstitutional, dangerous, and destructive of the freedom of American legislation."

Congress was now ready to take up the report, offered October 12, of the committee appointed to bring in a plan for carrying into effect the non-importation, non-consumption, and non-exportation agreements, which together now began to be called the plan of the Association. Both the name and the form appear to have been derived from the Virginia Association of August, 1774. It seems to have been generally supposed that the battle over the substance of the Association was at an end, that only the form and minor details would require further discussion. Those who thought thus had reckoned, however, without South Carolina. The resolution in favor of non-exportation (September 30) had in fact been carried only after some compromises to meet the demands of Virginia, Maryland, and North Carolina, and against the protests of the South Carolina delegation in particular; for the exportation of rice and indigo was essential to the commercial life of that colony. Now, upon a renewal of the discussion, that delegation (four of them at least, the Rutledges, Lynch, and Middleton; Gadsden seemed quite willing to yield) laid down an ultimatum that, unless the South Carolina staples, rice and indigo, should be excepted from the non-exportation provision, they would not sign the Association; and those delegates did in fact withdraw from Congress for the time being.

This was on the 20th of October. Thereupon, to prevent the break-up of the union, a compromise was effected whereby the South Carolinians yielded their contention with regard to indigo on condition that an exception be made of rice. Thus it came about that, at the end of the fourth article of the Association, were appended the words "except rice to Europe". For the moment at least the crisis had passed, and the delegates proceeded to append their signatures to the Association. That not all the delegates signed of their own free will, to say nothing of full accord, Joseph Galloway at least gave later testimony. He had signed the Association, partly in the hope of "preventing the Congress from proceeding to more violent measures", but partly also, it would seem, from fear of violent measures toward himself personally.

In form the Association is a solemn agreement on the part of the several colonies to pursue a rigid policy of non-intercourse with Great Britain until the grievances complained of should be redressed. The introductory paragraph, wherein are set forth the reasons for entering into the agreement, opens significantly with a pious avowal of loyalty to the king, although it does not fail in the close to point an accusing finger at "a wicked ministry".

Besides the non-intercourse resolutions already agreed upon but here somewhat elaborated, the Association embodies other mutual pledges, which at first glance might seem to have but little relation to the main objective. The associators enter into a pledge, for instance, that they will use their "utmost endeavors to improve the breed of sheep, and increase their number to the greatest extent"; and, if any should find themselves overstocked with sheep, they will dispose of them to their neighbors, "especially to the poorer sort, on moderate terms". Further, they pledge that, in their several stations, they will "encourage frugality, economy, and industry, and promote agriculture, arts and the manufactures of this country, especially that of wool". All of which was rational enough, when it is borne in mind that the population was like to find itself presently subjected to many deprivations. But the associators went further still, promising to "discountenance and discourage every species of extravagance and dissipation, especially all horse-racing, and all kinds of gaming, cock-fighting, exhibitions of shews, plays, and other expensive diversions and entertainments." Nor was this all. The pious associators even prescribe a severe simplification of the mourning customs. The conclusion is inescapable that some of these associated frowns were motivated by ethical rather than economical purposes. The ancient, if not always honorable, sport of cock-fighting, for instance, could scarcely have affected the commerce between Great Britain and her colonies or otherwise have thwarted the great common cause.

So far the Association was no more than a pledge, even if the pledge did include promises that, if any vender of goods should by any device whatsoever violate this agreement, the colonies one and all would thereafter have no dealings with such a person. The associators did not for a moment deceive themselves into supposing that their covenant, however solemnly entered into, would enforce itself. There must be machinery for its enforcement, and in this manner was such machinery provided for:

That a committee be chosen in every county, city, and town . . . whose business it shall be attentively to observe the conduct of all persons touching this association; and when it shall be made to appear . . . that any person within the limits of their appointment has violated this association, that

[they] cause the truth of the case to be published in the gazette; to the end, that all such foes to the rights of British-America may be publicly known, and universally contemned as the enemies of American liberty.

Furthermore, if any colony should fail to accede to the Association or hereafter violate it, such colony would be held as "unworthy of the rights of freemen, and as inimical to the liberties of their country".

If there had ever been any doubt that the machinery devised would be efficient for its purpose, that doubt was speedily dispelled. Committees were everywhere set up and went to work with zeal to perform the duties assigned them. There was rioting and burning, tarring and feathering, until the story became monotonous. Nor did these valiant enforcement agencies limit their interest and their activities to the weightier matters of the Association; the injunctions respecting diversions and entertainments likewise received due attention. For instance, a lady was counseled to "decline" giving a proposed ball at her house, as contrary to the spirit of the Association; and some men who had taken part in a horse race were prevailed upon to express repentance and to promise "proper atonement" for their "enormity". Of course there were lamentations and groans from the victims. Growled one such: "If I must be enslaved, let it be by a KING at least, and not by a parcel of upstart lawless Committee-men. If I must be devoured, let me be devoured by the jaws of a lion, and not gnawed to deth by rats and vermin." What a pity we could not have escaped this sordid chapter of our "Glorious Revolution"!

The Association has nevertheless a much worthier place in the history of the American Revolution than this story of mobs gone wild and liberty run mad. As the Declaration of Rights was in an important sense a forerunner of the Declaration of Independence, so the Association stands out as an important step toward the creation of an organic union among the colonies. Though not a constitution, for it laid down no framework of government other than for its own enforcement, it was in a true sense an instrument of union and the first to be subscribed by all the colonies then participating.

The Association completed, there remained little to detain Congress except to put the finishing touches to the several memorials and addresses, including one to their own constituents, giving an account of their stewardship. Anticipating that all its labors in behalf of a restoration of rights might prove to have been in vain, Congress resolved on October 22 that, unless the desired redress of grievances had been obtained before the 10th of May, 1775, another congress of all the colonies should be convened in Philadelphia at that time. On the same day, because of the indisposition of Peyton Randolph, Henry Middleton of South Carolina was chosen president, and therefore it came about that most of the addresses were signed by Middleton as president. All the Virginia delegates except Washington and Richard Henry Lee took their departure October 23 to attend the House of Burgesses; accordingly Washington and Lee between them appended all the Virginia signatures to the petition to the king, Washington having subscribed those of Bland, Harrison, and Pendleton, while Lee wrote the name of Patrick Henry. Randolph's signature is not found on the petition. A letter to the colonial agents in London was then prepared, arrangements made for its despatch, and on October 26 the Congress adjourned itself.

That evening "all the Congress and several gentlemen of the town" gathered at the City Tavern for a last friendly communion and farewells. It is not recorded that the delegates fell upon one another's necks and wept, yet time was to reveal that many strong and lasting friendships had been formed during those eventful, if somewhat quarrelsome, weeks of discussion. Without doubt this mingling of minds from the separated colonies was fraught with consequences far surpassing any personal relationships. If it was the beginning of separation from the mother country, it was also the beginning of union among themselves.

As the delegates wended their several ways homeward, many a mind must have been weighted with serious reflections upon the probable outcome of this congress of the colonies—the weal or the woe, may be the woe and the weal. So, no doubt, the mind of John Adams, chief among the chroniclers, if not also chief among the actors in that drama. Yet, however somber may have been his reflections, it was a gladsome note that John Adams chanted as he began the jog back to his beloved Boston (pity that his chant was buried in his diary):

Took our departure, in a very great rain, from the happy, the peaceful, the elegant, the hospitable, and polite city of Philadelphia. It is not likely that I shall ever see this part of the world again, but I shall ever retain a most grateful, pleasing sense of the many civilities I have received in it, and shall think myself happy to have an opportunity of returning them.

A few short but anxious months, nevertheless, and John Adams would find himself once more in Philadelphia, in the midst of its abounding and charming civilities—but not less amid redoubled perplexities.

CHAPTER IV

THE PRAYERS OF THE COLONIES UNAVAILING
THE SECOND CONGRESS ASSEMBLES

We therefore earnestly beseech your majesty, that your royal authority and interposition may be used for our relief; and that a gracious answer may be given to this petition.

That your majesty may enjoy every felicity through a long and glorious reign over loyal and happy subjects, and that your descendants may inherit your prosperity and dominions 'til time shall be no more, is and always will be our sincere and fervent prayer.

Such are the closing words of that petition which, on the 25th of October, 1774, the Congress, on behalf of the colonies, preferred to their "Most Gracious Sovereign". The petition was not, however, all honeyed words and fervent prayer. There were sharp accusations, bitter complaints. That the royal ear would be attuned to professions of "affectionate attachment to your majesty's person, family, and government", that it would be attentive to the assertion that "Your royal authority over us and our connexion with Great Britain, we shall always carefully and zealously endeavour to maintain", was scarcely to be doubted; but that the "royal indignation" would, as the petition besought, turn upon those "designing and dangerous men" who had interposed themselves "between your royal person and your faithful subjects . . . prosecuting the most desperate and irritating projects of oppression", not many of the petitioners dared to hope. Indeed there was too much reason for believing that the royal person and the designing men were actually cooperating in those irritating projects of oppression. As for the assertion of the petitioners that such of their sentiments as might disturb his majesty's repose had been "extorted from hearts that much more willingly would bleed" in his majesty's service, no doubt the king thereupon took a pinch of salt.

Significantly, the king did not return a gracious answer. Why should any one have supposed that he would? In fact, he was so ungracious as not to answer the petition at all. What was of even greater significance, the eyes and minds of the king and his faithful ministers were drawn to another document, emanating from the same body at the same time, to wit, the Association. That document had, in effect, thrown down the gauntlet at the foot of the throne and hurled defiance into the teeth of the ministry. So at least it was interpreted on and about the throne. "The New England governments", spake the king, "are now in a state of rebellion; blows must decide whether they are to be subject to this country or independent." To be sure, there were mild efforts in behalf of some sort of conciliation; even Lord North submitted a plan to that end; yet even such warm friends of America as Chatham, Burke, and Barré, however much they reprobated as unjust and inexpedient the measures that had been taken, were one in the view that the British Parliament was supreme over the colonies, that the authority of the empire could not be surrendered. Moreover it soon became evident that the government was abundantly supported by popular opinion, in so far at least as popular opinion was expressed through Parliament; for an address from the two houses to the king clearly pointed to an approval of measures of coercion.

Meanwhile the American pot—rather, the thirteen American pots— continued to boil. As extra-legal assemblies, under the name provincial congresses or conventions, had for the most part chosen the delegates to the congress of the continent, so similar bodies were called together to pass upon the acts of the Congress, with the result that before long all the colonies except New York and Georgia had adopted the Association, and local committees were busy with its enforcement. Even in New York and Georgia committees here and there went ahead with the business, with only the sanction of the general Congress. Some of the colonies did not wait to learn the effect in Great Britain of the action of Congress, but proceeded at once to choose their delegates to the Congress conditionally scheduled to meet in May, while in others provincial congresses or conventions were called for that express purpose. These revolutionary bodies were, in fact, pretty generally supplanting the regular governments and were taking measures to resist any attempts at enforcement of the coercive acts. Had not the Congress, in its address to the inhabitants of the American colonies, bidden them to extend their views "to the most mournful events, and be in all respects prepared for every contingency"?

The colony of Massachusetts in particular, as was to be expected, did not neglect to prepare for every contingency, or even to extend its views to mournful events. (To what degree it may also have been preparing the contingency is an open question.) Not only were the people being armed and trained, their will to resist any attempt at coercion was being assiduously stimulated. For a time General Gage sat twiddling his thumbs in Boston, watching uneasily the seething commotion all about him. The city of Boston was indeed under his control—for so long as he could keep it so—but all the rest of the colony was giving its allegiance to the revolutionary Provincial Congress. So long as Gage should do no more than twiddle his thumbs, the seething depths were but an admonition, a contingency; but if he should suddenly thrust out his arm, the wild winds would be loosed and mournful events would ensue.

Nor was Massachusetts alone in this ardor of preparation, in kindling the flame of resistance. Down in Virginia also the county militia was organizing, and, when the Virginia Convention, which had met to choose delegates to the second Continental Congress, extended its views to the contingency of war, suddenly the eloquence of Patrick Henry swept down upon that assembly. Whether it was by virtue of their reason or through their emotions, the orator convinced his hearers that reconciliation was hopeless, that war was inevitable. "The next gale from the north", Henry exclaimed, "will bring to our ears the clash of resounding arms." No exact record of the speech has survived, but the closing words, "Give me liberty or give me death!" has become one of the most cherished mementos of the struggle for independence.

Patrick Henry proved himself a true prophet as well as a superb orator. The next gale from the north did bring to their ears the clash of resounding arms. The exasperated Gage had all at once stopped twiddling his thumbs and had thrust out his arm to seize two of the so-called ringleaders of sedition, Samuel Adams and John Hancock, and to destroy the military stores thought to be concealed at Concord. This was on the night of the 18th of April, 1775. There is no need to retell for the thousandth time the story of that memorable April 19th; it is sufficient to observe that a goodly number of Gage's troops did not march back to Boston, and those that did failed to bring with them the cherished military stores. As for the general himself, he had probably at least gained something in wisdom.

Who had fired the first shot, whether one of Gage's soldiers or some American country bumpkin, is one of those small historical questions that have never been solved; and it matters very little. The fact of prime importance—to an imagination given free reign—is that the shot was "heard round the world". Of more immediate purport, however, were the reverberations throughout the length and breadth of the colonies. The news of Lexington and Concord swept through the country as "on the wings of the wind". Four days brought it to New York, five to Philadelphia. Sweeping southward across Maryland, Virginia, and North Carolina, it was at Charleston by May 8 and at Savannah two days later. In due time the news had also crossed the Atlantic, and wherever it went, close upon its heels followed a mongrel brood of exaggerations and falsifications of the truth. The Americans believed what they would believe, the British what they were told; and each obeyed emotion rather than reason. On the one side were redoubled efforts to resist the oppressor; on the other, still firmer resolves to suppress this sedition.

It was opportune that the second Congress was about to assemble. The distraught colonies could look to it hopefully for counsel and guidance. The 19th of April found some of the delegates already on their way thither, and the morning of May 10 saw those from Pennsylvania southward except Georgia, together with those from New Hampshire, on the ground, eagerly awaiting the arrival of others from the northward. For these latter it had been a triumphal march almost every mile of the way. From Stamford in Connecticut to Horseneck on the border the Massachusetts and Connecticut delegations (the Rhode Islanders, having lagged behind, missed all this glory) had been attended by a military guard, thence to New York City by another; and, not content to await their arrival in the city, "a great number of the principal gentlemen of the place, in carriages and on horseback", met them at Kingsbridge. Then, three miles out of the city, appeared the city militia, some eight or nine hundred in number, "a tollerable band of music", and "thousands of spectators". One of the spectators recorded that "the roads were lined with greater numbers of people than were ever known on any occasion before", and that the arrival of the delegates was announced "by the ringing of bells and other demonstrations of joy".

This was on Saturday, May 6. On Monday morning, crossing over into New Jersey, where they were joined by the New York delegates, they rode proudly on, escorted always by military guards and received by cities and towns with bands of music and other demonstrations of applause.

Philadelphia was not of course to be outdone by any lesser town in the measure or the fervor of its welcome. Early on the morning of May 10 the word was spread that the procession was approaching, and "a great number of persons rode out several miles" to hasten their greeting. Writes one chronicler, perched at some vantage point in the city, "About eleven o'clock the cavalcade appeared." "The public entry of the Bostonian delegates into this city", wrote Caesar Rodney, ". . . was very grand." (It might be the Bostonians to whom all these honors were paid, but Eliphalet Dyer of Connecticut seems to have derived as deep a satisfaction from these demonstrations as any man of Boston born and bred.)

Escorted into the city by officers, militia, a band of music, and "many thousands more", they were ushered into the City Tavern, "among Crouds of Spectators who dismissed us all besmeared with Sweat and dust and with 3 Cheers". All this was "a Strong Testimony of the Spirit and Unanimity of the people through out our long journey". Earlier that May morning Richard Henry Lee had given like testimony: "There never appeared more perfect unanimity among any sett of men." But Lee and the rest were thinking then mainly of objectives. Presently, when they had got down to ways and means, the unanimity would be anything but perfect.

The second Congress was made up in large part of the same men who had appeared in the first, with a few additions and a few substractions. Noteworthy among the additions were John Hancock from Massachusetts, Benjamin Franklin and James Wilson from Pennsylvania, and Thomas Jefferson from Virginia; although Jefferson, substituted for

Peyton Randolph, who had been compelled temporarily to withdraw, would attend only after Congress had been in session six weeks. The New York delegation underwent the greatest alteration, for that colony had now straightened out somewhat its political tangle and had constituted for itself a Provincial Congress, which chose the delegates. Although most of the New York delegates who had attended the Congress of 1774 were chosen for the new congress, including that Simon Boerum who was reputed to have lifted himself into the former Congress by his own bootstraps, five others were added, namely, George Clinton, Francis Lewis, Robert R. Livingston, Lewis Morris, and Philip Schuyler. Before many months had passed there would be numerous other changes, in several instances changes significant of shifting political power in the respective colonial electorates. One other addition was particularly gratifying, a delegate from the colony of Georgia, which had not been represented in the former Congress. True, this delegate, Lyman Hall, was deputed by only one parish in Georgia, but his coming was an earnest of what Georgia was about to do, join her sister colonies and so complete the ring.

Taken as a whole, the instructions of the delegates to this second Congress had much less to say than in the former instance about the objects of the Congress, for those objects were now generally well understood. New Hampshire merely authorized her delegates "to consent and Agree to all Measures, which said Congress shall deem necessary to Obtain redress of American Grievances". Massachusetts, on the other hand, again citing in general terms the grievances and the objectives, gave her delegates full power, in concert with the other delegates, to "direct and order such farther measures, as shall to them appear to be best calculated for the recovery and establishment of American rights and liberties, and for restoring harmony between Great Britain and the colonies". Connecticut's instructions were very brief and very broad: "to join, consult, and advise . . . on proper Measures for advancing the best Good of the Colonies". Rhode Island, using the same language as before, called for the repeal of the obnoxious acts and the establishment of the rights and liberties of the colonies "on a just and solid foundation". In the instructions (but not embodied in the credentials) was a further significant injunction, that the delegates should "endeavour to procure a regular annual Convention of Delegates or Representatives trom all the Colonies . . . for the Promotion and Establishment of the Peace Welfare and Security of the said Colonies".

New York's objectives were essentially the same as those set forth by Massachusetts, with a like emphasis upon the restoration of harmony between Great Britain and the colonies. New Jersey was content merely to require that her delegates report their proceedings to the next session of the General Assembly. Pennsylvania simply directed her delegates to attend the Congress, "unless the present Grievances of the American Colonies shall before that Time be redressed". Delaware specified her main objectives as "the accommodation of the unhappy differences between Great Britain and the Colonies, on a constitutional foundation".

Maryland conferred on her delegates "full and ample power to consent and agree to all measures, which such Congress shall deem necessary and effectual to obtain a redress of American grievances", but it also stipulated that "this Province bind themselves to execute, to the utmost of their power, all resolutions which the said Congress may adopt". The Virginia delegates laid before Congress only the certificate of their election. North Carolina, without naming specific objectives, gave a pledge similar to that of Maryland, investing her delegates "with such powers as may make any Acts done by them, or any of them, or consent given in behalf of this Province, obligatory, in honor, upon every Inhabitant thereof". South Carolina refrained in this instance from enumerating the grievances, but, in nearly the same language as before, empowered her delegates, in concert with those of these other colonies, to prosecute such measures as shall be "most likely to obtain a redress of American grievances".

The colony of Georgia had refused to adopt the Association, preferring to remain outside the pale, but the parish of St. John's had for itself chosen the other horn of the dilemma and had deputed Lyman Hall to represent it in the general Congress, pledging that its inhabitants were "determined faithfully to adhere to, and abide by the Determinations of him, and the other Honourable Members of the Same".

To all intents and purposes, the new Congress was only an adjourned meeting of that which had sat from September 5 to October 26 in the preceding autumn. The same men, Peyton Randolph and Charles

Thomson, were chosen as president and secretary, respectively, and the same rules of conduct in debating and determining questions were adopted (May 18). The rule of secrecy was, however, reinforced "under the strongest obligations of honor". Additional appointments were a doorkeeper and a messenger.

The recollection of the manner in which the Rev. Jacob Duché had so thrilled the previous Congress with the fervor and eloquence of his prayer, was still fresh in most of their minds. Accordingly, when the organization had been completed, it was voted to request Mr. Duché to open Congress the next morning with prayers. Mr. Duché did not disappoint them. He "made a most pathetic and pertinent prayer", wrote Silas Deane; and Congress was so well pleased that it deputed a special committee to express that body's thanks to Mr. Duché "for his excellent prayer so well adapted to the present occasion". Silas Deane was probably still under the influence of that prayer when he wrote (May 12): "The scenes before us are so vast that I can give no kind of judgment as to the term we shall be detained here, and I tremble when I think of their vast importance. May the God of Wisdom preside!" How vast a scene would soon be opened up beyond that wilderness the fringe of which they were entering, neither Deane nor any one else then dreamed.

The first item of business was the reading of a letter from the colonial agents in London, relating in what manner the petition had been rejected, and otherwise explaining the situation of affairs in England as of February 5. But all that was an old story. The next item was likewise an old story, except for the details. It was the reading of a mass of documents pertaining to the eventful doings of April 19, and the evidence offered was sufficiently stirring and sufficiently convincing to induce Congress to resolve to go into committee of the whole on the following Monday, to take into consideration the state of America. The state of America would occupy the time and thought of Congress for a good many days; but before that assembly had come to any definite conclusions, their thoughts had been quickened by events and their deliberations had been lured into unexpected fields.

One such event was the capture of Ticonderoga on Lake Champlain in the early morning of May 10, the very day on which the Congress was assembling itself. That important intelligence reached Philadelphia on the night of May 17, and on the morning of the 18th was laid before the assembled Congress by its president. It was thrilling news, and it also called for speedy and strategic action. That notable enterprise is definitely associated with the name of Ethan Allen, the same who later won fame as the leader of another enterprise, but one that gave to the Continental Congress many a headache. Yet it is for the capture of Ticonderoga that he is best remembered.

> .... Ethan—Ethan Allen,
> That when with fight he fills a quart
> He ups and gulps a gallon.

What American has not thrilled to Ethan Allen's peremptory demand of the British officer to surrender "in the name of the Great Jehovah and the Continental Congress"? Grave doubts, it is true, have been cast upon the authenticity of that phrase, particularly the invoking of the name of the Continental Congress; yet there is little reason to question that he did at least invoke the name of Jehovah, even if in more characteristic phrase.

Important as was this taste of glorious achievement at the beginning of the struggle, the capture of Ticonderoga and of other posts that speedily followed—Crown Point and St. John's—was of immense value for two other reasons; first, because of the much needed military stores that thereby fell into the hands of the Americans, and second, because the possession of this line of forts opened the way into Canada, in the event that the acquisition of that colony by force should be deemed advisable. Indeed even then Congress played with the Canadian temptation for a spell, but came to the decision (June 1) that, "as this Congress has nothing more in view than the defense of these colonies", no expedition or incursion ought to be undertaken against Canada. That decision did not, however, forestall them from purposing to use their utmost powers of persuasion upon the Canadians to convince them that they were in the same boat with their fellow-Americans to the south of them, that they too were "devoted by the cruel edicts of a despotic administration to common ruin". "We yet", so Congress told the Canadians (May 27), "entertain hopes of your uniting with us in defense of our common liberty". The reversal a little later of this decision not to interfere with Canada was to bring one of the first serious shocks to these hopes for a friendly union.

The little war flurries along Lake Champlain, far from being planned by Congress, had been unexpectedly tossed into the lap of that body while in the midst of its meditations. When those meditations had matured, Congress would have a general policy to offer, but in the interval it could but hand out to one or another or all of the colonies tentative and fragmentary bits of counsel. Although the colonies had not as yet collectively asserted their independence, they were acting both individually and collectively much as if they had already attained it. The authority of the home government was being pretty generally flouted, and whatever government existed was centered in the revolutionary assemblies, the provincial congresses or conventions. Congress had been called together primarily to formulate a general plan of action, but while it pondered a plan of concert, specific problems were arising in one colony or another upon which the advice of Congress was desired.

It was these specific questions, insistently thrust upon Congress, that, more than any formulated plans of its own, little by little drew the frail bark of this ambassadorial body of representatives out into the stormy sea and made it the flagship of the colonial political fleet. New York, for instance, asked the advice of Congress respecting the course it ought to pursue in the event that ministerial troops should arrive there; and, before Congress had quite made up its mind upon a general course of procedure, it was suggesting ways and means of defensive operations. So also the capture of the Champlain forts had resulted in requests to Connecticut and New York to furnish troops for the defense of those places. A petition from Massachusetts was presently to have consequences nothing less than momentous on the character of Congress.

We have business enough before us [wrote John Adams, June 10] to detain us until the 31st of next December. No assembly ever had a greater number of great objects before them. Provinces, nations, empires are small things before us. I wish we were good architects.

And Silas Deane, a few days earlier, had groaned (June 3): "Our business has run away with us."

From the 15th to the 26th of May, with only two or three interruptions, Congress sat as a committee of the whole, considering the state of America; and for a month or more thereafter it was the state of America—in general or in particular—that chiefly engaged the time and thought of that body. One small interruption, May 24, was the election of a new president in place of Peyton Randolph, who, as speaker of the Virginia House of Burgesses, withdrew to attend that assembly. The choice first fell upon Henry Middleton, who had been president for the last few days of the previous Congress; but when Middleton declined on account of his health, John Hancock of Massachusetts was elected. The chief significance of the election was that John Hancock was thereby thrust toward a pinnacle of fame that is peculiarly his own.

In this same interval a question was stirred whether Congress ought not to betake itself to some point "near the seat of Action", near, but not too near; say, to some point in Connecticut. The advocates of the removal appear, however, to have been cooled by the advice of a Connecticut statesman, Titus Hosmer. "I *fear*", wrote Hosmer, "were you near us you would have too many questions referred to you, and too much business cast upon you by the New England Colonies, to leave you the leisure you ought to have to digest and perfect matters of greater importance." At all events, Congress did not choose to plant itself any nearer to the scene of action, and a few weeks later even refused to establish a committee of its own body there.

Among the applications of the individual colonies was one from New Jersey (May 26), not a request for advice, but rather itself counseling action. The House of Assembly of that province, having observed Lord North's plan of conciliation as embodied in the resolution of the House of Commons, February 20, deemed it proper to transmit that resolution to Congress, with an expression of its own desire "of making use of all proper Means to effect a Reconciliation", and with a recommendation of the plan to the consideration of Congress. Congress would in time get around to giving very particular consideration to that House of Commons resolution, but just now it was deeply pondering, on its own initiative, the problem of reconciliation and was on the point of adopting certain resolutions which the committee of the whole had been maturing.

The first of these resolutions was no more than an assertion that, by sundry acts of the British government, the colonies had been "reduced to a dangerous and critical situation"; the second was a decision that "these colonies be immediately put into a state of defence"; the third was the expression of an ardent wish "for a restoration of the harmony formerly subsisting between our Mother country and these colonies" and a decision that "to the promotion of this most desirable reconciliation, an humble and dutiful petition be presented to his Majesty"; and the fourth was a resolve to enter into negotiations to that end. The first three of these resolutions are recorded as having passed unanimously, but that was evidently by colonies only; that there was individual opposition to this second petition to the king soon became abundantly clear.

For the next few weeks Congress would be mainly engaged in carrying into effect the second resolution, namely, to put the colonies in a state of defense. Some steps in that direction had already been taken in the requests to Connecticut and New York to man the Champlain forts; whilst other colonies were taking their measures without waiting for the advice of Congress. The New Hampshire congress, for instance, had resolved to raise two thousand men. They "could have desired to consult a General Congress" before taking such an important step, if time had allowed. But the case seemed "too urgent to be delayed". They were anxiously waiting "to hear the united plan of the Colonies in the General Council, which we pray and trust may be under the influence of Heaven". Massachusetts was of course feverishly preparing for eventualities and deeply anxious to know whether the other colonies would come to her assistance. On the 16th of May the Provincial Congress, then sitting at Watertown, despatched a communication to Congress, requesting the advice of that body on two specific points: Should the colony of Massachusetts take up and exercise the powers of civil government? Would Congress take over the army then forming about Boston? On the first point the Provincial Congress declared that, although it was ready to submit to such a plan as the general Congress might direct, it was convinced that it was "absolutely necessary for the salvation of our country" that their colony should establish such a form of government as would promote their own advantage and the union and interest of all America as well. On the second point it was suggested that, since the army collecting from the different colonies was for "the general defense of the right of America", its operations might more effectually answer the purposes designed if Congress should take over the regulation and direction of it. The answer of Congress to these two questions would in great measure determine the course and the character of the coming contest.

It was on the 2d of June that these disturbing queries were laid before Congress. They were in fact so disturbing that they were left lying on the table until the next day, when they were referred to a committee. A few days earlier John Adams had felt confident. "The Congress will support the Massachusetts", he wrote. "There is a good spirit here. . . . The Military spirit which runs through the continent is truly amazing." But when the question had been posed directly he felt less sure. "The Congress will support us", he ventured to say, "but in their own way. Not precisely in that way which I could wish, but in a better way than we could well expect, considering what a heterogeneous body it is." Silas Deane agreed that Congress was "a very unwieldy Body"—thirteen colonies whose situations and circumstances were so various that unanimous approbation of any proposition was rare and difficult. He could thank God, however, that "Unanimity . . . hitherto prevails to a most surprising degree". Evidently Deane would not be surprised if thereafter unanimity should not prevail.

While Congress was endeavoring to masticate the Massachusetts gristle it was unexpectedly offered a morsel to roll delightedly under its tongue. In the evening of June 7 a certain Major Philip Skene arrived in Philadelphia, having come from England by ship, while at the same time, all unknown to him, had come private letters intimating that Major Skene might be "a dangerous partizan of Administration", come to do devilment to the colonies generally, that he was even "charged with a power from Administration to influence the members of the Congress by arguments drawn on the treasury". Skene was therefore arrested and his papers examined, whereby it developed that he had a commission as governor of Ticonderoga, Crown Point and the Lakes, surveyor of the woods, and what not. Thereupon all Congress broke out into a loud guffaw. "It has happened", spoke staid John Morton, "so that the said Governor has no Government to go to, the New England Men having some time since taken possession of those important

Places." Opined John Adams, "He must dispute for his government with Arnold and Allen." "How amazingly was he Chagrined", chuckled Eliphalet Dyer; ". . . the dunce Imagined he should have easy work to settle the whole Controversy. . . . that he should soon get into his Kingdom att Crown Point", a good salary for that, another as surveyor of his majesty's woods, the command of a Canadian regiment, his great plantation—"all this . . . had opened his Views amazingly but the whole prospect was suddenly closed." "As we have no occasion for his services at the forts", wrote another delegate complacently, "and do not intend to deal in his reasonings, he remains a prisoner upon parole." Skene must have possessed a sense of humor, for he seemed "to brave it out tolerably well".

Having had its laugh at Major Skene and having deposited him under the watch-care of Governor Trumbull of Connecticut, Congress could now turn to more serious business. And what more serious or urgent than the response to Massachusetts? The committee on that subject had just offered its report when Major Philip Skene had bobbed up to distract attention. Two days of discussion, and the answer of Congress to the first question was ready, even if it did hedge somewhat and decline to go the full length of satisfying Massachusetts. Said Congress to the colony of Massachusetts, no obedience is due to the act of Parliament for altering the colony's charter, nor to a governor or a lieutenant-governor who will not observe the directions of the charter but endeavor to subvert it; therefore the governor and lieutenant-governor of that colony are to be considered as absent and those offices vacant. Furthermore, as the suspension of the powers of government is intolerable, especially at a time when General Gage was actually carrying on hostilities against his majesty's peaceable and loyal subjects of that colony, therefore, "in order to conform, as near as may be, to the spirit and substance of the charter", it is recommended to the provincial convention (provincial congress, the Massachusetts people called it) to summon an assembly of representatives, that these elect councillors, and that the assembly and council exercise the powers of government, "until a Governor, of his Majesty's appointment, will consent to govern the colony according to its charter".

This was not quite what the Massachusetts delegation desired. They would have preferred that *"the present provincial congress"* choose the councillors, and thus avoid delay in setting up their government. Still, if not quite a whole loaf, it was better than a half loaf or less, and they would endeavor to be content—for a while at least. John Adams was irked nevertheless at what he construed to be the prevailing disposition in Congress "to keep open the Door of Reconciliation—to hold the sword in one Hand and the olive Branch in the other". Quoth he: "I am myself as fond of Reconciliation, if we could reasonably entertain Hopes of it upon a constitutional Basis, as any Man. But . . . the Cancer is too deeply rooted, and too far Spread to be cured by anything short of cutting it out entire." "However", he continued, "this Continent is a vast, unwieldy Machine. We cannot force Events." Samuel Adams, though eager as any man to propel things forward at a more rapid pace, took a like view. "The Spirit of Patriotism prevails among the Members of this Congress", he declared, "but from the Necessity of things Business must go on slower than one could wish. It is difficult to possess upwards of Sixty Gentlemen at once with the same Feelings upon Questions of Importance that are continually arising."

If Congress had been cautious in answering the first of the Massachusetts queries, it behooved that body to be even more so in answering the second. The question of taking over an army and directing the contest in behalf of the united colonies was something to be pondered deeply and to be discussed from every angle. That would be tantamount to setting itself up as a government, and certainly it had not been called together for such a purpose. Congress would, however, so President Hancock wrote the Provincial Congress June 10, take the matter into consideration very soon. As a matter of fact, it was even then being carefully considered by the members, whether or not it had been debated on the floor. The very first step taken by Congress after assigning the Massachusetts letter to a committee seemed to be in the direction of the goal pointed out by Massachusetts. This was the appointment of a committee for the purpose of borrowing six thousand pounds, for the repayment of which Congress pledged itself (not the colonies) to make full and ample provision; and, further, the appointment of another committee to bring in an estimate of the money necessary to be raised.

The plan of making a loan, as will presently be pointed out, soon went out the window; for Congress hit upon another means of providing itself with money, abundance of money, money to give away, money to burn. It is also to be observed that Congress specified the purpose for which it desired the loan; it was to purchase powder. If there was to be fighting, powder was essential, and powder was exceedingly scarce. Already urgent calls for powder were pouring in upon Congress—soon to become an insistent cry: "Powder! powder! God send us powder—and Guns!"—and Congress relayed the call to all the colonies, urging the collection of existing supplies, the setting of powder mills in operation, even the search far and wide for those essential ingredients, saltpetre and brimstone. And all this before Congress had decided whether it would take over the conduct of the struggle or merely cheer on the several colonies with advice, counsel, and consent.

These measures were taken on the 10th of June. On that same day John Adams wrote to wife Abigail: "In Congress we are bound to secrecy. But, under the rose, I believe that ten thousand men will be maintained in the Massachusetts, and five thousand in New York, at the Continental expense." So many things were whispered under the rose in those days that the rose, even had it been snow-white, must have turned red with blushes. Still, upon the whole, members kept their pledge of secrecy more faithfully than might have been expected. It was a sore temptation to tell tales out of Congress, especially when the weal or woe of the home colony was involved. Was it any real violation of the pledge to mention what one had heard "out of doors", or to drop broad hints, such that even a wayfaring man could not fail to comprehend?

However these things may be, by the time the astute and cautious Abigail up in Braintree had received this token from the garden of silence, Congress had done just what her dear John had predicted, only better. Within the next twelve days Congress had taken measures to organize an army of fifteen thousand men, a little later increased to twenty thousand. On June 14 it was resolved that six companies of expert riflemen be raised, two each in Pennsylvania, Maryland, and Virginia; then a few days later Pennsylvania's quota was raised to six, making ten companies in all, and these were to be speedily despatched to Boston. They were to be recruited from those back-country men who were famous for their marksmanship. "They can kill with great Exactness at 200 yards Distance", declared John Adams shortly afterward; "they have Sworn certain death to the Ministerial officers. May they perform their oath."

On June 15 it was resolved, "That a General be appointed to command all the continental forces, raised or to be raised, for the defence of American liberty", and George Washington was unanimously chosen to that command. The next day Washington gave his acceptance, and on the same day a general plan of organization was laid down: two major generals, five brigadier generals, one adjutant general, one commissary general, one quartermaster general, one paymaster general, one chief engineer in the grand army, a chief engineer in each separate department, secretaries to the general and the major generals, aides-de-camp, deputies, assistants, and finally a commissary of musters.

What days of exultation for the Massachusetts; what days of glorious vision for the other colonies; what days of swelling greatness for the Continental Congress, as it put forth its hand to guide and control the fighting forces of the thirteen colonies! This initial plan of organization was undoubtedly designed with an eye single to military needs and efficiency; but if the Sons and Daughters of the Revolution have conceived the notion that the eye remained single and fixed upon these objectives, let them not delude themselves. Political as well as military objectives thrust themselves into the foreground; patronage as well as patriotism furnished its quota of motives; sectional jealousies as well as general welfare supplied their abundant springs of conduct. In the very beginning of the nation's struggle for existence there was an undue admixture of such influences—and the nation has never overcome the habit.

Even in the choice of Washington as commander-in-chief political expediency had its part—the need for assuaging a deep sectional jealousy. The New Englanders, naturally enough, since the operations, in their beginnings at least, would be centered about Boston, might be expected to prefer a commander of their own; and they already had one in the person of General Artemas Ward. On the other hand, the colonies south of New England felt a strong reluctance to putting their forces under a New England general. Almost alone among the Massachusetts delegates John Adams was long-headed enough to perceive the wisdom of giving the chief command to a southerner, and he labored a good many days to bring the fruit of that policy to a proper ripening. He must, however, notwithstanding the hesitancy of his own colleagues, have had encouragement from his people back home. For as early as the 4th of June, Elbridge Gerry had written to the delegates: "I should heartily rejoice to see this way the beloved Colonel Washington, and do not doubt the New England generals would acquiesce in showing to our sister colony, Virginia, the respect, which she has before experienced from the continent, in making him generalissimo." And he added that Dr. Joseph Warren agreed with him. The motion for the appointment of Washington was made by Thomas Johnson of Maryland and seconded by John Adams in a speech which, if his own later account may be accepted, not only was skilfully designed to effect the main purpose, but was just as skilfully framed to prick the bubble of John Hancock's vanity. For, strange as it may seem, Hancock had conceived the notion that his nimble pen could be fashioned into a mighty sword. Not often in these days that tried men's souls did John Adams exhibit a sense of humor, but on that particular day humor was moving him mightily, and even down to his old age he could not restrain a chuckle when he remembered "the sudden and striking change of countenance" in the face of the President of Congress, when the name pronounced was not John Hancock but George Washington.

Not all the conflict of opinion was, however, centered about the commander-in-chief; there was also a contest over who should be the second in command. By all the rules of faith and logic that choice would necessarily fall upon General Ward; yet many voices arose in behalf of another, one Charles Lee, a half-pay British officer recently come to America, who, by means of a facile tongue, had impressed many people with a belief in his extensive knowledge, experience, and superior military abilities, to say nothing of his parading as the most rampant rebel in America. Logic nevertheless won, and Artemas Ward was chosen "first major-general", Charles Lee "second major-general". "Nothing", wrote John Adams to James Warren (June 20), "has given me more Torment, than the Scuffle We have had in appointing the

General Officers. We could not obtain a Vote upon our Seat for L[ee].
Sam and John fought for him, however, through all the Weapons.
Dismal Bugbears were raised. There were Prejudices enough among
the weak and fears enough among the timid, as well as other obstacles
from the Cunning: but the great Necessity for officers of skill and Experience prevailed." For adjutant general was chosen another ex-
English officer, Horatio Gates. General Ward was destined soon to fade
out of the Revolutionary picture; General Lee would dash furiously
across the stage a few times, then disappear in the wings, where, for a
brief space, he would furnish some annoying thunder, but little light-
ning; General Gates would strut a stellar part for a longer period but
in due time he would stumble through a trap door, and so vanish from
the military scene.

In other appointments also, politics and sectionalism had their full
share of influence. A good many, if not most, of those fundamentals
later known as state rights quite early manifested themselves in the
cooperative enterprise of the American colonies, and one of those manifestations was a disposition in each colony to insist upon its due quota
of generals. Two major generals and five brigadier generals might meet
every requirement of the war machine, but they were insufficient to
meet the demands of the political machine. The number of major generals was accordingly increased (June 19) to four and that of the brigadier generals to eight. Of the two additional major generals New York
obtained one, Philip Schuyler, and Connecticut the other, Israel Putnam. New York was thoroughly justified in her Schuyler, even if, as
Eliphalet Dyer of Connecticut averred, he was chosen "to sweeten and
keep up the spirit in that Province"; and Connecticut was content to do
honor to her Putnam, even though it was pride in his past rather than
hope in his future that furnished the motive.

Of the brigadier generals Massachusetts won three, Connecticut two,
New Hampshire one, Rhode Island one, and New York one. And of
these eight hostages to performance and to fame, whose name led all the
rest? Seth Pomeroy of Massachusetts. The firm of "Adams and Adams"
strove mightily to obtain the appointment of James Warren, "But Notions, narrow Notions prevented it . . . fear of disobliging Pomroy
and his Friends". It was a barren victory, for Pomeroy soon withdrew

into quiet and obscurity. Of that colony's other two brigadiers, William Heath and John Thomas, their subsequent careers were honorable, even if not among the most distinguished. Indeed Thomas's career was cut short by death when the war had barely begun (June 2, 1776). Connecticut, on the other hand, found little reason thereafter for gratification in her two prizes, David Wooster and Joseph Spencer. Both presently withdrew into their tents to sulk and pout, contributing to the colony and state of Connecticut more of tribulation than of glory. It was the fate of New York's brigadier, Richard Montgomery, second on the list, to fall in leading a forlorn hope in Canada, thereby embalming his name in the reverential memories of his countrymen. New Hampshire's John Sullivan failed of unquestioned distinction in the field, but subsequently rendered valuable services in Congress. It was the last of the list—"one Green of Rhode Island", as Roger Sherman reported—who eventually went to the head of the class.

The appointment of the general officers did not of course complete the framework of the army. There must be a numerous body of subordinate officers, and these were to be nominated by the provincial congresses to General Washington, who would fill in commissions provided by Congress. Abundant room for more jealousies and more bickerings.

CHAPTER V

CONGRESS ORGANIZES FOR DEFENSE
LOOKS ASKANCE AT PERMANENT UNION

During all the more or less orderly preparation for a probable war Congress did not fail to stipulate the salaries to be attached to the several offices it had created, as it likewise gave assurance, through its president or otherwise, that all sundry services and things called for were to be "at Continental expense". And yet, not until the day the brigadiers were designated had Congress come to a decision whence should come the funds so liberally promised. It was not, however, as if Congress had made promises that were baseless, for some financial wizards had been dazzling the eyes of Congress with the vision of a marvelous money-tree, which Congress itself might grow and from which it might pluck at will whatever sums were needed. The vision was exhibited in the form of an elaborate plan sent down from New York, now known to have been drawn by the fertile brain and artistic hand of Gouverneur Morris.

This bountiful tree was by no means unknown to the gentlemen composing the Continental Congress, for all the colonies had grown it, at one time or another, sometimes with results that appeared to be fairly satisfactory, sometimes indeed with results that were not so satisfactory. The chief question that arose was whether the colonies jointly, through their common assembly as then constituted, could grow the tree successfully and gather its fruits without the danger of its succumbing to the blight that so commonly infested it. But Gouverneur Morris was a most persuasive person. With the simple quill of a goose, a little ink, and the English language, he could ofttimes do marvels in bringing the minds of men into unison, and his would seem to have been the chief influence in this instance. Perhaps the feat was not difficult, for he had only to point to the open road, the inviting way. In short, what was proposed was that Congress should issue paper money.

In the plan as offered to Congress three modes of issuing the needed sums of paper money were discussed: first, that each colony should strike for itself such a sum as might be apportioned by the Continental Congress; second, that the Continental Congress should strike the whole sum necessary, and each colony become bound to sink its proportionable part; third, that the Continental Congress should strike the whole sum and apportionate (that is the word used) the several shares to the different colonies, each colony becoming bound to discharge its proportionate part, the colonies jointly to discharge that part which any particular colony should be unable to pay. The author of the plan did not fail to recognize that there were obstacles to giving the money a ready and immediate currency and to providing ways and means for sinking it, but he gave reasons for believing that both obstacles might readily be overcome. One suggestion put forth is particularly deserving of attention. Such a currency, it was argued, would "be a new bond of union to the Associated Colonies, and every inhabitant thereof will be bound in interest to endeavour that ways and means be fallen upon for sinking it."

Congress was evidently strongly inclined toward the paper money idea, yet it did not embrace the plan with any sudden rashness. In fact, much of twenty days was occupied in seriously debating the project. Meanwhile other colonies besides New York were stirring the question whether the heavy expenses to which they were subjected, presumably in the common cause, might not in some form be made a common obligation. Massachusetts, for instance, at the same time that she was soliciting advice about setting up her own government, raised the question whether Congress would undertake to "give a credit" to her provincial notes; in other words, underwrite her obligations. New Hampshire also, in a letter laid before Congress at the same time (June 2), mentioned the "vast expense" that the colony was incurring and suggested the advisability of falling upon "some general plan for bills of credit", or "such other methods as shall appear just and equal, in apportioning the expense of the common cause".

By June 17, James Duane could write to the New York Provincial Congress, "Your great complaint of the want of money will, I hope, be soon removed"; for the committee of the whole, he was permitted to reveal, had resolved on an emission of Continental paper currency. Other members, with a like permission, hastened to inform their respective governments of this momentous action by their grand Continental Congress. Not however until the 22d of June was the resolve made definitive, a resolve that, in effect, adopted the third of the proposed plans:

Resolved, That a sum not exceeding two million of Spanish milled dollars be emitted by the Congress in bills of credit, for the defense of America.

Resolved, That the twelve confederated colonies be pledged for the redemption of the bills of credit, now directed to be emitted.

The ways and means of redemption are not otherwise recorded in connection with these resolutions (they are, however, specified with particularity at the time of the next emission), but Caesar Rodney stated at the time, "The money is to be sunk by all the 12 colonies in 7 years according to their quotas which are settled in proportion to the number of inhabitants in each Colony." "We . . . must, I suppose", wrote John Adams, "vote to issue a great deal more"; but, even if Adams had given the loosest rein to his imagination, his "great deal more" would still have fallen far, very far short of what Congress did in a little more than four years actually emit. Scarcely any one at that time could have been induced to believe that the contest was to be drawn out across seven long and dreary years, and even then the end by no means certain; and none could have forecast the stupendous cost in money.

Congress had launched the vessel of its hopes upon the uncertain sea of paper money; but through what storms the ship would pass, at what far port it would land and in what condition, no man could foretell. For some little while nevertheless, it was a smooth and merry voyage.

Applications for some of the Continental began immediately to be laid on the table of Congress; and as the time required for the printing, numbering, and signing of the bills dragged on, the eager colonial governments grew impatient. "For God's sake", wrote the New Yorkers to their delegates, "send us money, send us arms, send us ammunition!" The clamor for Congress money and still more Congress money had begun, a clamor that would resound almost incessantly in the ears of Congress through four years of never-ending trials and tribulations.

Indeed it ceased not until a Continental was not worth a clamor—or even a shorter and more explosive expletive. While it lasted, however, the trek for Continental money was like unto the trek of the wild deer and the buffalo for the salt licks. And who among them, whether colonial or buffalo, could be persuaded that the springs would ever run dry? Such was the beginning of what in later times came to be known as the "federal trough", one of America's most imperishable institutions.

The money problem solved, Congress decided that on the morrow it would resume consideration of the state of America, then adjourned, counting this 22d of June as a day well spent. Suddenly upon this contentment broke the news that the state of America had taken a turn for the worse. At six o'clock that evening President Hancock seized a hurried pen to write to General Artemas Ward: "The Congress just up. . . . We have just a Report of a Battle. . . . We are anxious. No Express. God send us a good acco[un]t." It was the first news—quite indefinite—of the battle of Bunker Hill. Not until eleven o'clock of the night of the 24th (Saturday) did any substantial account of the battle reach Philadelphia, and it was Monday morning the 26th when the account was read to the assembled Congress. Meanwhile, on the morning of the 23d, General Washington, with Generals Lee and Schuyler, had set out for the scene of operations, the latter to take command at Ticonderoga. On their journey out of the city they were accompanied a little way by a throng of well-wishers. "All the delegates from the Massachusetts, with their servants and carriages attended; many others of the delegates from the Congress; a large troop of light horse in their uniforms; many officers of the militia, in theirs; music playing, etc. Such", so wrote John Adams to his wife, "is the pride and pomp of war." President Hancock, although undoubtedly sorely chagrined that it was not he who was the center of all this pride and pomp and loud acclaim, that it was not he who was being ushered forth on the road to military glory, with a band of music playing Yankee Doodle or something, bravely suppressed the ego and wrote of Washington to Joseph Warren, "He is a Gentleman you will all like." More than that, he suggested that at the end of the journey Washington be received with like pomp and circumstance. Eliphalet Dyer, who had at first doubted whether Washington's military knowledge and ability were any better than "some of ours", nevertheless acknowledged that he was "Clever, and if any thing too modest." Continued Dyer, "he seems discreet and Virtuous, no harum Starum ranting Swearing fellow but Sober, steady, and Calm." He imagined Washington would be "Very Agreeable to the Genius and Climate of New England".

Lexington and Concord had put the war machine in motion, Ticonderoga and Crown Point had propelled it a little farther down the slope, Bunker Hill threw it into high gear and turned on the power. Congress besought the committee of Philadelphia to send to Boston and Ticonderoga all the powder it could spare and at the same time redoubled the search for existing supplies of that necessary article, to promote its manufacture and transportation, and to obtain other needful implements of war as well. To be sure, there were still some who would apply the brakes, but John Adams was not one of them. *"Secret and Confidential, as the saying is"*, he wrote to James Warren (July 6). "The Congress is not yet so much alarmed as it ought to be." There were still hopes that the ministry and Parliament, on hearing of the battle of Lexington, would recede, but in his opinion they were much deceived. "We shall have nothing", he declared, "but Deceit and Hostility, Fire, Famine, Pestilence and Sword from Administration and Parliament. Yet the Colonies like all Bodies of Men must and will have their Way and their Humour, and even their Whims." Indeed the opinions of some colonies, founded as they were on hopes and fears rather than on reason and evidence, was bound, so Adams thought, to "give a whimsical Cast" to the proceedings of Congress.

You will see [Adams went on to say] a Strange Oscillation between love and hatred, between War and Peace—Preparations for War and Negociations for Peace. We must have a Petition to the King and a delicate Proposal of Negociation, etc. This Negociation I dread like Death: But it must be proposed. We cant avoid it. Discord and total Disunion would be the effect of a resolute Refusal to petition and negociate.

His own hope was that the ministry would be as much afraid of negotiation as we and would therefore refuse it. If they should agree to it, we should "have Occasion for all our Wit Vigilance and Virtue to avoid being deceived, wheedled, threatened or bribed out of our Freedom". Negotiation would effect nothing—unless to "gain Time and Powder and Arms". Besides the petition to the king, Congress was sending out another address to the people of Great Britain, another to those of Jamaica, and one to the people of Ireland. "You will see also," Adams forewarned, "a Spirited Manifesto." For his part, he would have the colonies "dissolve all Ministerial Tyrannies and Custom houses" and set up their own governments, then "confederate together like an indissoluble Band, for mutual defense, and open our Ports to all Nations immediately. . . . But the Colonies are not yet ripe for it—a Bill of Attainder, etc., may soon ripen them."

What this most forward of the forward party was protesting against was nothing less than an effort to carry out just the program that Congress had laid down in its resolutions of May 26; and the one item in that program that most irked him was the petition to the king. The leader of the party of conciliation was John Dickinson, and to him Congress had entrusted the drafting of the petition. On July 5 the petition, very much in the form that Dickinson desired, was agreed to, and three days later was signed by the members. "If Administration be desirous of stopping the Effusion of British blood," Dickinson wrote to Arthur Lee July 7, "the Opportunity is now offered to them by an unexceptionable Petition, praying for an accommodation. If they reject this application with Contempt, the more humble it is, the more such Treatment will confirm the Minds of our Countrymen, to endure all the Misfortunes that may attend the Contest." The address to the inhabitants of Great Britain was agreed to July 8, those to Jamaica and Ireland July 25 and 28, respectively.

More important than any of these addresses was what Adams termed a "Spirited Manifesto", but labeled by Congress the "Declaration on Taking Arms". The Declaration had its origin in the appointment, June 23, of a committee of five (John Rutledge, William Livingston, Franklin, Jay, and Thomas Johnson) "to draw up a declaration, to be published by General Washington, upon his arrival at the Camp before Boston". The committee offered a report June 24, but it was "referred for farther consideration"; and when the further consideration was undertaken (June 26), the brief record is sufficient to indicate that Congress was not satisfied with the committee's offering. Accordingly two additional members, Dickinson and Jefferson, were assigned to the committee, presumably in the confident expectation that these two would between them produce something better. Jefferson was a new member from Virginia, sent to take the place of Peyton Randolph, and had taken his seat only five days before, but the reputation of his pen had preceded him. The committee now requested him to draft the declaration, and he did so, but Mr. Dickinson thought some of his language was too harsh. Mr. Jefferson thereupon requested Mr. Dickinson to soften it. Mr. Dickinson did so, preparing, as Jefferson later testified, "an entire new statement, and preserving of the former only the last 4 paragraphs and half of the preceding one". Dickinson's production was then adopted by Congress (July 6) without alteration.

Let no one assume, however, that in mollifying the harshness of Jefferson's indictment Dickinson offered any soft explanation of the causes and necessity for taking up arms. It is a reasoned bill of indictment, designed to carry conviction and also to stir men to action in defense of their rights, though not to rashness and violence. Many of its phrases seem nevertheless, at this distance of time, harsh enough. Some of them indeed must have stuck in the craws of the ministry like rasping burrs. Upon the whole, however, it was well adapted to the purposes for which it was intended. Having set forth at some length the reasons why the colonies had taken up arms, the Declaration then seeks to animate the soldiers with a sense of the righteousness of the cause for which they were fighting and with confidence in its attainment:

> Our cause is just. Our union is perfect. Our internal resources are great, and, if necessary, foreign assistance is undoubtedly attainable. . . . With hearts fortified with these animating reflections, we most solemnly, before God and the World, declare, that . . . the arms we have been compelled by our enemies to assume, we will, in defiance of every hazard, with unabating firmness and perseverance, employ for the preservation of our liberties; being with one mind resolved to dye Free-men rather than live Slaves.

Then follows a passage designed rather for eyes and ears across the Atlantic:

> Lest this declaration should disquiet the minds of our friends and fellow-subjects in any part of the empire, we assure them that we mean not to dis-

solve that Union which has so long and so happily subsisted between us, and which we sincerely wish to see restored. . . . We have not raised armies with ambitious designs of separating from Great Britain, and establishing independent states. We fight not for glory or for conquest.

The declaration closes with a prayer, devoutly imploring "the impartial Judge and Ruler of the universe . . . to dispose our adversaries to reconciliation on reasonable terms, and thereby to relieve the empire from the calamities of civil war".

"We might easily have occasioned a Debate of half a Day", John Adams wrote a few days afterward, "whether it should be called a Declaration or a Manifesto"; and he grumblingly surmised that, "In exchange for these Petitions, Declarations, and Addresses, I suppose we shall receive Bills of Attainder and other such like Expressions of Esteem and Kindness." The address to the people of Great Britain would, he presumed, "find many Admirers among the Ladies and fine Gentlemen", but it was not to his taste. "Prettynesses, Juvenilities, and much less Puerilities become not a great assembly like this the Representative of a great People."

The more Mr. Adams thought of these efforts in behalf of conciliation, especially that so-called "Olive Branch" petition to the king, the pride of the proud Mr. Dickinson, the more exasperated he became, convinced as he was of the utter futility of them one and all. One day (July 24) when in an especially ferocious mood, he threw overboard all restraint, seized his pen and wrote to his friend James Warren:

In Confidence. I am determined to write freely to you this time. A certain great Fortune and piddling Genius, whose fame has been trumpeted so loudly, has given a silly Cast to our whole Doings. We are between Hawk and Buzzard.

And then he proceeds to explain what, with no doubt whatever in his mind, ought to have been done:

We ought to have had in our Hands a month ago the whole Legislative, executive and judicial of the whole Continent, and have completely modeled a Constitution; to have raised a naval Power, and opened all our Ports wide; to have arrested every Friend to Government on the Continent and held them as Hostages for the poor Victims in Boston, and then opened the Door as wide as possible for Peace and Reconciliation. After this they might have petitioned, and negotiated, and addressed etc. if they would.

Fate, alas! played a scurvy trick on Mr. Adams. As young Benjamin Hichborne, in whose pocket or saddlebags this confidential letter reposed, journeyed serenely toward Boston, he was suddenly halted by some British officers, and relieved of the precious letter. There was news in it for the British authorities, and there was amusement in it besides. It was published. Who the "certain great Fortune and piddling Genius" was, doubtless most who read the letter knew or soon found out. It was John Dickinson. Whatever struck John Adams to characterize Mr. Dickinson in that peculiar manner, probably no man knoweth to this day. Mr. Dickinson, privileged in due time to look upon this rude delineation of himself drawn by the corrosive pen of John Adams, was not charmed by the portrait or warmed toward Mr. Adams. Mr. Adams, for his part, chagrined over the exposure of his castigating remarks, would perhaps have sought to pour oil into the wound. Thereafter, meeting Mr. Dickinson on the street, Mr. Adams bowed and pulled off his hat. Mr. Dickinson neither bowed nor pulled off his hat, but "passed haughtily by". Mr. John Dickinson was intensely human. So was Mr. John Adams. Spake the proud Mr. Adams to his Diary: "We are not to be upon speaking terms nor bowing terms for the time to come."

Probably unknown to Adams, at the very moment when Congress accepted from Mr. Dickinson's hands the petition to the king, another concoction that might have been just as nauseous to him had been prepared for the gullet of Congress but was yet withheld, secreted in the pockets of certain members. The dose had been prepared in New York's political pharmacy, which had not even yet succeeded in winning the complete confidence of the other colonies, notwithstanding William Hooper of North Carolina had declared as early as May 23, that "the character of the New-Yorkers is no longer suspicious". In fact, nearly a month later (June 16) Eliphalet Dyer wrote Governor Trumbull that it was still "apprehended" that the "Cautious men" in New York were "for saving themselves and the Province a safe retreat if possable"; and he gave this as the real reason why Congress had requested New York to make application to Connecticut for troops to occupy certain posts on or near the New York border. "The more they are brought to move and Apply", said Dyer, "the more they will Involve themselves in the same Predicament with the other Colonies, which will give us a stronger Security for their future firmness in the General Cause." James Duane, however, gave to the Provincial Congress (June 17) a different reason: "It was found", said he, "that you made no progress in raising men."

Perhaps if Congress had known what some of the "cautious men" of New York were brewing, some would have been even more suspicious, particularly those who mistrusted any plan of conciliation. The Provincial Congress of New York had, in fact, for some time been agitating the question of having their delegates in the Continental Congress propose a plan of accommodation. The plan as finally agreed upon and despatched to the delegates at Philadelphia called for the repeal of the obnoxious acts of Parliament, but granted to Great Britain the right, "from the necessity of the case", to regulate the trade of the whole empire, "for the general benefit of the whole"; agreed that the colonies should support their own civil governments and assist, according to their respective abilities, in the defense of the empire, but maintained that they were entitled to "a free and exclusive power of legislation . . . in all cases of internal polity whatsoever, subject only to the negative of the sovereign." But the plan did not end there. It was further proposed that, for the purpose of raising and apportioning the respective colonial contributions, there be established "a Continental Congress, deputed from the several Colonies, to meet with a President appointed by the Crown". As a sort of excrescence upon the plan was an allusion to the "establishment of Popery all along the interiour confines of the old Protestant Colonies", with the consequent proposition that "neither the Parliament of Great Britain, nor any other earthly legislature or tribunal, ought or can of right interfere or interpose in anywise howsoever in the religious and ecclesiastical concerns of the Colonies".

It was submitted to the better judgment of the delegates whether the plan should be laid before Congress. The delegates for their part acknowledged "with the utmost Gratitude" the deference paid to their judgment and the delicacy of the Provincial Congress in leaving them unrestrained "in a point of all others the most essential to yourselves and your Posterity, to the Continent of America and the whole british Empire", and promised to give the plan their "most earnest and respectful Attention". Touching the religious question, however, they were unanimously agreed to keep silent. It would be highly imprudent, they declared, to run the risk of dividing the colonies by the introduction of disputes foreign to the present controversy. All the members of Congress had hitherto concurred "in a Desire of burrying all Disputes on Ecclesiastical Points, which have for ages had no other Tendency than that of banishing Peace and Charity from the World". Some of New York's statesmen at home may have been overcautious, but her delegates in the Continental Congress proved themselves men of wisdom. As the New York plan of accommodation arrived just at the time that Congress was agreeing to the petition to the king and was sending forth its Declaration on Taking up Arms, it would have only confused the situation to inject the New York proposal.

As for that shadowy suggestion of a permanent union of the colonies in a continental congress, that question, so John Adams later indicated, had at least been the subject of conversation, and before many days it was to become the subject of serious consideration. One member of the Congress (Benjamin Franklin) at least had been contemplating the problem, and had drawn up an instrument for the purpose, which he called "Articles of Confederation and Perpetual Union". He showed it to Jefferson, who highly approved it.

He shewed it to others [says Jefferson]. Some thought as I did; others were revolted at it. We found that it could not be passed, and the proposing it to Congress as the subject for any vote whatever would startle many members so much that they would suspect we had lost sight of reconciliation with Great Britain, and that we should lose much more ground than we should gain by the proposition.

It was agreed amongst those whom Franklin had consulted that the plan might be laid before Congress in order that the members might be "turning the subject in their minds", but the "timid members", as Jefferson characterizes them, were insistent that no entry relative to the instrument be made in the Journals. Accordingly, on the 21st of

July, Franklin did lay his suggested articles before Congress, stating that it was not offered as a finished plan but merely as a basis for a more perfect instrument when it should become necessary. Although, in accordance with the agreement, no entry was made in the regular Journal, Secretary Thomson did transcribe the Articles in what he called a "History of the Confederation", with the preliminary explanation that the "sketch" had been submitted for consideration by Doctor Franklin.

In a subsequent chapter will be found some examination into the character of Franklin's Articles and the extent to which his proposals found their way into the Articles of Confederation as eventually adopted; here we need concern ourselves only with their further round of adventures in the approximate period. Copies of the Articles were doubtless distributed among the members of Congress, for they soon made their way out into the colonies. James Duane, for one, had a copy, copies on their way to South Carolina were captured by the British and published, and it was reported that "the thing began to make some noise" down in Virginia. The plan appears also to have been laid before the convention of New Jersey, with the proposition that it be acceded to or rejected "in the lump", and it was rejected "in the lump".

William Hooper doubtless carried a copy with him to North Carolina in the beginning of August, for on the 24th of that month the Articles were laid before the Provincial Congress, with the suggestion that they be viewed "as a Subject which will be proposed to the Continental Congress at their next Session", and with the expressed wish that they might "be dispassionately Debated and approved or Condemned upon their own Intrinsick merits". On September 4 the Provincial Congress came to the decision "that the same is not at present Eligible"; that their delegates ought to be instructed not to consent to any plan of confederation until it had been approved by the Provincial Congress, that the Association ought to be further relied on for bringing about a reconciliation of the parent state, and, quite emphatically, that "a further Confederacy ought only to be adopted in Case of the last necessity".

It is not without significance that, on the day before the Franklin

Articles were laid before the Provincial Congress of North Carolina, that body had signed a profession of allegiance to the king and an acknowledgment of "the constitutional executive power of Government", at the same time declaring that Parliament did not have a right "to impose Taxes on these Colonies to regulate the internal police thereof", and "solemnly and sincerely" promising and engaging, "under the Sanction of virtue, honor, and the sacred Love of Liberty, and our Country, to maintain and support all and every the Acts, Resolutions and Regulations" of the Continental and Provincial Congresses, "because in both they are freely represented by persons chosen by themselves."

Altogether the prospect of the adoption of any plan of permanent union amongst the colonies seemed at the time remote, and long remained so. It is more than probable that, after some months, Jefferson decided to put out a feeler to test any change of sentiment in Congress. At all events, on the 24th of December a committee of which he was chairman, reporting to Congress on the items of unfinished business, included in their list the "Report of the proposed Articles of Confederation"; although the Articles were so far from being an item of unfinished business that the customary record in the Journal had been refused. Whether in consequence of this committee's report or otherwise, on the 16th of January, so we learn from Richard Smith's Diary, there were "considerable Arguments on the Point Whether a Day shall be fixed for considering the Instrument of Confederation formerly brought in by a Com[mitt]ee". Franklin in particular exerted himself in favor of his project, while Dickinson and some others did likewise against it. In the end it was negatived.

Congress was not yet, after six months of weighing and balancing, quite in the mood to slam the door of reconciliation, although its ire was rapidly rising, and ere another half-year had passed would slam shut the door with a bang. Then Franklin's Articles of Confederation would be eagerly drawn forth from their dusty pigeonhole to become the basis of that "something better" which Franklin had visioned. From those July days of 1775, however, when Congress had summarily rejected Franklin's propositions and in numerous other ways had striven so determinedly to carry water on both shoulders—with possibly another vessel, after the immemorial manner of water carriers, balanced on the top of its head—thence to June, 1776, was a far cry.

In those same July days of 1775, when Congress was so intent on keeping the olive branch extended, it was taking extraordinary measures none the less to strengthen its sword-arm. Despite all it could do in promoting the manufacture of munitions of war, if those supplies were to be had in any sufficiency, importation of them was imperatively necessary. Here, however, the colonies ran smack up against their own Association, with its non-importation and non-exportation stipulations. What was more, Great Britain had prohibited the exportation of arms and ammunition to the plantations, and had endeavored to prevent other nations from supplying the colonies. Very well; the colonies had had some experience in circumventing British prohibitions; and as for their own non-importation and non-exportation agreements, they had made them and they could break them. The decision of Congress was made.

On the 15th of July it was resolved that every vessel that would, within nine months, import gunpowder, saltpetre, sulphur, brass field pieces, or good muskets fitted with bayonets, should be permitted to load and export the produce of the colonies to the value of such powder and stores, "the non-exportation agreement notwithstanding". And in order the more effectually to promote the good purposes of this their resolution, the delegates of Pennsylvania were authorized to have the resolution printed in the form of handbills and to forward them to the West Indies and such other places as they thought proper; but under no circumstances must the resolution be allowed to get into the newspapers. This was the first breach into the Association, but, such were the exigencies in which Congress found itself involved, other and wider breaches would subsequently be made.

In fact, the whole question of opening or closing the ports had for some time been in ferment, and was to ferment still more furiously in days to come. The subject had been taken up in committee of the whole July 3, and on July 12 a committee had been appointed "to devise ways and means to protect the trade of these colonies". On the 21st (the same day that Franklin offered his plan of confederation) the committee made a report, including some propositions by Franklin and Richard Henry Lee; but on the following day, "after some debate, the same was postponed to be taken up at some future day". "We have had in Contemplation", snapped John Adams July 23, "a Resolution to invite all Nations to bring their Commodities to market here, and like Fools have lost it for the present." The advocates of the measure were able to obtain a resumption of its consideration July 31, but Adams's "fools" were still in the majority, and once more the subject was postponed "to a future day". Congress did nevertheless on August 1 resolve certain doubts that had arisen respecting "the true spirit and construction" of the non-exportation agreement.

However fiercely Mr. Adams might grumble over what Congress had left undone, one act at least, brought to a conclusion on the last day of July, must have given him great satisfaction; for he himself had a hand in bringing it about. This was the disposition of Lord North's plan of conciliation as set forth in the resolution of the House of Commons, February 20. The subject, it will be recalled, had been urged upon the attention of Congress by New Jersey as early as the 26th of May. Four days later Thomas Willing of Pennsylvania laid before Congress a document, said to have been written at the desire of Lord North by Mr. Gray Cooper, under-secretary of the British treasury, which began in a soft voice of personal suasion designed to induce the colonies to accept his Lordship's generous offer. "If the colonies are not blinded by faction", said Mr. Gray Cooper, "these terms will remove every grievance relative to taxation, and be the basis of a compact between the colonies and the mother country." But upon reading a little further, it appeared for all the world as if Mr. Secretary, while waving a small olive twig in one hand, held a threatening cudgel in the other. "The people of Great Britain", the paper went on to say, "are perfectly united in opinion and determined to pursue the most effectual measures, and to use the whole force of the Kingdom, if it be necessary, to reduce the rebellious and refractory provinces and colonies." *"Ordered* to lie on the table", is the crisp record of the Congressional decision; and on the table it lay accordingly, soon becoming buried under a pile of more insistent measures.

It might have seemed as if Lord North's plan of conciliation, as embodied in the House of Commons resolution of February 20, had by this time been given an effectual quietus. Congress had administered to it more than one severe blow, notably that dagger-thrust of the Declaration on taking up arms. But there were those who would not be content until they knew the corpse had been securely buried. New Jersey and Pennsylvania had each thrust a shovel into the hands of Congress; and next came Virginia to complete the interment and polish off the grave.

Virginia's part in the burial ceremonies had begun when Governor Dunmore called the assembly together for the express purpose of taking into consideration the joint address of the two houses of Parliament on which the resolution of the House of Commons of February 20 was founded. That assembly met on June 1, and on June 12 the House of Burgesses, in a committee report drawn by Thomas Jefferson, made its response. The Burgesses declared that for many reasons, which the report cogently set forth, it could not "close with the terms of that Resolution". They had "viewed it in every point of light" in which they were able to place it, and, "with pain and disappointment", they were brought ultimately to declare that "it only changes the form of oppression, without lightening its burden".

Immediately after presenting this report Jefferson departed for Philadelphia to take his seat in Congress; and he was particularly charged with presenting to Congress this response of the House of Burgesses. Just a month after he had taken his seat Congress came to a decision to appoint a committee "to take into consideration, and report on the resolution of the House of Commons, Feb[ruar]y 20, 1775, commonly called Lord North's Motion"; and Jefferson was placed on that committee, the others being Franklin, John Adams, and Richard Henry Lee. Of these four, John Adams could probably have found no more delectable task than to dig the grave of Lord North's conciliation plan and bury it so deep that no political Gabriel could resurrect it; yet, because the Virginia response was so much admired, it was Jefferson who was called upon to prepare the committee's report.

The report, as agreed to July 31, begins with the familiar thesis that "the colonies of America are entitled to the sole and exclusive privilege of giving and granting their own money", a privilege that involves the right to determine the conditions of the grant or to withhold it. Furthermore, this privilege of giving or of withholding is an important barrier against the undue exertion of prerogative, which, without such control, might be exercised oppressively. As for the proposition that, whenever any one of the American colonies shall make provision, according to its circumstances, for the common defense and for the support of civil government in the colony and such provision shall be approved by the king and Parliament, then the home government will forbear to levy any duty or tax applicable to that colony, except for the regulation of commerce, such a proposition, declares the committee, is both unreasonable and insidious: unreasonable, because to accede to it would be tantamount to agreeing to purchase the favor of Parliament without knowing what price Parliament might put upon its favor; insidious, because it would enable an artful ministry to divide the colonies by granting easier terms to one than to another.

As for the proposed suspension of the "pretended power of taxation", expressly made dependent upon the continuance of the colonial gifts, that would have the effect of making the revenue perpetual. Parliament itself had wisely avoided that danger by establishing the practice of granting supplies only from year to year. Moreover, the committee continued, what is proposed imports "only a suspension of the mode, not a renunciation of the pretended right to tax us". There is no proposal to repeal the obnoxious acts; on the contrary, at the very moment of holding out this proposition, other obnoxious measures are enacted.

Touching the question of making provision for the support of civil government and the administration of justice, the committee spoke with particular plainness: "The provisions we have made are such as please ourselves and are agreeable to our own circumstances. . . . While parliament pursue their plan of civil government within their own jurisdiction, we also hope to pursue ours without molestation." "Upon the whole", the report concludes, "this proposition seems to have been held up to the world, to deceive it into a belief that there was nothing in dispute between us but the *mode* of levying taxes"; and, more particularly, it appears to have been calculated "to lull into fatal security our well-affected fellow-subjects on the other side of the water, till time should be given for the operation of those arms, which a British minister pronounced would instantaneously reduce the 'cowardly' sons of America to unreserved submission." Upon an attentive consideration of all the facts, therefore, it is unlikely that the world will be deceived or will "hesitate to believe with us, that nothing but our own exertions may defeat the ministerial sentence of death or abject submission". Thus ended the first of Lord North's great efforts for conciliation.

While Congress was rejecting these proposals of conciliation as specious, it was not neglecting to take measures for defense. One such measure was to provide for treaties with the principal Indian tribes, and to that end the country was divided into three departments, northern, middle, and southern. Commissioners for the northern and middle departments were appointed July 13, those for the southern department July 19. For these negotiations good "talks" were necessary, and Congress appears to have found among its own members, or close at hand, persons skilled in the language of Indian diplomacy. From the field, the chase, the fireside, were drawn the terms in which to make clear to the Red Men how the quarrel with Great Britain had originated and to what a sorry pass it had come.

This recital of wrongs endured might well seem to have been designed to rouse the Red Men to go on the war path; but no: "We don't wish you to take up the hatchet against the king's troops. We desire you to . . . keep the hatchet burried deep." "Nothing but peace." That is the whole burden of their plea. "Brothers! We live upon the same ground with you. The same Island is our common birth-place. We desire to sit down under the same tree of peace with you: let us water its roots and cherish its growth, till the large leaves and flourishing branches shall extend to the setting sun, and reach the skies."

Another step taken in the closing days of July was the establishment of a continental postal system. On May 29, Congress had decided that the critical situation of the colonies rendered it "highly necessary that ways and means should be devised for the speedy and secure conveyance of Intelligence from one end of the Continent to the other", and had appointed a committee, of which Franklin was chairman, to investigate the subject and report. On July 26, Congress took the committee's report into consideration, and provided for the erection of a department, with a postmaster general at its head, and that, under his direction, a line of posts be established "from Falmouth in New England to Savannah in Georgia", with as many cross posts as the postmaster general should think fit. Benjamin Franklin, who had served in that capacity under the crown, was unanimously chosen postmaster general.

More directly in way of defensive measures were recommendations to the colonies to put their militia, which was to include all able-bodied men between the ages of sixteen and fifty, in a state of preparedness. Each colony was of course presumed to organize its own militia, but Congress proposed a general plan, specifying the composition of a company, the combination of companies into regiments or battalions, and the requisite officers of each. The companies were to choose their own officers, but the regimental officers were to be appointed by the provincial bodies—assemblies, conventions, or committees of safety. Something like committees of safety had for some time been functioning in most of the colonies, but Congress embraced this opportunity to recommend (July 18) that each colony appoint a committee of safety to superintend and direct all matters necessary for their security and defense in the recess of their assemblies or conventions. Thereafter such committees grew and waxed strong in every colony. At the same time Congress took occasion to recommend that each colony, "at their own expence", make such provisions as it deemed necessary for the protection of its harbors and sea coasts.

Just then came a letter from General Washington opening to the view of Congress some of the problems—some, but by no means all—involved in his task of bringing some sort of order out of that chaos called "the grand American army". One of his worries was a fierce squabble amongst the general officers over the question of relative rank—those of Connecticut in particular (Spencer, Wooster, and Putnam), and those of Massachusetts (Pomeroy, Thomas, and Heath) only in lesser degree. If the delegates of those colonies had had their worries over the appointment of these officers, as John Adams had plainly revealed, they were now driven to mortification and to distraction to patch up the quarrels.

But the army was in sore need of other officers besides generals—a commissary general, a paymaster general, a quartermaster general, a commissary of musters, a commissary of artillery, and possibly three brigade majors. There was unanimous agreement upon Joseph Trumbull of Connecticut as commissary general, upon James Warren of Massachusetts as paymaster general of the main army, and upon Jonathan Trumbull Jr. as paymaster of the forces in New York; but, as no one in Congress knew of suitable men for the other officers, it was decided to leave their appointment to General Washington. The decision was not, however, reached without opposition. The Massachusetts delegates in particular labored hard against it. Leaving to General Washington the "important and lucrative" offices of quartermaster general, commissary of musters, and commissary of artillery, declared John Adams, was "against every proper Rule and Principle", and he could "never sufficiently regret" that in doing so Congress had "acted so much out of Character". Those officers, he declared, were a check upon the general, and he upon them, and "there ought not to be too much Connection between them". This was one of the first definite manifestations of jealous fear of the commander of the army, but it was by no means the last.

Another urgent need of the army was a hospital establishment, and a committee was at once appointed (July 19) to prepare a plan. In later years there was nearly always a physician or two among the members of Congress; indeed the number from that profession chosen to the national body during its career is nothing short of extraordinary. But this plan for hospitalization in the army was entrusted to a group of laymen, Francis Lewis, Robert Treat Paine, and Henry Middleton. The establishment proposed by the committee, and adopted with but small modification July 27, deserves to be exhibited, as well as may be, to the patriots of these latter days.

Designed for an army of 20,000 men, the establishment was to comprise officers and attendants as follows: one director general and chief physician, salary four dollars per day; four surgeons, one and one-third dollars per day; one apothecary, one and one-third of a dollar; twenty mates, each two-thirds of a dollar; one clerk, two-thirds of a dollar; two storekeepers, each four dollars per month; one nurse to every ten sick, one fifteenth of a dollar per day, or two dollars per month; "Labourers occasionally". The list does not include a matron, but her duties are specified nevertheless, as are the duties of all the members of the hospital organization. The duties of the nurses were "to attend the sick, and obey the matron's orders". Dr. Benjamin Church of Boston was chosen to be director general and chief physician, and entrusted with the appointment of his subordinates. The capable Dr. Church was, however, to earn his chief distinction in the American contest, not as director of the army hospital, but as a purveyor of army secrets to the enemy.

When Congress first met it seemed to be the consensus of opinion that they would furnish the colonies the immediately needed counsel, then adjourn. Possibly it might depute a committee of its body to sit near the scene of action, or even betake itself thither. But some of the problems were not so easily solved as had been hoped, and new problems continually arose. A full month went by, and George Clinton wrote to John McKesson (June 10): "I wish I coud tell you when this Congress will break up; but this is a Secret I can by no means divulge and for the best Reason in the World because I do not know nor dare I even to Guess. . . . Business multiplies upon us by Expresses daily from different Quarters." Four days later (June 14) one of the Virginia delegates ventured the opinion, "The Congress will sit long." The opinion was no doubt founded on the practical certainty of a coming event; for on the morrow Congress would assume a new character. It would not abandon the rôle of advisor to the colonies collectively and individually, but it would take upon its shoulders the added task of defending and guiding all America. Thereupon all idea of definitely dissolving itself at any proximate date vanished; yet as business continued to drag heavily and the perplexities of their affairs to increase, members grew tired and began to yearn for a rest. "I begin to hope", John Adams wrote June 17, "we shall not sit all summer"; but Congress was "like a coach and six, the swiftest horses must be slackened, and the slowest quickened, that all may keep an even pace".

Before the end of the month members were once more playing with the idea of planting a committee near the army to keep watch, while Congress as a whole took a brief rest. Yet, as the days went by, the burdens grew heavier instead of lighter. There were some things that must be done. "As to the time of their rising", wrote a Virginia delegate July 5, "it is totally beyond conjecture. . . . At the same time such an impatience for home seems to possess us all, that nothing keeps Congress together but the visible certainty that till our military proceedings are got into a good train, their separation would endanger the common cause greatly."

Then, just when their hope of release was rising, they discovered that their military affairs were in anything but a good train. Indeed the "discord and confusion" in the army with which Washington was struggling was such that he besought Congress either to come nearer to Boston or to send a committee with whom he could take counsel. Benjamin Harrison, through whom Washington had made the request, presently reported to him (July 23) that he had proposed the removal, but that Congress had turned thumbs down on the suggestion. He then proposed sending a committee, but this proposition was also rejected. Although many members had long been talking of doing one or the other of these things, now, so Harrison reported to Washington, "the Gentlemen could not think of parting with the least particle of their power."

As for adjournment, it looked as if that might come about without a vote; for all the Maryland delegates had just taken their departure, and the Virginians were on the point of doing so. "Our going I Expect will break up the Congress", Harrison remarked; "indeed I think it is high time there was an End of it. we have been too long together." Eliphalet Dyer seemed to be of the same opinion. "We are all exhausted", he wrote (July 28), "sitting so long at this place and being so long confined together that we feel pretty much as a Number of passengers confined togeather on board ship in a long Voyage." In short, the members of the Congress had got on one another's nerves.

It was only a few days before this (July 21) that the bills of credit authorized a month ago began to come from the press, and that event must have started the financiers to figuring up the obligations already incurred by Congress. Those obligations totaled a considerable sum. The two millions of bills of credit would be exhausted almost by the time they were numbered and signed; and certainly the end of need was nowhere in sight. Straightway (July 25) Congress authorized the issue of another million. John Adams had thought they might have to issue as much as four millions; in fact, before the end of the year 1775 six millions had been emitted or authorized, and even that proved to be but a small beginning. Still, why worry? If all their problems had been as easily solved as the issuing of their promises to pay, they would have looked forth upon a bright, not a gloomy, world. And this time (July 29) Congress specified with a degree of definiteness the manner in which the issues should be redeemed. Each colony was to provide ways and means for sinking its own proportion of the bills, "in such manner as may be most effectual and best adapted to the condition, circumstances, and usual mode of levying taxes in such colony". The quotas were to be determined according to the number of inhabitants of all ages in each colony, "including negroes and mulattoes"; and, until the numbers of inhabitants could be definitely ascertained, Congress fixed upon the respective quotas for the three million dollars authorized. It was further provided that the redemption should be in four equal installments, payable on the last day of November of 1779, 1780, 1781, and 1782. Meticulous provision was also made for rendering the bills "unpassable" when redeemed, namely, by "taking care to cut, by a circular punch, of an inch in diameter, an hole in each bill". Furthermore, now that Congress had gone extensively into the money business it must have a treasurer—two of them, in fact, one to watch the other.

With only two or three more matters of pressing business—the payment of obligations already incurred, the remittance of money to the paymasters of the two armies, putting the last touches to the answer to Lord North's proposals of conciliation—Congress was ready to disband for a while, and on July 29 it was resolved, "That this Congress will, as soon as the public business permits, adjourn to the 5th of Sept[embe]r next." On the morning of Wednesday, August 2, "after the fatigue of many days", Congress adjourned accordingly. And let it be recorded to their credit that, instead of scampering toward their respective homes, most of them "immediately set of[f] for the Camp at Cambridge". They would fain see with their own eyes how the contest for their rights and liberties was progressing.

CHAPTER VI

THE WITHERED OLIVE BRANCH
CONGRESS BECKONS TO CANADA

The day to which Congress had adjourned, September 5, saw very few of the members in Philadelphia ready to resume their seats. Late assembling was, in fact, destined to become a chronic dereliction of Congress. By the 12th there was a quorum of members, but no president. Mr. Hancock had "a Touch of the Gout" and did not appear until the next day; then business began in earnest. One encouraging fact was that another colony, Georgia, had joined its twelve sisters in the contest, having chosen as representatives of the entire colony Archibald Bulloch, John Houstoun, Noble Wimberly Jones, and the Rev. John Joachim Zubly, in addition to Lyman Hall, who had hitherto sat as a delegate for the parish of St. John's only. Mr. Noble Wimberly Jones did not, however, attend under this election. Virginia also had made a new choice of delegates, retaining Harrison, Jefferson, Richard Henry Lee, and Peyton Randolph, and adding Thomas Nelson, George Wythe, and Francis Lightfoot Lee, the latter, a brother of Richard Henry, in place of Richard Bland, who had declined on account of age and infirmities. Maryland had likewise held a new election, but had returned all her former delegates. New Hampshire was sending Josiah Bartlett in place of John Sullivan, who had gone into the military service, and North Carolina had chosen John Penn in place of Richard Caswell, who had declined. But both the New Hampshire and the North Carolina delegates were belated in their coming.

While Congress was dallying with measures, John Adams, as was his wont, turned his surveying eye upon the men about him, then took time from sleep to set down his impressions. Adams's estimates of men are usually pointed and tolerably accurate—unless it happened that one of them was obstructing one of his cherished objectives; and the flashlight pictures he has left of the principal characters in this reassembled

Congress serve as a useful guide, as we endeavor to trail along after a Congress plodding, sometimes clumsily, sometimes wearily, at times indeed recklessly, through a hitherto unexplored country, knowing only the goal at which it aimed, but with uncertain knowledge of the way thereto. Some of these men Adams had sketched before. What he mainly did now was to sharpen outlines, add touches of color. Samuel Chase was violent, boisterous, tedious upon frivolous points. Edward Rutledge was very uncouth and ungraceful as a speaker, given to disagreeable bodily contortions, talked through his nose—"as the Yankees sing". His brother John was not much better, and "both of them spout out their language in a rough and rapid torrent". Eliphalet Dyer was "long-winded and round-about, obscure and cloudy, very talkative and very tedious, yet honest; means and judges well". Roger Sherman's manner was stiffness and awkwardness itself. "Hogarth's genius could not have invented a motion more opposite to grace" than the characteristic gesture of this Connecticut statesman.

All these were old-timers. Of the newcomers from Virginia, Thomas Nelson, a fat man, but alert and agile for his weight, was "a speaker", meaning doubtless a good speaker. Adams failed for some reason to describe George Wythe physically, merely recording that he was a lawyer of the first eminence. Francis Lightfoot Lee was "sensible and patriotic, as the rest of the family". Of the Georgia delegates, the Rev. Dr. Zubly not only was a very learned man, but was possessed of a warm and zealous spirit. John Houstoun, a young man and a lawyer, seemed sensible and spirited, but inexperienced. Archibald Bulloch drew all eyes upon himself by being clothed in American manufacture —a genuine tribute to the Association. It is not at all surprising that Adams should interject among his jottings respecting personalities a note of vexation that, in the debates, some members were showing "a remarkable want of judgment"; at the same time he is willing to testify that "the Congress . . . feels the Spirit of War, more intimately than they did before the Adjournment. They set about Preparations for it with Seriousness and in Earnest."

Chief among the serious, even delicate, problems propounded to Congress by General Washington was that of a thorough organization of the heterogeneous forces under his command. That would require the appointment of many officers, and these appointments would in turn involve innumerable colonial contentions and jealousies. Congress pondered the general's communications several days, then decided (September 29) to send a committee to the camp at Cambridge to confer not only with General Washington, but also with the executive authorities of Massachusetts, Connecticut, Rhode Island, and New Hampshire, "and such other persons as to the said Committee shall seem proper", with a view to determining "the most effectual method of continuing, supporting, and regulating a continental army". The committee, chosen September 30, consisted of Thomas Lynch of South Carolina, Benjamin Franklin of Pennsylvania, and Benjamin Harrison of Virginia. For instructions to the committee, the general purpose outlined in the resolution was not sufficient, therefore another committee was designated to prepare the instructions. These were adopted October 2. Upon the whole, the committee was limited to making inquiries and reporting its findings, although in a few particulars it might, in concert with the general, take certain definite measures.

In one important particular Congress stopped just short of sending to General Washington through the committee positive instructions. The committee was to declare to General Washington "the Sense of the Congress respecting an Attack on the Ministerial Troops at Boston and on Bunkers Hill". If it appeared likely that the enemy could be defeated and driven out of Boston by the last day of December, it was the sense of Congress that the attack should be made. If the present force was insufficient, the general might call in as many minute men as he thought necessary. If, however, such an attack should not be deemed feasible, it was the desire of Congress that the army be reduced in numbers and the pay of the men be lessened to five dollars per calendar month. That the defeat of the British forces was an essential preliminary to the redress of grievances, which was still the objective of the colonies, could scarcely then be gainsaid; but the colonies and their Congress had yet much to learn respecting the requirements of an efficient fighting force.

The committee took its departure from Philadelphia October 4 and arrived at headquarters October 15. "This Embassy", Samuel Adams wrote to James Warren (October 3), "I conjecture will be attended with great and good Consequences." Mr. Lynch, he remarked, was "a Man of Sense and Virtue". Colonel Harrison's character he was not, apparently, ready to vouch for to the same degree. Franklin was too well known of course to need any encomiums from Samuel Adams. "I hope", Adams continued, "these Gentlemen will be treated with all the Respect that is due to the publick Character they sustain."

The committee were not long in reaching the conclusion that the army, instead of being reduced, should be substantially increased, an opinion in which not only General Washington and the sundry other officials coincided, but likewise "every officer we conversed with on the subject"; and, what was more, "that every moment's delay was big with danger". There was a like unanimity of opinion, "not only that any reduction of pay was absolutely impracticable, but that a bare proposal of this nature would cause such discontents, if not mutinies, as would, perhaps, prove the ruin of the army."

The outcome of nearly ten days of consultations were: a proposal immediately to re-enlist the present army for a year and to make such additions, from militia and other .recruits, as necessary to bring the force at Boston to not less than 20,372 men; a thorough reorganization of the whole; and a material strengthening of the rules and regulations governing the army. In addition the committee went minutely into the matter of rations, the methods of supply, and numerous other matters pertaining to the organization and maintenance of the army.

The committee returned and laid its report before Congress, November 2; whereupon John Adams ventured to say (November 5), "They are pretty well convinced, I believe, of several important points, which they and others doubted before." It was, in fact, the committee's task to bring Congress to a way of thinking to which it had not been wont when the committee departed for Cambridge; and in that undertaking they were eminently successful, for their recommendations were approved by Congress almost item by item. Indeed, in addition to strengthening the army about Boston, Congress resolved to keep up three battalions in South Carolina and one in Georgia for the defense of those colonies. "I am happy to inform you", Thomas Lynch wrote to Washington November 13, "that Congress has agreed to every Recommendation of the Committee and have gone beyond it in allowing the additional pay to the Officers". He rejoiced at this, yet could not think with patience "that Pittyfull wretches who stood cavilling with you when entreated to serve the next Campaign should reap the Benefit of this addition." The Articles of War had also been amended in accordance with the committee's recommendation, and he hoped that the general would not now suffer his officers "to sweep the Parade with the skirts of their Coats or bottoms of their Trowsers, to cheat or mess with their Men, to skulk in battle or sneak in Quarters". Mr. Lynch may have conceived a favorable opinion of the Massachusetts colony in general, as both Samuel and John Adams believed was the case, but he certainly was not very favorably impressed with the conduct of a good many officers in the army.

In the midst of these efforts to consolidate the colonial forces into an efficient army, there was one discordant note. Samuel Adams had learned from Elbridge Gerry that Massachusetts was about to organize its militia, and he took occasion (October 29) to suggest to Gerry that the assembly might well be cautious of putting the militia under the directions of the generals of the continent, "at least until such a Legislative shall be established over all America as every Colony shall consent to." "The Continental Army", he went on to say, "is very properly under the Direction of the Continental Congress", and it might be that the national legislative, when and if it should be established, ought to have control of the military power of the individual colonies, but until then it seemed to him prudent that "the Militia of each Colony should be and remain under the sole Direction of its own Legislative which is and ought to be the sovereign and uncontroulable Power within its own limits or Territory." Gerry was essentially in agreement with Adams. "We already see", he remarked, "the growing thirst for power in some of the inferior departments of the army, which ought to be regulated so far as to keep the military entirely subservient to the civil in every part of the United Colonies."

Adams and Gerry were for the moment chiefly concerned with the question as it related to the militia, but the same conflict of doctrines was manifesting itself in Congress in connection with the reorganization of the army. The idea of making the army wholly Continental, Samuel Ward wrote to his brother (November 21), was leading to many alterations that were disgusting to both officers and men. "I have often told the Congress", he remarked, "that, under the idea of new modelling, I was afraid we should destroy our army. Southern gentlemen wish to remove that attachment, which the officers and men have to their respective colonies, and make them look up to the continent at large for their support or promotion." For his part, he never thought the attachment to the colony injurious to the common cause, but, on the contrary, "the strongest inducement to people to risk every thing in defence of the whole, upon the preservation of which must depend the safety of each colony." He would not therefore seek to eradicate that sentiment but to regulate it so as to conduce to the benefit of the whole. It was just such a formula for which Congress would soon be seeking, not for application to the army alone, but to the whole organization of the colonies.

Although Congress was naturally most concerned about the main army under General Washington at Boston, it could not overlook the lesser army under General Schuyler at Ticonderoga. Accordingly on the very day that the committee sent to Cambridge returned, Congress decided to send a committee with a similar purpose "to the northward". The committee chosen in this instance were all New Englanders: John Langdon of New Hampshire, Robert Treat Paine of Massachusetts, and Eliphalet Dyer of Connecticut. Dyer, however, asked to be excused, and Robert R. Livingston of New York was substituted. The committee of five designated to draw up the instructions for the committee of conference was given a wider geographical distribution, ranging from New York to South Carolina. The principal motivating influence in sending this committee to the northern army was to take needful measures for two expeditions to Canada, one against Montreal under General Richard Montgomery, the other against Quebec under the command of Colonel Benedict Arnold. The former had been set on foot by General Schuyler, the latter by Washington and Schuyler in concert.

General Schuyler had for some time been endeavoring to prevail on Congress to send a delegation of its body to confer with him respecting the Canadian expeditions and other problems, but Congress had declined to do so, "at least for the present". The general was nevertheless given quite explicitly the views of Congress with regard to Canada. Writing to General Schuyler by the hand of President Hancock (October 11), Congress said:

What they expect from your Endeavours is, that the Canadians be induced to accede to an Union with these Colonies, and that they form from their several Parishes a Provincial Convention, and send Delegates to this Congress. . . . You may assure them that we shall hold their Rights as dear as our own, and on their Union with us, exert our utmost Endeavours to obtain for them and their Posterity the Blessings of a free Government, and that Security to their Persons and Property, which is derived from the British Constitution. And you may further declare that we hold sacred the Rights of Conscience, and shall never molest them in the free Enjoyment of their Religion.

When finally Congress had decided to despatch a committee to Ticonderoga, this language respecting the Canadians, with scarcely the change of a word, was incorporated in the committee's instructions. That Congress did not, however, entirely underestimate the difficulties involved in the effort to persuade the Canadians to join their brethren of the south, is evidenced by that same letter of October 11, in which Schuyler is told, "The Temper, the Disposition and local Circumstances of our Brethren in that Colony must be known, before we can form a proper Judgment on so important a question."

The committee departed on its mission November 12. On that day Montgomery had taken possession of Montreal, although Congress would not of course learn of that event until a good many days thereafter. Apart from its mission at Ticonderoga, the committee had been assigned an additional function of inspecting the fortifications in the Highlands, then being erected under the general supervision of the New York authorities, and accordingly visited those fortifications on its way northward. From Albany, November 23, the committee sent back to Congress a factual report respecting the fortifications, diffidently offering some suggestions, one of which was that Congress would do well to obtain the opinions of persons more capable than the committee of passing judgment upon such matters. A month later the committee appears to have been able to throw off its diffidence, for, in a further report December 23, this advice was pressed upon Congress "with the utmost earnestness".

Meanwhile, on the 29th of November, came the news that Montgomery had taken Montreal. It was an exultant hour for Congress, for was not one of its dearest hopes about to burst into full bloom? A committee of three, James Wilson, William Livingston, and John Jay, each of whom was reputed, in the language of that day, to possess a very fine pen, was immediately appointed to draft letters of thanks to the three general officers in the northern department, Schuyler, Montgomery, and Wooster. "It is with the utmost Satisfaction", says the letter to General Schuyler, "that the Congress received your Information of the Surrender of Montreal, and the general Success which has attended the American Arms in the Province of Canada", and it was the unanimous resolve of that body that the general's conduct and perseverance merited their thanks. But General Schuyler had requested leave to retire, and the letter, written in the name of President Hancock, is largely devoted to an exhortation to him to reconsider his request. "Consider", Congress appeals to him, "that the road to glory is seldom strewed with Flowers, and that when the black and bloody Standard of Tyranny is erected in a Land possessed by Freeman, Patriots cease to remain inactive Spectators of their Country's Fall." And more of like kind. Schuyler was indeed to learn that his own road would be strewn with more thorns than flowers. To Montgomery, as was fitting, were offered more particularly the plaudits of the hero; but as he likewise had intimated a wish to retire, he too was exhorted "to persevere in the Cause, and to continue gathering fresh Laurels". Wooster was briefly thanked for his important assistance in reducing St. John's, "and spreading the Banners of Freedom over the greatest part of Canada". Strange to say, while these letters were sent forth bearing the date November 30, it was not until the 12th of December that they were actually reported to Congress and approved.

Had the letters been delayed only a few days longer, probably Congress would have been disposed to delete some passages in them, particularly that in the letter to General Montgomery declaring that "The Victories already gained in Canada afford us a happy Presage of the

Smiles of Providence on the farther Designation of the Continental Arms in the North". For on December 18 came letters from Montgomery and Arnold that indicated anything but a happy presage of the smiles of Providence; and five days later John Langdon, one of the committee to the northward, returned and laid before Congress a report from that committee that deepened the gloom, The committee informed Congress, for one thing, that Montgomery had had great difficulties in the first instance in persuading the troops to follow him to Canada, and, despite all his efforts, he had been unable to keep more than a fraction of them there. Not only had Montgomery's little army melted away to a pitifully insufficient force, the committee were convinced that it would be impossible for them to remain longer in that country in their present condition, "some of them", so the committee declared, "being half nacked, and those of the New York Troops, who are best Clad, haveing only a Coat, nearly worn out, and linnen under Cloaths."

If the committee had begun its mission with a degree of diffidence, it concluded it with a report that is by no means lacking in boldness. Not only is Congress admonished that it had made insufficient provision for clothing troops employed in the harsh Canadian climate in midwinter, to say nothing of its failure to take into consideration the extra-arduous and extra-hazardous nature of the expedition, the committee had counseled General Montgomery to endeavor to conceal and to disregard certain resolutions of Congress relative to pay and clothing. From what the committee had been able to learn, Arnold's force was in much the same condition as that of Montgomery. Arnold had nevertheless made his way through the wilderness, under incredible hardships, and, some days prior to the time this report was laid before Congress, had planted his small force in front of Quebec, where Montgomery presently joined him.

The late news from Canada might well have deflated the buoyancy of Congress, yet that ever buoyant assembly seems not to have been greatly perturbed. The whole subject was merely passed on to a committee for a further report, and about all that was done at the moment was the proposal of a committee that once more, through General Montgomery, the Canadians be invited to form a general convention

and send delegates to Congress. Even that proposition appears, however, to have been laid aside, while Congress went on with other business; for there was other urgent business demanding attention.

For one thing, a report of a committee on the condition of the treasury
revealed the need for more money. It is a fact well worth noting that
the committee recommended (December 26) that Congress issue no
more paper money but borrow the sums necessary on treasury notes
bearing interest. The consideration of that proposition was "referred
till Tomorrow"—a tomorrow that seems never to have come, and
the decision was taken to issue another three millions of bills of credit,
with provisions for redemption as in the case of the previous issue, except that the redemption of this latest issue was to be in the period
1783-1786. For another thing, Congress had for some time been planning the creation of a small Continental navy, and only on December 22
had brought the plan to a conclusion by the appointment of officers for
the little fleet.

Of greater concern, however, was the problem of trade, that question of opening the ports, to which Congress had devoted a good deal
of time before the adjournment, and on which there had been innumerable discussions since. The question whether to trade or not to trade
was, in fact, deeply agitating the assembly, when, on January 17, came
the startling news that, on the last day of December, General Montgomery had attempted to storm Quebec and had been killed; that
Colonel Arnold had been wounded and carried off the field, and that
thereupon the American forces had retreated.

It was a rude awakening from a hopeful dream. Congress had set
its heart upon drawing Canada into the orbit of the thirteen, and this
both for practical and for sentimental reasons. From a military point of
view it was of great importance to close that open door to invasion
from Canada, whereby the eastern colonies might be cut off from the
others. Besides, it would add much to the chances of success for their
cause if all the British colonies in North America should present a
united front, whether their objective be the redress of grievances or
something more. Unfortunately Congress had injured its own case
by its attack on the Quebec Act and its other anti-Catholic activities
and utterances, and it would probably require more of honeyed words

and beatific smiles than Congress could command to remove the bitter taste of the past. To make matters worse, at the very moment when Congress was setting before the Canadians its dishes of sweet persuasion, the conduct of its own soldiers in Canada appeared to give evidence of a lack of good faith.

Notwithstanding its mortifying failure thus far, Congress was not to be deterred from making another trial of its persuasive powers; and to this end determined (February 15) to send a committee to Canada to endeavor to win over that obstreperous colony. Declared John Adams, "The Unanimous Voice of the Continent is Canada must be ours; Quebec must be taken." And a little later (April 6) Robert Morris put the case quite concretely to General Gates: "I jump in Opinion with you, that Country must be ours at all Events; shou'd it fall into the hands of the Enemy they will soon raise a Nest of Hornets on our backs that will sting us to the quick."

The choice of the committee was of course a matter for very careful consideration. Franklin's "masterly Acquaintance with the French Language, his extensive Correspondence in France, his great Experience in Life, his Wisdom, Prudence, Caution; his engaging Address", to say nothing of other qualifications, pointed him out, says John Adams, "as the fittest Character for this momentous Undertaking." Next named for the mission was Samuel Chase of Maryland, chosen probably because he was "very active, eloquent, Spirited, and capable", and because he was strongly convinced of the importance of securing Canada. For the third member of the committee Congress went outside its own body and chose Charles Carroll of Carrollton, also of Maryland, distinguished for his high character and his zeal for the American cause, but chosen more particularly because he was a Catholic and might therefore more readily obtain the ear of the Catholic Canadians. Then, to further strengthen the Catholic influence in its mission, Congress prevailed upon Carroll's brother, John Carroll, a Catholic priest, to accompany the committee.

Whilst placing great confidence in the effective abilities of its committee, Congress was not disposed to trust to suasion alone. It would likewise despatch to Canada as strong an army as it was able and it would place in command of it the man whom many in Congress believed to be the most capable general in their service, Charles Lee. He had acquired a reputation for "great experience and skill" in the grim business of war; he was known to be very active and to possess "address"; and, not the least of his qualifications for this particular undertaking, he spoke French with fluency. Although these appointments were made in mid-February, it was not until March 25 that the ambassadorial committee took its departure from Philadelphia, to begin one more chapter in the story of the futile efforts to add a fourteenth member to the American union.

If there was anxiety in Congress on that March 25 over the outcome of the mission to Canada, there was great rejoicing over another event that to some in that assembly was scarcely equaled in importance. For immediately upon its assembling that Monday morning Congress was greeted with a letter from General Washington carrying the joyful intelligence that on the 17th the enemy had evacuated Boston. It was indeed a consummation for which to be devoutly thankful, even to be commemorated with a medal of gold. And what made the consummation all the more happy, it had been accomplished almost without bloodshed.

Ever since the preceding October, Congress had been rather insistent upon the general's undertaking the enterprise of driving the enemy out of Boston, if he perceived any hope of success, and had even gone the length of instructing him to disregard the possibility that the town might be destroyed in consequence of the attack. At first Congress seems scarcely to have realized that the enterprise would require not only heavy artillery but a good deal more powder than the army possessed. To overcome these deficiencies Washington obtained, by dint of extraordinary exertions on the part of Colonel Henry Knox, some heavy guns from Ticonderoga, and Congress scurried around and found some powder. Thereupon preparations were made for the siege.

Fortunately for the Americans, the British army was about as eager to get out of Boston as the American army was to get in. The winter's sojourn there had been anything but agreeable for the soldiers, and now their supplies of rations had run short. A sufficiency of rum alone consoled them for their deprivations. When, therefore, to these arguments were added some frowning guns on Dorchester Heights, General Howe decided to withdraw. The destination of his army was Halifax, Nova Scotia, and thither also went a small army of Loyalists, a thousand or so, who decided that the discretion of departure, while depart they might, was preferable to the valor of remaining to endure, at the hands of angry patriots, the ills they wot not of.

By this time, however, many kaleidoscopic changes had come over the American scene. Congress had had many things to think about, of more ultimate importance perhaps than the evacuation of Boston or the conquest of Canada. Whatever lingering hope there had been for reconciliation had, by the beginning of October, pretty well evaporated. Summarizing the latest intelligence from England, Samuel Ward wrote to his brother, October 11, "In a word all hopes of a speedy reconcilliation are over, and we unanimously determine to push the war with the greatest vigour." A month later came news that drove that conviction deeper into every mind. It was a letter from the colonial agents in London dated September 2, received by Congress November 9, conveying the information that the petition to the king had been handed the secretary of state for America for presentation to his majesty, and the secretary, when pressed for an answer, had replied, "As his Majesty did not receive it on the throne, no answer would be given." To most Americans this contemptuous scorning of their petition was probably not wholly unexpected, to some it was perhaps not unwelcome. John Adams at least must have derived a certain comfort from the knowledge that his opinion had been justified by the event.

The refusal of the petition was not, however, to be alone in bringing conviction to Congress and to the country that no smooth road to their goal was to be opened to them; for, by the same vessel had come further confirmation of the administration's purposes.

Terms of Accommodation [wrote Samuel Ward November 11], that is the Terms upon which they are willing to receive Us and our Posterity for their Slaves are to be committed to the General and that they will treat with Us in no other Way. . . . If Administration succeeds they are determined . . . to extirpate the New England Colonies. an Army from Canada and the 20000 men from england they suppose capable of doing this.

Such threats, he declared, would only animate all in their country's cause. "Every private View, Passion and Interest", he went on to say, "ought to be buried; We are embarked in one common Bottom, if She sinks We all perish; if She survives the Storm, Peace and Plenty (the offspring of Liberty), and every thing which will dignify and felicitate human Nature will be the Reward of our Virtue." Then came the king's proclamation of August 23, declaring the American colonies in a state of rebellion and threatening condign punishment to the authors, perpetrators, and abettors of those traitorous designs.

It was indeed high time the country was bracing itself for a contest other than of words. By no means unaware of this fact, Congress still put great faith in the potency of words. They might not be effective weapons against the enemy, but they could be used to win friends at home and abroad; rightly used they could be made to strengthen the spirit and stiffen resolve. There must be a reply to the letter of the colonial agents, and a first-rate answer to the king's proclamation was much to be desired. A reply to the colonial agents was approved November 29, just when Congress had learned of Montgomery's success at Montreal, and Congress did not neglect to point to the operations in Canada as sufficiently evincing "what little success is likely to attend ministerial exertions for bringing the Catholics of Canada and the savages of the wilderness to war on the defenceless women and children of unoffending America". Happy it was for mankind "that ministers can form destructive plans with much more facility than they can execute them". The manner in which "the last dutiful petition to his majesty" had been received and the subsequent proclamation were only "further proofs of those malignant councils, that surround the sovereign and distract the British Empire". Nevertheless Congress clung to the hope that "the spirit and virtue of a sensible nation will soon be exerted to procure justice for the innocent oppressed colonies and to restore harmony and peace to the British Empire".

To frame a proper retort upon the king's proclamation was a more difficult and delicate undertaking. On November 13 a committee had been appointed "to prepare a declaration in answer to sundry illegal proclamations that have lately appeared in America", and it was that same November 29 that the committee laid the product of its labors before Congress. It was ordered to lie on the table "for the perusal of the members". If the members did not peruse it at once, they must have done so three days later, when still another proclamation fluttered down before the eyes of Congress, to stir its individual and collective wrath. This was Lord Dunmore's proclamation of martial law and worse down in Virginia. Well then, if the British administration and its henchmen in America were out to win the contest with proclamations, Congress also could indite proclamations, declarations, and all such. In fact, they had one ready and waiting. On December 6 it was debated by paragraphs and adopted and ordered to be published.

This declaration of "the thirteen United Colonies in North America" is principally a disclaimer to the charge that the colonies were in rebellion; but it is in a measure also a retort upon that part of the king's proclamation that called upon all and sundry "to disclose and make known all treasons and traitorous conspiracies which they shall know to be against us, our crown and dignity", in which category of condemnation were included "all persons who shall be found carrying on correspondence with, or in any manner or degree aiding or abetting the persons now in open arms and rebellion against our Government". It is a somewhat labored defense, yet it has much of the root of the matter in it.

We are accused [the colonies declaim] of "forgetting the allegiance which we owe to the power that has protected and sustained us". Why all this ambiguity and obscurity in what ought to be so plain and obvious, as that he who runs may read it? What allegiance is it that we forget? Allegiance to Parliament? We never owed—we never owned it. Allegiance to our King? Our words have ever avowed it—our conduct has ever been consistent with it. We condemn, and with arms in our hands—a resource which Freemen will never part with—we oppose the claim and exercise of unconstitutional powers, to which neither the Crown nor Parliament were ever entitled.

Touching the other phase of the proclamation, the declaration of Congress had several things to say, among them that "a correspondence between the inhabitants of Great Britain and their brethren in America, produced, in better times, much satisfaction to the individuals, and much advantage to the public." By what criterion was a correspondent now to regulate his conduct? The law is silent on the subject, and "can proclamations, according to the principles of reason and justice, and the constitution, go farther than the law?" In the event that these principles should not prevail, "we must resort to arguments drawn from a different source." There is no threat of independence anywhere in the declaration—quite to the contrary—yet it is evident enough that the leaven of independence was at work. In fact, just at this moment there were efforts, presently to be referred to, to extract the leaven before it should leaven the whole lump.

The preparation of these utterances of Congress was probably, in part at least, responsible for the germination of an idea that was to have far-reaching consequences in the conduct of the business of Congress. On the same day (November 29) that the declaration and the reply to the colonial agents were laid before Congress that body resolved to appoint a committee of five "for the sole purpose of corresponding with our friends in Great Britain, Ireland, and other parts of the world". The significant feature of this decision was that the committee was to act chiefly upon its own initiative, the only restriction being that the committee should lay its correspondence before Congress when directed. With just as little restriction Congress pledged itself to pay the committee's expenses, including the payment of any agents that the committee might find it needful to employ; and on December 11 three thousand dollars were put into the committee's hands. As at first constituted, the committee consisted of Benjamin Harrison, Benjamin Franklin, Thomas Johnson, John Dickinson, and John Jay; but two months later (January 30) Robert Morris was added. Called at first the Committee of Correspondence, the committee itself soon added the word "secret", and as the Committee of Secret Correspondence it was thereafter designated until, on April 17, 1777, Congress resolved that "for the future, it be styled the Committee for Foreign Affairs". Such was the beginning of what is now known as the Department of State.

The creation of a committee of secret correspondence was not quite, however, the first instance in which Congress permitted to one of its committees a degree of discretionary power, for another committee, self-directing and with rather broadly defined authority, had been functioning for some six weeks. On September 18 Congress had decided to set a committee to work contracting for the importation of powder and munitions and on the following day had designated nine of its members for the purpose. On the 6th of October the committee was empowered to export produce in payment for its purchases, and on November 8 that power was further extended. At that time it was called the Secret Committee, and that name clung to it until July 5, 1777, when it likewise received a new christening, under the name of the Committee of Commerce. By March, 1776, the Secret Committee and the Committee of Secret Correspondence were closely cooperating, and, because each carried the word "Secret" in its title and because the membership of the two was partly identical, they were sometimes confused with one another. The Committee of Commerce, as it came to be designated, functioned through the greater part of the war essentially as an executive department of Congress—indeed it was sometimes so secretive in its operations that it carefully concealed them from Congress—still it did not, as did some others of the standing committees, blossom into a full-grown department under the new government of 1789.

Closely related to the Secret Committee in origin and to some extent in purpose was what came to be called the Marine Committee, which in time developed into the Department of Marine, the progenitor of the later Navy Department. The Marine Committee, however, did not have a single origin. On October 5, 1775, a committee of three was appointed to prepare a plan for the interception of two British vessels laden with arms and powder; on October 13 another committee was appointed to carry out the plan and was assigned the additional function of fitting out two swift sailing vessels; and on October 30 it was instructed to fit out two additional vessels, while its personnel was enlarged from three to seven. This committee was for a time referred to by the cumbrous phrase "the committee for fitting out armed vessels", but soon came to be designated as the Naval Committee. It was this Naval Committee that formulated the "Rules for the Regulation of the Navy of the United Colonies", adopted by Congress November 28, and it was the same committee that, on December 22, submitted to Congress a list of officers for the Continental fleet of four armed vessels— the *Alfred,* the *Columbus,* the *Andrew Doria,* and the *Cabot.* But this was nearly the last of its performances. The Naval Committee, so called, does not appear to have been a standing committee but one of limited scope and purpose, and, having completed the task for which it was appointed, perhaps also because its membership had dwindled in consequence of absences, it was allowed to die a natural death.

Meanwhile a more comprehensive plan for creating a navy was under consideration, having its origin in quite a different source. On October 3 the Rhode Island delegates laid before Congress an instruction from their House of Magistrates, urging "the building and equipping an American fleet". The subject was debated from time to time until December 11, when a committee of one from each colony was appointed "to devise ways and means for furnishing these colonies with a naval armament". This committee reported a plan December 13, and on the following day a committee, again one from each colony, was designated to carry the plan into execution. It was the committee of December 14, which, as it happened, was nearly identical with that of December 11, that became the Marine Committee.

In the domain of finance, although the development presently culminated in the establishment of a standing committee of Congress whose function was to superintend the business of the treasury, that committee was less directly than in the cases previously mentioned an outgrowth from committees of lesser scope. The functioning of committees of accounts and claims did indeed have a part in the development, but more specifically the treasury department had its beginning in the appointment of two treasurers (July 29, 1775), who were not members of Congress. The characteristic step of placing the general supervision of the treasury and all matters of finance in the hands of a standing committee of Congress was taken February 17, 1776, when five members were assigned to that task. Although there were subsequent reorganizations, some of them very thoroughgoing, the committee form was retained until 1781.

Nearly a month before this initial step toward the creation of a department of finance a committee was appointed (January 24) "to consider the propriety of establishing a war office, and the powers with which the said office should be vested". How earnestly and how extensively the committee considered the question is not known, but it was not until June 12 that it was prompted to offer a report. At that moment the country was deeply stirred over the question of independence, and there was every reason to believe that Congress was destined to have a good-sized war on its hands. Accordingly it was resolved (June 12) to establish a war office, to be presided over by a committee of Congress, with the title "A Board of War and Ordnance", to consist of five members. Congress would in time learn that every attempt to carry on its administrative business through the instrumentality of groups of its own members was doomed to disappointments, failures, inefficiences; and among the earlier of these lessons was that no group of men whose chief concerns were legislative and political were fitted to plan and conduct a war. There ensued in consequence much puttering with the board of war, and always without distinguished success. Congress itself was an experiment and must needs in its turn do a lot of experimenting in whatever it set its hand to do. Not until a decisive crystalization of the fundamentals of government should take place in Congress itself would the leaven of permanency and efficiency begin to work in its branches.

CHAPTER VII

CONGRESS OFFERS COUNSEL
THE COLONIES LOOK TO THEIR OWN HEARTHS

If there was one chaos at the center, which was Congress, there were thirteen confusions at the rim, which were the colonies. Massachusetts had early besought Congress to advise the colony to set up its own government, but Congress had counseled tentative steps only. Then, in October, 1775, New Hampshire, finding herself in a "convuls'd state", with worse confusion threatened, instructed her delegates to use their utmost endeavors to obtain the advice and direction of Congress "with respect to a method for our administering justice, and regulating our civil police". To John Adams, long eager to have all the colonies fortify themselves behind governments of their own making, the New Hampshire request was as a stimulating draft. "I embraced with joy", he wrote at a later time, "the opportunity of haranguing on the subject at large, and of urging Congress to resolve on a general recommendation to all the States [he should have written *Colonies*] to call conventions and institute regular governments."

Notwithstanding the many reasons that Adams offered, as he avers, for pursuing that course, Congress was not persuaded. The advice it did give New Hampshire must, nevertheless, have been nearly all that the statesmen of that province hoped for. That advice (November 3) was, in effect, that the Provincial Convention call "a full and free representation of the people", and that this latter body "establish such a form of government, as, in their judgment, will best produce the happiness of the people, and most effectually secure peace and good order in the province, during the continuance of the present dispute between Great Britain and the colonies."

The arguments on this matter [wrote the New Hampshire delegates that same day] . . . were truly Ciceronial, the eminent Speakers did honour to themselves and the Continent; carried by a very great majority. . . . You'll see that the government is limited to the present contest: To ease the minds of some few persons who were fearful of Independence, we tho't it adviseable not to oppose that part too much, for once we had taken any sort of government nothing but Negotiation with Great Britain can alter it.

The delegates' own counsel was "not to proceed as far as Governor at present, tho' the Door may be left open for that purpose." Samuel Adams expressed the belief that all the New England governments would soon be on the same footing. "I am of opinion", he wrote to Elbridge Gerry (November 4), "it will not be long before every Colony will see the Necessity of setting up Governments within themselves for Reasons that appear to me to be obvious." John Adams wrote to James Warren in similar terms, and both cautioned their correspondents to say nothing of the matter until they should see it published. New Hampshire accordingly went on her way rejoicing—for a little while at least; although it was not long before querulous voices had arisen in that colony, with the result that New Hampshire again appeared at the bar of Congress, with a plea to that body to settle the dispute amongst them.

It so happened that the chairman of the committee that drew the advice to New Hampshire was John Rutledge of South Carolina, and he now made a like request in behalf of his own colony. There appears to have been no hesitancy in offering South Carolina the same counsel that had been given New Hampshire, with the addition only of a discretionary proviso, "if the Convention of South Carolina shall find it necessary", a proviso deemed essential because of the distance of that colony from the main fountain of advice.

If there was any expenditure of Ciceronial eloquence, it was on the part of John Adams, who once again, so he avers in later recollections, endeavored to get the resolution enlarged to the extent of recommending to all the colonies to institute governments. He even strove to have the words "province", "colony", "colonies", expunged, words that he "mortally hated", and "state" or "states" substituted. "But the child was not yet weaned." He did succeed, he says, in getting the phrase "Mother Country" dropped, but he was not so successful in his efforts to have the word "dispute" cast into the discard and to put in its place the word "war". But "what plan of government would you recommend?" members asked. Well, he had plans aplenty. His mind was fairly wriggling with plans. "I had in my head and at my tongue's end", he declared, "as many projects of government as Mr. Burke says the Abbé Sieyès had in his pigeon-holes"; but he was chary of offering more than general suggestions.

No doubt Adams and others of the "forward-looking" group in Congress were much encouraged when, a month later, a third colony appeared to have turned its back upon the past and grasped at what the immediate future offered. On December 2 word came to Congress from Northampton, Virginia, that the governor, Lord Dunmore, had "Erected his Standard at Norfolk", and from on board ship had issued a proclamation, declaring martial law, inviting the negroes to join him, and offering them their freedom. The proclamation had been issued as long ago as November 7, and since then the governor had been stirring up trouble in a number of ways both for Virginia and for Congress. As concerned itself, Congress took immediate measures to meet the emergency, and two days later recommended to the inhabitants of Virginia "to resist to the utmost the arbitrary government intended to be established therein by their governor". Then, without waiting for an application from Virginia, Congress went a step further and recommended to the Virginia Convention, if that body should find it necessary, to establish such form of government as in their judgment would best produce the happiness of the people, etc., couching the recommendation in the same language that was used in the cases of New Hampshire and South Carolina. "Gentlemen seem more and more to enlarge their views", Samuel Adams wrote to James Warren the next day, "and we must be content to wait till the fruit is ripe before we gather it." The Virginia Convention, for its part, was not slow in taking measures to nullify or check the activities of the royal governor; it even countered his proclamation with one of its own (December 13).

A strong current of supplication seems now to have set in toward Congress as a focal center; yet at the very moment when Congress was boldly offering its counsel to the Virginia Convention, oddly enough it found itself in the position of a suppliant to one of the colonies. On the

27th of November the New Jersey assembly then sitting at Burlington, appointed a committee to draft a petition to the king, "humbly beseeching him to use his interposition to prevent the effusion of blood; and to express the great desire this House hath to a restoration of peace and harmony with the Parent State, on constitutional principles". When news of this movement came to Congress, that body forthwith

> *Resolved unanimously,* That in the present situation of affairs, it will be very dangerous to the liberties and welfare of America, if any Colony should separately petition the King or either house of Parliament.

And it further resolved to send a committee of three members to confer with the New Jersey assembly on the subject. The committee chosen were John Dickinson, George Wythe, and John Jay, who proceeded to Burlington the following day (December 5) and made their plea before that assembly.

Respecting the outcome of this mission the Journals of Congress are strangely silent; and the record of proceedings in the New Jersey house reveal only that, when the proposed petition was taken up that same day in committee of the whole, it was resolved that it "be referred", on the ground that a petition was already before his majesty and that an answer to the former petition ought to be awaited before presenting another. It was thus that the New Jersey assembly saved its face, while yielding to the persuasion of Congress.

Some record nevertheless of the representation made by the committee of Congress has been preserved, in a communication from Governor Franklin to Lord Dartmouth just a month later. "After the draught of an address was prepared, which would probably have passed the House", Governor Franklin wrote, "a Committee of the General Congress at Philadelphia came in great haste to Burlington, desired admittance into the Assembly, which being granted, they harangued the House for about an hour on the subject, and persuaded them to drop the design." A gentleman present had taken down the substance of the remarks made by members of the committee, particularly those of Mr. Dickinson, and the governor was enabled to send his Lordship a copy of those notes. Mr. Dickinson briefly summarized the course of the controversy up to the time when the petition to the king had been rejected, then argued that it was the policy of Great Britain to divide the colonies and that she would therefore encourage separate petitions. For that very reason it behooved the colonies to avoid them. It had become necessary to convince Britain that we would fight and were not "a rope of sand". If the country stood united, it could not be conquered. "He spoke", says the memorandum, "more than half an hour." Mr. Jay declared that "we had nothing to expect from the mercy or justice of Britain", therefore, not petitions, but "vigour and unanimity" were the necessary means to the end. Then he shrewdly pointed the assembly to a way out of their dilemma, by remarking that the petition already presented ought to be relied on and that others were unnecessary. "He spoke about twelve minutes." And the memorandum concludes, "Mr. Wythe spoke about eight minutes, to the same purpose."

The governor's letter, with its enclosures, did not, however, get very far on its way toward London and Lord Dartmouth; for on the following day the messenger was overhauled near Elizabeth Town, at the instance of Lord Stirling, and relieved of his packet, which was despatched to Congress. In what manner the New Jersey hurdle had been overcome was no doubt already well known to Congress, for the committee upon its return must have given a satisfactory account of its mission.

What the governor himself had to say, however, on this and other subjects, was by no means lacking in a fresh interest for Congress. For one thing, he stated that several petitions had been presented to the assembly at its recent session, "praying them to discourage any attempt to promote an Independency on Great Britain". One such petition, from thirty-two freeholders of the county of Burlington, laid before the assembly November 23, expressed great alarm "at the sentiments of independency which are openly avowed by too many people at this time", in response to which the assembly came into a series of resolutions (November 28):

1. That the reports of Independency, in the apprension of this House, are groundless.

2. That it be recommended to the Delegates of the Colony to use their utmost endeavours for the obtaining a redress of American grievances, and

for restoring the union between the Colonies and Great Britain, upon constitutional principles.

3. That the said Delegates be directed not to give their assent to, but utterly to reject any propositions, if any should be made, that may separate this Colony from the Mother Country, or change the form of Government thereof.

In his letter to Lord Dartmouth, Governor Franklin had expressed the opinion that the majority of the people of New Jersey, and of Pennsylvania as well, were opposed to independence; "But", said he "the danger seems to be that the design will be carried on by such degrees, and under such pretences, as not to be perceived by the people, in general, till too late for resistance." At the opening of the session the governor had addressed the assembly on the subject of the rebellion amongst the colonies, and when the assembly came to respond to that address (November 30), it reiterated the statement, "We know of no sentiments of independency that are, by men of any consequence, openly avowed", and emphasized its own sentiments as expressed in its resolutions two days before.

Earlier in that same month (November 9) the assembly of Pennsylvania had given the delegates of that province instructions similar to those emanating from the New Jersey assembly, that they use their "utmost endeavours" to obtain a redress of grievances, at the same time strictly enjoining them utterly to reject any propositions that might lead to a separation from the mother country or to a change in the form of government. Following the publication of these instructions there was a prolonged discussion of the question pro and con in the Philadelphia papers, wherein one or another of the writers made allusion to Governor Franklin's pronouncements on the subject.

It was not long before Maryland, acting through a colonial convention sitting at Annapolis, pursued a course similar to that of New Jersey and Pennsylvania, although with a degree of caution and with provisos that found no place in the actions of those two colonies. On the 11th of January the Maryland Convention adopted a carefully drawn body of instructions to guide the conduct of their delegates in Congress "in certain points". First of all, it was declared to be the ardent wish of Maryland for a reconciliation with the mother country, "upon terms that may ensure to these Colonies an equal and permanent freedom"; therefore the delegates were admonished to keep constantly in view "the avowed end and purpose for which these Colonies originally associated—the redress of American grievances, and securing the rights of the Colonists". Accordingly, "should any proposition be happily made by the Crown or Parliament, that may lead to or lay a rational and probable ground for reconciliation", the delegates were to use their "utmost endeavours to cultivate and improve it into a happy settlement and lasting amity, taking care to secure the Colonies against the exercise of the right assumed by Parliament, to tax them, and to alter and change their Charters, Constitutions, and internal polity, without their consent."

Touching the question of independence, the injunction was not, as in the cases of New Jersey and Pennsylvania, "utterly to reject" such a proposition; rather, the delegates were instructed not to assent to any propositions for independence, alliance with a foreign power, or even a confederation of the colonies such as might lead to a separation from the mother country, without the previous knowledge and approbation of the convention—that is, unless a majority of the delegates should be convinced that the measure proposed was "absolutely necessary for the preservation of the liberties of the United Colonies". The instructions were not at the time revealed to Congress, but one of the delegates, Robert Alexander, himself much pleased with them, showed them in confidence to John Dickinson and others, presumably moderates only, who declared, "they breath that Spirit, which ought to govern all publick Bodies, Firmness tempered with Moderation".

Thus three colonies, one after another, had shaken a monitory finger at Congress, admonishing that body not to do that which, severally and collectively, it had long been vociferating that it had no intention of doing. A fourth colony, New York, seemed to be in a like mood with the other three, although not yet quite able to resolve its mental confusion, stumbling with tangled footsteps, fumbling inconsistently, stuttering incoherently. In time that colony would find itself, although belatedly.

It would seem as if the passing of the old year and the coming of the new had given an impetus of its own to the thought of independence.

On the 8th of January had come the king's speech of October 27, in which the colonies were definitely charged with aiming at independence. On the 9th, Congress had a look at a similar charge by Governor Franklin, along with the proceedings in New Jersey. Then, on the 11th, followed the action of the Maryland Convention, although Congress as a whole would probably not learn of that action for some time. But why should the negative theme be played with the loud pedal, unless to drown the overtones of the affirmative?

With these loudly reiterated charges pouring down upon the head of Congress, it was high time, thought some members, that the issue be clarified. If the colonies did not aim at independence, if Congress had no such purpose, then their constituents, the whole world in fact, should be told so in express terms. On the 9th of January, accordingly, James Wilson of Pennsylvania made a motion to that effect, prompted no doubt by the statement of Governor Franklin that had just been read. There was opposition of course, nevertheless a day (Friday, January 12) was fixed for going into that affair. "Several Members", so Richard Smith recorded in his Diary, "said that if a Foreign Force shall be sent here, they are willing to declare the Colonies in a State of Independent Sovereignty."

There was good reason for pointing to the possible use of a foreign force, for there were persistent reports that the British ministry had been scouring Europe for mercenary troops with which to suppress the American rebellion; and that very day it was reported that a fleet, with 5000 troops on board, had been sighted at sea. Wilson's motion was not taken up January 12, not in fact until the 24th; but on the 15th, Samuel Adams opened his mind somewhat on the subject to John Adams, then absent. The motion, he said, alarmed him. He thought that Congress had been explicit enough and might by this motion be drawn on to dangerous ground. He and others had labored to have the matter postponed and had even sought to prevent the fixing of a day for its consideration. For once, however, he had become doubtful about the wisdom of his own course.

The discussion on January 24, in which "much was said about Independency and the Mode and Propriety of stating our Dependance on the King", resulted in the appointment of a committee to prepare such an address, and the drafting of the document was, naturally, entrusted to James Wilson. It is well to remember that it was on this same January 24 that Congress began seriously to consider the propriety of establishing a war office, and that it was just one week earlier that the failure of the Canadian expedition had become known. Wilson laid the product of his labors before Congress on February 13. The proposed address, Richard Smith recorded, was "very long, badly written and full against Independency". Then he adds parenthetically (a remark evidently interpolated at a later time), "Wilson perceiving the Majority did not relish his Address and Doctrine never thought fit to stir it again." In his assertion that the address was "very long", Smith did not exaggerate, for it runs to some 6000 words; and on the score of quality, it drags its weary length along quite heavily. On the other hand, the opinion of the New Jersey delegate that it was "full against Independency" is scarcely justified. At all events, Congress ordered the address "to lie on the table". Wilson himself declared at a later day (to James Madison) that "it was meant to lead the public mind into the idea of Independence, of which the necessity was plainly foreseen by Congress"; and, in an address to his fellow-Pennsylvanians in 1780 (*Pennsylvania Evening Post,* October 17), he explained that at the time he drew the address the delegates of Pennsylvania were expressly restricted from consenting to independence, and that, although he had early foreseen that independence "could not but be the ultimate end", his "uniform language in Congress" had been that he would not vote for it without the authority of his constituents.

Whatever may have been Wilson's immediate purpose, if the address had actually found its way to the public, a wakeful and persevering reader would in the end have come upon a climacteric conclusion to a story of the contest that might well have led him to vision independence through the mists. The address closes with these words: "That the Colonies may continue connected, as they have been, with Britain, is our second Wish: Our first is—that America may be free." This sentence at least made an impression upon some members, for the words were echoed the very next day in a letter of John Penn of North Carolina: "My first wish is that America may be free; the second that we may be restored to peace and harmony with Britain upon Just and proper terms." Indeed Penn's colleague, William Hooper, who was a fellow-member with Wilson on the committee, may have been the author of the expression; for he had used almost the identical phraseology on February 6.

In the statement to Madison referred to above Wilson remarked that, at the time the address was presented, "the language became evidently short of the subsisting maturity for that measure", meaning independence. The truth of this statement is beyond a peradventure; for it was just during those days when Congress set about its endeavor to quiet the anxious minds of the people and soothe constituent nerves on the question of independence that that blazing comet, Thomas Paine's *Common Sense,* was beginning to sweep its fiery perihelion course across the American skies. It was one more of those new-year propulsions toward independence, and the most powerful of them all. Published on the 8th of January, 1776, it was soon being read by everybody in America. Within three months, it has been asserted, one hundred and twenty thousand copies had been sold, and it was reprinted over and over again. And wherever it was read it was extravagantly lauded, or as extravagantly denounced. That it had a tremendous influence in crystalizing sentiment in favor of independence is unquestionable.

It is not to be doubted that members of Congress were amongst the earliest readers of Paine's inflammatory appeal, or to be presumed that they had failed to follow the discussions of it in the Philadelphia papers; yet for some time they kept strangely silent respecting it. The pamphlet was more than a month old when the first of them, so far as discovered, timidly ventured to point it out to friends back home. On the day that Congress rejected Mr. Wilson's address, Joseph Hewes of North Carolina wrote to Samuel Johnston: "The only pamphlet that has been published here for a long time I now send you; it is a Curiosity; we have not put up any to go in the Waggon, not knowing how you might relish independency. The author is not known; some say Doctor Franklin had a hand in it, he denies it." At the same time Hewes's colleague, Penn, sent a copy to Thomas Person, along with that letter (February 14) in which he voiced as his first wish that

America may be free. It was a few days earlier that John Adams, journeying back to Congress after an absence of two months, came upon the pamphlet in New York and sent a copy of it to his wife. Writing to her on February 18, he remarked that "the further encroachments of tyranny, and depredations of oppression" would probably soon make the doctrines expounded by Paine "the common faith".

If, on the other hand, members of Congress were as yet disposed to keep only eyes and ears open, the mouth tightly closed, not so some who were outside that circle of caution. On January 24 (the day on which James Wilson and his fellow-committeemen were instructed to draft the explanatory address) General Charles Lee wrote to Washington:

Have you seen the pamphlet *Common Sense?* I never saw such a masterly, irresistible performance. It will, if I mistake not, in concurrence with the transcendent folly and wickedness of the Ministry, give the coup-de-grace to Great Britain. In short, I own myself convinced, by the arguments, of the necessity of separation.

If Washington had not then read the pamphlet, he had done so by January 31, when, in a letter to Joseph Reed, he spoke of "the sound doctrine and unanswerable reasoning" of the author. Ten days later he opened his mind to Reed more explicitly on the subject of independence. For his part, he wrote, he had "never entertained an idea of an accommodation" since the measures taken by the British government after the Bunker Hill fight, and the king's speech had but confirmed those sentiments.

If every man was of my mind [Washington declared], the ministers of Great Britain should know, in a few words, upon what issue the cause should be put. . . . I would tell them, that we had borne much, that we had long and ardently sought for reconciliation upon honorable terms, that it had been denied us, that all our attempts after peace had proved abortive, and had been grossly misrepresented, that we had done every thing which could be expected from the best of subjects, that the spirit of freedom beat too high in us to submit to slavery, and that, if nothing else could satisfy a tyrant and his diabolical ministry, we are determined to shake off all connexions with a state so unjust and unnatural. This I would tell them, not under covert, but in words as clear as the sun in its meridian brightness.

It was by no means as a new convert that Washington had been brought by *Common Sense* to espouse the doctrine of independence; the rather, Paine's disquisition had produced only a deepening of his convictions, with possibly a clarification of his reasoning. Similar doubtless was the case of Nathanael Greene, who had written to his brother as early as December 20: "We are now driven to the necessity of making a declaration of independence"; and to Samuel Ward in Congress on January 4: "America must raise an empire of permanent duration, supported upon the grand pillars of truth, freedom, and religion, based upon justice, and defended by her own patriotick sons." In deep sincerity therefore he recommended a declaration of independence and a "call upon the world, and the great God who governs it, to witness the necessity, propriety, and rectitude thereof". Greene was certainly not one of Paine's converts. Neither was that writer down in North Carolina, calling himself "A British American", who wrote December 28:

Thanks be to Heaven, though our case is bad, (not so bad that Britain cannot make it worse,) there is yet a way open for us, not only to escape the threatened ruin but to become a happy, wealthy, powerful, and respectable people. If it be asked how this great work is to be effected ? I answer, First, by declaring an immediate Independency.

He adds nine other recommendations, but they are of less immediate pertinency.

There were, naturally, professions of downright conversion as a result of reading Paine's pamphlet. One such convert, concealing his identity behind the mask "Essex", addressed an open letter to the author to say that the arguments of *Common Sense* had convinced him of the necessity of independence, and to offer some contribution of materials "for that great building, the grand charter of American liberty". Unfortunately Paine's plans for "the great building" to be erected on the foundations of independence were forgotten in the excitement of laying those foundations, and the contributions of "Essex" went to the rubbish heap. More characteristic perhaps was the case of Joseph Hawley of Massachusetts, who wrote to Elbridge Gerry (February 18) that, having read *Common Sense,* "every sentiment has sunk into my well-prepared heart; in short, you know that my heart before was like good ground well prepared for good seed; and that without an American independent Supreme Government and Constitution, wisely devised and designed, well established and settled, we shall always be but a rope of sand; but that well done, invincible." Returning to the subject two days later he added: "Independence, in short, is the only way to union and harmony, to vigour and despatch in business . . . any thing short of it will . . . be our destruction, infallible destruction, and that speedily."

Paine was indeed a sower who had gone forth to sow at the appropriate seedtime, finding ready for his seeds a congenial soil and well prepared. The colonists had pleaded their cause until they were weary and hoarse of voice. They had spun and refined their arguments to gossamer threads, and seemingly to no purpose. And all the while the bonds that bound them to the mother country had become more and more attenuated, more and more frayed, until only a common impulse was needed to snap them asunder. Paine's pamphlet *Common Sense* had supplied that impulse. Logic and reasoning seemed to have come to the end of their tether; life-old sentiments had vanished or were fading; new emotions were clamoring to be loosed. It was Paine's part to stir these new emotions into action.

To accomplish these things Paine relied mainly upon two means: demolishing respect for the crown, and undermining colonial admiration for the British constitution. The colonial writers and moulders of thought had freely denounced the supremacy of Parliament but had stoutly maintained, even to this hour, that Americans stood faithful to their allegiance to the crown. True, the latest words that had come forth from the mouth of the king were as hot lava to that faith, and Paine's added scorn would reduce it to ashes. Divine right of kings! exclaimed Paine; just cast your eye upon William the Conqueror. "A French bastard landing with an armed banditti, and establishing himself King of England against the consent of the natives, is, in plain terms, a very paltry, rascally original—it certainly hath no divinity in it." In fact, "Government by Kings . . . was the most prosperous invention the Devil ever set on foot for the promotion of idolatry"; and Paine therefore takes his readers through a course of Hebrew history to prove his point. As for hereditary succession, it is not only an absurdity, it is in many ways an evil; and here Paine rehearses the history of the British monarchy to prove that point. "Of more worth", he declared, "is one honest man to society, and in the sight of God, than all the crowned ruffians that ever lived."

Having heaped ridicule and contempt upon the kingship, Paine proceeds to belittle the lauded perfection of the English constitution, whose glories had been one theme in nearly every declamation, whether from assembly or from individual, since the controversy began. The component parts of the English constitution, Paine declared, are but "the base remains of two ancient tyrannies, compounded of some new Republican materials". The remains of those two ancient tyrannies were the king and the peers; the new republican materials find place in the Commons, "on whose virtue depends the freedom of England". It is said that the Commons have a check upon the King; but the King likewise has a check upon the Commons; and it is that part of the constitution that has the greater weight that will in the end govern. The Commons may "clog", but they can not effectually check the King, "the giver of places and pensions". "Though we may have been wise enough to shut and lock a door against absolute Monarchy, we, at the same time, have been foolish enough to put the Crown in possession of the key." A union of three powers, reciprocally checking each other? "Farsical . . . the different parts, by unnaturally opposing and destroying each other, prove the whole character to be absurd and useless." "The so much boasted Constitution of England", he continued, ". . . was noble for the dark and slavish times in which it was erected. . . . But that it is imperfect, subject to convulsions, and incapable of producing what it seems to promise, is easily demonstrated."

If now he had sufficiently weakened the two main pillars of the bridge by which the sentimental ties between the colonies and the mother country were maintained, his next step was to demolish the whole bridge and clear away the debris. Much had been said of the advantages of reconciliation, "which, like an agreeable dream, hath passed away and left us as we were", but he challenged the warmest advocate of reconciliation to show a single advantage that the continent could reap by a connection with Great Britain. "Every thing that is right or reasonable pleads for separation. The blood of the slain, the weeping voice of nature cries, ' 'Tis time to part.' " Even the distance set by the Almighty between the two countries was proof that Heaven had never designed that one should have authority over the other. "The utmost stretch of human wisdom" could not compass a plan, short of separation, that could promise the continent even a year's security. "Reconciliation is now a falacious dream. Nature hath deserted the connection, and Art cannot supply her place." Faith had been destroyed, and affection "wounded through a thousand pores". "Ye that tell us of harmony and reconciliation", he exclaimed, "can ye restore to us the time that is past? Can ye give to prostitution its former innocence? Neither can ye reconcile Britain and America. The last cord is broken." All arguments had been ineffectual, therefore "the period of debate is closed. Arms, as the last resource, must decide the contest." That appeal was the choice of the king, and the continent had accepted the challenge. The sun had never shone upon a cause of greater worth. It was not the affair of a city, a county, a province, or a kingdom, but of a continent. It was not the concern of a day, a year, or an age; "posterity are virtually involved in the contest. . . . Now is the seed-time of Continental union, faith, and honour." Then this impassioned appeal:

O ye that love mankind! Ye that dare oppose not only the tyranny, but the tyrant, stand forth! Every spot of the old world is overrun with oppression. Freedom hath been hunted round the globe. Asia and Africa have long expelled her. Europe regards her like a stranger, and England hath given her warning to depart. O! receive the fugitive, and prepare in time an asylum for mankind.

It was with such phrases that Paine appealed to America to declare her independence, and it was this part of his message that sank deeply into the American mind and heart. He did not, however, content himself with the counsel of independence. Now, he declared, is the time to consolidate the union and to form a government for all America. "Let slip the opportunity", and, instead of making laws for ourselves, we may have to receive laws from our conquerors. "But where, says some, is the King of America? I'll tell you friend, he reigns above; and doth not make havoc of mankind like the Royal Brute of Great Britain." Let the world know that "in America the Law is King. For as in absolute Governments the King is Law, so in free countries the Law ought to be King; and there ought to be no other." He proceeds then "modestly" to offer some "hints" as to what sort of government the colonies should set up and how they should go about it. On a backward view the most important of these hints was that a "Continental Conference" should be held, whose business it would be "to frame a Continental Charter, or Charter of the United Colonies". But if the many thousands who read the earlier parts of Paine's preachment ever plowed through to the end—and there is tedium enough in much of Paine's discourse—the crowning words of his appeal, that America should not merely tear down but should also build, and that on newer and better foundations, this final appeal, it would seem, failed to find lodgment in their minds. Stirred by Paine to an intense fervor for the demolition of the old, they would be less concerned about his plans for the new. Soon others would be suggesting a similar procedure, the calling of a continental conference, or what came in time to be called a constitutional convention, but all such suggestions would long fall upon dull, even deaf, ears. Only a new crisis would stir these ideas to life again.

Paine's attack upon the kingship was not, however, long in winning converts, with the result that his doctrine had a brief inning in Congress. On the 22d of March, when a measure relative to privateering was under consideration, Wythe and Lee of Virginia, doubtless sensing the trend of opinion in their colony, offered a sort of rider to the privateering measure to the effect that the king, instead of the ministry, was "the Author of our Miseries". The proposition was opposed, says Richard Smith, "on Supposition that this was effectually severing the King from us forever". It was "ably debated" for four hours, then postponed "till Tomorrow". The discussion was not resumed, and the king was permitted yet awhile to pose as the innocent victim of ministerial machinations, but not for long. Rapidly others began to perceive substance in the doctrine, so that by the middle of May, Congress was ready to couple the king with Parliament in the indictment for crimes against American liberties, and a few weeks later would ruthlessly exhibit to the country the stark deficiencies of the kingly robe and endeavor to expel every lingering odor of sanctity from the royal person.

Paine was not of course left to cultivate the field alone, but was speedily joined by many able helpers, while the wind and weather of political events added their stimulating force to the rapid growth of the idea of independence. And the British government itself was not the least of these contributing factors; for, by an act of Parliament December 22, 1775, the colonies were removed from the protection of the crown, trade with them prohibited, and seizure and confiscation of American ships at sea authorized. It was in the last days of February that an advance copy of the act came by surreptitious means under the eye of Congress, and its effect was to propel the colonies violently toward independence. Oliver Wolcott spoke of it as "the late pirating act", and declared, "it behooves us therefore to take care of ourselves." "I fear", wrote Joseph Hewes, "it will make the Breach between the two Countries so wide as never more to be reconciled. . . . Nothing is left now but to fight it out." "I know not", John Adams wrote to General Gates (March 23), "whether you have seen the Act of Parliament call'd the restraining Act, or prohibitory Act, or piratical Act, or plundering Act, or Act of Independency, for by all these titles is it called. I think the most apposite is the Act of Independency, for King Lords and Commons have united in sundering this country from that I think forever."

Adams was inclined to think it fortunate that the act of independence should come from the British Parliament rather than from the American Congress, and declared it "very odd" that Americans should hesitate in accepting the gift. In fact, he could not resist emitting a snort of disgust. "Independency is a Hobgoblin of so frightful Mien, that it would throw a delicate Person into Fits to look it in the Face." Three days later Elbridge Gerry was beseeching James Warren to "originate instructions", that is, instructions from the General Court to the delegates in Congress, "expressed in decency and firmness . . . in favour of independency". Gerry was certain that it would "turn many doubtful minds" and probably bring about a reversal of the contrary instructions that some of the colonies had given their delegates. "Some timid minds", said Gerry, "are terrified at the word Independence. If you think caution in this respect good policy, change the name."

The question of independence would of course have to simmer; but

Congress did not long delay taking action in consequence of the British Prohibitory Act. The British government would seize and confiscate American property on the high seas, would it? Well, that was a game that Congress also could play and would. In fact, Congress was in a manner poised for just such action before ever the prohibitory act had thrust its ungainly head inside the door. As early as February 13 Samuel Chase had given notice that he would move for orders to Admiral Hopkins to seize all ships of Great Britain and for a recommendation to all the colonies to fit out privateers.

At first Congress was rather cool toward the proposition, and the motion was delayed; but one of the first consequences of the British measure was a rain of petitions to Congress praying that body to grant letters of marque and reprisal. Soon the current toward privateering was running strong, and by March 13 Richard Smith could record that "many Delegates were for the Thing", although a few still had their scruples of one sort or another. Franklin was of opinion that there ought at least to be a declaration of war before launching upon such a policy, whereas Jay and others "contended for discriminating Foes from Friends". On March 19 Congress came to a decision "That the inhabitants of these colonies be permitted to fit out armed vessels to cruize on the enemies of these United Colonies", together with such other resolves as were needful for elaborating the particulars of the measure. Then, on the 23d, a preamble or declaration was prefixed, citing at some length the actuating motives. It was at this stage of proceedings that Wythe and Lee sought to have the finger of accusation pointed at the king as "the Author of our Miseries", but succeeded only in obtaining a milder degree of condemnation of the monarch for having treated their petition "with scorn and contempt".

Letters of marque and reprisal were not, however, the only answer of Congress to the British act. For a good many months Congress had debated, sometimes almost fiercely, whether to throw open the ports or to close them. The Association had not done its perfect work in bringing Great Britain to terms, consequently the argument for reversing that policy at least to some extent began to gain strength. Still there was hesitancy, chiefly, so John Adams averred, because opening the ports was considered as "a bold step to independence". For that

very reason, among others, he himself had urged it. But now, when
the British government suddenly announced that it would slam shut
the door of trade, Congress was not long in deciding that when it
came to opening and closing trade doors, that too was a game the
colonies could play. They would put their collective shoulder to the
door and open it wide to all the world—all, that is, except Great Britain
and her dominions. The decision was made on the 6th of April, yet not
even then without controversy, because some members still saw in the
measure a movement toward independence, for which they or their
constituents were not yet prepared.

The question of trading with the rest of the world was necessarily
bound up to a great degree with that of the relationship which the
colonies might be able to establish with the nations of the world. Early
in the autumn of 1775 Congress came to realize that its feet were entangled in a mesh from which it would not be easy to extricate itself.
"A more intricate and delicate Subject", John Adams declared in the
beginning of October, "never came into any Man's thoughts than the
Trade of America. The Questions that arise when one thinks of it, are
very numerous. If the Thirteen united Colonies should immediately
Surcease all Trade with every Part of the World what would be the
Consequence? In what manner, and to what degree, and how soon
would it affect the other Parts of the World?" Would the ships of
foreign countries venture to come here? Would foreign courts offer
their assistance? And if we should "assume an intrepid Countenance",
and send ambassadors at once to foreign courts, would they be treated
with contempt and our proposals rejected? Furthermore, what should
the colonies on their part offer? Treaties of commerce? Alliances?
These were ticklish and vexatious questions, and Congress was by no
means ready to answer them, except that on November 1 certain limitations were placed upon exportations. "We shall by the Spring know
the full Effect of our Non-exportation Agreement in the West Indies",
Samuel Adams wrote November 4; "Perhaps Alliances may then be
formed with foreign Powers, and Trade opened to all the World, Great
Britain excepted."

Still hesitant, still in doubt respecting the attitude of European powers toward the American affair, in the closing days of November Congress appointed the secret committee of correspondence for the express purpose of probing sentiment abroad and obtaining other information useful to the colonies in their contest. In pursuit of its main objective, on the 12th of December the committee addressed a specific request to Arthur Lee, then in London, to learn, if he could, the disposition of foreign powers towards the Americans, warning him at the same time that "great circumspection and impenetrable secrecy" were essential. It was of course especially important to know the attitude of France, and the committee was not long in obtaining encouraging intimations from a Frenchman, named Bonvouloir, who had mysteriously turned up in Philadelphia, professing to be merely "a traveler out of curiosity". It is now known that this Bonvouloir had actually been sent by the French government for the purpose of making observations, although disclaiming any official status. Bonvouloir gave the committee to understand that the French government was sympathetic with the colonies and would probably not put any obstacles in the way of their obtaining in France the supplies of which they were in urgent need.

There were accordingly during the next few months three parallel developments, each intimately related to the others: the growth of the spirit of independence, the increase of opinion in favor of opening the ports to world trade, the conviction that a foreign alliance, particularly with France, was essential. Foreign aid in any sufficiency seemed to point to independence as a prior requisite, a foreign alliance, necessarily so; and opening wide the ports was generally interpreted as leading straight to independence. In mid-February talk of a foreign alliance broke out openly in Congress. Writing to a North Carolina correspondent February 14, John Penn declared that "Matters are drawing to a crisis". Great Britain seemed determined to persevere, he said, and was forming alliances against us. "Must we not", he asked, "do something of the like nature? ... The consequences of making alliances is perhaps a total separation with Britain and without something of that sort we may not be able to provide what is necessary for our defence." Two days later, in the course of a discussion of the still unsettled problem respecting trade, Wythe of Virginia injected a proposition that the colonies had a right to contract alliances with foreign powers. "An Objection being offered that this was Independency", Richard Smith recorded in his Diary, "there ensued much Argument on that Ground."

The question was postponed at that time, but two weeks later (February 29) it arose again, and when trade was once more the topic under consideration. Four hours, says Richard Smith, were spent on the subject without any conclusion. "By a former Resolve", he goes on to say, "Trade opens Tomorrow under the Restrictions of the Association. the Points now agitated were the Expediency and Probability of contracting foreign Commercial Alliances and chiefly with France and Spain, and the Advantages and Disadvantages of attempting to carry on Trade in our present Circumstances." He adds that "much was said about declaring our Independency on G. Britain", but the discussion was brought to a halt by the fact that the delegates of some five or six of the colonies were under instructions not to agree to independence without further consultation of their own governments.

Although Congress might shy away from suggestions of soliciting foreign alliances, there was nothing to prevent the two secret committees from approaching foreigners in behalf of the colonies or being approached by them. Early in January two Frenchmen, Penet and Pliarne by name, having first approached General Washington, appeared at Philadelphia and entered into negotiations with the so-called secret committee (that which later became the committee of commerce), to supply munitions of war and other goods, dropping broad hints the while that the French government would connive at colonial trade with that kingdom. Other Frenchmen came offering cargoes of powder. All this added up with the intimations given by Bonvouloir to the secret committee of correspondence a little while before.

On the strength of these intimations accordingly the secret committee decided to send an agent to France to endeavor to procure supplies, and chose for this purpose Silas Deane, until recently a member of Congress. Thereupon the committee of secret correspondence, composed in part of the same members of Congress, gave to Deane a further commission to undertake the delicate task of probing the mind of the French minister, Vergennes, respecting the American colonies. The commission of the secret committee bears the date March 1, that of the secret committee of correspondence March 2, and the latter's instructions March 3.

Naturally every effort was made to surround Deane's mission with all needful secrecy and appropriate camouflage, neither of which proved to be as impenetrable as the sponsoring committees had fatuously believed. Events were to make Deane's mission the first chapter in the checkered story of our Revolutionary foreign relations, a story that was to have many chapters of tribulation before it reached a happy consummation. For Deane himself the story was to have a genuinely tragic dénouement. Deane took his departure within a few days, but because of an accident to his vessel was compelled to return and did not finally get away until about the 3d of April. By that time Congress had virtually reached its long-deferred decision to open wide the ports to the trade of all nations except Great Britain.

It was in the closing days of March, already crowded with events of great import, that another ambassadorial mission was begun, one that if successful would immensely brighten the colonial skies, but failing would only deepen the gloom. It was not thought of by Congress as a venture in foreign relations, which it essentially was, but rather as an effort toward a completer harmony and cooperation within the family circle. This was the mission, already alluded to, of Franklin, Chase, and the Carrolls to Canada. It was a delicate mission, for both Congress and its servants had grievous sins to answer for, and it would call for every blandishment of which Congress was capable to induce the Canadians to forget the past and clasp the extended hand of Congress. What should be said to them, and how? What should be left unsaid, and why?

Tell them, Congress instructed the commissioners, that we sent our armies into that province "for the purpose of frustrating the designs of the British court against our common liberties"; and you may add that "we shall put it into the power of our Canadian brethren, to pursue such measures for securing their own freedom and happiness, as a generous love of liberty and sound policy shall dictate to them". "Inform them, that in our judgment, their interests and ours are inseparably united; That it is impossible we can be reduced to a servile submission to Great Britain without their sharing our fate." On the other hand, if we shall obtain a full establishment of our rights (and we have never a doubt that we shall), "it depends wholly on their choice, whether they will participate with us in those blessings, or still remain subject to every act of tyranny, which British ministers shall please to exercise over them." To convince them that, "if we wisely and vigorously co-operate with each other", it is impossible that the war should be concluded to the disadvantage of these colonies, "urge all such arguments as your prudence shall suggest".

It was of no less importance to convince the Canadians of the uprightness of intentions toward them on the part of Congress, and to this end the commissioners were to declare that the people of Canada might set up such a form of government "as will be most likely, in their judgment, to produce their happiness", to assure them in the strongest terms that it was the earnest desire of Congress to adopt them into the union as a sister colony, "and to secure the same general system of mild and equal laws for them and for ourselves, with only such local differences as may be agreeable to each colony respectively." "You are further to declare", the commissioners were instructed, "that we hold sacred the rights of conscience, and may promise to the whole people, solemnly in our name, the free and undisturbed exercise of their religion". The clergy were to retain "full, perfect, and peaceable possession and enjoyment of all their estates, and all other matters relating to religion were to be "left entirely in the hands of the good people of that province". There was only one reservation, namely, "that all other denominations of Christians be equally entitled to hold offices, and enjoy civil privileges, and the free exercise of their religion, and be totally exempt from the payment of any tythes or taxes for the support of any religion".

Yes, one thing more: "Endeavour to stimulate them by motives of glory, as well as interest, to assume a part in a contest, by which they must be deeply affected; And to aspire to a portion of that power, by which they are ruled; and not to remain the mere spoils and prey of conquerors and lords." Inviting them, then, to come into the union on terms similar to those on which the other colonies were united, the commissioners were to "promise in the names of the United Colonies, that we will defend and protect the people of Canada against all enemies, in the same manner as we will defend and protect any of the United Colonies", and assurance was to be given them that their commerce with foreign nations should be placed on an equal footing with that of the United Colonies. Besides being authorized to assist the Canadians in setting up their government, the commissioners were in general vested with full powers to effect the purposes of Congress.

After more than a month of pondering, laboring, and debating, on March 20 the instructions for the Canadian mission were completed and adopted, and on the 25th the commissioners set out upon their mission. In the message of Congress to the Canadians there was never a suggestion of possible reconciliation with Great Britain, never a word of independence; yet at that very moment Congress was poised almost at the threshold of a declaration of independence, while at the same time listening intently for new offers of conciliation. Instead, however, of the sought-for hand-clasp and friendly cooperation, ere long it began to appear that the Canadians might offer them fight and turn loose a horde of Indians on them to boot.

Although it was not until June 11 that two of the commissioners, Chase and Carroll, returned to report that there had been "many and great abuses and mismanagement in Canada", Congress had already (May 18) received "the dismals" from that quarter, news of an ignominious defeat. But all the heaped-up dismals together served only to arouse Congress to stiffen the upper lip and to lay out (June 18) an elaborate program for the conquest of Canada. For one thing, "an experienced general" was to be immediately despatched thither, "with the powers of a Roman Dictator". And who could that be but General Gates? Meanwhile, that diligent search would be made for a scapegoat was one of the inevitables, and it was nearly as inevitable that, as Samuel Adams put it, "the Saddle has been laid, or attempted to be laid on the wrong horse". That horse appears to have been General Wooster, with the result that no little acrimony was set astir. To be sure, a committee offered the opinion (July 30) that the miscarriages were mainly attributable to short enlistments, want of hard money, and small pox, and Congress concurred therein; nevertheless the heats raised in that body did not subside until the summer was far spent.

CHAPTER VIII

THE TORRENT OF INDEPENDENCE
CONCILIATORS AVAUNT!

In mid-February, 1776, just when Congress was maturing its plans for approaching the Canadians, rumors began to stir that the British government was about to send over commissioners to treat with Congress. "All this news", wrote Oliver Wolcott (February 19), "makes no impression on firm Whigs. It is considered an insidious manoeuvre." Within a few days, however, the thickening reports had taken on a degree of form and substance; for it was learned that the very act of Parliament that was designed to quell the rebellion by destroying the commerce of the rebels carried as a sort of "rider" a proposition to send to America commissioners who would seek to bring about reconciliation. In short, the sword that Great Britain was flourishing in front of the colonies had a small olive branch tied to the handle thereof.

But who were the commissioners and what their powers no one could learn with certainty—and for the best of reasons, because they had not yet been appointed. And still the rumors multiplied and flitted hither and thither with ever greater rapidity. One bit of information crossed the Atlantic in a button of the coat of William Temple, but the button was found to contain nothing about commissioners for conciliation; it was merely a scrawl from Arthur Lee to the effect that troops were sailing from Ireland. From the mouth of the said Temple, however, appears to have come another story. Twenty commissioners, headed by Lord Howe and General Amherst, were already on the high seas; they would first try their hand with individual colonies, even with counties and towns, making every effort to avoid recognizing the legality of Congress; although, rather than fail completely, they would, as a last resort, approach the Continental Congress itself.

Some believed commissioners would really come, others were skeptical; but, since the act of Parliament merely authorized the king to appoint commissioners to receive submissions and grant pardons, they might as well stay on their own side of the water. They would not, declared Oliver Wolcott, "be ever able to execute their trust". "Though no man of understanding expects any good from the Commissioners", Joseph Reed wrote to Washington (March 3), "yet they [Congress] are waiting to hear their proposals before they declare off." And a few days later (March 15) he added: "To tell you the truth, my dear Sir, I am infinitely more afraid of these Commissioners than of their Generals and Armies. If their propositions are plausible, and behaviour artful, I am apprehensive they will divide us. There is so much suspicion in Congress, and so much party on this subject, that very little more fuel is required to kindle the flame." Because of this growth of "private pique, prejudice, and suspicion", Reed was of opinion that it was "high time for the colonies to begin a gradual change of delegates".

Reed was not a member of Congress, but he evidently knew a good deal of what went on within those supposedly sound-proof walls. At nearly the same time (March 20) Joseph Hewes of North Carolina wrote:

We do not treat each other with that decency and respect that was observed heretofore. Jealousies, ill natured observations and recriminations take the place of reason and argument. Our Tempers are soured. Some among us urge strongly for Independence and eternal separation, others wish to wait a little longer and to have the opinion of their Constituents on that subject.

In short, the tension in Congress had become so high that once more the members had got on one another's nerves.

Meanwhile a small ingredient had been dropped into the conciliation pot by Lord Drummond, yet without perceptibly altering either the odor or the flavor of the brew. Thomas, Lord Drummond, a scion of the Melfort Drummonds, had come to America in 1768, being then twenty-six years of age, to look after the estate of the earl of Melfort. In that same year he was elected a member of the Society of St. Andrew of New York, and in 1773 became its president for a year. The meat of Lord Drummond's proposal was that a member or members of Congress should be sent to England to lay the American case before the

British ministry, and early in the year 1776 he had sought, through Thomas Lynch, member of Congress from South Carolina, to interest General Washington in the plan. Lord Drummond had recently returned from England, where, so he told Lynch, he had had "many conversations" with the ministry, and indicated that they approved of his plan.

Without waiting to learn the result of Lynch's intercession, Lord Drummond had made application to the British General Robertson in Boston for passports for such as might be appointed under his plan. The application was not, however, sent direct to General Robertson, but to General Washington, with a view to its being forwarded by the latter to its desired destination. Washington, very naturally, chose instead to transmit the document to Congress. On the 5th of March, Congress actually discussed the matter in committee of the whole for four or five hours, when Wythe of Virginia offered a set of propositions to the effect that "no Public Bodies or private Persons other than the Congress or the People at large ought to treat for Peace." It is significant of the state of mind of Congress at that time that Wythe's proposition was negatived, so Richard Smith recorded, by eight colonies to three. As for his lordship's plan, General Washington was "not without suspicion of its meaning more than the generous purposes it professes"; and Congress, agreeing in sentiment with the general, merely ordered Lord Drummond's proposition filed among its papers.

In the following August his lordship made a second trial at negotiation, this time meeting with a definite rebuff. Although under parole from the New York committee of safety and thereby bound to hold no correspondence with the enemy, he had conferred with Lord Howe on the subject of his propositions and thereafter had some correspondence with him relative to his plan. Having transmitted this correspondence to General Washington, he received a prompt reply from the general, stating that he found himself under the disagreeable necessity of objecting to the mode of negotiation proposed, "while your Lordship's line of conduct appears so exceptionable". Washington at once submitted all the papers to Congress, and that body was equally prompt in voicing approval of the manner in which the commander-in-chief had "checked the officious and intemperate zeal of his Lordship", and in declining to take "any public or further notice of his Lordship or his letters". Lord Drummond's wand had broken in his hand. It had raised no big wind, and it had failed just as utterly in stilling any of the wild waves then beating on the American shores. His lordship subsequently took up his residence in Bermuda, where he died in 1780, probably still cherishing hopes of ultimate reconciliation between the Americans and their mother land.

While Congress pricked up its ears for further news of the commissioners on conciliation bent, speculation on what they might or might not propose, if and when they should come, went on apace. "We continue still between Hawk and Buzzard", John Adams, in deep disgust, wrote to James Warren (April 2). "Some people yet expect Commissioners, to treat with Congress, and to offer Chart blanc. All declare if they do not come empowered to treat with us, and grant us our Bill of Rights, in every Iota, they will hesitate no longer." "Where the plague are these Commissioners?" Robert Morris wrote to General Gates, April 6. "If they are to come, what is it that detains them? It is time we should be on a certainty and know positively whether the Libertys of America can be established and secured by reconciliation, or whether we must totally renounce connection with Great Britain and fight our way to a total independence." He wished them to come, but he dreaded nothing so much as even an appearance of division amongst ourselves.

It was on that same day that Congress had resolved to open the ports of America to all the world, a measure that rejoiced John Adams to such a degree that he was ready to snap his fingers at conciliators of every hue. On April 15 he wrote his wife:

We are waiting, it is said, for commissioners; a messiah that will never come. This story of commissioners is as arrant an illusion as ever was hatched in the brain of an enthusiast, a politician, or a maniac. I have laughed at it, scolded it, grieved at it, and I don't know but I may, at an unguarded moment, have rip'd at it. But it is vain to reason against such delusions.

To Mercy Warren the next day he termed the story of the commissioners "a Bubble", their errand "an Insult". By this time Oliver Wolcott, who two months before appears to have had little doubt of their

coming, had come to a like conclusion with Adams. "The ideal Phantom of Commissioners Comeing over to settle our Disputes", he wrote
his wife (April 17), "has almost vanished—indeed I do not know any
one could be serious in such Expectation. A final Separation between
the Countrys I consider as unavoidable."

As hopes of restoring the old bonds with the mother country on terms
that were tolerable dwindled and the ranks of those who had set their
hearts on reconciliation thinned, the forces for separation and independence were recruited accordingly. In a letter to Josiah Quincy in
mid-April, Franklin put the situation in a nutshell. Quincy had asked
when the Congress, *"by general consent"*, was to be formed into a supreme legislature, with alliances, defensive and offensive; and Franklin
replied:

> I can only answer at present, that nothing seems wanting but that "gen-
> eral consent". The novelty of the thing deters some, the doubts of success,
> others, the vain hope of reconciliation, many. But our enemies take con-
> tinually every proper measure to remove these obstacles, and their endeav-
> ours are attended with success, since every day furnishes us with new causes
> of increasing enmity, and new reasons for wishing an eternal separation;
> so that there is a rapid increase of the formerly small party, who were for
> an independent government.

At the same time (April 16) Samuel Adams was writing to James
Warren that the salvation of the country depended upon the proclaiming of independence and that speedily. "Every Day's Delay", he declared "trys my Patience." As for those commissioners, with their offers
of reconciliation, "This is all Amusement. I am exceedingly disgusted
when I hear it mentioned. . . . Reconciliation upon reasonable Terms is
no Part of their Plan: The only Alternative is Independency or
Slavery." And then he muses: "The Child Independence is now struggling for Birth. I trust that in a short time it will be brought forth and
in Spite of Pharaoh all America shall hail the dignified Stranger."

In his rôle of midwife for the delivery of the child Independence,
Samuel Adams appears to have been not quite accurate in his calculations and expectations because of the numerous imponderables in the
case. Among these just now were some lingering hopes of reconciliation

that refused to down. Thomas Stone of Maryland, for instance, not many days later (April 24) opened his mind to Daniel of St. Thomas Jenifer thus: "If the Commissioners do not arrive shortly and conduct themselves with great Candor and Uprightness to effect a Reconciliation, a Separation will undoubtedly take place." Yet, for his part, he wished to conduct affairs with a view to a just and honorable reconciliation, or else to arrive at a pretty unanimous resolution to fight it out for independence. "You know", he said, "my Heart wishes for peace upon terms of Security and Justice to America. But War, anything is preferable to a Surrender of our Rights."

A similar though stronger note was struck by Carter Braxton of Virginia. Braxton was a newcomer in Congress, having taken his seat as late as February 23, although he had been elected in the preceding December. Whether true or not, as was asserted, that a group of Virginians had obtained his election to Congress for the express purpose of turning the tide against independence, he was at least endeavoring to delay the movement, at the same time that his fellow-Virginians in Congress were turning their faces away from reconciliation and toward independence. "Independence and total seperation from Great Britain", he wrote to Landon Carter April 14, "are the interesting Subjects of all ranks of men and often agitate our Body. It is in truth a delusive Bait which men inconsiderately catch at, without knowing the hook to which it is affixed." It was an object, he asserted, to be wished for by every American, when it could be obtained with safety and honor, but this was not the moment. In the first place, public honor required that Congress await the terms to be offered by the commissioners. In the second place, America was in too defenseless a state for a declaration of independence, having no alliance with a naval power or any fleet of her own of any consequence. As for the belief that France would come to our assistance, "Would such a blind precipitate measure as this be justified by Prudence, first to throw off our connexion with G. Britain and then give ourselves up to the Arms of France?" Moreover, before these efforts for "Lugging us into Independence" could succeed, the numerous internal dissensions must needs first be healed and harmony prevail. "A grand Continental League", he declared, "must be formed and a superintending Power also." When these necessary steps had been taken and "a Coalition formed sufficient to withstand the Power of Britain, or any other", then he would be for an independent state and all its consequences.

Furthermore, Braxton believed he had penetrated one of the chief reasons why a certain group in Congress sought to hasten steps toward independence, why they pooh-poohed the idea of commissioners coming with offers of reconciliation. They were afraid to await the arrival of commissioners, lest the dispute should be accommodated, even upon the admission of our own terms. "For however strange it may appear", he continued, "I am satisfied that the eastern Colonies do not mean to have a Reconciliation."

In view of all this agitation it is rather strange to find Francis Light-foot Lee writing to Landon Carter, April 9: "Who in the name of Heaven, cou'd tell you, that Independency had been 3 times thrown out of Congress? You may be assured the Question has never been before the Congress, and it is probable they will wait till the people bring it before them: which event is not far off, from the best accounts from the different parts of the Continent." Certainly the measure for opening the ports adopted three days before had been strenuously opposed by some elements in Congress on the ground that it was a long step toward independence. Joseph Hewes might assert that the measure embodied "nothing looking towards Independency", yet at the same time John Adams could jubilantly exclaim: "What signifies a word?"

You say [Adams wrote to James Warren, April 16] the Sigh's for Independence are universal . . . Independence? Have we not been independent these twelve Months, wanting Three days? Have you seen the Privateering Resolves? Are not these Independence enough for my beloved Constituents? Have you seen the Resolves for opening our Ports to all Nations? Are these Independence enough? What more would you have?

In the latter part of March, Elbridge Gerry had suggested to Warren that the General Court of Massachusetts send instructions to the delegates of the colony in favor of independence; and now Adams reiterates the suggestion. "Why don't your Honours of the General Court, if you are so unanimous in this, give positive instructions to your own Delegates, to promote Independency? . . . The S[outhern] Colonies say you are afraid."

It was not so much that Massachusetts was hesitant or that the delegates needed prodding; rather it was thought that such instructions would be good leverage in promoting like instructions from other colonies. Some of the Virginia delegates were thinking in like terms. "You ask me", Richard Henry Lee wrote to General Charles Lee, April 22, "why we hesitate in Congress. I'll tell you my friend, because we are heavily clogged with instructions from those shamefully interested Proprietary people, and this will continue until Virginia sets the example of taking up Government, and sending peremptory Orders to their delegates to pursue the most effectual measures for the Security of America." The people of those colonies, he declared, would then force their governments to take action, "after which Adieu to Proprietary influence and timid senseless politics." On the 11th of May, Delegate Lee was reiterating to General Lee the same sentiments, although by this time Congress was applying pressure of its own upon the colonies, proprietary and other, to take up government.

First of all, Congress had administered a sedative dose to that furor over the conciliation commissioners. On March 24, 1776, not many days after he had taken possession of Boston, General Washington had requested Congress to inform him what course he should pursue in the event that the commissioners should land in Boston, as they probably would do; and after a long delay, induced no doubt by the difficulties in making up the Congressional mind, Congress got around to taking action on the general's request. On the 6th of May it was resolved:

That General Washington be informed, that Congress suppose, if commissioners are intended to be sent from Great Britain to treat of peace, that the practice usual in such cases will be observed, by making previous application for the necessary passports or safe conduct, and on such application being made, Congress will then direct the proper measures for the reception of such commissioners.

In short, Congress would cross that bridge if and when it came to it. According to John Adams's later recollections there had been "much debate" over the measure. One faction had "endeavored to insert in the resolution ideas of reconciliation; we carried our point for inserting peace. They wanted powers given to the General to receive the commissioners in ceremony; we ordered nothing to be done till we were solicited for passports." And so, he relates, "Upon the whole we avoided the snare, and brought the controversy to a close, with some dignity."

The skepticism with regard to the commissioners had in fact by this time become pretty general. "As to Commissioners coming to treat of peace", William Floyd wrote May 9, "we have little or no hopes of it, therefore we ought to be in a situation to preserve our Liberties another way." And two days later his colleague, James Duane, wrote to John Jay that the coming of commissioners was "not founded on any authority nor credited". It chanced nevertheless that on that same May 6 on which Congress had adopted its tentative resolve the British monarch had put his seal to the appointment of Lord Howe and General Howe as "Commissioners for restoring peace to his Majesty's Colonies and Plantations in North America, and for granting pardons to such of his Majesty's subjects there, now in rebellion, as shall deserve the Royal mercy."

Already that *vox populi* for which Congress had been listening, voices calling for independence, had begun to swell into a general chorus. To be sure there were as yet numerous voices of protest, overtones and undertones of denial, but they would soon be muted by a resourceful hand, drowned in the louder clamor.

The first of the colonies to speak out in unmistakable tones was North Carolina. The Provincial Congress had assembled at Halifax on April 4 and had taken into consideration letters of the colony's delegates in Congress of February 12 and March 1, wherein the situation of the colonies was set forth. On the 12th of April, 1776, after citing the wrongs inflicted on the colonies by the British ministry, the Provincial Congress came to this decision:

Whereas the moderation hitherto manifested by the United Colonies and their sincere desire to be reconciled to the mother country on constitutional principles, have procured no mitigation of the aforesaid wrongs and usurpations, and no hopes remain of obtaining redress by those means alone which have been hitherto tried. . . .

Resolved, That the Delegates for this colony in the Continental Congress be impowered to concur with the delegates of the other Colonies in declaring Independency, and forming foreign alliances, reserving to this Colony the sole and exclusive right of forming a Constitution and laws for this

Colony, and of appointing delegates from time to time (under the direction of a general representation thereof), to meet the delegates of the other Colonies for such purposes as shall hereafter be pointed out.

On the following day the Provincial Congress took a similarly firm position with regard to the commissioners said to be coming over to America, declaring that "unless such commissioner or commissioners shall produce a commission to treat with the Continental Congress", he or they should be "required to return immediately on board the vessel in which he or they arrive", and that if any of them should at any time be found on shore within this Province, their persons should be seized and immediately sent to the Continental Congress.

At nearly the same time the Provincial Congress of South Carolina, which had been sitting since the beginning of February, brought its session to a close. On the 23d of March it had "authorized and empowered" the colony's delegates in the Continental Congress "to concert, agree to, and execute, every measure which they or he, together with a majority of the Continental Congress, shall judge necessary, for the defence, security, interest, or welfare of this colony in particular, and of America in general." Three days later, acting upon advice given by the Continental Congress in the preceding November, the Provincial Congress had adopted "a constitution or form of government", which, as explained in an address April 1, "looks forward to an accomodation with Great Britain (an event which, though traduced and treated as Rebels, we still earnestly desire)". Then, on April 6, the Provincial Congress took its fling at the commissioners reported to be coming to treat with the several colonies. It was resolved that South Carolina "should not enter into any treaty or correspondence with the Court of Great Britain . . . but through the medium of the Continental Congress"; and further, if any such persons should arrive by water, they would not be allowed to remain longer than forty-eight hours, "wind and weather permitting", or to hold communication with any person in the colony; and, if they should arrive by land, that "they should be forthwith carefully escorted out of the Colony".

By the first of May the action of the two Carolinas was known in and about Congress, and in that house of zeal there was great rejoicing.

South Carolina had "behaved nobly", Elbridge Gerry wrote to James Warren, and North Carolina had "unanimously voted to follow their example". "Virginia", he added, "is always to be depended upon; and so fine a spirit prevails among them that, unless you send some of your cool patriots among them, they may be for declaring Independency before Congress is ready." Similarly John Adams wrote to Warren (May 8), "I am afraid they [the southern colonies] will all get the start of Congress in declarations of Independence. We are certainly ripe here for the grand resolution."

To be sure, South Carolina was yet halting betwixt two opinions, but the watchers in Independence tower could scarcely doubt what her ultimate decision would be. Had these same watchmen in the tower known of the action taken in Georgia, they would have had further reasons for encouragement. Like South Carolina, that colony had not yet been wholly converted to the doctrine of independence, but those who had their hand on the helm were cautiously watchful, with a weather-eye toward the north. On the 2d of February the colony had made a new choice of delegates to Congress—Archibald Bulloch, John Houstoun, Lyman Hall, Button Gwinnett, and George Walton—and on May 20, Hall and Gwinnett would come to take their seats, bringing a letter of instructions, dated April 5, wherein the delegates were essentially authorized to exercise their own judgment. Before the close of April the colony had adopted a temporary constitution and form of government.

The eager advocates for independence were not, however, content that Congress should wholly wait on events, while the colonies slowly made up their minds. They would quicken events, if might be. John Adams at least thought he knew a thing or two about how to help the colonies to make up their minds, how to coax the hesitant into the path leading to the great open spaces that he beheld in his visions. Were some of the colonies lame or halt? He would teach them how to walk erect and tread with firmness. Were any blind? He had a remedy for colonial blindness. Besought for counsel, he resolved "to borrow a little Time from his Sleep" and compound his prescription. He called it "Thoughts on Government", and it met with such approval that it was printed and spread abroad among the colonies. In particular, declared Richard Henry Lee, it made clear that the business of framing government was easy and necessary, whereas unthinking people had imagined it to be unnecessary and difficult.

And it was just that business that Adams and his fellow-laborers were bent on having the colonies undertake, such as had not already done so. Having on May 6 disposed of the question of peace commissioners until such time as they might actually present themselves, Congress thereupon resolved itself into a committee of the whole to take into consideration the state of the United Colonies. In the course of three days the committee had evolved a resolution, the formal consideration of which was, however, at the request of a colony postponed until the following day. On May 10 accordingly the resolution was offered and adopted,

That it be recommended to the respective assemblies and conventions of the United Colonies, where no government sufficient to the exigencies of their affairs have been hitherto established, to adopt such government as shall, in the opinion of the representatives of the people, best conduce to the happiness and safety of their constituents in particular, and America in general.

Thereupon a committee, consisting of John Adams, Edward Rutledge, and Richard Henry Lee, was appointed to prepare a preamble. Writing to Jay the next day, Duane remarked that the resolution "waits only for a preface and will then be ushered into the world. This in Confidence as *res infecta*." Then he ventured to add, "A Business of still greater moment is on the carpet." John Adams, who in concert with Richard Henry Lee had introduced the resolution into the committee of the whole, regarded its passage "as an epocha, a decisive event". For, as he later declared, it was a measure which he had "invariably pursued for a whole year, and contended for, through a scene and a series of anxiety, labor, study, argument, and obloquy."

If, as John Adams avers, this resolution of May 10 was adopted "with remarkable Unanimity", not so the preamble, over which a heated debate raged for three or four days. The preamble, which Adams maintained had been fashioned by his dextrous hand alone, begins with the usual recitation of the wrongs committed against the colonies by king and Parliament, including the charge that "the whole force of that kingdom, aided by foreign mercenaries, is to be exerted for the destruction of the good people of these colonies". Then comes the significant passage:

And whereas, it appears absolutely irreconcilable to reason and good conscience, for the people of these colonies now to take the oaths and affirmations necessary for the support of any government under the crown of Great Britain, and it is necessary that the exercise of every kind of authority under the said crown should be totally suppressed, and all the powers of government exerted, under the authority of the people of the colonies, for the preservation of internal peace, virtue, and good order, as well as for the defence of their lives, liberties, and properties, against the hostile invasions and cruel depredations of their enemies; therefore, resolved, etc.

The brunt of the opposition was borne by James Duane of New York and James Wilson of Pennsylvania; and it is to none other than John Adams that we are indebted for the preservation of their remarks. Duane took his stand first of all on the New York delegation's want of powers to vote on the question, and, secondly, on the implied premise that it was a matter for each colony's own determination. In short, he insisted, it was not the business of Congress to determine how justice should be administered in the respective colonies. "Why all this haste?" he asked; "why this urging? why this driving? Disputes about independence are in all the colonies. What is this owing to but our indiscretion?" He supposed, however, that the advocates of the measure had already taken a poll of the members and had their majority. Samuel Adams observed that the first object of New York was without doubt the establishment of their rights, but that the gentleman from New York had not offered an objection to the preamble itself; he had merely contended that he had not a right to vote for it.

Arose then James Wilson, whose colony was placed in much the same position as New York. Wilson began by saying that he had been one of the committee that some months before had reported the same advice to Massachusetts, New Hampshire, South Carolina, and Virginia, and that the advice given had had his hearty concurrence. But "those Colonies", he pointed out, "were royal governments; they could not subsist without some government." It was a maxim that "all government originates from the people", and the members of Congress were servants of the people, acting under a delegated authority. Some of them had been put under restraints by their constituents, among them the delegates of Pennsylvania, who had not been authorized by any public act to vote upon the question. As the assembly was convening in a few days, would the cause suffer much if publication of the preamble were delayed until that time, if the resolve were published without the preamble? In this Province, he asserted, if that preamble should pass, there would be an immediate dissolution of every kind of authority; the people would instantly be in a state of nature. "Why then precipitate this measure?" he asked. "Before we are prepared to build the new house, why should we pull down the old one, and expose ourselves to all the inclemencies of the season?"

The arguments of Duane and Wilson were unavailing. No doubt, as Duane had remarked, the votes had already been numbered, and it remained only to register them. On May 15 the preamble was adopted. Straightway the father of the measure broke forth in exultant, unrestrained halleluiah. "This Day the Congress has passed the most important Resolution that ever was taken in America", John Adams wrote to James Warren. Speaking of it at a later day he said, "Mr. Duane called it to me a machine for the fabrication of Independence. I said, smiling, I thought it was independence itself, but we must have it with more formality yet." Not perhaps so exultant, but equally convinced of its real meaning, was Oliver Wolcott of Connecticut, who wrote (May 16): "A Revolution in Government, you will perceive, is about to take Effect. May God grant a happy Establishment of it, and secuerety to the Rights of the People. . . . May the supreme Ruler of the Universe carry us thro the hardy Conflict to Liberty safety and Peace." Caesar Rodney, whose colony was yet poised at the forks of the road, had never a doubt of the utility of the measure, of "the Necessaty of immediately laying the foundation of a new Government", for "the Continuing to Swear Allegiance to the power that is Cutting our throats", so he wrote to Colonel John Haslet (May 17), " . . . is Certainly absurd"; and he set about at once devising means for effecting the new organization in Delaware. As for the ultimate implications of the resolution, "Most of those here who are *termed the Cool Considerate Men*", he wrote to his brother the same day, "think it amounts to a declaration of Independance. It Certainly savours of it, but you will see and Judge for Your Self." The note sounded by Duane was, as was to be expected, decidedly sour. To his absent colleague, John Jay, who was likewise endeavoring to steer between Scylla and Charybdis, he wrote: "Compare them [the resolution and the preamble] with each other and it will probably lead you into Reflections which I dare not point out."

More bitter in his reflections and more outspoken was Carter Braxton (May 17). If, as had been charged, he had come to scoff, he remained to praise. In due time he would enroll himself among the American immortals by signing the Declaration of Independence; but, like Robert Morris and others, he objected to undue haste in pushing measures designed to precipitate independence without first giving all the colonies a chance to speak their minds and without taking needful measures for maintaining independence. Every one, he said, knew that some of the delegates could not, consistently with their instructions, come into the proposed measure, as every one also knew that, if the reported commissioners did not soon arrive and with terms that were "free and honourable", then "America with one united Voice would have joined hand in hand to repell the haughty Invaders and to have rejected with disdain their future superiority. But," he added with biting sarcasm, "the wise Men of the East and some from the *South* thought it a reprehensible delay which might give a turn to their favourite plan and defeat those pursuits they had so nearly compleated and the plan for which they had so wisely and so long laid down in their own minds." The assumption of government, he declared, was necessary, and little objection had been made to that resolution;

but when the Preamble was reported much heat and debate did ensue for two or three Days. At length, I think by 6 to 4, it was determined to be accepted and accordingly published. Maryland withdrew after having desired in vain a Copy of the proceedings and their dissent; and gave us to understand they should not return nor deem our farther Resolutions obligatory, untill they had transmitted an Acc[oun]t of their Proceedings to their Convention and had their Instructions how to act or conduct themselves upon this alarming occasion. This Event is waited for with Impatience and while it is in agitation the assembly of this Province will meet and it is not impossible but they may join in this extraordinary proceeding. What then will be the consequence God only knows.

Consequences there were, and that right speedily. "The order of Congress concerning taking up Government under the people", Josiah Bartlett wrote May 19, "has made a great noise in this province" (that is, Pennsylvania). There was to be a meeting of the City and Liberties the next day, and he looked for a dissolution of the assembly and the calling of a convention. "In this Colony", Elbridge Gerry wrote the following day, "the spirit of the people is great, if a judgment is to be formed from appearances." And Richard Henry Lee wrote on the 21st that the resolve of Congress had "wrought a great change hereabouts". Very soon, he was confident, the public affairs would wear a different aspect and be directed with better spirit. In fact, just as James Wilson had forewarned, Pennsylvania was having a small revolution of its own; while the stirrings in several other colonies might also be characterized as revolutionary. Everywhere, in fact, among the people, in their colonial assemblies, called by whatever name, in their common Congress, all minds were pondering deeply the question, shall America declare its independence?

Let it not, however, be supposed that Congress had, during this eventful period, been concerning itself solely with the question whether and how soon the several colonies would or should set up their own governments, or with the intimately related question whether the movement toward independence was to be accelerated or retarded. A multitude of other questions, great and small, had pounded incessantly on the Congressional door, demanding a hearing, and it is one of the marvels of that era that Congress was able to answer so many of them so wisely.

Much of our time [Joseph Hewes wrote to James Iredell, May 17] is employed in raising men, making Cannon, muskets, and merely finding out ways and means of supplying our Troops with Cloathes, provisions and ammunition. We appear to have everything we want. We resolve to raise regiments, resolve to make Cannon, resolve to make and import muskets, powder and cloathing, but it is a melancholly fact that near half of our men,

Cannon, muskets, powder, cloathes, etc., is to be found nowhere but on paper. We are not discouraged at this; if our situation was ten times worse I could not agree to give up our cause.

Joseph Hewes was a man of business and perceived more clearly than did many of his contemporaries, likewise than many of his successors, that of themselves resolutions, acts, appropriations, do not fashion a nation's defenses, that brave words alone do not transform themselves into implements of war.

To John Adams, impatient to get ahead with the great project of having the colonies assert complete control over their own governments and then join together in declaring their independence, all other things, big or little, seemed but the tithing of mint, anise, and cumin. Late in life he even charged that "Little things were designedly thrown in the way of great ones . . . so that we could only now and then snatch a transient glimpse· of the promised land." That Congress did putter much and sometimes mightily with things trivial, perhaps even futile, is evinced with all needful clarity even to a wayfaring browser through some pages of its Journal. Such a browser might, however, easily underestimate the weight of an item because it seemed small. Was it, for instance, a trivial thing for Congress to instruct its committee to take care that the chests of medicines and instruments to be furnished to the North Carolina battalions should be of the same value as those recently supplied to the Pennsylvania regiments? On the contrary, that provision is to be accounted unto Congress for rightness, if not also for righteousness. Later such niceties in the balancing of perquisites and privileges would not be so imperative. Eventually also sheer necessity would drive Congress to devise ways and means of shifting from its own shoulders the intolerable burden of multiplied little things, likewise to more competent shoulders many of the weightier matters of administration. These, however, were problems that could be solved only by experience and the slow growth of wisdom.

The momentous decision of Congress (May 10, 15, 1776) to advise the colonies to suppress every authority under the crown and assume the powers of government under the authority of the people gave to Adams the fullest vision of the promised land that had yet been offered him. What was more, Congress appears to have convinced itself that the period of marking time in its preparations for the contest had come to an end, that it must needs gird itself for a real war. Accordingly, on May 16, General Washington was requested to come to Philadelphia, "in order to consult with Congress upon such measures as may be necessary for the carrying on the ensuing campaign". On May 24 and 25 the general had conferences with Congress, and thereupon a committee of fourteen, two from Virginia and one from each of the other colonies, was appointed to concert a plan of military operations for the ensuing campaign. To add immensely to the importance and seriousness of the problem, within two days after the request for General Washington's attendance on Congress deeply disturbing news began to pour in from the Canadian expedition—and worse was yet to come. "This Day", John Adams wrote to James Warren, May 18, "has brought us the Dismals from Canada—Defeated most ignominiously. Where shall we lay the blame? America, duped and bubbled with the Phantom of Commissioners, has been fast asleep." More than that, definite information had taken the place of rumor that the British government was hiring German mercenaries to aid them in subduing the rebellious Americans. Could anything do more to stir American wrath and rouse its fighting spirit?

While Congress waited to hear the unmistakable voices of the colonies with regard to independence, and now and then, as occasion seemed to require, gave attention to some matters that John Adams thought trivial, it did earnestly endeavor to exclude from consideration all else than its preparation for defense until that problem should be determined upon. Despite the dismals from Canada, Congress was determined to press forward with that undertaking. "There are still laurels to be acquired in Canada", President Hancock wrote to General Thomas, informing him that he had been chosen to that command. "Laurels are still to be reaped in Canada", Samuel Chase wrote to General Gates (June 13), intimating that many members of Congress had "cast their eyes" upon him to lead that great enterprise. Chiefly, the outcome of these deliberations was to employ 6,000 militia for the reinforcement of the army in Canada, 13,000 for the reinforcement of the army in New York, and to establish a flying camp of 10,000 men, apportioning these contributions of militia amongst the colonies from New Hampshire to Maryland inclusive, excepting Rhode Island.

Pondering this extraordinary call upon the people to arm for battle, Congress came to a resolution (May 29), "That an animated address be published to impress the minds of the people with the necessity of their now stepping forward to save their country, their freedom and property", and designated Jefferson, Wythe, Samuel Adams, and Edward Rutledge to prepare it. During the long course of the struggle for independence Congress seldom failed to embrace any good opportunity for appealing to the people in an animated address; yet, strangely enough, this proposed address seems not to have been published, although a fragment from the pen of George Wythe attests that at least its preparation was begun. At all events, the letter of President Hancock to the several colonies (June 4), accompanying the proceedings of Congress, was sufficiently animated, a sufficiently "solemn Appeal", to meet every requirement. "The Militia of the United Colonies", wrote President Hancock, "are a Body of Troops that may be depended on. . . . They are called upon to say, whether they will live Slaves, or die Freemen—they are requested to step forth in Defence of their Wives, their Children, and Liberty, and every Thing they hold dear. The Cause is certainly a most glorious one, and I trust that every man . . . is determined to see it gloriously ended, or perish in the ruins of it."

One other element of the preparations for the contest, namely, the financial, is not to be overlooked. On May 6, Congress reached a decision that ten million dollars would be required for carrying on the war during the current year, and three days later authorized the issue of one half that sum. A little more than two months and the other half was required, and long before the end of the year still another five millions were ordered (November 2). By that time depreciation, with its concomitant rise in prices, was creating a new problem for Congress. The more money issued, the more was required. It was extremely annoying.

As yet however that worry had scarcely been felt. In May money in abundance for every need seemed to be within easy reach. The great compelling questions were whether and how soon the colonies that had not done so would set their own governments in motion, and whether and how soon they would pronounce for a separation from Great Britain and all its works. If on May 15 John Adams had glimpsed the promised land, five days later he had ascended the sublime heights. "Every Post and every Day", he wrote to James Warren, May 20, "rolls in upon Us, Independence like a Torrent." The delegates from Georgia had made their appearance that day with unlimited powers, "and these Gentlemen themselves are very firm"; South Carolina had given her delegates ample powers, "and they are firm enough"; North Carolina had repealed her instructions against Confederation and independence. Moreover this day's post had brought a multitude of letters from Virginia, "all of which breathe the same Spirit".

"Here are four Colonies to the Southward", he continued, "who are perfectly agreed now with the four to the Northward. Five in the Middle are not yet quite so ripe; but they are very near it." "The middle colonies", he wrote a few days later, "have never tasted the bitter cup; they have never smarted, and are therefore a little cooler; but you will see that the colonies are united indissolubly." New York, New Jersey, Pennsylvania, and Delaware would, he was convinced, take decisive measures soon. Maryland was "so eccentric a Colony—sometimes so hot, sometimes so cold", that he scarcely knew what to expect from it. "What", he asked, "do you think must be my Sensations when I see the Congress now daily passing Resolutions, which I most earnestly pressed for against Wind and Tide Twelve Months ago? and which I have not omitted to labour for a Month together from that Time to this?" Perhaps not the least of his delectations was over the conversion of his long-time critic and opponent, John Dickinson. "What do you think must be my Reflection", he wrote to Warren, "when I see the Farmer himself now confessing the Falsehood of all his Prophecies, and the truth of mine. . . . ?"

Only the zeal of an Adams could have taken such full assurance from the expressed attitudes of Georgia and South Carolina, although he was not alone in his opinion that they would "readily accede". In the cases of North Carolina and Virginia he was on firmer ground. Indeed the New England colonies had not all yet spoken with that degree of definiteness that Adams assumed. The action taken by Rhode

Island May 4, and laid before Congress May 14, for instance, by no means authorized its delegates to vote for independence, although a letter of Governor Cooke that accompanied the act of the assembly suggested that the delegates would be warranted in pursuing that course. "I observe", Stephen Hopkins wrote to the governor in reply (May 15), "that you have avoided giving me a direct answer to my Queries concerning dependance or independance. However, the copy of the Act of Assembly which you have sent me, together with our instructions leave me little room to doubt what is the opinion of the Colony I came from." The New Hampshire delegates likewise, though they themselves were scarcely less eager than were the delegates of Massachusetts, had not yet received positive instructions from their government.

Even the attitude of Massachusetts was an inference, rather than a certainty based on explicit instructions. On May 10 the House of Representatives had called upon the several towns to express themselves, whether, "if the honourable Congress should, for the safety of the said Colonies, declare them independent of the Kingdom of Great Britain, they, the said inhabitants, will solemnly engage, with their lives and fortunes, to support them in the measure." Through the month of May, and indeed on through the month of June, the towns were responding, some briefly, others effusively, but almost uniformly, that they would solemnly engage to support the measure "with their lives and fortunes". Almost uniformly, but not quite. In the town of Barnstable, for instance, "It passed in the negative"; although many of the inhabitants of the town immediately registered a protest. The response from the town of Boston (May 23) was, as no one doubted it would be, all that either of the Adamses could desire. Nor had Connecticut yet given positive instructions, although there was no reason for skepticism respecting the course that colony would adopt. Altogether John Adams had substantial justification for his high optimism, even though it was an exaggeration to say that independence was then rolling in upon Congress like a torrent. Such a torrent would indeed soon descend upon Congress, but it was now only gathering. It had not yet begun to roll.

What was taking place in Virginia might very well nevertheless be characterized as torrential. As early as April 20, three weeks before

John Adams and Richard Henry Lee had brought into Congress their proposition for advising the colonies to take their own governments in hand, Lee had written to Patrick Henry to invite his attention to "the most important concerns of our approaching convention". "Ages yet unborn, and millions existing at present", Lee wrote, "must rue or bless that Assembly, on which their happiness or misery will so eminently depend." Virginia, so Lee declared, had hitherto taken the lead in great affairs, and many were now looking with anxious expectation to the spirit, wisdom, and energy of her councils. A prime necessity to America, he argued, was an alliance with a friendly power, therefore he besought that the convention give peremptory instructions to Virginia's delegates in Congress "to take every effectual step to secure America from the despotic aims of the British Court by Treaties of alliance with foreign States, or by any means that shall be thought most conducive to that end." Yet no European state, he was convinced, was likely to treat or trade with the American colonies so long as they considered themselves subjects of Great Britain, not until they should take rank as an independent people. "This", said he, "I take to be the time and the thing meant by Shakespeare when he says, 'There is a Tide in the Affairs of men'. . . ." Jefferson, who returned to Congress, May 14, after an absence of four and a half months, took much the same view. A foreign alliance, he wrote (May 17), was the only measure that could promise a prospect of importing the essential supplies. "For that measure", he remarked, "several colonies, and some of them weighty, are not yet quite ripe. I hope ours is, and that they will tell us so."

Virginia had, in fact, so spoken two days before. When the convention assembled on May 6, a stream of petitions from county after county poured in upon it, calling for instructions to the delegates in the Continental Congress to cast off the British yoke and declare the colonies independent. Some of the counties did not hesitate to register their wrath along with their convictions and their instructions. Charlotte County, for instance, declared that the ministry and Parliament had "added insult to their injustice and cruelty, by repeatedly pretending to hold out the olive-branch of peace in such a way as teacheth us that they are determined to persist in their hellish designs, and that nothing is intended for us but the most abject slavery." Cumberland

County would show the British monarch the door with no more than the minimum of ceremony. "We therefore your Constituents", reads an essential part of their instructions to the county's delegates in the Convention, "instruct you positively to declare for an independency; that you solemnly abjure any Allegiance to his Britannick Majesty, and bid him a good Night forever." Some of them, while advocating alliances with foreign powers, at the same time cautioned their representatives to beware of other than commercial alliances. In general the counties urged a confederation of the colonies. Augusta County, for instance, would have its delegates represent "the necessity of making the Confederacy of the United Colonies the most perfect, independent, and lasting; and of framing an equal, free, and liberal Government, that may bear the test of all future ages."

By the 15th of May, therefore, the Virginia Convention was ripe for action, a ripeness manifested by the following resolution, unanimously adopted:

That the Delegates appointed to represent this Colony in General Congress be instructed to propose to that·respectable body to declare the United Colonies free and independent States, absolved from all allegiance to, or dependence upon, the Crown or Parliament of Great Britain; and that they give the assent of this Colony to such declaration, and to whatever measures may be thought proper and necessary by the Congress for forming foreign alliances, and a Confederation of the Colonies, at such time and in the manner as to them shall seem best: *Provided,* That the power of forming Government and the regulations of the internal concerns of each Colony, be left to the respective Colonial Legislatures.

Further, for the colony itself, it was resolved, likewise unanimously, "That a Committee be appointed to prepare a Declaration of Rights, and such a plan of Government as will be most likely to maintain peace and order in this Colony, and secure substantial and equal liberty to the people."

Not only did Virginia go forward with the establishment of her own government, adopting (June 12) a notable Bill of Rights and a Frame of Government (June 29); but, without waiting on action by the Continental Congress, proceeded to declare her own independence. This Declaration, be it noted, was written by the same hand that, a few days later, would draw up the National Declaration of Independence. It was embodied in a preamble to a constitution for Virginia which had been offered by Jefferson, then in Philadelphia. The convention had, however, previously agreed on a constitution and therefore chose to make use of only Jefferson's preamble.

On May 27 the Virginia Convention's resolution of May 15, which had been transmitted not only to the Virginia delegates in Congress but also to the other colonies, was laid before Congress. At the same time the North Carolina delegates laid before Congress the like instructions of April 12 from their colony. Reporting these proceedings to President Meshech Weare the next day, the New Hampshire delegates expressed the opinion that South Carolina and Georgia would "readily accede", adding the further remark: "The Proprietary Gov[ernme]nts will be the last to agree to this necessary step. The disafected in them are now exerting themselves but these exertions are no more than the last strugles of expiring faction."

So it proved; yet it required a robust faith to believe that the resolutions of the Maryland Convention that had been laid before Congress May 24 were the struggles of an expiring faction. That convention had, in fact, unanimously resolved (May 15):

That as this Convention is firmly persuaded that a reunion with Great Britain on constitutional principles would most effectually secure the rights and liberties, and increase the strength and promote the happiness of the whole empire, objects which this Province has ever had in view, the said Deputies are bound and directed to govern themselves by the instructions given to them by this Convention in its session in December last, in the same manner as if the said instructions were particularly repeated.

This resolution certainly seemed decisive, for the time being at least, and the instructions given to the delegates were equally positive. "Maryland has passed a few eccentric resolves", commented John Adams, "but these are only flashes that will soon expire." The other middle colonies likewise failed to rush headlong to embrace independence with the speed and fervor expected by the enthusiasts.

CHAPTER IX

LAUNCHING THE NATIONAL SHIP
THE DECLARATION OF INDEPENDENCE

The resolutions of the Virginia Convention, May 15, 1776, calling for independence lay on the table of Congress like a bomb with a sputtering fuse. Not long could it be ignored, even if any were disposed to ignore it. Just then, however, Congress was deeply engrossed in the plan of defense that had been concerted with General Washington and was being wrought into system by a committee. Therefore, impatient as were the chief leaders of the movement for independence to press the question upon Congress, they were held in check until the military arrangements had been completed. On June 4 the plan was transmitted to the several colonies, whereupon these leaders made ready for action.

Richard Henry Lee, in compliance with the mandate of the Virginia Convention, had ready for submission a resolution embodying the convention's demands. On the 2d of June he wrote to Landon Carter:

The infamous treaties with Hesse, Brunswick etc. of which we have authentic copies and the Ministerial reply to Graftons motion leave not a doubt but that our enemies are determined upon the absolute conquest and subduction of N. America. *It is not choice then but necessity that calls for Independence, as the only means by which foreign Alliance can be obtained;* and a proper Confederation by which internal peace and union may be secured.

On June 6, Samuel Adams wrote to James Warren:

You know my Temper. Perhaps I may be too impatient. . . . However, to-morrow a Motion will be made, and a Question I hope decided, the most important that was ever agitated in America. I have no doubt but it will be decided to *your* satisfaction. This being done, Things will go on in the right Channel and our Country will be saved.

On the same day Josiah Bartlett wrote to Nathaniel Folsom that the affair of declaring the colonies independent must be decided soon, "whatever may be the opinion of the Delegates of New Hampshire on that matter". The delegates, he added, regarded it their duty to act agreeably to the minds of their constituents, and, in an affair of such magnitude, besought, as they had done previously, the explicit directions of their legislature.

On the 7th of June, Richard Henry Lee offered his resolution, embodying three distinct propositions:

That these United Colonies are, and of right ought to be, free and independent States, that they are absolved from all allegiance to the British Crown, and that all political connection between them and the State of Great Britain is, and ought to be, totally dissolved.

That it is expedient forthwith to take the most effectual measures for forming foreign Alliances.

That a plan of confederation be prepared and transmitted to the respective Colonies for their consideration and approbation.

It might seem from the order in which these propositions stand in the resolution that forming foreign alliances and creating a confederation were but corollaries to a declaration of independence; but Lee himself, stanch advocate of independence though he was, appears to have been thinking of independence as a means to an end rather than the goal itself. Such at least would seem to be the import of his statement to Landon Carter quoted above. On the other hand, John Adams, the "Atlas of Independence", as he was called, who had seconded Lee's motion, held to a somewhat different doctrine.

It has ever appeared to me [he wrote to Patrick Henry, June 3] that the natural course and order of things was this; for every colony to institute a government; for all the colonies to confederate, and define the limits of the continental Constitution; then to declare the colonies a sovereign state, or a number of confederated sovereign states; and last of all, to form treaties with foreign powers. But I fear we cannt proceed systematically, and that we shall be obliged to declare ourselves independent States, before we confederate, and indeed before all the colonies have established their governments.

It was now pretty clear, he added, that all these measures would follow one another in rapid succession, "and it may not perhaps be of much importance, which is done first." Probably few members of Congress could have been induced to believe that, once independence had been declared, it would still be nearly two years before the first foreign alliance would be consummated and nearly five years before the confidently expected confederation would become a reality. Perhaps it were well for their greater peace of mind that they had not this prevision.

Even the lively hopes of the Adamses that the question of independence would be decided without delay were destined to experience a severe chill. First, consideration of the resolution was postponed for one day; then, on June 8, Congress resolved itself into committee of the whole for the purpose, but came out of committee with only a decision to resume the consideration on the following Monday, which was June 10. That Saturday night at the hour of ten, Edward Rutledge of South Carolina sat him down to pen a hurried and somewhat vitriolic note to John Jay.

The Congress sat till 7 o'clock this evening [he wrote] in consequence of a motion of R. H. Lee's rendering ourselves free and independent States. The sensible part of the House opposed the Motion—they had no objection to forming a Scheme of a Treaty which they would send to France by proper Persons and uniting this Continent by a Confederacy; they saw no Wisdom in a *Declaration* of Independence, nor any other purpose to be enforced by it, but placing ourselves in the Power of those with whom we mean to treat, giving our Enemy Notice of our Intentions before we had taken any steps to execute them and thereby enabling them to counteract us in our Intentions and rendering ourselves ridiculous in the Eyes of foreign powers by attempting to bring them into an Union with us before we had united with each other.

No reason, he declared, could be assigned for pressing this measure, except "the reason of every Madman, a shew of our spirit". For his part, he meant to move, when the discussion was renewed, that it be postponed for three weeks or months. Meanwhile the other proposals, the plan of confederation and the scheme of a treaty, might be pushed forward. Altogether the opposition to the resolution in behalf of independence encountered on that first day of its consideration in Congress might well have damped John Adams's enthusiasm; but no; he arose that following Sunday morning with spirits as exuberant as a bubbling fountain.

Objects of the most stupendous magnitude, and measures in which the lives and liberties of millions yet unborn are intimately interested [he wrote to William Cushing], are now before us. We are in the very midst of a revolution, the most complete, unexpected, and remarkable, of any in the history of nations.

A few more things to be accomplished, and he would think he had answered the end of his creation and then might sing his *nunc dimittis*. The more important of these objects were that every colony should institute a perfect government, the colonies must confederate together in a solemn band of union, Congress must declare the colonies free and independent states, and ambassadors must then be sent to foreign courts to solicit their acknowledgment of us as sovereign states and to form with some of them at least treaties of commerce and friendship.

Came Monday, June 10, and the conservative element succeeded in having the question of independence postponed until July 1, although they were overborne to the extent of making prior provision for the eventful day—"and in the meanwhile, that no time be lost, in case the Congress agree thereto, that a committee be appointed to prepare a declaration to the effect of the said first resolution". The committee to prepare the declaration, which was appointed on June 11, consisted of Thomas Jefferson, John Adams, Benjamin Franklin, Roger Sherman, and Robert R. Livingston. On the same day it was further resolved that a committee be appointed "to prepare and digest the form of a confederation to be entered into between these colonies", and another "to prepare a plan of treaties to be proposed to foreign powers". The two latter committees were appointed June 12, that on the confederation consisting of a member from each colony, that on the plan of treaties being five in number, namely, Dickinson, Franklin, John Adams, Benjamin Harrison, and Robert Morris.

Edward Rutledge states that the whole argument on June 8 in opposition to an immediate adoption of the resolution for independence was sustained by Robert R. Livingston, James Wilson, John Dickinson, and himself, that on the other side "by the Power of all N[ew] England, Virginia, and Georgia". Jefferson, in his notes of the debates, names the opponents as Wilson, Livingston, Rutledge, Dickinson, "and others", and the principal advocates as John Adams, Richard Henry Lee, George Wythe, "and others". In these notes Jefferson has recorded a summary of the arguments presented on the one side and on the other.

The opponents argued that, although they were friends of the measure and recognized the impossibility of ever again being united with Great Britain, they were against a declaration of independence at this time. For one thing, we should wait for the unmistakable voice of the people, without which a declaration of independence could not be carried into effect. For another thing, the middle colonies "were not yet ripe for bidding adieu to the British connection", although "they were fast ripening, and in a short time would join in the general voice of America". The resolution of May 15 had thrown these colonies into a ferment, and "they had not yet accommodated their minds to a separation from the mother country". Some of them, in fact, had expressly forbidden their delegates to consent to such a declaration, and others had not yet given instructions on the subject. Yet most, if not all, of those colonies were on the point of doing just that thing. The assembly of Pennsylvania and the convention of New York were then sitting, those of New Jersey and Delaware were about to meet, and it was altogether probable that these bodies would shortly declare to their delegates the voice of their colony.

Suppose, ran the argument, a declaration of independence should now be agreed to in Congress. The delegates of those colonies would have to retire, and their colonies might secede from the union; and such a secession, it was contended, "would weaken us more than could be compensated by any foreign alliance". In that event, foreign powers would probably refuse to join themselves to our fortunes, or else they would make use of "that desperate declaration" to demand terms "proportionably more hard and prejudicial". As for obtaining France and Spain as allies, there was good reason to suppose that they would "be jealous of that rising power which would one day certainly strip them of all their American possessions". It was more likely that they would join with Great Britain in a scheme to partition America. Better at all events to wait until we should receive certain information of the disposition of the French court, and also until we should have fixed among ourselves the terms on which we would form an alliance.

The other side, according to Jefferson, concerned itself mainly with answering the arguments of the opposition point by point. "The question was not whether, by a declaration of independence, we should make ourselves what we are not; but whether we should declare a fact which already exists." The colonies always had been independent of the British Parliament, so these speakers maintained, even if they had at times acquiesced in Parliamentary restraints on their trade; our connection had been federal only, and that connection had now been dissolved by the commencement of hostilities. In like manner the former bond of allegiance to the king had been dissolved by his declaring us out of his protection. "Allegiance and protection are reciprocal, the one ceasing when the other is withdrawn."

As for the want of instructions, or instructions to oppose the measure, only the delegates of Pennsylvania and Maryland were absolutely tied up, and they only by a reservation by their colonies of a right of confirming or rejecting the measure. Besides, since those instructions were issued, those of Pennsylvania in particular, "the face of affairs has totally changed". If those two colonies were backward, it was partly because of proprietary influence and partly because they had not yet been attacked by the enemy or were likely to be soon. In any event, it would be vain to wait weeks or months for perfect unanimity—an impossible condition. Moreover, there was good reason to suspect that it had been from the beginning the settled policy of some colonies "to keep in the rear of the confederacy, that their particular prospect might be better, even in the worst event."

The advocates of an immediate declaration of independence were but little apprehensive of any danger from a secession of some of the colonies; and as for a foreign alliance, "a declaration of independence alone could render it consistent with European delicacy for European powers to treat with us, or even to receive an ambassador from us." France and Spain may, as it had been argued, be jealous of our rising power, but—and here they pointed to the probable alternative in the event the colonies should be overcome in the contest—they would expect that power to be "much more formidable with the addition of Great Britain". Indeed, these speakers acknowledge, the present campaign may be unsuccessful, and that is good reason why "we had better propose an alliance while our affairs wear a hopeful aspect". To attempt to settle the terms of alliance before we had determined that we would enter into an alliance would be sheer waste of time. In fact, the want of supplies made it necessary to lose no time in opening trade. It was a misfortune that we had not entered into an alliance with France six months ago. Finally, they declared the sum and substance of the whole matter to be, "the people wait for us to lead the way . . . *they* are in favour of the measure, tho' the instructions given by some of their *representatives* are not." It was therefore for "those colonies who had thrown themselves forward and hazarded all from the beginning, to come forward now also, and put all again to their own hazard." Thus argued the advocates of an immediate declaration of independence.

The debates had made it clear, Jefferson further records, that New York, New Jersey, Pennsylvania, Delaware, Maryland, and even South Carolina were "not yet matured for falling from the parent stem, but that they were fast advancing to that state", and it was accordingly "thought most prudent" to wait a while for this maturing process. The New Englander, Elbridge Gerry, similarly stated, in a letter to James Warren, June 11, that the postponement to July 1 was "in order to give the Assemblies of the Middle Colonies an opportunity to take off their instructions and let their Delegates unite in the measure." It was a fact nevertheless that two of the New England colonies, New Hampshire and Connecticut, had not yet spoken officially on the subject, although the New Hampshire delegates in particular had repeatedly besought their government to do so, and now (June 11) once more pressed their entreaty.

It was the middle colonies of course upon which all eyes were now turned. On June 8 the New York delegates, without waiting for further discussion of the question, had sent at once an express to their convention to say: "Some of us consider ourselves bound by our instructions not to vote on that question, and all wish to have your sentiments thereon." The Maryland delegates, for their part, promptly after the debates of June 10 despatched to their committee of safety a request that the convention of the province be called together as soon as possible "to give the explicit Sense of the Province on this Point".

We wish [wrote the Maryland delegates, June 11] to have the fair and uninfluenced sense of the people we have the Honour to represent in this most important and interesting Affair, And think it would be well if the Delegates to the Convention were desired to endeavour to collect the Opinion of the People at large, in some Manner or other previous to the Meeting of the Convention.

In Pennsylvania a revolution was already under way. On June 8 new instructions to the delegates in Congress had been adopted, not indeed authorizing them point blank to vote for independence, but removing the former restrictions and authorizing them to concur with the other delegates in Congress in forming further compacts between the colonies, in concluding treaties with foreign powers, and in adopting such other measures as should appear necessary for promoting the liberty, safety, and interests of America, but reserving to the people of Pennsylvania the sole and exclusive right of regulating their internal government and police. It was not, however, until June 14 that these instructions were embodied in a letter to the delegates. This was not all that was desired by the party of independence, but they watched the Pennsylvania struggle expectantly. "We seem at present to be in the Midst of a great Revolution", Oliver Wolcott wrote to his wife, June 11, and four days later reiterated the sentiment. Exclaimed John Adams (June 16): "Great things are on the tapis. These throes will usher in the birth of a fine boy."

The wheel of authority in Pennsylvania had indeed revolved a little way, but not far enough to suit the element that would forsake the old government and steer their course for a new one. Fiercely therefore they seized the wheel, wrenched it out of the hands of the former pilots, and within ten days had brought it around to the desired point. To use political rather than nautical language, the radicals had set up a revolutionary body, called the Provincial Conference, assumed to be expressive of the will of the people, and had taken control of the colonial government. On the 24th of June accordingly the Conference adopted a declaration including these words:

We the Deputies of the people of Pennsylvania . . . in behalf of ourselves, and with the approbation, consent, and authority of our constituents, unanimously declare our willingness to concur in a vote of the Congress declaring the United Colonies free and independent States, provided the forming the government, and the regulation of the internal police of this Colony, be always reserved to the people of the said Colony.

To be sure, the colony's delegates in Congress might have some doubt as to which was the real authority in Pennsylvania, the old Assembly or the new Conference; but theirs was the fate of all who doubt; they could but make their choice.

Meanwhile Delaware had trod close upon the heels of Pennsylvania. The same day on which the Pennsylvania delegates had received their revised instructions (June 14) the Delaware House of Assembly adopted instructions to that colony's delegates in like terms, and thereupon set aside the royal authority and took steps to set up the colonial authority instead. The former restrictions being now removed, the delegates might assume, if they chose, that they were authorized to vote for independence.

On the following day (June 15) the Provincial Congress of New Jersey took a long stride in the same direction, having ousted William Franklin from the governor's chair and ordered his arrest and confinement. Thence it was but a short step to the goal. On the 21st new delegates were chosen—Richard Stockton, Abraham Clark, John Hart, Francis Hopkinson, and Dr. John Witherspoon—and instructions given them

to join with the Delegates of the other Colonies in Continental Congress, in the most vigorous Measures for supporting the just Rights and Liberties of America; and, if you shall judge it necessary or expedient for this Purpose, we empower you to join with them in declaring the United Colonies independent of Great Britain, entering into a Confederacy for Union and common Defence, making Treaties with foreign Nations for Commerce and Assistance, and to take such other Measures as may appear to them and you necessary for these great Ends; promising to support them with the whole Force of this Province; always observing, that, whatever Plan of Confederacy you enter into, the Regulating the internal Police of this Province is to be reserved to the Colony Legislature.

Thus the gap was rapidly closing. Having received prior intimation of what New Jersey was about to do, John Adams declared that the new delegates would "vote plump". "Maryland", he added, "now stands alone. I presume she will soon join company; if not she must be left alone." (He appears to have forgotten about New York.) Then, on the 24th, when he had learned of New Jersey's positive instructions and its appointment of five "independent souls", he wrote, "I hope that before Monday morning next we shall receive from Maryland instructions to do right." Now that New Jersey's five new delegates had been "high charged" with instructions for independence, as Elbridge Gerry wrote exultantly (June 25), there appeared to be not even a doubt of any colony on the continent except New York and Maryland. "These", he added, "will not impede us a moment. . . . I think the contest is pretty nearly at an end."

The New England ranks, never really in doubt, had meanwhile been securely closed. The legislature of Connecticut had taken action on June 14, instructing the colony's delegates to propose to Congress "to declare the United American Colonies free and independent States, absolved from all allegiance to the King of Great Britain, and to give the assent of this Colony to such declaration, when they shall judge it expedient and best." Further, the delegates were authorized to give assent to whatever measures Congress might think proper and necessary for forming foreign alliances and instructed to move and promote "a regular and permanent plan of Union and Confederation of the Colonies, for the security and preservation of their just rights and liberties, and for mutual defence and security". In making the customary reservation of the internal concerns of the colony from the control of any 'confederation that might be formed, Connecticut broadened its scope with the stipulation,

saving that the administration of Government and the power of forming Governments for, and the regulation of the internal concerns and police of each Colony, ought to be left and remain to the respective Colonial legislatures, and also that such plan of Confederation be laid before such respective Legislatures for their previous consideration and assent.

On June 15 the New Hampshire legislature took similar action on the subject of independence, "solemnly pledging our faith and honour that we will, on our parts, support the measure with our lives and fortunes". No longer disturbed over what would be his duty and his privilege when the question should come to a vote, William Whipple could now (June 24) write: "The Middle Colonies are getting in a good way. Next Monday, being the 1st of July, the grand question is to be debated, and I believe determined unanimously. May God unite our hearts in all things that tend to the well-being of the rising empire."

But would the decision be unanimous? Would Maryland and New York be betimes with new and consenting instructions? The Maryland Convention had assembled on June 21 and had sent a request to Congress that the consideration of the resolution for independence, a foreign alliance, and confederation be postponed beyond July 1 in order to allow the colony more time for determining upon its position. Congress declined the request, on the ground that the proposed vote on July 1 had obtained wide publicity; and the Convention was accordingly confronted with the date July 1 as an ultimatum. Like New Jersey, Maryland still had a royal governor, and one of the first essentials, if the colony was going to set up in business for itself, was to dispose of this relic of its former dependence. The Convention and Council of Safety had no difficulty, as it turned out, in disposing of Governor Eden gently but effectively by permitting him to go aboard a British man-of-war.

In the meantime, in accordance with a suggestion of the Maryland delegates in Congress, June 11, some of the delegates to the Convention, particularly Samuel Chase and Charles Carroll of Carrollton, were busy collecting the sentiments of the people—and just as busily promoting the growth of the kind of sentiment that they were eager to collect. "I have not been idle", Chase wrote to John Adams, June 21. "I have appealed *in writing* to the people. County after County is instructing." Exactly one week later Chase again wrote to Adams. His note, hurried and brief, was dated at Annapolis, June 28, "Fryday

Evening 9 o'Clock", and its principal message was this: "I am this Moment from the House to procure an Express to follow the Post with an Unan: Vote of our Convention for Independence etc. etc.— see the glorious Effects of County Instructions—our people have fire if not smothered."

On this same Friday on which the Convention of Maryland was coming to its momentous decision in Annapolis, in Philadelphia Congress was anxiously waiting for that decision, most of the members eager and hopeful, a few of them apprehensive. Wrote Joseph Hewes of North Carolina that day: "On Monday the great question of independency and total separation from all political intercourse with Great Britain will come on. It will be carried, I expect, by a great majority, and then, I suppose we shall take upon us a new name." Wrote his colleague, John Penn: "The first day of July will be an era of great importance . . . there is no doubt but a total separation between Britain and her Colonies, that were, will take place as all the provinces but Maryland are for it, and the inhabitants there are coming over fast. . . . I don't doubt but we shall have spirit enough to act like men. indeed it could no longer be delayed." (Penn likewise appears to have overlooked New York.)

Edward Rutledge of South Carolina, on the other hand, sounded a lugubrious note. Writing to John Jay (June 29) to beseech him to give his attendance in Congress, if possible, on the following Monday, Rutledge said: "A Declaration of Independence, the form of a Confederation of these Colonies, and a Scheme for a Treaty with foreign Powers will be laid before the House on Monday. Whether we shall be able effectually to oppose the first and infuse Wisdom into the others will depend in a great measure upon the exertions of the honest and sensible part of the Members."

On Monday morning, July 1, "just as we were entering on the great debate", so John Adams wrote to Samuel Chase later in the day, the resolution of the Maryland Convention was brought into Congress, and straightway Congress resolved itself into a committee of the whole "to take into consideration the resolution respecting independency". Both Jefferson and Adams record that the debate consumed most of the day; "an idle mispence of time", Adams declares, "for nothing was said but what had been repeated and hackneyed in that room before, a hundred times, for six months past." When the question was at last put to a vote, the exultant party of independence discovered unexpected opposition. Both Pennsylvania and South Carolina cast their votes in the negative, while Delaware, having but two members present, was divided. South Carolina had been confidently counted among the advocates, at least until Edward Rutledge had flared up in criticism of an immediate declaration; and so also had Pennsylvania after the alteration of that colony's instructions to its delegates. For a like reason it seems to have been assumed that the Delaware delegates would vote *aye*. On the contrary, the delegates of Pennsylvania and Delaware voted their individual sentiments, and it happened that the majority of the Pennsylvania delegation were opposed to the measure.

Inasmuch as the vote in the committee of the whole gave a majority for the resolution it was so reported to the House; whereupon, "at the request of a colony", the determination was postponed until the next day. The request came from Edward Rutledge, who stated that, although the South Carolina delegates were opposed to the resolution, he believed they would join in it for the sake of unanimity. At one stage of the proceedings the New York delegates stated that, since they were forbidden by their instructions from assenting to the measure, they could and would refrain from voting. Even so, if unanimity were to be obtained, the votes of Pennsylvania and Delaware, as well as that of South Carolina, must be changed. "The Pennsylvania delegates", said Francis Lightfoot Lee (July 1), "indulge their own wishes, tho they acknowledge, what indeed everybody knows that they vote contrary to the earnest desires of the people." And John Adams thought it possible that on the morrow "one or two gentlemen may possibly be found, who will vote point-blank against the known and declared sense of their constituents."

Between what took place in Congress on the 2d of July and what on the 4th there is no little confusion. The Journal record of the proceedings July 2 is simply: "The Congress resumed the consideration of the resolution agreed to by and reported from the committee of the whole; and the same being read, was agreed to as follows"; that is, that part of the resolution offered June 7 relating to independence.

Henry Wisner, one of the New York delegates, wrote immediately after the vote had been taken, "the question of independance has been put in Congress and Carried in the afirmative without one desenting vote." And John Adams wrote July 3 that the resolution passed "without one dissenting Colony". Jefferson, in his Notes, after mentioning that, on July 2, South Carolina had concurred in the measure, says: "In the meantime a third member had come post from the Delaware counties and turned the vote of that colony in favour of the resolution. Members of a different sentiment attending that morning from Pennsylvania also, their vote was changed, so that the whole 12 colonies who were authorized to vote at all, gave their voices for it." The statement that the change of Pennsylvania's vote was in consequence of the coming of new members is known from other sources to be incorrect. The new delegates for Pennsylvania were not elected until July 20, and only on that day attended Congress. According to Thomas McKean, what took place was that, on July 1, Morton, Franklin, and Wilson voted in the affirmative, Dickinson, Morris, Willing and Humphreys in the negative; on the 4th Dickinson and Morris voluntarily absented themselves, leaving the vote of the colony three to two in the affirmative. Doubtless it was on July 2, not July 4, that Dickinson and Morris first absented themselves.

The change in the vote of Delaware was in consequence of the arrival of Caesar Rodney, who voted with McKean in the affirmative, against Read in the negative. McKean states that, in response to a message from himself, Rodney had ridden from Dover to Philadelphia through the night, arriving in time to cast his vote. Confusing the vote for the formal Declaration July 4 with the vote on the resolution July 2, McKean has Rodney arrive on July 4. Rodney himself wrote July 4: "I arrived in Congress (tho detained by Thunder and Rain) time enough to give my Voice in the matter of Independence"; but he does not state whether he refers to the vote of July 2 or that of July 4. The best evidence is that it was July 2.

If it should seem that Wisner and Adams were in a manner equivocating when they declared that there had not been one dissenting colony (and Caesar Rodney made a like assertion in his letter of July 4), it is to be borne in mind that New York had not actually dissented; the delegates had merely refrained from voting. In reply to their letter of June 8 they had received from their Provincial Congress a letter (dated June 11), declaring it to be the unanimous opinion of that congress that the delegates were not authorized to give the sense of the colony on the question of independence, but that measures were then pursuing to ascertain the sentiments of the inhabitants of the colony on that important question, and that the earliest opportunity would be embraced to instruct the delegates in Congress thereon.

The measures pursuing were the calling of a convention. July 1 the delegates took occasion to lay this letter before Congress, and it clearly warranted them in making to Congress the statement, as recorded by Jefferson, that "they were for it themselves and were assured their constituents were for it". On June 17 the delegates had assured the Provincial Congress that they had hitherto taken no steps inconsistent with the intentions of that congress as expressed in their letter, "by which we shall be careful to regulate our future conduct". Then, in the morning of July 2, before the question had been resumed, they reiterated this assurance: "We know the Line of our Conduct on this Occasion; we have your Instructions, and will faithfully pursue them." It came about therefore that, when later in the day the roll of the colonies was called, New York did not respond with either an aye or a no. The question was carried without a recorded negative.

Thus at last did Congress, on the 2d of July, 1776, after long hesitation and not a little squirming, resolve that henceforth the United Colonies should be free and independent states. To all intents and purposes this resolution was the conclusion of the whole matter. So at least thought the man who had mainly led the forces of independence to victory. In the morning of July 3, John Adams wrote to his wife: "Yesterday, the greatest question was decided, which ever was debated in America, and a greater, perhaps, never was nor will be decided among men." As the hours went by his spirit rose to yet loftier heights, and in the evening of the same day he again seized his pen to pour out to his beloved Abigail more of the precious news and more of the joy that filled his soul.

The second day of July, 1776 [he wrote], will be the most memorable epocha in the history of America. I am apt to believe that it will be celebrated by succeeding generations as the great anniversary Festival. It ought to be commemorated, as the day of deliverance, by solemn acts of devotion to God Almighty. It ought to be solemnized with pomp and parade, with shows, games, sports, guns, bells, bonfires, and illuminations, from one end of this continent to the other, from this time forward, forevermore.

Who can blame him if his heart was now filled to overflowing with gladness and his soul was lifted to the seventh heaven?

You will think me transported with enthusiasm [he continued], but I am not. I am well aware of the toil and bloodshed and treasure that it will cost us to maintain this Declaration, and support and defend these States. Yet through all the gloom I can see the rays of ravishing light and glory. I can see that the end is more than worth all the means; and that posterity will triumph in that day's transactions, even although we should rue it, which I trust in God we shall not.

The colonies through their Congress had indeed declared their independence, but the bare assertion of independence was not sufficient. The reasons therefor must be set forth explicitly, must be marshalled in a form and a manner that would not only convince Americans, but would inspire them to go to the hazard of its maintenance. Moreover, the facts must be submitted to a candid world, for the good opinion of the candid world might well prove to be essential to the success of their cause. The committee that, according to the well-laid plan, had been appointed to prepare such a declaration had presented the product of its labors on June 28, and the proposed declaration was accordingly under the consideration of Congress when the debates on the resolution took place on July 1 and 2.

The Declaration as reported to Congress was principally the work of Thomas Jefferson. He had been named first on the committee and would therefore normally have been expected to prepare the committee's report; but he was named first probably because he had come to Congress with a reputation for possessing an incisive and eloquent pen. Jefferson himself afterward stated simply that the committee had desired him to draw the Declaration, and that he had done so. Something more than custom and polite acquiescence must, however, have operated to entrust so important a task to one of the youngest members of

Congress. John Adams, who had been the most persistent and vigorous advocate of independence, might well have seemed the most appropriate choice for giving definitive expression to this momentous decision. In the course of his life Adams gave more than one account of how the task came to be entrusted to Jefferson rather than to himself, and that which he gave in lively and dramatic form four years before his death may be as accurate as any other. It is to be observed, however, that, according to Jefferson, there was no subcommittee, as indicated by Adams.

The committee met [Adams wrote in 1822], discussed the subject, then appointed Mr. Jefferson and me to make the draught, I suppose because we were the two first on the list. The subcommittee met. Jefferson proposed to me to make the draught.

I said, "I will not."

"You should do it!"

"Oh! no."

"Why will you not? You ought to do it."

"I will not."

"Why?"

"Reasons enough."

"What can be your reasons?"

"Reason first—You are a Virginian, and a Virginian ought to appear at the head of this business. Reason second—I am obnoxious, suspected, and unpopular. You are very much otherwise. Reason third—You can write ten times better than I can."

"Well, if you are decided, I will do as well as I can."

"Very well. When you have drawn it up, we will have a meeting."

The gentle controversy between the two that was provoked by Adams's account it is not incumbent upon us now to pursue. It is nevertheless a beguiling reflection that the fiftieth anniversary of the Declaration of Independence, which followed close upon this joust of memories, found the spirits of these two foremost creators of the Declaration crossing the Great Divide at one and the same time, and it is pleasing to indulge the hope that they then and there joined in friendly converse, harmonized their recollections, and happily adjusted their old-time differences, whether these differences revolved about the Declaration of Independence or any other subject.

Immediately upon the adoption of the resolution of independence, Congress again resolved itself into a committee of the whole to resume consideration of the declaration, and the discussion continued through the greater part of the next two days. When the document finally came out of the committee of the whole it had undergone numerous emendations of phraseology—for better, upon the whole, but sometimes for worse—and two important excisions. One of the rejected passages was a severe censure upon the people of Great Britain. "The pusillanimous idea", says Jefferson, "that we had friends in England worth keeping terms with, still haunted the minds of many", therefore those passages were struck out lest they give offence. Another passage was a caustic condemnation of the slave trade. This, says Jefferson, "was struck out in complaisance to South Carolina and Georgia, who had never attempted to restrain the importation of slaves, and who on the contrary still wished to continue it." Then he adds: "Our northern brethren also I believe felt a little tender under those censures; for tho' their people have very few slaves themselves yet they had been pretty considerable carriers of them to others."

In the evening of July 4 the debate was closed, the amended declaration reported by the committee of the whole to the house, and the vote taken. The situation in Congress was then essentially, if not precisely, the same as on July 2. Twelve colonists voted in the affirmative, while New York kept silent. To one listening at the keyhole the vote doubtless sounded unanimous; and this absence of any resounding NO, it may have been, that led Caesar Rodney to write that same evening: "It is determined by the Thirteen United Colonies, without one decenting Colony."

With the political philosophy of the Declaration of Independence, with its literary quality, or even with its form and substance, we need not here be concerned. It is needful only to observe that it was definitely designed to aid and promote the American cause, to justify the colonies in severing all ties with Great Britain and establishing their own governments; and it served that purpose in a manner that could not have been surpassed. Its immediate effect was to rally even hesitant forces to the American standard, and its statement of the fundamental principles of government is so clear and succinct that it has given enduring character to the nation of which it laid the foundation.

While the debate of July 4 was still in progress Abraham Clark of New Jersey wrote to Elias Dayton that he expected the Declaration to pass Congress that day, "after which it will be Proclaimed with all the State and Solemnity circumstances will admit". "It is gone so far", he added, "that we must now be a free independent State, or a Conquered Country". Clark was by no means wont to preen the wings of his imagination for ethereal flights, but when he contemplated the part he was taking in the establishment of a new and great nation, his severely practical mind leaped its accustomed bounds. "I am among a Consistory of Kings", he exclaimed. Then, as if he might have seemed over-bold in his claims, he added: "I assure you Sir, Our Congress is an August Assembly, and can they Support the Declaration now on the Anvil, they will be the greatest Assembly on Earth." Ten days later, when he had no doubt given further serious reflection to the consequences of the Declaration, he wrote: "A few weeks will probably determine our fate—perfect freedom, or Absolute Slavery—to some of us freedom or a halter." And a little later still (August 6): "As to my title, I know not yet whether it will be honourable or dishonourable: the issue of war must settle it. Perhaps our Congress will be exalted on a high gallows. We were truly brought to the case of the three lepers: If we continued in the state we were in, it was evident we must perish; if we declared Independence we might be saved—we could but perish."

When the Declaration had been adopted Congress ordered that it be authenticated and printed, and that copies "be sent to the several assemblies, conventions and committees, or councils of safety, and to the several commanding officers of the continental troops; that it be proclaimed in each of the United States, and at the head of the army." On July 5 and 6 accordingly President Hancock transmitted the copies, authenticated in the customary manner, that is, by the signatures of the President and secretary, with the request that the Declaration be proclaimed "in such a Mode, as that the People may be universally informed of it". General Washington was requested to proclaim it at the head of the army "in the way you shall think most proper". One paragraph found in most of President Hancock's letters may appropriately be emphasized:

Altho it is not possible to foresee the Consequences of Human Actions, yet it is nevertheless a Duty we owe ourselves and Posterity, in all our public Counsels, to decide in the best Manner we are able, and to leave the Event to that Being who controuls both Causes and Events to bring about his own determinations.

At the same time neither President Hancock nor the Congress was lacking in the conviction that it was equally their duty to come to the help of the Lord against the mighty.

Naturally the Declaration was first proclaimed in Philadelphia (July 8), and it was in the presence of "a great crowd of people". "Three cheers rended the welkin", so wrote John Adams. "The battalions paraded on the Common, and gave us the *feu de joie,* notwithstanding the scarcity of powder. The bells rang all day and almost all night. Even the chimers chimed away." In the evening of July 9 it was proclaimed before the army at New York, and General Washington reported to Congress that "the measure seemed to have their most hearty assent; the Expressions and behaviour, both of Officers and Men testifying their warmest approbation of it." Thereafter proclamations followed one another in rapid succession. With such speed as the times afforded copies of the Declaration were transmitted to the remotest corners of the thirteen now sovereign and independent states, and in many of these hamlets there were guns and bells, bonfires and illuminations, pomp and parade, such as would have gratified the yearnings of even John Adams himself. Nor were the solemn acts of devotion to God Almighty wholly lacking. The Declaration was published, for instance, in the churches of Boston; and throughout the country there were prayers, such, for example, as that of Meshech Weare of New Hampshire, who, in a letter to President Hancock (July 16), voiced the fervent desire "That He who putteth down potentates and setteth up States may guard and protect the United States of America."

In some places those who listened to the reading of the Declaration responded with "pleasing countenances" or with "three huzzas", often with demonstrations of "joy and applause by all ranks". Where it was possible the joy was further manifested by the firing of thirteen cannon or by thirteen volleys from such military organization as was available. It was the good fortune of Providence, Rhode Island, to be able to add thirteen volleys from the ships in the harbor. Many communities were not content to celebrate the event with noise alone, whether in threes or thirteens, or with noise and illumination combined; they must have a "collation" or an "elegant entertainment", whereat they could drink toasts to appropriate sentiments, such as, "Liberty to those who have the spirit to preserve it"; "May Liberty expand her sacred wings, and, in glorious effort, diffuse her influence o'er and o'er the globe"; "May the Crowns of Tyrants be crowns of thorns"; "May the Union of the States be established in justice and mutual confidence, and be as permanent as the pillars of nature". In most instances, whether it were volleys or toasts, the number thirteen was sacred. In one celebration, however, the toasts were twenty-four in number (possibly because there were twenty-four people who must at all hazards be allowed to speak), and one of the toasts was: "May the freedom and independence of America endure until the sun grows dim with age and this earth returns to chaos."

Not a few of these celebrations were climaxed by the burning of such insignia of royalty as might be available. For instance, in Providence, "Towards evening the King of Great Britain's Coat of Arms was taken from a late publick office, as was also the sign from the Crown Coffee-House, and burnt." In Baltimore, "At night, the Town was illuminated; and, at the same time, the effigy of our late King was carted through the Town, and committed to the flames, amidst the acclamations of many hundreds—the just reward of a tyrant." In New York the celebration was given a particularly practical turn; the leaden statue of George III was pulled down and melted into bullets. In reporting these celebrations the newspapers usually took care to relieve any possible anxieties on the part of their readers with a statement of the general tenor that "the whole was conducted with the utmost decorum".

While news of the Declaration was spreading and formal proclamations of it were multiplying, a confidently expected development had taken place in the colony of New York. There, after much maneuvering, the protagonists of independence had securely got their hands on the pilot's wheel, with the result that, on July 9, the new convention adopted a resolution, "That the reasons assigned by the Continental Congress for declaring the United Colonies Free and Independent States, are cogent and conclusive", and that now "we approve the same, and will, at the risque of our lives and fortunes, join with the other colonies in supporting it". This resolution was laid before Congress on Monday, July 15; accordingly it was now entirely truthful to entitle the Declaration "The Unanimous Declaration of the Thirteen United States of America", as Elbridge Gerry, in a letter to James Warren that day, predicted would be done. Four days later (July 19) Congress resolved that the Declaration should be engrossed on parchment with that title and that, when engrossed, it should be signed "by every member of Congress". It was not until the 2d of August that the engrossed copy was laid before Congress; then, so the Journals of that day record, "The declaration of independence being engrossed and compared at the table was signed by the members."

From these records in the official Journal of Congress it ought to be perfectly clear that not until July 15, when the adherence of New York was duly registered in the proceedings of Congress, could the Declaration be truthfully termed unanimous, and that not until July 19 was the title officially ordered to be prefixed to it. It would likewise seem to be just as clearly indicated that there was no signing of the Declaration by members of Congress prior to August 2, and then only in accordance with the order of July 19. The order of July 4 "That the declaration be authenticated and printed" can not be rationally interpreted as signifying any more than that this act of Congress be authenticated in the customary manner, that is, by the signatures of the president and secretary. The texts then printed in newspapers and such other official copies of that time as have survived are so authenticated.

Notwithstanding these facts, ere long it became the prevailing idea that, immediately following the adoption of the Declaration of Independence, the members of Congress then and there appended their signatures to the instrument. Strangely enough, this idea found lodgment in the minds of even some of the men who had taken an active part in the proceedings; and, stranger still, notwithstanding the fact that this erroneous notion was, within twenty years of the event, cor-rected by one of the signers of the Declaration, the error has persisted even to our day. What did more than anything else to promote this false idea, if indeed it did not originate the idea, was a fiction in the Journal record itself. In the Journals as published the Declaration ap-pears under the date of July 4 with its label, "The unanimous Declara-tion", etc., without any record of the qualifying fact that such a title was not actually adopted, and could not have truthfully been applied, until July 19. Then, following the text of the Declaration, is the further fiction that "The foregoing declaration was, by order of Congress, engrossed, and signed by the following members"—with a complete list of the signers. A reader of the printed Journals, with no other guide, could not indeed have escaped the conclusion that on that fourth of July the Declaration of Independence was signed by the very men whose names he found there appended to it.

The error of this conclusion was first pointed out in a semi-public manner, by Thomas McKean in the summer of 1796; although McKean chiefly concerned himself with combating the notion that "the fifty-five Gentlemen, whose names are there printed and none other, were on that day personally present in Congress and assenting to the declara-tion". A good many of the signers, he pointed out, were not actually in Congress on July 4; some of them, in fact, were not even members of Congress at the time; and, furthermore, some of the signers had actually given their individual votes in opposition to the Declaration. McKean's statement in 1796 appears to have won little attention; but twice subsequently (1813 and 1817) he reiterated his assertions, with some amplifications. The chief effect of these later statements was, however, to cause some skeptical eyebrows to be lifted, among them those of John Adams, and to stir Thomas Jefferson to retort upon the deficiencies of McKean's memory as compared with the superior ac-curacy of his own notes, taken in his seat at the time, and reduced to form "on the final conclusion".

As a matter of fact, Jefferson's notes, as they have come down to us, are a summary of the proceedings respecting the measure from June 7 to July 4, but embodying nevertheless references to the later adherence of New York (July 15) and to the attendance from Pennsylvania of "Members of a different sentiment". The latter occurrence he places, however, at July 2, whereas the new delegation from Pennsylvania did not attend until July 20, having only on that day been chosen. These references clearly prove that Jefferson's notes were reduced to their present form at some later time. Moreover, there is in them no definite statement that the Declaration was signed on July 4, although Jefferson afterward interpreted the following passage in his notes as carrying that implication:

The debates having taken up the greater parts of the 2d 3d and 4th days of July were, in the evening of the last, closed; the declaration was reported by the comm[itt]ee, agreed to by the house; and signed by every member present except mr Dickinson.

It may very properly be questioned whether Jefferson originally meant to convey the meaning that every member present except Mr. Dickinson had signed the Declaration "in the evening of the last", or only that ultimately every member except Mr. Dickinson had signed it. Incidentally, he was in error in assuming that Dickinson was present on July 4, for it is otherwise known that the Pennsylvanian had purposely absented himself on that day. Furthermore, it would seem probable that Jefferson had before him, when he appended that statement, a copy of the *Journals,* with the list of the signers and observed the absence of Dickinson's name. This conclusion derives definite support from a letter of Jefferson to the editor of the *Journal de Paris,* August 29, 1787, in which he asserts, in much the same language as used in his notes, that, in the evening of the 4th, the debates were closed and "the instrument approved by an unanimous vote and signed by every member, *except Mr. Dickinson"*. To clinch his argument he says, "Look into the Journal of Congress of that day, Sir, and you will see the instrument, and the names of the signers, and that Mr. Dickinson's name is not among them." What Jefferson did not know was that that list of signers was not as contemporaneous as he had supposed, but had actually been taken from the engrossed copy of the Declaration.

When, as a result of McKean's letter of 1817, it was brought to

Jefferson's attention that a good many of those whose names are appended to the Declaration were not actually in attendance on July 4, that one of them, Matthew Thornton of New Hampshire, had first taken his seat as late as November 4, Jefferson was ready with an explanation of most of the belated signatures, which he set forth in a letter to Samuel Adams Wells, May 12, 1819. The New York delegates were not of course authorized to sign until after the resolution of their convention on July 9 and the receipt of that resolution by Congress on the 15th. Concerning the Pennsylvanians, he allows that those newly appointed July 20 could not have signed earlier, but maintains that the three that had been reappointed, namely, Franklin, Morris, and Wilson, had actually signed on July 4. How it came about that Matthew Thornton was permitted to sign as late as November 4 he would not undertake to explain, but he did not doubt that it was "for some particular reason".

It was not until the Secret Journals were printed in 1821 that the discrepancies in the record as hitherto published were made to appear. It was then discovered that the earlier printed Journals were not by any means the complete proceedings of Congress, and, what was actually astounding, some of the essential facts respecting the Declaration of Independence had remained hitherto unknown. That Congress, on July 4, had ordered only that the Declaration be authenticated and printed, that on July 19, Congress had first ordered the Declaration to be engrossed and then signed by the members, and that only on August 2, so far as the Journals recorded, was the Declaration signed by the members—all these facts were revelations. In the period that had elapsed since 1776 the notion that the signing of the Declaration had all taken place on July 4 had taken deep root in the public mind, even, as has been pointed out, including some of the signers themselves. Franklin appears to have had such a notion in 1786, as Jefferson certainly did in 1787; and John Adams as well as Jefferson remained unconvinced even by the revelations of McKean in 1813 and 1817.

When the new publication of the Secret Journals came under Jefferson's eye, revealing those hitherto unknown entries of July 19 and August 2, he was evidently startled, although he refused even then to yield his convictions. He drew out his copy of his letter of May 12,

1819, to Samuel Adams Wells and added a postscript, dated August 6, 1822, to record his reading of those two important entries and to set down his own interpretation:

That is to say the copy engrossed on parchment (for durability) was signed by the members after being compared at the table with the original one signed on paper as before stated. I add this P.S. to my letter to mr Wells to prevent confounding the signature of the original with that of the copy engrossed on parchment.

It was doubtless at the same time that Jefferson inserted on a copy of the Declaration the following interlinear note: "The Declaration thus signed on the 4th, on paper, was engrossed on parchment, and signed again on the 2d of August." On the same sheet he pasted a note referring to his letter of May 12, 1819, to Samuel Adams Wells, giving his explanations of "Some erroneous statements of the proceedings on the declaration of independence" that had latterly got before the public.

Only by the assumption that the first signed copy of the Declaration was on paper and that it had been engrossed on parchment for durability could Jefferson reconcile the entries of July 19 and August 2 with his firm conviction that the Declaration had actually been signed on the 4th of July by all the members present "except Mr. Dickinson". Aside, however, from the fact that no previous mention of a copy "signed on paper" has come to light, and even if, in the face of the evidence already adduced, such an assumption could be accepted, there is contemporaneous documentary evidence proving as conclusively as could be that no general signing of the Declaration, on paper or otherwise, took place prior to August 2. It is not necessary here to cite more than two instances of such testimony. Samuel Chase of Maryland, one of the signers, who had labored valiantly and successfully, in those critical days preceding July 4, to bring his colony into line for independence, but had not been able to come to Congress to cast his own vote for the measure, wrote to John Adams, July 5: "I hope ere this the decisive blow is struck. . . . How shall I transmit to posterity that I gave my assent?" To which Adams replied, July 9: "As soon as an American seal is prepared, I conjecture the Declaration will be subscribed by all the members, which will give you the opportunity you wish for, of transmitting your name among the votaries of independence."

Most certainly, then, on July 9 the members had not subscribed their names to the Declaration, although it was in contemplation that they would presently be offered that privilege—or duty. On July 21, Elbridge Gerry, who had been present in Congress on July 4 and had voted for independence, but had taken his departure July 16 (the day after Congress had been informed of the adherence of New York), wrote to his colleagues, Samuel and John Adams: "Pray subscribe for me the Declaration of Independence, if the same is to be signed as proposed. I think We ought to have the privilege when necessarily absent of voting and signing by proxy." Gerry had evidently been informed of a proposal to have the Declaration signed by the members, probably of the order of July 19. Beyond question, if there had been an opportunity of signing the instrument between July 4 and 16, Gerry would never have made such a request.

In 1823, a little more than three years before John Adams's death, the question of the Fourth of July signing was posed before him (as had been done several times in the preceding decade), and his answer was, "I am incapable of Searching for Books or dates, and my memory may not be depended upon", but according to his recollection the Declaration was signed on the 4th of July by all the members then present. If he had searched his own files of correspondence, he would doubtless have found the letters mentioned and by them have been brought to an acknowledgment of the error of his memory. So also, if the same evidences could have been laid before Thomas Jefferson, there can be little doubt that he too would have professed conviction. Both Adams and Jefferson had been misled by the erroneous record in the Journals, neither had before him the corrective facts, and time had inevitably blurred their recollections.

One episode in the story of the Declaration of Independence needs yet to be mentioned. When Abraham Clark foresaw the possibility that Congress might "be exalted on a high gallows", he expressed a genuine fear felt by himself and other members of Congress. The Declaration was, in fact, an act of treason, and, if it were not made good, those who had signed it stood a good chance to incur the penalty meted out to traitors. Those names were accordingly long withheld as a secret and sacred record. Not until January 18, 1777, did Congress come to a decision to share that record with any other body than itself. On that day it was ordered

That an authenticated copy of the Declaration of Independency, with the names of the members of Congress signing the same, be sent to each of the United States, and that they be desired to have the same put upon record.

In complying with this order President Hancock, on January 31, addressed a circular letter to the states to accompany the respective copies of the Declaration, and, not content with merely citing the order, he added some elucidation of its purport and purpose:

As there is not a more distinguished Event in the History of America, than the Declaration of her Independence—nor any, that, in all probability, will so much excite the Attention of future Ages, it is highly proper, that the Memory of that Transaction, together with the Causes that gave rise to it, should be preserved in the most careful Manner that can be devised . . . that it may henceforth form a Part of the Archives of your State and remain a lasting Testimony of your Approbation of that necessary and important Measure.

CHAPTER X

GIRDING FOR THE CONTEST
THE PLAN OF TREATIES

With the passage of the Declaration of Independence, Congress became, to borrow a phrase of John Adams, "high-charged" with a new and strong purpose. Whether the struggle would be shortened or prolonged in consequence of the Declaration, no man could foretell; but the chief aim and purpose of the contest were now beyond question. Redress of grievances might mean one thing, or it might mean many things; independence, on the other hand, was a goal clear-cut and unmistakable. There could thenceforth be no middle ground; there was no longer a place for the lukewarm and the hesitant. The Declaration was a trumpet call to the Continent: Choose you this day whom ye will serve; henceforth he that is not with us is against us. Or, in speech more modern, "He that hesitates is lost, he that doubts is damned."

And straightway the people parted to this side and to that. There were those who, like the Adamses, could scarcely restrain their exultations over the consummation for which they had striven with a zeal that never abated. There were others who, exalted in spirit, flush with hope, nonetheless did not fail to count the possible cost; men like Abraham Clark, who, when the Declaration of Independence was barely one month old, came to doubt whether the fate in store for those who had promoted it was "freedom or a halter". Still others there were, such as Robert Morris, who long maintained that the Declaration was at best premature, yet, despite their convictions, once the die had been cast, threw their whole might into the cause of independence. Nor can it be doubted that many took their decision only after much searching of the heart and with deep anguish of soul. Others than Abraham Clark doubtless had visions of a halter.

And what of those who took their stand on the other side? For they also were many. In some camps perhaps these were actually more numerous than the combined adherents, of whatever degree of faith, to the cause of independence. As events proved, however, they were deficient in that boldness and enterprise that characterized the major portion of their antagonists, the boldness to take quick possession of the political implements of the contest. Perhaps also those who refused to break their allegiance to the old sovereignty and espouse the new were wanting somewhat in that intensity of zeal that is so characteristic a propelling force in a new faith. Yet it can not be said that they were lacking in the courage of their convictions. Many of them fought valiantly under the old banner, while the fate of many others was exile and the confiscation of their property, ofttimes indignities that were worse than either. In many instances, no doubt, theirs was the more courageous course.

And who are these whom we behold at the last moving sorrowfully back across the divide between the rival contending hosts? These are they who, with fervor and with zeal, had come thus far in the march of protest, they whose labors and whose hope had been for the redress of grievances, the righting of wrongs, and then a happy reconciliation; whose convictions and whose consciences forbade them to journey farther on the road chosen by the party called patriot. The standard of revolt they would not follow. The zigzag road of rebellion, leading none knew where, they refused to pursue. For them the patriot call, "To your tents, O Israel!" was a call to remain steadfast in their ancient allegiance, to forsake not the government of their fathers.

For one and all, however, the adoption of the Declaration appeared to mean, to borrow once more the language of John Adams, "the river is passed, and the bridge cut away". Nevertheless it came about that the doubting and the hesitant were yet to have a further brief day in court, and that speedily. The Declaration of Independence was scarcely a week old when the chief of the heralded peace commission, Admiral Lord Howe, whom the Americans held in affectionate esteem, arrived with authority to endeavor to effect a reconciliation between the mother country and her disgruntled daughters. He had confidently believed that within ten days after his arrival he would be able to consummate a peace, and he was therefore grievously disappointed that he had not come in time to try his persuasive powers before the adoption of the Declaration of Independence. Indeed there is good reason for believing that the proponents of independence had pushed that measure all the more vigorously for the very purpose of forestalling the possibility of reconciliation.

The first act in this drama of reconciliation was a little game of punctilio between his lordship and General Washington. Under instructions to do nothing that could be construed as recognition of the United States of America, its Congress, or its officers, my lord addressed a communication to "George Washington, Esq."; but his messenger was politely informed that such a person was unknown to the American army. A few etceteras were then added to the address and a second attempt made to deliver the communication, with the explanation that the etceteras "meant everything"; but it was again declined, because "etc.", one or more, did not spell Commander-in-Chief of the Armies of the United States. In rejecting the communication, General Washington had, so Congress declared, "acted with a dignity becoming his station".

Having failed in his frontal attack Lord Howe now essayed a flank movement. He had come equipped with letters from Englishmen to sundry Americans, subtly designed to promote the cause of reconciliation, and these, together with letters from his own hand, including a "Declaration" of his powers, he sent forth upon their mission of persuasion. It chanced that a formidable batch of them was intercepted and in due time was laid upon the Congressional table. Congress was accordingly now privileged, unhampered by punctilio, to deal with the matter as it chose. First of all, it was observed that his lordship's powers were limited to granting "free and general pardons" to such as "may have deviated from their just allegiance" and were now willing, "by a speedy return to their duty, to reap the benefits of Royal favour"; but there was the further broad intimation that "due consideration" would be given to the "meritorious services" of those who would assist in restoring public tranquillity. For the majority of Congress the revelation of these limited powers was sufficient. "The Temper of the House", said Robert Morris, "was plain." Congress chose merely to order the publication of Lord Howe's circular letters and declarations, that the good people of these United States may be informed of what nature are the Commissioners, and what the terms, with the expectation of which, the insidious court of Britain has endeavoured to amuse and disarm them, and that the few, who still remain suspended by a hope founded either in the justice or moderation of their late King, may now, at length, be convinced, that the valour alone of their country is to save its liberties.

It was on that same day, July 19, and perhaps not uninfluenced by these attempts at conciliation, that Congress ordered the Declaration of Independence to be engrossed, "with the title and stile of 'the unanimous declaration of the thirteen United States of America', and that the same, when engrossed, be signed by every member of Congress". As for those who had remained "suspended by a hope" of reconciliation, they too appear to have become convinced and to have taken their decisions accordingly.

Notable of these amongst the members of Congress was Robert Morris.

I am sorry to say [Morris wrote to Joseph Reed, July 20] there are some amongst us that cannot bear the thought of reconciliation on any terms. . . . I think with you that if the Commissioners have any proposition to make they ought to be heard. . . . If they can offer Peace on admissible terms I believe the great Majority of America wou'd still be for accepting it.

Nonetheless, he stood fast by an opinion long formed, "that it is the duty of every individual to act his part in whatever station his country may call him to in times of difficulty, danger, and distress . . . that the individual who declines the service of his country because its councils are not conformable to his ideas, makes but a bad subject; a good one will follow, if he cannot lead."

The attitude of the majority, on the other hand, not a little exultant, is exemplified by the comment of William Ellery of Rhode Island: *"Odi Danaös, etiam Dona ferentes"*, exclaimed he. . . . "The Truth is the Door is shut. . . . We have been driven into a Declara[tion] of Independency and must forget our former Love for our British Brethren. The Sword must determine our Quarrel." In a friendly letter to Lord Howe (August 20), Franklin put the matter thus:

The Temper of the Colonies as professed in their several Petitions to the

Crown was sincere. The Terms they proposed should then have been closed with, and all might have been Peace. . . . But the Contempt with which those Petitions were treated . . . and the cruel Measures since taken, have chang'd that Temper. It could not be otherwise. To propose now to the Colonies a Submission to the Crown of Great Britain, would be fruitless. The Time is past. One might as well propose it to France, on the Footing of a former title.

It chanced that this little drama was presently booked for a return engagement and that the sword, which had hung suspended while these negotiations proceeded, was to serve as the chief agency of the booking. The military plan of the British was to sever the states by the line of the Hudson river, and a first essential of that plan was to gain possession of New York. While his brother was seeking to adjust the quarrel, General Howe refrained from attacking the American army, but when the futility of those negotiations had been demonstrated, the general proceeded with his plans. Having defeated Washington in the battle of Long Island, he found one of the American commanders, General John Sullivan, a prisoner in his hands. Perhaps, reflected Lord Howe, the Americans will now be more amenable to offers of peace; accordingly he sent General Sullivan to Congress with another olive branch.

His lordship was right. Despite the carping of such men as John Adams that Sullivan was only a "decoy duck . . . sent among us to seduce us into a renunciation of our independence", Congress was disposed to lend an ear to proposals of peace and to take a look at the proffered olive branch. That branch did indeed appear to be somewhat more substantial than the one previously offered and it bore an olive of a sort, but was the olive sufficiently mature to accord with the Congressional taste? General Sullivan interpreted something that Lord Howe had said as an intimation that the obnoxious measures would be rescinded, but in the conference that ensued his lordship asserted that the general had misunderstood him. What he actually requested was that he might have opportunity to converse an hour or two with some members of Congress as private gentlemen: with Congress as such he could not treat.

That body accordingly devoted some four days to solemn debate over what they should do in the matter. Some were for outright rejection of the proposition, others for hearing what his lordship had to offer, but none hoped for peace. John Adams, as was to be expected, to the utmost of his abilities opposed taking any notice of it. Dr. Witherspoon declared that, since no one would "admit a thought of giving up the independence we have so lately declared", not only would no benefit be derived from the conference, but that, on the contrary, it would be "almost a certain forerunner of disgrace"; that it would embolden the Tories, who were already exulting, further discourage the friends of independence, and produce "a timorous and despondent spirit" in the army. Josiah Bartlett likewise thought it would "lessen the Congress in the eye of the publick . . . when they see us catching hold of so slender a thread to bring about a settlement"; yet a refusal of the conference, he feared, would give rise to the representation that Congress was "obstinate" and "desirous of war and bloodshed".

It was on the 2d of September that Sullivan delivered his message to Congress; on the 5th that body finally decided that, as "representatives of the free and independent states of America", it could not with propriety send any of its members to confer with Lord Howe "in their private characters", but would send a committee of their body "to know whether he has any authority to treat with persons authorized by Congress for that purpose, in behalf of America, and what that authority is, and to hear such propositions as he shall think fit to make respecting the same". Congress adopted this course, declared Caesar Rodney, "with a view to satisfy some disturbed minds out of doors, rather than expectation of its bringing about peace." On the following day Franklin, John Adams, and Edward Rutledge were designated for the conference, and three days later these gentlemen ventured on their mission. Four days of solemn deliberation were followed by another four days of anxious waiting. Debate within doors gave place to eager discussion and speculation without.

"Blessed is he that expecteth nothing" saith the proverb, "for he will not be disappointed." The committee went, conversed with Lord Howe for three hours, then returned (September 13) to report to Congress that his lordship required as a first essential "that the colonies should return to their allegiance and obedience to the government of Great

Britain"; that done, he had power "to confer, advise, and consult"
Further, however, he ventured "assurances, that there was an exceed
ing good disposition in the king and his ministers" toward the colonies,
and that this would probably eventuate in the removal or mollification
of the offensive measures. The committee, on its part, represented to
his lordship that Congress had adopted the Declaration of Independence "after long and great reluctance, in obedience to the positive instructions of their constituents", and that it was now not in the power
of Congress to undo that act. To this they added their private opinions
that America would never treat except in the character of independent
states. As for his lordship's "assurances", they were "too uncertain and
precarious to be relied on".

The whole affair, John Adams declared, was but "a bubble, an ambus-
cade, a mere insidious manoeuvre"; at the same time, he acknowledged, "the interview will do no disservice to us". Josiah Bartlett hoped
that it would at least "stop the mouths of the weak and credulous";
William Williams was sure it would "strike the Torys dumb"; while
John Penn of North Carolina was confident the people would now
realize that "we have no alternitive for our safety but our spirit as
Soldiers". "Our reliance continues, therefore", Edward Rutledge wrote
to Washington, "to be, under God, on your wisdom and fortitude, and
that of your forces."

Thus had independence passed through its first ordeal and come
forth with an increased vigor. The advocates of the measure were
everywhere strengthened in their purposes. Even if they were not as
yet, by means of argument, able to dispel all doubts or soothe all hesitancies, they had at least the will to smother the doubts—or to remove
the doubters—and they did both with fervor and efficiency.

If Congress was now stirred with new energies, buoyed with hopes
relumed, few if any of that body failed to realize that there was much
work to do if they were to make good that independence upon which
they had so solemnly embarked. Rightly intent upon answering the
question, whereunto had it been called, Congress might well at the
same time have reflected more seriously upon that other question,
whereof was it made? Better still had the constituent states earlier
taken into earnest consideration the essential means for attaining the

great objective. Was the Congress as constituted a fit body for such an undertaking? Would it be able to adapt itself to the exigencies of a war or would it create the efficient agencies which were requisite for the contest? In time both the states and their Congress came to ponder these questions deeply, but both learned their lessons slowly; in fact, they learned their most essential lessons only in consequence of manifold failures, only after the heart-burnings of successive defeats. Defeat of their armies on the field of battle they might—and usually did—seek to lay at other doors; but responsibility for failures in organization and administration, to which the defeats on the field were often directly traceable, this responsibility Congress could not easily escape.

The question whether Congress would be able to cope with the problems incident to the conduct of a war began to manifest itself immediately that Congress stepped out of the character of an advisory council to the colonies and assumed that of a governing body; and in the months following the Declaration the question was even more insistent. Yet beyond that loomed a question of still greater significance. Would the Congress as constituted meet the need of a central government of the states, whether it were a government for war or a government for peace? Would Congress be able to unify the wills of thirteen or more distinct, often antagonistic, political entities? In short, could such a body lay securely the foundations of the new nation that was to be?

To these questions had come the answer, even before independence itself had been resolved upon, and that answer had been an emphatic no. To call themselves "The United Colonies" was not sufficient; the name had little significance unless supported on a solid foundation of fact. Galloway's plan of union of 1774 had been summarily rejected; Franklin's propositions of July, 1775, had been thrust to one side; but as the thought of independence grew and took on form and substance, so did the idea of a bond of union—confederation, it came to be called—as a necessary implication of independence, a bond more explicit, more permanent than that embodied in the existing Congress. Indeed the sentiment for a confederation outran that for independence, winning many adherents who revolted at the idea of separation from the mother country, or else stood hesitant and aloof. The colonies had a common cause, and that cause could be effectually promoted only through the instrumentality of a firm union.

Nor was this all. A conviction had also taken hold of many minds that, whether the aim were to be independence or something less, America would probably need help from outside; and what chance was there of the colonies obtaining aid from a foreign power unless they themselves were firmly bound together? It came about therefore that, in the resolution offered by Richard Henry Lee, June 7, and adopted July 2, independence, confederation, and foreign alliances were put forward as three aspects of one purpose, three roads to one and the same goal. As John Adams remarked, all were essential, "and it may not perhaps be of much importance which is done first."

As hitherto pointed out, Congress had been so confident of an affirmative decision on the resolution for independence that committees were appointed to draft each of the three measures contemplated in the resolution, one (June 10) to draft a declaration of independence, another (June 12) "to prepare and digest the form of a confederation", and a third, the same day, "to prepare a plan of treaties to be proposed to foreign powers". One month later, that is, on July 12, 1776, the committee on confederation reported a draft of "Articles of confederation and perpetual union", and six days later (July 18) the committee on foreign alliances reported an elaborately drawn "Plan of Treaties".

Inasmuch as the latter project was sooner brought to maturity, it may appropriately be first considered. Of course the foreign power that was foremost in every mind as the one with which America should seek to form an alliance was France; and the "Plan of Treaties" as first presented to Congress bespoke "a firm, inviolable, and universal Peace, and a true and sincere Friendship between the most serene and mighty Prince, Lewis the Sixteenth, the most Christian King, his Heirs and Successors, and the united States of America", etc., etc. When, however, printed copies of the plan were struck off for the use of the members, as was done on July 20, it was ordered that "the names of persons, places and states, be omitted". Accordingly the texts in the hands of the members did not mention France or the United States by name, but substituted the phrase, "between A. and B. and the subjects of A. and of B.", and this language was retained in the introductory paragraph of the project as finally adopted, September 17, although in the articles of the proposed treaty "the Most Christian King" and "the United States" reappear. Indeed the adopting resolution (September 17) reads, "that the following plan of a treaty be proposed to His Most Christian Majesty."

The "plan" was only to a minor extent a creation of the committee; rather it was compounded of ingredients which the committee found ready to its hand in sundry eighteenth-century European treaties. John Adams, who penned the original draft and has left some account of the committee's labors (though written many years after the event), records that Franklin had put into his hands a printed volume of treaties wherein he had marked certain articles. "Some of these", Adams remarks, "were judiciously selected, and I took them, with others which I found necessary, into the draught, and made my report to the committee at large, who, after a reasonable examination of it, agreed to report it."

Joseph Hewes of North Carolina thought the report would be "the subject of much debate before it is agreed to"; if so, however, little record of such debate has survived. The few allusions to the subject by members of Congress in their correspondence are chiefly indicative of an eagerness that the project be brought to a conclusion. For instance, Samuel Adams wrote July 14 to Richard Henry Lee, then absent, "It is high time for us to have Ambassadors in foreign Courts. I fear we have already suffered too much by Delay." Congress did debate the plan for two or three days in committee of the whole, but made no extensive emendations. John Adams declares that "Many motions were made to insert in it articles of entangling alliance, exclusive privileges, and of warranties of possessions", but that "the treaty passed without one particle" of these stipulations. This "Plan of Treaties" as drawn up in Congress is, with a few modifications, the treaty of amity and commerce signed with France in 1778; as it was also the model for nearly all the treaties of the United States prior to 1800.

The plan was adopted September 17, but two further steps were necessary, before Congress would be ready to dangle the treaty before the eyes of the statesmen of France; these were the appointment of an agent or agents to do the dangling, and the adoption of instructions for their guidance. The instructions were adopted September 24, and two days later three commissioners, Silas Deane, Benjamin Franklin, and Thomas Jefferson, were appointed to undertake the mission. Deane was already in France as the agent of the "Secret Committee", Jefferson presently declined, and thereupon (October 22) Arthur Lee, who had for some time resided in London and had been in intimate correspondence with Congress and sundry of its members, was appointed in his stead.

The members of Congress were realistic enough to know that their commissioners, negotiating on the farther side of the Atlantic, hampered by slow and precarious communication, must needs be equipped with some powers of discretion if they were to achieve the main objectives of their mission. They were instructed to use every means in their power for concluding the treaty conformably to the Plan; but in the event of difficulties they might make sundry concessions, both by way of subtraction and by way of addition. Some articles might be waived with little concern, others were to be pressed, unless the treaty should thereby be endangered, whilst certain stipulations were to be strenuously insisted upon.

The great objective was to obtain the aid of France. In the Adams draft was a stipulation that "if France to favour the said united States shall join them in their present war against Great Britain, they shall not make a separate peace". This was eliminated from the plan as adopted, but the commissioners were authorized to promise that the United States would never acknowledge allegiance to the government of Great Britain, and further to stipulate that, in the event France became involved in a war with Great Britain in consequence of the treaty, neither the United States nor France would make peace with the enemy "until the expiration of six calendar months after the negotiation for that purpose shall have been duly notified" by the one party to the other. That the stipulation was fraught with danger Congress was evidently not unaware; but in how bitter a wrangle that body was destined to become involved thereby, and to what extent the stipulation would bedevil the final negotiations for peace, Congress could not foresee. The commissioners were further instructed to solicit from France an immediate supply of arms and ammunition, and also to engage "a few good engineers". This latter request likewise was to bring its quota of plagues; for it became the signal for the descent upon Congress of a horde of French officers, clamorous for commissions and perquisites, and the soul of that much-enduring body was greatly tormented thereby. Just when Franklin was about to take his departure for France the commissioners were further directed (October 22) to procure from the French court, either by purchase or by loan, eight line-of-battle ships, "well manned and fitted in every respect for service", and that they "expedite this negotiation with all possible diligence".

It was an alliance with France primarily for which Congress was most eager, yet to the minds of a good many of those venturesome statesmen it seemed worth while to try if they could not also draw other European powers into their new national orbit. Next to France among European powers, in the concern of the United States, was Spain; and Congress first took a squint at that power by authorizing the commissioners to the court of France "to give the strongest assurances" to the Spanish monarch that he need be in no apprehension of molestation by the United States in his South American dominions. No doubt that monarch felt little need of such assurances with regard to his South American possessions, even if for those bordering upon the United States he would in time justifiably feel a deep concern Then, not many days later (October 16), Congress made a further tentative venture into the chilly waters of European diplomacy in adding to the commissioners' instructions that they should endeavor, when they should "find occasion fit and convenient", to obtain from other European powers recognition of the independence of the United States and to conclude with them treaties of peace, amity, and commerce; that they should at least, to the utmost of their power, prevent those princes and potentates from taking part with Great Britain in the war. In every such treaty care was to be taken that the United States should not become a party in any war that might happen in consequence.

With three representatives commissioned to spy out the European land, and now about to sit them down in that capital wherein the most important diplomatic undertaking would of necessity be carried on, Congress might well have been content to wait until those watchmen had answered the question, What of the night? But the restless spirits in that body, stirred to activity and led on, so we are told, by the Adamses and the Lees, were not content to wait for invitations; it was for a free and independent republic to "crash" those courts.

Possibly the new situation in which Congress presently found itself had the effect of aggravating this impatience. On the 12th of December, 1776, Congress became so uneasy lest the British descend upon Philadelphia and capture the Congress itself, that they adjourned to Baltimore, where they reassembled on the 20th. If their cause was not to be undone, there was all the greater need of aid from foreign powers; and the committee of secret correspondence made haste to assure the commissioners at Paris that, although "all views of Accomodation with Great Britain but on Principles of Peace as independent states" were "totally at an End", nevertheless, "if France desires to preclude the Possibility of North America being ever reunited with Great Britain now is the favourable moment for establishing the Glory Strength and commercial Greatness of the former Kingdom by the Ruin of her ancient Rival". If only Congress had those eight line-of-battle ships which the commissioners had been instructed to procure, the contest might be decided "at one stroke."

At all events, Congress had barely settled down in Baltimore as best it could in a town so small and lacking most of the conveniences and comforts to which they had been accustomed in Philadelphia, when it was prevailed upon (December 24) to appoint a committee of five "to prepare and report a plan for obtaining foreign assistance". Four days later (December 28) the committee brought in its report, and Congress occupied some part of two days, in committee of the whole, debating and amending it. The meat of the decision, December 30, was in a brief resolve, "That Commissioners be forthwith sent to the courts of Vienna, Spain, Prussia and the Grand Duke of Tuscany"; but there were added elaborate new instructions to the several commissioners, those already appointed and those yet to be appointed, wherein the United States definitely offered to France and Spain, if those powers would join in the war against Great Britain, assistance in drawing their respective American chestnuts out of the British fire— to France a share in the Newfoundland fisheries and territorial conquests, to Spain the town and harbor of Pensacola. As for those other powers, they were to be especially solicited to prevent Great Britain from sending foreign troops to America.

Upon mature deliberation of all the circumstances [the committee of secret correspondence wrote to the commissioners at Paris the same day] Congress deem the speedy declaration of France and European Assistance so indispensibly necessary to secure the Independence of these States, that they have authorized you to make such tenders to France and Spain, as they hope, will prevent any longer delay of an event, that is judged so essential to the well-being of North America.

The tenders to Spain were regarded as of such importance that Franklin was at once (January 1, 1777) appointed commissioner to that court (in addition to his French mission) and directed to proceed thither to transact the business intrusted to him. The other appointments were delayed some four months, then Arthur Lee was designated (May 1) for the Spanish mission in place of Franklin, while Ralph Izard was appointed (May 7) commissioner to the court of Tuscany, and William Lee (May 9) to those of Berlin and Vienna.

With what majority Congress reached its decision to go a-begging and a-offering amongst the minor courts of Europe it can not be known, for the yeas and nays were not in those days ever recorded. It is known, however, that there were critics of the whole business. For instance, William Hooper wrote to Robert Morris, December 28, 1776 (the day Congress took the question into consideration in committee of the whole):

We have been holding forth new lines to France by offering what we have not to give and provided they will conquer the whole of Newfoundland and secure the fishing, that we will most bountifully and most graciously give them one half of it for their trouble. We have found out that the Duke of Tuscany is a potentate of much consequence, while some of us are such ignoramuses as to think him very insignificant in the naval and military line and in this respect not worthy attention and that in commercial matters his interest will attach him to us without much sollicitation.

Probably, however, neither Hooper nor any of his confreres of the opposition fully foresaw to what a series of fiascoes this venture was to lead. To none of them was it given to foretell that most of their diplomatic Don Quixotes would be unhorsed tilting against creaking political windmills, and that the least serious of the consequences of these somewhat frantic gestures would be to bring Congress into ridicule. Far from finding every European power eager to make common cause with the United States, it came about that Congress must needs pass through a long period of bitter anxiety before even the most important of these objectives, an alliance with France, would be realized. Not until independence had been won did the other European powers manifest an inclination to clasp to their bosoms this newcomer among the nations. That accomplished, court after court offered to treat with the United States, and thereupon Congress's "Plan of Treaties" entered one diplomatic sanctuary after another as the model on which these treaties were formed.

CHAPTER XI

UNITED WE STAND, DIVIDED WE FALL
WHAT PRICE CONFEDERATION?

In making its elaborate plans for negotiating treaties with foreign powers Congress blithely proceeded upon the assumption that the states, as the one-time colonies now called themselves, would soon be bound together in some sort of organic union; and apparently with good reason, for the business of forging the project of union had been going forward alongside that of the plan of treaties.

The committee "to prepare and digest the form of a confederation", appointed, as has already been mentioned, on June 12, 1776, had set earnestly about its task, entrusting the work of drafting the instrument to John Dickinson. In view of the fact that, when in January, Franklin had again stirred the question of a confederation, Dickinson had taken his stand in opposition, and in view of the further fact that, at the moment he was appointed as the member for Pennsylvania on the grand committee to prepare a confederation, he was opposing a declaration of independence, it might appear somewhat strange that he should be designated by the committee to be the draftsman of the instrument which they would propose.

On the face of things it would appear that Dickinson was drafting a plan for a union in which he did not believe and for political units which he still hoped would not become free and independent states. Since January, however, much water had flowed beneath the bridge, and, as has already been pointed out, sentiment for a union of the American colonies, whether or not they were ever to become free and independent states, had gathered immense strength. Dickinson, it would seem, had at length been converted to the doctrine of confederation, even if he was not yet prepared to embrace the gospel of independence.

The choice of Dickinson to be draftsman of the instrument of union may have had in it something of a political maneuver (the advocates of independence in Congress were not unskilled in political finesse); but there was at least one other sufficient reason: of all the members of that committee he had scarcely an equal as a facile wielder of the pen. It needs nevertheless to be borne in mind that Dickinson's participation in the formation of the Articles of Confederation was for the most part limited to the process of drafting, and to participation in such deliberations of the committee as took place prior to July 4. For on that day he appears to have taken his departure from Congress, and to have sat no more in that assembly until after the Articles of Confederation had been framed.

Of what took place in the committee but few revelations have come down to us, but those few are significant of the difficulties encountered. On June 17, 1776, only five days after the appointment of the committee, one of its members, Josiah Bartlett, wrote to John Langdon that, "all the members of all the Colonies" were unanimously agreed that there should be a confederation, yet that some difficulties had arisen, and he feared it would take some time to settle them. "The affair of voting", he remarked, "whether by Colonies as at present, or otherwise, is not decided, and causes some warm disputes." At nearly the same time (June 21) John Adams took occasion to say that, although there was diversity of sentiment concerning a declaration of independence, the colonies and their representatives were "extremely well united" on the importance of framing a permanent constitution and obtaining foreign aid. Adams was not however a member of the committee. It was Edward Rutledge who has left the clearest indication that all was not harmony in the committee. On June 29 he wrote to John Jay: "I have been much engaged lately upon a plan of a Confederation which Dickenson has drawn; it has the Vice of all his productions to a considerable Degree; I mean the Vice of Refining too much"; and he went on to say that the plan involved "the Idea of destroying all Provincial Distinctions and making every thing of the most minute kind bend to what they call the good of the whole". Unless it were greatly curtailed it could never pass, for the ultimate consequence would be "nothing less than Ruin to some Colonies". "I am resolved", he declared, "to vest the Congress with no more Power than is absolutely necessary, and to use a familiar Expression, to keep the Staff in our own Hands; for I am confident if surrendered into the Hands of others a most pernicious use will be made of it." Rutledge may have been unduly alarmed over the threat to the self-direction of the colonies, nevertheless a few months later a like alarm for the independence and sovereignty of the states would again raise its head in Congress and would then work the salvation of that deeply underlying principle.

Both the Franklin and the Dickinson plans provided that the general expenses of the confederation should be met from a common treasury supplied by the colonies, the taxes therefor being laid in each colony by its own legislative authority; but whereas Franklin proposed that these expenses should be apportioned in accordance with the number of male polls between sixteen and sixty years of age, the Dickinson plan provided that it should be in proportion to the number of inhabitants of every age, sex, and quality in each colony, except Indians not paying taxes. For this purpose the Dickinson plan would have a triennial census taken, "distinguishing the white Inhabitants" (an emendation of "the Inhabitants who are not slaves", as first proposed).

In providing for the common assembly of the confederated colonies the Dickinson plan departed from that of Franklin in several important particulars. For instance, the name "Congress", or "General Congress", used in the Franklin plan and also in the Dickinson plan as first written, was for some reason deleted in the latter, and "Meeting of the States" substituted. According to the Franklin plan the time and place of meeting were to be determined by "the next preceding Congress", and, further, it was "to be a Rule, that each succeeding Congress be held in a different Colony till the whole Number be gone through, and so in perpetual Rotation; and that accordingly the next Congress after the present shall be held at Annapolis in Maryland". The Dickinson plan, on the other hand, fixed Philadelphia as the place, "until otherwise ordered by the United States assembled", and the first Monday in November as the time. Each plan provided that the delegates should be chosen annually by the respective colonies; but, whereas Franklin would have had the number of delegates from each colony regulated by the number of male polls between sixteen and sixty years of age, one delegate being allowed for every 5,000 polls, Dickinson would leave the number at the discretion of the colony.

Likewise, in pursuance of the same idea of proportional representation, Franklin proposed that each delegate should have one vote and, if necessarily absent, might designate another delegate from the same colony to be his proxy. Dickinson's plan, on the contrary, provided that "in determining Questions each Colony shall have one vote". Franklin would have one half of the members returned constitute a quorum, whereas Dickinson's plan would require an affirmative vote of seven colonies to determine any question except that for adjourning, while certain determinations should require the affirmative vote of nine colonies. Franklin offered no limitation upon the length of time a delegate might serve, presumably leaving that question to be determined by each colony as it saw fit, whereas Dickinson's plan stipulated that "No Person shall be capable of being a Delegate for more than three Years in any Term of six Years."

Franklin's enumeration of the powers and duties of Congress are only in very broad and general terms: determining war and peace, sending and receiving ambassadors, forming alliances, settling disputes among the colonies, "and the Planting of new Colonies when proper"; matters pertaining to the general welfare to which particular colonies are not competent, general commerce, general currency, establishment of posts, regulation of the common forces, appointment of general officers, civil and military. There is no negative counterpart, no category of things forbidden to the common Congress. Here Dickinson's committee found it necessary to particularize, and it was in this article that they laid a powder train that subsequently came near to blowing up the whole works.

Franklin had offered two articles concerning relations with the Indians, one of them forbidding any colony to engage in offensive war with any Indian nation without the consent of Congress; the other providing, first of all, for an offensive and defensive alliance with the Six Nations, but also for ascertaining and securing to them and the other Indians as well the boundaries of their lands, for their protection against injustices, and for the relief, at public expense, of their wants and distresses; and, finally, that "all Purchases from them shall be by the Congress for the General Advantage and Benefit of the United Colonies". In the Dickinson draft, Franklin's proposition took form as follows:

Regulating the Trade, and managing all Affairs with the Indians—Limiting the Bounds of those Colonies, which by Charter or Proclamation, or under any Pretence, are said to extend to the South Sea, and ascertaining those Bounds of any other Colony that appear to be indeterminate—Assigning Territories for new Colonies, either in Lands to be thus separated from Colonies and heretofore purchased or obtained by the Crown of Great-Britain from the Indians, or hereafter to be purchased or obtained from them—Disposing of all such Lands for the general Benefit of all the United Colonies—Ascertaining Boundaries to such new Colonies, within which Forms of Government are to be established on the Principles of Liberty.

The language of the clause wriggles rather widely, but its principal bomb was in the phrase, "are said to extend to the South Sea".

One feature of Franklin's plan, destined to be embodied in the definitive Articles of Confederation, although in a much modified form, was that providing for an executive council. This council, under Franklin's plan, was to consist of twelve members of Congress, chosen by that body and put into three groups of four each in such a manner that one-third of the members would be changed annually; and it was further provided that "each Person who has served the said Term of three Years as Counsellor, shall have a Respite of three Years, before he can be elected again". The chief business of the Executive Council was "to manage the general continental Business in the recess of Congress", executing "whatever shall have been enjoined thereby". In the Dickinson plan the name is changed to Council of State and its constitution changed to one delegate from each state, "to be named annually by the Delegates of each Colony, and where they cannot agree, by the United States assembled", and its functions more amply particularized. In the end the name was once more changed, to the Committee of the States, and its appointment lodged in Congress alone.

When it came to providing for amendments, Franklin's foresightedness recognized that "all new Institutions may have Imperfections which only Time and Experience can discover", and therefore stipulated that the General Congress might from time to time propose amendments to this Constitution and that such, when approved by a majority of the Colonial assemblies, should be "equally binding with the rest of the Articles of this Confederation." The Dickinson plan, on the contrary, provided that no alteration should be made "unless such Alteration be agreed to in an Assembly of the United States, and be afterwards confirmed by the Legislatures of every Colony".

In providing for possible inclusion in the Confederation of other than the thirteen colonies Franklin nearly went the limit of his imagination. He proposed that "any and every Colony from Great Britain upon the Continent of North America", not at present "engag'd in our Association", might join the Association and be received into the Confederation and thereby become "entitled to all the Advantages of our Union, mutual Assistance and Commerce"; and he specified the West India Islands, Quebec, St. Johns, Nova Scotia, Bermudas, and the East and West Floridas. On second thought, he would even open the door to Ireland. Dickinson and his committee evidently thought it not worth while to leave the door ajar for any outsider except Canada. For Canada the latchstring remained on the outside until the close of the war.

The concluding clause of Franklin's propositions calls for particular notice. Drawn up at a time when the majority of Americans were still thinking primarily of a redress of grievances, of a possible reconciliation, Franklin's plan of union kept that possibility firmly in the foreground. The union established by the proposed Articles of Confederation was therefore "to continue firm" till the terms of reconciliation proposed in the last petition to the king had been agreed to, the obnoxious acts of Parliament repealed, and reparations made for the various injuries done the American colonies. "On the Arrival of these Events the Colonies shall return to their former Connection and Friendship with Great Britain: But on failure thereof this Confederation is to be perpetual." Within the year that had elapsed when the Dickinson plan was offered, hopes of reconciliation had all but wholly vanished. Therefore the plan of July, 1776, could only propose that, when the Articles of Confederation had been ratified by all the states, it should be inviolably observed by every one of them and the union be perpetual.

It will thus be seen that Franklin's Articles of Confederation, although themselves once disregarded, if not outright rejected, by Congress, were in large measure incorporated in the plan of confederation proposed by Dickinson's committee and through the latter made important contributions to the Articles of Confederation as finally adopted, which, in turn, furnished a great part of the substance that went to make up the Constitution of the United States.

It was on the 12th of July, 1776, that the committee laid its draft of "Articles of Confederation and Perpetual Union" before Congress; and thereupon Congress ordered "eighty copies, and no more" to be printed and put the printer and every member of Congress under the most rigid injunctions of secrecy respecting it. Until printed copies of the Articles were in the hands of the members probably the majority of them had but imperfectly clarified ideas of the provisions of the instrument, and particularly of its implications; yet the general expectation appears to have been that it would be "speedily digested and be made ready to be laid before the several States for their approbation". On July 22, Congress took the Articles into consideration in committee of the whole, and some part of nearly every day for twenty days was devoted to it.

On that first day (July 22) Josiah Bartlett wrote that "by reason of so much other business, [the Confederation] goes on but slowly". His colleague, William Whipple, itching to go home, tarried nevertheless to hear the debates. A week later both Whipple and Bartlett had begun to grow anxious. "Brother Whipple is here yet", Bartlett wrote July 29, "and will not set out for home till the Confederation is settled, which may possibly take a week or ten days' time . . . the sentiments of the members very different on many of the articles. . . . I see it will not be settled agreeable to my mind." A note of genuine alarm was at almost the same moment sounded by Joseph Hewes of North Carolina. Writing to Samuel Johnston, July 28, he said:

Much of our time is taken up in forming and debating a Confederation for the united States. what we shall make of it God only knows. I am inclined to think we shall never modell it so as to be agreed to by all the Colonies. a plan for foreign Alliances is also formed and I expect will be the subject of much debate before it is agreed to. these two Capital points ought to have been setled before our declaration of Independence went forth to the world. this was my opinion long ago and every days experience serves to confirm me in that opinion. I think it probable that we may split on these great points, if so our mighty Colossus falls to pieces.

John Adams likewise pointed to a probable rift. "If a confederation should take place", he wrote to his wife, July 29, "one great question is how we shall vote. Whether each colony shall count one? or whether each shall have a weight in proportion to its number, or wealth, or exports and imports, or a compound ratio of all? Another is, whether Congress shall have authority to limit the dimensions of each colony, to prevent those, which claim by charter, or proclamation, or commission to the south sea, from growing too great and powerful, so as to be dangerous to the rest."

Another dejected spirit was Samuel Chase of Maryland, who wrote to Richard Henry Lee, July 30:

I hurried to Congress, to give my little assistance to the framing a Confederacy, and a plan for a foreign alliance—both of them subjects of the utmost importance, and which, in my judgment, demand immediate despatch. The Confederacy has engaged our close attention for a week. Three great difficulties occur: Representation, the mode of voting, and the claims to the South Sea. The whole might, in my opinion, be settled, if candour, justice, and the real interests of America were attended to. We do not all see the importance, nay, the necessity of a Confederacy. We shall remain weak, distracted, and divided in our councils; our strength will decrease; we shall be open to all the arts of the insidious Court of Britain, and no foreign Court will attend to our applications for assistance before we are confederated. What contract will a foreign State make with us when we cannot agree among ourselves?

Chase was not quite accurate in referring to representation as one of the three controverted points, for representation and the mode of voting were but two aspects of one and the same problem. Rather, the question was on what basis the several quotas of expenses should be adjusted.

Abraham Clark of New Jersey, after listening for a whole week to the jowering, and participating to a small extent himself, was on the verge of despair. The difficulties to which these questions had given rise struck him as "very Alarming". "Nothing but Present danger", he wrote, August 1, "will ever make us all Agree, and I sometimes fear that will be insufficient." Two days before, when his colleague, Dr. Witherspoon, had just remarked on the floor of Congress, "The greatest danger we have, is of disunion among ourselves", Clark had risen to his feet to exclaim: "We must apply for pardons if we don't confederate." Already perhaps he had had that vision of which he wrote a few days later, the vision of a high gallows and a long row of halters, one for each signer of the Declaration of Independence.

That the central government of the union should take the form of such a Congress as then existed, an assembly of delegates from the several states, was generally accepted; but how the votes in that assembly should be determined stirred irreconcilable dissensions. The larger states naturally wished to exercise a power in the general voice in proportion to their actual weights, whatever the criterion by which those weights might be determined. In the first Congress, upon the insistence of the smaller colonies, all were placed on an equality, each colony being given one vote. The smaller states again stoutly held out for the retention in the confederation of that principle of equality, mainly on the ground that it was essential to their self-preservation: Quoth they, "Is not our all at stake as well as yours?" The larger states, on the other hand, sought not only to preserve their own relative importance, but also to safeguard their preservation against a possible combination of the lesser states.

The second question, though less vital and therefore less controversial, involved nonetheless its difficulties and its delicacies. Should the criterion for contributions be population or wealth? If wealth, should it be land values or some broader measure of property values? If population, what about slaves? Should they be counted as a part of the population or as property? Though the determination of the latter question may not have seemed of so vital a consequence as that of voting, nevertheless, here, at the very beginnings of the nation, was sounded an alarum bell that may well have roused the deepest slumberer. It would ring out again and more insistently when the Federal Convention should assemble, and yet once more a few years later, even "as a fire bell in the night".

The third question, as the first and the second, essentially concerned an equitable adjustment of relative weights among the members of the union. As propounded it was whether the Congress should be empowered to limit the boundaries of the states; but in essence it was a question whether the states which laid claim to large tracts of unsettled land in the west were to be permitted to utilize those lands for their own expansion or profit or be required to place them in the common stock for the behoof of the union. In these earlier stages of the controversy, uppermost in the minds of the statesmen who wished to make the west common property of the Union was the conviction that, if the claimant states were permitted to retain those lands, they would derive therefrom enrichment and enhanced power, while their lesser colleagues in the union would become impoverished. But even thus early there began to germinate another idea that was destined to grow until it overshadowed every other idea relating to the western territory, indeed to become the most vital force in the building of the nation. This was the idea that from this territory that stretched on and on toward the western horizon should be carved new states, to the enlargement, the enrichment, and the strengthening of the Union.

Of the earlier debates on these questions, from July 25 to August 2, both John Adams and Jefferson left notes, and these notes have been the basis of the most that has been known or said concerning the views of the delegates or the attitudes of their respective states upon the points involved. The question concerning the Western territory, or claims to the South Sea, came up July 25, when Samuel Chase took the position that "no Colony has a right to go to the South Sea"; that "it would not be safe to the rest". Wilson of Pennsylvania likewise declared that those claims were "extravagant", that "the grants were made upon mistakes". Pennsylvania, he said, has no right to interfere in those claims, but she could not confederate unless those claims were cut off. Jefferson protested the right of Congress to limit the boundaries of the states, but did not doubt that the colonies would limit themselves.

The discussion was renewed on the 2d of August, when Chase repeated his contention, while Sherman of Connecticut, one of the claimant states, thought that the bounds ought to be settled, but would add a proviso that no lands be separated from any state which are already settled or become private property. Harrison of Virginia stood stoutly upon the position that "by its charter Virginia owns to the South Sea", therefore there was no more reason why Maryland should wish to pare away Virginia than that Rhode Island should wish to pare away Massachusetts, or Delaware should wish to pare away Pennsylvania. Huntington of Connecticut declared that "a man's right does not cease to be a right because it is large". "Admit that there is danger from Virginia", he said, "does it follow that Congress has a right to limit her bounds? The consequence is, not to enter the confederation." Stone of Maryland, standing with his colleague, Chase, declared: "The small Colonies have a right to happiness and security; they would have no safety if the great Colonies were not limited."

The debates July 30 to August 1 were upon the questions of representation and taxation. Franklin insisted that votes should be in proportion to numbers; but that if the colonies must have an equal vote, then let them bear equal burdens, let them give equal money and men. At the time of the union between England and Scotland, he said, the latter had made the objection which the smaller states now do; it had been prognosticated that "it would happen again as in times of old that the whale would swallow Jonas"; but the prediction had been "reversed in event", and "Jonas had swallowed the whale". Middleton of South Carolina proposed that "the vote should be according to what they pay: Witherspoon took the position that "every Colony is a distinct person"; that "nothing relating to individuals could ever come before Congress; nothing but what would respect the colonies"; therefore the colonies should have an equal vote; "if an equal vote be refused, the smaller states will become vassals to the larger". Nevertheless, said he, "We all agree that there must and shall be a confederation for this war." Chase now suggested a compromise, "that a discrimination should take place among the questions which would come before Congress; that the smaller states should be secured in all questions concerning life or liberty, and the greater ones in all respecting property". Accordingly he proposed "that in votes relating to money, the voice of each colony should be proportioned to the number of its inhabitants".

John Adams, representing as he did one of the larger states, insisted that voting should be in proportion to numbers.

We stand here [he said] as representatives of the people . . . reason, justice, and equity never had weight enough on the face of the earth to govern the councils of men. it is interest alone which does it, and it is interest alone which can be trusted . . . therefore the interests within doors should be the mathematical representatives of the interests without doors.

Replying to Witherspoon he asserted that "the individuality of the colonies is a mere sound. Does the individuality of a colony increase its wealth and numbers? if it does, pay equally."

The question is not [he continued] what we are now but what we ought to be when our bargain shall be made. The confederacy is to make us one individual only; it is to form us, like separate parcels of metal, into one common mass. . . . it has been objected that a proportional vote will endanger the smaller states. We answer that an equal vote will endanger the larger.

Benjamin Rush of Pennsylvania pointed to the deplorable consequences of voting by provinces in the Dutch Republic, and argued that, since "a part of our rights is deposited in the hands of our Legislatures", another part in the hands of Congress, representation in the latter ought to be of the same character as in the former. Moreover, voting by colonies tended to keep up colonial distinctions, whereas "We are now a new nation. . . . The more a man aims at serving America, the more he serves his Colony. . . . If we vote by numbers", he declaimed, "Liberty will be always safe." He disclaimed that he was pleading the cause of Pennsylvania. "When I entered that door, I considered myself a citizen of America."

Rush's remarks provoked Stephen Hopkins of Rhode Island to speak up for the smaller colonies. The colonies, he said, fell into three classes, "four larger, five lesser, four stand indifferent". The four largest, containing more than half the population of the whole, he asserted, would have it in their power to govern the others as they pleased. "It can't be expected that nine Colonies will give way to be governed by four." Rush had spoken deprecatingly of keeping up colonial distinctions. Declared Hopkins: "The safety of the whole depends upon the distinctions of colonies."

To the question raised by Hopkins, whether nine colonies should put it in the power of four to govern them as they pleased, James Wilson of Pennsylvania replied: "I invert the question and ask Shall two millions of people put it into the power of one million to govern them as they please?" It had been said that Congress is a representation of states, not of individuals; "I say that the object of its care are all the individuals of the states." "It is strange", he continued, "that annexing the name of 'State' to ten thousand men, should give them an equal right of forty thousand . . . as to those matters which are referred to Congress, we are not so many states; we are one large state. we lay aside our individuality whenever we come here." Exclaimed Wilson: "I defy the wit of man to invent a possible case, or to suggest any one thing on earth, which shall be for the interest of Virginia, Pennsylvania, and Massachusetts, and which will not also be for the interest of the other states."

During the discussion on the 1st of August, Roger Sherman offered a new suggestion. He took his stand firmly upon the proposition that "we are representatives of States, not individuals", nevertheless he suggested that "The vote should be taken two ways; call the Colonies, and call the individuals, and have a majority of both." This, though vague in form, is possibly the germ of that compromise in the Constitution, credited to Sherman, whereby the states were given equal representation in the senate and proportional representation in the house.

In the debate, July 30, upon the provision that the quotas should be fixed by the number of inhabitants, Samuel Chase injected into the discussion that tormenting question about slaves. He moved to insert the word "white" before "inhabitants". He did not regard the number of inhabitants as a perfect criterion of property, but it was the best rule that could be laid down, with the exception that negroes, being property, should not be included in the numbers of population. "If negroes", he said, "are taken into the computation of numbers to ascertain wealth, they ought to be in settling the representation." John Adams observed that it was "of no consequence by what name you called your people whether by that of freemen or of slaves . . . it is the number of labourers which produce the surplus for taxation, and numbers therefore indiscriminately are the fair index of wealth."

Followed then much discussion of the relative productivity of free and slave labor, with pretty general agreement in favor of the former;

still, contended Adams and others, slaves were population and should be counted as such. "The negroes are wealth", declared Samuel Chase. "Negroes are goods and chattels, are property", asserted William Hooper; he wished to see the day nevertheless that slaves are not necessary. So also spoke Edward Rutledge: "I shall be happy to get rid of the idea of slavery." If it is to be debated whether our slaves are our property, declared Rutledge's colleague, Thomas Lynch, there is an end of the confederation. "Our slaves being our property, why should they be taxed more than the land, sheep, cattle, horses, etc.?" Retorted Franklin, there is "some difference between them and sheep; sheep will never make any insurrections."

Here Benjamin Harrison of Virginia brought the discussion to a head sharply with a new proposition. He doubted whether the labor of two slaves was more effective than that of one freeman, therefore he proposed that two slaves be counted as one freeman. His proposition was doomed to the discard for the present, nevertheless it would in time reappear and, in the proportion of three to five, instead of one to two, would become one of the notable compromises of the Constitution. It was now contested, by James Wilson principally, on the ground that "if this amendment shall take place the Southern colonies would have all the benefit of slaves, whilst the Northern would bear the burthen", and that it would greatly encourage slavekeeping. To an argument by Wilson that the southern colonies taxed slaves, therefore the Confederation might reasonably do so, Dr. Witherspoon replied that the cases were not parallel. "In the Southern colonies", he said, "slaves pervade the whole colony; but they do not pervade the whole continent." Witherspoon's chief contribution, however, was an emphasis upon the inadequacy of population as a criterion of a state's ability to pay. The method proposed, he said, was imperfect in itself and unequal between the states. The true barometer of wealth was the value of lands and houses. Divided on the question of counting slaves and unable to agree on "numbers" as the basis for determining quotas, it was to Witherspoon's proposition that Congress would eventually turn.

Thus argument continued to be piled upon argument, day after day uttered speech, and night after night brought no decision. "We make slow Progress in [the Confederation]", wrote William Williams of

Connecticut, August 7, "as every Inch of Ground is disputed, and very jarring Claims and interests are to be adjusted among us, and then all to be agreed to by the sev[era]l Legislatures, so that between both, I almost Despair of seeing it accomplished." And a few days later he wrote, "it seems to labour hard, and I fear a permanent one will never be settled." Similarly Samuel Chase wrote August 9, "when we shall be confederated States, I know not. I am afraid the Day is far distant." Another day or two, and Chase's hopes had dropped to zero.

The bold and sonorous Chase (and some or all of his Colleagues) [William Williams wrote August 12] solemnly protest against the Taxation Article etc. and declare that they consider Maryland as having no further Concern in it, and that his Colony never will nor never shall agree to it. They are all gone home, except Mr. Stone, to attend (they say) their Convention which sits this Day. Most of the Southern Colonies are as uneasie as they, but dont scold so hard. What will be the event of Things God only knows.

Mr. Chase had not only shaken off the dust of his shoes as a testimony against Congress, the manner of his departure was as though he had thumbed his nose at that august assembly.

Congress had, in fact, come to a deadlock. The iron, too hot to hold, was dropped, and it was more than a week before it had sufficiently cooled to be taken up again. "We have done nothing with the Confederation for some Days", Edward Rutledge wrote to Robert R. Livingston, August 19, "and it is of little Consequence if we never see it again; for we have made such a Devil of it already that the Colonies can never agree to it." Rutledge's welling gorge brought forth nevertheless one pertinent, even if not an immediately fertile, idea. "If my opinion was likely to be taken", he wrote, "I would propose that the States should appoint a special Congress to be composed of new Members for this purpose—and that no Person should disclose any part of the present plan. If that was done we might then stand some Chance of a Confederation, at present we stand none at all." In short, what Rutledge was proposing was what has come to be called a constitutional convention. Whether the idea was wholly original with him or whether he had drawn it from Paine's *Common Sense,* is not revealed. Paine had offered the counsel, "Let a continental conference be held . . .

to frame a Continental Charter, or Charter of the United Colonies";
but there is little evidence that, at the time it was uttered, this almost
incidental remark of his caught any one's attention.

Others than the Maryland delegates, having lingered in Congress in
the hope that the Confederation might soon be completed, had by this
time given way to despair, if not to disgust, and had taken their depar-
tures. That of itself naturally had an adverse effect on the progress
toward a solution of the problem. Despite these strongly antagonistic
views, however, there appears to have been a prevailing belief that in
some way or other the obstacles to union would be overcome. A confederation was essential to the success of their great cause, therefore
ways would be found, ways must be found for reconciling their differences. "Unless we confederate, we perish", was an almost universal
sentiment.

On the 20th of August the discussion of confederation was resumed
in committee of the whole, the preliminary revision completed, and
the results laid before the whole Congress, which would of course once
more thresh over the entire subject. "What alterations will be made
of them", Josiah Bartlett wrote a week later, "I know not; but am
afraid none for the better." That most members of Congress had convinced themselves nevertheless that the measure would be speedily
pushed to a conclusion is evidenced by the fact that on the same day
a committee, consisting of Benjamin Franklin, John Adams, and
Thomas Jefferson, who had been appointed to bring in a device for
a seal for the United States of America, laid their report before Congress. The preparation of a seal might, however, just as well wait; it
would be some time before there would be any use for it; for the Congress, acting in its own proper rôle, made no progress in disentangling
what, in the capacity of a committee, it had entangled. All that Congress then accomplished was to order a new printing of the Articles as
revised by the committee of the whole.

It was at this point that there intervened the conference with Lord
Howe, whose propositions had stirred in some minds renewed ideas
of a possible reconciliation. That conference at an end, and hopes of a
reconciliation on acceptable terms likewise at an end, the thought of
Congress once more turned to confederation as an essential means of

carrying on the contest. It is perhaps significant that Edward Rutledge, one of the committee to confer with Lord Howe, from an attitude of indifference if not of coolness toward the confederation, now became one of its warmest advocates. Writing to Robert R. Livingston, October 2, he said: "Our Confederation has been neglected for many weeks because the states have been unrepresented. Necessity requires that it be immediately past. If I am not much mistaken the salvation of your State depends upon something being soon done in this business." In his zeal he had obtained a resolution calling upon absent members to return. The dearth of representation was not, however, the sole, probably not even the principal cause of the neglect of the confederation. It is scarcely to be doubted that most members of Congress hesitated to renew a discussion which would but bring out once more and in perhaps a more virulent form the discordant views which had so pointedly manifested themselves in the debates in the committee of the whole. For antagonisms had not been reconciled; they had only in some degree been temporarily smothered. At all events, for a period of more than six months a profound silence falls upon the whole business of the confederation.

CHAPTER XII

EXODUS AND EXILE

WHICH WAY SALVATION?

While all were agreed that, for the successful promotion of their common purpose, an effective union of the states was a prime essential; still, if the states could not agree on a plan of confederation, then they must make the best of their case without it. They had acquired a common war and they must somehow find common ways and means of waging it. It was inevitable therefore that Congress should find its hands full of many problems and its shoulders burdened with many and heavy burdens.

For one thing, their army had not been driving the enemy before it in headlong flight. Something must be wrong with their military arm. There were not lacking men in Congress who were disposed to lay the blame on the commander-in-chief; and there can be no doubt that Washington himself did have much to learn from experience. Indeed in his acceptance of the command he had disclaimed any superior military knowledge and skill. On the contrary, he had frankly called Congress to witness that he did not consider himself equal to the task entrusted to him. He could only promise to exert every power that he possessed in the performance of that important trust.

Again and again Washington, on his part, had given warning to Congress that, without a well-organized and well-disciplined army, he could not hope to win battles. He had pointed out that short-term enlistments, to say nothing of desertions, perpetually left him paralyzed at critical moments. This lesson, which Washington had long sought to teach them, Congress, for its part, was at last beginning to learn, even if the men who controlled the states had not yet taken that lesson deeply into their hearts. In September, 1776, Congress authorized the commander-in-chief to enlist eighty-eight battalions to serve during the war, and, to encourage enlistments, offered bounties of money and lands. A principal aim of the measure was of course to create an army that would be more directly under the control of Congress and the commander-in-chief, less subject to state whims and jealousies, and therefore more efficient. To that end a provision was included that the officers of these regiments should be commissioned by Congress. The adoption of the measure did not, however, end the problem for that sorely perplexed body. Serious difficulties arose with some of the states, difficulties that called for compromises and gentle stroking of state fur, one of the compromises providing for an alternative enlistment for a period of three years. These enforced negotiations with recalcitrant states had at the same time the effect of stirring some members to recrimination and bitter denunciation. A remark of William Whipple, though mild enough, is significant: "This affair", he wrote, "has caus'd more perplexity and uneasiness than any thing that has happened in my time."

One sectional jealousy was, in fact, beginning to seethe at this time that would in the course of events blow the lid off the pot. It was mainly between the New England states, on the one hand, and New York, on the other. The New Englanders were finding fault with General Philip Schuyler of New York, as commander of the northern army, yet, curiously enough, it was not a New Englander that was set up as the champion antagonist to General Schuyler, but a Virginian officer, General Horatio Gates, who would eventually be promoted to a championship against General Washington himself. Sectional jealousies even bored their way into the business of provisioning the army, which was otherwise, in these autumn days of 1776, vexing the soul of Congress exceedingly. Indeed, from the beginning of the war to its end, never for more than an occasional brief interval of self-satisfying blindness did that problem cease to vex and bedevil. Altogether, the story of supplying the army of the Revolution is not, upon the whole, one that is calculated to lift the soul into the rarefied atmosphere of unalloyed patriotic exaltation. What particularly shocked Congress to learn about the end of September was that, despite the heroic efforts of the commissary-general, Joseph Trumbull, the soldiers were not obtaining their proper rations; that they were sustaining themselves almost entirely on bread of a sort and meat of a sort; no vegetables, no vinegar, no "greens". To be sure, it was not possible for Congress to escape all blame for these conditions; neither could that assembly escape all blame for the "jobbing and cheating" discovered to be rife in the business.

All these worries, added to a lack of harmony, even an atmosphere of suspicion, pervaded the Congress hall at the very time when the wisest of the men who sat there were convinced that a solid bond of union was among the first essentials. Then, to cap the climax of obstacles to the calm deliberation requisite to the perfection of the instrument of union, it came about that in mid-December, 1776, Congress was impelled to flee Philadelphia to escape capture by the British and to take refuge in Baltimore. The very thought of flight was of itself exceedingly depressing to the spirits of men engaged in the mighty effort to save a great cause; so depressing, in fact, that, when a rumor crept abroad that Congress would flee, General Washington was instructed (December 11) to contradict the "scandalous report" that Congress was "about to disperse", adding the solemn declaration: "Nor will they adjourn from the city of Philadelphia . . . until the last necessity shall direct it."

To the minds of a majority of the Congress, the last necessity did direct it the very next day. Declared William Whipple, "The near approach of the enemy to that city struck such a panick in all orders of the people there, except Tories . . . that the contagion seized the nerves of some members of C[ongress]." It is not to be overlooked that, in the process of departure, some betook themselves to the northward rather than to the southward. Once the members found themselves in Baltimore, so many of them as had chosen that alternative, the first impression seems to have been that the public business could now be conducted "with the undisturbed Deliberation that its Importance demands", and some of them even thought that the air was so much purer than that of Philadelphia that the "weak nerves" of Congress would be braced up. On the score of results, Samuel Adams declared on January 9, 1777, "We have done more important business in three weeks than we had done, and I believe should have done, at Philadelphia, in six months." At all events Congress had been immensely cheered and encouraged by the news of Washington's brilliant stroke at Trenton the night before Christmas.

At the moment of departure from Philadelphia, Congress took an extraordinary resolution "that, until the Congress shall otherwise order, General Washington be possessed of full power to order and direct all things relative to the department, and the operations of war." On December 27, Congress extended those powers, expressed in more precise terms, for a period of six months, "unless sooner determined by Congress". The resolve vested in the general "full, ample, and complete powers" to raise and officer sixteen battalions, along with most of the powers that would be exercised under martial law, as, for instance, "to arrest and confine persons who refuse to take the continental currency". "This measure", wrote William Whipple, December 31, "was thot absolutely necessary for the Salvation of America." Declared Benjamin Rush, "General Washington must be invested with dictatorial powers for a few months, or we are undone. The *vis inertiae* of the Congress has almost ruined this country." Samuel Adams, whose qualms on that score were probably as great as those of any man in Congress, explained to James Warren (January 1, 1777) that the resolution had vested in Washington "large powers . . . for a limited time"; yet he added, "It became in my Opinion necessary".

Although members at the time spoke of these powers as "almost dictatorial", as including "most" of the power of Congress, not long afterward there appeared a disposition to minimize those powers. For instance, in April, John Adams took occasion to declare that the report, "industriously circulated", that Congress had made General Washington dictator was false. Congress had only empowered the general, he said, to raise and officer some battalions and to commandeer supplies. "But no more. Congress never thought of making him dictator, or of giving him a sovereignty." Adams was not himself in Congress when the resolve was adopted, and he had probably not read it.

But there was another side to the story of Congress while it sat in Baltimore, and it is that other side that seems chiefly to have impressed members of Congress. Among the mildest of the complaints were that the town was exceedingly expensive, and exceedingly dirty, that at times members could make their way to the assembly hall only on horseback, through deep mud. "We live here", wrote Benjamin Rush (February 8), "in a Convent, we converse only with one another. We are precluded from all opportunities of feeling the pulse of the public upon our measures." And so they sat there through the gloomy winter, much of the time no more than a "rump" Congress, not quite despairing, yet weighted with eternal uncertainties. The temptation to members to mount their horses and ride back home was great, and many yielded to the temptation. The inducement to those at home to take the road to Baltimore and to the Congress, to endure there a winter's siege, was anything but alluring, and few there were that took it. One of those few was John Adams, who made his appearance as winter was on the verge of receding, and he forthwith sat him down to moan: "I have the mealancholy Prospect before me of a Congress continually changing, untill very few Faces remain, that I saw in the first Congress. . . . Mr. S. Adams, Mr. Sherman, Coll. Richard Henry Lee, Mr. Chase and Mr. Paca, are all that remain. The rest are dead, resigned, deserted or cutt up into Governors, etc., at home."

Samuel Adams to the contrary notwithstanding, that little group of patriots in Baltimore was much occupied with the not unprofitable and perhaps the not altogether undelectable tasks of chewing the Congressional cud. One such cud was the question of regulating prices, and it is not at all improbable that the exceedingly high prices encountered in Baltimore lent its impetus to the discussion. John Adams, upon his arrival, speedily added his voice to the general clamor and just as speedily joined his mind to other minds in the search for a solution of the problem. It proved to be the hottest discussion that Congress had handled since it dropped the problem of confederation.

What had immediately given rise to the debate was the proceedings of a committee of the four New England states, held in Providence, December 25, 1776, to January 2, 1777, the outcome of which was a recommendation for the rigid regulation of prices. These proceedings were laid before Congress on January 28 and at once produced sharp differences of opinion. Were the excessively high prices due to "the pernicious artifices of the enemies of American liberty"; in short, to what, in these latter days, has been termed a conspiracy of the "economic royalists"; or were they but the inevitable result of an excess of paper money? In either event, was attempt at regulation the proper remedy? Would regulatory acts, either by Congress or by the states singly or in groups, be successful? The debate was waged hotly for more than two weeks, while Congress halted betwixt two opinions, sometimes veering toward the one, sometimes toward the other.

Oddly enough some phases of the discussion have a very modern tang. By this time few members of Congress failed to realize that the excessive issues of paper money were chiefly responsible for the evils that had come about; but how else could they meet the costs of the war? In any case, thought some, prices could be controlled. Declared Samuel Chase (February 14, 1777), "It must be done. The mines of Peru would not support a war at the present high price of the necessaries of life." "It is absolutely necessary", asserted Richard Henry Lee, and the new governments instituted in every part of America would enable all classes of people to carry the measure of regulation into execution. Said James Wilson, "There are certain things Sir which Absolute power cannot do." "Remember", ventured Dr. Witherspoon, "laws are not almighty." John Adams, who perceived the working of inexorable economic law in the rise of prices, opined that after a time the evils would break out with all the greater violence. "The water will flow with greater rapidity for having been dammed up for a time." Spoke Dr. Benjamin Rush: "The continent labours under a universal malady. From the crown of her head to the Soal of her feet She is full of disorders. She requires the most powerful tonic medicines. The resolution before you is Nothing but an *Opiate*. It may compose the continent for a night, but She will soon awaken to a fresh sense of her pain and misery." No; retorted Richard Henry Lee, "The learned Doctor has mistook the disorder of the continent. She labours under a spasm, and Spasms he knows require *palliative* medicines." In the end (February 15) the action of the New England states received a qualified approval, while the middle and southern states were counseled to hold similar conventions for the consideration of the question.

In all this dreary winter scarcely a breath was emitted respecting the great problem of confederation, although, when the Confederation is again definitely brought under consideration, relief to the sinking currency becomes the keynote of the discussion. For one thing, the prolonged dearth of representation made a renewal of the debate impracticable, but there seemed to be a general avoidance of the subject, as yet too hot for successful handling. There are evidences nevertheless that the idea of confederation continued to seethe in the back of a good many minds. In the discussion of the proceedings of the New England convention, for instance, Congress made a sort of perihelion sweep around that blazing sun, then went off into space, evading the fateful plunge.

Aside from the primary question respecting the regulation of prices, there was injected into the discussion the further question whether two or more states had a right to take action upon continental subjects without the prior or subsequent approbation of Congress. William Ellery, in whose state the New England committee had held its conference, wrote, February 15: "After a long metaphysical Debate which took up Part of three Days Congress were equally divided. All the Members agreed that the meeting was right considering the Circumstances; but split upon the Question of Right hinted at." John Adams maintained (February 4) that

Altho' we were not confederated the same principles of equity and reason should govern us as if we were united by a confederacy—that the four New England States bore the same relation to the Congress that four counties bore to a single State. These four counties have a right to meet to regulate roads, and affairs that relate to the poor, but they have no right to tax or execute any other branch of legislation. In like manner the four New Eng[lan]d States, or any other four States have a right to meet upon matters wholly indifferent, but they have no right to touch upon Continental Subjects—that the committee from the 4 New Eng[lan]d States have touched upon continental Subjects, therefore the *Meeting* stands in need of the Approbation of the Congress.

Dr. Benjamin Rush, replying to Adams, remarked:

The *Meeting* is full of great and interesting consequences, and should be regarded with a serious and jealous eye. Their business was chiefly continental, and therefore they usurped the powers of congress as much as four counties would usurp the powers of legislation in a state sh[oul]d they attempt to tax themselves. The committee have in one instance in regulating the price of goods contravened an express resolution of Congress, and lastly tho' the meeting was necessary and no injustice intended or done by it to any state, yet it becomes us to remember that arbitrary power has often originated in justice and necessity.

Thus did Congress for some months skirt the subject of confederation, with little more than a look askance in its direction. On February 27, Congress adjourned from Baltimore to meet in Philadelphia on March 4, but was not able to assemble a quorum earlier than March 12. The return to Philadelphia was, however, soon to have one favorable result, namely, the scattered sheep began to flock back to that good old comfortable fold, so that, by April 8, every state had a representation in Congress. And that condition brought another result, a resolution to take up the Articles of Confederation once more and to devote two days in each week to the subject, "until it shall be wholly discussed in Congress". Some members interpreted this phrase to mean, until the Articles should be completed; and that appears to have been for a little while the general hope. By the 21st the discussion got under way, but it was not long before it had encountered obstacles. One of the first of these was the question of state sovereignty. Most members appear to have overlooked the fact that, as drawn by Dickinson, and even as left by the committee of the whole, the plan of Confederation reserved to the states little more than the regulation of their internal government. If it should seem strange that state sovereignty, which every state had deemed the tower of its salvation, the shield of its deliverance, was about to be surrendered, it was certainly not from any failure of universal regard for that cardinal doctrine. Most members of Congress, so it would seem, were scarcely aware of whither they were being led. It fell to the lot of Thomas Burke to sound the alarm and call the errant statesmen of Congress back to their fundamental faith; and the story of that re-direction can not be better told than in Burke's own words. Writing to Governor Caswell April 29, 1777, he said:

We have agreed to three articles: one containing the name: the second a declaration of the sovereignty of the States, and an express provision that they be considered as retaining every power not expressly delegated; and the third an agreement mutually to assist each other against every enemy. The first and latter passed without opposition or dissent, the second occa-

sioned two days debate. It stood originally the third article; and expressed
only a reservation of the power of regulating the internal police, and consequently resigned every other power. It appeared to me that this was not
what the States expected, and, I thought, it left it in the power of the future
Congress or General Council to explain away every right belonging to the
States and to make their own power as unlimited as they please.

He therefore offered an amendment whereby the state retained its
sovereignty and independence and all powers not expressly delegated.
The radical alteration produced by his amendment may readily be seen
from a comparison of Article II of the definitive Confederation with
Article III of the Dickinson draft or as reported by the committee of
the whole. Burke goes on to say that the real meaning of his amendment "was so little understood that it was some time before it was
seconded", but it was at last seconded by South Carolina. Strangely
enough, there was opposition to it on the part of James Wilson and
Richard Henry Lee, but when it came to a vote, there were eleven ayes,
one no (Virginia), while New Hampshire was divided.

Previously, in discussions of other questions, relating indirectly to
the Confederation, Burke had found occasion to enunciate the doctrine
since known as state rights and to stand forth as the champion of
checks upon governmental power, whether in a confederation of the
states or otherwise. He had observed, he said, a tendency to increase the
powers of Congress, even a tendency in Congress to assume powers,
and he voiced his protest, declaiming against "the Delusive Intoxication
which Power Naturally imposes on the human Mind". "Unlimited
power", he declared, "can not be safely trusted to any man or set of
men on earth."

Within a week three articles had been agreed upon, and there was
hope that "the whole would soon be passed". Those hopes, however,
were destined to be dashed on the same rocks that had wrecked their
earlier endeavors. On May 11, Burke wrote: "It goes on very slowly,
and I fear, the difficulty of preserving the independence of the States,
and at the same time giving to each its proper weight in the public
Council, will frustrate a Confederation."

Burke had, in fact, been trying his hand on a plan of his own. The
plan is of especial interest for the reason that it provided for a sort of

bicameral body. There was to be a General Council composed of delegates chosen by the several states, and a Council of State consisting of one delegate from each state and likewise chosen by the states. Every edict and ordinance must be moved in the General Council and assented to by "a majority of all the voices of which the Council ought to be composed", and must also be assented to by a similar majority of the Council of State. A declaration of war, however, was to require three-fourths of the voices of the General Council and nine voices of the Council of State; and then, "every State dissenting from such war shall be no further bound thereby than to refuse any aid or protection to the enemy with whom the other States may be at war". Burke appears to have offered his plan as an amendment to the Articles about May 5, when the question was put whether the Congress should consist of two houses. That having passed in the negative, the whole was dropped.

In the close of May, John Adams wrote to Jefferson, "The great work of Confederation drags heavily on, but I dont despair of it. The great and small states must be brought as near together as possible." Then came other and more immediately pressing problems to thrust confederation to one side. There was a sharp controversy respecting General Schuyler that must, if possible, be adjusted; and there was a problem respecting the region called Vermont, vexatious enough even in its earlier stages of fermentation and destined to torment the Continental Congress from time to time until its last hours. "A kind of fatality", lamented Samuel Adams (June 26), "still prevents our proceeding a Step in the important affair of the Confederation." Four days later he wrote more hopefully. There were but two or three things, he thought, which would be the subject of further debate, and upon these most of the members, he was confident, had already made up their minds.

Two or three things, yes! But it was just those two or three things that stood as all but insurmountable obstacles to the confederation. However little controversy other questions might stir, these would most certainly produce much debate. One of these things, Adams continued, was the question of voting, and that, he was inclined to believe, would be determined the next day. It was not determined the next day nor for many, many days thereafter. On that same day (June 26) a motion appears to have been offered that "Each State have a right to send one representative in Congress for every 30,000 inhabitants, contained within the said State. That each member in Congress shall have a voice in determining questions". If, however, the motion received any attention at that time it is not recorded. Another New England member, William Williams, indicated a few days later (July 5) that a strenuous contest over the question had been in progress between the larger and the smaller states. On July 2, Congress resolved to take the confederation into consideration "tomorrow"; yet tomorrows came and tomorrows went, a goodly number of them, without bringing the subject back upon the tapis.

Meanwhile attendance thinned—one of those eternally recurring obstacles to progress in any important measure; and on July 17, Congress made an effort to toll the absent members back to their seats for the special purpose of resuming consideration of the confederation. Sometime in the course of the wrangling there also appears to have arisen renewed snarling over another old bone of contention, the claims to the South Sea. "Almost every member of Congress", wrote Charles Carroll of Carrollton, August 12, "is anxious for a Confederacy, being sensible that a Confederation formed on a rational plan will certainly add much weight and consequence to the united States collectively and give great Security to each individually, and a credit to our paper money; but I despair of such a confederacy, as ought, and would take place, if little and partial interests could be laid aside." Once more, on August 16, a day (August 18) was assigned for the subject, but the assignment was not kept. On September 2 there was a motion to have the confederation made a part of each day's business, but the motion was negatived.

It was certainly not indifference that had stalled progress on the confederation, for at no time since the preceding summer had there appeared to be a more intense earnestness to press forward with the problem, even though at times it must have seemed as impossible of solution as that of fitting thirteen spokes of different materials, lengths, and sizes into a serviceable wheel. But there were "ten thousand interruptions", and beyond doubt the sorest of them in this dragging summer of 1777 was that invasion of foreign officers, seeking commissions in the American army. Too many of them, so it seemed to Congress, were actuated by quite other motives than a desire to aid in a noble cause; too many of them merely professional soldiers, attracted by the "fine war" over here.

This invasion had begun long before, but by now Congress was held virtually under siege. As early as July, 1776, Thomas Jefferson had written to John Page: "I would not advise that the French gentlemen should come here. We have so many of that country, and have been so much imposed on, that the Congress begins to be sore on that head." And two months later (September 21) the Committee of Secret Correspondence had written to William Bingham in Martinique: "Officers unacquainted with our language cannot be useful; therefore we do not wish to encourage such to come amongst us . . . if too many come over, the Congress will not know what to do with them." Another month, and Josiah Bartlett was writing to John Langdon (October 19): "great number of foreigners, especially French officers, are almost daily arriving here, and requesting to be employed in our army, many of whom are well recommended."

By the middle of February, 1777, these foreign volunteers for service in behalf of American freedom (at least for service in America's war) had become a veritable nuisance. "I must also request you", Robert Morris wrote to William Bingham (February 16), "to spare me all you can in the Introduction of French Officers to me . . . coud I speak the Language and had spare time it woud be a pleasure but it is now too much the reverse." Hitherto, he said, he had obtained appointments for all whom Bingham had sent, "but really they are flocking over in such Numbers from every Port by every Ship that I don't know what we shall do with them (all this in Confidence)." On March 13, 1777, an irked Congress screwed up its courage sufficiently to direct the Committee of Secret Correspondence "forthwith to write all their ministers and agents abroad, to discourage all gentlemen from coming to America with expectation of employment in the service, unless they are masters of our language, and have the best of recommendations." So far so good; but soon it seemed that the line drawn against such as did not understand our language was being "construed as a patent for those who do". "Nothing", declared James Lovell (July 4), "is more dreaded than such a Construction."

Copies of the resolve were transmitted by President Hancock to both General Washington and General Schuyler. (As if there were anything those generals could do about it!) To the latter Hancock wrote (March 18): "The Number of Foreigners already employed in the Army of these States is a prodigious Weight upon the Service; and the Evil is likely to encrease unless a speedy Stop can be put to it." The very next day, while its courage was still at the sticking point, Congress politely declined the proffered services of one General de Kalb. (Some months later, when that officer should present himself in person, his services would be accepted.) Meanwhile a good many other such proffers of services were accepted, with a bestowal of commissions; although other considerable numbers obtained only perquisites (a tidy sum, in the total, these perquisites), together with injunctions, as polite as circumstances permitted, to return to those lands whence they came.

So numerous, however, were those who descended upon the army, with commissions in their pockets, that, in May, General Washington ventured to inquire of Richard Henry Lee what Congress expected him to do "with the many foreigners they have at different times promoted to the rank of field officers". Were these appointments made to oblige the adventurers of a nation which we want to interest in our cause, or was it to get rid of their importunity? Lee replied (May 22) that the motives were "military and political meerly", in no sense to get rid of importunity. The adventurers, he said, were of three classes: those who had come early and without recommendations but with apparent zeal, those who had brought recommendations (as for instance, from the General of Martinique or Mr. Bingham), and those who had come from France, generally under agreement with the commissioners—"or one of them at least".

The "one of them" was Silas Deane. Congress had indeed instructed its commissioners in France to endeavor to obtain the services of "skilful engineers not exceeding four", and the commissioners had accordingly made inquiry for such artists. That inquiry had been only too successful. Applications for the service had poured in, and with recommendations from persons of so much importance in France that it became "quite necessary not to neglect them". Deane, for his part, appears to have put a very broad interpretation upon his commission, and so proceeded to make contracts with individuals and groups, to the great embarrassment of Congress and ultimately to his own undoing.

In the course of Deane's negotiations for the services of foreign officers one contract appears to have been wangled out of him that Congress could not quite stomach, because it not only set the American officers by the ears but likewise roiled those French engineers with whom Franklin and Deane had jointly made a contract in accordance with their instructions. The obnoxious contract was with one Du-Coudray, an officer of artillery, whereby he was to be given the rank of major general and made commander of the whole of both artillery and engineers, subject only to Congress and the commander-in-chief of the army. No sooner had DuCoudray, in the beginning of June, 1777, presented himself with his demands, than the wrath of Congress rose to the boiling point, while that of several officers in the army boiled over. Sullivan, Greene, and Knox all wrote caustic letters to Congress declaring that they would resign if the agreement with DuCoudray should be ratified. Congress thereupon found itself in a pretty pickle. Some among them, including John Adams (June 19), thought that the "Interest" of DuCoudray was "so great and so near the Throne, that it would be impolitick, not to avail ourselves of him". Others at the same time were convinced that to do so would unquestionably throw the army into confusion. Besides DuCoudray himself there was "a large Train of under Officers of various ranks who are with him, for whom also he has made appointments", so William Williams complained (July 5). He did not expect the contract to be ratified in full. Then, fearing that he might be transgressing the rules against divulging matters *"sub Judice"*, he remarked: "I forbear to say many things. The City swarms with French Men."

Throughout the entire summer the affair kept both Congress and the army seething. Finally a sort of compromise was effected. Congress voted to make DuCoudray inspector general of ordnance and military manufactures, with the rank of major general, then DuCoudray and the officers who had accompanied him offered to serve as volunteers.

On the day that Congress accepted this offer (September 15) DuCoudray was drowned crossing the Schuylkill. "This dispensation", wrote John Adams (September 18), with evident satisfaction, "will save us much altercation."

The story of another Frenchman who came a-knocking at the door of Congress this same summer of 1777—it was about midway the Du-Coudray beseigement—runs a very different and a much longer course, not one short chapter, but many. It must suffice, however, to note here briefly no more than the prologue. It was on the morning of July 27 that a party of Frenchmen, including the Marquis de Lafayette and Baron de Kalb, arrived in Philadelphia, having come up from George-town, South Carolina, where they had landed six weeks before. Having presented to President Hancock their recommendations and contracts (for they had contracts, signed by Silas Deane), they were given an appointment for the next day with James Lovell, chairman of the committee on foreign applications, member of the committee for foreign affairs, and almost, if not quite, the only member of Congress who had a command of the French language.

Much of Mr. Lovell's time during several months had been taken up by this multitude of Frenchmen, not merely in his capacity as interpreter, but also as counsellor to them and to Congress; and he had grown exceedingly weary of the whole business. "These Frenchmen have used me up quite", he wrote to a friend, June 30; and only three days before the coming of Lafayette, Kalb, and their group he had found it needful to set forth at length for the information of General Washington a history of the DuCoudray business, with interpretation and commentary. Unquestionably Mr. Lovell's nerves had become frazzled and raw, and clearly he had come to the conclusion that one good service he could render his country would be to shoo as many of these Frenchmen as possible away from Congress. Out from the Congress chamber he came, on shooing tactics bent, to where Lafayette and his friends waited. He did not invite them to any inner office for conference; instead he said to them, not too politely, that French officers seemed to have a great fancy for entering the American service without being invited, that Congress had already obtained all the French officers desired, and more. Whereupon he turned upon his heel and

strode back to his seat. Such in essence is the account left by the
Chevalier Dubuysson, one of the Lafayette party. The Chevalier did
give Mr. Lovell credit for speaking excellent French, but he was by
no means complimentary of that gentleman's manners. Lovell had
treated them, declared Dubuysson, "like a set of adventurers".

Lafayette was quick to act. Suspecting that his papers had not even
been read, he immediately sent a note to the president of Congress expressing a desire to be permitted to serve in the American army as a
volunteer and without pay. Nor was Congress slow to recognize that
here was a Frenchman of a different calibre from most of those by
whom it had long been bedeviled. On the 31st of July that body
adopted the following resolution:

Whereas, the marquis de la Fayette, out of his great zeal to the cause of
liberty, in which the United States are engaged, has left his family and connexions, and, at his own expense, come over to offer his service to the United
States, without pension or particular allowance, and is anxious to risque his
life in our cause:

Resolved, That his service be accepted, and that, in consideration of his
zeal, illustrious family and connexions, he have the rank and commission
of major general in the army of the United States.

To be sure, a rather delicate question was soon protruding itself in
front of the army and in front of Congress: just what was intended by
the bestowal of that commission on the Marquis. Benjamin Harrison
insisted (to Washington, August 20) that every member of Congress
had understood the commission to be "merely Honorary"; but Lafayette persisted in his solicitation to be given a command, and, after
much mulling over the problem, Congress informed General Washington on December 1 that "it is highly agreeable to Congress that the
Marquis de la Fayette be appointed to the command of a division in the
continental army". Congress was a bit more cautious in the case of
Baron de Kalb, but on September 15, he also was made a major
general.

Not all the Frenchmen questing glory in the American war—if glory
was indeed their quest—were nuisances by any means. Many proved
themselves capable officers and rendered great service to the American

cause. The foreigner who outdistanced all the rest in the worth of service rendered was not a Frenchman, although he made his entrance into the American army under much the same auspices as the French officers. This was Baron Steuben, who came over under the sponsorship of Franklin and Deane, and, from Boston in January, 1778, offered his services to Congress "in the quality of a volunteer". Congress "cheerfully" accepted his offer and directed him to repair to General Washington's headquarters. The baron appeared at York in person in the beginning of February, and a few days later presented himself to General Washington, who speedily discovered that Steuben could be made a valuable acquisition to the army. He accordingly proposed that the baron be made inspector-general, and on May 5 he was so commissioned. It would appear that a bit of deception was practiced on Congress by the baron with regard to his rank and prior military services, a deception in which Franklin seems to have had a share, but because of Steuben's great services to the Revolutionary cause Americans have not been disposed to cavil with either him or Franklin on that account.

All these agonizings over the troublesome Frenchmen were a sore hindrance to progress in that all-important business of confederation; yet they were by no means the sole hindrance. Not far from where Congress sat and sought to deliberate the contending armies were maneuvering back and forth. The British army was uncomfortably near to Philadelphia, and it might almost any day threaten or even take the city. It was on September 2, it will be remembered, that Congress negatived a motion that the confederation should be made a part of each day's business. On September 7, Eliphalet Dyer of Connecticut wrote to Joseph Trumbull: "I think Congress now are in a pretty good Temper to do business—if this plaguy fellow of an How does not disturb us. We are now very Sulky and determine not to move for him if we can help it. How long our courage may last I know not."

Whatever its temper, with commendable courage Congress continued to keep its nose to the grindstone of business, while at the same time keeping its ears cocked for the approach of the British army and not neglecting to make provision for its own swift departure. On September 14, it was resolved, "That if Congress shall be obliged to remove from Philadelphia, Lancaster shall be the place at which they shall meet." It was not long before General Howe, the "plaguy fellow", did disturb them. In the afternoon of September 18, Henry Laurens was writing to his friend Gervais down in Charleston concerning the contemplated removal and lamenting that fright had "driven some great Men" to do precipitantly what he himself, so he avers, had strongly urged as necessary to do coolly and deliberately. "Some who smiled at the proposition", Laurens remarked, "are gone in a hurry, embarrassed—others are now on the wing. We keep enough to make a Congress and that's all." Just then in came a member to announce, "in a burst of Laugh", that Congress was to meet at six o'clock that evening and on the morrow "enter upon the weighty business of the Confederation". Laurens took up his pen again to say, "Fright sometimes works Lunacy."

There was perhaps a dearth of cool deliberation, there may have been a modicum of fright, but there can be little doubt that a larger wisdom propelled the Congress to its exodus. The capture of the guiding body of the nation might well have proved disastrous. "The movement", declared Thomas Burke, "was made not by a Vote but by universal Consent, for every Member Consulted his own particular Safety." Through the night members continued to filter out of the city, and at three o'clock the morning of September 19, the few laggards, routed from their beds, hurriedly gathered their belongings and took the road to Lancaster—and beyond. That their road was leading them to new tribulations, new adventures, new endeavors, none were so dull as not to comprehend; that it was also destined to lead them to a brighter vista in the far distance, all earnestly hoped and most believed.

CHAPTER XIII

CONGRESS IN LABOR.
BIRTH OF CONFEDERATION

On the 27th of September, 1777, nine days after the dispersion at Philadelphia, a quorum of the members gathered at Lancaster, Pennsylvania, the appointed rendezvous, held one session, then hurried across the Susquehanna to York, where they proceeded to establish themselves for such time as might prove to be necessary. At Lancaster "hearts were still fluttering in some bosoms", so Henry Laurens afterward asserted (October 20), and it was deemed the part of wisdom to put a good-sized river, in addition to the many miles, between them and the British army. "Here", wrote James Duane (October 3), when they had got themselves seated at York, "we are at least sufficiently *retired* and can deliberate without interruption."

If the urge to confederate had been strong before the dispersion, it was stronger still amongst the diminished group now huddled at York. That urge had at no time been propelled solely by the desire to perfect the system of government for the American states of which they had made but a tentative beginning, noble as was that incentive and strong as was that impulse. From the beginning there had been another impelling motive, a motive now become more immediate. Confidence in unaided might had lost something of its virtue. If therefore they were to succeed in their great enterprise, there was not only the utmost need of that power which close unity alone could bestow, there was likewise need of outside help, such help as they could not hope to obtain unless the states were more effectually bonded together. Hitherto Congress had inclined to feel that it was captain of its soul and master of its fate. Now it was not so sure of either. Of one thing however they were sure: even while they wrangled over the terms of the union, they were firmly agreed one with another, we *must* confederate, or else we perish.

Accordingly the members had scarcely become adjusted to their new seats, when, a few routine matters out of the way, they adopted a crisp resolve, "that the articles of confederation be taken into consideration to morrow morning, at eleven o'clock". Once again began a procession of tomorrows, vacant of anything pertaining to the confederation until, on October 7, Congress actually obeyed its own injunction of the day before, that "to morrow morning, at 11 o'clock" it would take into its consideration "that part of the confederation that relates to the mode of voting in Congress".

It was evidently a strenuous discussion and revolved around the question whether the votes should be "by States" or "by Voices". A proposition from those in favor of "voices" that there should be one representative for every fifty thousand inhabitants and another that the ratio should be thirty thousand, were overwhelmingly defeated in succession, as was another proposition that representation should be proportioned to contributions of money or taxes. On the question whether each state should have one vote, Virginia alone among the states was in the negative, although there were single noes from Massachusetts (John Adams), North Carolina (John Penn), and South Carolina (Arthur Middleton).

Without doubt several of the states had at the last cast their votes for that method because there appeared to be no alternative between that and no confederation, some of the members uttering as they did so not only lamentations but dire prophecies. And now, having settled —for so long as it would remain settled—the most crucial of all the problems respecting the confederation, they hurried on to the adjustment of the other "pivotal points". Next in importance, so at least it seemed at the moment, was the apportionment of the general expenses, or, as members sometimes called it, taxation. Should the contributions of the states be in proportion to population, or to land values, or to general property values? Both in the Dickinson draft and in the report of the committee of the whole the quotas were to be determined in proportion to population. The problem was attacked on October 9. On the 10th, Henry Laurens wrote to his son John:

We are now upon the Confederation—have surmounted one vast point— the Votes are to be by States and not by Voices. the present question is the mode of Taxation. Two days have been amused in conning it, some sensible things have been said, and as much nonsense as ever I heard in so short a space. I have not contributed to either. I mean to expose my inabilities this Morning in a very few words because I think very few are necessary and very few would be made if we were about to Tax one State in which all are Interested. Candour and genuine honesty ought then to be our guides.

Four days more the discussion went on; then, on the 14th came the decision, in favor of land values with their improvements. The vote was five states to four, with two divided. The South was solidly in the affirmative, New England solidly in the negative. Of the middle states, New Jersey lined up with the southern states, whilst New York and Pennsylvania were divided, Duane of the former and Roberdeau of the latter voting in the negative. This decision also, as well as the method of voting, was destined to rise up to plague Congress in the days to come.

On the same day (October 14) were settled the minor questions respecting the number of delegates a state might send to Congress and the length of the term. The number of delegates was fixed at not less than two nor more than seven, and the length of term, as in the Dickinson draft, at three years in any period of six. By this measure Congress effectively inoculated itself with the germ of pernicious anemia.

On the following day (October 15) came on the third of the great tugs of war, that respecting the so-called claims to the South Sea. The Dickinson draft had provided that Congress should have power of limiting the bounds of those colonies having such claims, of ascertaining any other indeterminate boundaries, of disposing, for the common benefit of all the colonies, of the lands thus or otherwise obtained, and even of assigning territories to new colonies. The committee of the whole had, however, "postponed" these propositions. Now an effort was made to restore them, and in a more positive form. Three several motions to that end were successively made and successively negatived. The first was, "That, in order to render the present union and confederacy firm and perpetual, it is essential that the limits of each respective territorial jurisdiction should be ascertained by the articles of confederation"; and therefore would call upon the claimant states for "proofs" of their claims. The second would grant to Congress "the sole and exclusive right and power to ascertain and fix the western boundary of such states as claim to the South Sea, and to dispose of all land beyond the boundary so ascertained, for the benefit of the United States." The third proposition substituted for the last clause of the second: "and lay out the land beyond the boundary, so ascertained, into separate and independent states, from time to time, as the numbers and circum stances of the people thereof may require."

On the first motion eight states were in the negative, three in the affirmative, the latter being New York, Pennsylvania, and Maryland, although Williams of Connecticut voted *aye,* and Smith of Maryland voted *no.* On the second motion the yeas and nays are not recorded. It is significant that the third proposition obtained only the solid vote of Maryland, with one aye (Jonathan Elmer) from New Jersey. Congress was accordingly denied the power to limit the western boundaries of the states. But that decision likewise was to become a festering thorn in the flesh of Congress until the time when it would be heroically plucked out.

The three great questions having now been determined, what mattered it about the rest? Long eager to get back to their own firesides and their own chores, members forthwith began to take their flight (some had even departed while yet the tempest raged), and those who took the contrary journey were as yet not sufficient to fill the gaps. "Our House", wrote Laurens, October 16, "will be reduced in a few days to barely twenty or twenty one Members." Of those who departed immediately were the two stoutest delegates of Maryland, Samuel Chase and Charles Carroll of Carrollton. Among those who tarried but a few more days were three of the Massachusetts stalwarts, President Hancock and the two Adamses. Hancock had resigned the presidency October 31; and on November 1, Henry Laurens of South Carolina was elected to the office.

Notwithstanding these defections, the valiant remnant went right on energetically and even enthusiastically with their constructive enter prise, to erect the several wings to the main structure. With energy and with earnestness they took up the remaining articles of the report of the committee of the whole, revising, striking out, substituting, but pressing ever forward toward the completion of the instrument. Of the changes that were made it is not necessary here to speak, except to

mention one rather radical alteration. Just when their labors were almost at an end, it was decided to substitute for the proposed Council
of State a Committee of the States, that is, a committee of one from
each state, eliminating the whole of the article that described the
powers of the Council of State and substituting therefor the simple provision that the Committee of the States should have only such powers,
in the recess of Congress, as Congress by the consent of nine states
might vest them with. It came about that this Committee of the States
was never called into existence until the summer of 1784, when it made
a brief appearance before the national footlights, but, halted in its performance by the withdrawal of some of the actors, was never again
called upon to play its part.

Not perhaps a serious interruption to the labors on the Confederation, yet a sore disturber nevertheless of spiritual repose, was what
Henry Laurens dubbed "a very long apologetic expostulatory Cen
sorious, Rascally epistle from the Ir-Revd. Jacob Duché", transmitted
to Congress by General Washington and laid on their table October 20
The letter, dated Ocotber 8, 1777, and addressed to General Washington, was some three thousand words in length and certainly contained an abundance of the apologetic, the expostulatory, and the cen-
sorious, likewise elements which most members of Congress would
not have hesitated to term rascally. Boiled down to its residuum of
dregs, however, it sought to persuade General Washington that the
struggle for independence was hopeless, exhorted him to turn his back
squarely upon the American cause, and induce Congress to rescind the
Declaration of Independence and penitently seek reconciliation with
Great Britain.

In transmitting the letter to Congress, Washington had put upon his
pen such restraint that his comment was surely no measure of his indignation. Almost gently he remarked that the letter was of a very
"curious and extraordinary nature", a "ridiculous, illiberal performance". The Congressional vocabulary stirred to activity by Duché's illiberal performance included much harsher terms than curious, extraordinary, ridiculous, and illiberal; and the fact that the letter contained
remarks uncomplimentary to Congress was in nowise conducive to
either milder terms or softer tones.

It would doubtless have been so in any event. There is small likelihood that Congress could have been persuaded to listen to a counsel of defeat, had the gloom been never so deep nor so dense. But the gloom had just then lifted. For it so befell that almost at the precise moment that Duché's letter was spread before Congress, news had come of the surrender of General Burgoyne at Saratoga. With the sounds of victory ringing in their ears, who would listen but with scorn to whimpers of defeat? Congress was no longer in the depths. Congress was on the delectable heights.

And who was this "Ir-Revd. Jacob Duché", who now bade them stretch out their necks once more for the yoke and the bow? None other than he who, in those crucial days of the first assembling of Congress in September, 1774, had led them in storming the very gates of Heaven in defense of their rights. Standing before them, he had uttered a prayer in their behalf "as pertinent, as affectionate, as sublime, as devout" as was ever "offered up to Heaven", a prayer of such fervency and eloquence, of such a sensibility of the crisis, that it melted the hearts of all who heard it, "filled every bosom present". Thereafter Mr. Duché had served as the spiritual guide to Congress, its chaplain. So great was the contrast between that one-time intercession with Heaven and the present proffered intercession with what Congress could not but deem the powers of evil, that no wonder Reverend Jacob Duché was now denounced as a "Judas", an "apostate", a "traitor", "the first of villains". "Poor man!" bewailed John Adams; "I pity his weakness and detest his wickedness." Once again the Reverend Mr. Duché had "filled every bosom present".

In after years Mr. Duché must have reflected in sorrow how sadly he had missed his cue. If only he had delayed a few days the writing of that letter, it is inconceivable that he would ever have written it at all, and in that event he would have continued to be held in high regard as one of the bright particular stars of that troublous time. But he had snuffed out his own torch.

Congress, for its part, officially ignored Duché and his letter, and the members did not long bother their brains about him, but forged ahead with their efforts to complete the Articles of Confederation, pausing only to call upon the states (October 31, November 1) to set apart a day of thanksgiving "for the signal success, lately obtained over the enemies of these United States". On Friday evening, November 7, the Confederation was thought to have been finished, barring perhaps a bit of verbal and phrasal polishing for the benefit of diction, "without altering the sense". A Committee of the States had been substituted for the Council of State previously provided for, and a slight alteration had been made in the provision whereby Canada might, with a minimum of formalities, pull the latchstring and join the fraternal party—Canada only. Any other initiate into the fraternity would require the assent of nine states. Thereupon Mr. Samuel Adams and Mr. John Adams, who had been waiting only for these finishing strokes, sought and obtained leave of absence to visit their families.

Evidently, however, some members had cogitated and reconsidered over the Saturday and the Sabbath; for on Monday afternoon "sundry propositions . . . in addition to the articles of confederation" were laid before Congress. The committee to whom these propositions were referred reported (November 11) in favor of seven additions, some of which were adopted, others rejected, still others modified.

First among these new propositions was one providing for freedom of speech and debate in Congress and immunity of members from arrest. This was made a part of Article V, as the Articles were newly arranged. The earlier failure to include this fundamental of liberties was probably a mere oversight. Three of the new propositions, namely, one providing that the free citizens of each of the states shall be entitled to all the privileges and immunities of free citizens of the several states, one respecting extradition of fugitives from justice, and one requiring that full faith and credit be given by each state to the records, acts, etc., of every other state, were incorporated as article IV in the final arrangement. A provision respecting the settlement of controversies concerning the private right of soil claimed under different grants of two or more states was incorporated into Article IX; and a provision that the United States, when organized in pursuance of the Articles of Confederation, should assume all the obligations incurred under the authority of the prior Congress became Article XII.

On the 15th of November, 1777, the several Articles of Confederation were arranged and recorded in the Journals. There were of course many disappointments and dissatisfactions, yet there was a general feeling of relief that at last, for better or for worse, the great task had been accomplished. There was likewise an earnest desire that the Articles should speedily be ratified by the several states, and, upon the whole, the members of Congress appeared to be confident that this would be done, although there were not lacking some misgivings with regard to the outcome. It is even related that then, or at an approximate time, was uttered the prophecy that the Confederation as formed would prove to be no better than a rope of sand—a prophecy that, in the years to come, would be echoed over and over again.

Thomas Burke of North Carolina, though he had departed Congress a month before the completion of the Articles, declared that as the plan could "never be suited to the States . . . nothing decided on it is of consequence." In his view "a time of peace and tranquility" was the only "proper time for agitating so important a concern". Burke's colleague, Cornelius Harnett, wrote him (November 13): "The child Congress has been big with, these two years past, is at last brought forth—(Confederation). I fear it will by the several Legislatures be thought a little deformed—you will think it a Monster." A little later Harnett declared, "This has been the most difficult piece of Business that ever was under taken by any public Body." Then he added, "it is the best Confederacy that could be formed especially when we consider the number of states, their different Interests, Customs, etc., etc." Of course there were growlings over particular features of the plan, such, for instance, as that of Nathaniel Folsom of New Hampshire, who saw no justice in the plan adopted for determining quotas of the general expense, and he did not doubt that the states would take as much time for their deliberations on the measure as they might deem just and necessary. Most of the states did, in fact, take their time.

No doubt the circular letter which Congress despatched to the states alongside the Articles of Confederation voiced the prevailing sentiment of that body. The plan proposed, said Congress to the states, was "the best which could be adapted to the circumstances of all"; and the states were besought to review the Articles candidly, dispassionately, "under a sense of the difficulty of combining in one general system the various sentiments and interests of a continent divided into so many sovereign and independent communities", communities "differing in habits, produce, commerce, and internal police", and also "under a conviction of the absolute necessity of uniting all our councils and all our strength, to maintain and defend our common liberties".

Let them be examined [the appeal continues] with a liberality becoming brethren and fellow-citizens surrounded by the same imminent dangers, contending for the same illustrious prize, and deeply interested in being forever bound and connected together by ties the most intimate and indissoluble; and finally, let them be adjusted with the temper and magnanimity of wise and patriotic legislators, who, while they are concerned for the prosperity of their own more immediate circle, are capable of rising superior to local attachments, when they may be incompatible with the safety, happiness, and glory of the general Confederacy.

Further the states were entreated to reflect that the consummation of the union would "confound our foreign enemies, defeat the flagitious practices of the disaffected, strengthen and confirm our friends, support our public credit, restore the value of our money, enable us to maintain our fleets and armies, and add weight to our councils at home, and to our treaties abroad".

The pen that drew this forceful appeal to the states was that of Richard Henry Lee, and the same pen, in a private letter, cogently expressed the same sentiment. "In this great business dear Sir we must yield a little to each other, and not rigidly insist on having everything correspondent to the partial views of every State. On such terms we can never confederate."

It has been endeavored here, by the light of such expressions as have been left to us by the chief participants, flickering and spasmodic though these glimpses may be, to follow the progress of the Articles of Confederation through their manifold vicissitudes on the floor of Congress, to their completion there, and their despatch to the states for acceptance or rejection. Such a story of the Confederation is not of course the whole story; it is only a sort of airplane view of the contest as it was waged on the fighting front. The "home front", the seethe and surge of ideas and their expression among the people, it has not been sought here to envisage. As for the second act in the drama, the appearance of the instrument of union before the thirteen state legislatures, those stern courts of appeal which were to sit in judgment upon them, those scenes were yet to be enacted. It is permissible nevertheless to give a moment's consideration to the instrument which had cost so much thought and labor and whose mission amongst the states was so potent for good or evil.

To what extent this instrument of union, called the Articles of Confederation, would be effective for the purposes for which it was designed; whether it would stand the strain of antagonistic views and interests; whether it would endure even for the period of the war; these events were in the laps of the gods. Most members of Congress evidently believed, and the majority of the people presently came to believe, that, whether or not, in the language of the title, the union would be perpetual, it would at least make for efficiency in the accomplishment of what was all-important, the prosecution of the war to a successful conclusion and the achievement of independence. Few of them ventured to push their predictions farther than that, although there were those among them who lifted their eyes and peered through the mists toward a goal which they hoped and believed lay beyond that uncertain horizon where the war would end.

Because the Articles of Confederation, on account of certain inherent weaknesses, proved inadquate to its purposes and had in the end to be cast aside for a new-forged constitution, it has been much the practice to heap criticisms upon it and even to treat it with a measure of scorn. Whatever the defects of the Articles of Confederation, they constitute nevertheless an important, a necessary, stage in the development of an efficient constitution, even as the confederation under them was an important, a necessary step in the progress toward a more perfect union. There has been too little appreciation of the difficulties encountered in the formation of the Articles, too small an appraisement of the obstacles to even this tentative union. The generations that have lived under the noble instrument of government that has proved so adequate to our needs have viewed the period of the Confederation, as they could hardly have escaped from viewing it, in the concentrated light of subsequent history and have been all too prone to impatience with the men of that time, because, forsooth, their foresight was not as broad and as deep and as far-reaching as our hindsight! A closer view of the conditions of that period, a warmer contact with the men of those times, a more sympathetic consorting with their thoughts and feelings, not only will give us a fuller comprehension of the conditions under which they labored, of the materials with which they worked, but will surely lead us to a better understanding of what they wrought.

Those men had been called upon to yield much of what for their individual centers of political life had very great and very definite value, and all in return for that quite vague and ill-defined, that altogether problematical thing, "the benefit of the whole". Is it any wonder that they were hesitant and cautious? The rather, all things considered, it is to be marveled at that the men of that time went as far as they did toward merging their own political units, which hitherto had encompassed their lives and to them were very real, into a union whose figure was not only dim and whose value was uncertain, but which might in the end turn and destroy its creators. Were there local prejudices? They could be worn away only by a period of cooperation. Were there sectional jealousies? They could be assuaged only by the softening process of time. Were there fears of one another? Those fears must needs be overcome through friendly cooperation—or perhaps by fears more potent. The struggle to make good their Declaration of Independence must become more desperate; the iron must be brought to a whiter heat before a perfect welding could be accomplished. That so great a part of all this had even now been effected, is proof beyond peradventure that, in the two and a half years that had elapsed since Franklin had hesitantly suggested his tentative plan of union, there had come an enlargement of vision, an expansion of political horizons. And yet, before even this imperfect union of the states could become an accomplished fact, there must be more yielding one to another; there must be other surrenders of partial views and separate interests; there must be a still further enlargement of vision, a still greater expansion of horizons.

CHAPTER XIV

IN THE WILDERNESS
THE MANNA OF SARATOGA

Just when Congress was approaching the end of its long and arduous struggle to put the Articles of Confederation into acceptable form, it experienced one of its highest moments of triumphant joy, albeit in that same moment there was laid upon its table another problem that would sorely vex its spirit and tax its wisdom to the utmost. On the 16th of October, 1777, came news that the northern army, under General Gates, had won a victory over General Burgoyne; glorious news, if true, and Congress strained its ears for confirmation by circumstantial despatches. Four days the eager ears were listening, only by roundabout ways to learn that the whole British army under General Burgoyne had surrendered prisoners of war. Even so it was glorious news, glorious enough to set all the bells in York to ringing and to keep them ringing "for hours", and authentic enough for General Washington, who had earlier received the intelligence at his headquarters, to order thirteen cannon to be fired. But the measure of joy was not full. Not a line had yet come from the commander of the American forces, General Horatio Gates, and until that general's despatches, giving authentic and specific facts, should be received, exultation could but be held in leash. Another four days and members of Congress grew irritable, nervous. "We have had Rumours", John Adams wrote in one letter October 24, "which lifted us up to the Stars." In another the same day he grumbled, "We have been in a state of tormenting uncertainty concerning our affairs to the northward. . . . To this moment we have no express from Gates nor any authentic confirmation." Richard Henry Lee consoled himself with the reflection that Gates was *"slow* but *sure* moving". Three days more, and still no word from Gates—three days, growled John Adams, of "soaking and poaching in the heaviest rain that has been known for several years", but they were nothing to the gloom of soaking and poaching for ten days or more in intensified suspense. "We are out of patience", Adams burst forth. "It is impossible to bear this suspense with any temper." More equable tempers than that of John Adams had need of sweetening. It afforded some relief to learn, October 28, that Colonel James Wilkinson, deputy adjutant-general, was on the way with despatches from General Gates.

It was not, however, until October 31 that Congress had a sight of any of those despatches, and even then was compelled to content itself for the most part with a recital by Wilkinson, who begged for further time in which to "digest and arrange" the papers that he had brought to lay before Congress. This was on a Friday. By utilizing the intervening Saturday and Sunday, Wilkinson was enabled to accomplish the needful digesting and arranging of his papers and to write out a brief message from General Gates, which he had brought thither in his head only.

Congress did not, however, wait to read those despatches before resolving to call upon all the people to acknowledge with gratitude their obligation to the superintending providence of Almighty God "for benefits received, and to implore such farther blessings as they stand in need of", to give thanks that it had pleased Him "to smile upon us in the prosecution of a just and necessary war, for the defence and establishment of our unalienable rights and liberties; particularly in that he hath been pleased in so great a measure to prosper the means used for the support of our troops and to crown our arms with the most signal success". It was accordingly recommended that Thursday, December 18, be set apart as a day of thanksgiving and praise. The despatches having been read on November 3, on the 5th the newly elected President, Henry Laurens, wrote to General Gates: "the glorious Intelligence is now extending from City to City diffusing Joy in the heart of every Loyal American to the remotest State in the Union."

As for that long delay that had so irked the spirit of Congress, the loitering of the messenger with his precious despatches, the explanation of it was very simple. Young Colonel Wilkinson (he was only twenty at the time) had tarried by the way to conduct a siege of his own. Happily, the lady capitulated and the convention was duly consummated. Such at least was one story that gained circulation. Wilkinson ascribed the delay to his seizure by a "convulsive colic". May be so. In any event, Wilkinson received from Congress no rebuke for his loitering. On the contrary, because he had brought good news from Saratoga to York, and because his general had commended him to Congress with warm, even fulsome, praise, Congress rewarded him with a brevet of brigadier-general. It was nevertheless asserted in after years that Samuel Adams, with solemn countenance but with inner mirth, proposed that Congress express its appreciation of the merits of Colonel Wilkinson by presenting him with a pair of spurs.

Congress may seem to have smacked its lips over the Saratoga Convention as the most delectable dish that had been set before it since first it had launched upon that difficult and uncertain quest for independence; how shocking it was to come suddenly upon something very distasteful in that otherwise exceedingly palatable repast! For, when the articles of capitulation were carefully scanned, it was discovered that, although the Americans had been victorious in the contest of arms, a goodly part of that victory seemed to have been forfeited by the pen. It was stipulated, for instance, that Burgoyne's troops should march to Boston, whence they should be transported to England in British ships; and that they should not be again used in the American contest. Congress at once perceived, what Gates seems not to have realized, that there was nothing in the terms of surrender to prevent those troops taking the places, in England or elsewhere, of other British troops, who might in turn be employed in America. Realizing that these possible replacements might very well be on hand in time for the spring campaign, Congress began to scratch its collective head and to agitate its collective brain to see whether that very disturbing possibility might in some way be averted.

Congress might of course have taken the bull by the horns and have repudiated the Convention; in the course of the controversy that followed a good deal was said about the possibility that Great Britain might not ratify it; but for Congress to repudiate the Convention would have been to repudiate their general, who at that moment was perched on a high pedestal as the greatest hero the war had yet produced. To repudiate such a hero was unthinkable. But Congress could quibble, and quibble it did.

It ought not to be difficult to find minor infractions of the Conven
tion, real or apparent, and it suited the purpose admirably to discover
that probably not all the military accoutrements and colors had been
delivered up according to the stipulations; and to these might be added
other constructive infractions. For instance, Congress could demand a
minutely descriptive list of all the noncommissioned officers and privates of the surrendered army. It was when such a list was demanded
that Burgoyne gave to Congress just such a handle as it had been
seeking to fashion for itself. He uttered protests against it and made
difficulties about complying with the demand. An even more effective
contribution to the same end was made by General Howe when he
sought permission to embark the troops from some other port than
Boston. On several grounds that permission, in accordance with Washington's advice, Congress peremptorily refused to grant. Rightly or
wrongly, there was a suspicion that General Howe might utilize that
permission to incorporate the Convention troops into his own army

Finally, because of the unsatisfactory accommodations furnished his
officers in Boston, Burgoyne petulantly let out the accusation: "the
public faith is broke". Congress was quick to turn that accusation to
its own use. On the 27th of December, in committee of the whole,
Congress came to a resolution that the embarkation of General Burgoyne and his troops should be suspended "till a distinct and explicit
ratification of the convention shall be properly notified *to these States*
by the Court of Great Britain".

This resolution was, however, only a first tentative step in the course
that Congress was making up its mind to pursue, a course that was at
best devious. On the same day instructions went forth to General
Heath, the American commander at Boston, to determine by a meticulous investigation whether the transports for the troops were sufficiently provisioned (another good reason for delaying the embarkation
might develop thereby); and particularly to require a complete liquidation of all accounts, with payment of all amounts due, in gold or silver
according to a specified rate. These "essential Acts" General Heath
was to perform with all possible expedition, in anticipation of certain
resolutions that had not yet been given their finishing strokes; although

the general was not left in doubt respecting the essential purport of those resolutions.

Heath was, in fact, furnished a letter from President Laurens, written by direction of Congress and given only the date "January 1778", instructing him specifically to suspend the embarkation until further orders. If, when the necessary acts had in so far as possible been completed, Heath had not received the intended resolves, he was to disclose to General Burgoyne the contents of the letter, and thereupon peremptorily prohibit the embarkation until further directions. "You will understand", President Laurens wrote, "the motive for dating that Letter January 1778, and leaving a Blank for the day to be properly and carefully filled by yourself." Respecting the "essential acts" Laurens remarked: "These Acts which Congress judge indispensibly necessary to be performed before an embarkation can take place will employ some days and gain so much time without subjecting the Honour of the House or of its Constituents to any unfavourable imputation from the world." For those acts and resolutions were being prepared not only for Heath's further direction but "for public Information on both sides the Atlantic".

Then, and none the less thereafter, Congress strove mightily to give to its course of action a coating of righteousness, and doubtless it did in some measure succeed in accomplishing its own deception. A goodly quantum of the needful casuistry was furnished by the Rev. Dr. Witherspoon, whose speech on the question is the only one known to have been preserved. In the course of his speech Dr. Witherspoon found reason for citing the Roman example of the Caudine Forks; and, curiously enough, Burgoyne himself later made use of that same comparison, although by way of contrast, calling Parliament to witness that in his case he had saved a British army.

None, however, labored more zealously for the measure at the time, and afterward in behalf of a conviction that the action of Congress was "just and necessary", than did Henry Laurens. Indeed Laurens advanced the claim that he "had set or encouraged to be set in motion" the whole business. Just about the time, however, that the affair began to develop excessive heat, Laurens was sent to bed by a severe attack of the gout, and, in despair of being able to return to Congress speedily, on December 12 he besought Congress to relieve him of the presidency and choose a successor; because, he said, business was piling up upon his table faster than he was able to give proper despatch to it. Congress declined to accede to his request—an act, Laurens later declared, that "seemed and indeed was very kind and a little flattering"; accordingly he continued to carry on the official correspondence from his bed.

He mentions (December 30) "one particular Nights discipline", when he "kept the Pen in hand till one in the morning and resumed it again before five". In all this time, so he wrote his friend John Lewis Gervais, the "great affair" had been the subject of his "meditation and con-templation through several painful and Sleepless nights and Days". ("Believe me my dear friend I have been obliged to pause here a minute to wipe away a falling tear.") By the day after Christmas the steam in the Congressional boiler had reached the danger-point, and the ailing president was besought to return to his place, if it were anywise pos-sible, not so much as president, but as the only representative of his state.

This address to a State [he asserts] made an impression which would not have been felt, if it had been directed to the president . . . the summon ani-mated my Soul . . . "South Carolina shall not be quite unrepresented. I will be carried into Congress." I was *carried*—two whole days trenching deep upon each Night were passed in a Committee of the whole. late Satur-day Night the business was so far matured as to enable me to dispatch a special Messenger to General Heath at Boston. . . . the great business is not yet completed on our part. God only knows what will be the final end of it.

He had "laboured hard very hard", he declared, to advance the measure to its present state; and the labor of the next several days was probably just as arduous; for he must needs continue to be carried back and forth, and, even while he sat in the presidential chair, to have "both feet and Legs bound up in a blanket". He had no doubt that the act to which he had already put his signature would "be brought before the Tribunal of the whole Civilized World", but whatever the verdict of the world, he knew that "the Act is great and great good or evil will follow as its consequences". If his own countrymen should be of opinion with "a few in this House who appear to me to be timerous dunces", he would be very unhappy.

A similar strain runs through numerous subsequent letters. The act "must undergo the Criticism of all the Politicians of the Civilized World", he acknowledged in one letter, but, for his part, he would be happy "to have the approbation of those in our own Country". "The Justice and good Policy of the Act", he declared in another, "will be acknowledged by every disinterested Court in Europe." "Perhaps", he wrote to Baron de Kalb (February 11, 1778), "there is not an Instance in History of a General's having so completely betrayed himself the Dupe of his own policy. Mr. Burgoyne's duplicity will be quoted as a precedent by future Writers, while the resentment of Congress will be recorded as an example of sound policy."

Other members of Congress also, in their endeavors to bolster up the decision of Congress, had sent to Philadelphia for books on the law of nations—"Vattell, Puffendorf, Grotius"—and, whether or not their perusal of these authorities was done with all diligence, Congress did maintain that some of its conclusions at least were "sanctified by the judgment of the most distinguished writers on the law of nations", as well as by precedent.

And who were the "timerous dunces" who had not agreed with the majority upon the rectitude of the measure? The few records of yeas and nays do not quite reveal the degrees of timorousness, but they point quite definitely to four who stoutly resisted to the last, and to a fifth who appears to have yielded only at the last. The four were Francis Dana of Massachusetts, William Ellery of Rhode Island, Eliphalet Dyer of Connecticut, and John Harvie of Virginia; the fifth was Abraham Clark of New Jersey. Of these William Ellery alone has left otherwise an expression of his views.

I am suspicious [he wrote to Governor Cooke, January 14, 1778] that the enemy will consider the suspension of the embarkation of General Burgoyne and his troops as an infraction of the convention, attempt to rescue those troops, and at the same time pour their resentment on our State.

The "intended resolutions" were finished on January 8, 1778, and the essential item was of course the order that the embarkation be suspended "till a distinct and explicit ratification of the convention of Saratoga shall be properly notified by the Court of Great Britain to

Congress". This was, however, preceded by three other resolutions, one charging a failure to deliver all the military accoutrements as required, another respecting Burgoyne's refusal to furnish the descriptive lists demanded, and a third was focused upon Burgoyne's accusation of a breach of public faith. It was the latter that was made to serve as a springboard from which Congress took its grand leap. Such a charge, declared the resolution, was "not warranted by a just construction of any article of the convention"; moreover it was "a strong indication" of Burgoyne's intention and afforded "just ground of fear, that he will avail himself of such pretended breach of the convention in order to disengage himself, and the army under him, of the obligation they are under to these United States". The resolutions were transmitted to General Heath on January 14 and by him delivered to General Burgoyne on February 4, the letter having been given the date January 8 to accord with that of the resolutions. Thus was effectually prevented the embarkation of the "Convention Troops", as they came to be called, and presumably the dreaded substitution of other troops in their stead. Those same Convention Troops were nevertheless to give Congress several headaches before the termination of the war put an end to the whole unsavory episode.

Although by its resolution of January 8, Congress had prohibited General Burgoyne himself as well as his troops from embarkation until the Convention of Saratoga had been ratified by the Court of Great Britain, there followed an act of leniency, so far as the general himself was concerned. General Burgoyne had sent his aide, Captain Wilford, to Congress with two letters, the one a remonstrance against the suspension of the embarkation, the other a polite request that he, with certain officers of his family and their servants, be permitted to embark for England without further delay, one ground for this request being the state of his own health. The second letter was to be presented to Congress only after it had given its reply to the first; but Captain Wilford must have been made aware of what the purport of the answer to the first would be, therefore, without waiting, he presented the second letter, leaving Congress to deal with the two letters at once, as it deemed just.

To the first letter, so Henry Laurens wrote his son John (March 3), "we shall return a very laconic and decisive answer"; with regard to the second he thought good might be produced "from this Political condescension" and more particularly by acceding to Burgoyne's "appeal to humanity, or in the General's own term to our Generosity" The "very laconic and decisive answer" (March 2) to the first letter was that nothing in Burgoyne's letter and papers was "sufficient to induce Congress to recede from their resolves of the 8th day of January last, respecting the convention of Saratoga". The answer to the second (March 3) was a permission to General Burgoyne and his officers, with certain exceptions, to embark immediately, but to be put upon parole to return to America upon demand, in the event that the embarkation of the troops should be unexpectedly prolonged, and "re-deliver themselves into the power of Congress".

The surrender of General Burgoyne at Saratoga had other consequences besides that of the sorry squabble over the terms of the surrender. First of all, it lifted the country for a brief space out of the slough of despond; secondly, it led directly to the French alliance, the most important consequence of all; and, thirdly, one of its fruits was the enticement of a good many Americans, however well-intentioned, into one of the sorriest messes of the whole contest—so unsavory, in fact, that several worthy patriots had much trouble thereafter in ridding their political habiliments of a malodrous smell. This episode, known as the Conway Cabal, had for its main objective the displacement of Washington as commander-in-chief of the army.

The cabal against Washington did not have its beginning in the events of Saratoga, but those events did give a powerful impetus to all the contributory forces, open or secret, whose aim or tendency was to discredit Washington, elements of intrigue that had long been asquirm. mainly beneath the surface. To a superficial observer Washington had accomplished almost nothing but a long series of failures. Congress, had indeed learned, albeit imperfectly, during a year of tribulations, something of what was required to create an efficient army, and its provincial constituents were even more sadly behind in their lessons Washington had long pleaded for more effectual measures of enlistment, organization, and supply, and Congress had gone through the motions of partially and grudgingly complying, but the states had largely neglected or even declined to go through the motions. To the contrary, the commander was hampered at every stage by the very authorities that should have rendered him all possible aid. The underlying motive of all this disinclination and neglect was not merely the failure of understanding, there was everywhere a positive dread of creating an efficient army. That dread of a military dictatorship manifested itself very definitely when, in December, 1776, the whole cause was in such imminent danger of collapse, that Congress conferred upon Washington for a limited time almost dictatorial powers. It was done only as the lesser of two evils, and, on the part of many members, with feelings scarcely short of anguish.

This jealousy of the military power broke out in a pronounced form in the following February (1777), when Congress became involved in a debate lasting several days over the promotions of certain general officers. The question was essentially whether the promotions should be made on the recommendation of General Washington, and it stirred not only jealousy toward the commander-in-chief but all the old colonial jealousies of one another. Benjamin Rush, who was later to take a prominent hand in the cabal against Washington, although hiding behind anonymity, declared (February 19) that, if the motion should pass, he would immediately move "that all the civil power of the continent may be transferred from our hands into the hands of the army"; whilst John Adams spoke up to say:

I have been distressed to see some members of this house disposed to idolise an image which their own hands have molten. I speak here of the superstitious veneration that is sometimes paid to General Washington. Altho' I honour him for his good qualities, yet in this house I feel myself his Superior. In private life I shall always acknowledge that he is mine. It becomes us to attend early to the restraining our army.

A few days later (February 21) he remarked, "For my part I will vote upon the genuine principles of a republic for a new election of general officers annually." At the close of the discussion Thomas Burke wrote (February 24): "There appeared upon this whole debate a great desire in the Delegates of the Eastern States, and in one of New Jersey to Insult the General." The New Jersey member was Jonathan Dickinson Sergeant, from whose pen an especially bitter criticism of Washington will presently be mentioned.

The consequence of the situation, as it had developed in the autumn of 1777, was that, when hoped-for victories had not been won, a numerous group in and out of Congress were disposed to cast the blame for these failures on the commander-in-chief. This dissatisfaction began to come to a head when, in September, Washington lost Philadelphia to Howe, and Congress had perforce to scamper to safety and take refuge behind the Susquehanna River in the small town of York. The members of Congress had, in fact, barely settled down in their uncomfortable chairs in York when the sneering campaign got under way. It was inevitable that Washington's defeat at Germantown (October 4, 1777) should give rise to critical comment. In mid-October, President Laurens was pained to hear fall from the lips of one member of Congress after another, although in a casual gathering, caustic criticisms directed at the conduct of the army, all uttered in the confident assumption by the several speakers of their own superior military knowledge and skill.

It was at this precise moment, when the country was sunk in gloom, and when the commander-in-chief was the object of incessant sniping, that the Reverend Jacob Duché addressed to Washington the long letter already alluded to, seeking to persuade him that the American cause was lost and that therefore Congress should seek to make terms with Great Britain. The erstwhile spiritual counsellor of Congress had for the moment drawn down upon himself the fires of Congressional wrath, ridicule, and contempt, yet there was scarcely an abatement in the grumblings against the commander-in-chief. If some one thought to justify Washington's tactics by characterizing them as "Fabian", that arch-grumbler James Lovell retorted (he was writing to General Gates), "Our Affairs are Fabiused into a very disagreeable position", adding, more pointedly, that Washington had marched his soldiers hither and yon to no avail other than to wear out their shoes and breeches. He even went so far as to declare, "I have reason to think the battle of Germantown was the day of salvation offered by Heaven to us." What else could this mean but that Germantown would probably mark the downfall of the incompetent Washington, making way for the more capable Gates?

It was nearly at the same time that Lovell received a letter from Jonathan Dickinson Sergeant, a member of Congress but absent since early September (the letter is dated November 20, 1777), wherein Washington was denounced for his feebleness and for "such blunders as might have disgraced a soldier of three months' standing." It is perhaps not without significance that this letter now reposes among the papers of Samuel Adams, and that Adams took the utmost pains to obliterate the signature, all unmindful of the fact that Sergeant's handwriting sufficiently identifies the writer.

It was inevitable that some of these grumblings would come to the ears of General Washington. "I am informed", he wrote President Laurens (November 17), "that it is matter of amazement, and that reflections have been thrown out against this army, for not being more active and enterprising than, in the opinion of some, they ought to have been." If the charge is just, he said, the best answer is a comparison of the numbers of serviceable troops at his command with those under General Howe. What was more, great numbers of his own troops were practically without clothing. "The wonder will be", he concluded, "how they keep the field at all."

Indicative of the critical, even hostile, attitude of a majority of Con gress is a series of resolutions adopted December 10, 1777, in which Congress voices its "deep concern" that the principal supplies for the army since the loss of Philadelphia had been drawn from distant quar- ters at great expense, that the army had been but irregularly and scantily supplied, while at that very time large quantities of stock, provision, and forage remained in the neighboring counties, supplies that, by the fortune of war, might soon fall into the hands of the enemy Congress could only impute the general's forbearance in exercising the extraordinary powers vested in him by the resolutions of September 17 and November 14 "to a delicacy in exerting military authority on the citizens of these states; a delicacy, which though highly laudable in general, may, on critical exigencies, prove destructive to the army and prejudicial to the general liberties of America." It was therefore "the desire and expectation of Congress that General Washington should, for the future, endeavor as much as possible to subsist his army from such parts of the country as are in its vicinity", etc. Follow, then, specific orders to the commander-in-chief for commandeering, removing, or destroying such supplies. Chuckled James Lovell in a letter to Samuel Adams a few weeks later, "You could not expect more smartness in a Resolve which was meant to rap a Demi-G over the knuckles."

Reluctant as Congress had been to vest extraordinary powers in General Washington, that body was now making a show of impatience that he had forborne to use them. Moreover the orders to the commander-in-chief were not quite the whole of this particular proceeding As a companion measure, the legislature of Pennsylvania was earnestly recommended to enact a law requiring all persons within the state at a distance of seventy miles and upwards from Washington's headquarters to thresh out their grain promptly; "and, in case of failure, to subject the same to seizure by the commissaries and quarter masters of the American army, to be paid for at the price of straw only." There were to be, naturally, possible exemptions.

"Congress", so Washington wrote to President Laurens, December 15, 1777, "seem to have taken for granted a Fact, that is really not so." All the forage for the army, he went on to say, had been constantly drawn from the region specified, "insomuch that it was nearly exhausted and entirely so in the Country below our Camp". Similarly, all the supplies of flour had been obtained "that circumstances would admit of". "The Millers in most instances", he asserted, "were unwilling to grind, either from their disaffection or from motives of fear." A small quantity had been obtained by compulsion. Touching the question of "delicacy" in making use of his extraordinary powers, his remarks are exceedingly pertinent:

I confess I have felt myself greatly embarrassed with respect to a vigorous exercise of Military power. An Ill placed humanity perhaps and a reluctance to give distress may have restrained me too far. But these were not all. I have been well aware of the prevalent jealousy of military power, and that this has been considered an Evil much to be apprehended even by the best and most sensible among us. Under this idea, I have been cautious and wished to avoid as much as possible any Act that might improve it.

He then remarks that, "if the Civil Authority in the Several States thro' the recommendations of Congress, or their own mere will, seeing the necessity of supporting the Army, would always adopt the most spirited measures, suited to the end", he would be happy.

The people at large [he says in conclusion] are governed much by Custom. To Acts of Legislation or Civil Authority they have ever been taught to yield a willing obedience without reasoning about their propriety. On those of Military Power, whether immediate or derived from another Source, they have ever looked with a jealous and suspicious eye.

Not many days later (December 22, 23) Washington was calling the attention of Congress to an even more serious situation.

It is with infinite pain and concern [he wrote], that I transmit Congress the Inclosed Copies of Sundry Letters respecting the State of the Commissary's department. If these matters are not exaggerated . . . unless more Vigorous exertions and better regulations take place in that line, and immediately, this Army must dissolve.

One of his generals had written: "Three Days successively we have been destitute of Bread. Two Days we have been intirely without Meat. . . . The Men must be supplied, or they cannot be commanded." Others had revealed similar situations. He had done all in his power, General Washington declared, "by remonstrating, by writing to, by ordering the Commissaries on this Head, from time to time; but without any good effect, or obtaining more than a present scanty relief." The very next day there were "fresh, and more powerful reasons" for returning to the subject, and he added:

I am convinced, beyond a doubt that unless some great and capital change suddenly takes place in that line, this Army must inevitably be reduced to one or other of these three things. Starve, dissolve, or disperse, in order to obtain subsistence in the best manner they can; rest assured Sir this is not an exaggerated picture.

One thing that he had just learned from the only commissary in camp was that he had "not a single hoof of any kind to Slaughter, and not more than 25 Barls. of Flour"; neither did the commissary know whence to expect additional supplies. Another was that a mutiny because of the lack of food had only with difficulty been suppressed and that the danger was not at an end. Further, he learned that the enemy were foraging uncomfortably near his encampment. All that he could do under the circumstances was to send out small detachments to harrass the enemy and other parties to collect what provisions they could find. This condition of things led him to the conclusion either "that the present Commissaries are by no means equal to the execution [of the office] or that the disaffection of the People is past all belief".

That there was an abundance of disaffection among the people round about him he was soon to learn, as he was also to learn that in any event they preferred to sell their provisions for British gold than for depreciated Continental money. Concerning the inefficiency of the commissariat he was ready right now to speak out boldly, for he went on to say:

I have been tender heretofore of giving any opinion, or lodging complaints, as the change in that departm[en]t took place contrary to my judgment, and the consequences thereof were predicted; yet, finding that the inactivity of the Army, whether for want of provisions, Cloaths, or other essentials, is charged to my Acct., not only by the common vulgar, but those in power, it is time to speak plain in exculpation of myself; with truth then I can declare that, no Man, in my opinion, ever had his measures more impeded than I have, by every department of the Army. Since the Month of July, we have had no assistance from the Quarter Master Genl. and to want of assistance from this department the Commissary Genl. charges great part of his deficiency.

This was indeed plain language and strong to be thrown into the teeth of Congress; for the quartermaster-general pointed at with the finger of accusation was none other than General Thomas Mifflin, at that moment thought by many to be deeply engaged in the plot to supplant Washington.

Moreover, with equal severity Washington was condemning a pet measure of Congress. There were, in fact, two measures governing the supply business, one regulating the department of quartermaster-general (adopted May 14, 1777), the other regulating the department of commissary-general (adopted June 10), and taken together they constitute perhaps the most complicated piece of legislation that ever came from the mill of the Continental Congress, which has a good many extraordinary legislative concoctions to its credit—or debit. The regulations of the commissary department run to approximately seven thousand words and to such minutiae of detail that, if regulations could have furnished supplies, the army storehouses should have been bursting with a superabundance.

Heaven knows there was abundant reason why the officers of the commissariat should be compassed round about with every proper safeguard against maladministration; but this measure proved to be beyond the power of mortal man effectively to administer. It may suffice to point to one of the requirements:

That every Creature purchased for the Use of the Army shall immediately thereafter be branded with the initial Letters of the purchasing Commissary's Name and the first Creature purchased by such Commissary shall be branded on the Horns with the Figure 1, the second with the Figure 2 and so on.

One of the difficulties, although not the sole one by any means, was that hogs have no horns. Does any one doubt that there was a sequel? It is solemnly recorded in the Journals of Congress, under the date of October 4, 1777, and should be duly set down to the credit of that body, and most appropriately as an item under the denomination of sackcloth and ashes.

And whereas it is represented that it will be exceedingly difficult to comply with the regulations of Congress, for branding and numbering cattle on the horns [Congress carefully avoided any mention of hogs]:

Resolved, That the purchasers of live stock be respectively directed to adopt such other modes for marking the same as they shall judge expedient, and to transmit to Congress, by the earliest opportunity, the regulations for that purpose by them adopted.

This, to be sure, was a good beginning, but the cup of repentance was not yet full, and it would require some months of disastrous experience before it would run over. In the beginning of the following February, Elbridge Gerry stated that in all these months the commissary-general of purchases (William Buchanan) had afforded but little assistance and that little could indeed be expected of him, since he had been prevented from appointing his deputies. "But you well know [he was writing to Samuel Adams] from whence this Part of the Plan originated, and for what purpose it has been obstinately supported. Its advocates have finally given it up, after distressing the Army, Congress, and the Continent with it for six or eight Months."

About the middle of December, Washington had drawn his army into Valley Forge, where, as it was subsequently determined, it would go into cantonment for the winter. The movement of the army away from Philadelphia and the probability that the general would not undertake a winter campaign but would stand on the defensive, gave some uneasiness to New Jersey and Pennsylvania, and the council and assembly of the latter state sent a remonstrance to Congress against the cantonment. This remonstrance was presented to Congress on December 17, 1777. The preceding day a committee, appointed November 28 to consult with General Washington upon "the best and most practicable means for carrying on a winter's campaign with vigour and success", had made its report.

The committee had held a conference with the general at Whitemarsh, had taken the opinions of the commander-in-chief and the general officers, had carefully examined into the situation, and had come to the definite conclusion that an attack upon the enemy at that time was "an enterprise too dangerous, and not to be hazarded but in case of absolute necessity"; that an attempt to recover Philadelphia, so much desired by Congress, was for like reasons fraught with danger; that because of the impossibility of obtaining during the winter sufficient reinforcements and the want of clothing and blankets among the soldiers, as well as for a number of other reasons, it was inadvisable to undertake a winter's campaign. It was therefore the committee's counsel that the army take up a post where it could obtain the requisite supplies and keep watch on the enemy. That report was merely ordered to lie on the table, although some recommendations, offered in a letter to General Washington, were afterward (January 5, 1778) taken into consideration by Congress.

While Congress appears to have given little heed to the committee's report of December 16, it did, however, give heed to the Pennsylvania remonstrance of December 17 and proceeded to ask General Washington pointedly whether he had come to a fixed resolution to canton the army, and, if so, what measures he was taking for the protection of New Jersey and of Pennsylvania east of the Schuylkill, informing him at the same time that, in the opinion of Congress, "the State of New Jersey demands, in a peculiar degree, the protection of the armies of the United States", that "the struggles which have been made by the brave and virtuous inhabitants of that State, in defence of the common cause, cannot fail of exposing them to the particular resentment of a merciless enemy".

"We find Gentlemen", wrote Washington in response (December 23), "without knowing whether the Army was really going into Winter Quarters or not (for I am sure no resolution of mine would warrant the remonstrance) reprobating the measure as much as if they thought men [the Soldiery] were made of Stocks or Stones and equally insensible of frost and Snow." Those very gentlemen, he said, were very well apprized from ocular demonstration of the nakedness of the troops.

I can assure those Gentlemen [he continued] that it is a much easier and less distressing thing to draw remonstrances in a comfortable room by a good fire side than to occupy a cold bleak hill and sleep under frost and Snow without Cloaths or Blankets; however, although they seem to have little feeling for the naked, and distressed Soldier, I feel superabundantly for them, and from my soul pity those miseries, wch. it is neither in my power to relieve or prevent . . . and it adds not a little to my other difficulties, and distress, to find that much more is expected of me than is possible to be performed, and that upon the ground of safety and policy, I am obliged to conceal the true State of the Army from Public view and thereby expose myself to detraction and Calumny.

It is gratifying to find one of the Pennsylvania delegates, Daniel Roberdeau, as soon as he heard Washington's letter read in Congress, writing to the President of the Pennsylvania Council (December 26):

This is no time for recrimination, otherwise I could trace our present distress to other sources, and indeed Genl Washington speaks out for the first time and charges the principle difficiency viz., in the Commissary's department, to the arrangement made by Congress. I foresaw the Consiquences and withstood the measure, but in vain.

Three days later, anticipating that a committee of Congress would recommend that "the most vigorous measures" (meaning the commandeering of supplies) be taken *"immediately"*, Roberdeau wrote: "My situation is extremely delicate on this occasion; the ruin of our Army, or the interference with the police of the State, I apprehend will be the alternative set before me."

A committee, consisting of the board of war and three members of Congress, was, in fact, on that same day (December 29) "fully empowered to take the necessary measures for supplying the army with provisions and other necessaries"; while on the following day Congress resolved that certain extraordinary powers previously vested in General Washington for limited periods be extended until the 10th of April, and also directed that one month's extraordinary pay be given to the soldiers in recognition of "their soldierly patience, fidelity and zeal, in the cause of their country". Further, Congress assured the soldiers that they "are exerting themselves to remedy the inconveniences which the army have lately experienced from the defects of the commissary and clothier's departments."

In consequence of measures taken by the committee the immediate wants of the army were relieved, but General Washington warned Congress (January 5, 1778) that "the small seizures made . . . in consequence of the most pressing and absolute necessity, when that or to dissolve was the alternative", had "excited the greatest alarm and uneasiness even among our best and warmest friends", and that coercive measures must not be repeated, as they would inevitably spread disaffection and fear among the people as well as "raise in the soldiery a disposition to licentiousness, to plunder and robbery". What must be done was to take measures "for removing the difficulties and failures in the Commissary line".

At nearly the same time (January 3, 1778), in a circular letter to the states, President Laurens took occasion to remark:

The house have been for many days past laboriously engaged not only in matters of the very highest importance within their proper sphere, but also obliged from some unaccountable deficiency in the several departments of Quarter Master General, Clothier General and Commissary General to interfere immediately and personally in the procuring of Wagons, Clothing, Meat, and Flour for the Army, which otherwise from all appearance and from the Representation of the General, would have been dispersed.

The allusion in the first clause of this extract was to the problem raised by the Saratoga Convention. Congress had been for some time and still was desperately trying to save its Saratoga victory, its Saratoga hero, and its own face all at one stroke. In the sequel the victory was saved, the hero was preserved (for the time being at least), but the Congressional face was not as satisfactorily salvaged as was at the moment assumed.

CHAPTER XV

CONFUSION OF TONGUES
DISCONTENT, INTRIGUE

The extraordinary political disturbance that revolved about General Washington in the winter of 1777-1778 has been variously called an intrigue, a conspiracy, a cabal. All those terms, with others akin to them, were used by contemporaries to designate the thing they had observed, and the names then bestowed have come down to our day by a legitimate line of transmission. It may be that no one of those names precisely connotes the character of the thing so named, but, as best we are able from surviving fragments to reconstruct it, it had in it elements of all three—intrigue, conspiracy, cabal. Looked at from this distance of time, however, and with a due regard for the niceties of language, the term intrigue seems most aptly to fit its predominant character.

That some sort of intrigue involving General Washington was a-brew is substantiated by too much evidence, is testified to by too great a cloud of witnesses, to be whiffed away as the baseless fabric of a distorted vision. A mere huff and a puff can not blow the house down. There may be, there have been, doubts respecting the aims and purposes of those who planned and plotted, for they pursued darkly clandestine ways, as in the nature of the case they would do, and the secret springs and obscure ways have never since been wholly revealed. There may not have been, there probably was not, amongst the participants of whatever degree of activity, a complete unity of purpose; yet it is clear enough that they had in common one animating impulse—distrust in the competency of General Washington as commander of the army.

A good many people were involved in the affair in one way or another, and some of them have left ineradicable trails. Most of the latter, as well as others toward whom suspicion was directed at the time, denied then having any part in the plot and persisted in the denial thereafter. But, whatever the individual or collective purpose, had a new commander been placed at the head of the army, can there be any doubt that many of these same protesters of innocence would have put forth vociferous claims to a share in promoting the new order? The character and degree of participation no doubt varied with the individual. Henry Laurens aptly characterized the participants as "prompters and actors, accommodators, Candle snuffers, Shifters of scenes and mutes".

In truth, there is nothing extraordinary about such plotting. Every great crisis in world events, as well as many a lesser crisis, has had its quota of intrigues and conspiracies; every great figure in history has been the center of plot and counterplot. It would have been nothing short of a marvel if Washington had escaped. Any failure to accomplish as much as was expected of him would have been an incitement to the disappointed, any successful accomplishment of more than was desired would have been a signal for the disgruntled. Be the error one of too little or too much, the error must if possible be retrieved, the erring must in any event be punished. Came a time when many people were convinced that Washington had egregiously failed; straightway into minds thus prepared came the conviction that Gates had achieved a great success. In such a conjunction, what could be more natural than the desire to displace Washington with Gates?

If it may seem to some that the so-called cabal was but a minor incident in the contest for American independence, it should be borne in mind that the voyage of the ship of state is not all full speed ahead. The ship's log will record many vicissitudes, among them storms, breakers, and adverse winds. The cabal, though perhaps never threatening the destruction of the ship, did for the period of its duration seriously retard its progress.

Because for a time the opposition to Washington mainly centered about Thomas Conway, an Irishman long in the service of France, who had come to America to try his military fortunes, as so many real Frenchmen were doing, the affair came to be known as the Conway Cabal. At many of the French volunteers Congress gagged quite vigorously; Conway, on the other hand, appears to have captured the confidence and esteem of at least a numerous group in Congress and was, with little delay, made a brigadier general (May 13, 1777). As such Conway proved himself a capable officer, but his promotion over the heads of American officers created among them much dissatisfaction, as it was likewise displeasing to Washington himself. After his manner, Washington made the best of the situation with such patience as was possible; but, when word came to him that Congress contemplated making Conway a major general, that was too heavy a tax on his patience and he protested, not directly to Congress, but in a private letter to Richard Henry Lee (October 17).

By this time, however, Gates was becoming the real focus of the movement, and, when the victory of Saratoga made him the great and shining light amongst the military figures, all the eager eyes were naturally turned toward him. It happened that Congress had recently undertaken one of its much-needed executive reforms, namely, the creation of a board of war to be composed of others than members of Congress. Sadly needed as was a better organization of the department of war, the reform was bound to involve an important question: would it be so constituted as to aid the commander-in-chief or to thwart him? Such a board would properly have a measure of supervisory powers over the operations of the army, and the critics of Washington quickly perceived that it could be shaped admirably to fit their purposes. It was only necessary to fill it with the proper men.

The measure establishing the new board of war, which was to consist of three non-members of Congress, was adopted October 17, but it was not until November 6 that the men were chosen, namely, General Thomas Mifflin, who only a few days before had resigned his office of quartermaster general, Colonel Timothy Pickering, and Colonel Robert H. Harrison. Harrison presently declined, whereupon (November 27) three additional members were chosen, General Gates, Joseph Trumbull, and Richard Peters. Gates was designated by Congress as president of the board, while Peters, who had served as secretary of the old board, became secretary of the new. Joseph Trumbull, on account of failing health, did not take his seat, and in April, 1778, resigned. With Gates and Mifflin definitely hostile to Washington, and Pickering at best lukewarm, the board was heavily weighted against the commander-in-chief. Peters, who professed to love Washington "to a degree of Adoration", had nevertheless to defend himself against charges of being inimical to the general.

Ten days prior to the final constitution of the board, but in definite anticipation of that precise consummation, Lovell had written to Gates (November 17): "Prepare yourself for a jaunt to this place. Congress send for you. I have ten thousand things to tell." Then, immediately upon Gates's election, Lovell seized his pen and wrote (November 27): "This present Carryer will perhaps throw you into a dilemma. We want you in different places, but most of all in a third which you are not called to ballance about. We want you most near Germantown." The significance of the last expression would seem to be clear enough. Gates was wanted to supplant Washington.

Lovell probably did not yet know that, while this scene was enacted in or about Congress, another scene was unfolding outside those precincts that was destined to bring the whole architectural jumble of the conspirators down upon their heads. For Conway had stumbled, Gates had tripped over Conway, and between the two in their efforts to regain their feet, they knocked down the pillars of the flimsy structure. It began with a letter from Conway to Gates, containing severe strictures on Washington. So long as that letter was known only to Gates and his intimate friends, its chief effect was probably nothing more than the swelling of Gates's egotism. But one particularly juicy expression in the letter got abroad, although in somewhat garbled form. It appears that James Wilkinson, tongue loosened and mind befuddled by liquor, blabbed it to one Major McWilliams, McWilliams blabbed it to Lord Sterling, and my Lord, being a warm and devoted friend to Washington, went straight with it to the commander-in-chief.

Hitherto Washington had refrained from opening his mouth concerning the plot, which he knew was all about him; but now was the time and the opportunity to unmask the plotters. All he did at the moment was to address to General Conway the following crisp letter, dated November 9, 1777:

Sir,

A letter, which I received last Night, contain the following paragraph. In a Letter from Genl. Conway to Genl. Gates he says: "Heaven has been determined to save your Country; or a weak General and bad Counsellors would have ruined it."

I am Sir Yr. Hble Servt.

This bombshell, exploding in the camp of the conspirators, set them scampering to cover. There were denials that such a letter had ever been written, or at least had contained any such expression; there were accusations and counter accusations, charges and counter charges, and, before the affair was entirely at an end, a near-duel between General Gates and his former aide-de-camp, now Brigadier General Wilkinson, and an actual duel between General Conway and General John Cadwalader, in which Conway was all but mortally wounded.

It is not, however, for this chronicle to pursue the meanderings and the maneuvers of the affair on the outskirts of the Congressional domain. It needs only to be noted that General Gates, after resorting to numerous subterfuges and much devious squirming to clear himself, demanded of General Washington to know who had been treacherously snooping among his private papers professing to have found there the obnoxious statement of General Conway, and was calmly informed by Washington that the revelation had come from none other than his own aide and intimate, General Wilkinson. Gates thereupon turned furiously upon Wilkinson, who had meanwhile been made secretary of the board of war of which Gates was president, and denounced him with such blistering language that Wilkinson challenged his old general to meet him on the field (or back alley) of honor. Gates must have missed his calling in not becoming an actor, for there, with the tears and the tenderness of a fond father for a wayward son, he disarmed his irate antagonist and sent him away completely reconciled. That is, until Washington subsequently took occasion to show him the entire correspondence; whereupon Wilkinson could only exclaim upon such "a scene of perfidy and duplicity". The time was to come, however, when he would obtain to the full, so he afterward professed, the satisfaction denied him on the field of honor. That was when, at Camden in 1780, Heaven precipitated Gates "from the pinacle of undeserved fame to the abyss of humiliation". Of course it is not to be overlooked that some part of this story rests upon the after testimony of Wilkinson himself, whose subsequent career does not establish him as the most credible of witnesses.

If the backfire started by Washington could have been confined to the military fringes, it might soon have burnt itself out; but the new heats generated by Washington's letter to Conway were bound to communicate themselves to the already simmering Congressional pot and to set it fiercely to seething. Something of the course of the intrigue, its intensity, its dangerous proportions, its manifold ramifications, its baneful, often paralyzing effects on every part of the body politic, may be gained from the letters of Henry Laurens in the early weeks of 1778. Writing to his son John Laurens, aide-de-camp to Washington, January 8 (this was the same day on which Congress had taken its definite action on the Convention of Saratoga), he poured out his bitter lamentation:

Our whole frame is shattered; we are tottering, and without the immediate exertion of wisdom and fortitude we must fall flat down. among the Causes of this melancholy state are to be found some Men in whom your friend [Washington] reposed an implicit confidence. I do not mean in the Army. . . . We must include Characters of whome your friend entertains the most favorable sentiments. these taken together for a Club whose demands upon the Treasury and the War Office never go away ungratified. Candour obliges me to say that some of them respect your friend, and I am persuaded would not wittingly be concerned in a plot against him, but they "want the honour to defend". in all such junctoes, there are prompters and Actors, accommodators, Candle snuffers, Shifters of scenes and Mutes.

Laurens's allusions to persons is cryptic; no names are mentioned, and not all of them can be identified. There was, for instance, that mysterious person whose "fawning mild address and obsequiousness, procured him toleration from great Men on both sides, a sort of favoritism from some; his Idleness, duplicity and criminal partialities in a certain Circle laid the foundations of our present deplorable State." "I am not quite sure of the fact", Laurens wrote his son, "but I believe you have hit the pivot upon which the late mischiefs have turned." From John Laurens's letter it appears evident that the "pivot" was General Mifflin; and there are several evidences pointing to Mifflin as the person cryptically referred to above.

It was almost at the same time that Dr. James Craik wrote to Washington: "Base and villainous men, through chagrin, envy, or ambition, are endeavouring to lessen you in the minds of the people, and taking underhand methods to traduce your character." He had been informed that a strong faction was forming against Washington in the new board of war and in Congress, and "that some of the eastern and southern members were at the bottom of it, particularly one, who had been said to be your enemy before, but denied it, Richard Henry Lee". He added that General Mifflin of the board of war was said to be a very active person in the plot.

This was neither the first nor the last charge that Richard Henry Lee was concerned in the plot. Lafayette, for one, definitely placed the plot, so far as Congress was concerned, at the doors of Lee and the Adamses. Whether or not Lee was taking an active part in the intrigue, the mere fact that he was on the most intimate terms with Mifflin, Gates, Lovell, and others of the central figures, to say nothing of the Adamses, would be sufficient ground in many minds for tarring him with the same brush. All the participants, however, whether of greater or lesser degree, ultimately denied most vociferously any participation in the plot. Even James Lovell, when Washington had become President and had offices to bestow, professed an unbroken loyalty to the commander-in-chief. He could not, we may be sure, have forgotten the letters he had written to Gates and others, but he evidently had confidence in the security of their hiding.

There was, naturally, an immense eagerness among the members of Congress to fasten their eyes on that notorious letter of Conway, from which Washington had quoted a single sentence. Conway himself had furnished President Laurens with a "translation" of the letter, "but in much softer language", Laurens asserted, than the quotation that was being bandied about. Conway even denied the existence of such a sentence as Washington had quoted, and averred that he had spoken of General Washington "in terms of respect". "However", Laurens adds, "there was *something* in the manner of his representation, which raised doubts in my mind."

Soon Conway himself was showing the letter to a select group in Congress, and through one of these Laurens was permitted a sight of it. "I have seen the letter", he wrote (January 26, 1778) to Isaac Motte down in South Carolina, "(in the hands of one of your *good sort of Men* who shews it only to proper persons. I gained a perusal by intreaty) . . . it is true Genl. Washington was misinformed, the letter does not contain the words which had been reported to him, but ten times worse in every view." Anxious that "the poison" should not be disseminated, for he was bending every effort to bring about at least a semblance of peace in Congress, he refrained from saying anything of the contents, but he did make one brief extract and pass it over to Colonel John Fitzgerald, who in turn passed it on to Washington. If that extract was the actual germ of the sentence as quoted by Washington, somewhere along the line of transmission was an unusual ability for effective expression; for that extract was: "What a pity there is but one Gates! But the more I see of this army the less I think it fit for general action under its actual chiefs and actual discipline. I speak to you sincerely and freely, and wish I could serve under you."

On the day preceding that on which Laurens was privileged to scan the letter that had so long been stirring both Congress and camp with the most avid curiosity, another document of mysterious origin though by no means of mysterious purpose was placed in his hands. In a brief letter to Washington, January 27, he relates the story of the document thus:

While I was sitting in Congress yesterday a Member came in and delivered me the inclosed paper just in its present State except the broken Seals. the Gentleman's declaration as he was putting the thing into my hand, that he had picked it up on the Stairs, was a sufficient alarm. I passed my Eye cursorily over the pages, put them into my pocket and intimated to the House that it was an anonymous production containing stuff which I must be content with, as perquisites of Office, that the hearth was the proper depository for such Records.

This anonymous document, nearly a thousand words in length, bore the title "Thoughts of a Freeman" and the date January 17. Its contents were a sort of summary of the principal criticisms against the conduct of military affairs, on which the opposition to Washington was based. Instead of concealing it from Congress, Washington counseled the opposite course.

As I have no other view than to promote the public good [he wrote Laurens, January 31], and am unambitious of honours not founded in the approbation of my Country, I would not desire in the least degree to suppress a free spirit of enquiry into any part of my conduct that even faction itself may deem reprehensible. The anonymous paper handed you exhibits many serious charges, and it is my wish that it should be submitted to Congress; this I am the more inclined to, as the suppression, or concealment, may possibly involve you in embarrassments hereafter; since it is uncertain how many, or who may be privy to the contents.

His enemies, he went on to say, took "an ungenrous advantage" of him. They knew that he could not combat their insinuations "without disclosing secrets, which it is of the utmost moment to conceal". Then he offered some reflections on the matter that deserve to be repeated:

But why should I expect to be exempt from censure; the unfailing lot of an elevated station? Merit and talents, with which I can have no pretensions of rivalship, have ever been subject to it. My Heart tells me it has been my unremitted aim to do the best circumstances would permit; yet, I may have been very often mistaken in my judgment of the means, and may in many instances, deserve the imputation of error.

It does not appear that Laurens ever followed Washington's counsel to lay the document before Congress; neither has its author ever been identified.

Another anonymous screed put forth about the same time and far more caustic in its criticisms of the commander-in-chief was not so successful in preserving its anonymity. It was a letter addressed to Patrick Henry, was dated January 12, 1778, was written from "Yorktown", where Congress was then sitting, and might therefore have come from within that assembly. The opening note was a deprecation of "idolatrous attachment", and without definitely pointing out the idol, left no doubt of its identity. The body of the letter was chiefly a bewailing of the inefficiencies and the failures of the main army. Said the anonymous writer:

We have only passed the Red Sea. A dreary wilderness is still before us; and unless a Moses or a Joshua are raised up in our behalf, we must perish before we reach the promised land. . . . We have wisdom, virtue, and strength enough to save us, if they could be called into action. The northern army has shown us what Americans are capable of doing, with a General at their head. The spirit of the southern army is no way inferior to the spirit of the northern. A Gates, a Lee, or a Conway, would in few weeks render them an irresistible body of men.

The writer identifies himself only as "one of your Philadelphia friends", but begs Henry, if he should recognize the handwriting, to burn the letter. He had evidently, however, mistaken the character of Patrick Henry. That worthy patriot did not recognize the handwriting, but did not burn the letter. Instead he sent it, with appropriate remarks to Washington, who appears to have had little difficulty in determining its authorship. "From a similitude of hands" Washington was convinced that the writer was Dr. Benjamin Rush, formerly a member of Congress and one of the signers of the Declaration of Independence, but at this time chief of the hospital service in Washington's army.

This man [Washington wrote to Governor Henry, March 28] has been elaborate, and studied in his professions of regard for me; and long since the Letter to you. My caution to avoid any thing, that could injure the service, prevented me from communicating, but to a very few of my friends, the intrigues of a faction, which I know was formed against me, since it might serve to publish our internal dissensions . . . but I have good reason to believe, that their machinations have recoiled most sensibly upon themselves.

Indeed by this time the recoil was an actuality; for it was now the end of March, and the plotters were casting about for ways of disentangling themselves. There would be a few more reverberations, a few more echoes of the affair, at least one more effort on the part of the faction in Congress to fling slurs at Washington; but the cabal was about to slink back into the darkness whence it had come.

Meanwhile, through that worrisome winter, the intrigue left other trails in Congress. In his letter to Congress, December 23, 1777, to which reference has already been made, Washington suggested that two or three members of the board of war, or a committee of Congress, should repair immediately to camp, where, in consultation with the commander-in-chief or a committee of his appointment, they should "prepare and digest the most perfect plan that can be devised, for correcting all abuses and making new arrangements". On December 31 the question of sending a committee to camp was taken into consideration, while

it was at once resolved, "That it is expedient to promote a speedy reformation in the army, as well for the purpose of discipline as oeconomy." There was, in fact, one reform that Congress was right then
ready to begin upon, for it had been discovered that the number of
officers was "out of all proportion to that of the privates"; accordingly
it was recommended to the several states to suspend filling up vacancies
in their regiments, "until they shall hear further from Congress on the
subject". The states might be slow in recruiting their quotas of privates,
but trust them to find plenty of officers.

On the 10th of January, 1778, Congress had resolved to send to Washington's headquarters a committee to be composed partly of members
of its own body but to include also the principal members of the new
board of war—Gates, Mifflin, and Pickering; and at the same time laid
down the lines of a program of reform. It was on the afternoon of the
19th that General Gates arrived at York, where he was received "with
demonstrations of joy", to take up his new duties as president of the
board of war. The very next day Congress was informed by the board
that General Gates "offered such strong reasons for his not going to
camp" as induced them to request that he be excused. Whatever may
have been the strong reasons assigned by Gates, certainly Washington's
exposure of the notorious Conway letter was sufficient to induce him to
shun Washington's headquarters.

As similar reasons applied to Mifflin and Pickering, they too were
excused from attendance at camp, ordered to take their places on the
board, and two other members of Congress were added to the committee of conference. The members of Congress previously chosen were
Francis Dana of Massachusetts, Joseph Reed of Pennsylvania, Nathaniel Folsom of New Hampshire, and John Harvie of Virginia. The
two new members now added were Charles Carroll of Carrollton of
Maryland and Gouverneur Morris of New York. On January 22,
James Lovell confided to Samuel Adams:

I think I have told you that the Members of the new board of war who
were to go to camp are found *necessary* here, which is the reason others
have been chosen in their stead—Mr. Carryl and Govr. Morris—but I left
out ostensible before reason. It is best as it will now be managed. The tale
is too long or I would tell you the why and the wherefore.

Of the proceedings of the committee sent to headquarters, some account will presently be given. Meanwhile it is necessary to observe the vicissitudes of a favorite project of the new board of war. On January 22 the board laid before Congress a proposition,

that an irruption be made into Canada, and that the Board of War be authorized to take every necessary measure for the execution of the business, under such general officers as Congress shall appoint, and apply for such sums of money as may be thought by them proper and requisite for the expedition.

In this resolution is more than meets the eye. Indeed what does not meet the eye was a greater motivating force than that which doth appear. There is no mention whatever of the commander-in-chief. An irruption into Canada, if only it could succeed, would appeal mightily to Congress; but an irruption into the military domain of which General Washington was as yet the head was probably an important element in the inspiration of the promoters. President Laurens went straight from Congress to his own desk that afternoon to make a brief addition to a letter he had written to Lafayette that morning:

P.M. Just returned from Congress, where a Report was made from the Board of War making out a separate Command for Major General Marquis delafayette. this will undergo debate this evening and probably you will very soon receive minute information from the Board of War or from the President of Congress.

The board of war had evidently offered its nominations of general officers for the expedition, along with its proposition, but the election was postponed until the next day, when the ballots showed that "major general the Marquis de la Fayette, Major General Conway, and Brigadier General Stark were elected". The ballots were actually 6 for Lafayette, 6 for Conway, 8 for Stark, and one each for McDougall and Glover. Laurens appears even thus early to have sensed trouble ahead and pretty soon his suspicions were deepened. Letters began to come to him from Lafayette protesting against having Conway as second in command, and speaking his preference for General McDougall; while

Gouverneur Morris, one of the committee at camp, with whom Lafayette had incautiously discussed the matter, wrote to President Laurens (January 26),

It deserves the Consideration of Congress whether in case an Accident should happen to the Commander in Chief it would be prudent to trust a Person whose object it is to push his Fortunes in France with an opportunity to imbue the Minds of the Canadians with a Love of the Grand Monarque who may as probably like Canada as any of his Predecessors.

On January 28 Laurens wrote to Lafayette:

I took the liberty of intimating that it would be decent if not necessary to consult your Excellency upon the Question of who should be your Second, but the thing had been not only preconcerted but apparently predetermined. indeed by some contrivance I was deprived of the honour, and the means of doing my Duty, of informing you Officially of the appointments.

Laurens had certainly by this time had his eyes opened. In fact it now began to appear to him that the irruption into Canada, with Lafayette in command, might actually depend on whether Lafayette would "condescend to accept Mr. Conway for his second", despite the fact that Lafayette continued to express his "utmost abhorrence" of Conway and to urge the appointment of either Kalb or McDougall.

Conway meanwhile, knowing of Lafayette's opposition, zealously hastened, with the help of the board of war, to get started on the expedition. That also, asserted Laurens, was "according to the plan of his friends", to "make a shew of his activity in having commenced the enterprise." The board of war facilitated his departure by obtaining an order that bills of exchange to the amount of thirty thousand French livres, drawn on the commissioners of the United States in France, be furnished to the Marquis de Lafayette, *or* the general officer commanding the expedition. "These", Laurens wrote his son John (January 28), "are facts which you and I may think of, but I have neither time nor inclination to paraphrase, which I would do and boldly too if I were on the floor."

Lafayette now hastened to York to press his own demands, and during four or five days, if we may accept his own account of the matter, appears to have made the atmosphere fairly sizzle about Congress and the board of war. In the evening of January 31 ("At half past nine") he wrote Laurens a hurried note:

I am coming from that board. I spoke to them with a great frankness and finished by telling them if they don't give me mgdougall or Kalb, and the french officers appointed according to my ideas I decline the appointment and will go to france with most all the french officers in the Army. I am sorry my dear sir, to think that two or three rascals oblige me to make out such a conditions and take such steps, tho Lee was I believe for me, duer quite against, the secretary charmed with that dispute, and the old fellow scratching his wigg—I think they'l beg Congress to meet tomorrow tho' it is Sunday—then my proposition and my leave in case of refusal will be layd down in the worst light possible.

The board of war as it was then functioning was a conglomerate of the old board and the new. Of the new board, Gates (the president) and Richard Peters (the secretary) were alone in attendance. Members of the old board (that is, members of Congress) in attendance appear to have been Francis Lightfoot Lee and William Duer. It was Secretary Richard Peters who was so "charmed" with the dispute. A few days after this (February 3) Peters took occasion to remark:

For my part I wish myself anywhere but in this disagreeable Scene. . . . Unless great Alterations take Place the first and most capital of which is Restoration of the personal Harmony, I don't expect much from an arrangement of this Department in which I confess, leaving myself out of the Question, I promised great Advantages to the Cause.

One dramatic episode of Lafayette's visit to York was his entertainment at a banquet given by General Gates, where he was wined and toasted as the coming conqueror of Canada. When it came his turn, he reminded the banqueters that one toast, the most important of all, had thus far been omitted; and he proposed the commander-in-chief. This was an unlooked for shock. The commander-in-chief was of all men the one who, according to the carefully laid plans, was to have least to say or do in the business. If Lafayette had not already laid down his ultimatum to the board of war, it was now abundantly clear what one part of that ultimatum would be.

Congress was not called together on Sunday, as Lafayette had expected, but on Monday, February 2, the board of war made a report essentially in accordance with Lafayette's ultimatum. The full extent of that ultimatum and the proceedings in consequence are best revealed in a letter from Laurens to John Rutledge of South Carolina (February 3). The Marquis had "discovered a noble resentment", Laurens wrote, for the affront offered to General Washington, to whom his appointment had not been intimated by Congress, declared that he would not go without a general officer of the rank of major general in whom he could put confidence, and demanded General McDougall or Baron Kalb, and that their appointment should be through General Washington.

Congress and the Board of War hesitated [Laurens continues]. The Marquis said if he was disappointed he must immediately go to France to account for his conduct, and that every foreign Officer would accompany him, had an Irruption of this nature taken place, the World at large must have been informed of the unmerited insult offered the General and Commander in Chief, and Censure must have followed both on Congress and the Board of War.

A good deal of struggle was made [Laurens added] to elude the Marquis's demands, [but] he was firm and succeeded, and this morning he took his leave of me and proceeded to the Camp in order as he says, to receive the Commands of his General, to take either Genl. McDougal or Genl. Kalb with him and go rapidly forward to Albany.

With Washington's blessing Lafayette was soon journeying to Albany, whence the expedition was to start to Canada—and toward glory, as the board of war had sought to have him believe, and as he no doubt did believe. What was his chagrin when, upon arriving at Albany (February 17), he speedily discovered that the whole project could scarcely have been anything else but a fraud and a farce. Two days later he was writing to Washington:

Why am I so far from you and what business had the board of War to hurry me through the ice and snow without knowing what I should do, neither what they were doing themselves? . . . your Excellency cannot conceive what I have seen since I left the place where I was quiet and near my friend, to run myself through all the blunders of madness or treachery, (God knows what).

He had found Conway, who had preceded him by only three days, "very active, and looking as if he had good intentions", but Conway's first words were that the expedition was impossible and Lafayette was soon convinced that Conway was right. Schuyler, Lincoln, and Arnold had all written to Conway that it was not possible under existing circumstances even to begin the Canadian enterprise. The troops, what few there were, were likewise "reluctant to the utmost degree".

I have consulted every body [Lafayette continues] and every body answers, it would be madness. I have been deceived by the Board of War. They have, by the strongest expressions, promised me three thousand men. Now, Sir, I do not believe I can find in all twelve hundred fit for duty. and the greatest part of these are naked, even for a summer campaign. I was to find General Stark with a large body, and indeed General Gates told me, *"General Stark will have burnt the fleet before your arrival"* Well, the first letter I receive in Albany is from General Stark, who wishes to know, "what number of men, from where, for what time, and for what rendezvous, *I desire him to raise"*.

He had sent to Congress, he said, a full account of the matter. "I hope it will open their eyes." "I am sent", he wrote again, "with a great noise, at the head of an army, to do great things. The whole continent, France, and, what is the worse, the British army will be in expectation." With pardonable pride he had written letters to France concerning the great enterprise of which he was the head. His humiliation was extreme, and in numerous letters he poured out his resentment over the deception that had been practiced upon him. One of his private letters to Laurens was opened by the board of war; "by mistake", declared the board; "piracy", asserted Laurens; and it gave no end of trouble. A good deal of diplomacy on the part of Washington and of Laurens, and finally of Congress was required to conciliate the marquis. In such a situation it was inevitable that Lafayette should give up the enterprise in disgust. Washington applauded the prudence of his renunciation, and Congress made ready to register its own repentance, although without donning sackcloth.

The intended Irruption into Canada [Laurens wrote to John Rutledge, March 11] ended before it commenced. in this business the Marquis dela-fayette has acted with wisdom which had gained him much reputation, but he is seriously chagrined with the planners of that amusement. if I have the honour of any Influence it shall be, I may say it has been exercised to dis-suade him from the resentment at this critical juncture.

Laurens goes on to remark, as he had done before, that originally he was "almost alone in opposition to that indigested romantic scheme", but now one could scarcely find a man in Congress who favored it. "Except my own", he says, "I do not remember three dissenting voices. Now— well, 'I never liked that Canada Expedition' is unanimous."

Of the presumptive three, one was doubtless the Reverend but hard-headed John Witherspoon, who foresaw as early as February 2 that "Some Difficulties are likely to arise in that Expedition." He was writing to Dr. Benjamin Rush, who appears to have sought appointment as chief medical officer in the enterprise. Another was Eliphalet Dyer, who wrote to William Williams (February 17): "You . . . may wonder among our many wants we should undertake this wild plan. The truth is Genll. Gates had laid the plan and made every preparation for Genll. Starks with a party under him at the proper season to make an irrup-tion into Canada."

On March 13, therefore, Congress "judged it proper, that the irrup-tion ordered to be made into Canada should be suspended", and author-ized General Washington "to order Major General the Marquis de la Fayette and Major General Baron de Kalb to join the main army with-out delay". Even this order, Laurens explained, was obtained only "by a side wind" and "not without debate".

The abandonment of the Canadian expedition and the recall of Lafayette and Kalb to the main army had left Congress with two puzzling problems on its hands. One was what disposition to make of Lafayette, the other was what to do with Conway; and, as it turned out, the two problems became annoyingly entangled. When it came to Lafayette's ears that Conway might be left "where he is", the proposi-tion struck him as adding insult to injury; for to his mind Conway was still the symbol of the plot. Thereupon he asked permission to return to France. This put Congress upon an exceedingly warm spot, and a special committee was set to preparing a letter to Lafayette (March 24) to assure him that Congress "have a very high sense of your merit and attachment to America"; that, in the arrangements made for General Conway there was no intention of doing anything injurious to Lafayette's honor; and, finally, to express the hope that "this declaration, and the disposition since made for General Conway, will make it unnecessary to grant the permission you request". The problem of what disposition to make of Lafayette was all the more puzzling because he was eager to be given a separate command. Congress thereupon went into a huddle. On April 8, Laurens added a postscript to a letter begun March 27 to say: "I have detained this Messenger 13 days, from day to day hoping the next would produce Commands from Congress, but the Committee to whom your Letter was referred have not yet Reported." In fact, the committee does not appear ever to have made a report.

The disposition made of General Conway (March 23) was to order him to join the army at Peekskill under the command of General McDougall. He did not like his new assignment, and he told Congress so in language of characteristic vigor, and threatened to resign. Then, when in obedience to the order of Congress, he had gone to Peekskill, and McDougall had ordered him back to Albany, he proceeded to blow off the steam of his wrath right in the face of Congress. The performance was, in fact, repeated at intervals; and, to add to his own discomfiture, in the course of his activities he wrote to Washington what the latter termed an "impertinent letter . . . *demanding* the command of a division of the Continental army".

Congress, as needs it must, resented the affront to its own dignity, and all the more perhaps because to Congress, as to Lafayette, Conway was the symbol of the Canadian project, which it would fain forget. Conway's resignation was accepted. The impulsive Irishman thereupon averred that he had not meant to resign; but, declared President Laurens, "the door is now shut". "His conduct respecting General Washington", Laurens added, "is criminal and unpardonable, severely censured by all the foreign officers." Later, Laurens wrote that the gentlemen of Congress "feel keen resentment for the unprovoked gross affronts . . . to our worthy Commander in Chief". This was in June, and it is significant that members who, a short few months before, welcomed affronts to the commander-in-chief, now resented them. Having failed to obtain a restoration of his commission, Conway begged for at least a "Recommendatory Certificate of his behaviour"; he succeeded mainly in losing the sympathy and rousing the anger of that irascible gentleman who presided over Congress. All thumbs were now down on Thomas Conway.

Had Conway been a little less impulsive, had he possessed a little more diplomacy, he might well have become one of the beneficiaries of the French alliance. He had probably been more sinned against than sinning, the victim of a not overscrupulous bunch of schemers and his own unbridled tongue. Oddly enough he was the only one of the group who ever offered the amende honorable to the commander-in-chief.

The last curtain on the so-called Conway Cabal was dropped on the fourth of July, 1778, when Conway was desperately wounded in a duel with General John Cadwalader. The curtain was raised for just a moment on the 23d day of July to allow him to make his final bow to the audience and to speak a few words of what he supposed to be his last farewell. It was a brief message and was addressed to General Washington:

Sir,

I find myself just able to hold the pen during a few minutes, and take this opportunity of expressing my sincere grief for having done, written, or said any thing disagreeable to your Excellency. My career will soon be over; therefore justice and truth prompt me to declare my last sentiments. You are in my eyes the great and good man. May you long enjoy the love, veneration, and esteem of those States, whose liberties you have asserted by your virtues.

I am with the greatest respect, etc.,

Thomas Conway.

Conway's career was, however, by no means so nearly over as he then believed. He recovered from his wound and a few months later returned to France, where in good time he won honors such as had eluded him in America, but where likewise he escaped other troubles such as ever had pursued him.

CHAPTER XVI

ARMS AND THE MAN
THE COMMITTEE AT CAMP, HALF-PAY

In the latter days of January, 1778, the committee appointed to repair to headquarters—Dana, Folsom, Reed, Harvie, and Morris, for Charles Carroll of Carrollton did not join the committee at any time—established itself at Moor Hall, near Washington's headquarters at Valley Forge, and at once applied itself to its duties, according to its comprehension of them. Two of the committee, Morris and Harvie, when on their way to the army, became concerned in an incident at Lancaster that had unfortunate consequences, indicating, for one thing, that the committee was inclined to stretch unduly its prerogatives. One phase of the incident was an interference with some British officers who were proceeding under a flag, in accordance with an arrangement between General Washington and General Howe, with clothing and medicines for British prisoners in American hands. The action of the committee constituted nothing less than a breach of faith and seriously complicated subsequent negotiations with General Howe for an exchange of prisoners. A first consequence was of course a remonstrance from Washington. Another phase of the incident amounted to an interference with the Pennsylvania police authority, and this not only brought remonstrances from the authorities of that state, but had later repercussions in a warm and protracted controversy between Gouverneur Morris and Joseph Reed, then become President of Pennsylvania. The committee had made a bad start in its mission of reform.

The first item of the committee's program was the promotion of good discipline in the army, to which was afterward added, through the efforts of some of the more pious members of Congress, "good morals"; the second was economy; the third was, remarkable to relate, "the most speedy and effectual measures . . . for reducing the number of regiments in the continental service"; and the fourth, which by all means should have been the first, was the reform of abuses, "which have too long prevailed in the different departments belonging to the army". Some of these reforms the committee were, by their instructions, to put into effect in concert with the commander-in-chief; others they were to report to Congress for its consideration.

The committee's sittings at camp continued until about the end of March, with General Washington frequently sitting with them and lending them every reasonable cooperation. It is evident nevertheless that there were disagreements. Indeed Elias Boudinot, then commissary general of prisoners but afterward a member of Congress, declared that the committee created much dissatisfaction in the army and finally returned to Congress in disgust. There can be little doubt that the committee thoroughly disgusted the officers of the army, as it also did many members of Congress, and was as successful in muddling as it was enterprising in meddling. Although its authorization was to endeavor to carry out the reforms "in concert" with General Washington, it appears to have assumed that that injunction need not be construed over strictly. The minutes of its meetings accordingly lead to the inference that a good many steps were taken without consultation with the general. The committee may well also have felt justified in attacking army problems without any particularly delicate consideration for the wishes of the officers; for, to say the least, Congress was in a very critical attitude toward the army. For instance, the Rev. John Witherspoon, who had "positively refused" to be placed on the committee, chiefly he declared (January 27) on account of his character and reputation, expressed the hope that the army officers would be "brought into Order".

Early in its career the committee came into conflict with Washington over his plan for a general exchange of prisoners, thereby bringing on a protracted and bitter discussion in Congress. Washington had negotiated with General Howe an agreement with regard to the principles upon which an exchange would take place, and commissioners from the two armies were about to meet for the purpose of carrying out the plan, when the committee at headquarters set about an effort to persuade the general practically to nullify his agreement and to take a course that Washington regarded as not only injudicious but dishonorable. The committee was unable to swerve Washington but they appear to have had no difficulty in persuading a majority of Congress to their way of thinking.

Congress first thrust its muddling hand into the business with a resolution (February 26) that, before any exchange could take place, all accounts chargeable for supplies furnished British prisoners must be liquidated. Although the President was "directed to intimate" to the general that "every proper precaution" was to be taken "against putting it in the power of the Enemy to take any unfair advantages in the exchange of prisoners" (Laurens to Washington, March 1), the resolution of February 26 does not appear to have been sent to General Washington. He first saw it in a Philadelphia paper on March 7, after he had arranged with General Howe for a meeting of their respective commissioners on March 10. Nothing was left for him to do but inform General Howe that "particular circumstances make it inconvenient for my commissioners to meet yours at the time appointed", and to suggest March 31 as the time for the meeting.

It was Washington's hope that by that time Congress could be prevailed on to rescind or modify its resolution, and he pointed out to Congress that the required liquidation "would more than exhaust all the ensuing summer". Further, he admonished Congress, he had supposed himself authorized "by the instructions and intentions" of Congress to act as he did, and that now the public as well as his own personal honor and faith were pledged for the performance. Moreover, "principles of genuine, extensive policy, independent of the considerations of compassion and justice", argued strongly for going ahead with the exchange as planned; for, if all the letters between himself and General Howe and the proceedings of Congress on the subject were published, "it would be difficult to prevent our being generally accused of a breach of good faith". In fact, Howe did conclude that the suspension of the arrangement, "without any reasons assigned, carries with it the appearance of something disingenuous".

Just at the moment when Washington discovered the resolution of February 26 and was in consequence compelled to postpone the meeting of the commissioners, the camp committee's campaign of persuasion seems to have attained something of a climax. The campaign appears to have begun with a letter from the committee to Washington on

February 11, written by Francis Dana, "by Order". Thereafter the minutes of the committee, day by day, usually record, "The General not present". Under the 19th of February the minutes record, "Mr. Harvey left the Committee". The reason is not assigned, but there is evidence that Harvie was out of sympathy with the committee, at least with the two dominating members, Dana and Gouverneur Morris, in the matter of the cartel. Finally, on or about the 9th of March, Dana and Morris between them concocted a long and labored argument to be laid before Washington. The letter was probably not delivered, for it is endorsed, "Superseded by a Conference".

Congress evidently debated Washington's letter relative to the proposed cartel for several days, with John Harvie, now returned to Congress, acting as chairman of the committee of the whole. In the end Congress did for the moment listen to reason, cast its thought upon "the unhappy sufferers now laboring under a cruel captivity", and authorized General Washington (March 18) to proceed with the exchange, "upon such principles as may appear to him most advantageous to the United States, and agreeable to the aforementioned resolutions". The latter clause was mainly a piece of face-saving, for the "aforementioned resolutions" (December 19 and February 26) were just what the authorization was setting to one side.

So far so good. Unfortunately, however, Congress was not yet through with the business. Some phases of the matter had been referred to the board of war, and that board was not likely to give Washington the heartiest support. It is also significant that Francis Dana of the camp committee had just then returned to Congress, and that his hand is manifest in what followed. On March 30 a committee was appointed to prepare instructions to the commissioners appointed by General Washington to negotiate a cartel, and Dana was placed on that committee. Those instructions must have been already prepared, for they were almost immediately reported. In a letter to General Howe (March 12), a copy of which he transmitted to Congress, Washington had remarked that there were "some ambiguities" in the measures taken by General Howe respecting General Charles Lee that justified "alarming surmises". The committee insisted therefore that it should be a preliminary in the proposed cartel that General Lee be "absolutely exchanged for Major General Prescott, and if refused, that no exchange could take place till the further order of Congress". There was a slightly less rigorous requirement with regard to the exchange of Ethan Allen. Further, General Washington was directed to instruct the commissioners not to contravene any of the resolutions of Congress, "particularly that of the 30 December, respecting such of the citizens of these states as may voluntarily join the enemy, and be taken in arms against these States." The commissioners were also to be instructed "positively to insist on" the exchange of citizens "without any relation to rank". Finally General Washington was directed not to permit any article of the cartel to be concluded without his express approbation.

Congress was no doubt unduly alarmed with regard to General Lee (a time came when that body probably wished that it had never redeemed General Lee from captivity); nevertheless what was at first alarm presently grew into violent wrath. The crux of the problem, however, was in the peremptory demand of Congress with regard to the exchange of citizens. The resolution of December 30, 1777, upon the enforcement of which Congress was insisting, reads:

That all persons, inhabitants of any of these United States, who have voluntarily inlisted, or shall so inlist with or join the enemy of the said states, and have been or shall be taken in arms, be confined in close gaols, subject to be delivered up to the respective states to which they belong, to be dealt with agreeable to the laws thereof.

In short, any Loyalists taken in arms Congress would hand over to the respective states, there to be dealt with as traitors.

When Washington received the resolutions of March 30, he wrote to President Laurens (April 4):

It gives me pain to observe, they appear to contain several implications, by which my sensibility is not a little wounded. . . . The Views of Congress seem to be very different from what I supposed them, when I entered into my late engagements with General Howe. Their Resolution of the 30th ulto. pointedly requiring a strict adherence to all former ones upon the subject, will in all probability render them impracticable. . . . In most respects they might be substantially complied with, but there are some points to which an exact conformity must of necessity destroy the Idea of a Cartel.

One of those points was that requiring the enemy to pay gold and silver on equal terms with Continental currency; another was that subjecting to trial and punishment, agreeably to the resolve of December 30, inhabitants of these states taken in arms against them. The first requirement, he said, was unfair, and to the second it was certain General Howe would never assent. It would be wise therefore if the law were "suffered to sleep". Before the resolve of March 30 had come to hand, so he informed Congress, the commissioners had "been in treaty two days, with a prospect of a favorable accommodation".

Probably no letter of Washington throughout his career was more effective than this in stirring the mud in Congress, dregs that had been accumulating through the long, bitter winter. To James Duane, President Laurens wrote, April 7:

The Letter has not yet been presented to Congress, but has undergone severe strictures from a knot of our friends who called here late at night and conned it over. I will give no opinion at present, yet I have the vanity to think if you were in York we should not differ, had you been present, certain ambiguities, I do not say contradictions, would not have taken place in our Acts—but this is under ground, I will wait the event of that debate which in three or four hours I shall *hear* in the multitude of Counsellors.

Washington's letter was presented to Congress that same day and referred to a committee of which Francis Dana was chairman. It was not until the 10th that the committee brought in its proposed answer to the letter, but meanwhile there was evidently much fretting, fuming, and frothing among the members. The dissatisfaction with Washington's contention was by no means, however, confined to his enemies. Some members who were generally friendly to him, men disposed as a rule to take a rational view of measures, were slow in coming around to Washington's point of view. Thomas Burke, for instance, remarking upon Washington's suggestion that "the Laws be suffered to sleep", wrote to Governor Caswell (April 9):

This proposal met with very great and almost general opposition and indignation in Congress. It appears to most of us that giving up a matter of this kind is betraying our independence and in effect giving a licence to the enemy to recruit in our country. If we suffer our citizens who adhere to our enemies, and actually take arms against us to be considered as prisoners of war, and subject to no municipal laws, I see not where our independence remains, and we cannot conceive that even Congress can dispense with such Laws much less a Cabinet Council of Military Officers. These are the sentiments, I believe of a great majority in Congress as well as mine, and I venture to say the matter will be peremptorily insisted on.

In a letter the same day to John Laurens, Henry Laurens leaves the impression that at the moment he was balancing between two opinions: "I am greatly distressed by circumstances now in agitation respecting your friend. I think I once said 'I hope he will never afford him or them his own consent to hurt him'."

The proposed reply to General Washington, which was drafted by William Duer, begins with a note of mild deprecation, but as it proceeds it takes on a rasping tone of anger, then rises in volume till it becomes almost a ferocious denunciation.

Congress with great Concern perceive [reads the first paragraph] that your Sensibility is wounded by their Resolutions. Placing the firmest Confidence in your Prudence, Abilities and Integrity, they wish to preserve that Harmony with you, which is essential to the general Weal: You may rest assured that far from any Intention to give you Pain, their Resolutions have no other Motives or End, but the public Good; they therefore hope that you will not in future be distrest by Apprehensions, as injurious to their Honor, as they are to your own Feelings.

The letter then proceeds at some length to controvert Washington's contentions, emphasizing the apprehensions of Congress respecting "the Duplicity of General Howe", and the "authentic Information" that the commissioners appointed by Washington "held Opinions repugnant to the Sense of Congress". These things had "constrained them . . . to express their Sentiments in an Explicit Manner: lest they might have only to lament, when it was out of their power to remedy, a Misapprehension on Points, deeply affecting, in their Judgment, the Safety and Honor of these States." Coming to the resolution of December 30, "a Measure naturally flowing from the Treason Acts", which the states had passed upon the express recommendation of Congress, the letter states:

On a Mature Deliberation, they are convinced that a Deviation from it would be subversive of our Character as an Independent People, and inconsistent with Sound Policy. No Act of Congress can suspend the Operation of the Laws of the different States, and therefore they cannot consent that any Measure should be adopted in the propos'd Cartel, which may contravene this Resolution. . . . The carrying this Resolution into Practice can depend only on the Will of the several States, who in this respect must be presumed to be governed by Principles of Policy, of which they must necessarily be com-- petent Judges.

Thus far the letter had pursued an argumentative strain, although not without occasional insinuations against the commander-in-chief and his commissioners. But when it came to take up the case of General Charles Lee, restraint was cast to the winds. Washington had informed Congress that General Lee was coming out on parole. But mere parole was not what Congress desired and had commanded. The exchange of General Lee for General Prescott was to have been "an absolute preliminary":

I am therefore directed to inform you [the letter proceeds; for it was assumed that the letter would be signed by the President "by order"] that it is the Unalterable Determination of Congress, that unless this Point is acceded to, all further Negotiation, whether for a general or Partial Exchange, (except in cases to be submitted to the opinion of Congress) should cease.

There was more of like kind, then a long final paragraph, the pith of which runs thus:

I am directed, Sir, by Congress to inform you, that in their opinion, the late Conduct and Correspondence of General Howe, render a strict Attention to the Support of the Dignity of these Free and Independent States, at this time peculiarly necessary . . . they therefore doubt not from your Zeal for the Honor of these States, that you will pay a strict Attention to this Matter.

By a vote of five states to three, and one divided (individually there were nine ayes and eight noes), these latter passages were stricken out, and the following comparatively innocuous passage substituted:

With respect to the Resolution concerning General Lee, Congress, at his Request, are willing that you should waive his Exchange for Major General Prescott as a Preliminary Article: it is however their Intention that no Cartel be acceded to unless it be expressly admitted therein that General Lee be exchanged for General Prescot.

As amended and finally approved on the 13th the letter, bearing the date April 14, was signed by President Laurens, "By order of Congress", and despatched to General Washington.

The letter actually sent to General Washington, although it could not be otherwise interpreted than as a severe rebuke, gives scarcely an inkling of the bitter contest involved in its making. The draft, however, with its extensive erased passages, clearly reveals with what ferocity of purpose certain elements in Congress sought to administer to the general a rebuke that would blister and sting him to the quick, while the recorded vote shows how narrowly they failed of succeeding. The dry, crisp record in the Journals seldom affords an intimation, much less a revelation, of even the fiercest wrangles in Congress, but for once the secretary dipped his quill into a bottle of corrosive ink. Significantly enough, Congress was holding a night session to try to finish the battle. Came the hour of ten, when a motion was made to adjourn.

While the states were calling [the secretary records] Mr. [Thomas] Burke, representing the State of North Carolina, after voting in the affirmative, declared the states might vote as they pleased, he would upon his honor adjourn himself; and thereupon he immediately withdrew; by which means Congress could not proceed to business.

Mr. [Edward] Langworthy, the delegate representing Georgia, having also withdrawn.

Ordered, That the messenger wait on the members, and desire them to attend Congress.

The messenger returned, and reported, That he had delivered the message of Congress to the members. That Mr. Langworthy replied he would return presently. That Mr. Burke replied, "Devil take him if he would come; it was too late and too unreasonable".

The secretary appears to have been slightly in error in quoting the first clause of Mr. Burke's response, for what Burke seems to have said was,

"Devil a foot will I go tonight", to which, a moment later, he added, "It is too late and too unreasonable." His abettor, Edward Langworthy, did, however, return to Congress that same night, offering the explanation that he had withdrawn under the impression that Congress was adjourned.

Thus endeth the first chapter. But there were other chapters to follow, some of which, while not without import in the formative years of the youthful nation, must have added likewise an element of gayety to the scene. As befitted a body presumed to represent the national sovereignty, if any such there was, the refractory member from North Carolina was next morning charged by Congress with a breach of order and called upon to defend his conduct, if he could. Mr. Burke could. He admitted that he had in a manner invoked the name of the Devil in his reply to the messenger of Congress (to Governor Caswell he afterward explained that his reply was intended for Mr. Duer, not for Congress); but he still maintained that he had been guilty of no rudeness to Congress, for Congress was then adjourned, and when Congress was adjourned it "ceased to be a body". He declined therefore to make any apology. If he had been guilty of any affront, it was to individuals, and that required a different kind of apology.

In the course of the grilling the Irish in Mr. Burke appears to have been stirred to such a degree as to bring from him a declaration that he would not submit to "a tyranny of a majority of this Congress, which would keep him here at unreasonable hours"; he would attend at all times he thought reasonable, but would not attend at times he thought unreasonable, "unless by force on his person". What power, he inquired, has Congress over its members anyway? For his part, if he had been guilty of misbehavior, he would answer to his own state. In a written statement that Burke presented to Congress he was somewhat less obstreperous, nevertheless he still stood stoutly by his main contention. "Until the laws of the State I represent shall expressly declare to the contrary", he asserted, "I shall hold myself accountable for my conduct in Congress to that State, and [to] no other power on earth." In so stating he was using "the freedom which according to my idea belongs to a Republican, and a representative of a Sovereign people".

There was, in fact, more method in Burke's course of procedure than is revealed in his statements before Congress. Shortly afterward (April 29) he wrote to Governor Caswell a circumstantial account of the affair, and later he laid a similar statement before the North Carolina assembly. He explained that, in the opinion of himself and several other members of Congress, the draft of the proposed letter to General Washington was "exceptionable in many parts, particularly in some Eulogisms on the whole Tenor of the resolutions of Congress relative to the Exchange of prisoners". Those passages, Burke and his associates declared, were "neither consistent with Truth or Modesty", and the "several charges against the General of suffering the Dignity and Honor of the United States to be Injured" were "void of all foundation". Indeed the whole proceeding appeared "to indicate in the framers a disposition not friendly to the General, nor such as so good, so Important, so public spirited and Disinterested a Character deserves".

One Paragraph [Burke goes on to relate] had taken up the whole afternoon in debate. The members of the Committee had let themselves very largely into many foreign matters, declaimed very vehemently but to no other purpose than confirming us in our former opinions, and fatiguing every faculty. At length the exceptionable parts of the Paragraph were expunged and it received a very different dress.

The committee urged that the letter be finished that night, although it was then after ten o'clock. The opposition thought it wiser to postpone the matter to the next day and accordingly moved an adjournment. Of himself Burke relates: "I labored under a very Distressing fit of an intermitting fever, which heightened by the part I was obliged to take in the Debate, and the noise of loud, incessant Declamation, occasioned so violent pain in my head that I was totally unable to attend any longer." Burke intimates nevertheless that he was influenced by more than his personal discomfort. There was a bare quorum present, and he conceived a plan to break the quorum. "The Question for adjournment was put", he says, "and before it came to me I was very apprehensive it would pass in the Negative and I determined to withdraw if no other way was left, to prevent our proceeding so improperly on business of such Importance."

Having failed to induce Mr. Burke to return to his seat that night,

Congress proceeded the next morning to administer to the recalcitrant member such castigation as it might.

The members of the Committee who had framed the letter [Burke related] now united, and labored strenuously to make a Mountain out of this Mole-hill, talked vehemently of the insolence of appealing to the States, declared their disposition to proceed to Commitment or to Expulsion and lamented that the circumstances of Congress made my presence Necessary and prevented them from moving to such purposes. They talked very much of the Contempt in calling any act of a majority of Congress a Tyranny.

The committee demanded an explicit acknowledgment of his error, but Burke declared that he "knew no power who could make a man change his opinion before he was convinced of his error", and, since he remained unconvinced of error he would not acknowledge it. Burke shortly afterward took his departure, in due course appealed to his own legislature, and not only obtained from that body a hearty approbation of his conduct, but was returned to Congress with an increase of prestige and confidence.

What an extraordinary situation! Congress contemplated committing Mr. Burke (presumably the York county jail might be borrowed for the purpose), or expelling him. Yet, before Congress could do either it would be necessary to compel his attendance, since without his attendance Congress could not function at all. For once that august assembly was in a most ridiculous dilemma. The question whether Congress could discipline one of its own members would arise again and would again throw that body into a like dilemma. A similar question, whether Congress could discipline one of its officers, was not, however, quite so perturbing. Congress could in any event give an officer "leave to attend to his private affairs".

As for the letter over which such a furor had been stirred in Congress, General Washington assumed to overlook the element of rebuke in its content and thanked Congress for the "fresh assurances . . . of their confidence". Meanwhile, however, in consequence of a deficiency in the powers of the commissioners acting in behalf of the British army, the negotiations for a cartel had already broken down. Thus, for the time being, the episode was closed. In Congress one result, so it would seem, of the wrangle in which Thomas Burke played so conspicuous part, was an extraordinary pledge on the part of the majority of the members that thereafter they would "not speak more than Ten minutes, seldom more than once, never more than twice", and that they would "unite in supporting order and preserving decency and politeness in debate"—a pledge that seems to have been honored more in the breach than in the observance.

At all events, when members had cooled down from the heats of that debate, the opposition to General Washington appears to have subsided. Occasionally one of the chronic growlers would break out, as, for instance, when James Lovell, in his characteristic manner, wrote to Samuel Adams (April 18):

Howe most evidently had rather have to do with any body rather than Congress; there being this difference, that he cannot induce us to believe him any thing better than a deceitful rogue, while some others confide altogether in his *honor* and often put themselves into situations to have their "feelings hurt" by our decisive Resolves, which are therefore wished to "sleep".

The general attitude that had come over Congress is perhaps better characterized by Henry Laurens, in a letter to James Duane (April 17):

By the bye—remember to whom I speak [that is, to a fellow-member of Congress]—a certain Club of which you are a Member have very fortunately got out of a scrape. you shall see the whole, except the latter stroke, in Print very speedily. I whispered to a friend, *this* may be passed to the credit of Providence.

Although the committee at camp, with its meddling, disgusted the army and the friends of Washington in Congress as well, it did present to Congress a number of constructive measures within the purposes of its appointment, measures chiefly prepared by General Washington or under his direction. In particular, the departments of quartermaster-general and commissary-general were reorganized, and the ablest men that could be found were placed at the head of them, General Nathanael Greene over the former, and Jeremiah Wadsworth over the latter. Aside from the character and the ability of the men chosen for these important posts, an exceedingly important element of the reform consisted in vesting these officers with actual responsibility, with the power of appointing their subordinates, and with freedom from outside control. By the time, however, that these things had been fully accomplished the winter had passed, and the worst of the crisis, so far as concerned the problem of supplying the army with necessities, was over.

With regard to the contemplated alterations in the arrangements of the army, one of the chief items of the committee's agenda, a new "regulation" or "establishment" of the army was, after a long delay, worked out and presented to Congress on May 18, nearly two months after the committee had left camp, and was adopted by Congress, May 27. The putting of this new arrangement into effect, which was passed on to another committee, was not, however, seriously begun until the close of the summer, and it had not been completed at the end of the year. So much for the "speedy reformation" that Congress had so zealously launched when the year was yet young.

Of all the proposals respecting the army that emanated from the committee sent to headquarters the measure providing for half-pay for life to the officers of the army had the greatest repercussion in Congress. The proposal did not originate with that committee, for the subject had been a matter of conference between General Washington and the committee that conferred with him at Whitemarsh in the preceding December, and the last mentioned committee's report, laid before Congress on January 5, 1778, recommended not only a half-pay establishment for officers but a pensionary establishment in favor of officers' widows. The subject had therefore received some consideration in Congress before the specific plan, worked out between Washington and the committee of conference at Valley Forge, was presented to Congress. Near the end of March two members of the committee, Dana and Folsom, returned to Congress for the express purpose of pressing the adoption of the measure, and the two remaining members, Reed and Morris, followed shortly afterward. Harvie had resumed his seat in Congress sometime earlier.

On March 26, Dana and Folsom laid before Congress their propositions, which included, beside the provisions for half-pay and widows' pensions, a provision to make commissions vendible. Congress at once divided into two opposing camps, the advocates of the measure having a bare majority, but with the opposition contesting every inch of ground. It was "a Question of such magnitude", declared William Ellery (April 5), that it ought to be referred to the states, and in due time he would move that that be done. If it should become necessary to give his vote before he should receive instructions, he hoped he would not be censured if he failed to "jump judgment" with his constituents. Henry Laurens, who was to become one of the most irreconcilable opponents of the measure, wrote to James Duane (April 7): "We are meanaced and not slightly, with the loss of all our good Officers unless a Peace establishment is made." A threat, this, that was "the worst adapted in the whole circle of ratiocination" of converting him. "The danger of losing 'ALL' 'ALL' your 'good' Officers, or that of getting *'no more'* Men, and 'losing those you have'." For his part, he could not believe it. If he could he would say, "every Man to his Tent!" It was a matter of indifference to him "whether the Tyrants name be George or Dick". In short, Laurens felt, as did others, that the chief actuating motive of the officers should be a spirit of patriotism. "There are many Thousands", said he, "whose hearts are warm with the reasonings which induced the original Compact and who have not bowed the Knee to Luxury nor to Mammon."

Ten days later Laurens was again writing to Duane to report that "long and warm debates for many a day had led us to the threshold of the Report from the Committee of the Whole", that they had "Entered fairly the Door", when they were "turned out by a New Motion". In short, the contestants were skirmishing for advantage, resorting to parliamentary maneuvers. Two days more of this skirmishing, and Laurens' temperature had risen to a new high. To Governor William Livingston of New Jersey he wrote (April 19):

Sir, We have within a Month past, improved many whole days and Some tedious Nights by hammering upon a plan for an half pay establishment . . . a most momentous engagement—in which all our labour has not yet matured one single Clause nor even determined the great leading questions to be, or not to be. the Combattants have agreed to meet to morrow *vis a vis* and by the point of Reason and by somethings proxies for Reason put an end to the Contest. I'll be hanged they do. had I heard of the Loss of half my Estate, the amount would not have involved my mind in such fixed concern as I feel from the introducing of this untoward project.

The arguments for the measure were, that officers were unable to support themselves on their pay and that great numbers of them were resigning their commissions and seeking those lucrative avenues of employment that the war was abundantly offering; therefore it was impossible to introduce adequate discipline, for the mere suggestion of discipline brought forth a resignation. To increase the pay would be but to inflate the currency, which would in turn result in further depreciation. It was urgently necessary therefore that officers be given a permanent interest in their commissions. Against the measure were brought two principal arguments, with numerous corollaries. First, that Congress lacked the power to create such an establishment; and, second, that it threatened the country with that dangerous institution, a standing army. "The fear of a standing Army arising from this establishment", declared Thomas Burke (April 9), "has no great weight with me. This War will make too many of our people Soldiers to leave us anything to apprehend from a standing Army in one generation." "But the most formidable argument", Burke went on to say, "is that the Congress being instituted only for the purpose of War have no power without particular instructions, to make any peace establishment." To this Burke's answer was: "the argument of want of power is no more conclusive against this than against borrowing money which must be paid and its interest in the mean time kept up by revenues which must continue long beyond the War."

General Washington, who initiated the measure and no doubt supplied at the outset the principal reasonings in behalf of it, continued, while the measure was under discussion, to reinforce his arguments. To President Laurens he wrote, April 10:

If my opinion is asked with respect to the necessity of making this provision for the Officers, I am ready to declare, that I do most religiously believe the salvation of the cause depends upon it, and without it, your Officers will moulder to nothing, or be composed of low and illiterate men void of capacity for this, or any other business. To prove this, I can with truth aver, that scarce a day passes without the offer of two or three Commissions.

Personally, he asserted, he had no interest in the decision of Congress, for he had before declared and now repeated that he would not receive the smallest benefit from the half-pay establishment. Nevertheless, apart from all other considerations, upon the single ground of economy and public saving, he would maintain the utility of the measure; for he had not the least doubt, that, "until officers consider their commissions in an honorable and interested point of view, and are afraid to endanger them by negligence and inattention, no order, regularity, or care, either of the men or public property will prevail." To John Banister, a delegate from Virginia, he wrote a few days later more intimately and more earnestly not only respecting the importance of this measure but concerning other aspects of a situation that had become, in his view, exceedingly critical. That letter was doubtless meant for more eyes and more minds than Banister's.

On April 16 the opposition endeavored to have the question referred to the states. The motion was defeated by a narrow margin, but it was enough, provided there should be no defections. The opposition began to lose hope, as is evidenced by a letter of James Lovell to Samuel Adams April 18, in which he alludes with his accustomed sneer to Washington's letter to Congress.

You may expect soon an half pay system upon which the existence of yr army this campaign is said, "religiously" at one time, and "devoutly" at another, to depend. It is said to be Oeconomy, Justice and Necessity. The latter really is not altogether fictitious, the second does not exist, and the first is quite problematical. Distinction ought however to be made between an *half-pay* establishment and a *military* establishment, the latter being a curse, the former a nuisance.

For nearly a month thereafter, nevertheless, the contesting factions tusseled back and forth almost daily. Meanwhile some members took their departure, defections began to threaten in one or more delegations, whereupon there was scurrying among the absentees for recruits. On May 13 the forces once more joined battle. The question was again whether the matter should be referred to the states and the success of that motion would be equivalent to defeat of the half-pay measure. But the motion failed by a vote of six states to five. Thereupon the minority came forward with a compromise, by which the provision should be for a period of seven years instead of for life; and in that form the measure was adopted (May 15), by the unanimous vote of the states, although with two individual negatives, James Lovell of Massachusetts and Oliver Wolcott of Connecticut.

Henry Laurens somehow found consolation in the result. "After two Months labor on a scheme for half pay to officers," he wrote to President Lowndes of South Carolina May 17, ". . . ridden by amendments and new Resolves, the original project by the Grace of God, was the day before yesterday rid to Death, and from the Ashes, the inclosed Act of Congress of the 15th May produced." Said the Connecticut delegates, who furnished Governor Trumbull with a summary account of the contest (May 18):

The inclosd Resolution of Congress is the result of the most painful and disagreeable question that hath ever been agitated in Congress. . . . It is allmost impossible to give a clear and full representation of the difficulties attending this debate, on both sides the question, to any gentleman who was not present. . . . If the inclosd Resolve is not the best measure the nature and circumstances of the case would admit, it is certainly the best that could be obtain.

The act provided that officers commissioned by Congress should, after the conclusion of the war, receive annually for the term of seven years, "if they should live so long", one half the present pay of such officers. But there were several provisos: They must continue in the service to the end of the war, must not hold any office of profit under the United States, "or any of them", must have taken an oath of allegiance to and actually reside in one of the states. There was a further provision that noncommissioned officers and soldiers who enlisted "for and during the war, and shall continue therein to the end thereof" should receive at the expiration of the war the further reward of eighty dollars.

Both the pros and the cons appear to have assumed that the question was settled once for all, even though every one knew perfectly well that what Congress had done Congress could undo. As it turned out, the close of the war was some time off, and each of the dragging years between was to bring, in one form or another, a renewal of the agitation, while the conclusion of the war would bring still another and even more violent contest. It was nevertheless of no small importance at the moment that the dispute between Congress and its own right arm had found a tolerable adjustment. The next task devolving upon Congress, that of effecting the new establishment of the army (May 18, 27), in so far as concerned the approval of the plan by Congress, would present no great difficulty, involve no angry debate, but putting the plan into actual operation would prove to be quite a different matter. Congress, perhaps more than most political bodies, was apt to be fertile in plans, but exceedingly unfertile in the performance of the tasks of administration. Administration was one of the things about which Congress still had a great deal to learn.

CHAPTER XVII

IN THE DEPTHS

THE SHADOW OF DEFEAT

The adoption of the half-pay measure, May 15, 1778, marks very nearly the close of one of the most trying periods in the career of that body that had chosen to be called—if and when the proposed instrument of union should be adopted—the United States in Congress Assembled. Indeed, with one exception, it was probably the most quarrelsome period in the whole fifteen years of that assembly's life of wrangle. The times were trying to their souls, the problems lay heavy on their shoulders, and no wonder tempers crossed and sputtered.

The blizzard raised by the half-pay measure was still raging when John Banister dropped the remark to Washington (April 16) that within Congress, where knowledge of military subjects was sorely needed, was "the greatest Ignorance in every Occurrence of that kind mixt with an inactivity that permits affairs of the greatest magnitude to lie dormant and give place to local Trifles". At nearly the same time (April 21) Charles Carroll of Carrollton made a similar comment: "The Congress do worse than ever: We murder time, and chat it away in idle impertinent talk: However, I hope the urgency of affairs will teach even that Body a little discretion."

John Mathews of South Carolina, who came to Congress only in late April, 1778, may or may not have held his grumbles in check at the time, but as soon as Congress had returned to Philadelphia he turned them loose. It was in a letter to Governor Rutledge (July 7):

I have wrote to you for leave to come home in December. For God's sake procure it for me, and I'll be dam'd if you ever catch me here again. Those who have dispositions for Jangling, and are fond of displaying their Rhetorical abilities, let them come. I never was so sick of anything in my life.

Even the summer months in Philadelphia failed to rid his spiritual system of the complaints contracted in York, for he wrote to Thomas Bee (September 22):

> Oh! my worthy friend, never was Child more sick of a school, than I am, of this same business, I am sent here upon. . . . I fully intended when I came into Congress, to have accustomed myself to deliver my sentiments upon every important Question, but I have found the thirst for Chattering so extremely prevalent, that it absolutely disgusts me, and frequently Seals my lips, least my conscience should upraid me with the commission of that very sin against our righteous cause, that I see daily committed by others, vizt. the loss of so much precious irretrieviable time.

More of like kind from the pen of John Mathews, more of like kind from other pens; complaints against long-winded speeches, the "very loud talker", the "Six-Deep Orator", as Henry Laurens once characterized the species; complaints also against those members who "have such a knack at starting questions of order, raising debates upon critical, captious, and trifling amendments, protracting them by long speeches, by postponing, calling for the previous question, and other arts." In short, the art of filibustering got an early start in our national history.

And why so much oratory before no more than a baker's dozen huddled in a small room? The time was to come when the Congress of the United States would attain high fame for its oratory; but in that later era the speeches were delivered before large audiences and were read by many thousands more. In the days of our national beginnings, however, speeches in Congress could not reach either the ears or the eyes of eager constituents. Furthermore, few of those speeches were ever put down upon paper, and fewer still have survived the ravages of time.

The time at which we are endeavoring to listen in on Congress is one that would seem to offer the least inducements to oratory. It is scarcely less than astounding that the states had permitted their Congress, which they had inaugurated with so great a flourish and with such magnificent hopes, to become reduced to no more than a frazzled fragment of itself. At the very beginning of the new year (January 3, 1778)

President Laurens had complained to the governor of Rhode Island of the "extraordinary and unreasonable" burdens of Congressional business that "fall heavily upon a very few Members from 17 to 21 who faithfully attend their duty at the expense of domestic happiness and the improvement of their private Estates"; while at the end of the month he was writing (to John Rutledge, January 30) that attendance often did not exceed thirteen, that sometimes, in fact, there were "barely 9 States on the floor represented by as many persons". A few days later (February 7) he wrote to John Lewis Gervais:

I could add a long and affecting paragraph on the subject of Non Representation. I could tell you truly, the House has been reduced to nine States represented in Units—that we have sometimes been stagnant from a want of Members—and oftener running whole days into weeks of unmatured conversations from a want of able Members.

On the same day Elbridge Gerry wrote: "The Business of Congress in the Winter Season is greatly increased on account of the necessary Reformation, Plans, and Preparation for the succeeding Campaign, and at this Time there is half the number of Members to transact it."

Individual appeals to absent members to come over to York and help them seemed to avail but little, therefore on March 12 Congress (rather the remnant thereof) decided to do a bit of official prodding. The states were informed that "the multiplicity and importance of the business of Congress, during the war, will require the constant attendance of at least three members from each State; that, from the want thereof, the health of members has been frequently impaired, and the public business greatly obstructed."

It was about the end of March that James Duane of New York, who had been in hibernation at his home since early in the preceding December, made inquiry of President Laurens what Congress was doing or going to do, particularly with regard to the defense of North River (he would naturally be much interested in that defense). Laurens replied (April 7):

If you and I were *téte á téte,* I might attempt to account for the amazing neglect of North River, I might add at least twenty other neglects, and possibly as many Acts which ought to have been neglected—make an aggregate of these and transfer the whole to the debit of the general Account of the thirteen *United free and Independent* States of America.

And then, with an accusing finger pointed directly at Mr. Duane, he asked:

What Representation had ye for upward of three precious Months, when those things were done which ought not to have been done, and those left undone which ought to have been done? Why—9 States—9 or 11 Members when we could collect them—seldom 15—17 made a very full House—you well know Sir, the unavoidable drudgery of Committees requires more *hands*—I am not competent to Lecture upon *heads*—nor need I attempt description to a Gentleman so well acquainted with the sagacity of the Stock which he left upon hand.

Laurens's retort upon Duane for New York's failure to keep up its representation was not the only one of its kind. It was on New Year's day that Nathaniel Folsom of New Hampshire received from his absent colleague, Josiah Bartlett, a letter criticizing certain measures pertaining to the promotion of general officers of the army, one of them in particular. Folsom defended the measure as founded in "Justice and equity", as well as good policy. He also defended himself and Congress.

You ask me [wrote Folsom] how I Could be Induced to Disgrace all the field officers in the northern army to which I answer if when you Say you if you mean Congress I will not answer for them . . . if you meen me Personally Considerd, and think you Could Do better hope you will in twenty four hours after Receiving this mount your horse and Come and Relieve me, and if you think you Cant Do So well would not have that Stop you as I have worne allmost all the flesh off my Bones being Exercised in my mind night and Day, and no time to Relax.

Not until more than four months later did Bartlett mount his horse for the journey to York. He came only when the political skies were clearing and gentle spring beckoned him to take the road. Gentle spring did, in fact, make no inconsiderable contribution to the patriotic impulses of those derelict members of Congress who had long sat snugly ensconced in their own chimney corners; and the fact was duly recorded by that member of Congress who scarcely ever failed to be in his seat when Congress was in session, and betwixt times plied with a like unfailing diligence his nimble goose quill. On the 18th of April, James Lovell had much to say to Samuel Adams in his customary grumbling tone, but he offered one gladsome note: "We are now come to the Season when certain birds of passage return who seldom appear in our flock during winter."

One potent reason for this baleful recreancy was the fact that Congress was actually in exile. York was a small town, well back in the interior of Pennsylvania and therefore comparatively inaccessible— that is, to the members of Congress. On the other hand, Henry Laurens intimated that it was just the accessibility of the place to the British army, the fear of "a sudden surprize by the Enemy", that prompted many members to speed their departure and to retard their return. Certainly, however, there were reasons that bore down upon most of the derelicts with greater weight.

Congress had been in York scarcely two months when Cornelius Harnett of North Carolina wrote (November 20, 1777) to Thomas Burke, then at home: "For God's sake endeavour to get some Gentlemen appointed in my stead. I can not stay here any longer with any pleasure." At the close of December he was writing another friend:

Believe me it is the most inhospitable scandalous place I ever was in. If I once more can return to my family all the Devils in Hell shall not separate us. The honor of being once a member of Congress is sufficient for me, I acknowledge it is the highest honor a free state can bestow on one of its members. I shall be carefull to ask for nothing more, but will sit down under my own vine and my own Fig tree (for I have them both) at Poplar Grove where none shall make me afraid except the boats of the British cruisers.

In fact, the little town was almost completely lacking in all the comforts, conveniencies, and cultural attractions that made Philadelphia so delightful a city in which to live and meditate on the problems of founding a nation. In York, members were from the very outset irked by the lack of suitable living accommodations, while, one and all, they found the cost of living excessive and usually "attended by very bad fare". "Here", James Lovell wrote to Joseph Trumbull in mid-April, "you can *command* no course of Diet. I am not Galen enough to say whether the Lime water which tears your Countrymen's Bowels out would not serve you. It has driven several Delegates home to their native springs." It was a few weeks later that Lovell, scanning the horizon for the return of what he had called birds of passage, beheld one of his own colleagues, Samuel Adams, flit down from the north. Adams presently picked up his pen to write: "I am happy to find C[ongress] in perfect good humour and attentive to Business, though so hard put to it in this place, as hardly to have a Room apiece in which to write a Letter to a Friend."

It was indeed a propitious time for the return of the birds of passage, or for the coming of other birds that had not hitherto been of the flock. The worst also of the stormy political weather that had prevailed for so long in and about Congress had pretty well passed by; the skies had cleared, the sun had come out again. The newcomers would escape most of the harsh bickerings that had been the dominating aspect of the Congressional dwelling-place. The poison of the Conway Cabal had at last been all but purged from the Congressional system. The committee sent to headquarters had ceased from bedeviling the army and, though they had climaxed their career of meddling by bedeviling Congress and the commander-in-chief over the matter of the cartel, on that score also they had been effectually squelched. If Congress had not been wholly successful in its pious effort to castigate the refractory member from North Carolina, it was at all events ready, for the time being at least, to cry quits. The tug of war over the half-pay question had winded the contestants on both sides, and they had come to terms. In short, those who came in the late spring and early summer not only escaped much of gloom and grumbling, they were, in fact, just in time to behold the coming of great events.

On the 18th of April, General Washington transmitted to Congress what purported to be a Parliamentary bill pertaining to America, which had been brought to his headquarters the day before.

Whether this insidious proceeding is genuine [Washington wrote] . . . or contrived in Philadelphia is a point undetermined and immaterial; but it is certainly founded in principles of the most wicked, diabolical baseness, meant to poison the minds of the people and detach the wavering, at least, from our cause. . . . I trust it will be attacked in every shape, in every part of the Continent.

President Laurens, into whose hands the document came (April 20), described it as the "spurious draught of a Bill insinuated to be Parliamentary, importing an intended proposition for reconciling differences and quieting disturbances in the Colonies", and ascribed its origin to General Howe and his "Emissaries". "I make no doubt", he added, "but that we shall return it decently tarred and feathered. I differ with Gentlemen who suppose the performance originated under authority in England", he wrote further; "it appears to me to be destitute of the most essential marks. . . . I believe it to be of Philadelphia manufacture probably under hints from the other side of the Water and sent abroad like a Sibyl's letter."

"Two opinions prevail here", Samuel Chase wrote to Governor Johnson (April 20); "some [think] that this insidious scheme originated in Philadelphia, others the far greater Number believe it came from the Ministry. The manifest Intention is to amuse us with a Prospect of Peace and to relax our Preperations." "I did intend Home", he wrote the next day, "but I believe I shall stay and see it out. The Hour to try the Firmness and prudence of Man is near at Hand. . . . I shall endeavor to act my Part well. My Soul has been chagrined at certain Conduct, but I love my Country. . . ." Said Chase's colleague, John Henry, who was also convinced of its genuineness, "I dread the impression it will make upon the minds of many of our people . . . it will prove more dangerous to our cause than ten thousand of their best Troops." Similarly the Virginia delegates wrote to Governor Henry that General Howe was industriously circulating the draft, "with a view no doubt of diverting the People of America from their grand object of Preparation and defense". Unless the "political stroke" were counteracted by proper "strictures", unless the subject should be placed "in its true Light before the people", there was danger that it might "mislead the ignorant and alienate the Minds of the wavering".

Congress was not, however, long left in doubt. Within two or three days convincing evidence had appeared that what they had before them was a genuine Parliamentary plan of conciliation, one part of which was to be a declaration of the intentions of Parliament with regard to the right of taxing the colonies, another for the appointment of commissioners to treat with the Americans, and a third embodying certain conciliatory propositions. Then came a speech of Lord North on introducing into Parliament his conciliatory motion. The latter had come to Washington two days after the transmission of the supposedly spurious draft and was at once sent on to Congress. Convinced now of the authenticity of these documents, Washington admonished Congress that they aimed at "objects of the greatest extent and importance", which would in one way or another "involve the most interesting consequences to this country". Washington shrewdly conjectured, as indicated in a private letter to Delegate John Banister (April 21), that France had recognized the independence of the United States and that Great Britain was hurrying action to forestall the arrival of the treaty with France. It was only necessary therefore to counteract the obvious design of the bills and to show the states what was the temper of their delegates. That done, independence was assured. And nothing short of independence, he insisted, should for a moment be considered.

Congress, for its part, did not wait for positive assurance of the genuineness of the bills, but went at once into action. A committee composed of Gouverneur Morris, William Henry Drayton, and Francis Dana was appointed to prepare a response, and the response the committee proposed (April 22d) was in good set terms. "Upon a supposition the matters contained in the said paper will really go into the British statute Book", says the report, "they serve to shew, in a clear point of view, the weakness and wickedness of the enemy." First, their weaknesses, which were four in number:

1. The fact that they now recede from their former claim that they had "a right to bind the inhabitants of these states in all cases whatsoever", shows their inability to enforce it.

2. Their prince had heretofore rejected the humble petition of the representatives of America; "now the same prince pretends to treat with those very representatives, and grant to the arms of America what he refused to their prayers."

3. Confident in their own strength they had labored to conquer the

continent, rejecting every idea of accommodation; now they had evidently lost that confidence.

4. Heretofore their constant language has been "that it is incompatible with their dignity to treat with the Americans"; now they are about to offer to treat.

Secondly, their "wickedness and insincerity". On these they were indicted on eight counts, elaborated at some length. Gouverneur Morris, whose pen drew the report (except "two clauses inserted by the house"), wrote to John Jay (May 3): "You may find perhaps some difficulty to discover how they shew the wickedness or insincerity of the Enemy"—and the points are somewhat labored. Besides the two clauses inserted (precisely what these were can not be determined), he goes on to say, one short passage was deleted, and "sundry smaller alterations were made, as is the case in Matrimony, for better, for worse". One item of wickedness at least deserves to be noted: that, if they really are receding from a part of their former claims, then they have "sacrificed many brave men in an unjust quarrel".

The marrow of the response was:

As the Americans united in this arduous contest upon principles of common interest, for the defence of common rights and privileges . . . so the great cause for which they contend . . . must derive its success from the continuance of that union; wherefore any men, or body of men, who should presume to make any separate or partial convention or agreement with commissioners under the crown of Great Britain, or any of them, ought to be considered and treated as open and avowed enemies of these United States.

And further . . . that these United States cannot, with propriety, hold any conference or treaty with any commissioners on the part of Great Britain, unless they shall, as a preliminary thereto, either withdraw their fleets and armies, or else, in positive and express terms, acknowledge the independence of the said States.

The report was unanimously approved and, as the "Observations" of Congress, was immediately published, together with Lord North's speech and the drafts of his bills. The "Observations", Charles Carroll of Carrollton wrote (April 23), "are not so perfect as they ought to be, but the hurry of business and the want of time must, and will, no doubt, sufficiently apologize with an impartial public for all their imperfections." "I trust", wrote John Henry, another Maryland delegate (April 24), "they will be sufficient to shew the wickedness of the Ministry."

I am glad [Henry Laurens wrote to his son, April 28] our Act of the 22d pleases you. It appears to me to be sufficiently energetic for the present purpose. the last paragraph one excepted will point out to the illustrious Commissioners from White Hall from whence to take their departure, and save much time which might otherwise have been spent in Ceremonious preliminary. my sentiment is, this little Clause of 7 Lines nullifies many Pages of their Instructions. it certainly contains a complete answer to the Laborious performances of Lord North and the Labours of the blood thirsty Tryon. The Tit for Tat, which your General lately gave to the Quondam Governor must exceedingly mortify a Man of his arrogance.

Laurens was evidently pleased with his own conceit about the place whence the commissioners should take their departure, for a week later he repeated his sentiments in a letter to Washington, specifying more precisely the place of departure as "the Tower of Independence". A colleague of Laurens, John Mathews, who had arrived just in time to hear the committee's report, transmitted a copy of the publication to Thomas Bee (April 26) with these remarks:

I imagine some parts will not a little surprise you. Compare the speech of the Minister with the last speech from the Throne. . . . When the Acts were posted up in Phliadelphia the officers tore them down in a most riotous manner, swearing they were all cheated, for they were promised the Rebels should be conquered and their Estates divided amongst them. The Physic begins to work you see. all we have farther to do, is to give them one good dose more this campaign, and the business is done. The speech and the Acts, the exchange of Lee . . . all serve to shew, those Dam'd Villains are heartily sick of the business. However Congress takes it up in a different point of View, as all meant to throw dust in our eyes, and are preparing for a Vigorous Campaign.

Not all the members, however, regarded the propositions as mere dust in the eyes. Gouverneur Morris, for instance, wrote to John Jay (April 28), "Great Britain seriously means to treat." Then he added:

Our affairs are most critical, though not dangerously so. If the minister from France were present as well as him from England, I am a blind politician if the thirteen States with their extended territory, would not be in peaceable possession of their independence three months from this day. As it is, expect a long war. I believe it will not require such astonishing efforts after this campaign to keep the enemy at bay. Probably a treaty is signed with the house of Bourbon ere this; if so, a spark hath fallen upon the train which is to fire the world. Ye gods! what havoc doth ambition make among your works.

Laurens was another who was convinced of the serious purpose of Great Britain behind the offers of conciliation, and not less of the need for America to take the offers seriously and make ready for the negotiation. To that end he offered a farsighted suggestion. To General Washington he wrote, April 27:

We are now verging towards a most important Crisis, when all the Wisdom of these States will be required. Permit me Sir, to lay before you my private Sentiments: If the time shall come for appointing a Deputation for treating with British Commissioners on terms for establishing Peace I hold it necessary that able Men be called forth for that purpose from any place within the Union without confining our election within any one State or Body.

With these ideas Washington was in substantial agreement. On the same day Laurens wrote in similar terms to Governor William Livingston of New Jersey. Then, on May 1, he wrote to President Rawlins Lowndes of his own state:

We shall probably soon be called upon to meet by a proper Deputation the Commissioners expected from White Hall. for this momentous interview, my private Sentiment is, that the Wisdom of the Union should be selected, that we should go beyond the bounds of Congress and of any particular State in our choice of Character[s]. it is probably too late to ask advice or Instruction, and if I do not misunderstand we shall find our Men in York Town.

Subsequently (in 1779) Laurens advanced fundamentally the same idea, suggesting the calling of a "grand council", or convention, to undertake the task of solving the serious problems of the union.

While it was generally accepted that the observations of Congress on the bills for conciliation were "judicious and spirited" and "much to their honor", there were those who feared that they might have been too spirited, that they might rebuff the expected commissioners too effectually, might drive them away entirely.

Some of our people here [Laurens wrote, April 28] have been exceedingly desirous of throwing abroad in addition to the Resolutions an intimation of the willingness of Americans to treat with G[reat] Britain upon terms not inconsistent with the Independence of these States or with Treaties with foreign Powers. I am averse. we have made an excellent move on the Table. rest until we see or learn the motions on the other side. the whole World must know we are disposed to treat of Peace and to conclude one upon honorable terms. to Publish therefore is unnecessary. it would be a dangerous Act, encourage our Enemies and alarm our friends.

It was probably in view of the movement to which Laurens alludes that Thomas McKean wrote to Caesar Rodney the same day:

Do Sir . . . press the General Assembly to send two more Delegates here, and inform them that you know with certainty I am determined never to give up the Independence of the United States, after so much expense of blood and treasure, whilst I have a breath to draw; that I shall neither be allured nor intimidated into it; and that, if this resolution should not meet with their fullest approbation, they would be pleased to remove me immediately. God grant us virtue and fortitude in this hour of trial.

If such was not the stoutheartedness of each and every member of Congress, if within some bosoms there were quiverings of fear for the result, such quiverings must be confined within their bosoms and in nowise allowed to affect the boldness of their voices. It is probably true that at this moment independence as a fixed and unalterable condition of terminating the contest dominated the American mind far more widely and more deeply than it had done even on that fateful July 4 of 1776. At the same time, it is probably just as true that doubts of the possibility of achieving independence had crept into many minds that once had felt supremely confident. The winter months just past had brought dark clouds of discouragement and but the glimmerings of hope. While the army had starved and frozen at Valley Forge,

Congress had quaked with fear and trembling at York, and each had glared at the other across the intervening rivers and hills, not always in a manner the most amicable, not always with the full comprehension that they were members of one and the same body. Promise of a better understanding and of a more sympathetic cooperation had nevertheless now begun to dawn.

Some idea of the doubts and fears that were about to be dispelled may be gained from a letter of Henry Laurens to James Duane in early April, before Congress had learned of the conciliation bills.

The United States [Laurens declared] have acted, and 'tis far from impossible may be whipped, like Children. . . . I still trust we are not quite too late . . . be it so; let us not be stricken by fear, let us be animated and Wise— there is Wisdom in America, let it be collected—strength and success will be the Issue—but no time is to be lost—I do not hold it impossible, we shall hear of some attempts to accommodation as a prelude to the ensuing Campaign . . . but we need not distress our minds by apprehensions that the very first article will be a confirmation of American Independency—and who can dry eyed contemplate submission.

Whether with dry eyes or with wet, whether with palpitating hearts or with stout, whether with trembling knees or with bold and confident mien, it was just that possibility that many Americans had begun to envisage, as they sought to penetrate the gloom that was all about them. When therefore, on the 2d of May, the treaty of alliance with France was suddenly laid before the anxious group at York, it was as the sun suddenly bursting through dark clouds and compelling them to scurry away. All at once they who had stood the anxious watch through a cruel winter looked into the national skies to behold them brightened, their erstwhile gloomy world suffused with gladness.

CHAPTER XVIII

ON THE HEIGHTS
FRANCE COMES TO THE RESCUE

When Lord North's conciliatory bills and his speech first appeared, in April, 1778, Washington was at once convinced that behind them was some impelling force more than met the eye in the speech and the bills, surmising that France had "ratified our independence". It is not surprising that Congress was deeply in the dark about what the commissioners in Paris had been doing, for not a scratch of the pen had come from them later than a letter written in the closing days of May of the preceding year and received some four months afterward. Almost a year and not one word.

Not that the commissioners had failed to write; the enemy had been all too successful in intercepting the correspondence. Late in March, 1778, word had come by a roundabout way that "an important packet" was on its way to Congress, but without a hint of its contents. On the 27th of April, just ten days after the bills had first come to Washington's hands, Congress had the benefit of something better than surmise; for on that day Congress heard read a letter to Robert Morris from George Johnstone (who would presently appear as one of the commissioners for conciliation), dated "House of Commons, February 5, 1778", wherein was dropped not only a hint of the propositions about to be made to Parliament by the ministry, but the further intimation that "some preliminaries of a treaty have lately gone to France" Johnstone offered the suggestion that, "in prudence", Congress should "do nothing hastily with foreign powers". Another letter of the same George Johnstone a few days later (February 13) appears to have spoken of a treaty between the United States and France as a definite fact.

Yet all this was quite unofficial. It might be mere conjecture. The committee for foreign affairs must write and try to find out what was doing. What they had learned of the British plan, so the committee wrote to the commissioners at Paris (April 30), "must shortly perplex us much, unless we receive dispatches from you to enlighten us as to your Situation and Transactions, of which we have had no information since the latter end of May"—meaning, of course, May of the year before. This letter from George Johnstone—imagine how solicitous we are to know the truth of this before we receive any proposals from Britain in consequence of the scheme in Ld. North's speech and the two Draughts of Bills now sent to you."

Unless the commissioners should have vastly better success than hitherto in getting their communications across the water, bright prospect Congress had of obtaining "shortly" a reply to this letter! At best a reply could scarcely be expected short of three months, and long before the expiration of that time the dreaded tussle with the British commissioners might become necessary—a tussle or a downright repulse, depending upon the tautness of the Congressional nerve.

Indeed a report was already abroad that those commissioners were right then in Philadelphia, preparing to spring upon them. Not only was Congress perplexed, solicitous, it may well be believed that members were nervous, distraught, not knowing what a day might bring forth. One and all, they were agreed that their affairs were in a critical state. True, the new offers of conciliation, in so far as they could yet be interpreted, went far beyond any concessions that hitherto had been made; true, Americans were not now denounced as rebels, and no nooses dangled in front of them, such as once obtruded upon their vision and sent chills down their spines; yet in all those offerings independence was missing. To independence they had made their vows, and to those vows they would remain faithful. But could they maintain them? They were no longer quite so sure as they once were. Faith in their purposes was still strong, but the foundations of their hopes were somewhat shaken.

Fortunately Congress did not have to wait for a reply to the letter of its committee for foreign affairs; for already an answer to that anxious inquiry had crossed the Atlantic and was at that moment speeding toward York—that is, with such speed as could be expected in those days. On Saturday, the 2d of May, Congress had adjourned over the Sabbath, and the members had dispersed to their several places of abode—or elsewhere. Suddenly that Saturday evening the members were summoned to return to the assembly hall to hear such joyful news as had not fallen upon their ears since Saratoga, if ever. For Simeon Deane, brother to Silas, had come a messenger direct from the commissioners in Paris, bearing two treaties with France, one of alliance, the other of amity and commerce, concluded on the 6th of February, 1778.

Having listened to the reading of the treaties, Congress again adjourned until Monday. In what manner the members gave expression to their joy that night is one of the things concerning which, alas! they have left no record; but on Sunday morning they seized their pens to spread the glad tidings. President Laurens sent off a messenger with the news to General Washington, although, as it chanced, Washington had learned of it the day before. For Simeon Deane, on his way to York, had paused at Bethlehem to send a note to Washington conveying the purport of his despatches; and Washington had told it to the officers about him. "I believe", Washington wrote to President Laurens (May 1), "no event was ever received with more heart-felt joy." He only awaited the authorization of Congress to announce the good news to the army and to celebrate the happy event in a suitable manner.

On the same day Lafayette wrote to Laurens:

houra, my good friend, now the affair is over, and a very good treaty will assure our noble independence . . . I hope a grand, noisy *feu de joy* will be ordered, it will give high spirits to our soldiers, it will run through the whole continent, it schall reach the ears of our good friends in philadelphia. I wish Mss Commissioners may arrive from england that very same day, where we schall let them know that we have discovered their jesuitical meanings, and *the Candor* of theyr propositions.

On the 6th of May the event was celebrated in the army with all the "grand, noisy *feu de joy*" that Lafayette could have desired. Said one of the eye-witnesses to the celebration: "I never was present where there was such unfeigned and perfect joy, as was discovered in every countenance."

When Congress reassembled on the 4th of May, the treaties were quickly ratified by a unanimous vote, although exceptions were taken to two of the articles, and France was to be asked to rescind them. Of the treaties as a whole most members had only the highest praise. The Virginia delegates wrote to Governor Henry (May 3):

In general we find that his most Christian Majesty has been governed by principles of Magnanimity and true generosity, taking no advantage of our circumstances, but acting as if we were in the plenitude of power and in the greatest security . . . with a strong Army, we shall, under God, be perfectly secure, and it will probably compel G[reat] B[ritain] to a speedy recognition of our Independence.

William Ellery of Rhode Island was similarly impressed with France's guarantee of our independence and possessions and with the fact that the treaties displayed "a spirit of magnanimity and a soundness of policy scarcely to be paralleled". A few days later (May 14) Ellery was thinking especially of the threatened encroachment upon Britain's commerce:

The old enfeebled *Lion* growls out as if at the aggression on his honour, while the *Cock* crows round him determined to pick up his share of the commerce. . . . Can Britain, will Britain submit that France should carry on an unmolested Commerce with these States? . . . Will she risk the Loss of her West India Islands, the Loss of Canada, the Loss of rank amidst the Empires of the world rather than acknowledge the Independence we are in *full possession* of? I think she will. *Quos deus vult perdere prius dementat.*

Samuel Chase, who, despite the fact that his soul had been "chagrined at certain conduct" and despite the unsatisfactory accommodations at York that had given him a strong impulse to go back home, was now lifted into the heights of exaltation. "America", he declared, "has now taken her rank among the nations." Yet, with all his "bold and sonorous" oratory, Chase retained still a sense of the practical. He hoped that the alliance would bring "speedy and liberal loans of money to the Continent and a respectable Army". Said Oliver Wolcott, the treaties "have been much approved of. . . . They are founded upon the broad Basis of Mutual Interest and Security, and Nothing in them which indicates any Design of obtaining any Advantage over us". And that mouthpiece of the whole Congress, the committee for foreign affairs, wrote, probably by the hand of Richard Henry Lee, to the commissioners at Paris (May 14):

We admire the true Wisdom and Dignity of the Court of France. . . . In those Treaties we see the Politician founded on the Philosopher and harmony of affections made the ground Work of mutual Interest. France by her open Candor has *won* us more Powerfully than any reserved Treaties could possibly *bind* us, and at a happy Juncture of Times and Circumstances laid the seeds of an eternal Friendship.

Whatever else might be involved in the treaties with France, whether in America or in Europe, one result seemed now to be beyond question: the independence of the United States was assured. Even Washington spoke (May 5) of the *"certain* prospect of success", although at the same time he applauded the wisdom of Congress in not relaxing their preparations for war. Indeed one of his first comments on the news of the alliance was the expression of a conviction that "one immediate good consequence" of the treaty would be "that the states will shake off their languor, and be stimulated to complete their battalions". Whether or not Congress was so stimulated, the plan for the reorganization of the army was adopted with reasonable speed and without serious friction.

Such parts of the treaties as Congress judged necessary, accompanied by a "proper publication" for the government of the conduct of commanders of vessels and for the information of the people, were at once published, and, in addition, Congress sent abroad (May 8) an address to the inhabitants of the United States, recommending that ministers of the gospel of all denominations read it or cause it to be read in their respective places of worship immediately after divine service. The address, which was written by Gouverneur Morris and is in his characteristic manner, painted in fervid terms the cruelties and ignominies that the people of America had suffered at the hands of their enemies and were certain yet to suffer if they listened to the insidious offers of peace with which the enemy was now endeavoring to ensnare them.

At length That God of battles, in whom was our trust [says one part of the address], hath conducted us through the paths of danger and distress to the thresholds of security . . . if we have courage to persevere, we shall establish our liberties and independence. The haughty prince, who spurned us from his feet with contumely and disdain, and the parliament which proscribed us, now descend to offer terms of accommodation . . . they now endeavor to ensnare us with the insidious offers of peace. They would seduce you into a dependence, which necessarily inevitably leads to the most humiliating slavery. . . . Is there a man who would not abhor a dependence upon those who have deluged his country in the blood of its inhabitants? . . . What, then, is their intention? Is it not to lull you with the fallacious hopes of peace, until they can assemble new armies to prosecute their nefarious designs. . . . Be not, therefore, deceived. You have still to expect one severe conflict. Your foreign alliances, though they secure your independence, cannot secure your country from desolation, your habitations from plunder, your wives from insult or violation, nor your children from butchery. . . . Arise then! to your tents, and gird you for the battle! It is time to turn the headlong current of vengeance upon the head of the destroyer. . . . Expect not peace, whilst any corner of America is in possession of your foes. . . . Trust not to appearances of peace or safety. . . . But, if you exert the means of defence which God and nature have given you, the time will soon arrive when every man shall sit under his own vine and under his own fig-tree, and there shall be none to make him afraid. . . . Thus shall the power and the happiness of these sovereign, free and independent states, founded on the virtue of their citizens, increase, extend and endure, until the Almighty shall blot out all the empires of the earth.

This is no more than a sampling of the address, from which several Fourth-of-July orations might be mined. Numerous copies of this address were sent out to the several states and to many officials besides, with the request that they "be dispersed as generally and as speedily as possible". For instance, fifty copies were transmitted (May 11) to General Washington, who was besought to direct a dispersion of them "so as most effectually to answer the purposes intended".

The address was calculated to establish a basis of popular support for the part Congress would take in the next act of the drama just about to be staged. Enter first, Lord Howe and General Sir Henry Clinton with the Parliamentary acts designed to bring about an accommodation. This was on the 6th of June. That Congress was not disposed to dawdle is made clear by the fact that the committee to whom the letters of Messrs. Howe and Clinton were referred were ordered to "retire into the next room, and prepare an answer". That the mind of Congress was already fixed is evidenced by the speedy adoption of the committee's recommendation, that the answer be a transmission of the act of April 22, adopted upon the first appearance of the drafts of the bills, with a brief, crisp addition:

Your lordship may be assured, that when the king of Great Britain shall be seriously disposed to put an end to the unprovoked and cruel war waged against these United States, Congress will readily attend to such terms of peace, as may consist with the honor of independent nations, the interest of their constituents, and the sacred regard they mean to pay to treaties.

Messrs. Howe and Clinton were not, however, to be thus rebuffed. Already, on June 4, the commissioners designated for carrying into effect Lord North's measures for conciliation, namely, the Earl of Carlisle, William Eden, and George Johnstone, had arrived in Philadelphia. Thereupon General Clinton requested of General Washington (June 9) a passport for Dr. Adam Ferguson, secretary to the commissioners, that he might repair to Congress with despatches from his principals. Washington declined, however, to grant the passport, "without being previously instructed by Congress on the subject". In this instance Congress was not quite so swift in its response, for that body was still in the midst of a third day's debate (June 13) on what answer should be given to General Clinton, when a packet was "ushered into the house" and delivered to the President. "This", President Laurens announced, holding up the packet in full view of the house, "this might prove an attempt to amend the whole."

The despatches, Laurens tells us, "were under a superb direction and triple Seals, the device of the latter, a fond Mother embracing returning Children". The packet was opened, the reading began, and had advanced to the second page without interruption; but when Congress heard the President read the words, "insidious interposition of a power, which has, from the first settlement of these colonies, been actuated with enmity to us both; and notwithstanding the pretended date or present form of the French offers", up rose a member (Gouverneur Morris) and moved that the reading proceed no further, "because of the offensive language against his most Christian majesty". The motion was not carried without debate, but in the end the President was ordered to seal up the packet, and Congress adjourned until the following Monday.

Evidently not all the members agreed with Gouverneur Morris that the "insolent letter" should be sent back "with contempt". Josiah Bartlett, for instance, deplored "the Zeal of some members" for sealing up the letters and sending them back without reading them, thereby delaying the reply. Samuel Adams, for another, declared that "Some Expressions in the Letter gave Disgust to all the Members", and he had no doubt that the subject would be treated "with becoming Spirit and Propriety"; but what especially concerned him was the plain design of the commissioners "to draw us back to a Subjection to their King". Richard Henry Lee in particular characterized the letter as "a combination of fraud, falsehood, insidious offers, and abuse of France, concluding with a denial of Independence", the *"sine qua non"*. Lee was nevertheless one of those who preferred to adopt a reasonably conciliatory attitude toward the commissioners, and he, as well as some others, including John Witherspoon and Secretary Thomson, tried his hand at drafting a reply to the commissioners' letter.

It was not until June 16 that Congress reached a decision to read the whole of the letter, and not until the 17th, after much discussion and the trial of several formulae, that the answer was at last agreed upon. Then, remarkable to relate, the vote was unanimous, not only of states but also of individuals, thirty-one in number. In the reply agreed upon was no lack of spirit, yet but small evidence of that offended dignity with which Congress had stopped the reading of the letter. "Nothing but an earnest desire to spare the further effusion of human blood", said Congress, "could have induced them to read a paper containing expressions so disrespectful to his most Christian majesty, the good and great ally of these states, or to consider propositions so derogatory to the honor of an independent nation." The reply concluded by stating that Congress would be ready to enter upon the consideration of a treaty of peace and commerce, "not inconsistent with treaties already subsisting", whenever the king of Great Britain should demonstrate a sincere disposition for that purpose, proof of which would be "an explicit acknowledgment of the independence of these states, or the withdrawing his fleets and armies".

If all the fine things now offered [wrote Henry Laurens to General Gates, June 17] had been tendered some time ago, admitting their solidity, there can be no doubt but that the people of America would joyfully have embraced the proposition, but now what answer can be given but that which was returned to the foolish Virgins—"the Door is shut" . . . here's a Boy's Card House tumbled down by a Breath.

Two days later he added: "One part of the Mission is to grant Pardons. Sing tantarara All Mad." For Thomas McKean it was an hour for exultation. "I have lived to see the day", he exclaimed, "when, instead of 'Americans licking the dust from the feet of a British Minister', the tables are turned."

Not only did the commissioners as a body plead earnestly with the wandering children to return to the family fireside, offering practically everything that had been asked short of actual independence, they plied their individual pens industriously to the same end. Chiefly in response to an order of Congress, a number of such letters were thrown upon the table, some of them a bit reluctantly, others with gestures of scorn. But how many more there may have been, to whom, and what the nature and the manner of their pleas, these, despite sundry intimations, are among the things that have remained unrevealed.

In addition, the commissioners came armed with eloquent pleas from men in England to their American friends. Said one such writer to a member of Congress: "Lose not the feelings of the Christian in the resentment of the man, and as you have nobly fought, act more nobly and forgive." Furthermore, let the full truth be told, the commissioners did not content themselves with persuasive appeals addressed to reason and brotherly love; they plied another sort of logic: offers of emoluments, offices, and other substantial rewards. "Be upon your guard with regard to letters from the Enemy", Thomas McKean wrote to Caesar Rodney (June 17); "they intend to seduce, corrupt and bribe by every method possible."

Congress itself, on that same day, issued a like warning to all the legislative and executive authorities. Ideas "insidiously calculated to divide and delude the good people of these states" were being disseminated by or through the commissioners, and these authorities were urged to take "the most effectual measures to put a stop to so dangerous and criminal a correspondence". Beyond adopting these recommendatory resolutions and ordering their publication, Congress did not at the moment extend an interfering hand in the matter of private correspondence, although some members made an effort to have Congress do just that thing. "Yesterday", Laurens wrote to Washington June 18, "there was an extraordinary Motion on our floor for calling upon Members to lay before Congress such Letters as they had received from the Commissioners or other persons, meaning persons in Great Britain on Political subjects." Laurens deemed it "a dangerous attempt to stretch the power of Congress", and, for his part, he could never consent to have his property taken from him by an order from his fellow-citizens "destitute of authority for the purpose".

The attempt not only involved the delicate question of Congressional prerogative, it involved the much deeper principle of personal liberty. In this instance the principle of personal liberty won; in a renewal of the contest a little later the victory was on the side of presumed expediency. So far however as regards the end aimed at by the commissioners and their aiders and abettors, it mattered little which of the elements in Congress won the bout; such was the manner in which individuals were approached and offers made that the result was the precise opposite of that for which the commissioners had hoped.

The curtain may here be let fall for a brief space upon the activities of Carlisle, Eden, Johnstone, and Company, while Congress enacts quite another scene in the unfolding of the drama. Before the end of May, Congress had begun to prick up its ears at rumors, reports, and surmises that the British were about to evacuate Philadelphia, and one and all they eagerly watched for signs in the air that would confirm that purpose. Reports, however, became more and more conflicting. "Here we are", James Lovell wrote to General Gates (June 9), "still the Sport of Lyars. One Day we are told the Enemy are filling their Ditches and preparing to leave Philad[elphi]a . . . in the next we are informed of new Works and fresh arrived Troops." In a similar vein John Wentworth, Jr., of New Hampshire wrote to John Langdon the next day, adding that the enemy's maneuvers were so various that it was impossible to guess what they would do. Upon the whole, however, it was the conviction that Philadelphia would soon be theirs again. The prospect was deeply satisfying. For more and more, during their enforced exile, Philadelphia had come to symbolize ways of pleasantness.

It was on June 19, two days after the commissioners had been informed "whence to take their departure", that Congress learned from General Washington that Philadelphia had been evacuated, and thereupon Congress began to make its own preparations to return to the city. On June 24 it was resolved to adjourn from York on Saturday, June 27, to reassemble in Philadelphia on Thursday, the 2d of July, and that on the 4th there should be a public celebration of the anniversary of the Declaration of Independence. More than that, it was resolved that on Sunday, the 5th, Congress would in a body attend divine worship, "to return thanks for the divine mercy in supporting the independence of these states".

Meanwhile there was urgent work to do where they sat. Congress had scarcely calmed itself after its first triumphant rejoicing over the alliance with France, when it bethought itself that, while the United States of America had acted as a nation in making treaties with another power, no organic union of the states actually existed, except in so far as such a union was manifest in a common assembly, the Congress, and that the power and authority of Congress was nowhere explicitly defined. Articles of Confederation designed to create the United States of America, with the treaty-making power embodied in just such an assembly as the existing Congress, were indeed then before the states but had not been accepted by them. At that moment therefore the union was without other bond than a vague and ill-defined general consent. What a humiliating state of affairs, when the minister of their ally was expected almost any day. The Articles of Confederation *must* be ratified. For Congress to receive the representative of their great and good ally otherwise than as the constitutional head of a perfected union, is unthinkable.

When the Articles of Confederation had been sent to the states at the end of November, 1777, the respective legislatures were eloquently besought to invest their delegates in Congress with competent powers to subscribe the Articles by the 10th of March, 1778; yet, when the 10th of March had come around, but few responses had been received, and only one state, Virginia, had offered to ratify the Confederation unconditionally, although New York shortly afterward took similar action. Most of the others did transmit their acts of ratification within the next few weeks, but nearly all these acts were accompanied by proposed amendments or other conditions, a few of the conditions having the character of ultimata. By the beginning of June, despite the fact that a few of the states had not signified their assent to the Confederation either with or without amendments, and notwithstanding some of them were without representation in Congress, there appears to have been a confident opinion that the Confederation would be "universally agreed to".

On the 9th of May, that is within a week from the receipt of the French treaty, at a time when only nine states were represented and only twenty-one delegates were on the floor, Congress ordered that the delegates of the several states lay on the table "for the perusal of the members", any objections or amendments that their states had to propose. Because, however, of the intervention of other urgent matters the Confederation became thrust to one side until the 20th of June, when Congress again called for reports from the various states; and within the next five days one state after another, all those with representation on the floor, laid its verdict on the table. New Hampshire answered the roll-call with unqualified assent, making a third to accept without conditions; but after that the line did not grow. Others offered objections or proposed amendments, some not very weighty, others extensive, and a few of them going to the very heart of the union.

Maryland in particular reiterated an objection that she had offered in the beginning, and now proposed an amendment whereby the United States in Congress assembled should have power "to ascertain and restrict the boundaries of such of the confederated States which claim to extend to the river Mississippi, or the South Sea". Once again Maryland's demand gave Congress pause, and for two days the question was warmly debated; the urgency, however, of immediate ratification was such, in the opinion of the majority, that Maryland's proposition was rejected by a vote of six states to five, with one divided. Said the Maryland delegation, George Plater and Charles Carroll of Carrollton, in reporting the matter to their general assembly (June 22):

A Confederation at this critical juncture appears to Congress of such momentous consequence, that I am satisfied a great majority are resolved to reject the amendments from every State, not so much from an opinion that *all* the amendments are improper, as from the conviction, that if *any* should be adopted, no Confederation will take place, at least for some months, perhaps years; and in that case many apprehend none will ever be entered into by all the present United States.

New Jersey took her place beside Maryland in the matter of the western lands and, in an elaborate "representation", offered other objections besides; whereof the fate was the same as the offerings of Maryland, only a little more so, the vote being six to three, and one divided. Hurriedly, almost frantically, Congress went through the long lists of objections and proposed amendments, putting a firm negative upon them one and all, notwithstanding the persistence of two or three dissentients.

In view of all the facts then before Congress it is surprising how confident members were that ratification would be unanimous and that very soon. Of two states not yet heard from, Georgia and Delaware, there was every reason to believe that Georgia would give her assent; but there were almost as strong reasons for concluding that Delaware would take her stand, as in fact she did, with Maryland and New Jersey. On the day that Congress took the Confederation into consideration (June 20) Richard Henry Lee wrote: "The friends to the future happiness and glory of America are now urging the Confederation to a close, and I hope it will be sighned in a few days." The small states, he was confident, would "undoubtedly fall in". Oliver Wolcott likewise believed (June 20) that ratification would take place "within about the Course of a Week". The Rhode Island delegates had a like conviction; "for this", they declared, "is the Grand Corner Stone".

Even President Laurens thought at one time (June 22) that "The whole will be ratified in the original form within three days".

Such indeed was the general confidence that Congress had "the form of a ratification prepared" and ordered the Articles to be engrossed, ready for the signing. All this was to be done before adjourning to Philadelphia. When, however, the engrossed copy was brought into Congress, almost at the moment of adjournment, it was found to contain "interlineations and mistakes". There was nothing to do but to quench the fires of hope for a few days and try to complete "this great work" in Philadelphia. It was just as well. No one as yet seems to have measured correctly the stoutness of resistance to come from Maryland and her allies.

Congress seldom had difficulty in adjourning, but hardly ever succeeded in reassembling at the appointed time. Eager as every one had been to get back to Philadelphia, many of them wandered hither and yon or loitered, with the result that not until July 7 was it possible to gather a quorum. "Various impediments", wrote President Laurens (July 15), had prevented an earlier assembling.

One was the offensiveness of the air in and around the State House, which the Enemy had made an Hospital and left it in a condition disgraceful to the Character of civility. Particularly they had opened a large square pit near the House, a receptacle for filth, into which they had also cast dead horses and the bodies of men who by the mercy of death had escaped from their further cruelties. I cannot proceed to a new subject before I add a curse on their savage practices.

In consequence of this situation Congress had been "shuffling from Meeting House to College Hall"; and that of itself was a serious obstacle to the facilitation of business.

There was nothing, however, to prevent those who had arrived betimes from joining in the celebration of the anniversary of independence, as Congress had planned before leaving York. It was a "grand festival", so one of the Philadelphia papers chronicled. It was "a very elegant dinner", wrote Samuel Holten. And after the dinner came the usual thirteen toasts, of which the first was "The United States of

America", and the last was "May the Union of the American States be perpetual". Between the two, and not to be overlooked, was "The Friendly European Powers". On the following day, which was Sunday, Congress in a body, so much of it as had been brought together, attended divine service; twice, in fact; at "church" in the morning, and at the Congregational meeting in the afternoon.

On the 9th of July the newly engrossed Articles of Confederation were laid before Congress, and the delegates of eight states thereupon appended their signatures to the instrument. Two states that had authorized ratification, namely North Carolina and Georgia, had no delegates present at the time, but completed their acts of ratification shortly afterward. The delegates of Maryland, New Jersey, and Delaware informed Congress that they had "not yet received powers to ratify and sign". And thus for a time the matter stood, three states outside the circle, the Confederation without effect.

Nathaniel Scudder, one of the delegates of New Jersey, undertook the task of trying to overcome the scruples of his state, for he regarded the affair as "of the most serious and alarming importance". He pointed out that the United States, "as a Confederated people", had entered into a treaty with the court of Versailles, and that a minister from that court was already on the coast, "with a powerful Fleet of Ships". "How must he be astonished and confounded", Scudder protested, "and what may be the fatal Consequences to America when he discovers (which he will immediately do) that we are *ipso facto* unconfederated, and consequently, what our Enemies have called us, 'a Rope of Sand'?"

Probably no state had been more desirous of extensive amendments to the Confederation than South Carolina, but in the end the delegates of that state, notwithstanding a doubt respecting their authorization, agreed to sign. John Mathews of that delegation was probably even more deeply impressed with the importance of completing the Confederation if possible, then and there, than was President Laurens.

This I am clear in, from what I have seen, and know, since I have been in Congress [Mathews wrote, July 7] that if we are to have no Confederation until the Legislatures of the Thirteen States agree to one, that we shall never have one, and if we have not one, we shall be literally a rope of sand, and I shall tremble for the consequences that will follow at the end of this War.

Others than Mathews dropped intimations that the idea of confederating with fewer than all thirteen states was already brewing. James Lovell, for instance, had no doubt (July 14) that Georgia, Delaware and New Jersey would sign; but "Maryland", he was sure, "will take airs and plague us, but upon our determination to confederate with 12 will do as she has always before done—come in without grace." Maryland proved to be a more stubborn dame than most members of Congress had supposed.

Congress could not of course be content to allow the three recalcitrant states to sulk in their tents without every effort being made to prevail upon them to dismiss their scruples for the time being and to complete the union that was so necessary to the attainment of their common purpose. Accordingly a committee was at once designated— Richard Henry Lee, Francis Dana, and Gouverneur Morris—to prepare an appeal to them. Congress, declared the appeal, had "never ceased to consider a confederacy as the great principle of union, which can alone establish the liberty of America and exclude forever the hopes of its enemies". It could scarcely be expected that any plan that might be formed would "exactly meet the wishes and obtain the approbation of so many states, differing essentially in various points"; yet Congress was "willing to hope that the patriotism and good sense" of these states, "influenced by motives so important", would induce them to instruct their delegates "to ratify the confederation with all convenient despatch; trusting to future deliberation to make such alterations and amendments as experience may shew to be expedient and just." Whatever may have been the arguments or the influences, in November, New Jersey relented, as did Delaware in January following. Maryland alone continued to stand out, and, contrary to the opinion of James Lovell, much grace would be required before she would cease to plague them or be persuaded to come in.

Before Congress had been able to settle down to business in any acceptable manner, while still "shuffling from Meeting House to College Hall", word came that a French vessel, the *Languedoc,* commanded by the Comte d'Estaing, with a fleet of twelve sail of the line and four frigates, had arrived in Delaware Bay, and, what was more, on board the *Languedoc* had come a minister plenipotentiary of his Most Christian Majesty, the Sieur Conrade Alexandre Gérard. Congress at once became all agog and all aglow. First of all General Washington must be requested to take measures for cooperation with the Comte d'Estaing in the execution of offensive operations against the enemy, and to that end he was empowered to call on certain of the states for aids of their militia. Nor was it of less importance that a suitable house be secured for the accommodation of the French minister and that a committee be appointed to receive him with proper honors and to escort him to his lodgings. He was met by the committee at Chester, with ceremonies of which Elias Boudinot has left a lively description, and escorted to the city, where there were other ceremonies.

All these things, however, were only a polite welcome. The public audience was yet to come. Meanwhile members of Congress hastened to pay their respects to the minister, then, upon returning to their lodgings, to write their friends their impressions of this representative of the mighty power that had come to the aid of America. The Massachusetts delegates had "paid him their Complements in Form", so Samuel Adams wrote to James Warren. He did not know whether any other state had observed that ceremony, but it had appeared to them as "highly proper". Apparently it lay in Adams's mind that the French mission was to the states individually as much as to the states collectively, especially since they were not yet confederated. "We were receivd with Politeness", Adams continued, "and heard some handsome Things said of the State we have the Honor to represent." He thought the minister's manners "would suit our country". After a subsequent interview Adams was more specific: "He is easy and polite in his Manners and converses freely without much Ceremony." Some spoke of him as "wise", some as "well-bred", some as "modest", and one declared that he was "as grave as a Frenchman can be."

Henry Marchant of Rhode Island found the interview "most cordial, generous and noble"; indeed "the most interesting interview that ever took place in America, or perhaps in the world", and his bosom was made to swell with ardor and with hope.

The Scene brightens [he exclaimed], grows more and more interesting, and calls for new and fresh Exertions of Senatorial Wisdom. We advance into the Circle and Standing of mighty Nations—Adepts in all the Policy of Peace and War. . . . I never was Witness to a more elevating and unspeakably joyous Interview than that between the Plenipotenteary of His most Christian Majesty, and the President of Congress in the Name and Behalf of the thirteen United States of America. It was reciprocally easy graceful Endearing and Noble. May it presage a happy Issue to the american Struggle and a growing and undecaying Glory that shall diffuse its grateful Influences thro' the World.

Not every one gave way to such rhetorical outbursts as did Marchant, but there can be no doubt that the dominant note in every mind was that it presaged a happy issue to the American struggle. A characteristic expression of that thought was furnished by the *Pennsylvania Packet:*

Who would have thought . . . that the American colonies imperfectly known in Europe a few years ago, and claimed by every pettyfogging lawyer in the House of Commons, and every cobler in the beer houses of London, as a part of their property, should in the course of three years of a war with Great Britain, receive an Ambassador from the most powerful Monarchy in Europe.

The public audience that must of course be given to the minister was a serious matter and must be deeply pondered and carefully planned. First of all that filthy State House would have to be renovated, cleansed of all reminders of its late occupancy by the common enemy. As to the ceremonies that should be employed, Congress was not a little perplexed. It was a new thing in the life of the youthful nation. Some members wished that they might get on without ceremony, yet this sort of thing, they supposed, was a necessary accompaniment to the part that the United States of America were about to take among the nations of the world, and certainly they must try to do their part with all decency and propriety. "Would you think", wrote Samuel Adams, "that one so little of the Man of the World as I am should be joynd in a Committee to settle Ceremonials? It is however of some Importance that we agree upon Forms that are adapted to the true *republican* Principles; for this Instance may be recurrd to as a Precedent in Futurity."

First of all, it devolved upon Congress to determine whether Gérard should be received as minister plenipotentiary or merely as "resident", for he had been commissioned to serve in either capacity, as Congress might prefer. He himself indicated a preference for the character of minister plenipotentiary, and Congress naturally accepted that preference. But the actual ceremonies to be followed in the official reception were not so easily settled. What salute, for instance, should an ambassador, minister plenipotentiary, envoy, or resident, receive upon his arrival within the United States? What military honors should be paid him? How many members of Congress should be deputed to wait upon him to inform him that Congress was ready to receive him? How many should accompany him to the assembly hall and how should they seat themselves in the chariot?

It was at first proposed to depute three members to act as escort, but that raised a troublesome problem of seating, therefore the final decision was, two members, the one to sit to the left of the minister, the other in the front seat. And what of the arrangements in the Congress chamber? How high, for instance, should the President's chair be raised above the common level? The answer, two feet. How high that of the minister? Answer, eighteen inches. Then, there were even more troublesome questions. Who shall introduce the minister? With what titles shall the Congress and its President be addressed? With what the minister? When shall the one or the other sit and when shall they rise? When shall they bow and to whom? And when shall they be bowed unto?

These and other like questions were mulled over a good many days "I assure you", wrote Richard Henry Lee, "it is a work of no small difficulty." Whatever the difficulties and differences of opinion, one provision, we may confidently assume, was accorded unanimous assent. It is recorded in these words:

All speeches or communications in writing, may, if the publick ministers choose it, be in the language of their respective countries. And all replies, or answers, shall be in the language of the United States.

Congress occupied much of its time for a week in settling upon the details of the ceremonial, it consumed two weeks in formulating the reply that the President would make to the speech of the minister, and it required a whole month to make the State House a fit place in which to receive the minister of their great and good friend and ally. At last, on the 6th of August, nearly a month since the minister's arrival, everything was in readiness—except that some members of Congress had not quite been able to puzzle out satisfactorily their own parts in the ceremony. Accordingly Congress devoted a long session the evening before mainly to clarifying the obscure points. The puzzling questions were chiefly those pertaining to the risings, the standings, the sittings, and the bowings. For another thing, it was decided that the door of the Congress chamber should be open during the audience, but that admittance be by ticket only, each member of Congress being allowed two tickets.

The audience, which began at high noon on August 6, appears to have been conducted smoothly through its appointed course. Followed then a banquet, "at which were present by invitation several foreigners of distinction, and gentlemen of public character", all "conducted with a decorum suited to the occasion". Gérard himself made a report of the affair to his government, stating that twenty-one toasts were drunk, amid the roar of cannon, including healths to the king and queen of France, the king of Spain, and toasts to the perpetuity of the union between France and America, and to the success of the combined arms. "It was an Important Day", wrote Henry Marchant; "An Important Transaction. . . . I think the Connection brought about by the Hand of Heaven, and that therefore, it promises to be as lasting as it is mutually beneficial, generous, and noble."

It is not however to be inferred that amid all this inundation of joy there was no rift in the lute, no voice but applauded the alliance, whether or not it might be entangling. There is much testimony at an earlier day that fears of such entanglements existed, just as at this moment there were those who had their anxious misgivings. Now, however, such fears were mainly stilled or thrust behind, and doubting voices mostly hushed. One of those who notwithstanding, in the intimacy of a private letter, ventured to lift the curtain upon his inner thoughts, even in the very midst of the general acclaim, was Andrew Adams of Connecticut.

I must freely own [he wrote to Oliver Wolcott, July 22] I dont feel myself so compleatly flush'd upon this Occasion as many do: I cant say that it may be attended with the happy Consiquences expected; but when I view the Matter upon a larger Scale sundry Questions suggest themselves for our Consideration; I was fully of Oppinion that the War was drawing to a speedy issue . . . upon this View of the Case I would quere whither the arrival of this Fleet will not be a Means of lengthening out the War, and also ley us under an Obligation of affording France an arm'd force in Case they Need it . . . besides would it not be much to our Advantage had we settled the present Controversy in our favour without a foreign Aid? Under such Idears I have never been fond of the Assistance of any foreign Power: However I am no Adept in Politicks . . . and leave the Decision to abler Politi[ci]ans or future Time.

Five weeks later the Connecticut member was again confiding his anxieties to Wolcott, and this time indulging in some speculations. Suppose a similar treaty should be made with Spain ("which perhaps may already be the Case"), and suppose France should possess herself of the West India islands, Spain of the two Floridas, and then France and Spain should unite for the extirpation of England: "a Quere would arise whether they would not expect our Assistance." "However", he added, "I confess this is looking forward some Ways."

Probably there was not a man in Congress who would not have opposed seeking foreign aid, if only he could have felt sure that without it the contest could be settled "in our favor". That was the great uncertainty that glared Congress in the face and would continue to glare to the end of the chapter. On the score of entanglements, Andrew Adams would in the end prove to have been no mean seer. Americans were, in fact, soon to discover that their great cause had become intricately entangled in the affairs of Europe, that their war for independence had become, so far as Europe was concerned, a skirmish in the struggle for supremacy between two great powers. As for the hearty encomiums so lavishly bestowed upon the French minister personally, before many months shall have gone by not a few of the encomiasts will be searching for words at the opposite pole of their vocabularies.

Congress may well have wished that it be left undisturbed while planning its own steps toward cementing the French alliance; but it was not to be. The discussion of those plans and the meditation upon expressions of sweet accord with the new-found friend of American independence were rudely broken in upon by those same British commissioners who had recently been summarily bidden to begone. They had indeed departed Philadelphia, along with the British army, but from their new base in New York they undertook a renewal of their campaign of conciliation, albeit the manner of their conducting it was more aggressive than conciliatory, and in consequence the more ineffective.

For some three months barrages and counter barrages of words went on, distracting enough in their noises and at times exciting in their verbal display, but with little or no effect on the front-line trenches of either side. The first of these essays of the commissioners was dated July 11 and was delivered to Congress on July 18.

If I dared to venture an opinion, from a very cursory reading of the performance [President Laurens wrote to General Washington, July 18], it would be, that this is more puerile than any thing I have seen from the other side, since the commencement of our present dispute, with a little dash of insolence, as unnecessary as it will be unavailing.

"Very silly, and equally insolent", declared Richard Henry Lee. "A curious letter", wrote John Penn. In view of all the facts, however, it was not so curious; certainly it was not puerile or silly; but that it had a dash of insolence, that it was at best undiplomatic, unwise, can scarcely be gainsaid.

Probably just at that time, when Congress was fondly embracing its ally, almost revelling in feelings of security and disposed to bid defiance to Great Britain and all her works, nothing that the commissioners could have said or done would have effected a reconciliation carrying the least semblance of dependence. But the commissioners had touched Congress in an exceedingly sore spot. They had, in effect, taunted Congress with the fact that the United States were yet unconfederated. "We likewise think ourselves", so wrote the commissioners, "entitled to a full Communication of the Powers by which you conceive yourselves Authorized to make Treaties with Foreign Nations." Then they went on to point out that, while the Articles of Confederation stipulated that Congress should have such powers, "under certain Restrictions therein specified", yet nowhere had they been able to find promulgated "any Act or Resolution of the Assembly's of particular States conferring this Power on you".

The action of Congress was a crisp resolution (July 18), "That no answer be given to the letter of the 11th inst. from the British commissioners". There was indeed a preamble, neither so short nor so crisp, wherein was reiterated the resolution of June 17, with its alternatives of withdrawing the fleets and armies or an explicit acknowledgment of the independence of the United States, neither of which had been complied with. The letter of the commissioners and the resolution of Congress were ordered published, and that was all.

It was not at all difficult for Congress to take refuge in official silence when there was a ready pen at hand that could be employed to make any desired retort, a pen sufficiently unofficial to have little need of restraint. Gouverneur Morris possessed just such a pen, and he proceeded to employ it, using the signature "An American". To the taunt of the commissioners that was especially nettling to Congress, "An American", addressing the Earl of Carlisle, offered this reply:

It is a most diverting circumstance to hear you ask Congress what power they have to treat, after offering to enter into a treaty with them, and being refused. But I shall be glad to know by what authority you call on them for this discovery. The Count de Vergennes had a right to it, but the Earl of Carlisle certainly has not.

The commissioners further intimated that they might also make use of the press with a view to appealing to the people against Congress; to which "An American" replied: "There is but one way to sink you still lower, and thank God you have found it out. You are about to publish! Oh my Lord! my Lord! you are indeed in a mighty pitiful condition. You have tried fleets and armies, and proclamations, and now you threaten us with newspapers." Not very dignified; not particularly convincing; not in the least calculated to calm the troubled waters; but it no doubt tickled patriotic fancy, made many a patriot grin.

To make matters worse it began to be bruited about that amongst the letters from one or another of the commissioners to individuals there were not only offers of honors and emoluments to those who would steer the vessel in the storm and bring her safely to port, such, for instance, as that of Commissioner Johnstone to Robert Morris, which the latter had laid upon the table of Congress on July 9, but there were letters more plainly intimating a readiness to bestow other substantial rewards. In particular it leaked out that the recipient of one such letter, Joseph Reed, a member of Congress from Pennsylvania, had been approached by an intermediary on behalf of commissioner Johnstone, with the suggestion that, if he would undertake to promote a re-union between Great Britain and America, he might have ten thousand pounds sterling and any office in America in his majesty's gift. Reed's reply to this proposition was that, "He was not worth purchasing, but such as he was, the King of Great Britain was not rich enough to do it." Accordingly Congress put forth (August 11) "A Declaration", citing in particular Johnstone's endeavors with Morris and Reed and closing with a resolution, "That it is incompatible with the honor of Congress to hold any manner of correspondence or intercourse with the said George Johnstone, Esq., especially to negotiate with him upon affairs in which the cause of liberty is interested."

Before this Declaration, destined to be sent by a flag to the commissioners, had been started on its journey, came a renewed remonstrance respecting the detention of the Convention troops, a remonstrance which must needs be countered with a suitable retort; and when, a few weeks later, General Clinton again adverted to the subject, he did so in such a manner that Congress did no more about it than to instruct the secretary of Congress (September 28) to inform the general that "the Congress of the United States make no answer to insolent letters". The rebuffs administered to the commissioners individually and collectively might seem to have been sufficient to reduce them to complete silence; but having, as they were convinced, a great purpose to subserve, they were not the men to relinquish their efforts so long as the remotest hope of accomplishing their purpose remained. It was perhaps as a last despairing effort therefore that, in the beginning of October, the commissioners issued a "Manifesto and Proclamation", offering a general pardon and adding intimations of the calamities that would ensue if their offers of conciliation were not accepted. "I believe", wrote Samuel Holten, "there is but few people here want their pardon."

It was learned that the manifesto was to be liberally spread abroad by means of flags of truce, clearly "a prostitution of the flag", Congress declared. It was "an insulting Paper", said Samuel Adams (October 16), "calculated to promote a Rebellion", and he suggested that the vessel bringing the paper to Pennsylvania be seized and the men be brought up blindfold, "to be dealt with according to the Laws of Nature and Nations". In the case of the batch of manifestoes destined particularly for the city of Philadelphia one of the laws of nature dealt with it so effectively as to obviate any need for invoking the law of nations; for the vessel was wrecked on the New Jersey coast, with some loss of men as well as of papers. "The Sea", said Richard Henry Lee, "has saved us the trouble by previously swallowing up these silly Missives."

Before many days, however, the sea disgorged two parcels of the silly missives, one marked Pennsylvania, the other Delaware, and both were presently laid before Congress. "Congress would take no cognizance of the waif", so President Laurens wrote to President Rodney of Delaware (November 1), adding that the president of Pennsylvania likewise "declined touching the Bundle" marked for his state. If President Rodney desired it, he was welcome to the Delaware bundle. Governor Livingston of New Jersey did receive his assignment, and he forthwith delivered himself of some characteristically caustic remarks upon it.

There were numerous responses, unofficial and semi-official, to the manifesto, and one official pronouncement by Congress (October 16), wherein "certain seditious papers, under the name and title of mani-festoes" were roundly denounced as designed "to stir up dissentions, animosities and rebellion, among the good people of these states", and the executive powers of the states were recommended "to take up and secure in safe and close custody" any persons concerned in their dis-tribution.

This pronouncement followed immediately upon the first appear-ance of the manifesto (October 16). But Congress was not through with it. There had been threats of dire consequences to America for having mortgaged herself to France, Britain's "natural enemy". These threats Congress could not pass by; accordingly, on October 30, that body promulgated a manifesto of its own, which began by proclaiming the justice of their cause, their confidence of success, their trust "in Him, who disposes of human events", their bounden love for their enemies, "as children of that Being who is equally the Father of All, their earnest endeavors in the past, "to alleviate the calamities of war"; proceeded to point out how, on the contrary, the conduct of the British armies had been "diametrically opposite", and how, having been foiled "in their vain attempt to subjugate the unconquerable spirit of free-dom", they had "meanly assailed the representatives of America with bribes, with deceit, and the servility of adulation"; and ended with a solemn declaration that, "if our enemies presume to execute their threats, or persist in their present career of barbarity, we will take such exemplary vengeance, as shall deter others from a like conduct".

By this time the commissioners, for their part, had become weary of a hopeless undertaking, and thereupon Messrs. Carlisle, Eden, and Johnstone returned to their own country, sadder no doubt, if not also wiser men. If they had failed, they had at least battled with all their might against overwhelming odds. In fact, the case was decided against them before ever they had set foot upon American shores. It had been a race between the British conciliation acts and the French treaty, which should capture the eye and ear of Congress first; and the French treaty had won the race. If the peace commissioners had ar-rived a few weeks earlier than they did, there is little doubt that the subsequent story of the American Revolution would have been very different from what it became.

CHAPTER XIX

CASTLES IN THE AIR
TRIBULATIONS AT HOME AND ABROAD

One of the first results of the French alliance was, naturally, that Congress should feel an impulsion to put its disheveled foreign relations into more presentable as well as more effective shape. Some tentative beginnings toward a solution of the problem had, in fact, been made prior to the arrival of the French treaties, and now, so great was the elation in Congress over the success in France, some members at least began to have visions of all the European powers lining up to consummate treaties of commerce, if not also treaties of alliance, with the new power that had suddenly loomed up in the western hemisphere.

Not only were the commissioners to the courts of Berlin, Vienna, and Tuscany to have new and enlarged instructions similar to those given to the commissioner at Paris (it mattered little that these other commissioners were still huddled in or near Paris, far from their respective courts), commissioners with like powers were to be sent to the courts of Lisbon, the Hague, Stockholm, Copenhagen, and St. Petersburg. "Two whole days", Laurens wrote to John Rutledge June 3, 1778, "the subject has been upon the anvil and very laboriously hammered." Actually the subject had been on the anvil or in the forge a good many more than two days, and there must have been a good deal of hammering, both in committee and in Congress. As early as April 21, 1778, Congress had resolved upon a course of study in its foreign affairs, and on May 7, three days after the ratification of the French treaties, it had been resolved that the commissioners appointed to the courts of Spain, Tuscany, Vienna, and Berlin, "should live in such style and manner . . . as they may find suitable and necessary to support the dignity of their public character", and that they "be empowered to draw bills of exchange, from time to time . . . upon the commissioners at the court of France."

The next step was to settle upon the new instructions to these commissioners, and it was these that Congress was hammering upon during the first two days of June. Laurens lamented that there was so little commercial knowledge in Congress, "not a Merchant present, and not a Book in Town to assist a speculatist". He himself, as the presiding officer, had to remain "a Silent Spectator and auditor", while Congress floundered. With regard, however, to persons to fill the various posts, there were some definite ideas. Arthur Lee, for instance, had been suggested for the court of Lisbon. Lee himself had meanwhile been harboring other plans, and among his suggestions was one that Dr. Franklin be sent to Vienna, "as the first, most respectable, and quiet" court, and that he himself be designated for France, which was bound to be "the centre of activity".

All this time other irons in the fire had been getting hot and required attention; accordingly the business of appointing new representatives for European courts and providing new instructions for those already appointed must be laid to one side, and before the discussion could be renewed the whole subject had taken on a new aspect. At his first conference with President Laurens, the French minister had intimated that the character he should assume, whether as minister plenipotentiary or simply as resident, would depend on "the determination of Congress respecting the public Character of their Minister or Ministers at the Court of Versailles"; and, when Congress decided to receive Gérard as minister plenipotentiary, it became necessary to give to their own mission in France the same rank.

Before, however, Congress was able to get around to taking the appropriate measures it developed that dissentions of a serious nature had broken out among the several representatives of the United States in Europe, with the result that Congress itself was being rapidly split into opposing factions. The immediately crucial controversy was between Arthur Lee and Silas Deane, a controversy that Congress began vigorously to probe immediately after the public reception to the French minister. Scarcely less acute was the hostility between Lee and Franklin—acute now and destined to attain a stage of positive virulence. Deane was destined soon to lose most of his support in Congress, whereas the distrust of Franklin was in the outset confined to a small group, and the confidence of the majority in Congress he would retain to the last.

On the 11th of September, 1778, Congress came to a decision "unanimously" "That it is essential to the interest and honor of the United States, that a minister plenipotentiary be, without delay, appointed to represent these states at the court of France", and on the 14th, Franklin was chosen to that post. The latter vote is not recorded, but there is every reason to believe that it was not unanimous, for two days later (September 16) Richard Henry Lee wrote to Arthur Lee, alluding to the latter's criticisms of Franklin, "The Doctor is old and must soon be called to account for his misdeeds; therefore bear with him, if possible." A committee was at once appointed to prepare a letter of credence and instructions for Franklin, but it was five weeks before these were ready for consideration by Congress. The letter of credence was adopted October 21, the instructions, in the main, October 22, with some alterations October 26.

First of all, the minister was to assure his Most Christian Majesty that the United States "entertain the highest sense of his exertions in their favour", that they considered his speedy aid "not only as a testimony of his Majesty's fidelity to the engagements he hath entered into, but as an earnest of that protection which they hope from his power and magnanimity". Likewise he was to assure the king and his ministers that, as, "without any the slightest assurance of foreign aid" (it was not meet to speak here of the secret aid received from France), the United States had, "during three bloody campaigns, persevered in their determination to be free", so would they remain inflexible in that determination, would "faithfully perform their engagements, and afford every assistance in their power to prosecute the war for the great purposes of the alliance."

These were such assurances and pledges as comity required. Then came instructions of a more specific nature. For instance, the 11th and 12th articles of the treaty of commerce, which, at the very first reading, Congress had found "inconsistent with that equality and reciprocity which form the best surety to perpetuate the whole", these he was to endeavor to have expunged. He was particularly to urge the ruining of the British fisheries on the banks of Newfoundland by the reduction of Halifax and Quebec; and a plan for effecting those objects accompanied the instructions. The plan of an attack on Canada would presently receive the further consideration of Congress only to be abandoned; but the question of the Newfoundland fisheries was destined to become, before many months, one of the most trouble-making problems with which Congress at any time had to deal. How near the fisheries were to the New England heart is made evident by a remark of Samuel Adams (to James Warren, November 3, 1778), apropos the instructions to Franklin on this head: "We never shall be upon a solid Footing till Britain cedes to us what Nature designs we should have, or till we wrest it from her."

It was inevitable that Congress should be harboring hopes of financial as well as military and naval aid from France, therefore the minister was instructed to lay before the court the deranged state of the finances, "together with the causes thereof". To assist him in that purpose some "Observations on the Finances of America", drawn up by Gouverneur Morris, were transmitted to him. Among these instructions is one of a rather curious nature; it was "to suggest" that the best means of striking a fatal blow at British commerce would be "by confining the war to the European and Asiatic seas", so that the coasts of America might be free to become "a safe asylum to the frigates and privateers of the allied nations and their prizes". Finally the minister was informed that he should take care not to make any engagements or stipulations on the part of America without having previously obtained the consent of Congress. Congress was by no means yet ready to put the destiny of America into the keeping of France.

A single minister at the court of Versailles having now been decided upon, it became a problem what to do with the other representatives in Europe, particularly John Adams, who was by this action left footloose. Appointed at the end of November, 1777, in place of Silas Deane, and now therefore only a few short months in Paris he had scarcely taken his place before, so to speak, his chair was jerked out from under him. Congress had no design to deal harshly or unfairly with its former commissioner, but it must needs take thought.

At the same time that the committee for foreign affairs wrote to Franklin for the purpose of transmitting to him his new instructions, they wrote to Adams (October 28):

Congress must and will speedily determine upon the arrangement of their foreign affairs. This is become, so far as regards you, peculiarly necessary upon a new commission being sent to Dr. Franklin. In the meantime we hope you will exercise your whole extensive abilities on the subject of our finances.

And Samuel Adams wrote him (October 25): "As Congress entertain great Expectations from your Services, you may depend upon Employment being allotted for you somewhere." In any event, "France must be our Pole Star". Richard Henry Lee also offered his consolations and encouragement (October 29): "It may soon happen that you be desired to visit Holland."

So it did eventually happen, although not soon. It was not until June, 1780, that Adams was authorized to visit Holland, in the interest of a loan, and not until December of that year that he was commissioned minister to that country. In the interval he had for several months been left somewhat afloat in France, then had a brief period of retirement at home. In September, 1779, he was chosen minister for the negotiation of peace, at that time believed to be in prospect, although, as it turned out, peace was still in the far distance, while the whole business of the foreign relations of the United States had begun to look like muddle piled on top of muddle.

Silas Deane, recalled in the late autumn of 1777, had lingered in Paris long enough to sign the treaties with France, then had returned to America in the same ship with the French minister. Now, in the summer of 1778, his conduct as commissioner was under investigation. Congress had been provoked to recall him largely because he had wildly, even if with the best of intentions, made agreements with French military adventurers, who had in consequence besieged Congress in such shoals, demanding commissions, that native officers protested in disgust, and Congress itself at length became jittery. In numerous instances there was nothing to be done but to decline the proffered services of the eager, clamorous Frenchmen and send them back to France—"at the expense of the Continent".

All criticisms of Deane on this score were, however, destined to be deeply smothered beneath a mass of more serious charges. For one thing, it was charged that he had overindulged in commercial ventures on the side and had misapplied public funds; but mingled with these charges was another that was destined not only to set Congress by the ears but to vex their successors for many years to come. It was, in effect, a simple question that might have seemed easy of determination; yet it was not satisfactorily determined then, persisted in bobbing up from time to time in later years, and, even after more than a century and a half, remains a bone to be picked on occasion. The question was whether the supplies secretly furnished through Beaumarchais prior to the alliance were to be a charge against the United States or were an outright gift from the French government. Deane maintained that they were to be a charge. Arthur Lee, that they were a gift. It was Arthur Lee who originated the charges against Deane and through his brothers and other friends in Congress zealously pressed for an investigation of Deane's conduct.

On July 28, shortly after his return to America, Deane requested an audience of Congress that he might give an account of their affairs in Europe and of his own conduct in particular. His first hearing was on August 15, and it had not proceeded far when a motion was made to require him to reduce his narrative to writing. The motion did not at that time prevail, but the debate upon it served to show clearly that Congress had already split into two factions on the subject, a split that was destined to widen with the months. Unless this rift could be closed there was the most serious danger that the whole American structure would come down in irretrievable ruin. "Your friend Deane who hath rendered the most essential services", Gouverneur Morris wrote to John Jay (August 16), "stands as one accused. The Storm increases, and I think some one of the tall trees, must be torn up by the roots." On the same day more particular evidence of the storm and the danger to tall trees was recorded by Henry Laurens in a letter to President Lowndes:

In this debate [wrote Laurens] I clearly discovered that my fellow labourers had as absolutely taken sides as it can be supposed Gentlemen are capable of in a *pure unbiased* Assembly. Were I to say as ever Attornies had taken at a Bar I might be charged in the modern term with aberation, nevertheless I have taken the liberty to recommend the fillet and scales of Justice to one of my worthy Colleagues who appears strongly attached to one of the parties, no doubt from conviction that that side is right . . .

Laurens regrets that "the Chair" had been a bar to the delivery of his own sentiments on the floor. Had he done so, his worthy colleague, William Henry Drayton, would doubtless have had abundant temptation to retort with a like recommendation of the fillet and scales of justice. Laurens correctly predicted that the mode adopted by Congress for dealing with Mr. Deane's case would "extend debates and often lead disputants into warm contests", and would open "a field without limits for Oratory and wrangle and finally for mutual dissatisfaction". Soon Laurens himself would find the restraints of the Chair too much for him, and he would descend to the floor with such a reverberating thud as to throw the whole Congress into confusion.

Even at this stage not all the charges were being leveled at Deane. There were "mutual recriminations", as Joseph Reed wrote to his wife (August 16), and some of them revolved about himself. It was one of those chances, or mischances, that so often play pranks in human affairs. Almost upon his first entrance into the Revolutionary contest Arthur Lee, with the best motive in the world, no doubt, had warned the leaders in America to "beware" of certain men. One such warning (dated June 3, 1776) pointed to Joseph Reed in particular. To follow the account given by Samuel Adams (November 23, 1778), the letter "was written on the inner Sides of the Outside Leaves of a small pocket Dictionary, and so neatly closd to the Covers as not to afford the least Suspicion if it should meet with the Fate of being taken by the Enemy." This dictionary, which was itself designed to serve as the basis of a correspondence in cipher with the committee of secret correspondence, with its concealed message, was delivered to William Carmichael, who was in turn to deliver it to the committee. This was in London. Passing over to France, Carmichael, in violation of Lee's confidence, delivered the dictionary to the commissioners in Paris, who chose to withhold a letter that pointed with such positive suspicions toward men generally held in confidence and esteem. In time nevertheless the dictionary found its way into the office of the committee of commerce, where it was deemed to be only a dictionary and nothing more.

It was just at this juncture, when Silas Deane was, in effect, being tried on charges preferred by his former fellow-commissioner Arthur Lee, that Lee's warning of more than two years ago came to light. It was a new piece of rancid fat thrown into the fire of the controversy, and it produced no small sizzling. Partly through its instrumentality a back fire was set against Arthur Lee, who would ere long find himself the center of a conflagration as fierce as that which was beginning to rage about Silas Deane. In fact, the whole affair degenerated into a struggle between the partisans of Lee and the partisans of Deane, with the welfare of America all but lost sight of.

After prodding Deane from time to time for more than a month, and listening to other complaining voices besides, Congress came to the conclusion (September 22) that "certain dissentions, detrimental to the public service" existed among the American commissioners in Europe, and set about to probe into those dissensions. It happened that William Carmichael, who had been in close contact with the commissioners during the past two years, much of the time in a semi-official capacity, was now at hand, and Congress proposed to begin its investigation by grilling him minutely. The result of the grilling, instead of clearing the views of Congress, was to leave that body more perplexed than ever. In a doleful and grumbling letter to Jefferson (October 9), Cyrus Griffin declared: "We are plagued to death with quarrels and recriminations relative to our Commissioners abroad; these men will involve the Continent in perdition."

Time and again Deane besought Congress to resume its inquiries of him and release him. Failing in this, he decided to go over the head of Congress and appeal his cause directly to the people. Accordingly, on the 5th of December, 1778, he published in the *Pennsylvania Packet* an address "To the Free and Virtuous Citizens of America", wherein he not only vigorously defended his own course but brought counter-charges against his chief accuser. The address threw some very inflammable fat into an already hot fire. Deane's opponents denounced his publication as an insult to Congress, while his friends saw in his appeal only the effort of a much wronged man to defend his own character.

This Appeal to the People [Henry Laurens wrote to President Lowndes, December 7], this rash unnecessary appeal I trust will this day be attended to in Congress, but as I am concerned in no intrigue nor Cabal, I am consequently ignorant of the designs of my fellow labourers. The honor and interests of these United States call upon every Delegate in Congress for support. If therefore other Men shall be silent, I will deliver my sentiments on this very extraordinary circumstance and I have in prospect the production of much good out of this evil.

The day on which Deane's address appeared was Saturday, and the members of Congress had probably not seen the paper when it was resolved to give him a hearing on Monday evening following. Came Monday and the Congress hall became the center of a cyclonic storm. The storm began when President Laurens laid before the house "informations . . . from Citizens of respectable characters" that Deane's letter had created anxieties in the minds of the good People of this City, and excited tumults amongst them". He himself had found the letter to contain articles "highly derogatory to the honor and interests of these United States", and he cited Deane's intimation that, following up his appeal to the people, he designed "giving them a course of Letters". He therefore deemed it "dishonorable to Congress" to hear Deane that evening as planned and accordingly moved for the appointment of a committee to report upon the contents of the letter. A motion that the letter be read in Congress was interjected, but was defeated by a vote of six states to five, chiefly, it would appear, upon the ground that the reading would be a waste of time. The consideration of the motion was prevented, so Laurens afterwards averred, by "spinning out time" until a certain order of the day might be called for. All that was then accomplished was an order to Deane to "report to Congress, in writing, as soon as may be" upon his own agency in Europe, together with any intelligence he deemed proper respecting the foreign affairs of the United States.

If the calm of the following day led members of Congress to assume that the storm had passed, when they reassembled on the morning of

December 9, they quickly learned that they had been mistaken. The journal record of the proceedings of that day is of the briefest. It is merely that "before any business was entered on" the President arose, "and having assigned sundry reasons why he could not continue longer to execute the office of President, he resigned, and immediately quitted the chair". Congress thereupon resolved that on tomorrow it would go into an election of a president, then adjourned. The startling effect of this action upon Congress is well indicated by Nathaniel Scudder, who hastened to add to a letter to Richard Henry Lee, "I am this Moment come out of Congress, where an extraordinary Event has taken Place." Time, he said, would not admit of an explanation of "the Causes of this Occurrence".

Laurens's "sundry reasons" became buried in oblivion, and in oblivion they remained for five score years and ten. It was not, in fact, until 1889 that his speech to Congress on that occasion first came to light, while his notes and his letters bearing on his resignation have appeared more recently. In a letter to President Lowndes of South Carolina on December 16, Laurens gives his motives concisely: "failing in my attempt to rouse Congress in the vindication of their honor, I felt for my own, and Resolved to descend from the Chair to the floor where I could be of most real service to my Country." His speech to Congress closed with a rebuke to that body that was evidently intended to sting:

Finally, Gentlemen, from the considerations above mentioned, as I cannot consistently with my own honor, nor with utility to my country, considering the manner in which business is transacted here, remain any longer in this chair, I now resign it.

"The party of Deanites", Laurens continued in his letter to Lowndes, "were pleased to catch at the concluding sentence", but he would not "for any consideration" have omitted it, because he was persuaded that "good consequences would follow the strong reproof, and perhaps continue at least a fortnight". James Duane, a good friend to Laurens, while favorably disposed toward Deane, thought the President's zeal had "transported him a little too far". Edward Langworthy, also pro-Deane, could but remark upon the President's "extraordinary Oration" and the "Phantasticability and absurdity" of his conduct, and was particularly pleased that "the House were of Opinion there should not be the least restraint on the Liberty of the Press". For his part, he would "rejoice to see more publications on the proceedings of Congress"; "a little gentle Satyr", he thought would be useful on many occasions; it would "restrain the Spirit of Intrigue and Cabal". Before many months Langworthy would be availing himself of the liberty of the press to make some contributions of satire (not very gentle, it is true) on proceedings in Congress.

Laurens himself continued to assert that his resignation was the best act of his life; yet, finding presently that he was "kept in a state of implied censure", on December 15 he "modestly" demanded a testimonial of his conduct in the chair, "intimating the honor and interests of Congress and the States" were as nearly concerned as his own. At the same time he offered a sort of apology for the phrase "the manner in which business is conducted here", on which he had been "Jockey'd" daily since its utterance. Congress was gracious enough to give him a vote of thanks.

It would be difficult to discover from the stormy and confused proceedings of Congress during the next few months wherein, by his descent from the chair to the floor, Laurens had contributed to the promotion of the "much good" on which he had set his hopes. No man in Congress ever decried "party" more vociferously or more scornfully than did Laurens, yet no man, barring the Lees themselves, became more tightly tied to the anti-Deane party than he, and his resignation of the presidency, with all its concomitant flurry, bound him to that party more strongly than ever. Indeed some of his later positions on measures can scarcely be explained on any other ground than that they were the positions assumed by the group to which he had become so closely attached.

Moreover he must have come to feel that one of the first results of his resignation was defeat of his aims; for his successor in the presidency was none other than John Jay of New York, a pronounced adherent of Deane. Others than Laurens were, however, oppressed by a sense of failure. Francis Lightfoot Lee, for instance, wrote to his brother Richard Henry Lee (December 22), "Publications still continue in abundance to blacken the Lees and make Deane the greatest man in the world." "Common Sense" (Thomas Paine) alone had dared to enter the lists in behalf of the Lees, and the Deanites charged that he was being hired to do so. What was more, Lee lamented, "the poor fellow got a beating from an Officer, it is said for having wrote the piece".

In accordance with the requirement of Congress, Deane wrote out his narrative, and on December 22 he was permitted to read so much of it as Congress found time to listen to. It was not until the last day of the month that the reading was finished, when Deane was informed that "Congress will notify to him their future orders". It was a good many months before he received those orders, and then they were that he should not depart America until he had the permission of Congress. Meanwhile a prodigious amount of muddy water had rushed down the channel, carrying all manner of noxious debris upon its surface.

There were to be many more and even fiercer contests within the Congress hall, but battles equally fierce would be waged just over the border of those sacred precincts, and they were already beginning. Though the contest centered about the characters and conduct of the two men, it was no longer a mere personal combat between Silas Deane and Arthur Lee, for Deane had his champions and Lee his co-horts, each side gathering new recruits as the weeks and the months went by, and the rival forces came to tilt in the pages of the Philadelphia press. Among the champions of Deane were "Senex", "Plain Truth", and other knights of the quill, who, with visors drawn, plunged into the fray. If, as Francis Lightfoot Lee bemoaned, "Common sense" was at the outset the sole or chief protagonist of the Lees, he was a match for any two or three that could be brought against him. Few or none could parry his skillful thrusts. However, Paine presently overshot the mark and brought down upon his head the wrath not only of the French minister but of Congress as well; for he had revealed secrets which, as secretary to the committee for foreign affairs, he was supposed to keep inviolable.

At all events, there was soon raging as furious a newspaper war as ever our Revolutionary forebears beheld, they who dearly loved such wars and knew so well how to wage them. From that battle of pens few would come forth without painful wounds and battered armor.

Deane would be discredited, Arthur Lee would lose prestige, if not something more, and, as Gouverneur Morris had predicted, other tall trees were uprooted or broken by the storm. Furthermore, other potent questions began to be stirred, questions other than whether Silas Deane was a peculator and despicable to boot, and whether Arthur Lee was a wise and capable diplomat or, to the contrary, was "jealous", "affrontive", and, in particular, was *persona non grata* at the court of Versailles.

As if Congress did not have worries enough, it became necessary just then, or so at least it seemed, that one of the military officers should be disciplined. The affair was of small importance except as it involved a test of the question whether Congress could maintain its own dignity and authority. The officer was General William Thompson, a prisoner of war on parole and just now seeking to have himself exchanged. Conceiving that the Hon. Thomas McKean had obstructed his exchange, General Thompson vented his wrath upon that gentleman and at the same time made, or was thought to have made, remarks concerning Congress that gave umbrage to that body. Accordingly he was haled before the bar of Congress, charged with having made use of "abusive, disrespectful, and contemptuous expressions" toward that assembly. The general attended as required, but when he had withdrawn, he proceeded to indite a memorial to Congress, containing, as was alleged, "opprobrious language against, and scandalous reflections upon" a member of Congress, towit, Mr. Thomas McKean, thereby offering "an insult to the honor and dignity" of Congress. Specifically General Thompson was charged with having called Congress a set of rascals or villains and to have applied those or worse epithets to the Honorable Mr. McKean, emphasizing the latter by means of appropriate prefixes.

Congress devoted a good deal of precious time to hearing the evidence pro and con, in the course of which the general averred that he had not applied any opprobrious terms to Congress, whose members he regarded as estimable gentlemen, and that the terms he had applied to Mr. McKean had reference to his private, not his public, character. For the general, the outcome was an acquittal; for Congress, the result was appropriately set down by Francis Lightfoot Lee, who declared, "Congress has no power, and every Villain whome they want to call to account, insults them." That closed the record for Congress, but it was not quite the end of the controversy between General Thompson and Mr. McKean. Having failed to obtain his exchange and being, as he said, "about to return to captivity", General Thompson took occasion "to declare to the world", through the pages of the *Pennsylvania Packet* (December 29), that Thomas McKean had "behaved like a Lyar, a rascal, and a coward". Mr. McKean thereupon took occasion to make suitable response; but he did so in his private, not his public, character.

The Thompson affair was little more than the temporary though irksome fraying of the Congressional nerves; the Deane-Lee imbroglio was a virulent poison in the blood-stream, destined seriously to affect the body politic for years to come. Meanwhile the bitter wrangling would seem to have all but driven from the mind of Congress the beneficent results promised by the partnership with France. Thus far, in truth, the alliance had accomplished almost nothing to which Congress might point as a tangible achievement.

Even before the French minister had set foot in Philadelphia, Congress had hastened to take measures for the support of Comte d'Estaing in a projected attack upon New York, and both Congress and General Washington had indulged themselves in high hopes of the success of that undertaking; but they were doomed to disappointment. Because of an insufficient depth of water on the bar, Estaing was unable to get at the British ships in New York harbor; therefore he turned and put out for Rhode Island. It is said that he had scarcely turned his back upon New York when a strong wind drove water in abundance over the bar; but the water was behind time, the French fleet was already gone. Congress had at the outset proposed as an alternative an attack on the British squadron in Rhode Island waters, and all hopes were now transferred thither. Washington stripped himself of troops to co-operate with Estaing. But new troubles began to brew (or old troubles new-brewed); there was delay in the arrival of the troops, there was a quarrel between the Americans and the French, then, while the French and British fleets were maneuvering, there entered an element over which neither Congress, General Washington, the Comte d'Estaing, nor Admiral Howe had any control; it was a hurricane that scattered the fleets, severely damaged them, and even wrecked the camps on shore. Instead of renewing the attack, Estaing decided against the pleadings of the American offices to go to Boston to repair his ships.

Americans generally became almost sick of the alliance; still they gulped their disgust and passed a few complimentary exchanges, however perfunctory. Washington at least did his part diplomatically, and Congress did its utmost to wear the best possible face in a most mortifying situation. By a majority of nine states to three it quashed a proposition to make an inquiry into the failure of the Rhode Island expedition, and instead adopted votes of thanks to one or another of those concerned, and in particular directed (September 10) that a letter be written to the Comte d'Estaing expressive of the continued trust reposed in his "proved abilities, zeal and bravery" and in his attachment to the joint interests of France and the United States. While regretting the misfortune by which he had been overborne, Congress would still "look forward, in hope of Events more consonant to the wise intentions of His Most Christian Majesty, the Glory of his Fleets, and the security and Interest of the United States". Later (October 17) Congress would add a laudatory resolution, then move on to consideration of plans for the future.

One very ambitious plan had just been laid upon the table of Congress, a plan for an attack upon Quebec, and it so far found approval in Congress that the plan was transmitted to Franklin, just then made minister plenipotentiary at the court of Versailles, with instructions that he present it to the French ministry for their consideration. Despite the collapse of the expedition projected early in the year, a number of members of Congress, particularly the New England delegates, still clung to hopes of eventually bringing Canada into the Union, and that hope had been accentuated by the arrival of a memorial from Nova Scotia within a few days after the coming of the French treaty. "Nova Scotia", wrote the committee for foreign affairs to William Lee (May 14, 1778), "has long ago expressed its wishes to be adopted by us, and now afresh solicits. Canada will be greatly affected by the news of our alliance with its former parent State."

The new plan appears to have originated with Lafayette, who had been chagrined over the failure of the previous project, which he was to have led, and he evidently had no difficulty in obtaining a qualified approval in Congress. It was needful of course to obtain General Washington's opinion of the project. "You know more of the Subject", Gouverneur Morris wrote to Washington (October 26), "than all of us put together." For his part, Morris had "already had a great Deal of Trouble with it". Washington expressed to Congress (November 11) his disapproval of the plan, chiefly upon military grounds; but in a private letter to President Laurens (November 14) he opened his mind with regard to certain possible dangers of a political nature. In brief, if France once obtained a strong foothold in Canada, there was more than a mere possibility that she would choose to remain, with results that would be diametrically opposed to the interests of the United States. She might engage in the business "with the purest intentions", but afterward alter her views. "Men are very apt to run into extremes", Washington wrote; "hatred to England may carry some into an excess of Confidence in France; especially when motives of gratitude are thrown into the scale." "But", he added, "it is a maxim founded on the universal experience of mankind, that no nation is to be trusted farther than it is bound by its interest; and no prudent statesman or politician will venture to depart from it." For his part, he would wish to avoid, so far as possible, asking assistance of any foreign power that is not indispensable. In fact, Washington's objections to "entangling alliances" have an earlier origin than is ordinarily ascribed to them.

Laurens was heartily in accord with Washington's views, and did not doubt that Congress would be in accord with his official observations. "I am much mistaken", he wrote, "if every Member in Congress is not decided in his opinion in favor of them." The committee to whom Washington's letter had been referred did indeed report, and Congress agreed to the report, "that the Reasons assigned by the General against an Expedition to Canada appear . . . to be well founded"; nevertheless, the report went on to say, it was highly probable that the British would shortly evacuate the posts that they held in the United States, and, in view of that probable event, it would be advisable to take the needful measures for carrying out the plan. When this report was forwarded to Washington he at once suggested (December 13) that Congress call him to Philadelphia for a personal conference, in which he might discuss with them the whole situation as concerned the army. As a result of the conference, which lasted from December 22 to the end of January, it was decided, January 1, that the proposed plan "for the emancipation of Canada" be abandoned.

During these earlier months of his mission the French minister had for the most part concerned himself with observing the ways of the body with which he had to deal, with informing himself upon the ideas and the motives that actuated it, and in familiarizing himself with the characters of the men who composed the American Congress. He soon discovered that there were a good many men in Congress who were by no means friendly to the alliance, and he seems to have conceived a fear that these men desired a reconciliation with Great Britain. On this score he was doubtless mistaken, but he deemed it necessary to obtain from Congress a more positive commitment to the alliance than that body had yet given. Gérard had already received instructions to this effect from Vergennes, and in compliance, through a letter to President Laurens, December 7, 1778, he pressed Congress for a definitive expression of America's fidelity to the alliance. The letter was referred to a committee of five, but that committee was not very prompt in reporting, therefore on January 10, 1779, Gérard again urged it upon Congress "to give to this subject a ready, formal, and explicit declaration". In his reports to Vergennes, Gérard explained that, in his efforts to obtain this response from Congress, he had had especial difficulties with a group of delegates led by Samuel Adams. Despite this opposition, however, on January 14, Congress at length complied in a resolution that is recorded as unanimous:

That as neither France or these United States may of right, so these United States will not conclude either truce or peace with the common enemy, without the formal consent of their ally first obtained, and that any matters or things which may be insinuated or asserted to the contrary thereof tend to the injury and dishonor of the said States.

So far so good; but there would come other bitter fights over the precise implications of this pledge.

Almost simultaneously Gérard had drawn Congress into another commitment, one that led a good many members to the suppression of groans which they scarcely dared to utter. In the course of the controversy that had been raging both within and without Congress over the contradictory assertions of Silas Deane and Arthur Lee, Thomas Paine, who was secretary to the committee for foreign affairs, but unofficially, using his pen name "Common Sense", had taken up the cudgels in behalf of Arthur Lee, asserted that documentary evidence in his office definitely proved, as Arthur Lee maintained, that the supplies furnished through Beaumarchais had been a free gift from France. So long as it was a free-for-all unofficial quarrel Gérard might affect to ignore the whole business. When, however, such an assertion was made by an official of Congress and official documents were cited in evidence, it was time for the French minister to intervene. Whatever the facts, France could not afford to admit that, prior to the alliance, she had been furnishing secret aid to the Americans.

Immediately following Paine's publications, therefore, Gérard called upon Congress (January 5, 1779) for a categorical denial of Paine's assertions. Although probably everybody knew who "Common Sense" was, Congress proceeded upon the business in an orderly fashion. Mr. John Dunlap, printer of the *Pennsylvania Packet,* was called in and asked who was the author of those certain articles signed "Common Sense", and, when he had answered "Thomas Paine", Paine was in turn summoned and straightway avowed the authorship. "Debate ensued", John Fell recorded in his Diary of that day (January 6). "Letter read from Thos. Payne", Fell recorded January 7; "debate concerning him lasted all day." "Letter read from T. Payne, with Resignation", Fell recorded January 8; "debates on the subject lasted till Past 4 oClock." January 9, "debate concerning Mr. Payne lasted till 5 P.M."; but the day was not wholly devoted to Mr. Paine. The 10th was the Sabbath day, and quiet prevailed in the hall of Congress. Monday, January 11, "Debates concerning Mr. Payne [and one other matter] lasted till near 6 oClock."

It is evident both from Fell's brief record and from the Journals that Congress had been deeply stirred and violently agitated by the affair. A variety of motions were made, and no doubt there were numerous impassioned speeches, although only one such (by Gouverneur Morris, January 7) has survived. A misadventure of Henry Laurens, late President of Congress, served to add to existing complications. In his letter of January 8, Paine professed to have learned from the Journals of the preceding day that Congress had refused him a hearing. How could Paine have known anything of the proceedings of Congress, supposed to be kept in strict secrecy? What had Mr. Secretary Thomson to say about that? The secretary declared that Mr. Paine could not have had a sight of the Journals of January 7, for he had taken the record home with him, and not even the clerks of his office had seen it. Some member, then, must have told tales out of Congress. Who could it have been? A motion was made (January 8) that the members be "separately examined by the President on their honour", whether they had communicated the resolutions of yesterday to Mr. Paine. Thereupon up rose Mr. Henry Laurens to acknowledge having informed Mr. Paine that a motion to give him a hearing had been negatived, but he had not told him that he was not to be heard. Further, he had referred Mr. Paine to Mr. Thomson and the Journals.

By this time the tempest was too big for any Congressional teapot, nevertheless on January 12, Congress came to a resolution "unanimously" that the President be directed "to assure the said Minister, that Congress do fully, in the clearest and most explicit manner, disavow the publications referred to in his said memorials", and that they were "convinced by indisputable evidence that . . . the great and generous ally of these United States, did not preface his alliance with any supplies whatever sent to America". This latter clause, with some further particulars, was not in the resolution as first framed and was probably inserted to satisfy the Deane faction. The Lee faction must have reflected that, since, as they viewed it, the whole thing was a falsehood, they might as well go the limit while they were about it. The essential thing just then was not to jeopardize the alliance. The cause of independence was probably at stake. Gérard, for his part, doubtless felt, in view of the two strong commitments he had obtained from Congress, that he had prevented the alliance from going on the rocks, and that was well. He was to learn nevertheless that there were other breakers ahead and that even more skillful steering would be required of him.

CHAPTER XX

NEW WINE IN OLD BOTTLES
THE BUBBLE OF "CONTINENTAL"

However averse most members of Congress had been to an alliance with any foreign power until the very salvation of their cause seemed to hinge upon it, and however deeply they might yet be concerned to keep the United States from becoming unnecessarily entangled with France, few of them were the least averse to seeking loans or other financial aids from France—or elsewhere. Since France had intimated early in the contest a willingness to furnish a variety of military aids, it seemed to some members of Congress that a loan of money on such good security as the United States of America was in nowise a chimerical project, and, but for discouragements from their agent in France, an application for a loan would have been made earlier than was done.

It sometimes happens that a lesser discouragement is overcome by a greater, and so it must have been with Congress. The necessity of fleeing to Baltimore in December, 1776, was assuredly one of those greater discouragements. At all events, on the 23d of December, three days after Congress had gathered at Baltimore, it was resolved that the commissioners at the court of France be authorized to borrow on the faith of the thirteen United States a sum not exceeding two millions sterling, for a term not less than two years. Two impulses were propelling Congress into this bold measure: one was to bolster a domestic loan of five millions resolved upon a few weeks earlier (October 3, 1776), the other to sustain the sinking Continental currency.

Partly in desperation, partly because many members seemed to think it such a simple and easy thing to do, Congress was induced to proceed with the expenditure of its foreign loans without waiting to see whether the lenders would lend; in short, to draw bills of exchange on its ministers in France, in the hope that the bills would be accepted. An elaborate proposition to this end was submitted by a committee in

June, 1777, and, on September 10 following, Congress solemnly resolved to pay interest on loan office certificates in bills of exchange drawn on the commissioners at Paris.

There were doubts respecting the wisdom of the measure, likewise sharp warnings of its unwisdom. One of the doubters was John Adams, who declared (to James Warren August 18, 1777), "But Taxation, My dear Sir, Taxation, and Oeconomy, are our only effectual Resources" Less doubtful was James Lovell, but he also was of opinion that "Taxes are indubitably our only wise plan for a continuance; and every day we omit to tax we pass a precious opportunity." The warnings against the measure appear to have come chiefly from Henry Laurens. During the discussion he set forth at some length, in a letter to John Lewis Gervais (September 5, 1777), his criticisms of the proposition.

> I cannot persuade Gentlemen [he wrote] to believe that Bills of Exchange on France bearing 6 Per Cent Interest is a further emission of paper Money, but so much more dangerous than an emission of Square Dollars by the Interest which will accumulate to be repaid abroad and thereby in effect mortgaging to a foreign Crafty power so much of our Soil. . . . If we have not virtue enough to Save our Selves, easy access to the Treasury of France will only hasten our ruin. . . . I compare our present attempt to the folly of a Young Man borrowing Money from a designing Sharper upon the Credit of an expected Heirship.

Much more upon specific aspects of the measure he wrote to Gervais before final action had been taken by Congress. When the resolve had been adopted he wrote in similar terms to President Rutledge. Drawing bills of exchange, he remarked, "is putting our debt out of sight for a little but it will infallibly return upon us with accumulated force"

It is worth observing that the vote on this measure was among the first recorded in the Journals and that of the twenty-five members present only six were in the negative, one of whom was Henry Laurens The two doubters above mentioned both voted in the affirmative. Commenting upon the measure more than a year later (November 20, 1778) Laurens again laments the "Mortgaging these States to foreign powers", adding the remark: "Our Bills for that Interest are now floating in imminent danger of dishonor and disgrace".

The proposition of September 10, 1777, was, in effect, an attempt at a forced loan. On the 3d of December following, Congress took steps to obtain a voluntary assent before the blows of the forced loan should fall; in other words, to clear a landing field for its bills of exchange. It was resolved that the commissioners at the courts of France and Spain be directed to exert their utmost endeavors to obtain a loan of two millions sterling, on the faith of the thirteen United States, for a term not less than ten years. There were stipulations, promises, provisos, but they are of minor importance.

It is not to be forgotten that Congress had heard not a word from its commissioners in France since the preceding May, and that another May would come before any communication from these commissioners would be received. Nothing daunted, when spring had followed a winter of deep, exasperating silence on the part of the commissioners in France, Congress once again went adventuring into the domain of bills of exchange on France, proposing now to make an even wider use of them than had been contemplated in the preceding September. They would be used not merely to pay the interest on domestic obligations already incurred, but likewise on a further loan by which some twenty millions of the first emission of bills of credit were to be sunk. Those bills of credit, *alias* Continental money, had got quite out of hand, and something must be done about them.

Nor had the idea of a foreign loan been by any means dismissed. Only the day before the arrival of the treaty with France, William Henry Drayton, usually at almost violent odds with his colleague, Henry Laurens, introduced a motion that once more the commissioners to France and Spain be instructed to press their respective courts for a substantial loan, even to urge upon those courts an immediate declaration of war against Great Britain. Drayton would even instruct the commissioners to "demand a categorical answer of France and Spain to this point". No doubt the immediate coming of the treaty of alliance put a quietus on this movement for the time being.

There is nothing particularly surprising in the efforts of Congress to obtain a loan from France, or even from Spain; but it is nothing short of astonishing that these efforts should have extended also to Italy. That even the most visionary members of Congress could have deluded themselves with hopes of borrowing money from Italy is beyond comprehension, except that Mr. Ralph Izard, upon accepting the mission to Tuscany (October 6, 1777), had led the committee for foreign affairs to an act of faith pure and simple. With an air of sublime assurance, therefore, Congress instructed the commissioner at the court of Tuscany (February 4, 1778) to endeavor to obtain a loan of money, not exceeding one million sterling, "on the faith of the thirteen united states of America, for a term not less than ten years". As in the case of the like instructions of December 3, 1777, to the commissioners to France and Spain, Mr. Izard was instructed "to keep as secret as the nature of the thing will admit" whatever loan he should obtain. Nothing could have been easier for the commissioner to the court of Tuscany than to conform to this latter clause of his instructions, for the loan obtained could be measured only in zeros.

If faith is the substance of things hoped for, the evidence of things unseen, then the faith of Congress in a forthcoming loan from Tuscany was no more baseless than its faith in the preposition *at*. For Commissioner Izard was not then or ever afterward *at* the court of Tuscany. He was then sojourning in Paris, and in Paris he continued to cool his heels throughout the duration of his mission. How tenaciously nevertheless the idea of such a loan clung to some minds in Congress, even long after Mr. Izard himself had been made aware of its hopelessness, is evidenced by a suggestion of Richard Henry Lee to Thomas Jefferson as late as October 5, 1778, that, if James Madison should be sent to Genoa as secretary to Philip Mazzei, there might be "a good chance" of borrowing that million.

How immensely the expectations of Congress were buoyed by the consummation of the treaties with France may be gauged by the fact that, within three days after the ratification of the treaties, the commissioners to the lesser courts were authorized to live as became their station and to draw on the commissioners at Paris for their expenses. All this was of course but one more headache for the commissioners at Paris. "You have drawn so many bills of exchange upon us", John Adams wrote to Lovell, July 9, 1778, "that I assure you I am very uneasy concerning our finances here." Meanwhile, however, the commissioners were diligently exploring every market for loans.

But why should Congress be seeking so desperately for loans in Europe, when its own printing press was in such good working order? That old printing press was, in fact, the chief source of these anxieties. When, in December, 1777, Congress undertook its active campaign for loans from abroad, the committee for foreign affairs wrote to the commissioners at Paris (December 2):

We shall have emitted twenty-eight millions of dollars by the close of this year, exclusive of provincial currency. The quantity is too great, and of course the quality is injured. The slow operations of taxes will not afford adequate remedy, and the offer of sterling interest does not fill the loan offices so quickly as the necessary expences call for supply. If a loan of two millions sterling could be obtained, the high exchange would enable Congress, by drawing on that fund, to call so large a quantity of paper presently out of circulation as to appreciate the rest, and give time for taxation to work a radical cure. Without this remedy of the evil very pernicious consequences will follow ere long.

Very pernicious consequences were, in fact, already upon them. In short, the superabundance of "Continental", plus the state issues, had produced the inevitable depreciation, with its consequent rise of prices. These results were by no means surprising, for there was scarcely a member of Congress who did not know that large issues of fiat money would cause a decline in its value, and some of them at least knew well enough that the corresponding rise of prices was but the obverse of the shield; and almost without exception they uttered frequent and loud groans over the calamity that had befallen them.

But what were they to do? May be by means of legislation, state as well as Continental, supplemented by several sorts of moral suasion, in the application of which they had had a good deal of experience, they might hold the money at somewhere near its face value. Their success was exceedingly poor. They tried the other horn of the dilemma, the regulation of prices; but that worked much in the manner of a boomerang. Domestic loans had all along proved disappointing in results, while lotteries, tried from time to time, had scarcely furnished pin money. If American commodities—tobacco, rice, indigo—could only be sold in Europe for cash, that would go a long way toward meeting the costs of the war. "You may be assured", Richard Henry

Lee wrote to his brother Arthur, May 12, 1778, "that Congress are ready and willing to send powerful remittances to Europe in the way of commodities, but the attempt now would be only supplying the enemy, whose cruisers are so numerous on our Coast and in our Bays, that almost every vessel is taken." Loans therefore, as was reiterated over and over again, were urgently needed to sustain the credit of the paper money.

If the committee for foreign affairs, in its letter of December 2, 1777, actually stated the emissions at the close of 1777 as twenty-eight, instead of thirty-eight millions, it had miscalculated, for they stood at twenty-five millions at the end of 1776, nineteen millions having been added in that year to the six millions issued in 1775, and to these twenty-five millions thirteen more were added in 1777. If Congress had become uneasy over thirty-eight millions of its promises to pay at the end of 1777, what must have been its state of mind a year later, when to this sum had been added sixty-three and one half millions, plus three hundred dollars thrown in for small change? (An extra hundred had been added to each of the three last emissions to fit the scheme of denominations.) And, if that were not sufficiently terrifying, the year 1779 would have to be inaugurated by an additional issue of fifty millions and four hundred dollars. By this time it was clear to everybody that "Continental" was plunging toward an abyss and might well carry Congress with it into avernus. But of all this, more anon.

The struggle with the continental finances had begun early in the year 1778, but had for the most part been suspended after the arrival of the treaty until the French minister had been formally received and Congress had adjusted itself somewhat to the new situation. Such however was the zeal and determination of Congress that on August 12 it was resolved to set apart two days in every week for the consideration of the affairs of the treasury and finances, and "that no other business, excepting the reading and disposing of public letters, be taken up on those days without the unanimous consent of the house", until that business had been finished. On the 13th an additional day was assigned to the purpose. These resolutions were not very religiously adhered to, nevertheless Congress did devote a great part of its time during the next five months to efforts to find some sort of solution for its financial muddle. On the 27th of August a committee of five (Robert Morris, Elbridge Gerry, Richard Henry Lee, John Witherspoon, and Gouverneur Morris) was appointed to take the whole business of money and finances into consideration and report from time to time. On September 19, 1778, an extensive report, drawn by Gouverneur Morris, was laid before Congress, then the debating began.

The financial reports that were the bases of discussions in Congress are usually very interesting documents, and this one is especially so. "It will be proper", says the report, "to negociate as soon as possible a Loan of five Millions Sterling in Europe." "Agreed 29 Sept." (Such is the marginal notation on the report). "It will be proper to borrow twenty Million Dollars on Loan in the Confederal Fund at 4 per cent", etc. "Postponed". "It will be proper to borrow ten Million Dollars on Loan Office Certificates at 6 per cent Interest", etc. "Postponed 29 Sept." "It will be proper to call on the several States to pay in their Quotas of ten Million Dollars." "Agreed 6 Oct." (It was seldom deemed improper to call on the states to pay in their quotas, but calling was not necessarily collecting.)

There were other though lesser measures that the committee deemed proper, then it advanced to propositions which might be termed feelers: one was that the states be called upon for permanent funds amounting to two million dollars annually for ten years; another, that a poll tax of half a dollar a head be laid on all inhabitants; a third, that a duty of two per cent be laid on imported commodities to be paid to the continent (a proposal of that nature would again and again be brought forward, and the time would come when the national life would seem to hang on just that slender thread); and still another, "That the Emissions of the several States be cried down as a Currency and loan office Certificates issued for the Amount."

Other propositions there were affecting the states directly, and one of them would try the metal of the states to the utmost. It was a bone that had hitherto been much gnawed upon and had excited some rather harsh growls. It was "that the several States having large uncultivated Territory, beyond what is in their Power to govern, be called on to cede the same to the United States", on certain terms, one of which was:

That it be covenanted with the States that the Lands set off shall be erected into separate independent States to be admitted into the Union, to have a Representation in Congress, and to have free Governments in which no Officers shall be appointed by Congress, other than such as are appointed through the other States.

But what had this to do with·the finances? The committee proposed that, these cessions having been made, a tract of twenty to forty million acres be set off and disposed of in shares; then, if that plan did not work out satisfactorily, that another similar tract be set off and disposed of in a different manner, there particularized. Finally the committee recommended that Congress appoint two committees, one to go to the northward, one to the southward, to negotiate with the state legislatures respecting the principal propositions presented.

This report was guarded by Congress with more than the normal secrecy. Sixty copies were to be printed for the use of the members and the printer was placed under oath to return every scrap of paper relating to it to the secretary of Congress and not to divulge any part of the report. A similar injunction was placed on the members. Some one wished to add "except to the assemblies of the respective states", but that exception was denied. The consequence was that members for the most part refrained from mentioning in their letters details of the propositions or discussions, limiting themselves to lamenting the seriousness and the difficulties of the problem. Roger Sherman does seem to have forgotten the injunction of secrecy in so far as to reveal to Governor Trumbull (October 27) some of the questions then under discussion. His chief conviction appears to have been that "the members in general seem to be at a loss what can be done" to restore the credit of the paper money.

No member offered a more illuminating comment than did Nathaniel Scudder of New Jersey. Scudder was a physician, a profession that furnished Congress many of its worthiest members; but in one respect he is in a class by himself. After serving two years in Congress he became a colonel of New Jersey militia and was killed in a skirmish at Shrewsbury, October 16, 1781, three days before the surrender of Cornwallis at Yorktown. Other members of Congress turned soldier, but Scudder was the only one to give his life in battle. Scudder's remarks were penned after the financial debates had been raging for some four months, and were written (December 9) to Richard Henry Lee, then absent from Congress:

What shall I say as to the great Business of our Finances? I cannot yet determine that I have learned any Thing concerning them, much indeed I have unlearned; for although an amazing Deal of Time has been spent on this important Subject; tho one Hypothesis has been piled upon another like Pelion on Ossa; tho Scheme has been tacked to Scheme, and System succeeded System, while the speculative Genius and playfull Fancies of some of our Brethren have again and again in amendments and a variety of Substitutes exhausted themselves, and finally, when all their pretty wiredrawn Plans were crumbled away in the handling, have often in common Consent assisted to sweep away the rubbish, and begin *de novo;* I say tho we have ranged in this Way the boundless Field of Finance and with great Labor and Diligence too, I have for my own Part obtained no more than to determine what will *not do* for the Support of our public Credit and the prevention of a general Depreciation. When I shall be happy enough to determine what *will do* Heaven only knows—my Enthusiasm alone remains.

During the last half of December the discussion had in large part revolved about the question whether to burn or not to burn Continental. In the financial report brought in early in April there had actually been a proposition that all the issues from June 22, 1775, to July 22, 1776, totaling 20,010,000, be "borrowed" on loan office certificates, then destroyed. In October the committee on finance also proposed a large destruction of bills, but this committee proposed to take out of circulation and destroy all bills issued prior to April 11, 1778, except bills of small denominations, the whole being placed at 46,500,000. This proposition was once agreed to, but afterward rejected. There was general agreement on the committee's proposition, "That to support the War, it is indispensibly necessary to restore the Value of the Money by reducing the Quantity"; the difficulty was in determining how much to destroy and what particular emissions.

On December 16 came still a different proposition, namely, to take out of circulation the whole of the emissions of May 20, 1777, and April 11, 1778, meaning the series of emissions bearing those dates, of which the total was 41,500,000 dollars. This was adopted, and so became a part of the measure as essentially completed on December 31, 1778, and put into finished form on January 2, 1779. The mode by which the specified bills were to be removed from circulation was definitely set forth: they were to be brought in by the first day of June following and not thereafter to be redeemable; they were receivable for Continental debts and taxes, for state taxes, or might be deposited at loan offices as loans or exchanged for bills of like tenor or loan office certificates; then they were to be "crossed and struck through with a circular punch, of one inch diameter, to be afterwards examined and burned, as Congress shall direct". An equally important provision of the measure was that the states be called on to pay in their respective quotas of 15,000,000 dollars for the year 1779, and of 6,000,000 dollars annually for eighteen years thereafter, as a fund for sinking the emissions and loans of the United States to the end of the year 1778.

The effort to have Congress "cry down" the state emissions had failed, because some members considered it an unwarranted interference with the rights of the states. Thomas Burke, for one, objected also to the whole scheme of cancellation on a similar ground. Congress could not, Burke maintained, prevent the currency of money that the states had made legal tender, "because that implies a power to suspend or repeal our Laws". The selection of those particular issues for cancellation on the ground that they had been much counterfeited was, he asserted, all a pretense. At all times a stanch protagonist of state rights, Burke further declared that he "always was averse to giving the powers of borrowing and emitting to Congress by the Confederation", a power which, he was persuaded, would "always be used for purposes partial, and unjust, and either to serve particular States, or Individuals to the prejudice of the whole community". On other grounds, moreover, he had fears of the results of the measure. Said William Floyd of New York: "Some gentlemen appear very sanguine that they [the resolves] will have their desired good effects; I wish they may; but must confess I have great doubts." Floyd's colleague, James Duane, who had taken an important part in shaping the measure, particularly in its later stages, was much more hopeful.

If the different legislatures heartily support the arrangement proposed by Congress [he wrote to Governor Clinton, January 3, 1779], I flatter myself the public credit will be restored: for sufficient and known funds being once established for sinking the debt in a reasonable period, the good sense as well as monied interest of America will be on the side of government. The danger lies not in the past; but the future increase of paper money, should the war unhappily be protracted.

As the war was unhappily protracted Duane's utmost fears rather than his hopes were realized.

A carefully prepared preamble, giving an explanation of the underlying reasons for the measure and the purposes that it aimed to accomplish, was prefixed to the resolves, but Congress was not quite content that the measure should go out to the states without a special Congressional benediction, therefore the board of treasury was instructed to prepare a circular letter to accompany the resolves. This "Address to the People on the Currency", which was adopted January 13 and sent forth over the signature of the President the next day, vigorously defends the issue of bills of credit and places much of the blame for their depreciation, much but not all, on the enemy, who, "in despair of subduing the free spirits of America by force of arms or the intrigues of negociation", had had recourse to fraud. "Their emissaries have been employed in a variety of artifices to debase our money, and to raise the price of commodities." In fact, "our enemies of the highest rank" had not hesitated to counterfeit the bills of credit and disperse them throughout the United States. One further step remained to be taken: new bills must be issued to be exchanged for those to be taken out of circulation—and for supporting the war a little longer. Accordingly, on January 14, an emission of 50,000,400 dollars was ordered.

There is good reason to doubt whether the people at large were greatly inspired by the address or had greater faith in the measure than did some of its critics in Congress. Like the latter, they were probably inclined to give to the claim of counterfeiting a minimum of weight and assign to it several of the proverbial grains of salt. At all events, in a much shorter time than it took Congress to frame the measure all the flourishing hopes of its adequacy had gone a glimmering.

CHAPTER XXI

THE GENERAL SPEAKS TO THE CONGRESS
"HALF-PAY" AGAIN, LIKEWISE HUNGER

As previously stated (Chapter XIX), General Washington had indicated, in a letter of December 13, 1778, his desire for a personal conference with Congress, that he might lay before them "more minutely
the state of the army, the condition of our supplies, and the requisites
for carrying into execution an undertaking that may involve the most
serious events". Congress accordingly "directed" the general to attend
as soon as practicable; and on the morning of December 24 the President announced that General Washington had arrived in town "pursuant to their orders". From the point of view of Congress there was
no doubt good reason why the initiative should appear to have been
taken by Congress, and the conference should take place in pursuance
of their orders. The civil was supreme over the military power, and
there must be nothing in the record to suggest the contrary.

When Washington was presently introduced to Congress, he was
informed that Congress had directed his attendance "in order, among
other things, to confer with him on the operations of the next campaign". A committee of conference was at once appointed, consisting
of James Duane of New York, Jesse Root of Connecticut, Meriwether
Smith of Virginia, Gouverneur Morris of New York, and Henry
Laurens of South Carolina. One of Washington's immediate purposes
was to persuade Congress to abandon the proposed irruption into
Canada (the "undertaking" alluded to in his letter), an aim that was
soon accomplished. That done, the general was free to enter upon a
discussion with the committee of the real needs of the army.

In view of the dissatisfaction with the commander-in-chief that had
so largely prevailed in Congress only a few short months before, it is
interesting to observe how readily the committee and Congress now

fell into accord with his proposals. It is none the less interesting to take note of Washington's impressions of the Congressional scene in the midst of which he now found himself. In a confidential letter (December 30, 1778) to Benjamin Harrison, an intimate friend and a former member of Congress, he opened his mind quite freely:

I have seen nothing since I came here (on the 22d Instt.) [he wrote to Harrison] to change my opinion of Men or Measrs. but abundant reason to be convinced, that our Affairs are in a more distressed, ruinous, and deplorable condition than they have been in since the commencement of the War. . . .

If I was to be called upon to draw a picture of the times, and of Men; from what I have seen, heard, and in part know I should in one word say that idleness, dissipation and extravagance seem to have laid fast hold of most of them. That Speculation, peculation, and an insatiable thirst for riches seems to have got the better of every other consideration and almost every order of Men. That party disputes and personal quarrels are the great business of the day whilst the momentous concerns of an empire, a great and accumulated debt; ruined finances, depreciated money, and want of credit (which in their consequences is the want of every thing) are but secondary considerations and postponed from day to day, from week to week as if our affairs wore the most promising aspect.

He spoke, he said, as "one who wishes the prosperity of America most devoutly and sees or thinks he sees it, on the brink of ruin."

Your money [he continued] is now sinking 5 pr. Ct. a day in this City; and I shall not be surprized if in the course of a few months a total stop is put to the currency of it. And yet an assembly, a concert, a Dinner, or Supper (that will cost three or four hundred pounds) will not only take Men of[f] from acting in but even from thinking of this business while a great part of the Officers of your army from absolute necessity are quitting the Service and the more virtuous few rather than do this are sinking by sure degrees into beggery and want.

"This is not an exaggerated acct.", he went on to say, but "that it is an alarming one I do not deny, and confess to you, that I feel more real distress on acc[oun]t of the pres[en]t appearances of things than I have done at any one time since the commencement of the dispute." For his part, he had "no resentments", and he had been given reason to believe that he stood well in the estimation of Congress.

It was under such a weight of discouragement, even of gloom, that the commander-in-chief set about his endeavors to procure measures that, if actually put into effect, would give promise of an army capable of accomplishing its purpose. At the outset he laid before the committee of conference what would probably nowadays be labeled agenda, but which he called "Minutes of heads of matters requiring attention", matters which he elaborated on from time to time during the conference.

In planning for the campaign it was of course essential first of all to determine whether the campaign should be offensive or only defensive, and Washington reasoned upon the possible and probable results of these campaigns, respectively, and their requirements. An idea appears to have gained lodgment in the minds of Congress that the British were on the point of evacuating their posts on the continent, and the result was a disposition to mark time and wait upon events. This disposition Washington found it necessary vigorously to combat. "If", he argued, "we were to take our measures on the presumption of an evacuation, and this should not happen, we might be ruined by the Mistakes." It was safest, he insisted, to suppose that the enemy will not "leave us", and to prepare accordingly. His own conclusion was that the prospect of any capital offensive operation was so slender that of necessity they must remain entirely on the defensive, except for such lesser operations against the Indians as might become absolutely necessary.

Whatever might be the plan of campaign fixed upon, the problem of filling the ranks of the army and keeping them filled was most acute and therefore must first be attacked. Two modes of recruiting were suggested, one of them to enlist for the period of the war all men now in the army, encouraging them by means of large bounties, the other a draft, such as he had suggested the winter before. If the campaign were to be offensive, the two modes must be united; if defensive, only the former need be employed. The question of bounties was seriously complicated by the practice then prevalent among the states of offering large bounties, which, by their "inequality, interference, and competition", had already greatly injured the recruiting service. Washington favored a large Continental bounty only in the event that the state bounties could be abolished.

On January 23, 1779, about a week before the conference with the committee was brought to a close, Congress adopted one feature of Washington's proposal, essentially in the terms suggested by him. To each soldier who would voluntarily re-enlist "during the war" a bounty was offered "according to the circumstances of his present engagement, but not to exceed in any case 200 dollars", and to each new recruit who should enlist in any of the Continental battalions, likewise "during the war", "such a bounty as the Commander in Chief shall judge proper", but not to exceed two hundred dollars. It was not, however, the soldiers alone who were to receive bounties. The recruiting officers also were to be given "such reward as the Commander in Chief shall think fit", those appointed to "re-inlist" to have not exceeding ten dollars for each able-bodied man who should pass muster, those appointed to recruit new levies to have not exceeding twenty dollars per man, with three dollars a day for expenses. The committee offered a further proposition that, whereas the partial bounties granted by the state legislatures, "al-tho' well intentioned", had "occasioned a Competition hurtful to the Service and productive of Dissatisfaction and Complaints", and "where-as by the blessing of divine Providence the extraordinary exertions of the several States individually are in this respect no longer necessary", it be recommended to the states to revoke all such bounties. But Congress rejected the proposition, doubtless for the reason that a majority of the members foresaw that their states would decline to heed the recommendation. Indeed some of the states thereafter went from bad to worse, offering larger bounties than ever before.

After Washington had taken his departure it was resolved (February 4) that he proceed, "in such manner as he shall judge expedient", to complete the arrangement of the army. Among the problems discussed between Washington and the committee had been one pertaining to the rank of officers; and it was determined at the same time to give the commander-in-chief a free hand to settle questions of relative rank under the degree of brigadier, but agreeably to the rules laid down in an act of November 24, 1778.

No sooner however had the measure of January 23 been tried out than it became evident that Washington and the committee had been right in their view that the crux of the problem lay in the prevalence of large state bounties. Accordingly, on March 9, Congress repealed that part of the measure that pertained to new enlistments and the re-enlistment of those whose terms were about to expire, and substituted a straight bounty of two hundred dollars to each recruit who, after the 23d of January, "hath inlisted, or shall inlist" for the duration of the war, with a proviso that, if the state had granted as great or greater bounty, then the two hundred dollars should be passed to the credit of the state. At the same time Congress earnestly recommended it to the states to complete their respective battalions "by draughts, or in any other manner they shall think proper", and to have them ready to take the field without delay.

The respective battalions alluded to were those provided for in a measure adopted earlier the same day. On May 27, 1778, Congress had adopted what was termed the "Establishment of the American Army", that is, the number of companies constituting a battalion, with the requisite officers for each battalion of infantry, artillery, cavalry, etc., and from time to time during the succeeding months had enacted sup-plementary or explanatory provisions. In planning for the campaign of 1779 it was necessary to consider how large an army would be needed, and the decision reached in the conference between Washington and the committee was that the infantry should be composed of eighty batta-lions, to be provided by the several states in determined quotas, from fifteen battalions assigned to Massachusetts to one each from Delaware and Georgia. This provision was included in the committee's report January 23, but was not actually adopted until March 9.

An indication of the hopeful mood of Congress at this time is the tone of President Jay's circular letter to the states, March 12, 1779, transmitting the resolutions of March 9. "As there is great reason", says the letter, "to expect that this Campaign, if successful, will be the last", there was every confidence that the states would cheerfully adopt every measure necessary "to render the Issue of it honorable to the American arms, and auspicious to American Liberty and Independ-ence". Francis Lewis expressed a similar conviction that "this year must one way or the other determine our fate"; and he based his conclusion on the near-exhaustion of Great Britain's resources of money and men, adding, "and . . . ours is in the same predicament". "One more good campaign and victory is ours", had ever been and would continue to be the Congressional theme-song. Deeply discouraged the members of Congress often were and well might be, but the note of despair they forever refused to utter.

Another of Washington's proposals to the committee of conference (January 29) was a renewal of his recommendation of the year before of a provision for half-pay for life to the officers of the army. The compromise measure that had been adopted, half-pay for seven years, had, he asserted, by no means given satisfaction; for, although in his opinion the majority of the officers would probably not live beyond the seven years, certainly most of them expected to do so, and it was just those last years of their lives that most greatly concerned them. But for the hope of a speedy termination of the war, greatly encouraged by the French alliance, the discontents among the officers would probably ere this time have reduced the army to a shadow; now, however, that temporary consolation had subsided, and all the former dangers from those discontents had become imminent. Washington cautioned the committee, nevertheless, that, unless it should appear clear that Congress would approve the measure, it would be best not to agitate it at all. The committee appears to have convinced itself that the measure would be defeated; and the fate of a motion, May 24, in behalf of such a provision proved the correctness of that view. The motion, made by Gouverneur Morris and seconded by William Carmichael, obtained only the votes of those two members.

Not many days afterward (June 12, 1779), an event unlooked for by Congress stirred that body to anxiety. It was a memorial from a group of officers in behalf of such a provision, and its tone was such that Congress by a unanimous vote referred it to the committee of conference, with instructions "to report speedily upon a further provision for the army of the United States". The committee doubtless used such speed as seemed advisable, for there was an evident uncertainty respecting the attitude of the states, although some of them had already enacted similar measures of their own. For instance, James Duane, chairman of the committee of conference, wrote to Governor Clinton the day the memorial was presented, stating that Pennsylvania and Maryland had, without waiting for the opinion of Congress, given their officers half-pay for life, and he desired to know the sense of his state in the matter. General John Armstrong, an army officer lately become a member of Congress, declared (June 25) that the business would meet with more opposition in Congress than he had imagined. "Many declaim against the policy of that measure", he wrote, "but say they are ready to agree to something tantamount, by reducing the necessaries of life to a moderate price, and making the pay good from the beginning as tho' there had been no depreciation: which of these modes Congress ought to adopt, I am at a loss to know." By the 14th of July the committee had made up its mind and brought in a report in favor of half-pay for life.

At the outset of the discussion came a curious motion by Dickinson and Drayton that a body of militia be collected to join General Washington and that thereupon "Congress immediately adjourn to the place where the Army shall be, and that the members shall respectively join the Militia, and act with them in such important operations as shall be judged most expedient for advancing the welfare of these States." Just what may have provoked a motion that could scarcely be regarded as anything but a joke does not appear, but it drew from Henry Laurens the scoffing remark, "This shews more valour in those Gentlemen than of the wisdom and reflection of grave Senators, but who can restrain the ardor of fighting Men when an opportunity offers?"

If the committee had been slow in reporting, Congress was still slower in acting. The question was taken under consideration July 30, and apparently not again until August 11. By this time the opposition had become convinced, as James Lovell declared August 17, that they would be able to combat the measure only by recommending it to the states "to do justice by Half pay for Life *or* such other Provision as they find adequate" to the purpose, which was "to keep the army together". It was by just that means that the opposition won the fight (August 17); and they added the further recommendation that the states make such provision for the widows of officers and soldiers "as shall secure to them the sweets of that liberty for the attainment of which their husbands have nobly laid down their lives". Then, on the following day, Congress voted some increases in the salaries of officers.

Some of the states that had not already done so complied with the recommendation of Congress by passing laws extending half-pay for life to their own officers; but, as officers who held their commissions from Congress could not hope to benefit thereby, and, as there were many officers also who did not benefit by the new increases in salaries, Congress soon began to be bombarded by memorials from such officers, so that once again the measure of half-pay for life was proposed (December 1, 1779), but once again it failed of passage. Thus the matter stood until the following summer, when Washington once more essayed the task (August 20, 1780), and so persistently and so persuasively, with the aid of the alarming conditions that had arisen, that he was at last successful (October 21, 1780).

It was just when Congress found itself in the midst of this new wrangle over the half-pay question, and probably because of it, that the committee of conference was called upon (July 26, 1779) to render an account of its proceedings during the past several months, which it did on the 16th of August. It might be supposed that Congress should have known what had been done, was doing, or in prospect; for all had been matters of report and record. For one thing, however, during the seven months since the conference had begun, members had gone and members had come, with the result that nearly one half the membership had changed. There were therefore many new mental thirsts that needed to be quenched. For another thing, and perhaps of even greater importance, through the whole of the spring and summer Congress had been deeply engrossed in problems pertaining to its finances and even more serious problems pertaining to its foreign relations, over which it had become so rent and torn by faction and personal quarrels that but a modicum of its attention could be bestowed on matters pertaining to the army.

Meanwhile General Washington had occasion more than once to lament, in private correspondence, that he was left uninformed of matters he needed to know for his better guidance, particularly with regard to the temper and designs of our allies and the general complexion of affairs in Europe. Fuller knowledge of these things, he wrote to Edmund Randolph August 1, "would in many cases determine the propriety of measures, which under a cloud of darkness can only be groped at". At that moment, he declared (to John Armstrong, May 18, 1779), he was as totally unacquainted with what was going forward "in the great national council", as if he were an alien. Echoes of the disputes and dissensions in Congress had nevertheless come to his ears, and he had pleaded that it was high time for them to subside, that the hour had come "when every Man (especially those in office) should with one hand and one heart pull the same way, and with their whole strength".

And thus spring dragged into summer, and summer into autumn, when it became necessary to begin again the perennial planning for the next campaign. Accordingly in a communication dated November 18, 1779, Washington laid before Congress the status of the army, together with his suggestions for filling the eternally depleted and depleting ranks. His specific plan was essentially a repetition of his proposition of February, 1778, and of January, 1779, namely, an annual draft, although he now proposed a small modification of his earlier plans. This was that each state be informed of its real deficiency of troops and be called upon to make up that deficiency by draft, unless Congress should decide that a lesser number would suffice: that the men thus drafted should join the army by January 1 to serve for a full year; and that the officers of the states from which the troops came be directed to endeavor to enlist them for the duration of the war, under the same bounties as offered in the act of January 23, 1779. Once more also Washington urged that all state, county, and town bounties be abolished if practicable.

The committee to whom Washington's letter was referred brought in two reports (December 7 and 14) essentially in accordance with Washington's suggestions, but the result, after a month of discussion, involving among other things the perpetual controversy over the adjustment of state quotas, was merely a resolution that the states "be required to furnish, by draughts or otherwise, on or before the first day of February next, the deficiency of their respective quotas of 80 battalions of infantry", as apportioned by the act of March 9, 1779. The committee had proposed, in accordance with Washington's suggestion, an earnest recommendation to the states to abolish their bounties, but again Congress declined to press the states to that extent. It could employ the word "required" in its resolution, though knowing full well that the states would comply or not comply, as they saw fit, just as, in deference to sovereign states, it must qualify the method proposed by the addition of the words "or otherwise". Another year and, strangely enough, Congress would be setting about reducing the army rather than enlarging it: that is, until wisdom should overtake that unstable body and bring it to a right-about-face.

The problems of recruiting and organizing the army were of course only the beginning; the army must be supplied with the necessities of life, to say nothing of the requisite fighting implements. In this period it was food and clothing that constituted the most crucial problem, for there were frequent serious deficiencies of both. Under Jeremiah Wadsworth as commissary general and General Nathanael Greene as quartermaster general the business of supplying the army had been conducted to such a degree of satisfaction that for several months there was a subsidence of those complaints which theretofore had been chronic, and Congress had interfered comparatively little in the conduct of their respective departments.

In the late autumn of 1778, however, difficulties began to develop and murmurs to arise. For instance, on the last day of October, 1778, a member announced that he had heard of frauds and abuses on the part of certain individuals in the quartermaster general's department, and a committee was appointed to make a strict inquiry into the charges. This particular incident appears to have been without importance except as the beginning of complaints that soon grew in volume and in force. Five days later (November 5) Washington drew the attention of Congress to representations from both the commissary general and the quartermaster general respecting distresses in the army for want of provisions, and to the related problem of going into winter quarters. In this matter the cooperation of the states was particularly necessary, and a committee was designated to take such measures as it thought proper. Then, on November 10, came a letter from Quartermaster General Greene touching problems in his department that called for action on the part of Congress.

Congress now decided that it was necessary not only to take vigorous measures for the regulation of the two great supply departments but also itself to give a more constant attention to those departments. Accordingly the committee already designated was vested with broad general powers to superintend those departments. This committee, albeit with some changes of personnel, continued its activities for somewhat more than a year, when its functions were turned over to the board of war (November 25, 1779).

The persistence of reports of abuses in the public departments led to the appointment January 25, 1779, of a committee of five to effect a remedy for these evils; but, if this particular committee ever remedied any abuses, there is no certain record of it. Probably it withdrew into quiescence because of the activity of the committee of November 5 and 10, 1778, and the fact that Gouverneur Morris was a member of both committees furnishes an additional explanation. That there was no dearth, however, of reforming zeal is shown by the appointment on May 28, 1779, of two other committees, with related functions. The immediate impetus to these appointments was some representations of the treasury committee that had been strung along for the past two months. One general proposition of the treasury committee was that it would be impracticable to carry on the war with paper emissions.

Congress did not need any admonition from its committee of the treasury to be made aware of the dangerous quagmires into which paper emissions had led it. Had it not already been racking its brain and tearing its hair to find some way out of the mess? But what was more to the point, the treasury committee pointed the accusing finger at what it believed to be one of the prime causes of the enormous, the alarming expenses of the different departments. It was that long prevailing practice of rewarding purchasing agents by commissions on purchases. Of course when the higher the prices paid the more the purchasing agents were able to put into their own pockets, there was anything but a disposition to keep prices down. Two years before this, sage old Roger Sherman had decried the practice and had declared that it was "such a temptation as an honest man would not wish to be led into". Congress nevertheless persisted in the practice, and some men who counted themselves honest were led into it. A modern instance of a like blunder inevitably thrusts itself into the mental foreground—that evil-working device of the ten-per-cent-plus adopted by our government at the beginning of the World War.

At all events, declared the treasury committee, the departments ought to be thoroughly overhauled. It was doubtless these treasury reports that led Daniel of St. Thomas Jenifer to write (May 26, 1779):

I believe the Quarter Masters and Commissaries have had their share in the Depreciation of our Currencies. An enquiry into their Conduct is now on foot, and if I can touch them up over the left shoulder they may depend that I will do it. perhaps their Tens of Thousands, and hundreds of thousands that they have made, may be brought down to Units before we have done with them. But the peculators are the Vermin that have been the great cause and source of our misfortunes in this respect.

Accordingly one committee (Dickinson, Sherman, and Scudder) was assigned the task of making a strict inquiry into the expenses of the departments, boards, etc., and another (Dickinson, Huntington, and Burke) instructed to report a plan for putting those establishments on a different footing with regard to the expenditure of public money. Thus it had come about that there were now four committees having to do with one phase or another of the public departments and all aiming at some sort of reform. Between the last two committees the Journals do not always make a clear distinction, as the designations applied to them respectively are by no means uniform. The fact that Dickinson was chairman of both committees helps to add to the confusion.

Despite their general efficiency, indeed sometimes because of it, both Wadsworth and Greene had become the objects of much criticism and unpopularity, and both threatened to resign. Greene had done so in April, declaring that the jealousies, suspicions, and obloquy to which he was exposed were such that he could not continue in office unless he could do so consistent with his reputation. In the beginning of June, Wadsworth for a second time declared his intention of resigning, and at the same time gave such an alarming account of the condition of his department that Congress made haste to declare (June 7), in a resolution recorded as unanimous, its full confidence in the integrity and abilities of the quartermaster general and the commissary general, while averring nevertheless that there was reason to believe that abuses had been committed by inferior officers in their respective departments, adding significantly that it was the intention of that body to take measures speedily "to distinguish such of them as have been faithful from such as have been otherwise, and thereby cause justice to be done to all". Declining to accept Wadsworth's resignation, Congress admonished him that if he and his principal officers should quit the service at so critical a period, it would not only arouse the resentment of the country but actually be a dangerous step. Similar admonitions were given Wadsworth by his fellow-countryman of Connecticut, Samuel Huntington, with the further intimation that some new regulations would be set up for the two great departments purchasing on commission.

Greene and Wadsworth were both prevailed upon to remain in office for the time being, while Congress went lumbering on in its confused efforts toward reform, and while new troubles were continually added to old. One particularly annoying complication was created by an act of New Jersey, whereby the officers of the quartermaster general's department became subject to a tax as Continental officers. It was a sad state of affairs of course, very detrimental to the public service, when a particular state could exercise a power to tax the staff officers in the Continental service, merely as such; and if the practice should spread to the other states, it would be little short of disastrous. Yet there was nothing Congress could do about it except to appeal to New Jersey to revise its law or its practice, while Congress, for its part, was duty bound to promise indemnification to its staff officers; for a state had "an undoubted right . . . to tax all property therein however or wherever acquired", and in any manner that it saw fit. So at least a committee reported (August 6); but Congress, having listened to the report, went on to other business, and when later (October 22) that matter was brought up again, Congress once more chose to go on to other business.

This last incident befell almost at the moment when Congress had come to something like an impasse in its efforts to evolve new regulations for the departments. On the 9th of July, 1779, about the time when the New Jersey problem first impinged upon the Congressional consciousness, although at that time it had not pricked the Congressional conscience, Congress found it possible to agree upon one measure that might possibly lead to at least a modicum of reform, namely, that the executive powers of the states be earnestly requested instantly to make the strictest inquiry into the conduct of every person employed within the state in connection with any of the supply departments, and, in the event that "any kind of misbehaviour or strong suspicion thereof" should be made to appear, that such persons be removed or, if deemed proper, prosecuted "at the expense of the United States". The committee that reported this resolution made other offerings, to which Congress does not appear to have taken so kindly, among them a proposition that every deputy commissary should "brand or inscribe plainly and legibly so that the same cannot be rubbed out, his Christian and Sirname at full length" upon every barrel that came to his hand. Then, on July 23, another of the reforming committees (probably the second of those appointed May 28) laid before Congress an elaborate plan for regulating the departments.

That Congress meant to give careful study to the plan is evidenced by the fact that sixty copies of the plan were ordered printed. Those who drafted the measure clearly aimed to leave no contingency unprovided for; but the very minutiae of its requirements would probably have defeated its purposes. Whether or not members of Congress were able to comprehend its intricacies, it was not until October 18 that it was taken into consideration in committee of the whole, there debated during some part of two days, with "no resolution thereon", then disappeared until December 4, when it was passed over to a new committee.

It was just then that Wadsworth definitely gave in his resignation, which this time was accepted (November 29, 1779), and Ephraim Blaine was appointed in his stead (December 2). Not many days later Greene likewise resigned, but again Congress refused (December 17), because a change of officers in the department at that time was thought to be "dangerously critical". In fact, what had chiefly led to these resignations were the difficulties experienced in obtaining supplies for the army in any manner, difficulties caused in great part by the deranged conditions of the finances and become so serious that all plans for reforms were cast into deep shadow.

Nevertheless the new committee that had taken over the great project of July 23, 1779, did make a report on January 20, 1780; but then the business took the curious turn of being referred to three commissioners, one of whom at least was to be a member of Congress, who should repair to headquarters and, in conjunction with General Washington, carry out various retrenchments and reforms, or report their recommendations to Congress. The member of Congress chosen was General Schuyler, not then in attendance, the outside members of the commission being Mifflin and Pickering, the latter at the time a member of the board of war.

Schuyler came to Congress early in March, 1780, but declined to serve on the commission, although he did consent to be one of a committee of Congress whose purpose should be to consult with the commander-in-chief and the heads of the several civil departments of the army and to adopt such measures as would have "a probable tendency" to effect the great object that Congress had in view. Schuyler drew some subtle distinctions between service as a member of Congress and acting in a capacity that carried the implication that he was a servant of Congress; but a decisive factor in his decision appears to have been a determination not to be placed in a position of assisting Mifflin and Pickering, who, he believed, not only were unfriendly to Washington but would probably attempt measures designed to injure the general. Mifflin and Pickering were accordingly instructed to proceed with the business, while a committee of Congress was appointed to advise with them, and Schuyler was placed on the committee. This Schuyler regarded as an act of indelicacy toward him, and he refused to have anything to do with either the committee or the commissioners. Thereupon the two commissioners, together with the other two members of the committee, Sherman and Allen Jones, proceeded to work out an elaborate project of reforms, particularly for the quartermaster's department; and on March 27, 1780, they laid their plan before Congress.

Schuyler called it (April 5, 1780) "a voluminous system", although only the first part had as yet been reported. A second part was to pertain to the business of the commissary general of issues, and a third to the hospital department. How voluminous it was may be judged from the fact that the plan for the quartermaster's department occupies thirty-six pages of manuscript and eighteen pages of printed text. General Greene, who had a conference with the committee the day the report was presented, wrote to Washington (March 28):

The best people in Congress think the new system for drawing supplies from the States, will be found totally incompetent to the business. . . . The scheme is too complex and tedious, for such heavy and pressing demands as are frequently made upon the Department. . . . General Schuyler and others think it will starve the Army in ten days.

A few days later (March 31) he added, "The more I view it the less I like it."

Greene was of opinion that the plan had been devised partly to disgrace and injure him, while he and Schuyler both were convinced there was also a design to embarrass Washington. These suspicions were of course pointed at Mifflin, the chief author of the plan, who in a letter to General Gates, ascribed to himself the character of "State Cobbler", and stated that his plan was founded on some of the old ideas of that general. It came about therefore that one more ambitious plan to reform the departments went into the discard, and the actual reform would devolve upon the committee sent to headquarters in May, of which Schuyler was a member, and would, in accordance with Schuyler's proposition in the early days of March, be worked out in conjunction with the commander-in-chief.

Thus many months had gone by since that October day in 1778, when Congress had started out confidently if not blithely to correct some abuses, small or large, in the public departments. It had stumbled into one blind alley after another, and at every step had found itself more and more entangled in the complexities of its finances, of its economics, and even of its own administration. As the year 1779 approached an end, the end also of one campaign, such as it had been, and the time to lay plans for another, if there were to be another, the condition of the existing army became desperate. Streams of supply were drying up, magazines were empty or fast emptying, hunger began to stalk through the army, mutiny and dissolution to threaten. The chief officers of the supply departments, finding themselves at the end of their resources, were resigning or threatening to resign. The worst of the entanglements, the chief source of all the troubles, was of course the terrible depreciation of the Continental money, the awful rise in prices. To find a solution for that problem Congress had been struggling desperately for a good many months, with the result of only sinking deeper and deeper into the mire. Something must be done and done quickly, else there was an end to all hopes. It is no wonder that now and again some member would loose the distressful cry, "Congress are at their wit's end."

Even at such times, however, there was always some member who had the wit to devise a plan that he believed would be a potent remedy for the ills that did so mightily beset them and the persuasive power to obtain a trial of its efficacy. So it happened in this instance. If, some fertile brain concluded, individuals could carry on their transactions by barter, as was at that time to some extent being done, why not Congress? Would it not be a comparatively simple thing for the states to furnish directly to the army, without the intervention of money, the actual supplies that were needed? It was so resolved. On December 11, 1779, certain of the near-by states (Virginia, Maryland, Pennsylvania, Delaware, New Jersey, and Connecticut) were requested to furnish designated supplies, some immediately, others by the first of April. Then, on the 14th, the requisition was made general, with the promise that these specific supplies should be credited in lieu of money quotas. Naturally it would require some investigations and careful calculations to determine just what specific supplies should be asked of each state, in what quantities, and at what prices. Meanwhile Congress could only promise that due care would be taken to suit the convenience of the several states and that the accounts should finally be compared and adjusted, "so as to do equity to all the states".

The responses from the near-by states were, upon the whole, generous, but the supplies were insufficient, and Washington found it necessary to resort to impressment or the threat of it. To General Irvine he wrote January 4, 1780, "of the scanty pittance we have distributed to the army the last is nearly exhausted, and without a prospect of any adequate and immediate succour." Then, on the 9th, he added, "Our Affairs are in so deplorable a condition (on the score of provisions) as to fill the Mind with the most anxious and alarming fears . . . Men half starved, imperfectly Cloathed, riotous, and robbing the Country people of their subsistence from shear necessity." Explaining to the magistrates of New Jersey the necessity for his requisitions upon the counties of that state for supplies of grain and cattle, he wrote (January 8):

The present situation of the Army with respect to provisions is the most distressing of any we have experienced since the beginning of the War. For a Fortnight past the Troops both Officers and Men, have been almost perishing for want. They have been alternately without Bread or Meat the whole time, with a very scanty allowance of either and frequently destitute of both. They have borne their sufferings with a patience that merits the approbation and ought to excite the sympathy of their Countrymen. But they are now reduced to an extremity no longer to be supported.

About the same time General Greene laid before Washington a picture of the situation as it affected his department. "The cloud thickens", he wrote, "and the prospects are daily growing darker." His agents were loaded with heavy debts, perplexed with half-finished contracts, people clamorous for their pay and refusing to proceed in the public business until their present demands were discharged. He could see nothing ahead but "a general check if not an absolute stop" to every branch of the business. As for the new measure of calling for specific supplies, it fell far short of the requirements, and besides was sure to involve difficulties of adjustment between the different agents and between the different authorities as well, and he was apprehensive of "some jarring interests, many improper disputes, as well as dangerous delays". There was, in fact, "such a maze, from the mixed modes adopted by some states, and about to be adopted by others", that disorder and confusion were bound to follow. There was no deficiency in the resources of the country, Greene asserted; on the contrary, he had every reason for concluding that the country was more plentifully stored with every material necessary for the support of the army, than it had been for three years past. "The defect", he declared, "lies in the want of a proper means to draw them into public use." Similarly President Huntington, who had succeeded John Jay, September 28, 1779, sent forth a circular letter to some of the states January 12, 1780, urging them "in the most pressing manner, to send immediate supplies of provisions to the army", declared, "The Country abounds with the necessary Resources, but private gain seems the only Object of too many Individuals, without any Concern for the public safety."

That the measure in its first tentative and ill-defined form was something of a maze, as General Greene had characterized it, and that it would need to be brought down to particulars, was probably clearly understood by every member of Congress. The task was, however, a complicated one, well calculated to tax the ingenuity as well as the knowledge of Congress. Not only was it necessary to learn what were the existing or probable supplies in each of the states, but the solution of the problem called particularly for an adjustment of requirements to the respective capacities of the states and for an even more delicate balancing of their equitable proportions of the general burden. That rule-of-thumb by which state quotas had hitherto been apportioned in accordance with population had never been a satisfactory one, and for this particular purpose it seemed to some members of Congress to be especially unfair. Necessarily therefore the adjustment of the state quotas of supplies stirred no end of controversy, with its inevitable accompaniment of maneuvering and dickering among the delegations.

It was not until the end of February that an agreement was reached, and before that time one member, Elbridge Gerry of Massachusetts, had become so infuriated over what he termed injustice to his state that he quit Congress in a huff, and two and a half years thereafter was still refusing to be comforted. Most members, however, notwithstanding disgruntlements similar to Gerry's, urged upon their states a full and liberal compliance. The North Carolina delegates, for instance, insisted that the quotas assigned to their state, and to South Carolina as well, were "far beyond what is their supposed proportion", but they had given their assent because they regarded the measure as indispensable.

It is unquestionably clear [they wrote the governor, February 29] that a failure in any State, who furnishes considerable supplies, might be attended with consequences, in the last degree ruinous to the Cause we are engaged in; and which is now happily drawing to a glorious conclusion. In a word, Sir, the Exertions of Congress are no longer competent; and, unless the States exert themselves, the Cause is utterly lost; and we shall be left in a situation the most wretched among human beings—that is, exposed to all the Oppressions and Insults of enraged, Victorious, and avaricious Tyranny.

President Huntington, in transmitting the act to the states, voiced the general sentiment of Congress when he declared that the importance and necessity of a substantial compliance with the act of Congress were so obvious that nothing more seemed needful "to excite the most vigorous Exertions on the part of the several States to carry the same into Execution". To John Collins of Rhode Island, a former sea captain, the measure was "like takeing a leap in the dark—and Crouding the Ship through a Strait amongst Rock and Sholes in a thick fog. We may Run the Ship a Shoar she may *poke* through".

The fog was even then gathering thick and fast; the ship of Congress was entering the treacherous strait, amongst rocks and shoals; soon it would be a serious question whether she would be able even to poke through.

CHAPTER XXII

APPLES OF SODOM
COLLAPSE OF "CONTINENTAL"

The resolution of Congress on January 2, 1779, to cancel certain of its old bills of credit and substitute therefor bills of a new emission, although recorded on the day after New Year, may properly be regarded as a New Year's resolution; and, like many another New Year's resolution, it was not meticulously kept. The case of Congress may well be likened to that of the man who, after a prolonged inner struggle, firmly resolved that he would never drink again; then, exulting in the victory of the spirit over the flesh, rushed into the nearest saloon to take a drink to his good resolution.

The new emission which Congress ordered for the purpose of carrying out its plan of cancellation was fixed at 50,000,400 dollars, a few millions more than the quantum of bills to be taken up; but Congress would have plenty of use for these extra millions. If that had been really the end of continental emissions of bills of credit, Congress might reasonably have maintained that it had stopped the press and checked the flood of paper money. Within two weeks, however, the cry for money to meet the ever mounting expenses made a further issue imperative—so at least it seemed—and on February 3, the order went forth for the emission of an additional five millions, plus some small change. Another two weeks, and the amount was duplicated (February 19). Six weeks later (April 1) another like amount was put forth. And that was just the beginning. By June, 1779, when the condemned issues were supposed to be punched and ready for destruction, somewhat more than thirty-five millions had been added. What was more, despite diligent efforts on the part of Congress, a great quantity of those condemned issues were still wandering about, and Congress had perforce (July 2) to extend the time for redemption to January 1, 1780.

In fact, the flourishing hopes that had gathered around the redemption measure had flown out the window not many days after its enactment. On the last day of March the committee of the treasury boldly proclaimed its opinion that the war could not be carried on by means of paper emissions, that the quantity already issued was excessive and should be reduced, if the credit of the money was to be restored. To that pronouncement most members of Congress, if not all, responded amen!—and straightway ordered the emission of still more millions. In solemn truth, they could do no other; at least until they had found some other workable means; and to that even the financial wizards of the treasury were agreed.

To be sure, the treasury committee had remedies to propose, even though they could scarcely have hoped thereby to fill the insatiable maw of the monstrous devourer of the money. One remedy was a domestic loan (they would deck out loan office certificates in more attractive hues), another was a foreign loan (always a refuge in a time of storm), both of course exceedingly problematical. It would be some help if by some means the enormous expenses of the governmental machine might be reduced; and efforts to that end were made, although the eternal rise of prices made any actual reduction impossible. Another plan, promising more practical results, was being tried, although as yet with but partial success. This was the plan of obtaining from the states specific supplies in lieu of money quotas.

By the middle of May, 1779, so serious had the financial problem become, Congress was devoting three days out of each week to that problem alone. On the 21st Congress emerged from its welter of argument with a resolution that the states be called upon for their respective quotas of forty-five million dollars, to be paid into the treasury by the first of January, 1780; this in addition to the fifteen millions called for by the act of January 2. Even if these quotas could be collected, William Fleming wrote to Jefferson (May 22), it would not answer the end, without the aid of a foreign loan; for before the time allotted for the payment, emissions far in excess of forty-five millions would be necessary. Still, he added, "the very critical situation of our affairs seems to make it not only expedient, but absolutely necessary".

What, in effect, the act called for was the levying of heavy taxes by the states, and taxes were bound to be unpopular. Had not the Revolution started in a protest against taxation? Yet taxation, even "deep taxation", had long been advocated by some members of Congress, despite the known reluctance of the states to comply. But now the situation was grown desperate, and a great majority of Congress, so declared William Whipple, was in favor of this new measure. "The prevailing Opinion is", wrote Whipple (May 21), "that nothing will do but (I was going to say) *excessive* Taxes, but I will soften the ephithet and adopt the words *very high*. If a sufficiency can be raised by Taxes to support the War, farther emissions will be unnecessary." The greatest difficulty about taxes, he remarked, is in levying them on the proper persons. "If the whole sum", he declared, "could be drawn from those speculating miscreants, who have been sucking the Blood of their country, it would be a most happy circumstance."

In general, the Continental Congress was prone to a high degree of optimism, seldom failing to count a full hatching from every setting of eggs; but from this particular setting William Ellery's expectations seem to have exceeded all others.

A Stoppage of the press once effected [he wrote, May 25] our liberties are established and an end is put to the war. Our enemy's whole dependence now rests upon our being crushed with the weight of Rheams of depreciated paper money. Once remove that ground of Hope and they will offer us, as proud and haughty as they may be, honorable terms of peace.

Obviously a chief difficulty would be in obtaining the acquiescence of the states in a measure that touched them in a very sensitive spot, and then to prevail upon them to comply with its terms. They must therefore be appealed to in the most persuasive manner possible. Several members of Congress tried their hands at the preparation of the proposed address, but it was the pen of John Dickinson that found the language most acceptable to that always meticulous body, although some of Dickinson's most perfervid passages were deleted in Congress. The address, which was adopted May 26, 1779, is essentially an explanation and defense of the call for additional taxation, but it includes also some very frank admonitions, even sharp rebukes, to the states, as well as pleas of a very practical kind. It closes, as all such addresses must, with a stirring appeal:

Rouse yourselves, therefore, that this campaign may finish the great work you have so nobly carried on for several years past. What nation ever engaged in such a contest under such a complication of disadvantages, so soon surmounted many of them, and in so short a period of time had so certain a prospect of a speedy and happy conclusion? . . . Consider how much you have done, and how comparatively little remains to be done to crown you with success. Persevere, and you ensure peace, freedom, safety, glory, sovereignty, and felicity, to yourselves, your children, and your children's children. . . . Fill up your battalions . . . place your several quotas in the continental treasury; lend money for public uses; sink the emissions of your respective states . . . diligently promote piety, virtue, brotherly love, learning, frugality, and moderation; and may you be approved before Almighty God worthy of those blessings we devoutly wish you to enjoy.

"It is well drawn", wrote Charles Carroll of Carrollton, June 3, "but I think it comes too late by six months."

While waiting to see whether the states would rush to the rescue, it were well to see what might be done by way of loans. On May 28 a committee was appointed to report upon "the most advisable mode" of negotiating a foreign loan; likewise to what amount, and how it should be used. And while these presumed experts were brewing their special brew of counsel, it was resolved (June 11, 25, 29) to seek a domestic loan of 20,000,000 dollars—"on the faith of the United States of America", said the resolution; "on probable temptations", said one skeptical member. At the same time Congress avowed its intention "not only to avoid further emissions, but to diminish the quantity in circulation", that is, "provided the respective states, by correspondent and vigorous exertions, shall put it into their power to raise the necessary supplies". The question of a foreign loan was a much more ticklish business, consequently it dragged through several months before any definite plan was concluded upon. And while the committee and sundry more racked their brains for a plan that offered hopes of success, conditions went from exceeding bad to worse and worse. Daniel of St. Thomas Jenifer declared (May 24) that prices had increased one hundred per cent in three weeks. "This", said he, "has made those Vermins the Speculators become the object of resentment, and a Mob has assembled to regulate prices. What will be the issue God knows."

This City [Governeur Morris wrote May 30] is now the scene of policies high and low. I may add it is the scene of faction anarchy and distraction. Never were the affairs of any country in a better and a worse situation than those of America at this moment. A storm is gathering and will burst upon the heads of our enemies, perhaps of our own. Would to God that the desire of that great luxury to be free was the great desire of my countrymen, but other luxuries more alluring have influenced but too much upon their conduct. The torrent of *paper money* hath swept away with it much of our morals and impaired the national industry to a degree truly alarming.

"The inundation of money", wrote Richard Henry Lee (June 9), "appears to have overflowed virtue, and I fear will bury the liberty of America in the same grave. . . . The demon of avarice, extortion, and fortune-making seizes all ranks." Declared William Whipple (June 12), "If there is not virtue enough in the people to support the credit of the money, there can be but little dependence on their virtue to support the army without money."

That Congress would have more than a plenty of sage advice from outside its chamber was never to be doubted. Their own voices might be restrained within the compass of that chamber's four walls, but there was nothing to prevent the penetration of voices from without. Pens by the multitude were fluttering all about them. As far back as March, 1779, one writer, styling himself "A Customer", offered through the pages of the *Pennsylvania Packet* "A Speech which OUGHT to be spoken in Congress" upon the subject of the Continental money, wherein he proposed a foreign loan as the sovereign remedy for the dread disease that was so fearfully ravaging the country. It can scarcely be doubted that members read the speech, and one or another of them may have declaimed it textually or in substance in Congress assembled; but no official notice was taken of it.

It was a somewhat different case when, on July 3, 1779, another writer, signing himself "Leonidas", proposed a "SPEECH which *ought* to be spoken *to* the Congress on the same subject". The speech was loud and long and far from reverent, and without a doubt the nerves of Congress on the subject of its money had become not a little raw. "Leonidas" pressed upon Congress the need of making both foreign and domestic loans, and that speedily; above all, to stop the press.

I perceive by your late publication [spake Leonidas], that you are no strangers to the low value of your money. But why have you delayed so long to complain of this evil to your constituents? Why has the disease been suffered to run on to its last stage before you raised the cry of danger in the ears of your country? It is vain to blame the arts of your enemies, or the infamous practices of monopolizers and forestallers, The present depreciated state of your money must be traced only to the mistakes of Congress.

He concludes his speech to Congress with this impassioned appeal:

Rouse then, Gentlemen, to a sense of the danger of these infant States that are committed to your care. Let us read something more than the "Yeas" and "Nays", and questions for recommitting and postponing business in your journals. Your money—your money—demands every thought and every hour. You have more to dread from this quarter than you have from all the Britons, Hessians, New Levies, Refugees, Indians and Negroes that are now in arms against you. I conjure you therefore immediately to bind yourselves to each other by an oath, not to eat, drink or sleep till you have arrested your money in its progress toward destruction, and fixed it upon a permanent foundation.

These were stinging words, harsh accusations, to be hurled into the teeth of the Congress of the United States, and one member at least was exceeding wroth. Even as Congress was going through the morning grind of public despatches, Elbridge Gerry rose to a question of personal privilege and demanded that Mr. Dunlap, printer of the *Pennsylvania Packet,* be directed to attend at the bar of the House to answer such questions as should be propounded to him. "If such infamous Publications", vociferated the enraged Mr. Gerry, "are to pass without proper notice, 'tis time for Congress to go home and other men come in their stead"; and with like explosions of his wrath he occupied, according to the testimony of Henry Laurens, a good half hour.

Strangely enough most other members of Congress appear to have been of a different mind from that of Mr. Gerry. If it was a question of sustaining the dignity of Congress, said Thomas Burke of North Carolina, the only result of an investigation by Congress would be, not to elevate and sustain, but to bring lower still that prized attribute. It is not recorded that Burke reminded Congress of the incident; but it is altogether probable that, in the back of his head, was a recollection of the unavailing endeavor of Congress, some fifteen months agone, to maintain its dignity and authority as against him, Thomas Burke, the representative of a free and sovereign state.

Meriwether Smith, dubbed by some of his fellow-Congressmen the "oddity" of Virginia, likewise harangued Congress liberally, declaring that the speech of Leonidas "contained several good things", and closing with the flourish, "When the liberty of the Press shall be restrained, take my word for it, the liberties of the People will be at an end." John Penn of North Carolina was of like mind, and he even outdid Meriwether Smith as a prophet. "Gentlemen talk of imprisoning the Printer or the Author", he exclaimed. "I will undertake to say, if you have power, which I doubt, and were to imprison them for six Months, they would come out greater Men than they went in. What was it", he asked, "made Wilkes so great and popular a Man, but the imprisonment he suffered?"

Whether Mr. Gerry's wrath was cooled or heated by these preachments on the freedom of the press, he did not at that time take his disgustful leave of Congress, as he had threatened to do. (A few months later, on a different provocation, he did take a somewhat unceremonious leave, having first sulked for a while in his tent.) The rather, he tore a leaf from the book of the obnoxious Leonidas and offered Congress some plans of finance, foremost of which was one for making a foreign loan. This was on July 23. Gerry's scheme for obtaining a foreign loan was not, however, altogether new. He merely proposed that a plan which Congress had tried a time or two in a small way be employed on a more ambitious scale than hitherto. In its essentials the plan was to draw bills of exchange on the commissioners at Paris to the amount of 25,000,000 livres tournois, in denominations of 1000 to 15,000, and have the commissioners of the loan office sell the bills. Since they were to bear interest at six per cent and were payable in eight years, these bills were assumed to be an attractive investment. In the months to come Congress would from time to time seize upon the device of drawing bills of exchange on the commissioners at Paris as the only means of salvation; for the present, however, it was decided to try a different plan for bolstering up the collapsing currency.

For a long time Congress had been talking about limiting its emissions of bills of credit; and no longer ago than the 11th of June it had declared its intention of avoiding further emissions if possible; but neither the proposed domestic loan nor the requisitions on the states proved to be sufficient for requirements, and accordingly on July 17 the printing press was again called into service to the extent of 5,000,180 dollars. After months of wrestling with the question whether to resolve or not to resolve to quit its bad money habits, at last on the first day of September, Congress screwed its courage to the sticking point and took a pledge that "on no account whatever" would it emit more bills of credit than to make the whole amount of the issues 200,000,000 dollars. It was figured that at that time the issues fell short of the 200,000,000 by some 40,000,000 dollars, and it was further resolved (September 3) not even to emit those forty millions, unless it should become absolutely necessary.

In the vote on the main proposition there were very few negatives, but one of those was the vote of John Jay, then President of Congress and soon to be appointed minister to Spain. Jay had a special reason for voting no. In his view Congress had failed in its duty to the state of New York in the matter of the Vermont controversy; accordingly he wrote to Governor Clinton (September 2): "In the course of the debate, I intimated my doubts of their obtaining taxes from New York until Congress shall have decided the claims of Vermont." His advice to Clinton therefore was to "detain every shilling of it till justice be done to the State".

Jay had voted and was now writing as a representative for the state of New York. Observe, however, his conduct as president of Congress. On September 8 Congress requested the president to prepare a circular letter to the states to accompany the resolutions respecting the stoppage of emissions; and Jay rose to the occasion magnificently. The address, which was laid before Congress September 13, 1779, is about 4500 words in length and occupies nearly eleven closely printed pages in the *Journals*. Among the many state papers put forth by the Continental Congress it ranks among the first. The opening sentence particularly deserves to be quoted, because of its clear enunciation of basic principles and purposes.

In governments raised on the generous principles of equal liberty, where the rulers of the state are the servants of the people, and not the masters of those from whom they derive authority; it is their duty to inform their fellow-citizens of the state of their affairs, and by evincing the propriety of public measures, lead them to unite the influence of inclination to the force of legal obligation in rendering them successful.

Then, briefly summarizing the history of the contest, Jay advances to a statement of the necessity for issuing bills of credit, for the redemption of which "your faith was pledged". Follows a statement of the existing situation with regard to the bills, the resultant depreciation and the consequent rise of prices, the urgent need for supplies that could be provided only through loans and taxes, then the admonition: "To keep your battalions full, to encourage loans, and to assess your taxes with prudence, collect them with firmness, and pay them with punctuality, is all that will be requisite on your part."

The crux of the entire problem being the depreciation of the bills of credit, Jay proceeds to examine the causes of depreciation, which "is always either natural or artificial". "The latter is our case." Natural depreciation ensues and is in proportion to the excess of issues beyond the requirements of commerce; artificial depreciation, which is more serious, arises chiefly from distrust. Thence the main objective of his argument is to remove every sense of distrust of the ability of the United States to redeem their bills.

That the time has been [he asserts] when honest men might, without being chargeable with timidity, have doubted the success of the present revolution, we admit: but that period is passed. The independence of America is now as fixed as fate, and the petulant efforts of Britain to break it down are as vain and fruitless as the raging of the waves which beat against their cliffs.

In the last half of the address he considers three questions raised by the doubters:

1st. Whether and in what manner the faith of the United States has been pledged for the redemption of their bills:

2d. Whether they have put themselves in a political capacity to redeem them; and

3d. Whether, admitting the two former propositions, there is any reason to apprehend a wanton violation of the public faith.

For answer to the first query he points to the Journals of Congress, to the bills themselves, and to their actual acceptance by states and individuals, as sufficient evidence that "the people have pledged their faith for the redemption of them, not only collectively by their representatives, but individually".

To the second query, which takes its rise mainly from the argument that the Confederation has not been perfected, that the union may therefore be dissolved, Congress be abolished, and the several states resume all the rights of sovereignty, Jay's answer is unique among the arguments substantiating an actually existing union of the states. "For every purpose essential to the defense of these states in the progress of the present war, and necessary to the attainment of the objects of it", he maintains, "these states now are as fully, legally, and absolutely confederated as it is possible for them to be." The credentials of the delegates in 1774, 1775, and 1776, he asserts, "establish an union for the express purpose of opposing the oppressions of Great Britain, and obtaining redress of grievances". Then comes his pivotal argument:

On the 4th of July, 1776, your representatives in Congress, perceiving that nothing less than unconditional submission would satisfy our enemies, did, in the name of the people of the thirteen United Colonies, declare them to be free and independent states, and "for the SUPPORT of that declaration, with a firm reliance on the protection of Divine Providence, did mutually pledge to each other their LIVES, their FORTUNES, and their SACRED HONOR." Was ever confederation more formal, more solemn, or explicit? It has been expressly assented to and ratified by every state in the union.

So long, then, as any of the objects of this union remain unattained—and the redemption of these bills, the payment of these debts, are such objects—the union "cannot, so far as it may respect such objects, be dissolved, consistent with the laws of God or man".

The third query, Jay finds, "involves in it a doubt so injurious to the honor and dignity of America" that it is only "with great regret and reluctance" that he can prevail upon himself to take the least notice of it. Nevertheless he combats it with a two-fold argument: first, that

Congress, being the chosen representatives of the people, no more have it in their power "to annihilate your money than your independency, and that any act of theirs for either of these purposes would be null and void"; second, that the honor and pride of America would revolt against "the baseness or bad policy of violating our national faith."

The address closes, appropriately, with admonitions and appeals; and not the least pertinent admonition was: "Disdain to leave the whole business of your defence to your ally." Then this final appeal:

Rouse, therefore, strive who shall do most for his country; re-kindle that flame of patriotism which at the mention of disgrace and slavery blazed throughout America, and animated all her citizens. Determine to finish the contest as you began it, honestly and gloriously. Let it never be said that America had no sooner become independent than she became insolvent, or that her infant glories and growing fame were obscured and tarnished by broken contracts and violated faith, in the very hour when all the nations of the earth were admiring and almost adoring the splendor of her rising.

The address appears to have been so satisfactory to Congress that it was approved unanimously, and two hundred copies in English and the same number in German were ordered to be printed. Jay may have persuaded some people that a breach of faith on the part of Congress was unthinkable; but, if so, they were mainly outside of Congress, for within a few short months Congress was thinking that very thought, at least that repudiation in part was equitable. And then it was that Jay's doctrine was hurled violently into the teeth of Congress by an outraged public.

In his private letter to Governor Clinton (September 2) Jay had voiced the opinion that the whole sum required should be collected by means of taxes, "because we shall never be able to raise it with so little difficulty as at present"; and it chanced that on the very day the persuasive circular letter was approved a committee on ways and means reported a measure looking toward that end—*toward* only. It was a proposition to call upon the states for quotas of money in addition to those of Nov. 22, 1777, Jan. 2, 1779, and May 21, 1779; but it was not until October 6 that a decision was reached, and then the call decided on was for 15,000,000 dollars monthly from February 1 to October 1, 1780, the states to be charged interest on any deficiencies. When it came to fixing the quotas, there were, as always, difficulties, and a resolution was obtained, "That neither the present nor any former apportionment of quotas to the several states be considered as a precedent." The brief letter (drawn by Elbridge Gerry) that accompanied the act to the states carried a hope and a promise. The hope was "that the operation of taxes and other salutary measures in the course of the year will reduce the price of articles, and lessen the quotas required"; the promise was that "Congress, on their part, will endeavour to observe the strictest economy in the expenditures."

Although upon the whole the delegates earnestly besought their states to raise their taxes and pay their quotas promptly, most of them sounded notes of pessimism. *"Quere:",* ventured Cornelius Harnett (October 9); "Will it be paid? I believe not. The consequences, you must know, will be distressing indeed. The quota of our state is out of proportion, but this could not be avoided." "I would pour out . . . my earnest Supplications", wrote Gouverneur Morris (October 7), "by speedy vigorous and repeated Taxation to strike at the Root of a Disease which may prove dangerous if not fatal." "Taxation", John Armstrong wrote to Washington (October 15), "altho' the radical means of appreciation as well as of the payment of the publick debt, is a remedy too remote for our support, the disease has ran too long to be overtaken by a common cure."

The best financier, so Henry Laurens remarked just when Congress began the study of its latest measure, is one who can devise means of drawing the largest revenues from the people with the least murmuring; "for Taxes and murmuring more or less, are inseparable companions." Then he added, "when the burthens of Taxes fall heavily upon [our constituents], they will open their Eyes and enquire—and then—but here I draw a Veil." "Will the Chapter of Accidents again relieve us?" he queried a few days later (September 26); "God only knows." As for the plan adopted, he wrote to Governor Trumbull (October 19), "the medicine is rather rude, but if it be taken in time and in chearful spirits it may produce much relief, but cannot perform a radical cure." At best it would afford "a little time for breathing and recollection", and perhaps would stimulate the states "to look a little more narrowly into things which concern their temporal salvation". "But alas! alas!" he groaned, "we are threatened with an empty Treasury before the 1st day of December", and only the vigorous and virtuous exertions of the states, and that immediately, could "so far heal the wound given by rash, bad policy as to save us from a violent convulsion".

Under conditions so dire the thoughts of Congress once more turned toward a foreign loan. On September 27 John Jay was chosen minister to Spain. The main purpose of the mission was to negotiate a treaty of alliance and of amity and commerce with that power, but Congress could scarcely escape visions of a loan. Before taking his departure Jay deemed it prudent to inquire in what manner he was to be supplied with money for his expenses on his arrival in Europe. The answer was not long delayed. The minister at the court of France would be desired to take the most effectual measures for supplying the newly appointed ministers and their secretaries with the necessary funds, while at the same time he was to be assured that Congress would take measures immediately for replacing such sums, "as well as for establishing a fund in Europe for the future support of all the Embassies from these States". Establish funds in Europe, forsooth! At that moment not a soul in Congress knew whether there would be anywhere sufficient funds to buy the next week's provisions for the army.

But hold! May be the hopes of Congress were not so ill-founded after all; for the same committee that had reported the proper answer to Jay's query reported that there were reasons for hoping that a loan might be obtained from Holland. Those reasons were founded on a suggestion made about a year before by a Hollander, Lieutenant-Colonel J. G. Diriks, sometime in the service of the United States. At that time the reply had been "that Congress are not yet prepared to adopt the scheme of a negotiation for the loan proposed"; but a year had brought a change of needs and a change of mood on the part of Congress. There was now scarcely a moment's hesitation. Congress would be delighted to negotiate such a loan, and on October 21 appointed Henry Laurens to undertake that mission. On November 1 Congress decided to go a step further and designated Laurens as commissioner to negotiate a treaty of amity and commerce with the United Provinces.

This appointment was ultimately to have consequences of importance, although quite outside the present purposes of Congress. It was nearly ten months before Laurens actually departed on his mission, and then only to be taken captive by the British when he had barely begun his voyage. His destination was accordingly altered, from the court of the Netherlands to the Tower of London. Released from prison on the last day of December, 1781, he had previously been designated by Congress as one of the commissioners to negotiate peace. He had, however, only a minor part in those negotiations.

As had sometime before been forecast, the approach of December saw the treasury on the verge of exhaustion. Quotas paid in by the states had produced little more than a trickle. "Out of the 60 Millions which was heretofore called for from the States", Cornelius Harnett wrote October 9, "only 3 millions have been received. How the war can be carried on after [December] I know not." In mid-November there was an additional emission of somewhat more than ten millions, and on November 29 another emission of ten millions plus, bringing the whole of the emissions up to the dead-line of 200,000,000. These new emissions were, however, being swallowed up about as fast as the presses could print them. In such an emergency what better could be done than fall back upon the scheme of Elbridge Gerry of the preceding July—anticipate European loans by drawing bills of exchange? Gerry's proposed bills had, however, rather the character of bonds, payable in eight years. The plan now adopted (November 23) was to draw bills payable at six months' sight to the amount of 100,000 pounds sterling each on John Jay and Henry Laurens, to be sold at the current rate of exchange.

It mattered little that neither Jay nor Laurens was at his post in Europe, that Jay was in fact somewhere on the broad Atlantic and might never reach the other side, that Laurens had not even as yet taken to the water; it mattered less that former experiences in drawing bills of exchange with no funds to meet them were monitory warnings against the measure. All these heavy cons were nevertheless outbalanced by weightier pros. It would be a considerable time before the bills would be presented for payment, and at worst it would be a longer time before they could be coming back and knocking at the doors of the treasury. In that time they might be made to contribute most helpfully to feeding and clothing the army, might still the clamors of sundry debtors; indeed they might make it possible for some of the states to make advances to their delegates in Congress, not a few of whom were right then in dire need. And who could say what stroke of good fortune might meanwhile befall? In one way or another the bills appear to have found purchasers; and one of the distressful incidents in this sad chapter of Continental finance is that, long before Mr. Laurens ever left these shores, bills drawn on him were diligently seeking him in Europe, and he could not be found.

In Congress, and to some extent in the country as well, there appears to have been an expectation that stoppage of the press would halt the downward plunge of the money. It was supposed that the first of December, 1779, would mark the beginning of some degree of stabilization. But all such expectations were doomed to disappointment. The situation grew rapidly worse rather than better. In mid-December the device of supplying the army by drawing specific supplies from the states was hit upon, but the device was cumbersome at best, and it was a good while before it could be made to work with any degree of satisfaction. If Congress was tempted to disregard the limit set for its emissions, it did not yield, doubtless because it knew full well that yielding would only make bad matters worse. Congress did propose to itself (December 23) to borrow twenty millions of its own bills of credit on sterling bills of exchange to be drawn on Jay and Laurens, offering the most liberal terms; but it did not propose a new emission of bills. Nevertheless, when some financial expert produced figures to show that a mistake had been made in the calculations and that the actual issues fell short of 200,000,000 dollars, Congress did not inquire diligently into the accuracy of these figures. It accepted them instanter and ordered additional emissions accordingly.

As members of Congress beheld the "inconceivable" depreciation, the "enormous" rise of prices, and were painfully pinched by the "amazing" increase of the cost of living, a good many of them took refuge in flight. "The expense of living here", wrote Nathaniel Peabody, "is intolerable, beyond conception, and almost insupportable." "It seems", said William Floyd, "as if the Devil was with all his Emissaries let loose in this State to Ruin our money." Conditions were probably not much worse, if at all, in Philadelphia than elsewhere, yet on December 3, Congress resolved that in April it would remove to some other place, just where it was unable to decide.

Not only was Congress dissatisfied with some aspects of its environment, there were internal discomforts as well. Some members, like James Mercer of Virginia, disgruntled over one act or another of Congress, departed in disgust. Others, like Cornelius Harnett of North Carolina, or his colleague, William Sharp, stuck to their posts, but pleaded the while to be released from "the House of Bondage". As early as the beginning of October, Harnett had written to Thomas Burke:

> For God's sake come on to relieve me in Nov[ember], but at the furthest the very beginning of December. . . . I acknowledge it is cruel in me to wish you to return. . . . But you have this Consolation: that, should you fail of receiving your reward in this world, you will no doubt be singing Hallelujas in the next to all Eternity, Tho' I acknowledge your Voice is not very well Calculated for that business.

There is no blinking the fact that, in those December days of 1779, Congress was very unhappy; and it augurs well for the building of the nation that the builders, even at moments most critical, did not lose their sense of humor, held fast to their sense of proportion. Indeed at such an hour it behooved the Congress to cheer up, for worse, much worse, was yet to come.

It was just when thus beset by problems beyond their ken that, on the 9th of December, as sometime before appointed, Congress paused in its labors to join in consecrating that day to be

a day of public and solemn thanksgiving to Almighty God for his mercies, and of prayer for the continuance of his favor and protection to these United States; to beseech him that he would be graciously pleased to influence our public councils, and bless them with wisdom from on high, with unanimity, firmness, and success; that he would go forth with our hosts and crown our arms with victory . . .

It was altogether befitting that at such a time the people give thanks for mercies obtained and blessings bestowed, and it was likewise befitting that the nation implore Divine Providence for other blessings of which it stood in sore need.

The composition of this thanksgiving proclamation had been entrusted to Jesse Root of Connecticut, reputed to be powerful in prayer, and the fervor of his invocation, the sublimity of his appeal to the throne of grace, could not but touch the hearts and quicken the spirits of all who heard it. It was meet that thanks be rendered up to Heaven "for raising us . . . from deep distress to be numbered among the nations of the earth", and particularly that praise be given to the ruler of the universe "for arming the hands of just and mighty princes in our deliverance". To be sure, thus far only one such prince had come forward to champion the American cause, but that was a deficiency time no doubt would remedy. If in his fervor the supplicant was at times oblivious to the factual, if he seemed to be coursing at an altitude above the harsh and sordid conditions that cluttered the earthy plain, who but would respond with joyous acclaim? If he gave praise to the Lord for "blessing the labors of the husbandmen, and spreading plenty through the land", would any one complain that he did not at the same time point to a shivering and starving army? And if he gave thanks "that he hath prospered our arms and those of our ally; been a shield to our troops in the hour of danger, pointed their swords to victory and led them in triumph over the bulwarks of the foe", who would cavil and demand to know just when, in the year of grace, 1779, those swords had been thus pointed, or where might be those bulwarks that had been thus overcome? Most certainly all the people would join heart and soul in the climax of the prayer—"and finally, that he would establish the independence of these United States upon the basis of religion and virtue, and support and protect them in the enjoyment of peace, liberty, and safety." Thus far Congress was in hearty accord with the invocation. When, however, Mr. Root would have added, "as long as the sun and moon shall endure, until time shall be no more", then Congress voted an emphatic NAY. The gentleman from Connecticut might lift himself by his own bootstraps into the emotional stratosphere, but the other gentlemen of the Congress chose to keep their feet on the ground.

So long as the disposition prevailed to attribute the inordinately high prices to engrossers, forestallers, extortioners, and "those vermins the speculators", it followed as certainly as night the day that efforts would be made to regulate prices by law and by such enforcement of the law as might be possible. The attempt to regulate prices had begun early in the war. That was one of the first reactions to depreciation of Continental money and the rise in the cost of commodities. This attempted regulation began in the New England states in the latter part of 1776, was approved by Congress and recommended to the middle and southern states; then, after trial and utter failure, Congress recommended the repeal of the laws. Attempts at regulation, it was concluded, had only aggravated the evil. Now, however, in the face of the hitherto inconceivable, the sickening, fall in the purchasing power of the money, a new demand for regulation arose.

Early in October, 1779, New Jersey made a representation to Congress in behalf of such a measure, and at nearly the same time (October 20) a convention of the eastern states, including New York, met at Hartford with a like objective in view. Not only did New Jersey circularize all the states and the members of Congress in behalf of the proposition, but the Hartford convention likewise sent copies of its proceedings to the several states, and further recommended a similar convention of all the states as far south as Virginia to meet in Philadelphia the first Wednesday in January, 1780 (the 5th).

The Hartford proceedings were laid before Congress, November 10, when the New Jersey representation had been under consideration for about a month, and on the 19th, Congress came to a decision to recommend to the several states "forthwith to enact laws for establishing and carrying into execution a general limitation of prices throughout their respective jurisdictions", as also "strict laws against engrossing and withholding". It was figured that prices of articles of domestic produce ought not to exceed twenty fold the prices current in 1774, accordingly the prices of domestic articles were to be fixed on that basis, while prices of imported articles were to be "in due proportion

. . . making proper allowance for freight, insurance, and other charges". Salt and military stores were excepted from any limitation. February 1, 1780, was set as the date when all the state laws should go into effect. The New Jersey delegates were confident that, although some members of Congress had thought the ratio of prices too large, the measure would be universally adopted and would "produce an easy turn to the tide of depreciation, and make a further reduction in due time more natural and practicable". Since the resolutions had passed *"nem. con."* (so Roger Sherman asserted), it would appear that most members of Congress were of like opinion with those of New Jersey. "The good effect expected from them", declared Sherman (December 20), "is to reduce prices to a level in all the States, with the expectation that by the operation of taxes they may be kept so, and even be reduced below the limitation."

Later the enthusiasm of a good many members appears to have oozed out, and there was at least one skeptic at the time, Allen Jones of North Carolina, who had taken his seat in Congress shortly after the adoption of the measure. Said he (December 23), "I do not promise myself much relief [from the plan] as I am apprehensive it will not be generally adopted." In fact, Jones appears to have been skeptical of most of the financial schemes of the time, with which Congress had been busy. "From these Schemes likewise", he confided to Governor Caswell, "I fear nothing Advantageous will arise. We have found it dangerous from experience to tamper with our money. Every step hitherto taken to appreciate it, having had the contrary Effect." Allen Jones proved to be the best prophet of them all, for most of the states failed to enact the requisite laws.

Three several efforts were made between January and April, 1780, to hold the proposed convention in Philadelphia, with abortive results. By that time it seemed just as well to await the outcome of the recommendation of Congress to the states, November 19. Besides, Congress had become busy with a price-fixing measure that concerned itself alone, namely, to determine what prices should be set upon the various specific supplies called for from the several states, as well as to fix the respective quotas of the states. There had been no small wrangling over both features of the measure, and compromise agreements were reached (February 25) only because everybody recognized the desperateness of the situation.

If Congress was about to learn once more that regulation of prices, however vigorously attempted, failed to regulate, so it was learning even then that its brave efforts to stabilize the circulating medium had failed to stabilize. Instead of depreciation coming to a full stop with the stoppage of the press, it had hardly paused in its headlong course down the steep decline. Twenty for one seemed a fair valuation to set upon its money in mid-November, 1779; yet by the middle of March, 1780, the exchange was running at about sixty for one. It required from five to eight dollars just then to buy a pound of grass-fed beef; and it began to look as if some morning soon members of Congress would not be able to pay for their breakfasts, unless they happened to have stored up some Spanish milled dollars; and few of them had been that foresighted.

In early January, 1780, John Armstrong, with whom regulation of prices had been so favorite a remedy for the country's ills that he had written several long dissertations upon the theme, wrote to Washington:

On the subtile subject of finance my pretensions are truly small, but on the necessity of some different measures from any yet adopted what man can shut his eyes? To say nothing of the various aireal schemes that have ben thrown out, one thing is clear, that even such as have been tryed from their shew of more reason and solidity, either from their being inadequate in their nature, or too late in their application have palpably failed of the effect. For some time past we have resembled a Patient far gone in disease, given up by his Physicians and left to the mere efforts of nature.

Armstrong was by no means, however, ready to yield the argument. There were "grand difficulties" as well as "nicities" in the execution of such regulations, but they "ought not to be supposed insurmountable". At nearly the same time (January 14) Oliver Ellsworth was writing to Governor Trumbull, "The failure of that great resource, the press, gives as was expectable a violent shock, but it is hoped will prove a salutary one." His hopes for the better were based mainly on the system of taxation which was now "establishing itself fast".

Old doubts of the efficacy of regulation had already begun to reassert themselves, and their strength increased rapidly with the weeks. Congress began to squint at the problem from other angles, and at the end of February, when it had somewhat freed its hands from other projects, set about earnestly to devise a new remedy. The essence of the new remedy was a regulation of the money rather than of prices. Within two weeks the measure was ready and the decision reached. In its consequences the decision proved to be a momentous one, but it was likewise momentous for another reason: Congress was swallowing the bitterest pill of its whole career: it was going back on its solemn promises, was renouncing its plighted faith.

Through the past two years and more Congress had striven mightily to uphold the integrity of its money; the later emissions had been put forth against its own conscience; every one of them had been as a desperate charge in the face of a withering fire. The battle, for some time in doubt, now seemed utterly hopeless; now there was naught to do but raise the white flag and bury their dead with so much decency as might be possible. These were essential facts, even though Congress might still affect to be unconvinced of defeat, might avow the retreat to be strategic. Some members did remain unconvinced and would at least delay the obsequies until they had made trial of other methods, other tactics.

The date of these final ministrations was the 18th of March, 1780. Although in the preceding September, Congress had declared it unthinkable that the total of its outstanding obligations, bills of credit and all other, would not be redeemed at par, now that body was able to convince itself that, since the present holders at least had received the money at a depreciated value, justice and fairness required that it be redeemed only on such a basis of depreciation as might appear equitable. The basis determined upon as being essentially just was one fortieth of its face value. That would reduce at one stroke a nominal debt of 200,000,000 dollars to an actual debt of 5,000,000. The redemption was to be accomplished by the acceptance of the bills in payment of state quotas of taxes at the rate designated and destroying them. Congress could not stop, however, with the mere destruction of its bills, whether at forty for one or at any other rate; it must have funds to carry on the war.

To meet this need new bills were to be issued as the old were destroyed, but at a rate not to exceed one-twentieth part of the nominal sum of the bills brought in to be destroyed, and these new bills were to be redeemable in specie in six years. For this redemption the states were called upon to make provision by the establishment of specific funds. However, lest any state should, by the events of the war, be rendered incapable of redeeming its proportion of bills, the faith of the United States was pledged for their redemption. If any were so wicked as to charge that the faith of the United States had been impaired by this very act, Congress would have it understood that that faith was still robust—at least would be six years hence. Further, to strengthen the new issues they were to bear interest at five per cent, that interest likewise to be paid in specie upon the redemption of the bills, or (at the option of the holder) annually in sterling bills of exchange drawn by the United States on their commissioners in Europe. It was, to say the least, somewhat presumptuous for Congress to assume, or to endeavor, after all that had taken place, to persuade the public to believe that there would be funds in Europe on which to draw; but it was not the first or the last of such presumptions. At all events, it was not long before Congress was receiving an unmistakable response from the public; and it would not be much longer before it would receive an equally emphatic word from Europe. In the public mind the act was generally regarded as downright repudiation, a confession of bankruptcy; and not a few members of Congress joined in that view. Abroad, a particularly vigorous protest was voiced by Vergennes, the minister of France, to the effect that, whatever Congress might do as affecting citizens of the United States, foreigners, who had accepted the money in good faith, should have been excepted from its provisions. The protest of Vergennes did not of course come to the knowledge of Congress until many months later; and at worst it gave rise to only one of the minor wrestling matches with that minister of the great and good ally of these United States.

CHAPTER XXIII

THE RIGHTS OF COD AND HADDOCK

FISH OR FIGHT?

The year 1779, with a prefix and a suffix of a few weeks each, was for Congress a period of burdensome and vexatious problems; for the country as a whole a period of disappointments, anxieties, forebodings, even of groanings that could not be uttered. In the domain of arms it was a period of unusual barrenness, even though Congress might choose to give thanks for Divine help in pointing the swords of its army to victory and in overcoming the bulwarks of the foe. In the domain of finance it was a period of stress and strain, its contributions chiefly the lessons of failure. In the domain of diplomacy the most notable exhibits are party disputes, factional strife, even personal quarrels, with only a hesitant approach toward the settlement of issues vital to national independence and self-reliance.

In one particular, however, the year 1779 seems to stand out conspicuously among the five years through which the struggle had endured: scarcely a man amongst the leaders in America seems to have harbored so much as a thought of surrender. The future they saw but as through a glass darkly, yet they quenched not the spirit; they held fast to that which was good, they continued to hope for that they saw not. Even in the darkest days they could join in sentiment with William Churchill Houston: *Nesquam desperandum est de Republica.*

Although there was little doubt anywhere that the alliance with France had enabled Americans to look with greater confidence for the ultimate triumph of their cause, there had been and would continue to be many perplexities involved in the task of steering the alliance through the inevitable breakers. It is never easy to bring divergent purposes into convergence upon a common objective.

Attention has already been called (Chapter XIX) to two commitments of Congress in the beginning of the year, both of them obtained by the insistence of the minister of France. Shortly afterward arose another question respecting the interpretation of the alliance, sufficiently vexing to stir a controversy between Congress and the minister. It was mainly a question whether aid should be requested of the Comte d'Estaing for the defense of Georgia and South Carolina, which had been invaded by the British, and whether the United States should compensate France for such aid. Congress did resolve to make the application for aid, then, after a conference with Gérard, withdrew the proposed application, moved thereto, in part at least, by the fact of Estaing's recent repulse in the West Indies.

In the midst of this discussion came the anniversary of the alliance, February 6, 1779, whereupon the controversy was stilled for the moment, while the Honorable the Congress gave to His Excellency the Minister Plenipotentiary of His Most Christian Majesty a public entertainment in celebration of the great and notable event (at a net cost of 1086 dollars, presumably Continental). At this entertainment the first of the thirteen toasts was, naturally, "May the Alliance between France and the United States be perpetual", while another was, "Success to the allied arms". Declaimed the *Pennsylvania Packet* (February 9):

> The chearfulness which existed in the company upon the happy occasion of their being assembled, was not to be exceeded; and a thousand brilliances alluding to the Alliance were uttered. . . . The principles of the Alliance are founded in true policy and equal justice; and it is highly probable that mankind will have cause to rejoice in this union which has taken place between the two nations; the one, the most puissant in the old, and the other the most powerful in the new world.

Then back to the discussion of the question whether the United States should furnish compensation for any aid that the Comte d'Estaing might send to Georgia and South Carolina. "Long debates again" on the subject, John Fell recorded, February 8. Well, the easiest way to settle the problem was not to ask for the aid. The admiral was in no condition to furnish it anyway.

On the same day (February 8) Gérard informed the president that he had been ordered to communicate to Congress "subjects of the highest importance", and desired to know whether the communication should be to the president or to Congress "in an audience". Then, on the following day, Gérard communicated to the president another piece of intelligence of such great importance that, although it was not formally communicated to Congress until February 12, the purport of it was evidently whispered about, setting the members of Congress all agog. One after another they wrote that this intelligence would "put our affairs on a more respectable footing than ever", but that, being enjoined to secrecy, they could not reveal particulars.

Soon the whisperings ceased to be confined to Congressional circles, and rumors began to "run through the country in a variety of forms". In due time they reached the ears of General Washington, who expressed to President Jay his surprise that intelligence from Europe as important as this appeared to be had not been communicated to him. Jay replied (March 3) that it was of such a nature as to require secrecy, but that, with the consent of the minister of France, Congress had directed that the general be informed of it. It had accordingly been arranged that Doctor Witherspoon should communicate to him this confidential information in the course of a visit to New Jersey. It developed that the important secret was nothing less than the near prospect of Spain's adherence to the alliance. The lofty expectations so carefully nourished for a time were, however, destined to flop; for, although Spain did enter into an alliance with France, she did not include the United States in the same embrace.

But Gérard had other communications to make to Congress, and he must have concluded that now, while the bosoms of the members were still aglow with the pleasing anticipations and endearing sentiments called forth by the recent banquet, was a good time to bring them forward. Accordingly, "in a private audience and free conference" with the committee of the whole (February 15), he pointed out in terms polite but emphatic and urgent the importance of coming speedily and definitely to a decision respecting those matters that would necessarily be involved in any peace settlement. How far, for instance, were the United States prepared to go in the prosecution of the war? What among the things claimed or desired would they be willing to relinquish? For what things in particular were they disposed to fight on? In short, what would be their ultimata? There was of course the general question respecting the boundaries that the United States would wish to hold out for, there was a more specific question, pertaining to the Floridas, and there was that other exceedingly important question of the navigation of the Mississippi River. The last two questions particularly concerned Spain, their prospective ally.

On February 23 a committee consisting of Gouverneur Morris of New York, Thomas Burke of North Carolina, John Witherspoon of New Jersey, Samuel Adams of Massachusetts, and Meriwether Smith of Virginia, to whom had been assigned the task of making a preliminary examination of the subject, brought in a report recommending that, as "a ground and preliminary" to any treaty or negotiation for peace, "the liberty, sovereignty, and independence, absolute and unlimited, of these United States, as well in matters of government as of commerce, shall be acknowledged on the part of Great Britain"; then added six stipulations that should be of the nature of ultimata, namely, certain minimum boundaries, evacuation by the British forces, fishing rights on the banks and coasts of Newfoundland, navigation of the Mississippi River to the southern boundary of the United States, free commerce with some port or ports below that boundary, and lastly the cession of Nova Scotia, in the event that the allies would support the contention. The committee offered also six conditional stipulations, which might be utilized as "trading points" in the negotiations.

Upon some of the major as well as upon some of the minor provisions Congress fell into ready accord. Over others, however, the contest was to wax exceeding warm and to continue unabated for six months. Meanwhile Gérard from time to time prodded Congress with reminders that it was impossible to be too economical of time in coming to a decision.

I am afraid [James Lovell wrote March 1] of the Arts that are using to hurry us into a rash ultimatum. We are told that such is our *first* Business tho' . . . the Observations of a blind man may convince us of the contrary; but forsooth France and Spain are of that opinion fully as say the Lickspittles of the Plenipo.

Here is evidence enough that Gérard had become *persona non grata* to that considerable faction in Congress that was anti-Deane and pro-Lee. The discussion of the peace terms had, in fact, begun to revolve around the personality of Arthur Lee. Was he or was he not a fit person to conduct the peace negotiations? It might seem as if the disputants were more concerned about the qualities of the negotiator than the terms of the negotiation; yet it was just because of the deep concern for the outcome of the negotiations that the personality of the possible negotiator was deemed to be of prime importance. In short, the contest over the peace terms was in great part a contest between the pro-Gallican and anti-Gallican forces in Congress, and Arthur Lee had come to personify the anti-Gallican element in Congress, sometimes dubbed the Adams-Lee faction.

In their preliminary skirmishes for advantage, therefore, it was deemed by both parties to be important to determine the question respecting Arthur Lee. The Adams-Lee faction was contending that Arthur Lee was acceptable to the French court, the opposition that he was not; and in this contest Gérard was caught between the two fires. In April, two of the anti-Lee faction, William Paca of Maryland and William Henry Drayton of South Carolina, obtained from Gérard a statement that Arthur Lee did not have the confidence of either the court of Versailles or that of Madrid. Lee's integrity was in no wise impugned, but such was his disposition and such had been his conduct that those courts did not consider him a proper person to whom to entrust the delicate negotiations for peace. Condemnation of his manner and his methods was in fact quite severe. Vergennes was quoted as saying frankly, "I confess to you that I fear Mr. Lee and those about him."

When this statement of Gérard was revealed to Congress (April 30, 1779), it naturally threw the friends of Arthur Lee into a fury. The result was that the hostility between the two factions was greatly intensified, that Gérard himself became the object of gibes and sneers from the protagonists of Arthur Lee, and, what was worse, all this bitter rivalry and distrust were carried over into the discussion of peace terms and seriously retarded the decision of Congress. It was a month after the revelation of the "Paca-Drayton Information" before Gérard once more ventured upon his admonitions to Congress, warning that body that they were incurring the risk of fatiguing Spain by these delays, of "cooling the good will" of his Catholic Majesty, and even of alienating him.

The decision with regard to the boundaries had in a manner been reached on March 19; but the debates over the fisheries and the navigation of the Mississippi raged on. On these two questions Congress divided for the most part along geographical lines, the New Englanders standing stoutly for the fisheries, the Southerners for the navigation of the Mississippi, while the intervening states cast their votes partly with the one side, partly with the other. The fisheries had long been a favorite industry in New England, therefore the delegates of those states strenuously insisted upon holding fast to what they regarded as both a natural and a historic right. In this contention they had the aid of two southerners in particular: Richard Henry Lee, until he took his departure late in May, and Henry Laurens, who stood stanchly with them from the beginning to the end.

The struggle over the fisheries, which was begun in early February and continued almost without cessation until the middle of August, was one of the most protracted, as it was probably the most hotly contested parliamentary battle ever waged in Congress. Without question no other contest stirred so violently the great deeps of Congressional bile. The words "arduous", "strenuous", pertinaceous", sometimes used to characterize it, were all too mild. "This subject", declared John Mathews when the battle had ended, "was twisted and tortured in all the variety of modes human ingenuity could invent, to gain and to oppose, this important object." Burke of North Carolina asserted that the aim of the opposition was at all times "to prevent every obstruction to peace but such as were unavoidable", to make the direct operation of every resolution "plain and unequivocal"; in short, to strip every proposition "of every artificial Coloring until it was brought down to the Simple Question 'Shall the War be continued merely for that object?'"

On the 23d of March, by a substantial majority in which most of the New Englanders joined, a resolution was adopted, demanding an acknowledgment of "a common right in these states to fish on the coasts", etc., "provided always that the allies of these States shall be in circumstances to support them in carrying on the war for such acknowledgment", but with the additional proviso, "that in no case, by any treaty of peace, the common right of fishing as above described be given up". The first of these provisos was a sop to the Southerners, the last to the New Englanders, so that, in effect, it was a compromise measure not quite satisfactory to either. On second thought the pro-fisheries group decided to call for a reconsideration, with a view to circumventing the argument that, since the fishing rights had apper-tained to the Americans only as British subjects, by severing their con-nection with Great Britain they had lost those ancient rights. In this effort they were successful (March 24). The opposition thereupon turned their endeavors to an undertaking that might be likened to the delicate art of extracting the egg without breaking the shell, in which they were fairly successful (May 27), by reducing the demand to the simple proposition, "that in no case, by any treaty of peace, the common right of fishery be given up".

It was now the turn of those who wished to make the fishing rights an ultimatum to see if they could not put the egg back into the shell in a manner as dextrous as their opponents had used in extracting it. The operation was first undertaken on June 3 by means of an explana-tory resolution, but some of the middle-state members who had hitherto for the most part voted with the New Englanders refused their sup-port, and the motion failed. On June 19 the effort was resumed through a series of five propositions offered by Elbridge Gerry, shrewdly calcu-lated to sap the works of the enemy and tumble the walls of his fortress about him.

Gerry's first proposition declared it essential to the welfare of the United States that the inhabitants "continue to enjoy" their common right of fishing, etc., thereby preserving inviolate the treaties with France; his second, that France should be asked for a more explicit guarantee of that right; his third, that in the treaty of peace with Great Britain, a stipulation be demanded that the inhabitants of the United States should not be disturbed in the exercise of that right; his fourth, that the faith of Congress be pledged to the states that, without their unanimous consent, no treaty of commerce be made with Great Britain previous to such a stipulation; and his fifth, that in the event that neither the guarantee by France nor the stipulation on the part of Great Britain as called for in the second and third propositions be obtained, the minister conducting the business should sign no treaty of peace until further instructions from Congress. The first and second propositions were carried without great difficulty; but when the third was thrown into the arena, July 1, it was the signal for a renewal of the struggle.

In the meantime occurred an event, of little real concern to the United States, yet one that might avail to soften the asperities of the contest that was raging. The king of France announced to Congress the birth of a royal princess, whereupon Congress, as an ally of that monarch, did its duty well and nobly in responding to that announcement, requesting (June 15, 1779) his Most Christian Majesty "to oblige us with portraits of yourself and royal consort, that by being placed in our council chamber, the representatives of these states may daily have before their eyes the first royal friends and patrons of their cause".

It likewise befell that the Fourth of July (rather the fifth, for the fourth fell on Sunday) broke into these heated discussions over the terms of peace, and Congress paused to celebrate the anniversary of the Declaration of Independence with an entertainment, at which the minister of France was the principal guest. As was appropriate, there were toasts to "His Most Christian Majesty, THE PROTECTOR OF THE RIGHTS OF MANKIND", "The Queen, Princess, and Royal Family of France", "His Most Catholic Majesty and the other Branches of the Royal House of Bourbon", "The allied arms of France and America", and, significantly, "May *affection* cement the union which wisdom has formed between France and America".

At the time when Gerry's propositions were presented to Congress, Gouverneur Morris had made the charge that "our pretended private business" was no secret, that it was "known and talked of in every one of the States"; and other members offered testimony that probably more than one of that body had told tales out of Congress. Evidence enough that such was the case was then all about them, and much more was soon to follow. In the *Maryland Gazette* of May 28, 1779, some one, said to have been a former member of Congress, charged that an "execrable faction" in Congress had been responsible for peace not having been made in the spring. In the *Pennsylvania Gazette* of June 23, "Americanus" particularly attacked the proposition to make the fisheries an ultimatum in the peace negotiations; and this drew forth other screeds more or less vitriolic and eventually led to episodes of violence not limited to words. One such scribe, screening himself behind the lugubrious *nom de plume,* "O Tempora! O Mores!", all but bearded Congress in its own den. He particularly pointed the finger of denunciation at a "Junto", in Congress, who "meet regularly, debate upon, and adjust the manner of their proceedings", and thus "have at last brought it about that a minority, and a small one too, can retard, delay, and even obstruct every proceeding". One of his specific charges was that the insistence of the New England delegates upon making the right to fish on the banks of Newfoundland a *sine qua non* of peace was chiefly responsible for the exasperating delay. The article was first printed in Philadelphia, July 9, although it had previously appeared in the *Maryland Journal* of June 29, and, because of the writer's intimate knowledge of the doings of Congress and his keen thrusts at some who sat there, there were wrung withers and much wincing. No one, however, not even Mr. Gerry, who had beforetime wished to bring the vitriolic Leonidas to book, proposed to ferret out the mysterious writer and hale him before the bar of Congress. One of the New England delegates was asked why Congress had taken no notice of the screed, and the delegate had replied, "Because it had too much of truth in it."

At this juncture Gérard asked for an audience, in the hope that he might break the deadlock. The audience was given on July 12, but the deadlock, for the time being at least, remained unbroken. On July 17, when Gerry's fourth proposition came under discussion, Dickinson endeavored to still the troubled waters by a pouring on of oil in the form of carefully drawn instructions to the minister who should be appointed for the peace negotiations. It seemed to be good storm-quelling oil, yet it was not immediately effective. On the 22d, the proposition was adopted, although weighted with a lumbering amendment. Finally, on July 29, Gerry's fifth proposition was set aside, and in its stead was adopted a resolution that, if after the treaty of peace Great Britain should molest the inhabitants of the United States in taking fish on the banks, etc., Congress would deem it a direct violation and breach of the peace, and that the force of the Union would be exerted to obtain redress for the parties injured. This resolution, in effect the substitution of a *casus belli* for an ultimatum, obtained the solid votes of all the states from New Hampshire to Delaware inclusive, against the solid votes of all the states from Maryland southward.

When, two weeks later (August 14), Congress came to decide on the instructions to be given to the minister who should negotiate the peace, the heats generated by the contest had somewhat cooled, reflection had entered in, and there appears to have been a general acquiescence in the proposed instruction that, although it was of the utmost importance that the common right to the fisheries, as also the acquisition of Canada and Nova Scotia, be guaranteed, "yet a desire of terminating the war hath induced us not to make the acquisition of these objects an ultimatum on the present occasion". The advocates of the fisheries were probably the more ready to agree to this instruction because they still hoped to name a man of their choice to negotiate the treaty.

The commissioner to negotiate the treaty of peace was further empowered with the consent of France, to agree to a cessation of hostilities, provided it be stipulated that all the forces of the enemy should be immediately withdrawn from the United States. The instructions conclude with this significant passage:

In all matters not above mentioned, you are to govern yourselves by the Alliance between his Most Christian Majesty and these States, by the advice of our allies, by your knowledge of our Interests, and by your own discretion, in which we repose the fullest confidence.

The question concerning the navigation of the Mississippi, while actually longer on the carpet than that of the fisheries and itself productive of much skirmishing and some hard-fought contests, was never the object of such fierce battles as were waged over the latter. When the subject was brought up in Congress, March 24, Burke and Drayton, delegates of North Carolina and South Carolina respectively, sought to qualify the demand by adding "provided that the allies of these

United States shall declare themselves in circumstances to afford effectual assistance for carrying on the war until said acknowledgment and ratification shall be obtained", a proposition entirely consistent with the attitude that these southern members had previously taken on the question of the fisheries. Both the amendment and the main proposition were, however, overwhelmingly defeated, and the Mississippi question was allowed to sleep until that respecting the fisheries had been settled.

The subject was resumed August 5, when an effort was made to have the minister to Spain endeavor to obtain not only the free navigation of the Mississippi, but the Floridas as well. This also failed; and on September 9, Gérard ventured the warning that, if Congress hoped for the aid of Spain, it were best not to ask that power to yield two such cherished objects as the Floridas and the navigation of the Mississippi. Thereupon, there was a movement to make these demands conditional and propose a number of *quid pro quos*. A proposition was even made that the United States assist Spain in the conquest of the Floridas, but it gained few adherents. The outcome was a resolution on September 17 that, if Spain would join hands with France and the United States, and if perchance Spain should secure the Floridas, the United States would guarantee them to her, "provided always, that the United States shall enjoy the free navigation of the river Mississippi into and from the sea". In less than a month, however, some members began to fear that even this was demanding too much, and it was proposed that the minister to Spain be privately instructed to recede from the demand on condition that Spain would grant a free port. But the majority stood by the proposition as adopted.

The peace terms decided, after a fashion, it was next in order to choose the person or persons to conduct the negotiations. There was first an effort on the part of a few members to obtain a "self-denying ordinance", cast in these general terms, "that Congress will not appoint any person, being a member of Congress, to any office under the United States, for which he or another for him, is to receive any salary, fees, or emolument of any kind"; but it failed now, as did when proposed again some weeks later. The partizans of Arthur Lee, who were in the main also the pro-fisheries group, were eager to have him designated for the peace mission; but they speedily found the support altogether too feeble. The chief contest for the mission accordingly arose as between John Adams and John Jay; but after some maneuvering the adherents of the two men entered into a combination whereby Jay was made minister to Spain, while Adams was chosen to negotiate the treaties of peace and commerce with Great Britain (September 27). The next day Jay's place as President was filled by the election of Samuel Huntington of Connecticut.

The friends of Arthur Lee were, naturally, sorely chagrined. "God's will be done!" exclaimed Henry Laurens—probably meaning something quite different. One of the warmest of Lee's adherents, James Lovell, concluded that he might as well take his defeat philosophically. Quoth he: "I am freed from a Load. For I have long practiced upon David's Rule, away with Sackloth and Ashes when evitables become inevitable." Then, looking about over the opposition, he mused, "Some of us look as calm as if we were sure we had *laid the Devil*. Others look as much relieved as David was when he became *certain* that the little Innocent was beyond hope, dead."

During the last several months the French minister had found his mission anything but a bed of roses, and now that the peace terms had been settled, even if not entirely to his satisfaction, he was eager to return to France. He had, in fact, been holding on tenaciously, despite bad health, for just this consummation. His successor, La Luzerne, had arrived at Boston about the middle of August and would soon be in Philadelphia. Gérard accordingly made ready to depart, and on September 3 transmitted to Congress the address with which he proposed to take his leave. When it came to adopt the response which Congress was in duty bound to make, there were not a few members whose lukewarmness toward the minister led them to seek to spread the commendation of him no thicker than might be absolutely essential, while some would have sent him away with a downright snub.

Congress was not, however, wholly without wisdom, whatever might be the feelings of individual members. Was not the alliance their sheet anchor? Accordingly the speech with which Congress bade the minister adieu, September 17, while by no means lavish with praise, matched aptly enough the speech to which it was a response. John Dickinson, chairman of the committee to whom the task of drafting the response had been assigned, remarked in a letter to Caesar Rodney, "We have dismist him with as honourable Testimonial, respecting his public and private Conduct, as we could give." On the 18th of October, or there-abouts, the late minister of France and the newly elected minister to Spain went aboard the *Confederacy,* which a few days later sailed away.

A few days before Gérard had brought his endeavors with Congress to a conclusion, his successor, the Chevalier La Luzerne, arrived in Philadelphia (September 21), although he did not present his credentials until the 4th of November. At the same time, he transmitted to Congress a copy of the speech he proposed to make at his audience, and a committee was appointed to prepare the response which Congress should make. After the response had been approved by Congress, Luzerne transmitted a second speech, which he now desired to use instead of the one first transmitted, whereupon it became necessary that a new response be prepared. That done (November 13), Congress fixed Wednesday, November 17, for the audience.

The ceremonial of the audience was carried through essentially in accordance with that fixed for the first minister of France, but it appears to have created no such interest and enthusiasm as that stirred by the reception and audience of Gérard. Having first, from his seat, sent to the President, by the hand of the secretary of the embassy, his letter of credence from the king, the minister was then announced to the House, whereupon he arose and delivered his speech, which opened with these encouraging words:

The wisdom and courage which have founded your republic: the prudence which presides over your deliberations; your firmness in execution; the skill and valor displayed by your generals and soldiers, during the course of the war, have attracted the admiration and regard of the whole world. The King, my master, was the first to acknowledge a liberty acquired amidst so many perils and with so much glory. Since treaties dictated by moderation have fixed upon a permanent base the union of France with the American republic, his majesty's whole conduct must have demonstrated how dearly he tenders your prosperity, and his firm resolution to maintain your independence by every means in his power.

Further, he remarked that the alliance was becoming "daily more indissoluble" and that he considered it the happiest circumstance of his life that he had been sent upon a mission "to a nation whose interests are so intimately blended with our own."

The response given by the President was not less graceful and suave.

The early attention of our good friend and ally to these United States is gratefully felt by all their virtuous citizens; and we should be unfaithful representatives if we did not warmly acknowledge every instance of his regard, and take every opportunity of expressing the attachment of our constituents to treaties formed upon the purest principles. . . .

We well know, and all the world must acknowledge, the moderation and friendship of the most Christian King, in neglecting conquests which courted his acceptance for the benevolent pleasure of succouring his allies. In this, as in every other instance, we perceive his strict adherence to the principles of our defensive alliance. . . .

The prosperous course of the campaign gives a pleasing hope that the moment of peace may soon arrive, when the reciprocation of mutual good offices shall amply recompense our mutual labours and cares. . . .

The pronouncement by the President of that phrase, "the prosperous course of the campaign" must have been with tongue in cheek and have been reciprocated by the minister with a like gesture of complacence. Altogether, nevertheless, this exchange of compliments was in the approved manner of diplomatic amenities; and that done, they were ready to resume their parry and thrust.

CHAPTER XXIV

THE WHOLE *VERSUS* THE PART
THE COMMITTEE AT HEADQUARTERS

It is one of the many paradoxes discoverable in the proceedings of the Continental Congress that, at the very time when that body was seriously pondering the perennial problem of recruiting an eternally dissolving army, it should also, with equally serious purpose, consider taking just the opposite course; that is, reducing the army instead of increasing it. On January 8, 1780, while Congress still had under consideration, albeit somewhat laggardly, a measure designed to promote enlistments, a movement was inaugurated to have General Washington dismiss all troops whose enlistments would expire on April 1, and to have the eighty-eight battalions reduced to sixty.

The motion was made by no less a personage than Robert R. Livingston of New York and seconded by John Penn of North Carolina. That such a movement would appeal strongly to many members of Congress was a natural result of the agitation then in progress for retrenchment and reform, and, because of that agitation, was not quite so paradoxical as it might seem. Nevertheless Livingston's motion had the immediate result of stirring the moribund measure for recruiting into new life.

An opinion has been lately suggested [Elbridge Gerry wrote to Washington, January 12, 1780], and I fear with too much effect, "that the Number of Men inlisted for the War is already sufficient, and that reinforcements are not necessary for the Army in this Quarter". Should this Sentiment prevail, or the Requisitions be much longer delayed, we shall probably lay the Foundation of an inactive Campaign, if not of greater Misfortunes; and renew the uneasiness of the Court of France, who last year remonstrated in very friendly but *expressive* Terms, against the Delays of our military preparations for that Campaign.

Gerry thought that "a fresh application" from the general was needed to bestir Congress to action. The fresh application was accordingly made by Washington (January 23), who also reinforced his arguments in a private letter to Gerry (January 29). The hopes indulged in from the beginning that peace would soon take place, Washington argued, had been the source of great expense and might well be the means of protracting the war. "There is nothing so likely to produce peace", he wrote to Gerry, "as to be well prepared to meet an enemy."

Gerry may have had private intimations of the probable uneasiness of the court of France; at all events Congress was not to be left long without positive expressions from the French minister, Luzerne. On the 25th of January, while Congress was yet halting betwixt two opinions, whether to increase the army or to reduce it, Luzerne admonished that body that "the present situation of the affairs of the alliance in Europe announces the necessity of another campaign, which is indispensable to bring England to an acknowledgment of the independence of the thirteen United States", and that "the only means of putting an end to the calamities of the war is to push it with new vigour; to take measures immediately for completing the army, and putting it in condition to begin an early campaign." Returning to the subject a few days later, with additional information respecting the European situation, and with renewed urgings that speedy and effectual preparations be made to prosecute the war with all possible vigor, he put to Congress a few pertinent questions: for instance, what force could the United States bring into the field the next campaign, and on what resources could they rely for their maintenance?

When it came to voicing confident expectations, Congress has scarcely ever had a peer among legislative assemblies. The response to the minister's queries was: "That the United States have expectations on which they can rely with confidence of bringing into the field an army of 25,000 effective men", with reinforcements of militia "sufficient for any enterprises against the posts occupied by the enemy"; that "supplies of provisions for the army in its greatest number", both that of the United States and that of their ally, could certainly be obtained in the United States, for which purpose Congress, with the cooperation of the several states, would take effectual measures; that "Congress rely on the contributions of the states by taxes, and on moneys to be raised on internal loans for the pay of the army".

All this should have been reassuring to the French minister, provided he could find sure ground on which to rest his faith, whether it be in the confidence expressed by Congress or in the wills of the states to co-operate. He had at least, with the aid of Washington and his military advisers, persuaded Congress to abandon for the time being (March 25) the thought of reducing the army, and instead to turn its face in the opposite direction, even though it did so with some grumbling. Growled one delegate, "We must cut Throats another year at least, and we ought to do it vigorously. F[rance] and S[pain] will persist in strenuous Cooperation for the Purpose of *securing* our Independ[en]ce and *indemnifying themselves.*"

Even Luzerne's short acquaintance with the American scene had probably taught him to accept such Congressional assurances with the proverbial grains of salt; at all events he would presently have occasion to recur to these assurances and to refresh the Congressional memory. In the meantime, however, he was to have the gratification of seeing the first essential steps taken toward the fulfillment of these promises; for on the 9th of February, Congress finally brought to maturity, although not without much bickering among the delegations over state quotas, the recruiting measure on which at intervals it had sometime been hammering. The essential feature of the measure was a demand upon the states that they "furnish by draughts or otherwise, on or before the first day of April next, their deficiencies of the number of 35,211 men, exclusive of commissioned officers, which Congress deem necessary for the service of the present year". With more than 35,000 as the goal, a promise of 25,000 was modesty itself; but Washington had more than once offered the admonition that there was "an essential difference between an army on paper, and its real efficient force".

That the promise of an abundant supply of provisions for an army of any size and of sure pay for the soldiers was mainly a case of wishful thinking, could scarcely have escaped the observant mind of the French minister; for at that moment Congress was engaged in a desperate effort to rescue its own sinking currency, was beseeching the states to tax, collect, and pay into the Continental treasury their assigned quotas of money, was soliciting, with little success, the loans so blithely promised as a source of funds, and was even striving to inaugurate a system of obtaining supplies of provisions directly from the states without the use of money. By February 25 a neat plan for this purpose had been laid down; but would it work? The ominous grumblings of various state delegations over what they regarded as unfair quotas did nothing to brighten the prospects of success. Followed the mighty effort (March 18, 1780) to stabilize the currency by offering new dollars for old at the rate of one for forty, which had mainly the effect of accelerating the already rapid depreciation. Indeed most of the affairs of Congress and of America were rapidly going from bad to worse. The assertion of one delegate that the Continental Congress as well as the Continental money was depreciating was not wholly without foundation.

To add to all the other causes of anxiety, there came a letter from General Washington calling the attention of Congress very emphatically to a critical situation that had developed in the army. "There has never been a stage of the War", he wrote (April 3), "in which the dissatisfaction has been so general or alarming. It has lately in particular instances worn features of a very dangerous complexion." A disposition had of late manifested itself among the men, and even to some extent among the officers, he said, "to enter into seditious combinations". The causes were various, but uppermost amongst them were "the diversity in the terms of enlistments, the inequality of the rewards given for entering into the service; but still more the disparity in the provision made by the several States for their respective troops". "It were devoutly to be wished", he said, "[that] a plan could be adopted by which every thing relating to the Army could be conducted on a general principle under the direction of Congress." As for the new system of state supplies, it had "proved in its operation pernicious beyond description".

The idea of sending a committee to headquarters with a view to carrying out, in cooperation with the commander-in-chief, a project of retrenchments and reforms had now and again appeared in Congress since the preceding autumn, and at the end of January an attempt had been made, as explained in an earlier chapter, to put the plan into operation, but it had broken down before ever it got started. At the time, however, when Washington's disturbing letter was laid before Congress, the idea had been given a new impetus at the hands of General Greene, quartermaster general, who was then in Philadelphia seeking to obtain important revisions of his own department.

On the very day that Washington was writing to Congress of the alarming situation in the army, Greene wrote to Washington:

I have advised many Members of Congress to send a committee of the best informed Members of their body to Head Quarters; and there with the Heads of the Departments and such General Officers as it may be necessary to consult in the business, fix upon a plan properly adapted to the Service, and the nature of the Country.

A committee to headquarters therefore appeared to be the obvious means of approaching not only the old problems that were pressing for solution, but also the new dangers that were threatening. Accordingly it was so decided (April 6); with a degree of promptness, to be sure, although not with unanimity. Luzerne, who, despite closed doors and supposed secrecy, had his own means of learning what went on in Congress, wrote to Vergennes that, when the proposition was offered, "warm debates ensued". Still warmer debates must have taken place over the instructions to the committee, which were adopted only on April 12.

Many members of Congress were, naturally, hesitant to share any substantial part of the direct authority of Congress, even with a committee of its own body, and that hesitancy was not a little enhanced by the chronic fear of strengthening the military arm at the expense of the civilian. To escape the concentration of authority in the hands of so small a group it was even proposed to send what was generally termed a grand committee, or one composed of a member from each of the states; but that was rejected because a committee of that size would be almost as cumbrous in action as the whole Congress. A committee of three was therefore resolved upon and empowered, in consultation with the commander-in-chief, to carry out various reforms, to institute regulations in a number of the departments, and to supervise the execution of plans adopted; and their action in every case to be reported to Congress. Extensive as these powers were, they nevertheless fell short of what Washington believed to be necessary for the efficient conduct of the business, and he soon had good reason for requesting that they be enlarged.

The committee appointed (April 13) consisted of Philip Schuyler of New York, John Mathews of South Carolina, and Nathaniel Peabody of New Hampshire, and it set about its tasks immediately by making some minor reforms in the civil establishments located in Philadelphia. Toward the end of April the committee proceeded to headquarters, where it began in earnest its attack upon the main problems for which it had been designated. It was just then that Lafayette returned from France, bringing the definite information, already vaguely rumored, that France was on the point of sending to the aid of the United States both a naval and a military force. Preparation to cooperate with these forces therefore became at once of first importance. To accomplish that purpose Washington believed that an unusual and decisive course was esential, and he confided his views to Joseph Jones and to James Duane:

It appears to me of the greatest importance, and even of absolute necessity [he wrote to Jones, May 14] that a *small* Committee should be immediately appointed to reside near head Quarters vested with all the powers which Congress have so far as respects the purpose of a full co-operation with the French fleet and Army on the *Continent*. The authority should be Plenipotentiary to draw out men and supplies of every kind and give their sanction to any operations which the Commander in chief may not think himself at liberty to undertake without it as well beyond, as within the limits of these States.

He proceeded to point out that such a committee could act with despatch and energy, and that the commander-in-chief could open to them his plans "with more freedom and confidence than to a numerous body—where secrecy is impossible, where the indiscretion of a single member by disclosing may defeat the project".

The conjuncture [he went on to say] is one of the most critical and important we have seen, all our prudence and exertions are requisite to give it a favorable issue. Hesitancy and delay would in all probability ruin our Affairs.... We shall probably fix the independence of America if we succeed and if we fail the abilities of the State will have been so strained in the attempt that a total relaxation and debility must ensue and the worst is to be apprehended.

It was accordingly decided between Washington and the committee that Mathews should return to Congress and endeavor to obtain for the committee a grant of essentially dictatorial powers. Lafayette also came on to Philadelphia to confer with Luzerne, whereupon that minister, having discovered that the projected aid from France was already known to the British authorities in America, straightway presented a memorial to Congress, explaining the plans of his government and emphasizing the necessity of sending to headquarters a committee equipped with ample powers.

Here was something to be truly thankful for, and Congress did not fail to instruct its President to communicate to his Most Christian Majesty, through his minister, "the grateful sense that Congress entertain of his unremitted attention to the interests of these United States, evidenced by his many great and generous efforts in their behalf". Nor did that body fail to manifest its gratitude in works—at least in laying a substantial foundation therefor in the form of a resolution. (May 19, 1780).

The states (all except the three southernmost, which more particularly had the enemy on their hands) were called upon for an extra contribution of ten million dollars, to be paid in within thirty days, for the special purpose of bringing the army into the field and forwarding the supplies. Whether any member of Congress believed for a moment that any considerable part of the ten millions would be available inside of thirty days may well be doubted; but President Huntington could at least in all truth say to the states: "Congress have no resources but in your Spirit and Virtue", and he was bound in all decency to add, "upon these they confidently rely". He could also make the inspiring appeal, "You know the Value of the prize for which you contend, nor need you be informed how much you are interested in a speedy Termination of this distressing and expensive War."

That the reliance upon the states was not without a reservation is evidenced by another decision at the same time; namely, that bills to the sum of twenty-five thousand dollars each be drawn upon Franklin and Jay, the ministers to France and Spain, respectively, at sixty days' sight and be offered for sale in six of the states in varying amounts, in Massachusetts twenty thousand, in Rhode Island three thousand, in Connecticut eight thousand, in Pennsylvania ten thousand, in Maryland five thousand, and in Virginia four thousand. In view of former warnings against drawing bills of exchange on non-existent funds in Europe and of promises of Congress to do so no more, the step was taken with reluctance and with profound apologies; but, declared the committee for foreign affairs, the crisis is great. It may not have been altogether unfortunate that a quarrel among the treasury officials considerably delayed the execution of the bills and their distribution for sale.

As for conferring additional powers on the committee at headquarters, that too was a serious question and must be pondered and argued. Congress did, however, on that same May 19, equip the committee with some further powers, useful indeed, yet not especially significant; certainly far short of what Washington had desired. Such as they were, however, Mr. Mathews obtained a copy of them and returned forthwith to camp. Robert R. Livingston, who on his way to New York had conferred with Schuyler on the subject and had returned to Congress expressly to use his efforts in behalf of the measure, wrote to Schuyler (May 21) that even the insufficient powers granted had been obtained with difficulty. Further light on these difficulties was thrown by Duane a few days later in a letter to Schuyler. What had been accomplished, Duane wrote, "falls vastly short of your views and my efforts, but it is the fate of deliberate bodies to move with caution"; adding, "Mr. Mathews will be able to inform you of the obstacles to a committee plenipo: they are deep-rooted in the human passions, and not to be surmounted on the first impression." Duane was of opinion nevertheless that every measure that the general thought necessary would, "on his own application", be supported by Congress with unanimity.

Washington had gently intimated privately a wish that the personnel of the committee at headquarters might be changed. No man, he said, could be more useful than Schuyler; of Mathew's understanding and integrity he had a very favorable opinion; and he would be willing to trust everything to the goodness of Peabody's intentions, although he had some doubts of his discretion; but he wished that Livingston or Duane might be in the appointment. He must, however, have realized that even two New Yorkers on the committee, to say nothing of three, would not for a moment have been countenanced by Congress. There appears to have been no attempt to change the personnel, and the additional authority given to the existing committee was mainly by way of instructions to expedite the drawing forth of supplies in accordance with the act of February 25, 1780, and, in the event that the supplies enumerated in that act proved insufficient, then, with the advice of the commander-in-chief, to apply to the states or to civil magistrates for the purchase of other supplies at the expense of the United States. Supporting this authorization to the committee was a resolution requesting the states to invest their executive authority, or some other persons, with such powers as would enable them, on the application of the committee, to draw forth the resources of the state.

At headquarters the question necessarily arose, in view of the limited powers of the committee, what course should be taken. General Greene counseled Washington to press Congress again for an augmentation of the committee's powers.

If you undertake the business upon the present footing [Greene argued, May 23], and exercise powers beyond the present Scheme, It will be asked why you did not ask for an enlargement of the Committee's powers, if you deemed them inadequate. And if you engage and fail for want of support, it will be asked why you embarked in such a business without being fully persuaded that the means were adequate to the end.

As a preliminary to any action, Greene further suggested that Washington obtain from the committee a written opinion respecting the competency of its powers, and this Washington appears to have done (May 24). No response from the committee is of record, but, since the committee began the very next day, with Washington's approval, the exercise of its functions, it may be inferred that Washington's decision was that the committee should proceed upon the basis of its present grant of powers. Indeed events soon proved that to have pursued the course advocated by General Greene would have been to court defeat at the outset.

The committee had been appointed in the first instance to assist the commander-in-chief and his staff in effecting certain urgently needed reforms in the military establishment, and to these tasks it presently applied itself. At the moment, however, the task more lately laid upon its shoulders was more pressing—that of obtaining supplies for the existing army. It had long been the opinion of those most competent to know that the plan of depending upon the states for specific supplies would be an utter failure, unless it should be pushed toward its goal by a more effective driving force than yet appeared. Schuyler and Greene in particular had insisted that the plan would ruin the army, and its defects were now manifesting themselves to a degree that justified their predictions.

Nearly two months before, when Congress became convinced that the states required a bit of prodding because of their laggardness in furnishing their quotas of money and supplies, a committee was appointed to draft a suitable letter. This was on March 28, and the committee was obtained, so Schuyler wrote Washington, only "after some altercation". When a draft was reported, April 4, "some Gentlemen", said Schuyler, "were averse at the decisive plainness" with which it was proposed that Congress should speak to the states, whilst others contended that the language of the address ought to be even more pointed. The subject was debated for a whole day, then passed on to another committee. And that was only the beginning. There followed further debates and other committees; until finally one member, William Churchill Houston, was entrusted with the arduous task of finding language with which Congress might properly address its constituents. Houston's draft, offered April 24, nearly a month after the beginning of the attempt, was accepted and despatched. The address was reasonably forceful, but it was not calculated to fire any state enthusiasms. It carried no live coals; and there are times when only live coals will stir the sluggish terrapin to open his shell and move.

What Congress, then, had failed to accomplish with its softened voice, the committee must endeavor to do, though its voice should rise to a pitch of rasping querulousness. Moreover, the committee could base its plaints and its pleas on a more acutely distressful situation. One of the most serious defects of the act of February 25 was the failure to provide for transportation to the army; for the states were only to gather the supplies into magazines within their respective borders. Accordingly this problem of transportation was one of the first attacked by the committee, in a circular letter to the states May 25, although it did not neglect to urge upon the states a speedy compliance with the requisition of February 9 for men. The letter was as forceful an appeal as the virile pen of the committee could well indite, and it failed not to point its moral with such facts as these:

That the Army was five months pay in arrears, that it has Seldom or ever, since it took this cantonement, had more than Six days provision in advance. That at present it is without meat and has been on half, and on quarter allowance for some days past. That the commissaries cannot give any assurances of doing more than bearly subsisting the Troops from day to day. That even then they apprehend a want of meat will frequently prevail . . . .

This was only the beginning of the committee's exhortations to the states. Before it came to the end of its career, near three months later, it had searched the whole domain of rhetoric for the language of appeal.

Nor did the committee limit its remonstrances to the governors and legislatures of the states. It made bold to thrust its admonitions into the very face of Congress itself. Observe, for instance, this exhortation addressed to President Huntington, May 28:

Persuaded, sir, that to be silent on such occasions would be criminal, We will address our Compeers with decency but with Freedom. We will advise them, that something more is necessary than mere recommendation, or they will lose an army, and thereby risk the loss of an Empire. Times and exigencies render it sometimes necessary for Governing powers to deviate from the strict lines of conduct which Regular Constitutions prescribe. . . . We intreat Congress seriously to consider Whether such times and exigencies do not now exist. If they do, shall Posterity say, that those who directed the affairs of America, at this era, were less intripid, more attentive to personal consequences than their Predicessors. Heaven forbid the thought!

Bold language, this, to be addressed to Congress. Spoken by a member on the floor of Congress, it would most certainly have provoked a flood of condemnation; it would almost certainly have drawn a none too mild rebuke to the speaker. But coming from a committee actually sitting at the headquarters of the army and not quite free from suspicion—the committee had best beware! The meaning of this admonition of the committee to the body of which it was a part is sufficiently clear: Do not wait for the states to grant you powers; take them. The suggestion will be put forth again, although from other sources and not with quite the same boldness.

Meanwhile we may fittingly observe the committee in the further pursuit of its aims. The committee's pointed statements in its circular letter of May 25 respecting conditions in the army were of course obtained directly from the commander-in-chief. At almost the same time, in a letter to Congress (May 27), Washington had made like revelations, and more: mutiny had already broken out in the army and threatened to spread. The prime cause was the arrears of pay and the prospect, if paid at all, of receiving only Continental money, of little or no value. What was more, the British were circulating among the troops inducements to desert.

On May 28, Washington wrote to Joseph Reed:

All our departments, all our operations are at a stand, and unless a system very different from that which has for a long time prevailed, be immediately adopted throughout the states, our affairs must soon become desperate beyond the possibility of recovery.... Indeed I have almost ceased to hope. The country in general is in such a state of insensibility and indifference to its interests, that I dare not flatter myself with any change for the better.

The committee, in its address to the states, had given "a just picture of our situation", he asserted, but he very much doubted its making the desired impression. It appeared to him that "motives of honor, public good, and even self-preservation have lost their influence upon our minds." Yet the moment was decisive, *"the* most important America has seen".

Three days later (May 31) Washington once more took occasion to lay before the committee a clear account of the situation of the army, pointing out that, in order to plan with any degree of certainty for cooperation with the expected French forces, it was of indispensable importance to know precisely what could be depended on in the way of men and supplies. At his suggestion the committee despatched letters to the states (exclusive of the three southernmost), requesting from each certain designated supplies, including transportation, deliveries to be made monthly and to begin July 1; likewise certain numbers of troops, to be delivered at designated rendezvous by July 15. The committee's solicitations were reinforced by an emphatic appeal from Washington himself.

Not content with these appeals, urgent and explicit though they were, and particularly because some of the states, it had been learned, were planning a less extensive augmentation of their forces than had been requested, Washington asked the committee to reiterate and further to emphasize the urgency of a compliance with their requisitions, especially the requisitions for troops. Then, when a week had gone by without a word of response from any of the states, they were once more earnestly entreated to take speedy and decisive measures and to inform the committee of their actions; for the fleet and army of our ally were hourly expected. Despite the exasperating negligence of the states, the committee restrained its impatience and indulged itself in such diplomatic language as: "From the well known indefatigable attention of Your State, to the welfare of the United States we cannot entertain a doubt of its exertions at this interesting Conjuncture". Amongst themselves the committee used a different language.

The offices of this committee of three members of Congress, near the headquarters of the army, rather than the floor of Congress, were thus becoming the real center of activities. Congress was, however, by no means idle. Many affairs of lesser importance, and now and then a few weightier matters, had been considered, debated, and decided in Congress assembled. One particularly noteworthy deed of that assembly had been to add (June 15) to the appeals of the committee and General Washington to the state authorities one more installment of its own argument and exhortation.

As first proposed by Robert R. Livingston, that exhortation was in part a scorching criticism of the states for their negligence and failures. It was "the supineness and false security of too many states", Livingston would have had Congress say, that had involved the country in its present difficulties. No, no! a majority of the members decided; Congress could not afford to make such accusations against the states. Delete those words and say: "Every state in the union is bound by the strongest obligations to afford us their aid." Nobody could object to that. That undeniable truth was nevertheless followed by some exceedingly pointed questions:

What, then, can justify any in withholding it? is the present ease or convenience of the subjects to be put in competition with the lasting happiness of millions? Do the rulers fear at this critical period to exert their utmost authority? Can they so far distrust the feelings and understandings of their people, as to believe that they will refuse a momentary submission to such vigorous exertions of government as are necessary to secure them from continued oppression and established tyranny?

Too pointed, too harsh. Substitute: "We trust . . . that the rulers of states will not hesitate to exert their utmost authority", etc. To urge, to beseech, to exhort—these were the only proper modes in which Congress might approach the free, sovereign, and independent states. And yet in the very next lines of the address, as approved by Congress, the exhortation is only perceptibly softened. Indeed, in one particular its admonition is even more pointed:

A Common Council [proceeds the address] involves the power of direction. Let not our measures be checked or controuled by the negligence or partial views and interests of separate communities, while they profess to be members of one body—too long have the dearest interests of America been sacrificed to present ease, too many of us have slept in false security. Let us awake before the season of successful exertion is passed.

The committee had urged, Washington had besought, and now Congress had once more exhorted; but would the states awake? "Distress and Calamity", James Duane declared (June 6), "will rouse us to a suitable display of *publick* Confidence and *private* Virtue."

It is especially significant that, in this address to the states, Congress should have made bold to intimate that the states should bestow upon their "Common Council" a larger "power of direction". The question was, in fact, being seriously considered at the time, mainly by a limited group in Congress; but the surprising thing is that Congress should have given its approval to this intimation. The agitation of the question appears to have been started, as was natural, by none other than the commander-in-chief. It is a mark of Washington's wisdom that he had taken the utmost care at all times not to assume any powers that had not been definitely bestowed upon him, but to work in harmony with Congress and through Congress. For, just as Congress had, upon the whole, come to realize that through Washington alone could the states succeed in their struggle, so Washington recognized that through Congress alone, as the common council of the union, could the cause of America, as he conceived it, be won.

Washington was, however, above all else, practical, and the clear stream of his thinking was never muddied by any political philosophy. In his view Congress, as the representative of the states in their united capacity, might properly have buttressed its own powers, vaguely defined though they were; instead, however, Congress had persistently catered to the hesitancies of the states and had thereby broken the staff in its own hands. This thought Washington cogently expressed to his friend Joseph Jones, member of Congress from Virginia, in a letter written the last day of May, when, as he had expressed it to other friends, America stood face to face with probably the most decisive moment of her history.

Certain I am [he wrote] that unless Congress speaks in a more decisive tone; unless they are vested with powers by the several States competent to the great purposes of War, or assume them as a matter of right; and they, and the States respectively, act with more energy than they hitherto have done, that our Cause is lost.

One state, he went on to say, would comply with the requisitions of Congress, another would neglect to do it, while a third would execute it by halves, with the result that "we are always working up hill, and ever shall be (while such a system as the present one, or rather want of one prevails) unable to apply our strength or resources to any advantage." These failures of cooperation he had had occasion to lament time and time again; what he was now emphasizing was the alarming centrifugal tendency among the states then threatening the union and all that the union stood for.

I see one head gradually changing into thirteen [he declared]. I see one Army branching into thirteen; and instead of its looking up to Congress as the supreme controuling power of the united States, are considering themselves as dependent on their respective States. In a word, I see the powers of Congress declining too fast for the consequence and respect which is due to them as the grand representative body of America, and I am fearful of the consequences of it.

A few men in Congress, and Joseph Jones was one of them, evidently saw eye to eye with Washington. Jones agreed with Washington (letter of June 19) that Congress had been "gradually surrendering or throw-

ing upon the several States the exercise of powers they should have retained and to their utmost have exercised themselves", until that body
had little power left except such as concerned foreign affairs. What
powers Congress once possessed had, for the most part, "from embarrassment and difficulties" been "frittered away to the States", and he
was convinced that it would be difficult to recover them. Certain steps,
however, Jones went on to say, had been taken in Congress with a view
to bringing about something of what was desired, and he pointed particularly to the resolution of June 17 requesting the states to inform
Congress what measures they had taken in consequence of certain
resolutions. "This", he thought, "may probably serve as a Basis for
assuming powers should the answers afford an opening." What Jones
was alluding to was probably not the resolution proper but its preamble, wherein it is stated to be essential that "the superintending
power" should be intimately acquainted with the measures that had
been pursued. Among the resolutions then before Congress having in
view the strengthening of the hand of Congress, one desired the states
"to give express powers" for calling forth men, provisions, and money
for carrying on the war; "others go to the assumption of them im-
[m]ediately." The first would probably pass Congress but "sleep with
the States"; the others would probably "dye where they are", for some
members of Congress were exceedingly cautious of offending the states
in this respect.

Congress did adopt several resolutions (June 21) once more emphatically calling upon the states to comply with the requisitions of
Congress and its committee at headquarters, and to inform them without delay what had been done. In particular the state executives were
urged to correspond weekly with the committee. It is significant that
these resolutions were taken in response to a memorial from the minister of France, calling the attention of Congress to those very positive
but as yet unfulfilled assurances given back in January that requisite
measures would be taken to cooperate effectively with the forces of
France, now on the point of arrival. The resolutions were sufficiently
forcible to stir the most sluggish of the states to action—if they could
be so stirred; yet the best conjecture would be that they also would
"sleep with the states".

Indeed so feeble was the faith in the states, it is not surprising that far-seeing statesmen should be seeking a concentration of power where it might be effectively used. Feeble and futile though it was, that endeavor at this time is particularly noteworthy because it is one of the first definite steps in that progress toward "a more perfect union" that found its haven seven years later. Unfortunately, because of the meagerness of information, it can not be determined how extensive that effort really was. Some light is thrown upon it by a letter of June 18 (the day preceding that on which Jones wrote to Washington) from Ezekiel Cornell of Rhode Island to Governor Greene:

The different policy of the several states, and too many of them turning all their views to their own advantage; without consulting the Common Good, Cause some able Politicians to think that our Political Salvation, in a great measure depends on a controuling power, over the whole, being lodged in some person or persons. I wish to have your Excellencys Sentiments upon this subject, before the matter is taken up in Congress which I think will be soon, as the Union is too much dissolved in some of our Sister States, whatever [your] sentiments may be will be my line of Conduct.

What the governor's response was, if any, does not appear; but a month later (July 21) Cornell wrote to General Greene: "There doth not appear to be the most distant wish for more powers, but rather on the contrary, a wish to see their States without control (as the term is) free, sovereign, and independent." If some one raises the question, what can we do? the answer is, "Why, we can do nothing; the States must exert themselves; if they will not, they must suffer the consequences". For his part, Cornell was at a loss to know the motives and views of Congress—"if they have any". "There appears", he said, "to be a languor that attends all our conduct, want of decision and spirited measures. The greatest part of our time is taken up in disputes about diction, comas, colons, consonants, vowels, etc."

What had taken place during that interval of a month? The one clue is an undated report, placed in the (printed) *Journals* under October 3, 1780, but evidently pertaining to the period now under consideration. It carries the title, "Report of the Com[mitt]ee for encreasing the powers of Congress—Application to the State Legislatures", and was drawn by Robert R. Livingston. Livingston was chairman of the committee appointed June 19 on Luzerne's memorial of June 18, to whom were also referred "certain resolutions" then moved. There can be little doubt therefore that this report "for encreasing the powers of Congress" emanated from the Livingston committee of June 19. Indeed it bears a close kinship with the resolutions adopted June 21 in response to the memorial of the minister; but more directly to the point are certain other propositions. A preamble to the most significant proposition states that it is "highly important to the interests of the United States that at this crisis the common council of America should be vested with sufficient powers to call forth from time to time the military resources of the said States"; then follows a proposed resolution "that it be recommended to the Legislatures of each of the United States to invest in Congress sufficient powers . . . for the common defence". Still another of the resolutions proposes, as Joseph Jones had remarked, the "assumption" of powers by Congress immediately. It reads:

Resolved that Congress by the authority which the nature of the trust reposed in them vests them with, will immediately take measures to procure the supplies of men provisions and carriages necessary to give vigor and success to the operations of the present campaign.

It is clear enough that the resolution died in its tracks, as Jones had predicted; that is, in so far as any immediate action by Congress was concerned. That the idea did not die, however, is just as evident; for it was again vigorously astir less than three months later.

The committee at headquarters meanwhile continued to prod and exhort, not the states alone but Congress as well, while General Washington plied his own forceful arguments and appeals. In a circular letter to the states at the end of June the General said:

Our allies would be chagrined were they to arrive today, to find that we have but a handful of men in the field and would doubt, it is more than probable, whether we had serious intentions to prosecute measures with vigor. If we do not avail ourselves of their succour by the most decisive and energetic steps on our part, the aid they so generously bring may prove our ruin.

It was not many days later, in mid-July, that the first division of the French naval and land forces arived—ten war vessels under the command of Admiral Ternay, and some six thousand men under the command of the Comte de Rochambeau. Washington had perforce to make the best of the situation. Unfortunately the French fleet became bottled up in Narragansett Bay by the British fleet under Admiral Graves, in consequence of which the French army was unable to render any service for a year.

The committee at headquarters, for its part, seized upon the occasion of the arrival of French aid to lay before Congress a long and detailed statement of the situation in the army, of what the various states had done or had not done toward complying with the requisitions upon them for men and supplies. It was not an inspiring picture. Some states had thus far made no responses whatever, although it had been learned indirectly that some of them had indicated a purpose not to complete their battalions to the extent requested. "The eyes of Europe generally, and those of all America", the committee wrote, "are intently turned to Congress, and to the operations of their Army in this Campaign. . . . We cannot contemplate without horror the Effects of disappointment." It is not a matter for surprise therefore that Ezekiel Cornell was shortly afterward writing to Governor Greene (August 1), "The necessity of appointing General Washington, sole dictator of America, is again talked of as the only means under God by which we can be saved from destruction." As yet the idea appears to have been confined to out-of-doors talk, but early in September, when John Mathews of the headquarters committee had returned to Congress, he offered such a motion, drawn out to particularities. It was "a most scandalous Motion", growled James Lovell, "a product of Camp Education"; but then, "if we have not a Supply of Money from the States, we must expect frequent Maggots about creating Omnipotencies."

At last, in the midst of this general gloom, assurances began to come from most of the states that they were actively assembling troops and supplies. For the moment the army had food; for the moment also many of its other problems had been solved or were quiescent. Accordingly optimism once more gained the ascendancy in Congress. The worst, so often predicted, had not come about after all; probably it never would. Some members even visioned, as had been their wont of old, a speedy conclusion of the "glorious contest". Unfortunately these rising enthusiasms were just then chilled in consequence of an old problem coming to a new climax.

Among the heavy tasks laid upon the committee at headquarters at its first appointment was an instruction to investigate and reform the staff departments, of which the quartermaster's department had long sorely vexed and perplexed Congress, as it had also been a matter of anxious concern to Washington. Latterly it had been taxing the ingenuity and wisdom of the committee at headquarters. Included among the committee's instructions was one "to pay a particular attention" to the plan for arranging that department which had been offered by Mifflin and Pickering at the end of March. The committee might nevertheless adopt, amend, or alter the plan, as to them should appear most advisable. There was no likelihood that the committee would approve the plan, for Schuyler in particular had already expressed his disapprobation of it. Quite naturally therefore the committee, under Schuyler's guidance and in consultation with General Greene and General Washington, drew up a plan of its own. In the middle of June, Schuyler returned to Philadelphia to present the committee's plan to Congress.

There, at intervals during nearly a month, the new plan underwent discussion. Even before it finally came forth from the Congressional mill (July 15), in Schuyler's opinion it had been so mutilated that its utility would in great measure be destroyed. Greene withheld his judgment until he should see the plan in its revised form, but, in a private letter, he gave utterance to a characteristic sentiment: "Congress always destroy with the left hand what they begin with the right"; to which he added the biting comment: "People that will not learn Wisdom by suffering and experience cannot be saved." If Greene could have confined his caustic remarks to private letters he would doubtless have saved himself much trouble, as in the sequel he was to learn.

A chief point of controversy (though by no means the only one) between Congress and its quartermaster general was over the question of his responsibility. At the outset of the discussion of the plan in Congress, Greene had stated, in a letter to Congress June 19, the degree of responsibility that he would assume; and, when he was given to understand that he would be held responsible for his appointments "in a very different manner" from that in which he had conceived himself bound, he wrote to the committee (July 14), "Nor would I hold the office upon such a footing for any consideration that could be offered me".

Congress declined to accede to Greene's demands, asserting, in a resolution of July 24, that it was "essential to the public interest, as well as incident to the nature of all offices entrusted with the disbursement of public monies, that those who exercise them should be responsible for such disbursement", and that Congress could not, "consistently with their duty to their constituents, by any general resolution, hold up a contrary maxim". Congress would, however, "determine on circumstances as they arise, and make such favourable allowances as justice may require". The general principle thus announced was certainly sound; it was rather the application likely to be made of it at which Greene balked. His contention, as it had been the contention of every other agent of Congress similarly placed, was primarily for a degree of discretionary power, that he might adapt measures to exigencies as they arose. And it was just this lesson in efficiency—discretion coupled with responsibility—that it had been so hard for Congress to learn.

Since Congress and its quartermaster general could not come to an agreement upon the terms on which the business of the department should be conducted, the result was necessarily Greene's resignation (July 26). In his letter of resignation Greene refrained from reiterating his general objections to the plan, except to remark, "I do not choose to attempt an experiment of so dangerous a nature, where I see a physical impossibility of performing the duties that will be required of me." Some particular criticisms, however, he did offer; among them a failure to make provision for his two assistants, John Cox and Charles Pettit, on whom he had greatly depended in the past and must continue to depend, if he remained in charge of the department. "Systems without agents", he remarked, "are useless things, and the probability of getting the one should be taken into consideration in framing the other."

Had Greene contented himself with this sage observation, the current of events would no doubt have flowed smoothly on, with scarcely more than a ripple or two; but he added a corollary that let the storm-winds out of the cave. Quoth he: "Administration seem to think it far less important to the public interest to have this department well filled, and properly arranged, than it really is, and as they will find it by future experience." Mildly critical, to be sure; yet what was there in the statement to loose the winds of wrath or to rouse drowsing dogs to ferocity? Simply the word "Administration"! Odious term, that, reminiscent of the early days of the struggle, when a hateful administration in Great Britain sought to plant its heel on colonial necks.

The offensive connotation of the word seems never to have entered Greene's mind when he used it. To a body so sorely nettled, however, it was like flaunting a red rag in the face of an already excited bull. General Greene had flung "gross insults" into the face of congress; and straightway there was a motion to disrobe him of all military rank. No; the less angry members cautioned; Congress ought to allow General Greene time "to see, acknowledge, and retract his error". Followed a motion, itself by no means mild, "that the Commander in Chief be directed to inform Major General Green that the United States have no farther occasion for his services, and that it is expected he will proceed immediately to the settlement of his accounts." Even that motion could not obtain the assent of a majority, and Congress presently contented itself, for the time being at least, with choosing (August 5) a new quartermaster general, Timothy Pickering.

Most members of Congress severely reprobated Greene's conduct in quitting the department and thus throwing it into confusion at a time of crisis, while even his best friends thought that he might properly, in view of the critical situation, have been less rigid in his demands. His friend Ezekiel Cornell, for instance, warned him (July 29) that Congress might yet hurt his feelings worse than they had hitherto done, that some members would be happy to do it, "and that soon". Even so judicious a man as Joseph Jones thought the manner of his demands and the peremptoriness of his terms had lessened him in the esteem of the public as well as of Congress, and he doubted, so he wrote to Washington, whether the matter would terminate with a mere acceptance of his resignation. Washington, who better understood Greene's difficulties and his scruples than did Congress, replied to Jones (August 13), "If by this it is in contemplation to suspend him from his command in the line (of which he made an express reservation at the time of entering on the other duty) and it is not already enacted, let me beseech you to consider *well* what you are about before you resolve." Without a more explicit knowledge of the facts, Washington stated, he would not untertake either to condemn or to acquit General Greene's conduct in resigning, but "you may find him treading on better ground than you seem to imagine".

Greene's resignation naturally had its repercussions upon the committee at headquarters, who were as much displeased with the alteration of their plan for the quartermaster's department as was General Greene himself. But the committee had not in the past been altogether diplomatic in their dealings with Congress—their superiors—and they now became less so. The committee undertook to ply Congress with arguments in General Greene's behalf, which had an unexpected result, if not the precise opposite of what had been hoped for. Even before Greene's resignation had been acted upon Congress sharply admonished the committee that the general himself had requested the sense of Congress on the important subject of his responsibility, therefore the committee "ought not to have interfered therein". Moreover, declared Congress in a frigid resolution (August 2), those certain memorials and applications "which seem to have employed [the committee's] time and attention, should have been made directly to Congress, and the committee should thus have informed the applicants".

It so happened that these resolutions reprimanding the committee for its manifest encroachments upon the authority of Congress and for a conduct otherwise derogatory to the latter's dignity were not promptly transmitted to the committee, which, in the interval of delay, had become reduced to a single individual, John Mathews. Peabody had been taken ill, and Schuyler had found it necessary to go to New York. Mathews was not wont to put restraints upon the freedom of his own speech, and, persuading himself that Congress was in need of admonitions, he proceeded to give that body a course of treatment in a manner all his own. "Convinced from long experience", he wrote to President Huntington, August 6, "that the decisions of Congress are not very rapid, tho on matters of the last importance, I am induced to address you on this subject"; and thereupon he launched upon a lecture at length and at large concerning the situation in general and the quarter-master's department in particular. All too pointedly he said:

It may be asked, whether Congress are to be dictated to, by their Officers? I answer without hesitation, that on the present occasion they must; necessity compels them to it, and it is a duty they owe their constituents, not to suffer punctilio, to militate against their essential interests. If there are men in the great council of this nation, capable of such a conduct, I will not say what I think are their deserts.

Then he went on to plead the cause of General Washington in his present trying situation. "Remember the Gentleman at the head of your Army. . . . For Gods sake! have some regard to his feelings."

This letter was written on the 6th of August, and, as any one except Mathews himself might have expected, when it was laid before Congress (August 11), a motion was immediately made that the committee be discharged from further attendance at headquarters and that they report their proceedings to Congress. The motion was carried by a vote of ten ayes to two noes and one (Virginia) divided, showing clearly that the committee had almost completely lost favor in Congress. Not yet, however, had Congress received the full measure of John Mathews' mind. Stung by the rebuke administered to the committee the 2d of August, and when he had not as yet learned of the committee's recall, he wrote a letter to Congress (August 16), couched in terms of such biting sarcasm that, when he resumed his seat in Congress, he was "made to *feel*", so he wrote to Washington, that the "rancour of these demagogues had risen to a height he could never have imagined. His colleague Nathaniel Peabody, recuperating in Morristown, appears to have taken the Congressional rebuke to the committee with amused aloofness. To Josiah Bartlett he wrote (August 6): "I once read of a people who were at times led by a cloud; And I have known a people whose *Grand Multiform'd Sanhedrin* were often times in the midst of a Fog." Peabody occupied himself for some time at Morristown with the preparation of the voluminous record of the committee's proceedings, but neither he nor Schuyler put foot inside the hall of Congress again.

The dismissal of the committee came at a very crucial moment. On

August 20, two days before he had learned of that dismissal, Washington found it necessary once more to lay before Congress at length an account of the "complication of embarrassments that menace us on every side with disappointment". At that moment he was under the painful necessity of dismissing part of the militia then beginning to assemble, although a month behind schedule, or else to "let them come forward to starve". "Every day's experience", he declared, "proves more and more that the present mode of obtaining Supplies is the most uncertain, expensive, and injurious that could be devised."

To me it will appear miraculous [he went on to say] if our affairs can maintain themselves much longer in their present train. If either the temper or the resources of the country will not admit of an alteration, we may expect soon to be reduced to the humiliating condition of seeing the cause of America, in America, upheld by foreign arms. The generosity of our Allies has a claim to all our confidence and all our gratitude, but it is neither for the honor of America, nor for the interest of the common cause to leave the work entirely for them.

Once again he urged the adoption of a peremptory draft for the duration of the war or for three years—if, he took pains to say, it could be effected. Once again he declared the system of short-term enlistments to have been "pernicious beyond description". It had been the cause of most of the misfortunes of the past, had led to an unnecessary prolongation of the war, and besides was enormously expensive. It is a long letter, replete with facts, arguments, and earnest pleas, and closes with this candid statement:

In this delicate and perplexing conjuncture which I cannot but contemplate with extreme inquietude, I have thought it my duty to lay my sentiments with freedom, and I hope I have done it with all possible deference, before Congress; and to give them the fullest and truest information in my power. I trust they will receive what I have said, with all the indulgence which must flow from a conviction that it is dictated by a sincere attachment to their honor, and by an anxious concern for the welfare of my country.

Washington had leaned heavily on the committee at headquarters, and he took the first opportunity (August 28) after its recall to testify his grateful sense of their "cheerful and vigorous exertions" during their residence with the army. "I feel myself", he said, "under the greatest obligations to them for having done all in their power to accomplish the objects of their appointment". For his own part, now that the committee had been extinguished, he redoubled his exertions with the states. On August 27 he addressed them in a circular letter, wherein he laid bare the situation even more intimately than he had done to Congress. During the past six days, he stated, the greater part of the army had been without meat, and at that moment there was only one day's supply of flour in the camp. By moving the army from place to place and stripping the country he had been able to obtain a scanty pittance; but that mode of subsistence was "in the highest degree distressing to individuals" and "attended with ruin to the Morals and discipline of the Army". If that were to continue, "we must assume the odious character of the plunderers instead of the protectors of the people".

Although the procuring of food for the army demanded action as swift as possible, Congress spent more than two weeks in devising even temporary measures. These were: a request of the bank in Philadelphia to finance a small purchase of cattle, a call upon the states of New Jersey, Pennsylvania, and Delaware to furnish an immediate supply of cattle to the army, and an order that warrants be drawn on sundry states for expense money. Despite the most vigorous and persistent efforts the committee at headquarters had fallen far short of its endeavors, but Congress was laggard even in feeble endeavors. Having, in a fit of righteous indignation, rid itself of the obstreperous committee, Congress seemed to forget the hunger of the soldiers. If there be doubt, hear the testimony of a member:

I have seen many new scenes before I came to this place [wrote Ezekiel Cornell, August 13]. But what I have experienced since, exceeds anything I have ever seen before. I never before saw a set of men that could quietly submit to every kind of difficulty that tended to the ruin of the country, without endeavoring to make one effort to remove the obstruction. I believe they wish their country well, but suffer their time almost wholly to be taken up in business of no consequence.

The clouds might lower never so darkly, but amongst them somewhere there must surely be a silver lining. Quoth Thomas McKean, when he had listened to the reading of Washington's letter of August 20:

"Si male nunc, et olim non erit", slightly misquoting Horace, who was reputed to be an authority on silver linings.

What Congress next beheld, however, as it watched and waited, was not a cloud with a silver lining; it was another cloud indeed, but its lining gave no silvery gleam. It was the news, which began to drift in early in September, that the second French squadron had been blockaded at Brest and was therefore not at all likely to reach America in time for such operations as had been planned. Washington at once gave up all idea of an effective campaign this season and decided to dismiss the greater part of the militia. It would save expense; besides, their periods of service would have expired before any use could probably be made of them.

So far as the main army was concerned, therefore, the season of 1780 seemed about to pass out without having to its credit any military operations worth speaking of. The southern field of activities had indeed produced results, but they had not been such as to prompt exultation or inspire hope. On the 12th of May the American forces at Charleston, under General Benjamin Lincoln, had been compelled to surrender, although it was a full month before Congress had definite confirmation of this untoward event. Georgia had for sometime been under British control, and now, with Charleston in their possession, the two southernmost states may well have seemed lost to the American union.

In fact, two months before the fall of Charleston it had been rumored that the British government would offer independence to the eleven northern states on condition that South Carolina and Georgia should be left in British possession; and, following the surrender of Charleston, a report gained currency that Congress was on the point of making peace by the cession of those two states. To silence that rumor Congress, on June 23, resolved unanimously:

That the said report is insidious and utterly void of foundation.

That this Confederacy is most sacredly pledged to support the liberty and independence of every one of its members; and, in a firm reliance on the divine blessing, will unremittingly persevere in their exertions for the establishment of the same, and also for the recovery and preservation of any and every part of these United States that has been or may hereafter be invaded or possessed by the common enemy.

Congress had, in fact, taken steps to make good this pledge before ever the pledge had been recorded. On June 13 it had appointed the hero of Saratoga, General Horatio Gates, to the command of the southern department, had authorized him to call on the states of Virginia, North Carolina, South Carolina, and Georgia for such aids of militia and supplies as he deemed necessary, to appoint all the necessary staff officers, and, lest some needful authority had been overlooked, had empowered him "to take such other measures, from time to time, for the defence of the southern states as he shall think most proper".

Hopefully Congress awaited the outcome. It would be a victory for the American arms of course. It could not be otherwise with the conqueror of Burgoyne in command. Listening eagerly for the good news, suddenly, in the early days of September, Congress got one of the worst shocks of its career. On the 16th of August, at Camden in South Carolina, Gates's army had been routed, almost totally annihilated. The general himself had escaped, had indeed more than escaped; he had put a swift two hundred miles, or near it, between himself and the British army.

But why had he sped to so great a distance from the scene of action? Why had he abandoned the remnant of his own army? Bristling questions, these, and they would not down. Among the devotees of Gates, faith in their favorite had been such as would remove mountains of doubt; but when satisfactory answers to these questions were not forthcoming, that faith dwindled and died. The legend of Saratoga, which had so long confused the councils of war, would bedevil Congress no more. After all, Camden no doubt had its compensations.

Gates's own explanation, that he had established himself at Hillsborough as the best center from which to undertake the rebuilding of his army, may have been logical, but it failed to carry conviction. On October 5, Congress ordered an inquiry into Gates's conduct, but it was not pressed, and on May 21, 1781, Congress entered into a resolution "that Major General Gates be informed, that he is at liberty to repair to head quarters, and take such command as the Commander in Chief shall direct".

Gates sought to have the inquiry accelerated, while some of his friends in Congress endeavored to obtain a repeal of the order for the inquiry. Writing to Jefferson, August 2, Gates said: "A Motion for rescinding the Resolve of the 5th of October has been several times made in Congress, but once to my astonishment was prevented being carried by a Mr. Maddison of this State, a Gentleman I do not know, and who I am satisfied does not know me." It was nearly at the same time (August 8) that General Greene offered his opinion that if Gates "was to be blamed for any thing at all, it was for fighting, not for what he did, or did not do, in or after the action". It was not however until a year later (August 14, 1782) that Congress was prevailed on to repeal the order for a court of inquiry.

Whatever may have been Gates's merits or demerits, whether or not he deserved, in the language of James Wilkinson, to be precipitated "from the pinacle of undeserved fame to the abyss of humiliation", the reflections of James Mitchel Varnum, in a sympathetic letter to Gates (February 15, 1781), are an appropriate comment on his situation: "Misfortune is construed into Wickedness or Weekness, and the shining Merits of Years are enveloped in the illfated Events of an Hour. How ungenerous is the human Heart when under the Controul of tumultuous Passions!"

The country was to receive one more shock from a near-disaster before any turn in the tide of its affairs would seem to lead toward fortune. For hard upon the heels of the southern debacle came the treason of Arnold. It was therefore in no mood of exultation that Congress paused to proclaim its annual day of thanksgiving and prayer. In the proclamation of the year before, Congress had offered up thanks for imaginary triumphs over the foe; but for the campaign of 1780, if not in a more chastened spirit, at least with a deeper regard for facts, Congress refrained from claiming victories, even in vague and general terms. The one thing in particular that called for "devout and thankful acknowledgments" was "the late remarkable interposition of his watchful providence in rescuing the person of our Commander in Chief and the army from imminent dangers, at the moment when treason was ripened for execution".

The proclamation was adopted on the 18th of October. Had Congress lingered only five days longer, how different would have been the language of thanksgiving! For on the seventh of October had occurred the glorious victory at King's Mountain, a victory of which Congress did not learn until the 23d. It was no large affair, judged even by the standards of the Revolution, but in its psychological effect it was a victory of the first magnitude. It went far toward dispelling the general gloom, it inspired the country with renewed hope, and it marked that turn of the tide for which all patriots had long been yearning. Measures were at once taken to rebuild the southern army, so sorely stricken at Camden, and not the least of the hostages given to fortune was the appointment of General Nathanael Greene to the command of that army.

It was time, too, to begin preparations for the next campaign of the main army, an undertaking that was at least begun every autumn, although the coming of spring usually found the task still unfinished. In the past, one year had repeated another. Would it be different this year? Washington would begin betimes with his plans and his requests for needful measures, Congress would dally over them for weeks, may be months, the states would procrastinate, and before the army could be got ready the fighting season would be over. Troops had come and troops had gone, but troops fit to fight and in sufficient numbers were seldom available. Supplies, costly and laboriously obtained, had been consumed; precious time had been lost. Wasted effort everywhere. Only heart-burnings and vexation of spirit.

CHAPTER XXV

MAKING BRICKS WITHOUT STRAW
CONFEDERATION AT LAST, BUT LAME AND HALT

The campaign season of 1780 had opened with rather large promises, and even with buoyant hopes. Spring had however brought its full quota of disappointments, summer had piled problem upon problem, heaped a Pelion of worries upon an Ossa of anxieties, and now autumn was pronouncing its verdict of failure upon months of endeavor. Vanished now every prospect of a major enterprise before the coming of winter.

Perceiving this with his usual clarity, Washington set vigorously about the task of building an army on which he could securely base hopes for the year to follow. Even before it had been learned positively that the second squadron of the French fleet had not succeeded in departing France, he had taken steps toward his goal. In his letter to Congress, August 20, 1780, he had squarely posed the problem and urged the needed measures. For once Congress actually speeded action, so that within a month (September 21) the project was ready for Washington's approval, and on the 3d of October it was adopted.

The essential feature of the measure, so far as concerned enlistments, was a recommendation to the states to recruit their regiments to their full quotas with men enlisted for the war, if this could be accomplished by December 1, otherwise with enlistments for one year. John Mathews, a member of the late committee at headquarters and willing enough to concede that, as James Lovell had charged, he had been inoculated with a large dose of "camp doctrine", wrote Washington (September 24) that he had stretched his abilities to the utmost and had exhausted every argument with which nature and his inquiries and observations had furnished him to get the fatal alternative, "or for one year", eliminated, and instead to call upon the states, "in the most forcible language", to fill up their regiments by drafts for not less than one year from the first of January, with the additional provision that, if not then relieved, they should be obliged to continue in the field until their places should be actually supplied by other drafts or enlistments for one year or for the war.

The vote was overwhelmingly against Mathews' contention, and it may well have been that his late excoriation of his fellow-members of Congress militated against his success. However this may have been, Mathews of all men ought by now to have learned that it was of small avail to address the states in "forcible language". Urgent requests, earnest solicitations, forceful pleadings, eloquent appeals from Congress to the states, had become as commonplace as changes of the moon, and about as effective for military purposes, whether the appeal were for men, for money, or for supplies.

It was quite as much the failure of supplies as of men that had broken the back of the last campaign. The device of specific supplies, adopted only as a desperate resort because a collapsed or collapsing currency had made a money economy all but impossible, had utterly failed to meet the requirements of the army. Something therefore must be done to obtain the necessary supplies, and something must be done to restore the sinking finances.

Both these problems had, in a manner, been attacked prior to that of recruiting. On the 11th of August a committee of ways and means was appointed to examine into both the problem of finances and that of supplies. In the weeks that followed the committee advanced a number of propositions, to say nothing of offerings by individual members, but only a modicum of the mass was able to run the gauntlet of Congressional scrutiny. On August 26, for instance, Congress adopted measures designed to support and make more effective the act of March 18, providing for the issue of new money in place of the old; but these measures did not prove effective for the resuscitation of dying Continental.

More to the purpose was a measure adopted November 4, 1780, the aim of which was to remedy the defects in the existing method of obtaining supplies. In essence it was a mixed system of specific supplies and monetary contributions. The states were called upon to levy a tax, "equal in value to six millions of silver dollars, to be paid partly in the specific articles and at the prices hereafter enumerated, and the residue in gold or silver, or bills of credit emitted pursuant to the resolution of the 18 March last". Each state was accordingly assigned certain quantities of beef, pork, flour, rum, and salt, at designated prices, to be delivered in quantities specified for each state by certain designated dates over the period from January 1 to July 15, the designated balances of money to be paid quarterly, beginning May 1, 1781. (The quantity of rum called for, be it known, was 299,999 gallons.) At first glance it might seem to be a complicated system, yet each state's share in the program is set down with a precision that could not be surpassed. Indeed it is an example of meticulously planned economy such as might well arouse envy in the bosoms of present-day leaders of that cult. There was just one crucial question: would it work?

"The success of this expedient", James Madison wrote to Joseph Jones (October 24, 1780), "depends on the mode of carrying it into execution." If, instead of executing it by specific taxes, he said, resort should be had to state emissions, commissary's and quartermaster's certificates, a worse species of emissions than Continental bills of credit, "what was intended for our relief will only hasten our destruction." A few days later, speaking of the alarming picture of the situation given by General Washington, Madison remarked that applications to the contiguous states on the subject had been repeated from every quarter, "till they seem to have lost all their force".

It was a matter of course that the requisition of November 4 should go forth to the states accompanied by a ringing appeal. In this appeal, which bears the date of November 9, there is observed, on the one hand, an unwonted tone of humility in the confession of Congress that "the events of the present year have not enabled us to speak the language of triumph". On the other hand, the finger of accusation, though not for the first time, is pointed at the states, when, in referring to the causes of these failures, Congress declares, "We cannot refrain from observing, that the unpunctuality of the states in their supplies of men, money, and provisions, is not one of the least."

The clear recognition of nearly every thinking person that requisitions upon the states, whether for men, money, or provisions, was an utterly inadequate basis for any efficient conduct of the affairs of the union, had led to the suggestion, as pointed out in the preceding chapter, that Congress seek from the states a grant of enlarged powers. A tentative advancement of the proposition had, however, quickly proved that such a request at that time was vain. Earnest minds in Congress thereupon began to grope for some other solution of the problem. During the consideration of that notable act of March 18, 1780, for instance, it had been proposed by the two North Carolina delegates:

That the states be requested to pass laws enabling Congress to levy an impost of one per cent on all exports and imports, as a fund for sinking the emissions for carrying on the present war, to continue until a sum equal to the whole of the said emissions shall be collected.

In the vote, however, only three other members stood with the proponents, Burke and Jones, namely, Peabody of New Hampshire, Houston of New Jersey, and Plater of Maryland.

Even so overwhelming a defeat did not, however, suffice to drive the idea completely from the field. In June, for instance, as pointed out in the preceding chapter, there was a movement for the acquisition of greater powers for Congress, at which time was probably presented some resolutions to that end prepared by Robert R. Livingston. (They are found in the *Journals* under October 3, 1780, doubtless misplaced.) Then, on August 22, Livingston offered another series of resolutions, this time along the line of the proposition of the North Carolina delegates. Two of the latter resolutions are particularly pertinent. One of them would recommend to the states to impose a tax of two and a half per cent on exports, the funds to be collected by officers to be appointed by Congress and to be used for the payment of the foreign debt and for the procurement of further credit. The other was to request the states to levy a duty of five per cent (at some stage altered to two and a half per cent) on vessels and cargoes captured from the enemy, the funds to be used solely for the maintenance of the navy. The propositions were turned over to the committee of ways and means, who chose, however, to make to Congress quite different recommendations (August 26), principally those already mentioned, the aim of which was to put some additional props beneath the act of March 18.

The committee was not, however, wholly unmindful of the Livingston propositions, for on August 28, Ezekiel Cornell, a member of the committee, wrote to Governor Greene of Rhode Island that the committee had in contemplation a recommendation to the states to lay a duty of two and one half per cent on all exports, or one and a half per cent on all exports and imports, and a duty of two and a half per cent on all prize goods, for the benefit of the navy. The committee's contemplation appears to have been rather protracted. More than a month later (October 4) Jared Ingersoll, in a letter to Joseph Reed, spoke of the measure as still "in Contemplation". "This however", he remarked, "is but a Scheme in Embryo. What will finally be thought of it I do not know." In fact another month passed before the committee offered its report on the subject (November 8), and then the report (drawn by John Henry of Maryland, not by James Madison, as stated in the *Journals,* p. 1035 n.) was little more than the Livingston resolutions slightly altered and extended. The duty on prize goods, for instance, was restored to five per cent, as Livingston had at first proposed.

Chief, however, among the elaborations was an instruction to the treasury to report an estimate of the value of the exports and imports of the several states, with the further proposition that copies of these estimates be transmitted to the ministers in France and Spain, who were to be empowered to enter into stipulations for the repayment, from funds derived from this source, of any sums they might borrow. In the nature of the case the source for such funds was exceedingly problematical, at best a long way off, and the need for funds to carry on the war was immediate and pressing. Accordingly the committee once more proposed to draw bills of exchange on Jay and Franklin. Upon that proposition, however, Congress turned thumbs down—for the time being anyway. "Experience has shown", say the instructions to Franklin (November 28, 1780), "that the negotiation of bills is attended with insupportable loss and disadvantage."

For some two months Congress had been pondering and debating a memorial to the court of Versailles "for the purpose of procuring aids and supplies for a vigorous prosecution of the war against Great Britain"; and now some one conceived the bright idea of turning this memorial into a direct appeal to the king, an affectionate letter to his Most Christian Majesty, whose heart might be touched by the distresses of his loving allies, even though a cold-blooded minister might not listen to their pleas. The letter was prepared and on November 22 adopted, beseeching his Majesty for a loan of at least twenty-five millions of livres as indispensably necessary for the prosecution of the war. For security, "we do hereby solemnly pledge the faith of these United States to indemnify, or reimburse your Majesty, according to the nature of the case, both for principal and interest, in such manner as shall be agreed upon with our minister at your Majesty's court."

While this memorial was yet under consideration a motion was made by the Georgia delegates (November 18), "That an Envoy extraordinary be appointed to go to the Court of Versailles, to make, in concert with Mr. Franklin, the public representations of the United States". The chief purpose designed by the Georgia delegates to be attained by the measure was a diplomatic one, presently to be mentioned; but the idea was at once seized upon as a means better calculated to obtain the desired loan from France than even the most tearful appeal by letter. Accordingly, on December 8, it was resolved, "That a minister be appointed to proceed to the Court of Versailles for the special purpose of soliciting the aids requested by Congress, and forwarding them to America without loss of time."

As first drawn the resolution was for the appointment of "an envoy extraordinary", and his solicitations were to be made "in conjunction with our Minister Plenipotentiary at that court"; but these phrases were stricken out in Congress. Some members of Congress were averse to sending a special envoy as indicative of a want of confidence in Franklin; but the faction that had no such scruples won in the contest. On December 11, John Laurens was chosen for the mission, and early in 1781 he sailed for France. There, with the invaluable cooperation of Franklin, and in spite of the undiplomatic methods of procedure into which his zeal had led him, he was successful to an extent which probably few members of Congress had dared to hope.

The proposal as first made to send a special envoy to France had taken its rise from the intimation that the belligerent powers in Europe might soon proceed to a negotiation of peace on the basis of *uti possidetis,* and that would probably mean that South Carolina and Georgia would be left in British possession. Some months earlier, in view of similar reports, Congress had been induced (June 23, 1780) to record a sacred pledge "to support the liberty and independence" of every one of the states. Now however the situation was even more acute. Spain was manifesting great obduracy with regard to the Mississippi, refusing to concede to the United States the free navigation of that river to the sea, for which Jay had been instructed to contend. If Spain could only be brought into the alliance, not only would the chances of military success be improved, but the weight of that power might in any event prevent a restoration to Great Britain of any part of the thirteen states. The essential part of the motion of November 18 by the Georgia delegates was therefore that the instructions to Jay be reconsidered and he be empowered to yield the point to Spain, if indispensably necessary, in return for an agreement on Spain's part not to accede to proposals of peace without the concurrence of the United States—and for a handsome subsidy or loan.

A chief obstacle to the alteration of Jay's instructions was the insistence of Virginia upon the free navigation of the Mississippi; but so real, in Madison's view, had the danger become, that he set about to persuade the Virginia assembly to rescind its instructions to the state's delegates respecting that matter. In that effort Madison was successful, and on February 15, 1781, Congress in turn instructed Jay not to contend unalterably for the free navigation of the Mississippi below the thirty-first degree of north latitude. "No doubt this event if it takes place", Joseph Jones wrote to Washington, "will give us more Credit in Europe but we pay dear for it." He was even inclined to believe the result would be an alliance with Spain and an acknowledgment of our independence. The expected results did not follow, and, when the present menace had passed, both Virginia and Congress returned to their original positions on the question. In the summer of 1786 the free navigation of the Mississippi River was destined to take its place once more as one of the hotly debated questions in Congress.

In this same period Congress made still another of its ventures into European diplomacy. The proposal of an armed neutrality sponsored by Russia appealed so strongly to the advocates in Congress of the so-called militia diplomacy that they became all agog for sending a minister to Russia, and this they were successful in accomplishing with but little opposition. This decision was taken December 15, 1780, and on the 19th Francis Dana was chosen for that mission, and his commission and instructions adopted the same day.

The great object of your negotiation [say the instructions] is to engage her imperial majesty to favour and support the sovereignty and independence of these United States, and to lay a foundation for a good understanding and friendly intercourse between the subjects of her Imperial Majesty and the citizens of these United States, to the mutual advantage of both nations.

Further, Dana was not only instructed to testify, "in the strongest terms", the approbation of Congress of the measures which her Imperial Majesty had matured for the protection of commerce and the rights of nations, but to "use every means which can be devised to obtain the consent and influence of that court that these United States shall be formally invited, or admitted, to accede as principals and as an independent nation" to the proposed convention of neutral and belligerent powers. In the sequel this venture would but add one more to the list of diplomatic fiascoes for which Congress had stood sponsor. It could scarcely have been otherwise, for it was a gamble against all the chances.

In the meantime, the long chase after a foreign loan, into which Congress had been led by one item in the committee report of November 8, 1780, and the other lures into the foreign field, had left the real kernel of that report, the proposal of an impost measure, somewhat neglected for a while, though not entirely lost sight of. In fact, a new committee on finance, with John Sullivan as chairman, had been appointed November 7; and this committee, having straightway convinced itself that, in the past "most of our difficulties have arisen from an Ignorance of Finance" (wherein the committee was probably correct), proceeded to delve deeply into the sources of financial knowledge. Particularly they dived into the *Essays* of David Hume, whence they brought forth a mass of financial reflections, most of them of but little applicability to the exigencies of Congress. In fact, the committee evolved a number of financial schemes that it did not even offer to Congress, and of those that it did offer, such as the establishment of a bank, the gathering in of plate, as well as coined and uncoined gold and silver, were, for the most part, pushed to one side.

Once more the kernel of this committee's report, which was laid before Congress, December 18, was a repetition of the impost measure, first broached by the North Carolina delegates March 18, then in an expanded form proposed by Livingston, August 22, again by the committee of ways and means, November 8, but now worked out in greater detail and with additions. As yet no one had been able to think of a more practicable plan. Over these propositions therefore Congress labored assiduously for some six weeks, during which time there was serious discussion whether after all Congress had not better ask the states for a power to regulate all foreign commerce.

Even after Congress had determined, in committee of the whole, upon the impost measure, Witherspoon of New Jersey and Burke of North Carolina offered a motion of wider scope (February 3, 1781), to which they hung numerous provisos. They were able, however, to obtain the votes of only two states besides their own, namely, Connecticut and New York, with a few scattering individual ayes. It is deserving of attention that one of the sponsors of this measure, Thomas Burke, had at an earlier day been one of the chief antagonists of proposals to increase the powers of Congress.

In this same period there had been discussion also of that possible source of funds on which longing eyes were always cast whenever Continental finances came under consideration, namely the unlocated lands. That source also was passed by for the moment, although, in consequence of the accession of Maryland to the Confederation just as the impost act was reaching completion, the unlocated lands presently began to loom large in the financial picture.

The 3d of February, 1781, is one of the outstanding dates in the history of Congress, because it marks the first definite effort by Congress to obtain from the states such an enlargement of power as would give it at least a measure of financial independence. The act as adopted that day recommended to the states, as indispensably necessary, that they vest in Congress a power to levy for the use of the United States a duty of five per cent *ad valorem* upon all imported goods, with certain exceptions, including prizes and prize goods, the moneys derived therefrom to be used for the discharge of the public debt, contracted or to be contracted, the act to remain in force until the debts should be fully and finally discharged.

At almost the last moment a few alterations were made in the measure as agreed to in the committee of the whole, one of them particularly significant. A provision that the moneys should "be paid quarterly into the hands of such persons as Congress shall appoint to receive the same" was stricken out. Another alteration was in the rate of duty; fixed in committee of the whole at four per cent, it was changed to five per cent. In the form approved by the committee of the whole it was recommended that the states "pass laws granting to Congress", etc. This was changed to read: "that they vest a power in Congress to levy".

Inasmuch as the acquiescence of all thirteen states was necessary, and since it was most improbable that South Carolina and Georgia, then in possession of the enemy, would in the near future be in a position to act on the measure, a resolution was adoted February 7 that, as soon as all the states "whose legislatures shall and may assemble" should consent, Congress would proceed to the execution of the powers.

It was estimated that the measure would produce 600,000 or 700,000 specie dollars per annum, "but a trifle when compared with our wants", wrote John Mathews; "the interest alone of the debt already contracted amounts to two millions of dollars annually". The general hope was nevertheless that the measure would do much "to retrieve the character of and give new confidence and importance to the United States". The chief question was whether all the states would give their consent and take the necessary action. "How it will suit the genius of the several states", wrote Cornell of Rhode Island, "I will not undertake to say." As it turned out, his own state of Rhode Island was the one out of the thirteen that decided the measure was not suited to its genius.

It was while Congress was maturing with confident hope this proposal to the states, and at the same time advancing toward needed reforms in its own household, that it was suddenly confronted by an exigency of the most ominous import. In the afternoon of January 3, 1781, when it was supposed that the daily grind had been finished, the members of Congress were startled by the news that, on New Year's day, the Pennsylvania line, stationed near Morristown, had mutinied, deposed its officers, placed a board of sergeants in control, and had marched off to Princeton. Congress immediately reassembled and appointed a committee (Sullivan, Witherspoon, and Mathews) to confer with the supreme executive of Pennsylvania in an effort to quell the mutiny.

The chief grievance was that men who had enlisted "for three years or during the war" were being held to service after the expiration of the three years, which the soldiers interpreted as the maximum time of their service. In addition, there was the complaint that they had not received their pay and promised clothing. It was at first feared that the soldiers meditated joining the British, but, so far from doing so, they arrested some spies sent by General Sir Henry Clinton to persuade them to that course, and later turned them over to the military authorities, by whom they were tried and executed. The negotiations of President Reed and the committee of Congress with the mutineers, which proceeded through several days, in the end effected a satisfactory adjustment of the difficulties; but the period of waiting was one of great anxiety for Congress. Without doubt nevertheless the experience afforded Congress and the states a valuable lesson. Washington had over and over again pointed out to Congress the danger of just such eventualities, and nothing short of actual mutiny seemed able to bring genuine conviction.

One outcome of the mutiny was a circular letter from Congress to the states (January 15), wherein the states were told in unusually plain terms that remissness on their part in complying with the requisitions of Congress had been responsible for the whole trouble. Followed, as a matter of course, a fervent appeal to the states to levy their taxes and pay their quotas. "Will a people", spoke the address, "whose fortitude and patriotism have excited the admiration of Europe, languish at the bright dawn of triumph, and endanger the public happiness by a selfish parsimony?" "For our own part", Congress asserted, "we have left nothing unessayed to render the operations of the war more vigorous and successful." It did not behoove Congress to confess to its constituents its own shortcomings; especially when the shortcomings of the states were so much more reprehensible. Congress had strenuously urged, the address asserted, the states alone could execute. It remained therefore for "an enlightened people, who know how to estimate the blessings for which we contend", to give to the measures recommended by Congress their full and seasonable effect.

Individual delegates added their own appeals, often with pertinent comment. The Connecticut delegates, for instance, wrote to Governor Trumbull (January 16): "The existence of a power (if it can be called such) constituted for national purposes, especially for directing the affairs of a war, not possessing any constitutional authority to command the smallest portion of property, is scarcely conceivable." There ought to be, the delegates went on to say, "a power vested in such as superintend national affairs to raise a revenue from such property as cannot with convenience nor advantage be subject to the controul of any particular State, and thereby extend public credit by establishing a revenue purely national." They wondered at the same time whether sentiments of this kind might not be thought improper. One of these delegates, Jesse Root, spoke a few days later (January 29, 1781) even more pointedly of "the miseries that flow from a want of system in government", of "that ruinous policy which influenced Congress to divide out to the different States the prosecution of the war". On the same day James Duane wrote to Washington in a similar tone.

The day is at length arrived [said he] when dangers and distresses have opened the Eyes of the People and they perceive the Want of a common head to draw forth in some Just proportion the Resources of the several Branches of the federal Union. They perceive that the deliberate power exercised by States individually over the Acts of Congress must terminate in the common Ruin; and the Legislature, however reluctantly, must resign a portion of their Authority to the national Representative, or cease to be Legislatures.

Duane had spoken of having exceedingly at heart the completion of those measures on which Congress was just then earnestly engaged, namely, the establishment of the chief civil departments under single executive heads, and "the procuring to Congress an augmentation of power and permanent Revenues for carrying on the War". Duane no doubt realized more clearly than most men in Congress that the impost measure, about to be sent forth for its trial among the states, would fall far short of furnishing Congress the full amount of needed revenue, and, what was more, that it certainly would not afford to Congress the full measure of power that was requisite for its purpose. Evidently also Duane had reached the conclusion that the people were at length more favorably disposed toward an augmentation of the powers of Congress than had been the case a few short months before.

Not so very long ago the suggestion that Congress petition the states for an enlargement of its powers was dismissed as wholly inadvisable, mainly for the reason that the states were too jealous of their freedom, sovereignty, and independence to share a modicum of their powers even with their own Congress. Similarly a proposal, as lately as the beginning of September, 1780, that extensive powers be conferred on the commander-in-chief encountered the scornful retort that, in the distressful situation of the country, such "frequent Maggots about creating Omnipotencies" were of course to be expected. Near disaster was indeed at last compelling the realization that a sound, strong hub was as essential to the governmental wheel as spokes and rim.

Apart from the movement that culminated in the impost act of February 3, 1781, another movement, having for its aim the essential strengthening of the hub, had been under way at the same time. The first impetus to the movement was given by a convention of New England states at Boston in August, 1780, by that convention imparted to the New York legislature, thence to the convention assembled at Hartford in November. Both the New York legislature and the Hartford Convention next endeavored to propel their proposition into Congress, with not altogether happy results, for, as it appeared in Congress, the proposal had a rather forbidding visage.

The New York legislature had adopted, October 10, 1780, a resolution instructing the delegates of the state in Congress to declare the earnest wish of the state

that Congress should during the War, or until a perpetual Confederation shall be completed, exercise every Power which they may deem necessary for an effectual Prosecution of the War, and that whenever it shall appear to them that any State is deficient in furnishing its Quota of Men, Money, and Provisions or other Supplies required of such State, that Congress direct the Commander-in-Chief, without delay, to march the Army, or such Part of it as may be requisite, into such State; and by a Military Force, compel it to furnish its deficiency.

It was further resolved that the commissioners of the state appointed to the convention called to meet at Hartford on the 8th of November, 1780, make a like proposition to that convention. This latter instruction was but in accord with a suggestion of the Boston convention of August, whence had come the call for the convention at Hartford.

Having received advance notice of the proposed action by the New York legislature, James Duane wrote to Washington, September 19:

I find with great Satisfaction that the Legislature of New York have fallen in with the Views of the Eastern Convention and particularly to strengthen the Hands of Congress, and enable them to enforce their Decisions: We can never manage the publick Interests with Success till this Disposition becomes general.

To which Washington replied: "I share with you the pleasure you feel from the measures taking to strengthen the hands of Congress. I am convinced it is essential to our safety, that Congress should have an efficient power. The want of it must ruin us."

When the resolutions of October 10 arrived, Duane declared (November 14) that, upon the whole, they did honor to the zeal and public spirit of the legislature; yet one item gave him pause. "The Compulsory Clause", he ventured to say, "is not perhaps proper for publick Inspection." He and his colleague, John Morin Scott, were agreed on "the Impolicy of producing" the clause in Congress. There was a certain hazard in doing so. They would wait for further instructions.

Despite the care taken by the New York delegates to conceal from Congress the compulsory clause of the proposition, about a month later (December 12) it made its appearance in Congress in all its stark nakedness. For, offered to the Hartford Convention by the New York commissioners and adopted by that body, it was laid before Congress, along with the whole of the proceedings of the convention. The reaction of John Witherspoon may not have been characteristic, but it was significant.

> Though it is well known to you [he wrote to Governor Livingston, December 16, 1780] that few persons have a higher opinion of or confidence in Gen. Washington than myself or a greater desire of having vigorous executive powers put into the hands of persons at the head of affairs either in the military or civil department, yet that resolution is of such a nature that I should never give my voice for it unless you or my constituents should specifically direct it, perhaps *even not then*. . . . What could induce that Convention to recommend such a measure is a mystery to me, but I believe it will have few advocates.

Quite as explicit and fully as significant, coming as it did from one who was not a member of Congress to one who was, was the expression of James Warren in a letter to Samuel Adams, December 4, written before the proceedings of the convention had reached Congress.

> I suppose [wrote Warren] you have before this seen the doings and Resolutions of the Hartford Convention, if one of them does not astonish you I have forgot my political Catechism. surely History will not be Credited when it shall record that a Convention of Delegates from the four New England States and from the next to them met at Hartford in the year 1780, and in the height of our Contest for public Liberty and Security solemnly resolved to recommend it to their several States to Vest the Military with Civil Powers of an Extraordinary kind and, where their own Interest is Concerned, no less than a Compulsive power over deficient States to oblige them by the point of the Bayonet to furnish money and supplies for their own pay and support.

General Washington, Warren went on to say, was "a Good and a Great Man", whom he loved and reverenced; yet no man, however great or good, should be vested with such powers. Besides, no one knew what manner of man his successor might be, much less could it be known "what Influence this precedent may have half a Century hence".

In February, 1781, Congress took into consideration sundry recommendations of the Hartford Convention, for there were numerous other recommendations respecting a proper organization of the government, recommendations that Congress could soberly consider; but the proposal to employ force against a delinquent state was not one of them. Frowned upon now, the proposition would nevertheless return from time to time, only to be frowned upon again; but it did not vanish altogether until the Federal Convention found a more acceptable substitute.

In this same period when Congress was rejecting propositions that it apply to the states for an augmentation of powers, when it was refusing to try its own hand, without so much as a by-your-leave of the states, at methods carrying the implications of dictatorship, still another method of solving the problem of giving to the union a power adequate to its purpose was tentatively broached. This was the suggestion that, instead of trying to mend the existing machine, a convention of representatives of the states be brought together to overhaul the entire system. The idea was by no means new, for it had been proposed by Thomas Paine in "Common Sense", was put forward by Edward Rutledge when the first attempts were made to frame the Articles of Confederation, and had twice at least been suggested by Henry Laurens in 1779. It was the form, the manner, and the situation in which the idea was now presented that lent to it a weight and a substance that it had not hitherto exhibited.

Greatly exercised over the inability of Congress to conduct the public business efficiently because of the failure of the states to lend their complete and ready cooperation, James Duane bethought himself to stir the fertile mind of Alexander Hamilton to find a solution. Hamilton's response, September 3, 1780, was a series of constructive propositions, among them that of a convention to new-frame the Articles of Confederation. It was a long way from 1780 to 1787, but it would seem to have been directly, perhaps chiefly, from this implantation by Hamilton that the Federal Convention of 1787 eventually grew. The suggestion appears to have been pushed to one side at the time by the planners in Congress, because that body had then fixed its eyes upon the device of an impost as offering the most hopeful means of obtaining the first essentials of an economic self-sufficiency.

Whether or not it was a direct growth from Hamilton's suggestion, the idea of a federal convention was soon taking hold of the most thoughtful minds in Congress. John Sullivan may or may not have seen Hamilton's communication to Duane, but on the 2d of Octobeɪ he remarked in a letter to President Weare that Congress had become "a Body without power and the States the Several Componant parts of a Monster with Thirteen heads", and he added that the only relief in such a situation was "to Call a Convention of the Several States to Declare what powers Congress is to possess and to vest them with authority to use Coercive measures with those States which Refuse to Comply with reasonable requisitions".

When, a little later, the Hartford proceedings would be laid before Congress, Sullivan would learn that any suggestion of using coercive powers against a recalcitrant state would meet with small favor in Congress, and probably just as little elsewhere. The idea of a convention would, notwithstanding, grow both within Congress and beyond The stone which the builders had rejected would in time, even though perhaps not in due time, become the head of the corner. For instance, Thomas Paine stepped forward to remind the country of the "hint" which he had thrown out in his pamphlet "Common Sense" in behalf of a continental convention. From the distant south General Nathanael Greene wrote in the autumn of 1780 to insist that "a convention of the states" be called to "establish a congress upon a constitutional footing". In the New York legislature, General Philip Schuyler. about to become the father-in-law of Hamilton, was actively engaged in promoting the plan. Some two years later, in cooperation with Hamilton, he would renew his undertaking in behalf of a convention, although once again the project would for the time being come to naught.

In these critical days when Congress was prescribing for its own ills and begging the states for the needful curative, it is not of record that any statesman was so bold as to say unto Congress, "Physician, heal thyself!" yet it is abundantly of record that Congress was becoming aware as never before that it had long been afflicted with ailments the specifics for which were in its own possession and that no other hand could administer them. That for many of its purposes Congress was not equipped with adequate powers, every man who thought with both lobes of his brain at the same time knew well enough; but for curing the ills of its own departments the powers of Congress were adequate to the fullest degree.

Zeal for the reform of the military departments, such as those of the commissary and quartermaster, had seldom been lacking, indeed had at times risen to an intensity that called for restraint. Now and then also would come a recognition of the weaknesses of the civil departments, those immediate instruments for carrying out the decisions of Congress, and efforts would be made for their renovation and reform; but only to be held in check by the doubting and the hesitant, long the dominant element in the body politic, fearing lest, by the touch of these new-constituted instruments of power, virtue would go out of the body of Congress.

Most of the administrative arms of Congress, such as those of war, treasury, foreign affairs, and marine, having begun as standing committees of Congress, had little by little been transformed into boards composed partly of members of Congress, partly of non-members. In consequence of the fluctuating membership of Congress, with corresponding fluctuation of committee membership, the conduct of the departments, for most practical purposes, came into the hands of the non-member personnel of the boards. Still, Congress long persisted in placing members of its own body on these boards; just as subsequently Congress resisted the demands on the part of the more businesslike members to go a step further and replace the boards with executive departments having a single, responsible head.

Conviction strong enough to lead to reform came first in the case of foreign affairs, which had remained in charge of a committee of Congress, called, since April, 1777, the committee for foreign affairs. In the summer of 1779 that committee had dwindled to one man, James Lovell, who frankly wrote to Arthur Lee (August 6, 1779): "But there is really no such Thing as a *Com'tee* of foreign affairs existing—no Secretary or Clerk—further than that I presevere to be the one and the other. The Books and Papers of that extinguished Body lay yet on the Table of Congress, or rather are locked up in the Secretary's private Box."

In the spring of 1780 the status of the committee had not much improved, and Congress had long neglected to do anything about it. What is more, Mr. Lovell, as he himself more than once acknowledged, had not been very attentive to the business of the committee, even if he did somewhat boastfully assert at one time (June 13, 1779) to Arthur Lee, "Quires of my Writing have been sunk in the sea, most of it near these Capes". On the other hand, almost unashamed he wrote to John Jay, July 11, 1780: "The weather is murderous hot, and I cannot go up and down to the offices, in search of those authenticated papers, which ought to be regularly forwarded to you, and other dignified officers abroad." Certainly high time that department was overhauled. Jay pertinently replied, "One good private correspondent would be worth twenty standing committees, made up of the wisest heads in America, for purposes of intelligence."

James Duane had long before come to a like conclusion and on May 15, 1780, had moved for the appointment of a committee to report a proper arrangement of the department of foreign affairs. The committee (Lovell, William Churchill Houston, and Duane) brought in a report on June 12, but for some undiscovered reason the report was not taken into consideration until December 15. That Congress was then induced to take up the report was because of a decided rise of temperature in foreign relations. Arthur Lee and Ralph Izard had returned from abroad, each with his bag of thunderbolts; it would be a good idea, some members thought, to send a minister to Russia just at this juncture; numerous letters from ministers already abroad, particularly from John Adams, the peace commissioner, were coming in; and, perhaps not the least of the new influences, there was a desire to obtain another loan from France. Abundance of work was cut out for an actively functioning department of foreign affairs.

The interval between May 15 and December 15 had not, however, been one of idleness either on the part of Congress or of its committees. On the 29th of August, on the motion of Robert R. Livingston and Joseph Jones, two men who were not only earnest advocates of strengthening the hand of Congress but likewise of introducing order and efficiency into the work of that hand, a committee of five was appointed to report a plan for the revision and new arrangement of the civil executive departments. Besides Livingston and Jones, the com-

mittee included Lovell, John Henry of Maryland, and Timothy Matlack of Pennsylvania. Livingston and Henry were both taking forward parts in the promotion of the impost measure, and Matlack
would presently have an important share in that undertaking. Mr.
Lovell could scarcely object to some sort of reconstitution of the department of foreign affairs, which he had for some time guided, or
misguided, almost alone; but when presently the plan for reforming
that committee included the removal of Mr. Lovell's own well-worn
seat from beneath him, he went sour.

The committee of August 29 appears to have set to work immediately, and it included within its scope the department of foreign affairs,
despite the fact that a report on that department by the committee of
May 15 then lay on the table of Congress. The committee had in contemplation, so Jones later explained (to Madison October 2), "to place
at the head of the Foreign Affairs the Admiralty and Treasury some
respectable persons to conduct the Business and be responsible. . . .
We shall never have these great departments well managed until
something of this kind is done." Progress in the plan was, however,
halted by the departure of members of the committee, one after another, until only Lovell was left. In November, however, the spirit of
reform appears to have taken a new spurt, for it was just then that the
New York legislature was advising Congress to assume the needful
powers, and the admonitions of the Hartford Convention a little later
no doubt gave a further impetus to that spirit. "All Publick Departments", John Sullivan wrote to President Weare, November 15, "are
now Arranging upon oeconomical Principles. The several and expensive Navy Boards will be Abolished. The War Office and Treasury
Board regulated." Just who were at this time working at that particular problem is not clear, for the old committee on the executive departments was practically dissolved.

Just one month later (December 15) Congress took into consideration the report of June 12, drawn by James Duane, on the department
of foreign affairs, but reached no decision. On January 6, 1781, four
new members, including Duane, were added to the committee on departments, and on the 10th the report of June 12, with additions, was
adopted. The act provided for a secretary for foreign affairs, whose

chief function was to carry on the correspondence with the ministers of the United States at foreign courts and with the ministers of foreign powers, to keep Congress informed concerning foreign relations, and, in order that he might explain his reports and himself be better informed, he was privileged to attend Congress. Because, however, of factional rivalries in Congress it was not until August 10 following that a secretary was elected, when the choice fell upon Robert R. Livingston.

On January 13, 1781, the reinforced committee on departments, chiefly dominated by James Duane, made its report with regard to the other departments, whereupon Congress went into a protracted discussion of the propositions. It was not until February 6 that a decision was reached, when it was resolved to place the three departments of war, marine, and treasury under individual heads responsible to Congress. Over the first was to be a secretary at war; over the second, a secretary of marine; and over the third, a superintendent of finance. On February 20, Robert Morris was chosen superintendent of finance; on February 27, Alexander McDougall as secretary of marine; while on the 28th, for various reasons, real and ostensible, the election of a secretary at war was postponed until October 1.

Robert Morris demanded as a condition of his acceptance of the office of superintendent of finance the appointment and control of his subordinates, and it was not without much demurring that Congress finally yielded in so far as to grant control, while reserving appointment to itself. On May 14, Morris assumed the office. McDougall similarly stipulated certain conditions respecting the retention of his rank in the army, and, when Congress refused to accede, he declined the office. In July, further efforts were made to elect a secretary of marine, but without success. Then, in August, Congress created the office of agent of marine, and a little later assigned the duties of the office temporarily to the superintendent of finance. The election of a secretary at war, which had been postponed to October 1, took place October 30, resulting in the choice of General Benjamin Lincoln.

Thus, almost when the war was coming to a close, Congress at last put its principal administrative and executive business upon such a basis as, if it had been done in the beginning of the contest, would have saved that devoted body from many blunders and would have proved of incalculable advantage in the conduct of its affairs. And not the least of those benefits would have been the release of the energies of Congress from the thousand and one petty annoyances to be devoted to the weightier matters of its legislative tasks. It is not to be assumed, however, that all members of Congress had even yet been weaned from their old-time jealousies of one-man power in any place and in any form. Some who now yielded, albeit doubtfully and reluctantly, would ere long be drawn back into alliance with the unreconcilables to undo much of the good work that had, however belatedly, been accomplished. Meanwhile, the reform movement was not limited to the four principal departments, but was extended to a number of the lesser administrative groups and offices.

Just when Congress was forging ahead with unaccustomed energy toward the completion of its program of renovations and reforms came an item of news that roused the majority of its members to a pitch of enthusiasm greater probably than they had known since the news of the French treaty. It was that Maryland was on the point of acceding to the confederation. So long had that state refused to join with the other twelve in subscribing to this written instrument of their union that hope of that consummation had dwindled and all but died. Maryland, for her part, had made it unmistakably clear what the conditions of her ratification would be, namely, the cession of western claims; and, so long as those cessions were stoutly refused, just so long and so stoutly would she reject the bonds which the Articles of Confederation prescribed.

In all this time the failure to complete the confederation had been felt as a severe handicap in the conduct of the war, and a continued failure to weld this bond seemed to forebode the dissolution of even such tentative union as existed, and the ultimate collapse of every hope and aspiration for founding an American nation. So strong was this feeling that even before the accession of Delaware, there was a movement to confederate with fewer than the thirteen states. Naturally Virginia, whose western claims were the chief obstacle to Maryland's accession, took the lead in this movement and instructed her delegates, December 19, 1778, to make such a proposition to Congress. It was not until May 20, 1779, that these instructions were actually laid before Congress, whereupon the Maryland delegates drew forth instructions of their own, adopted four days earlier than those of Virginia, and laid them beside the latter on the table of Congress. The Virginia delegates thereupon denounced the Maryland instructions as an "intemperate paper", "a very extraordinary, indecent performance".

Next Connecticut came forward (May 21, 1779) with instructions (dated April 7), similar to those of Virginia, but with a definite proviso that Maryland should not be excluded. North Carolina was on the point of taking similar action, when that state appears to have been checked in the proposed course by the argument of Thomas Burke (October 31, 1779) that "such partial Confederacy may lay the foundation of disunion", that it would probably have the effect of inducing the British to a longer continuation of hostilities, that even the appearance of divided councils would lead to confusion; in short, that a partial confederacy "would destroy the old union". There was therefore small ground for hope that a confederation without Maryland could be consummated. There was likewise just as little ground for expectation that Maryland, that "froward hussey", as William Whipple had dubbed her (February 7, 1779), would not persist in her chosen course. For the time being, then, a confederation either with or without Maryland appeared to be doomed.

At almost the moment, however, when Burke was offering his counsel to the North Carolina assembly (he was then in North Carolina, having left Congress in the middle of August), a step was being taken by Congress that bade fair to make matters either better or worse. Following a debate on memorials of some of the land companies Congress recorded the opinion (October 30, 1779) that the appropriation of vacant lands by the several states during the continuance of the war would be attended with great mischiefs, and accordingly recommended to Virginia that she reconsider a late act of her assembly for reopening their land office. The measure was promoted by the Maryland delegates, and North Carolina alone among the states stood by Virginia.

The Virginia assembly thereupon adopted a "Remonstrance" (December 14, 1779), in which was expressed a hope that the Confederation would soon be "made compleat on a plan free and liberal in its principles, secured on the most solid and permanent Basis". With regard however to the state's internal government, says the Virginia assembly, "We hope to be excused when we reserve to ourselves the sole power of determining every matter relative thereto." A rather curt rejoinder, but the remonstrance does not pause there. Probably after the war has been successfully won, it continues, "other states may incline to accede to our Union, and perhaps at a future Day one or more of the larger States already united may for their own Convenience and Accommodation effect a Division and claim a right of Representation in Congress for each State so divided." Here was the most encouraging note that had yet come out of the controversy. Virginia herself might yet come to the conclusion that it would conduce to her own welfare if some part of her vast land-holdings should be divided, erected into states that should become members of the union.

Meanwhile in an unexpected quarter a small breeze had started that would presently blow an offer of land cessions right into the front door of Congress. On November 30, 1779, just one month after Congress had besought Virginia to hold up on making grants of lands until after the war, Robert R. Livingston wrote to Governor Clinton that he found "a violent inclination in most of the States to appropriate all the western Lands to the use of the United States", and he was inclined to believe that, in proportion as the states felt the weight of taxes, the inclination would increase, "till I fear it will at last overpower us, unless we make a sacrifice of part to secure the remainder". Schuyler was of like opinion and proceeded to promote the gesture in the New York legislature.

The result was the passage of an act, February 19, 1780, designed "especially to accelerate the federal alliance" by relinquishing for the benefit of the United States some part of its western lands. Schuyler came down to Congress, March 7, and laid the act before that body, which only referred it to a committee; but the effect was to cause the Virginia delegates to bring forth the remonstrance of their assembly, which they had hitherto held back, and lay that before Congress. This was on the 28th of April, 1780, nearly two months after the appearance in Congress of the New York act, and there followed another two months of silence on the matter in Congress. Finally, on June 26, 1780, the New York act, the Virginia remonstrance, together with the Maryland instructions and declaration that had been laid before Congress more than a year before (May 21, 1779), were all referred to a committee, consisting of Duane of New York, Henry of Maryland, Jones of Virginia, Sherman of Connecticut, and Willie Jones of North Carolina. The committee brought in its report only four days later, but the report does not appear to have been the subject of discussion on the floor of Congress until the 2d of September, 1780. What Joseph Jones had to say of the matter the day the report was delivered is, however, significant. To Jefferson he wrote (June 30):

The present is the season for accomplishing the great work of Confederation. If we suffer it to pass away I fear it will never return. The example of New York is worthy of imitation. could Virginia but think herself as she certainly is already full large for vigorous government, she too would moderate her desires, and cede to the united States, upon certain conditions, her territory beyond the Ohio.

He expected, he said, that the committee would report (if not then on the table of Congress, the report had actually been drawn) a recommendation to the states having extensive western unappropriated claims "to follow the example of New York and by law authorize their delegates to make the cession".

The report of June 30, which was taken into consideration September 2 and again September 6, contains as its essential feature the recommendation indicated in Jones's letter to Jefferson; but some part of the language of the report deserves emphasis as indicative of the thought that animated the advocates of the measure. The committee was decidedly of opinion that a revival of the controversies that had taken place when the Articles of Confederation were debated would not now be conducive to conciliation, therefore its counsel was

to press upon those states which can remove the embarrassment respecting the western country, a liberal surrender of a portion of their territorial claims, since they cannot be preserved entire without endangering the stability of the general confederacy; to remind them how indispensibly necessary it is to establish the federal union on a fixed and permanent basis, and on principles acceptable to all its respective members; how essential to public credit and confidence, to the support of our army, to the vigour of our councils and success of our measures, to our tranquility at home, and our reputation abroad, to our present safety and our future prosperity, to our very existence as a free, sovereign and independent people.

Congress agreed to the report, adding an earnest request to the legislature of Maryland to authorize their delegates in Congress to subscribe to the Articles of Confederation. On the same day (September 6, 1780) Jones and Madison threw an additional weight into the scales by way of a motion to this effect:

That in case the recommendation of Congress . . . shall be complied with in such a manner as to be approved by Congress, the Territory so ceded shall be laid out in separate and distinct States at such time and in such manner as Congress shall hereafter direct. . . .

That all the Lands to be ceded to the United States and not appropriated or disposed of in bounties to the American Army, shall be considered as a common fund for the use and benefit of such of the United States as have become or shall become members of the confederation according to their usual proportions or quotas of general charge and expenditure, and shall be applied and disposed of for that purpose and no other whatsoever. . . .

There was, however, as was to be expected, a proviso that the expense incurred by any state "in subduing any of the British Posts within the Territory proposed to be ceded and in maintaining Garrisons and supporting civil government therein" should be reimbursed by the Continent. This of course had reference primarily to the conquest of the northwest by Virginia under George Rogers Clark.

Joseph Jones immediately returned to Virginia to promote the measure, while Madison, remaining in Congress, endeavored to guide proceedings there to the desired goal. Referring to the matter in a letter to Edmund Pendleton, September 12, Madison expressed himself as "pretty sanguine" that the states concerned would "see the necessity of closing the union in too strong a light to oppose the only expedient that can accomplish it". Pendleton was in hearty accord with Madison.

Said he (September 25): "I would not hesitate to yield a very large portion of our back lands to accomplish this purpose, except for the reason which Shakespeare has put into the mouth of his Hotspur:

> 'I'll give thrice so much land
> To any well deserving friend:
> But in the way of bargain, mark ye me,
> I'll cavil on the ninth part of a hair.' "

Madison found that there was some hesitancy in Congress to allow Virginia her expenses in maintaining garrisons and civil government in the western territory, therefore he suggested to Jones (September 19) that the expense had been inconsiderable and was not worth insisting upon. Further, it was his view that the states, in order to guard against misapplication, might annex what conditions they pleased to their cessions.

The North Carolina delegation, for their part, took an attitude of indifference. "Maryland surely has great Merit in the present Contest", Willie Jones wrote October 1, "yet I think it will be time enough for No[rth] Carolina to deliberate on the surrender of Western Territory, when the States have vigorously supported and finally secured her in her Eastern Territory." What was weighing on the mind of Willie Jones was the recent defeat of Gates, in consequence of which a goodly part of his state was at the moment being overrun by the British army.

Congress was not slow in agreeing to the principal propositions offered by the Virginia delegates September 6. On October 10 it was resolved:

That the unappropriated lands that may be ceded or relinquished to the United States, by any particular state . . . shall be disposed of for the common benefit of the United States and be settled and formed into distinct republican states, which shall become members of the federal union, and have the same rights of sovereignty, freedom and independence, as the other states: that each state which shall be so formed shall contain a suitable extent of territory, not less than one hundred nor more than one hundred and fifty miles square, or as near thereto as circumstances will admit . . .

That the said lands shall be granted and settled at such times and under such regulations as shall hereafter be agreed on by the United States in Congress assembled, or any nine or more of them.

Touching the question of reimbursement of Virginia for expenses incurred in the conquest of the Northwest territory, that also was agreed to, with only the qualification "necessary and reasonable expences".

While Virginia was still debating the question, Connecticut came forward with a cession of territory, reserving however the jurisdiction and stipulating other conditions such as, in Madison's phrase, "to clog the cession" and "greatly depreciate it". The reservation and conditions were "the more extraordinary", declared Madison (November 28), "as their title to the land is so controvertible a one". The Connecticut act, though passed in October, 1780, was not laid before Congress until the last day of January, 1781. Meanwhile, on the 2d of January, the Virginia assembly had passed an act ceding to the United States the territory northwest of the river Ohio. The resolutions were "not precisely conformable to the recommendation of Congress on the subject", so the Virginia delegates wrote to Governor Jefferson, nevertheless they flattered themselves "that the liberal Spirit which dictated them will be approved and that the public will not be disappointed of the advantages expected from the measure." Commented James Lovell: "Virginia *seems* to give away *Something* for the good of the Union and recommends to others to do the like."

Since all these acts and resolutions were designed primarily for the persuasion of Maryland to accede to the Confederation, the next question was, what would Maryland do? Were the measures taken by three of the claimant states and Congress of sufficient weight to turn the scales? The acts of Congress of September 6 and October 10 were laid before the Maryland assembly, November 22, and a joint committee of the two houses was appointed to draft instructions to the state's delegates in Congress. Precisely what took place in the Maryland assembly during the next few weeks is not altogether clear, but it is known that there were conflicting attitudes among its members. It has been generally assumed that it was the Virginia cession of January 2 that proved to be the deciding factor in bringing Maryland to a decision; but it has recently been brought to light that there was another weight thrown into the scales just then that was probably more potent than Virginia's belated concession to Maryland's demands. This new influence was none other than a word of admonition from the French minister, Luzerne. Finding herself in some difficulties in defending the Chesapeake Bay against the British sea power, Maryland, in the beginning of January, 1781, had applied to the French minister for aid; whereupon that minister, naturally much interested in the completion of the Confederation as essential to the solidity of the American union and therefore to the solidity of the alliance, availed himself of the occasion to urge upon Maryland the ratification of the Confederation. To be sure he was venturing quite beyond his presumed diplomatic limitations; yet if he succeeded, all would be well. And he did succeed. In the closing days of January and the beginning of February the assembly passed an act authorizing the state's delegates in Congress to subscribe the Articles of Confederation on behalf of the state.

The news of what Maryland was about to do reached Congress even before the definitive measure had been taken, and it naturally gave rise to great rejoicing. At that moment not a single delegate of the state was in attendance, and it was not until February 12 that Daniel Carroll, one of the newly elected delegates, took his seat in Congress and laid the act of his state before that body. The signatures of two delegates were, however, necessary, and there must needs be a further wait. Ten days later a second delegate, John Hanson, attended, and thereupon (February 24) Congress set March 1, at twelve o'clock, for the announcement to the public of "the final ratification of the Confederation of the United States of America".

So long had the Articles of Confederation lain waiting for these last signatures, an event of such importance as their final ratification ought by all means to be surrounded with an atmosphere of dignity, even of ceremonial formality. Although Congress declined to authorize all the ceremony that some members desired, there would of course be firing of cannon (a boom for each of the thirteen states) by the artillery on land and a like *"feu de joye"* from Paul Jones's frigate, the *Ariel,* then in the harbor; there would be ringing of bells; there would be banquets and the drinking of toasts to "The United States of America"; and at night there would be fireworks to enhance their joy.

The newspapers of the city likewise would well and handsomely, as befitted them, play their parts in the celebration. Exclaimed the *Penn-*

sylvania Packet, "Thursday, the first of March, will be a day memorable in the annals of America to the latest posterity, for the final ratification in Congress of the articles of confederation and perpetual union between these states"; and the *Pennsylvania Gazette* added, "A Union, begun by necessity, cemented by oppression and common danger, and now finally consolidated into a perpetual confederacy of these new and rising States". Throughout it all there would of course be no end of handshaking and congratulation upon so glorious a consummation so long deferred—and on the morrow the wise men of Congress would once again take up their long-time endeavor to find ways and means whereby this their instrument of government might be made more adequate to the exigencies of the union.

CHAPTER XXVI

CONGRESS TAKES THE MEASURE OF ITS STATURE
SHORT BY MANY CUBITS

Prior to the ratification of the Articles of Confederation, on March 1, 1781, the Congress of the thirteen states, although it had begun as only an advisory body to the states, had been impelled by the necessities of conducting the war to assume many of the attributes of sovereignty. Such functions of a national government as it exercised were, however, mainly by general acquiescence of the states or by assent from time to time obtained. In short, Congress had not theretofore acted without authority; it was merely that the extent of its authority had been but ill defined. The main purpose of the Articles of Confederation had, in fact, been to prescribe the form of the union and to define the powers to be exercised by the common representative body.

Theoretically therefore the status of Congress was not fixed until the instrument of union had been ratified by all the thirteen states; yet in practice Congress had, in most essential particulars, restrained itself within the limitations of that instrument from the time when it was first proposed to the states. The consummation of the Confederation by the accession of Maryland did not therefore effect any important change in the conduct of the government by Congress. Only the alteration of some minor details of practice was at the time thought to be required. What made the completion of the Confederation loom so large in the mind of Congress and in the public mind as well was that the bond long since forged had at last been given its definitive welding.

There was, to be sure, some recognition in the official record of the entrance upon a new régime. On February 28, 1781, all matters before Congress were "referred over, and recommended to the attention of the United States in Congress assembled". For, "The United States in Congress Assembled", a title drawn from the Articles of Confederation, was now to be the official designation of the body hitherto entitled simply "The Congress". Nevertheless it was the same Congress as before, composed of the same members, continuing to serve under prior elections. There was no new organization of any kind, not even the election of a new President. President Samuel Huntington continued his occupancy of that office with never a question of change. On July 6, President Huntington asked to be relieved on account of ill health, whereupon (July 9) a successor, Samuel Johnston of North Carolina, was chosen. On the following day Johnston declined the office, and Thomas McKean of Delaware was elected.

In one particular Congress did find it immediately necessary to give recognition to a requirement of the Confederation. Whereas under the old régime a single member might, if his state so directed, give the vote of his state, according to the Articles a state could not be represented by fewer than two members. It so happened that New Hampshire and Rhode Island had but one delegate each in attendance, therefore those states would be without effective votes. Accordingly, on the 2d of March, the delegates of those two states offered a motion that Congress adjourn to the first of June, constituting a committee of the states (in which one delegate might give the vote of his state) to sit in the interval. "The question", says Thomas Rodney, "passed off without a Division." It was, however, the general opinion of Congress, so Rodney further records, "that those Members might Continue to sit in Congress and Debate and Serve on Committees tho they Could not give the Vote of their States".

This endeavor of Congress to adjust itself to the Articles of Confederation led to a discussion (March 3, 4, and 6) of two other questions: One was whether the three-year term of a member, as prescribed by the Articles, should include his service prior to March 1 or only thereafter. Again no definite decision was recorded, but Rodney asserts that it was "the general sense of Congress that the Term of three years intended Should Commence with the Confederation". The second question was, what number of states in Congress were competent to do business? For measures of certain kinds, according to the Confederation, no fewer than nine states were competent; but what number should constitute a quorum in other cases? "This", says Rodney, "brought on a long and Learned Debate", so long, in fact, that mem-

bers became "tired out" and came to the tentative agreement that no
business would be undertaken except when nine states were represented, and would adopt no measure but with the assent of seven
states. Two months later (May 4), when general rules were adopted, a
quorum of seven states for ordinary business was established.

The problem of adjusting itself to the new situation, of confining
its activities within the metes and bounds now definitely marked, was
not therefore one to cause Congress much worry; what did give Congress deep concern was the clear impossibility of doing a national task
unequipped with the requisite national tools. For those tasks it must
needs be implemented; and that need was, if possible, more clearly
recognized after the adoption of the Confederation than it had been
before. Accordingly the echoes of rejoicing had scarcely subsided when,
on a motion of Varnum of Rhode Island and Root of Connecticut,
two of the strongest and most persistent advocates of enlarged powers
for Congress, a committee was appointed (March 6) to prepare a plan
to invest Congress "with full and explicit powers for effectually carrying into execution in the several states all acts and resolutions passed
agreeably to the Articles of Confederation."

On its face this action would not appear to have had in view any
amendment to the Articles, but rather to probe the question whether,
within the Articles, it were possible to implement Congress with a
power to enforce its own resolutions. The committee, which consisted
of Varnum, Duane, and Madison, all three supremely interested in
the object aimed at, was ready with its report within six days, and four
days later (March 16) laid the report, drawn mainly by Madison,
before Congress.

In one particular this report, because of two opinions therein set
forth, has a significant bearing upon our subsequent constitutional
history. One opinion was to the effect that the thirteenth article of the
Confederation contained an implied power in Congress to enforce every
provision of the Confederation; and a second was that, notwithstanding this implication, it was "most consonant to the spirit of a free
Constitution that on the one hand all exercise of power should be
explicitly and precisely warranted, and on the other that the penal
consequences of a violation of duty should be clearly promulged and

understood". The committee therefore recommended the proposal of an amendment to the Articles of Confederation authorizing Congress, in the event that a state should refuse or neglect to abide by a determination of Congress made in accordance with the provisions of the Confederation, "to employ the force of the United States as well by sea as by land to compel such state or States to fulfil their federal engagements". It was not until May 2 that Congress took the report into consideration on the floor, but expressions on the subject at large by individual members in the interval indicate the trend of sentiment and, to some extent, the clashes of opinion.

At the outset Thomas Burke had warned that any attempt so soon after the adoption of the Confederation to claim for Congress powers "not expressly given by that Charter" or to pervert it to increase their power, "would give a dreadfull alarm to their Constituents who are so jealous of their Liberty". John Mathews, in a letter to Governor William Livingston of New Jersey (March 6), expressed the hope that the new constitution would be the means of introducing a clearer understanding between Congress and the states, and anticipated "the most happy consequences"; nevertheless he presently proposed that the states be asked to vest Congress with the power to make and execute any laws deemed necessary for the prosecution of the war. John Sullivan was as firmly convinced as any that Congress ought to have more power, yet he was not very hopeful of results, even if the power should be granted; for it was his opinion, so he wrote to Washington (March 6), "that the old Members Should be in Heaven or at Home before this Takes place".

On the day that his committee made its report (March 16, 1781), James M. Varnum wrote to Governor Greene that, if Congress approved the committee's recommendation, as he hoped, and if the states then acquiesced, at least "the willing States would be greatly relieved." Writing again to Governor Greene, April 2, he was less hopeful:

The Articles of Confederation [he wrote] give only the Power of apportioning. Compliance in the respective states is generally slow, and in many Instances does not take Place. The Consequence is, Disappointment, and may be fatal. In the second Place, an extreme, tho perhaps well-meant Jealousy, in many Members of Congress, especially those of a long Standing, seems to frustrate every Attempt to introduce a more efficacious System. Prudent Caution against the Abuse of Power, is very requisite for supporting the Principles of republican Government; but when that Caution is carried too far, the Event may, and probably will prove alarming.

In this same letter Varnum reveals that the idea of a constitutional convention, set definitely in motion in the preceding September, was gaining strength.

If [said he] the kind of Government sufficiently energetic to obtain the Objects of Peace when free from invasion, is too feeble to raise and support Armies, fight Battles, and obtain compleat Victory, I know of but one eligible Resort in the Power of the United States. That is to form a Convention, not composed of Members of Congress, especially those whose political Sentiments have become interwoven with their Habits, from a long Train of thinking in the same way. It should be the Business of this Convention to revise and refraim the Articles of Confederation; To define the aggregate Powers of the United States in Congress assembled; fix the Executive Department, and ascertain their Authorities. Many other matters, subservient to these general Ideas Would come before them, and their Powers should be extensive in point of Ratification; But the System to be by them adopted should expire at a given or limited Time.

The recommendation of such a plan, he thought, would have to come from one of the states. It was unlikely that Congress would take the initiative, for it would probably "affect some Gentlemen in a Tender point". The mere mention of the three-year limit to membership in Congress as provided in the Articles of Confederation "offends them extremely".

John Mathews was in much the same mood as Varnum. There appeared to be no disposition in Congress, he wrote Washington (April 16), to remedy its own weakness. On the contrary, "Whenever the subject is brought forward, men seem to shrink from it as if the case was desperate." Thereupon he breaks forth, as was his wont, in impassioned speech:

And clear I am, in my opinion, that unless some effectual, vigorous, and decisive measures are speedily taken, to extricate us from the labyrinth of difficulty and distress into which we are at present plunged, all the generous blood that has been spilt in this glorious contest will have been spilt in vain, and the spirits of those who have nobly fallen will stalk through our land, seeking vengeance on those who have so infamously suffered their children to become slaves.

Just one month after the committee report had been laid before Congress Madison sent a copy of it to Jefferson (April 16) and solicited his views. Madison acknowledged that the committee had posed a very delicate question but argued at some length for the measure. The necessity, he wrote, of arming Congress with coercive powers arose from the shameful deficiency of states most capable of furnishing their apportioned supplies, while some of the less capable were in consequence exhausted by the military exactions of the enemy and our own troops. Moreover, he added, without such powers in the general government "the whole confederacy may be insulted and the most salutary measures frustrated by the most inconsiderable state in the union". The expediency of making the application to the states would of course depend on the probability of their complying with it. Still another important question was, what means Congress might employ in the exercise of such a power. He suggested that a small military force, "acting under civil authority", might easily accomplish the purpose; but a more efficacious mode, he thought, would be the use of the naval power against the trade of the recalcitrant state.

On the same day (April 16), Joseph Jones, then at home in Virginia, also wrote to Jefferson on the subject. Jones was as firmly convinced as was Madison that it was "indispensably necessary for the general welfare in time of war, that the Congress should be vested with a controuling power over the States sufficient to compel obedience to requisitions for Men and Money apportioned agreeable to the Rules laid down." Without such a power, he declared, "I know . . . we shall be a rope of sand and the Union be dissolved". Two questions in particular, however, disturbed him. One was, how a disobedient state should be punished; the other was whether it would not be better to obtain from the states a "voluntary declaration". "Such a Recommendation coming from Congress", he suspected, "wo[ul]d excite fears in the States, that there was a disposition in Congress to grasp dangerous powers."

Speculations of the sort were rife amongst the members of Congress before ever the committee report was taken from the table for debate. When this was at last done (May 2), the report was immediately referred to a grand committee, that is, one member from each state. When the grand committee brought in its report, July 20, every trace of a proposed coercive power in Congress had disappeared. What the grand committee proposed was that it be recommended to the states to pass laws empowering Congress to lay embargoes in time of war, but for a term not exceeding sixty days (this was but the revival of a proposition that, in one form or another, had been frequently made in the past); that moneys collected by the states in fulfillment of their quotas be "vested specifically" for the use of the United States; and that such taxes be paid by the collectors to persons appointed by Congress. The grand committee was thereupon discharged, and a new committee of three (Randolph, Ellsworth, and Varnum) was appointed "to prepare an exposition of the Confederation, a plan for its complete execution, and supplemental articles".

Unlike its two predecessors, this committee, whose report was laid before Congress, August 22, did not fasten its eyes upon the one problem of equipping Congress with much needed powers, but allowed its vision to sweep a rather wide field. To be sure, it began by asking to be excused from the exposition of the Confederation, because such an exposition, if coextensive with the subject, would be altogether too voluminous, and, besides, the omission to enumerate any powers of Congress would become an argument against their existence. Nevertheless the committee did indulge itself in the suggestion of twenty-one particulars in which the Confederation required execution, and seven additional powers that the states should be requested to grant to Congress.

The twenty-one particulars are of especial interest, for the reason that, in considerable part, they anticipate provisions of the Constitution of 1787. The twenty-first and last of these specifications, however, is more directly applicable to the committee's immediate problem, for it calls for "providing means for animadverting on delinquent States"

In its list of seven additional powers that Congress ought to possess, the committee answers the question it had raised by proposing that Congress be authorized "to distrain upon the property of a State delinquent in its assigned proportion of Men and Money". Other desired powers for Congress were: to lay embargoes in time of war without any limitation; to prescribe rules for impressing property; to appoint collectors of taxes imposed in accordance with the requisitions of Congress and to direct the mode of accounting for them; to admit into the federal union a part of an existing state, with the consent of the dismembered state; to stipulate with foreign powers for the establishment of consular service without reference to the individual states; and to vary the rules of suffrage in Congress, but with the proviso that, in determining certain important questions, the voices of two-thirds of the states shall be necessary.

As a sort of preamble to these recommendations, the committee declared that a general council is a necessary organ of the republic and that without the extension of its powers as suggested, "War may receive a fatal inclination and peace be exposed to daily convulsion." So elaborate a report and one to which so much thought had evidently been given would seem to deserve careful consideration by Congress, and it was made an order of the day "for to Morrow". There is, however, no record of its ever having been debated at any time. All that was salvaged from all these reports was a resolution adopted November 2, recommending to the states that the taxes laid for the payment of their quotas of money that day assigned be an item separate and distinct from any taxes for state purposes, and that they be paid to the commissioner of the federal loan office or to such person as the superintendent of finance might designate. For this request there was an excellent reason; for some of the states, having collected the taxes laid expressly for their quotas, had straightway appropriated the funds, in part at least, to their own use. Congress had asked for bread and had been given a stone.

One reason no doubt why Congress hesitated in its supplications to the states was that it had one important petition, that of February 3, 1781, then before them and thought it best to await the result of that before piling up other pleas for new powers. If Congress could then have known that ultimately, after waiting an exasperatingly long time, the modest request for power to levy import duties would be turned down, perhaps there would have been urgent requests for other grants of powers. In any event it was known well enough that it would at best be months before all the states could or would take action on the measure, and that financial problems would meanwhile be daily knocking at the door. Accordingly on the same day (March 6) that Congress set out upon its quest for additional power, it was resolved that three days of each week should be devoted to the subject of finance, "until the United States in Congress assembled, shall have come to a final decision on that subject". What Congress meant by *final* was doubtless any kind of financial plan that would offer a fair promise of tiding the country over the immediate difficulties.

To the dismay of Congress, a ghost thought to have been laid just one year before had reappeared upon the scene, riviving old anxieties and stirring new fears. In short, the whole plan of March 18, 1780, had gone awry. Those new emissions, every dollar of which was supposed to drive forty of the old emissions scurrying into oblivion, had encountered obstacles to their victorious march, and, when they did appear, had exhibited an unexpected feebleness for their appointed task. As perhaps ought to have been foreseen, the measures taken by the several states in carrying out the provisions of the plan were about as various as the states, each pursuing the course that its own exigencies or interests seemed to demand, whether in the redemption of the old money or the issuing of the new. One particularly disturbing result was that the states fixed various rates of exchange between the old and the new, which offered a magnificent opportunity to speculators; and the speculators were not slow to make use of it, gathering up the old bills where they were cheap and rushing them into other states where the exchange was higher. The speculators were swift, but the bills, in their headlong plunge, were ofttimes swifter. At the beginning of March, 1781, the rate of exchange was about 75 for one. A month later the old money had sunk to 135 for one and was continually sinking, while the new money, such of it as had actually been issued, was dragged downward with the old.

On April 8, 1781, Samuel Johnston of North Carolina wrote to

James Iredell, "Never was a poor fly more completely entangled in a cobweb than Congress in their paper currency. It is the daily subject of conversation in that body; but our situation is so very intricate and delicate that I have as yet heard no proposal that is not subject to numberless objections." Another month and the rate had gone to 225 for one. New Jersey attempted to fix exchange at 150, Pennsylvania at 175; but they might as well have tried to whistle down the wind. Every effort to check the fall apparently accelerated it. The effect of the Pennsylvania declaration, so Madison wrote to Jefferson, May 5, "has been a confusion among the people of this City approaching nearly to tumult, a total stop to the circulation of the old money, and a considerable stagnation and increased depreciation of the new." Three days later the Virginia delegates were writing Jefferson that depreciation of old Continental had swept on downward "from two hundred to seven, eight, and some say nine hundred for one"—had in fact thumped the bottom, while the new seemed about to share the same fate. "Very great convulsions and Dissatisfaction in this city" wrote Samuel Johnston the same day; "old continental dollars . . . still lie prostrate, nor is there the least probability of their ever rising."

Serious as was the situation, so serious that by May 5 traders were shutting up their shops, and the jailer even refused to take Continental money for a glass of rum, there was still a residue of good humor in Philadelphia, and one of the manifestations of it was the oft-told story of the inhabitants sticking Continental money in their hats "by way of cockades" and parading the streets, accompanied by a dog which they had smeared with tar and covered with a blanket of Continental bills. The disastrous swiftness of the fall is well illustrated by an instance related by Witherspoon. His son-in-law had sold some property in Virginia for paper money, amounting to "several thousand pounds", and before the money could be transported to New Jersey "it perished in his hand in one Week".

There was of course, as Johnston of North Carolina testified, no dearth of plans for the restoration and support of public credit. On March 16, Congress had recommended to the states the repeal of all tender laws, only one member of twenty-seven voting having given a negative voice. Such repeals were necessary, otherwise a debtor, provided he could overtake his creditor and hem him in a corner, could compel him to accept a handful of worthless paper in payment of the obligation. On the same day the states were called upon for their quotas of one and a half million dollars, payable quarterly, and Congress agreed to accept bills of the new issue at specie value.

A month later (April 18, 1781) a committee that had been appointed in February brought in a statement of the amount of the public debt and an estimate of the expenses for the current year, together with a historical résumé of the efforts of Congress to solve its financial problems, efforts almost invariably defeated by the "unpunctuality of the states" in complying with requisitions, or by machinations of the enemy. It was, for instance, asserted that the failure of the states to carry out the plan of March 18, 1780, was chiefly responsible for the present difficulties. The report concludes by emphasizing the necessity of the states immediately granting to Congress the duties on imports and prizes requested by the act of February 3, in order that Congress might have a permanent fund for meeting urgent requirements. One proposition of the committee, even though it failed to meet the approval of Congress, deserves attention; this was a recommendation that wheat or flour or beef be made the standard instead of money.

Among the various "schemes of finance" (a favorite phrase) were two, offered by Oliver Wolcott and Meriwether Smith, respectively (April 12, 1781), that gained such a degree of recognition that they were put into the form of ordinances and passed the first reading (April 25). Both plans were, in the main, elaborations upon that of March 18, 1780, but Smith's scheme in particular proposed a new emission of ten million dollars in bills of credit, with provisions for their redemption. In view of the act of March 18, however, any plan of redemption proposed by Congress was not likely to restore public confidence. Smith, with sublime confidence in his scheme, appended to it the admonition, "Let Congress adopt and pursue this plan and be great and happy." The majority of his fellow-members evidently chose, however, to achieve greatness and happiness by pursuing some other course.

In one particular the two proposed ordinances contain an identical

provision, namely, a provision for a form of compulsion upon a delinquent state, in the event of refusal or neglect on the part of a state,
without sufficient reason assigned, to comply with a requisition. In
such an event, it is provided that "a remonstrance shall issue under the
sign manual of the President of Congress for the time being, and
under the seal of the United States", against the delinquent state, demanding full payment of arrears at a day certain; if the state should
still refuse or neglect to comply, "a *prohibition* shall thenceforth issue
against the commerce both by sea and land of such delinquent State
or States . . . and the same shall be continued until full payment be
made as aforesaid, and justice duly rendered to the United States".
Congress had hitherto indicated a certain skepticism with regard to the
employment of force against a delinquent state, therefore it is not to
be wondered at that a like skepticism existed respecting the efficacy
of sign manuals, seals, remonstrances, and verbal prohibitions. The
formula for the solution of that particular conundrum was yet to be
discovered.

The proposals of Wolcott and Smith having been found unacceptable
(they were never given a second reading), the committee of ways and
means proceeded in its search for a method that would be acceptable
and possibly efficacious. Since the states neglected or refused to remit
their quotas, perhaps the end could better be accomplished by drawing
drafts on the states at one month's sight. This the committee proposed,
May 14, and on May 22 it was adopted, together with the forceful
statement that the states were expected to direct their treasurers to
accept those orders as soon as presented and to take effectual measures
to pay them punctually as they became due. During the course of the
discussion it was proposed to add the words, *"in real efficient money,*
that is to say, either in silver and gold, or in paper money equivalent
thereto"; but only three states, Pennsylvania, North Carolina, and
Georgia, were in favor of so rigid a requirement, and the words were
stricken out. In lieu of them, Congress contented itself with informing
the states that all calculations had been made "in solid coin", and with
the admonition that "any further delay in complying with the requisitions of Congress must prove ruinous". There was the further recom-

mendation that, if any laws yet existed making paper bills a tender, such laws be repealed; for experience had "evinced the inefficacy of all attempts to support the credit of paper money by compulsory acts".

On the same day that the committee of ways and means made this report (May 14), Robert Morris, recently elected superintendent of finance, gave in his acceptance of that office. As previously pointed out, Morris had insisted upon having the appointment of his subordinates as well as the control of them, since without that power it would be impossible, he maintained, effectively to execute the duties of his office. Congress was prevailed upon to grant to Morris the designation of the places to be filled and the control of all persons acting under him, but reserved the actual appointments to itself. Nothing short of desperation would probably have induced Congress to go as far as it did in entrusting its finances to one man. The dread of one-man power, particularly in the domain of finance, was in fact still so great that Morris's election could be recorded as "unanimous" only by virtue of the fact that the Massachusetts delegates, Samuel Adams and General Artemas Ward, declined to vote. That others had yielded despite their fears is evidenced by such expressions as that of Thomas McKean, who wrote (July 3) to Samuel Adams (then absent): "There are some amongst us, who are so fond of having a great and powerful Man to look up to, that, tho' they may not like the name of King, seem anxious to confer kingly powers, under the titles of Dictator, Superintendant of Finance, or some such, but the majority do not yet appear to be so disposed." In time, when it again appeared that Congress might somehow or other get along without a financial dictator, these critics would combine to depose Morris, even at the risk of demolishing the fair structure that he had erected.

The superintendent of finance began his task in the confident hope that, with a fair measure of cooperation on the part of Congress and the states, he would be able to bring some sort of order out of the existing financial chaos; but he afterwards declared that, although the aspect of affairs was anything but promising at the time, even so, "appearances were more favorable than the reality". For one thing, he appears not to have reckoned sufficiently upon the utter impossibility of prevailing upon the states to comply with the requisitions of Congress—and upon requisitions almost solely the whole financial structure had rested and continued to rest. The most facile pens in Congress, with Washington's persuasive logic added, had thus far failed to induce the states to a ready compliance; and now Morris was to find that the utmost of his powers of appeal would bring only meager results.

On the other hand, the disposition in Congress for a time was one of hearty cooperation, despite an occasional note of criticism. What a relief it was to have the tremendous burden of responsibility lifted in so great a measure from their own shoulders! Now they could just leave it to the superintendent of finance; he would find a way, if way could be found. This new arrangement might prove to be the salvation of the country. Unfortunately perhaps many came to regard Robert Morris as a sort of superman who could perform miracles of finance. Not so General Washington, who, always realistic, was wise enough to perceive that even Robert Morris possessed no "magic art", although he might "recover us by degrees from the labyrinth into which our finances are plunged".

Morris's first proposal was the establishment of a national bank, which he expected would be of especial assistance to him in the conduct of his financial operations. The plan was drawn up May 17, 1781, three days after he had entered upon his duties, was laid before Congress May 21, and was approved by Congress on the 26th, with the promise of support, including a charter of incorporation; yet it was not until the last day of the year 1781 that Congress adopted an ordinance for the incorporation of the bank. The delay had occurred mainly in consequence of doubts on the part of a good many members whether Congress was possessed of powers competent to incorporate such an institution. Finally, when subscribers to the bank insisted upon the fulfillment of the Congressional promise of incorporation, Congress was placed in a dilemma. On the one hand, says Madison, there was a recognition of the importance of the bank, while on the other was a supposed want of power and an aversion to assume it. "Something like a middle way", Madison explained to Edmund Pendleton (January 8, 1782), "finally produced an acquiescing rather than an affirmative vote. A charter of incorporation was granted, with a recommendation to the States to give it all the necessary validity within their respective jurisdictions." It had also been recommended to the states, when the project was first approved, to provide that no other bank or banker be permitted to operate in the state during the war, and it was further resolved that the notes of the bank would be receivable in payment of all taxes, duties, and debts to the United States.

On the 7th of January, 1782, the bank was opened for business. Before many months there would be attacks upon the bank and attacks upon the superintendent of finance by a group in Congress; but in midsummer, when the bank had been in operation only six months, the Connecticut delegates could write the governor (July 29, 1782): "The Financier's notes and bank bills are in full credit and paid on sight, and are rather preferred to money by the merch[an]ts here."

Events could not wait, however, on the slow maturing of the plan to establish a bank. At the moment of Morris's acceptance of the office of superintendent of finance had come a letter from General Washington setting forth that the army was again in a desperate condition for want of provisions. He had appealed particularly to the eastern states and had sent General Heath thither to endeavor to have the needful supplies, particularly beef-cattle, forwarded promptly. Unless that could be done speedily and regularly, he wrote to President Weare (May 10, 1781), "our posts cannot be maintained, nor the army be kept in the field much longer". Congress made its own urgent request of the states from New Hampshire to Pennsylvania (May 14), and President Huntington forwarded the resolution with a scolding letter of his own, besides stating bluntly that unless the states immediately sent forward supplies of provisions, of which it was known there was abundance in the country, the army would of necessity disband.

Here was work cut out for the superintendent of finance, and he applied himself to the task with characteristic energy. Convinced, as were Washington and most thoughtful members of Congress, that the system of specific supplies was inordinately extravagant and wasteful, he proposed to do away with the system, in so far as possible, and return to a cash basis. He found that at the very time when the army was in dire need supplies were lying here and there over the country perishing, but that the cost of their transportation to places where they were needed might alone be more than they were worth. Accordingly, in the beginning of June, Morris sought and obtained from Congress authority to dispose of these supplies for cash or by exchange, and a few weeks later he obtained authority to supply the army by contract. To adopt a cash basis was almost tantamount to resorting to the use of hard money, and this Morris sought by every means in his power to obtain—by borrowing at home, by importation through commercial transactions, and by means of his personal credit.

In the close of May, 1781, France had come to the rescue of the United States with a subsidy of six million livres turnois, mainly to be used for the purchase of clothing, arms, and stores in France, but some part of which was to be in cash at the disposal of Congress. The French minister suggested that this latter fund be entrusted to the superintendent of finance, and that was done (June 4). By these means Morris was enabled to relieve the country of its most serious embarrassments.

These new assurances from France had come in the nick of time. Early in April, Washington had written to John Laurens, who had been sent to France to solicit further desperately needed aid, "If France delays a timely and powerful aid in the critical posture of our affairs it will avail us nothing should she attempt it hereafter . . . it may be declared in a word, that we are at the end of our tether, now or never our deliverance must come." That members of Congress, that patriots everywhere, did not despair, is scarcely short of marvellous. From the beginning of the struggle, members of Congress, with probably few exceptions, had year after year deluded themselves with the belief that one more campaign would bring the contest to a fortunate conclusion, and the spring of 1781, despite the general gloom that enveloped them, was no exception. Somehow hope persisted, and whatever the difficulties, however grievous the failures, there were always a few members of Congress who never threw up their hands in despair, but strove on to find a way out of the morass of defective methods, of state negligence, of popular indifference.

Essential as was aid from France, Washington in particular had again and again warned the country against depending too greatly upon the exertions of our ally; and, although it sometimes seemed as if his warning fell upon deaf ears, as if even Congress was not always fully alive to the necessity for America's doing her own part, in this crisis a rallying note runs through most of their utterances. John Sullivan, for example, alluding to probable negotiations for peace, wrote to Washington, May 28, 1781, "we are called upon to make our last desperate Struggle to pave the way to that peace and Independance for which we have so long contended"; and he expressed a faith that Congress and the states would "exert every nerve at this critical moment". Said the New Hampshire delegation, writing to President Weare the next day: "We are now upon our last Campaign; if vigorous Exertions render it Successful we Shall Sit down Quietly in the Enjoyment of that Independance for which we have so Long contended but if Languid Efforts render our attempts unsuccessful we are ruined past relief." Washington himself, more hopeful now, in view of the promised aid from France, and encouraged in some degree by the better spirit arising in America, wrote to John Mathews (June 7), "We must not despair; the game is yet in our own hands; to play it well is all we have to do. . . . A cloud may yet pass over us . . . but certain I am, that it is in our power to bring the War to a happy conclusion."

The assurances of aid lately offered by France to enable Congress to act with greater vigor were indeed encouraging, but there were other assurances from the same source at the same time that were not a little perturbing; for the French minister had brought it to the attention of Congress (May 26, 1781) that the anticipated mediation by the courts of Russia and Austria on the basis of *uti possidetis* had actually been proposed; that the overtures had been eagerly embraced by Great Britain, that France had withheld full acceptation until the concurrence of her allies, the United States, could be obtained, but might later find it necessary to enter into the negotiations conditionally in behalf of the United States as well as for herself. It was therefore of great importance that Congress should at once decide upon the instructions to be given to the plenipotentiary of the United States for the negotiation of peace.

What especially perturbed Congress was the proposal that the negotiations were to be on the basis of *uti possidetis,* that is to say, on the basis of Great Britain retaining such parts of America as were then in her possession. At that moment the British forces were in control of the greater part of Georgia, much of South Carolina, some part of North Carolina, and also of New York City and vicinity, to say nothing of occupancies of lesser importance. Here was a danger to be averted, one that called for every ounce of exertion in the country's power, and for all the wisdom of all her statesmen.

First of all, Congress deemed it essential to lay the situation plainly before the individual states, which was done in a confidential letter June 1. The letter as first drawn up was from the hand of John Mathews of South Carolina, whose state was one of those vitally concerned, and it contained, as might be expected, a vigorous protest against having "obtruded upon us . . . the hard necessity of acceding to these overtures at a time when these states are in a less eligible situation to enter the negotiations for peace, than at any other period of the war." The clause was, however, rejected for one, not without force and vigor indeed, yet carrying a less pessimistic note. The states were besought to place the country "in such a situation as to enable our negotiators to speak a firm and decided language, becoming the character of the ministers of free, sovereign and independent states". "Congress have not a doubt in their minds", said the letter, "but that each State in the union is determined to support the Confederacy that has been so solemnly entered into, through every difficulty, and hand it down unimpaired to their posterity."

The clearing of all parts of the union of British occupation was not, however, the only problem that confronted Congress and the states; there was, besides, an especially delicate question which the French minister had posed for Congress: Would the plenipotentiary of the United States for the forthcoming negotiations be instructed to consult the ministers of France at all points and, what was especially crucial, conform to the advice of those ministers? The debate over the instructions ranged over a good many days, revolving about a variety of forms as well as the substance of their content. Two requirements were laid down as essential, namely, that the independence and sovereignty of the thirteen states should be effectually secured, and that the treaties with France should be left in their full force and validity. As for boundaries and other questions, it was decided to be "unsafe at this distance" to tie up the negotiators "by absolute and peremptory directions".

Along with the particular question that he had posed, Luzerne offered renewed assurances "that his Majesty will defend the cause of the United States as zealously as the interests of his own crown". That seemed to demand corresponding assurances on the part of Congress; accordingly the ministers for the negotiation of peace were instructed "to make the most candid and confidential communications, upon all subjects, to the ministers of our generous ally the king of France; to undertake nothing in the negotiations for peace or truce, without their knowledge and concurrence", and otherwise to rely upon his Majesty for support of whatever might be necessary for the security and future prosperity of the United States. So far very good, but still not quite up to the mark desired by Vergennes, whose instructions Luzerne was endeavoring to carry out. Accordingly Luzerne obtained a reconsideration of the instructions and the addition of the clause: "and ultimately to govern yourselves by their advice and opinion".

This addition was not, however, carried without vigorous opposition by a minority of Congress—all the delegates of Massachusetts, Rhode Island, and Connecticut, with two of Pennsylvania, and one of Virginia—nine out of the twenty-seven members voting. One-third of Congress was unwilling to subject the negotiators to the "leading-strings" of France. One of them, James Lovell, would confide his mortification to John Adams, but he must use caution; he must shroud his words in cipher. He may as well have kept his thoughts in his bosom, for Adams appears never to have been able to come at his meaning. "Blush! Blush! America", he spluttered; "Consult and ultimately concur in every thing with the Ministers of his Most Christian Majesty, the Independence of the United States according to the Tenor of our alliance kept sole ultimatum!"

The instructions were finally adopted on June 15, 1781. Already, on June 11, it had been decided to join two persons to John Adams for the negotiations of peace with Great Britain, and on the 13th, John Jay had been chosen as one of them. Then, on the 14th, before the second person to be joined to Adams had been designated, it was decided to add still two others, bringing the commission to five in number. Accordingly there were now three additions to be made to the commission, and the choice fell upon Franklin, Henry Laurens, and Jefferson. In part, Congress was actuated by a predilection for numbers as against a single individual for any purpose; but in large part this multiple commission was the outcome of factional rivalries and personal jealousies and suspicions. The known dissatisfaction of the court of France with John Adams likewise had its influence.

These instructions seemed to have an air of finality for the peace negotiations; yet, before the summer had ended, the project of mediation for which they were especially designed had proved to be but a bubble that had burst even while it was blown. Whatever hopes therefore had been inspired by the promised peace negotiations, flickered and vanished. Not so, however, the fears; for the instructions were to have another day in the court of Congress, again to be vigorously contested, and were destined eventually to perturb the peace negotiations, almost to their undoing.

CHAPTER XXVII

OUT OF THE DESERT INTO THE PROMISED LAND

YORKTOWN

In the beginning of September, 1781, John Laurens, who had been sent as a special envoy to France to solicit aid, returned with precious supplies and precious money and precious promises of more to come. Congress lifted its head high and walked proudly. "The affairs of the States", wrote Richard Howly of Georgia, "never bore so prosperous an appearance as at present."

What was far more thrilling, at that very moment Congress caught a glimpse of coming peace, not a peace by concession, not a peace through mediation, but a peace won by victory over the foe. For in these first September days the army of General Washington and the troops of our ally came marching through the streets of Philadelphia, pressing on into Virginia in the hope of a final triumph over the enemy. Cornwallis was down there in a corner, and if they could only trap him!

As from the State House door members of Congress watched the procession of the French troops, they received the royal salute, and their bosoms swelled with a pride they had not known for seven long years. The gentlemen of the Congress made the best response they could, they doffed their hats. Declared one of them: "The engaging figure and behaviour of the officers of all ranks, their dress, the cavalry, musick, arms, artillery, the figure and behaviour of the privates, and the uniform motion of the whole, afforded the most pleasing prospect of the kind I ever saw." If Mr. Samuel Livermore's goose quill squeaked a bit, it should be ascribed to his enthusiasm.

Members of Congress could know but little what was in the minds of the military chieftains, but from what they saw and what they could learn as the days passed swiftly by they could shrewdly guess what portended and where; and as news of fleets of enemy and of friend from day to day drifted into their ken, they became acutely aware that sea power also was destined to play an important part in the coming drama. "We are at the eve of great events", wrote President McKean (September 4), foreseeing a probable contest at sea: "May God grant them to be prosperous to us, and that they may terminate in securing to us, peace, liberty, and safety." Events ripened rapidly, and one of them, the junction of the two French fleets, was of auspicious import. Cornwallis would probably be penned between the French and American armies, on the one side, and the French naval forces on the other. And so it proved, and swiftly came the consummation.

Yorktown is not far from Philadelphia in terms of miles, but in terms of eighteenth-century travel it is a long, hard journey, requiring four to six days for expresses to travel the distance that lay between. On the 16th of October word came to Congress through private channels that Cornwallis had offered to capitulate but had been refused. On the same day came the joyful news of Greene's victory at Eutaw Springs in South Carolina on September 8. Followed five days of anxious waiting; then, at three o'clock on Monday morning, October 22, an express rode into Philadelphia with the message that on the 19th Cornwallis and his entire army had surrendered. At eight o'clock Elias Boudinot learned the news, whereupon he straightway broke open a letter he had written to his wife the day before and added a brief postscript to tell her of the glorious victory and to offer up a prayer of thanksgiving: "God be praised!" Two days later came Washington's official despatches, whereupon it was immediately resolved,

that Congress will, at two o'clock this day go in procession to the Dutch Lutheran church, and return thanks to Almighty God, for crowning the allied arms of the United States and France, with success, by the surrender of the whole British army under the command of the Earl of Cornwallis.

On the other side of the Atlantic, when the news of the surrender came to Lord North, he is said to have exclaimed over and over again: "It is all over! It is all over!" If that utterance could have speedily reached the ears of members of Congress, it would have given them a degree of assurance for the future that their restricted knowledge did not permit them to feel. Nevertheless it was the almost universal conviction in America that Yorktown marked virtually the end of the long struggle. "If these severe doses of ill fortune do not cool the phrenzy and relax the pride of Britain", Madison wrote to Edmund Pendleton, October 30, "it would seem as if Heaven had in reality abandoned her to her folly and her fate. . . . it seems scarcely possible for them much longer to shut their ears against the voice of peace." Until, however, there should be definite assurances of peace, the army must be maintained, Congress must continue at its appointed tasks.

It is needful to take note here of an incident, of no great national importance of itself, but one concerning which much has been written and upon which some unsubstantial claims have been based. On the morning of October 23, 1781, that is, the day following that on which he had been aroused from his slumbers to receive the glad tidings from Yorktown, President McKean offered his resignation, reminding Congress that, at the time of his election, he had given warning of the necessity for his retiring from the presidency in October at the latest. Congress at once accepted the resignation and set the next day for the election of his successor. Then Mr. John Witherspoon bethought him that the Articles of Confederation had provided for a federal year to begin on the first Monday in November, and that to abide by that provision a new president should then be elected. He accordingly moved that Mr. McKean be requested to continue in the chair until that time. The motion was unanimously adopted, Mr. McKean continued to preside through Saturday, November 3, and on Monday morning, November 5, Congress chose John Hanson of Maryland to be president. Hanson was accordingly the first of the presidents of Congress to begin his presidential service at the beginning of the federal year provided for by the Articles of Confederation. He was not, however, as has been maintained, the first president to serve under the Confederation, since both Huntington and McKean had served since the adoption of the Articles.

Quite in the dark as to how the present campaign would terminate, in mid-summer Congress had set about, as usual, to make plans for the ensuing campaign, and to that end decided (July 26) to despatch a committee (Carroll, Bland, and Varnum), together with a member of the board of war and the superintendent of finance, to headquarters to determine upon the arrangement of the army for the ensuing year. In addition to questions respecting enlistment and matters pertaining to regulations, an important problem was whether the good of the service might permit a reduction in the force, in order to curtail expenses. Just as these conferences started, however, plans for the march to Yorktown were quietly under way, and directly the army was in motion.

When the Yorktown undertaking had been completed, to the immense relief and deep satisfaction of Congress, of the army, and of the country at large, General Washington came on to Philadelphia and was thereupon given an audience in Congress (November 28), in order, as Secretary Thomson informed the General, "to give you a farther testimony of the high esteem they have for your person and services and to communicate their intentions respecting provisional measures for the next campaign." At the audience Washington was more particularly informed through the president that it was the expectation of Congress that he would remain for some time in the city to give his aid to the committee "appointed to state the requisitions necessary to be made for the establishment of the army." The interrupted conferences were thereupon resumed.

By this time there was a secretary at war to take part in formulating plans; for, after much squabbling, Congress had elected General Benjamin Lincoln to that office on October 30, and on November 26 he had indicated his acceptance. The decision of Congress (December 10) was that it was inexpedient to make any material alterations in the arrangement fixed upon in October, 1780, but, as it was learned that deficiencies existed in the quotas of the states as called for by that arrangement, the states were urged, "in the most pressing manner", to complete their quotas by the first of March following, and that new enlistments be for three years or during the war.

Whatever the size of the army, means must be found to support it, if it were to be kept together. A decision to this end had already been taken on the 30th of October, which was to call upon the states for their respective quotas of eight million dollars, to be paid quarterly, beginning April 1, 1782. The quotas were fixed November 2, this time including all thirteen states, and on the same day, as noted in the preceding chapter, the states were urged to make their levies of taxes for federal purposes separate and distinct from any taxes for state purposes, as they were likewise requested to pass laws requiring collectors to pay the funds into the hands of certain officers of Congress. The long-standing controversy over the rule by which the quotas were established was again stirred, but for the time being it was squelched, only to be resumed in greater earnest a few months later.

The superintendent of finance had meanwhile been struggling with might and main to make ends meet. To drag the cumbrous financial machine through the crucial period of the Yorktown campaign had taxed his abilities to the utmost, but by dint of extraordinary efforts he had succeeded. Washington had deemed it of great importance that his own army be given one month's payment in specie, for there had been grumbling, even as the soldiers marched through Philadelphia; and there was need of hard money for secret services besides. Some part of those needs, twenty thousand hard dollars, Morris was able, by means of his personal pledge, to borrow from the French military chest, until the money brought by John Laurens could be transported from Boston. Enthusiasm over the Yorktown victory had loosened voices and set bosoms to vibrating, but it failed to loosen purse strings or induce the states to relax the tight fist for the benefit of their union.

In the early part of 1782 Morris found his further progress practically blocked by a stonewall of negligence and indifference on the part of the states. Perhaps the banishment of fears by Yorktown had something to do with this indifference. Exasperated, the superintendent of finance, on February 11, laid the case before Congress in a statement of such unusual frankness and vigor that members of Congress, inured as they were to situations such as Morris portrayed, must have been stunned as they sat and listened to the reading of that extraordinary report.

Some of the states, said the superintendent of finance, had not yet taken any action on the request of Congress on February 3, 1781, for a grant of import duties for federal purposes; accordingly no provision had yet been made for the payment of interest on the public debt. Declared Morris, "Those, therefore, who trusted us in the hour of distress are defrauded." Under such circumstance, to expect that others would confide in the government would be folly; "and to expect that foreigners will trust a government which has no credit with its own citizens would be madness". He had hoped, after the brilliant successes of the last campaign, that additional funds might be obtained from France; but he had been repeatedly assured by the ministers of France that no further pecuniary aid would be extended; and as for loans from other European powers, that delusion had already passed away. Our reliance then must be upon ourselves. But what was the prospect? "I would to God that I could say that there were even the appearances of general vigor and execution." So far as he could learn not a single state had laid the necessary taxes to comply with the requisition of the second of November for eight million dollars. "There appears to be no solicitude anywhere for the support of arrangements on which the salvation of our country depends."

Morris did not of course fail to understand where the chief weakness lay. While the Confederation, he declared, had conferred on Congress "the privilege of asking everything", it had secured to each state "the prerogative of granting nothing". What moneys the states would grant and when they would grant them was "known only to Him who knoweth all things". This shameful negligence had "marked us to a proverb, while all Europe gazed in astonishment at the unparalleled boldness and vastness of claims blended with an unparalleled indolence and imbecility of conduct". For his part, nevertheless, he would not be deterred from endeavoring to wake those "who slumber on the brink of ruin", and he was not disposed to be particularly delicate in the mode of his waking. Supported by Congress he might perhaps do something, but without that support he would be but a useless encumbrance. Strong language this to be spoken to Congress by one of its own officers, but his ineffective appeals to the states had convinced him that it was no time for soft steps and soothing words.

Knowing that Morris had spoken solemn truth, unsavory though it was, Congress was deeply impressed and appointed a committee to confer with the superintendent of finance, the commander-in-chief, and the secretary at war, and to draft another of those inevitable appeals to the states. Perhaps five members of Congress could amongst them find language keen enough to penetrate the thick shells of state somnolence.

Daniel Carroll first tried his hand, producing a long factual but force-ful account of the backwardness of the states and of the pain that Con-gress had suffered therefrom. When, however, it was made to run the gauntlet of Congress, it was so badly broken and bruised that another committee was assigned the task of putting its pieces together and dressing it up in acceptable form. But that committee also failed to find favor in the sight of Congress; its proposed address was rejected, and Congress appears to have decided that it was a hopeless under-taking. Undiluted truth was too harsh for state ears, too strong for state stomachs.

The first of April, 1782, came and went and not a single quarterly installment of the eight millions called for the preceding autumn had been paid. Accordingly on May 16, Morris wrote another circular letter to the states, wherein he observed that, with the exception of five thou-sand five hundred dollars just received from New Jersey (less than one twenty-second part of the quarterly installment of the state's quota), not a shilling had been paid in for the services of the year 1782. The states, he complained, had been "deaf to the calls of Congress, to the clamors of the public creditors, to the just demands of a suffering army, and even to the reproaches of the enemy, who scoffingly declare that the American Army is fed, paid, and clothed by France." What was worse, there was danger that the army would have to subsist itself or disband.

Having written the letter he reflected that he might be exposing a situation that was all too delicate for general knowledge, and he took counsel with a committee of Congress. It was the opinion of the com-mittee, and Congress agreed, that, since the circumstances of the several states were different, it would be to better that members of Congress be deputed to make personal representations to each of the legislatures. Accordingly Morris's letter was suppressed, and two members (Rut-ledge and Clymer) were despatched to the southern states, except South Carolina and Georgia, and two (Montgomery and Root) to the eastward for the purpose. So critical was the situation that an effort was made to keep the whole affair in impenetrable secrecy—not with com-plete success.

In the beginning of June, while the two deputations were making their rounds of the legislatures, the superintendent of finance reported that the payments from the states had scarcely amounted to twenty thousand dollars, barely sufficient for one day's expenses. Nor was this the end of the story of glaring deficiency. On July 1, when 4,000,000 dollars should have been received from the states only a paltry 50,000 had been paid in, and on September 1, of the 6,000,000 then due only 125,000 had been received. Meanwhile the superintendent of finance not merely was encountering the grumbling that was to be expected, but was being subjected to a campaign of sniping from the faction that had always been hostile to a one-man dominance of public finances. Madison, among others, endeavored to parry the attacks on Morris. "Every member in Congress", he wrote to Edmund Pendleton, June 4, "must be sensible of the benefit which has accrued to the public from his administration; no intelligent man out of Congress can be altogether insensible of it."

On June 27, Rutledge and Clymer returned to Congress, bringing hopeful promises from Delaware, Maryland, and Virginia (they did not venture into North Carolina, because the legislature had adjourned), and "the strongest assurances" from the President of Pennsylvania. On July 18 the northern deputation reported that all the legislatures to the eastward "gave assurance that the several objects . . . should be attended to with that seriousness and despatch their importance demanded", yet none of them, so far as the committee could learn, had actually adopted the desired measures. Contrariwise, the committee discovered, several of the states that had laid taxes for their quotas were appropriating the proceeds to their own use. This had been done before and ought to have occasioned no surprise, but it shocked Mr. Montgomery into a complete revolution of his attitude. If the ground was to be trodden over again, he confided to Madison, he would take a very different part in Congress. He and Mr. Root nevertheless carefully refrained from inserting any reference to this state of affairs in their written report. Altogether the outcome of the visitations had not been very encouraging.

Accordingly, on July 22, Congress appointed a grand committee to report upon the most effectual means of supporting the credit of the United States. Before the committee had finished its explorations it

would have joined with the superintendent of finance in fixing the
attention of Congress upon the public lands as the source of salvation;
meanwhile Congress continued to look forward hopefully to the adoption by all the states of the impost measure of February 3, 1781. Those
hopes were strengthened on July 15, when it was learned that Maryland, the eleventh state, had acceded to the proposition, leaving only the
states of Rhode Island and Georgia as delinquents.

Georgia, long in possession of the enemy and only occasionally represented in Congress, was all but out of the reckoning. Rhode Island
therefore appeared to hold the key to the situation. Hitherto the delegates of that state (Varnum, Mowry, Ellery, and Cornell) had been
favorable to the measure, particularly Varnum and Mowry, who had
written to Governor Greene (August 14, 1781) that they were at a loss
to conjecture the reasons that had induced the state to delay complying
with that request of Congress. "It must be obvious", they said, "that
unless we can call forth the Resources of the respective States equally,
it will be impossible to execute any great Object, while the states who
do most will be the greatest Sufferers." On September 4 following, the
delegates repeated the inquiry to their governor, adding that not a
farthing had been paid into the treasury by any state, except Pennsylvania, for more than a year.

Whatever may have been the causes of Rhode Island's hesitancy in
the summer of 1781, in the year that ensued a new and dominating
personality had arisen in Rhode Island politics, and that dominating
personality David Howell had become a delegate in Congress. Howell
had taken his seat on June 7, 1782, soon to be followed by Jonathan
Arnold, who, for the most part, appears to have taken his cue from his
colleague. Howell, whose position in most particulars was at the farthest extremity of the doctrine of state rights, had lost no time in making
clear his hostility to all centralizing measures, and in particular occupied
himself with breathing denunciation against the impost measure and
all its kind. In early September it was learned that the Rhode Island
legislature had adjourned without taking action on the impost measure.

Not quite ready to give up hope, but because exigencies were pressing, Congress resolved (September 10, 1782) to make an emergency
call upon the states for one million two hundred thousand dollars, "as

absolutely and immediately necessary" for the payment of the interest on the public debt. What ground Congress could have had for expecting a new requisition to be paid while former requests remained unheeded it is difficult to understand; yet the characteristic scramble of nearly every delegation to shift part of its state's quota to some other state seemed to indicate a belief that real money was involved. The old device of last resort, drawing bills of exchange on Europe, so it seemed, was out of the question. There were no funds in Europe on which to draw and not likely to be any, for all expected funds had already been anticipated.

Just at that moment of deep anxiety, however, came word from John Adams that he was negotiating a loan in Holland. That good fortune gave to Congress such a fillip of elation that it straightway resolved to borrow four millions in addition to the loan Adams was negotiating, pledging "the faith of the United States of America" therefor. It was almost inevitable that these loans, like other foreign loans and aids, should be made use of before they were actually available. "Our Army is extremely clamorous", the North Carolina delegates wrote, October 22: "we cannot pay them—we can hardly feed them. There is no money in the Treasury and we are obliged to draw upon the Foreign Loans before they are perfected." "Never", these delegates declared, "was an army worse paid than they have been and are, to say nothing of the clothes and rations."

In the midst of its serious pondering how to make ends meet, Congress paused on Monday, November 4, as in obedience to its constitution it must do, to choose a new president and to indulge in a few other formalities presumed to be requisite to the inauguration of a new federal year. Among these formalities was the reading of credentials and recording the names of those in attendance. The credentials themselves are evidence that some of the states had not yet, in the terms for which their delegates were chosen, conformed to the provisions of the Confederation; but, however much the states might disregard the injunctions of their instrument of union, Congress must be obedient thereto. The choice for president was Elias Boudinot of New Jersey. Remarked Madison, with a touch of sarcasm, "The principle of rotation, altho' in no instance less proper, is applied with great firmness to the one in question by the states which have not yet filled the chair of Congress or which least expect a turn on any other principle."

The Holland loan, by a curious coincidence, was destined.to play a part in Howell's campaign against the impost measure; destined, in fact, to turn the spotlight on that gentleman in a manner much to his discomfort. On October 10 that grand committee which, since July 22, had been investigating ways and means of supporting public credit recommended that Congress call upon the states of Rhode Island and of Georgia for an immediate definitive answer whether they were going to comply with the request of Congress for power to levy an impost duty of five per cent; and the only nays to the question were from the two Rhode Island delegates and the one from Georgia.

No sooner, however, had Congress despatched its demand than the Rhode Island delegates followed with a counter plea (October 15), wherein the delegates waxed long, warm, and eloquent. "The object of a seven years war", they wrote, "has been to preserve the Liberties of this Country, and not to assume into our own hands the power of governing tyrannically." They would therefore quicken the governor's memory and awaken his feelings. Defeat the impost measure without fail, they counseled. "Should it once be adopted, the fatal dye is cast—it is to us irrevocable. Let no man therefore Vote in its favor with a single remaining doubt. . . . 'He that doubteth is damned if he eat'."

Among the evil results of the measure would be "a numerous train of Officers concerned in the Collection and after management of the revenue, the Tribes of half-pay Officers, Pensioners, and public credi-tors, whose number and influence might be increased from time to time at the Pleasure of Congress, would enlarge, extend and increase their power". The next step would be to add the land tax, the poll tax, and the excise, then the "bond of union" would be complete. Yes, the "Yoke of Tyranny" would be fixed on all the states, "and the Chains Rivotted". Moreover, that "great System of Government", the Con-federation, had pointed out the method of ascertaining the quotas of the states, and the equity and justice of the mode was not contested. Finally the delegates appeal to the legislature to reject the impost measure and thereby "preserve the Liberties of the United States and transmit them to posterity", at the same time erecting for themselves "a Monument more durable than brass".

This endeavor was of course quite within the rights and privileges of the delegates. The next day, however, Howell wrote a private letter in which he revealed more concerning the projected foreign loan than, under the injunction of secrecy, he was privileged to reveal. The loan John Adams was negotiating, he declared, "fills as fast as could be expected". Further, "Our foreign Affairs are in a good Train", and such is the credit of the United States that "they have of late failed in no Application for foreign Loans". That Howell should have made statements so utterly at variance with the facts as other members of Congress interpreted them, was astonishing enough; but when he went further and spoke of a secret proposal of Sweden to enter into a treaty, it was a direct violation of his pledge of secrecy. Other members of Congress had lapsed at one time or another from a strict regard for that injunction, but Howell's indiscretion presently became public; wherefore he thereupon found himself on the grill.

In the interval it was learned unofficially that the lower house of the Rhode Island legislature had, in the beginning of November, flatly refused to accede to the impost measure, whereupon Congress set about an effort to convert that stubborn little state, by voting to send thither (December 6) a deputation to intercede with the legislature. It was not until December 22 that the deputation set out for Rhode Island, and it had not gone far when it learned that Virginia had repealed her act of accession to the measure and that Maryland was about to do the same. The deputation therefore sadly retraced its steps to Philadelphia. And that was the end of nearly two years of hopes and endeavors.

It was on that same December 6 that the attention of Congress was called to a publication that not only was injurious to the finances of the United States, but involved the national character and the honor of Congress. This, as it turned out, was that letter of David Howell in which he had been all too free with the secrets of Congress, to say nothing of his misrepresentations of fact. Howell was from the first suspected of being the writer of the letter, but not until he was cornered did he acknowledge its authorship. Then, in a motion (December 18) which was seconded by his colleague, Jonathan Arnold, Howell endeavored to defend his conduct, taking refuge mainly under the provision of the Articles of Confederation that permits, as Howell explained, *"freedom of speech and debate in Congress,* and of course a free communication of such speeches and debates to their constituents, by the members of Congress, without being accountable to that body for the propriety of what is said, debated or communicated"; in short, that Congress had no power "to call any member of their body to account for any information which he may think proper to communicate to his constituents (the secrets only of Congress excepted)".

Howell was, in fact, taking his stand essentially on the same ground as that taken by Thomas Burke in April, 1778. Just as in Burke's case, Congress could do little else than administer to the gentleman from Rhode Island a severe rebuke; but that rebuke they were resolved to administer by transmitting to the governor of Rhode Island, a record of the proceedings, together with a statement of facts respecting applications for foreign loans and their results. This decision was reached on December 20, and on January 4, 1783, the secretary for foreign affairs, Robert R. Livingston, transmitted to the governor such a statement as completely controverted Mr. Howell's assertions.

Some indication of the mood into which Congress was thrown by Howell's conduct may be gathered from Madison's remarks in his notes of debates, December 18. Referring to Howell's motion and defense Madison declares:

The indecency of this paper, and the pertinacity of Mr. Howell in adhering to his assertions with respect to the non-failure of any application for foreign loans, excited great and (excepting his Colleagues or rather Mr. Arnold) universal indignation and astonishment in Congress; and he was repeatedly premonished of the certain ruin in w[hi]ch he w[oul]d thereby involve his character and consequence; and of the necessity w[hi]ch Congress w[oul]d be laid under of vindicating themselves by some act which would expose and condemn him to all the world.

For his part, Howell seemed to be glad enough to escape from his tormentors and return to Rhode Island, but the defection of Virginia placed him in a position to gloat over his chief critics and to deflect some part of the wrath of Congress from the smallest of the states to the most powerful. The causes of Virginia's defection meanwhile remained shrouded in mystery. Even the governor had known nothing of the movement for repeal until the act was laid on his table after the adjournment of the assembly. He was mortified over the act, but he could do naught but acquiesce. Madison besought Edmund Randolph to probe the mystery. "Many have surmised", he wrote to Randolph (January 22, 1783), "that the enmity of Doctor Lee against Morris is at the bottom of it"; and Randolph was convinced that such was at least one of the influences, although "the fatal repeal" was "wrapped up in more than common mystery; the motives being various as assigned by different persons". One of the reasons given, "that Congress ought not to raise a revenue by other means, than those prescribed in the confederation", was closely related to one of Howell's objections, namely, that it was unconstitutional. "Virginia", Madison went on to say, "could never have cut off this source of public relief at a more unlucky crisis than when she is protesting her inability to comply with the continental requisitions." He hoped that the state would yet be made sensible of the impropriety of the repeal and would make amends by a more liberal grant. Congress could not abandon the plan so long as there was a spark of hope.

The spark of hope for that particular measure had pretty well gone a-glimmering, nevertheless another trial would presently be undertaken, although by means of a measure of somewhat different character. The discouragement over that failure was increased by another at almost the same time. The idea of making the western lands a source of federal funds had long been floating around in a good many minds and now and then had been put forward, only to be pushed to one side for the best of reasons: Congress must first get possession of those western lands before they could be converted into available funds.

In fact, the suggestion that the western lands might be utilized for meeting federal obligations was an afterthought. Far transcending the financial aspects of the question and fundamental in the movement to obtain from the claimant states cessions of their western lands to Congress was the bearing that such cessions would have not only upon the relations of the states within the Union but upon the whole future of the United States. A fair beginning toward the solution of the problem was thought to have been made in the cessions of New York, Connecticut, and Virginia, sufficiently promising to induce Maryland to enter the Confederation; but conditions attached to those cessions were far from satisfactory to most of the other states, and the ink of the Maryland signatures to the Articles of Confederation was scarcely dry when efforts were begun to obtain modifications of those conditions.

The subject had numerous phases and complications, not the least of which were the claims of certain land companies, which served to confuse the councils of states and of Congress. For another thing, the claims of the states themselves were overlapping and varied greatly in validity. Questions of right and expediency likewise had their parts in the controversy. The states without such claims naturally pressed for cessions the most extensive and the least hampered by reservations and conditions. On the other hand, the claimant states were just as eager to conserve their own interests, to salvage of their holdings what they might with wisdom, or to utilize their claims as *quid-pro-quos*. The Virginia claim, being the most extensive and the most encumbered with claims of land companies, naturally gave rise to the sharpest and most prolonged controversy.

It was to this complicated aspect of the problem that Congress mainly addressed itself, although at wide intervals, during the greater part of the year 1781. First posed (May 14, 1781) by the committee of ways and means, as a general question whether Congress would fix and guarantee a western boundary to each of the states, then "declare the remainder the property of the United States as a fund of credit for their common interest and the general defense", the subject was taken up by a committee appointed to report upon the cessions of Virginia, New York, and Connecticut. It would be inexpedient, said the committee (June 27), to accept those cessions in the form offered, but recommended that Congress adopt resolutions of the tenor proposed by the committee of ways and means. By this time memorials from some of the land companies were troubling the waters, and attention became focused upon the character of the several claims and the deficiencies of the cessions, to the exclusion of the plan of utilizing these lands as a source of federal funds. On October 2 a further report offered by the committee, containing the additional recommendation that the ceded lands be laid out in separate states, was referred to a new committee. Between the latter committee and the Virginia delegates a warm controversy arose, chiefly respecting the Virginia title, a controversy that was carried to the floor of Congress and there produced a stalemate in the whole business. A report from that committee (November 3) recommended the acceptance of the New York cession and the rejection of those of Connecticut and Virginia, upholding the validity of New York's title and maintaining that the New York cession covered the territory proposed to be ceded by Virginia. The committee's decisions with regard to the claims of land companies were likewise obnoxious to the Virginians. The prospect of a harmonious adjustment of the controversy therefore seemed more remote than ever.

At all events the subject remained in a state of coma until April 16, 1782, when the report of November 3, 1781, was again taken into consideration. Both the Virginians and the New Yorkers had grown anxious to have the question settled, the Virginians that their assembly "may not again be left in uncertainty on that subject", the New Yorkers because they needed the acceptance of their cession to aid them in their contest over Vermont. Preliminary to a discussion of the question two of the Virginia delegates, Arthur Lee and Theodorick Bland, endeavored to obtain a requirement that every member of Congress should declare upon his honor whether or not he was personally interested in the claims of any of the land companies; but they were unsuccessful, as were Bland and Clark of New Jersey in a similar effort May 1. The report of November 3 was, however, now for the first time spread upon the Journal, although its consideration was postponed that day and again on May 6. The attempt to bring on the subject, Madison wrote to Randolph May 1, "produced all the perplexing and dilatory objections which its adversaries could devise". In particular, western cessions and the Vermont question had become badly entangled, inducing some strange political consortings. One more stalemate. To persist longer in fruitless applications to Congress, declared Madison, would be inconsistent with the self-respect of the delegates and the dignity of their state, therefore the assembly would certainly "be fully justified in taking any course with respect to their western claims, which the interest of the state shall prescribe".

This controversy, which had lasted almost exactly a year, had been initiated by a proposition that the western lands ought to be made a source of funds for the payment of the public debt; and it was a like proposition that was to bring the question again upon the carpet. On July 22, 1782, as previously mentioned, a grand committee was appointed to examine into ways and means of supporting public credit, and on July 31 the committee recommended as a first essential step to that end that Congress decide on the cessions of Connecticut, New York, and Virginia. This report coincided closely in point of time with a report from the superintendent of finance, dated July 29, discussing at length and from numerous angles the country's financial problems and possibilities and emphasizing the back lands as a fruitful source of funds. The latter report was laid before Congress, August 5, and referred to the committee just mentioned, who had probably already discussed the subject with the superintendent of finance. When the report of July 31 was offered, a motion to set a day for taking it into consideration was lost, but on September 4, the grand committee again offered its recommendation, although in a somewhat different form, namely, "that the western lands if ceded to the U.S. might contribute towards a fund for paying the debts of these States."

Thereupon a debate arose whether to accept the cessions of Virginia, New York, and Connecticut with the conditions named in the cessions, or to ask those states to reconsider their acts of cession with a view to making them conform to the recommendations of Congress, September 6 and October 10, 1780, while at the same time states that had made no cessions were to be asked to take the question under consideration. A set of resolutions to this effect was proposed (September 6, 1782) by Witherspoon and Howell, together with another, pledging that the determinations of states respecting private property and claims of land within the cessions should not be altered without their consent. The matter was referred to a committee of five (Witherspoon, Madison, Rutledge, Osgood, and Montgomery), who, on September 25, offered those precise resolutions as their report. The report failed of passage, however, and the subject was held in abeyance for another month. During the discussion Madison had written to Edmund Randolph (September 10): "Every review I take of the Western territory produces fresh conviction that it is the true policy of *Virginia* as well as of the United States to bring the dispute to a friendly compromise"; and he hoped that, if the decision of the state on the claim of the land companies could be saved, her other conditions would be relaxed.

The North Carolina delegates, Williamson and Blount, on the other hand, were not so ready to part with their western lands. "The smaller States", they wrote to Governor Martin October 22, 1782, "and some of the larger ones are extremely desirous to do something with the backlands. Their eyes are so eagerly fixed on those forests that they seem to stumble over the more obvious and productive subjects of Revenue which are nearer at hand." The debate on the subject, they continued, had only been dismissed for the present; it was certain to be revived whenever the northern and minor states should be better represented. "And as those lands are likely to prove the subject of warm and obstinate contention", they ventured to admonish the governor, "it may be proper to consider whether there is any middle path by which the State may equally consult its honor, its interest and the public peace."

The prediction of the North Carolina delegates was not long delayed in fulfillment. On October 28, Carroll of Maryland offered a motion that the cession of New York made March 1, 1781, be accepted, and on the 29th it was so resolved, the only negatives being Virginia, with Osgood of Massachusetts, Blount of North Carolina, and Rutledge and Gervais of South Carolina. On the following day Williamson of North Carolina and Bland of Virginia endeavored to have a proviso inserted that the resolve accepting the cession of New York should not be interpreted as operating to prevent the determination of any dispute concerning territory between New York and any other state or states; but the motion failed to obtain the requisite votes of seven states.

In a letter to Randolph, November 5, Madison gives an explanation of the proceedings. It was the outcome, he said, of a coalition of the middle states with New York, and the policy appeared to be to proceed from the vantage ground gained by the acceptance of the New York cession to a demand upon Connecticut and Virginia for amendments to their cessions. That Connecticut joined the coalition was a surprise to everybody, even to the Connecticut delegates themselves, who, after they had had time to reflect, so Madison asserted, "would gladly have revoked their error". As for New York, that state had, by good fortune or skillful management or both, "succeeded in a very important object: by ceding a claim which was tenable neither by force nor by right she has acquired with Congress the merit of liberality, rendered the title to her reservation more respectable, and at least dampt the zeal by which Vermont has been abetted."

Once again therefore the cessions of western claims, whether for the purpose of creating new states and enlarging the union or with the more immediate objective of making those lands a source of much needed funds, was brought for the time being to an impasse, although neither objective had by any means been given over as hopeless. One of the Delaware delegates, Samuel Wharton, writing to the council of his state, January 7, 1783, concerning the proceedings upon the acceptance of the New York cession, spoke with a degree of gratification of the manner in which he and his colaborers had, "by Assiduity, and private Arguments, deduced from Justice and policy, and corroborated by historical Truths", succeeded in removing the objections of some of the members of Congress until at length they prevailed, to the great irritation of the minority. It was their intention, he said, to press their advantage still farther, but the necessary withdrawal of the Connecticut delegates to attend the trial between that state and Pennsylvania prevented. For one thing, they were waiting for recruits to some of the delegations; for another, "There are many new Delegates in Congress, who are much uninformed upon the Subject of the vacant, and unappropriated Lands at the Revolution, and Therefore it is judged imprudent to make for firm and decissive Measures concerning Them, until proper Discussions have been *previously* had." The magnitude of the object, he declared, demanded that Congress should terminate the controversy with all prudent despatch, otherwise, he was persuaded, "They will have abundant Cause to deplore their Neglect".

The case of Vermont, sometimes called the New Hampshire Grants, had in its earlier stages been for the most part dissociated from the question pertaining to the western lands but had finally come to have a direct bearing upon the western problem in so far as that problem involved the erection of new states out of the territory proposed to be ceded to the United States. Beginning as a revolt from New York, it soon developed a dispute between that state and New Hampshire in particular, with Massachusetts involved to a minor extent. Having early in the war (1777) declared their independence, with the name of New Connecticut, the revolters sought admission to the union as a distinct state, but because of the vigorous opposition of New York to its own dismemberment, Congress could scarcely do otherwise than shy away from the problem. New York naturally wished to have the support of Congress in curbing the revolters and persistently pressed it upon that body to take some decisive step in the matter. In this effort New York was so far successful that, in September, 1779, Congress was prevailed on to "pledge their faith" that, if the disputant states would refer their differences to Congress, Congress would determine the questions according to equity and would support their decisions in the premises. The first of February, 1780, was set for the hearing, but when the time came around, Vermont was the only party to the controversy that was ready for the trial; and Vermont was ready only with an offer to become one of the states of the union and with a refusal to submit her independence to Congress.

It had now become a case of Vermont against all the rest, Congress included. The case was to be tried under the provision in the Articles of Confederation, which made the presence of nine states necessary; but when at last the states concerned were ready, Congress was unable to muster the requisite nine states. For once Congress was not disposed to grumble over deficient representation; there was no desire in that assembly, except among the interested parties, to fish in the Vermont pond; just as likely as not the catch would be a small war, and Congress had war enough on its hands already. New York continued nevertheless, from time to time, to make "the most warm and pressing representations" to prevail upon Congress, as the only body that could preserve the peace of the Confederacy, to come into some pointed resolutions censuring the Vermonters for their contempt of authority.

In the autumn of 1780 the affair was even uglier than before, for Vermont itself became involved in antagonistic factions. Madison, convinced that it was no longer possible for Congress to resort to "evasive expedients", sought (September 16, 1780) to have Congress lay down the fundamental principle "that every attempt by force to set up a separate and independent jurisdiction within the limits of any one of the United States, is a direct violation of the rights of such State, and subversive of the union of the whole, under the superintending authority of Congress". From the 12th of September the debate raged fiercely for nearly a month, when suddenly the independence party of Vermont threw into the Congressional camp (October 6) a bomb of the nature of an ultimatum. If Congress, the Vermonters in effect declared, are unwilling to receive us, there are other hovering wings beneath which we may find a welcome refuge. It was time for Congress to scamper to safety. The debates, James Duane presently reported (October 7), "took a Turn most injurious to New York"; whereupon, from pushing the matter "almost beyond the bounds of modesty", as one delegate declared, the "Yorkers" became quite willing to keep hands off for the present. Vermont had become a hot iron, and everybody hastened to drop it.

Instead of cooling, however, the Vermont business became hotter. For one thing, the Vermonters began to make encroachments upon New York on the one side and New Hampshire on the other, in consequence of which New Hampshire became as eager as New York to have Congress come to the rescue by fulfilling its promise of September, 1779. But a more potent argument than either New York or New Hampshire had been able to devise was suddenly brought to bear upon Congress by Vermont herself. The Vermonters had before dropped intimations that they might make their peace with Great Britain, and in July, 1781, came evidence that they were actually in negotiations with the agents of the British government.

Apart from all other arguments, many members of Congress now became convinced that there was need for a decision, and a quick one too, before Great Britain should be enabled to drive this dangerous wedge into the states. Accordingly on the 7th of August, Congress came to a resolution to enter into negotiations with Vermont concerning the terms of admission to the union, while at the same time offering guarantees to New York and New Hampshire with regard to boundaries. Just a week later agents of Vermont appeared bearing a commission that authorized them "to repair to the American Congress, and to propose to and receive from them terms of an union with the United States". The outcome was an act of Congress (August 20) stipulating "as an indispensible preliminary" to the admission of Vermont to the union, the explicit relinquishment of "all demands of lands or jurisdiction" outside certain defined boundaries. New York was far from being satisfied with the proposition, and Vermont less so. As for those lands and jurisdiction to which Congress had alluded, Vermont had her own plan for the adjustment of those territorial disputes. "The labouring Oar I think", wrote Samuel Livermore of New Hampshire (December 18, 1781), "is on Congress to support their own honour, dignity and authority; I wish to keep it so."

By this time Vermont had lost nearly all the friendly support she had had in Congress hitherto, but political motives soon found their way to the top again, even to the extent of palliating the intrigues with the British, and this despite the fact that evidences of those intrigues continued to accumulate. The interposition of Congress, Madison confessed (January 22, 1782), seemed to be indispensable; the chief question was whether it should be by way of military coercion or renewed overtures. It was a "thorny subject". It was while Congress was debating which way and what price the solution of this vexing problem that commissioners from Vermont again made their appearance in Philadelphia. "Some members of Congress", wrote Livermore (February 5), are much alarmed and all are embarrassed." The new commissioners had come with assurances that Vermont had fully complied with the terms laid down by Congress and offered to subscribe to the Articles of Confederation. One party in Congress would accept those assurances in good faith, throw a blanket of oblivion over the past, and open the arms of the union to the newcomer. Another party had serious doubts whether compliance had been genuine and complete, while some contended that Vermont's former refusal of the offer of Congress had absolved that body from its promise.

In fact, to admit or not to admit had come to be less a question of Vermont's merit than of Congressional politics. The Vermont question had become by now inextricably entangled with the whole problem of the western territory. The Rhode Island delegates, for instance, asserted (April 16) that "Some States will oppose their being admitted into the federal union because it might affect the balance of power by throwing an additional weight into the eastern Scale"; while, on the other hand, Madison declared (April 23), "The true secret is that the Vote of Vermont is wished for as an auxiliary ag[ain]st the Western claims of Virg[ini]a." New York of course had her own reasons for fighting admission with all her might. Into all this ferment was cast one other ingredient, a doubt whether under the Confederation, Congress was authorized to admit Vermont at all. About all that Congress seemed able to accomplish under these conditions was to put an end to the wrangle by postponing further consideration of the subject to some future time, when conditions might be changed. That done (April 18), the Vermont commissioners took their departure, probably sadder, but whether also wiser men, events only would determine.

In the early autumn of 1782 new disturbances in southeastern Vermont were interpreted by the New York delegates as an omen of Vermont's sinking cause, and that, together with recent changes in the membership of Congress, offered hopes that a decision favorable to New York might now be obtained. The report of a committee on the subject (October 17) was, however, a sore disappointment to the New Yorkers, since its chief proposition was a pious recommendation of peace and tranquillity. "A Milk and Water Peace of Business", snorted Ezra L'Hommedieu. The committee did, however, further recommend that Congress once more take into consideration the proposition of April 17 preceding for the admission of Vermont. What was actually obtained was some more debates and postponements. "Almost all agree", Gilman of New Hampshire declared (November 20), "that it is absolutely necessary to make a final determination of the matter, but are at a loss to know what is best to be done."

In the meantime depositions and memorials respecting the conduct of the Vermonters had been piling up, with the result that Congress was at last driven to desperation and decision. On the 5th of December, Congress came to a resolution denouncing the proceedings of Vermont as "highly derogatory to the authority of the United States", "dangerous to the Confederacy", and requiring "the immediate and decided interposition of Congress"; and further declaring that, unless full and complete restitution should be made without delay as respects both persons and property, the United States would "take effectual measures to enforce a compliance" with its resolutions. The New Yorkers could scarcely ask for an act with a better set of teeth in it; but there were evidently lingering doubts whether Congress would merely show its teeth or would, if the occasion demanded, vigorously use them. "It is done in pretty Spirited Terms", William Floyd was willing to say; yet at the same time Floyd and Hamilton confided to Governor Clinton (December 8) that they could not "absolutely rely upon the coercive part" of the resolutions in the event that an exertion of force should actually be required.

If Congress could indulge itself in a sharp rebuke to Vermont, so could that free, sovereign, and independent state retort in language equally sharp; and the retort was not long delayed. On the 4th of February, 1783, Congress listened to some remarks of Vermont's governor, Thomas T. Chittenden, and not a few Congressional ears were made to burn. One delegate reported that the address contained "animadversions on the conduct of Congress towards the Territory of Vermont"; another that the address exhibited "very little respect to this Body"; and a third (James Madison), one whose voice was normally judiciously restrained, declared it "an indecent and tart remonstrance".

As for those "effectual measures" that Congress had proposed to take to enforce compliance with its resolutions, Governor Chittenden intimated that he had no fears of the Continental army; and he was confident that Vermont could take care of New York unaided. The effect of Governor Chittenden's response was, upon the whole, to increase the alienation from Vermont; but at the same time no war fervor was aroused in Congress. All things considered, the best course to pursue seemed to be a policy of avoidance, at least until the questions respecting the western territory should be decided upon, or until the conclusion of peace. In July, Hamilton, who at first had advocated the application of force to the obstreperous Vermont, came to the conclusion that Congress would come to no determination in the matter except in the manner prescribed by the Articles of Confederation, and his counsel was accordingly that New York institute a claim according to the principles of the Confederation. "While Congress have a discretion", he wrote to Governor Clinton, July 27, 1783, "they will procrastinate; when they are bound by the Constitution they must proceed."

The suggestion of a constitutional adjustment arose doubtless from the fact that the dispute between Connecticut and Pennsylvania over the Susquehanna lands, usually referred to as the Wyoming controversy, had lately been settled, or was supposed to have been settled, in just that manner. The court for the determination of that issue, in accordance with the provision of the ninth article of the Confederation, had been constituted in August, 1782, had sat upon the case from November 12 to December 30, at Trenton, New Jersey, and on the 2d of January, 1783, had laid its verdict before Congress. Whatever the defects of the Confederation, here was one provision that seemed to offer a means for the amicable adjustment of the several existing controversies among the states and of those numerous other controversies that would likely arise. In one respect at least therefore the omens for the union were favorable.

In another particular, however, a serious question respecting the future of the new nation yet hung heavy over the heads of Congress. Did the near future offer peace and independence to the United States, or a renewal of the war? Expectations as well as hopes were generally for peace and independence, but the country must needs be on its guard against a renewal of the war. Indeed it was equally vital that the country be on its guard in defense of an acceptable peace. In June, 1781, as hitherto noted, in anticipation of the mediation of Russia and Austria, Congress had, despite strong opposition, voted to entrust the fate of the United States in great measure to the wisdom of their ally. The suspicion that France might in the end betray them, at least leave them to flounder and to struggle ashore as best they might, nevertheless lingered in some quarters, with the result that as early as January 8, 1782, a motion was made "that it is now expedient that Congress should enlarge their ultimata for concluding a treaty of peace". The motion was defeated by an overwheming majority; nevertheless it was not long before the question of the relative parts to be taken by the two allied powers in the negotiations was again brought forward, more precise in form and more definite in intent. In April, 1782, it began to appear that negotiations for peace were about to be entered upon but that Great Britain was seeking to drive a wedge between America and her allies, with a view to making peace with them separately. There were even reasons for suspecting that the British ministry harbored the thought of once more endeavoring to subdue the former colonies. In the face of these fears and suspicions, the French minister, Luzerne, re-iterated in strong terms the resolution of the French government "to adhere to the principles of the alliance, and to form no treaty of peace which does not secure to the United States the object of it"; and Congress, in its turn, reaffirmed its own purpose to conduct the negotiations "in confidence and in concert with his Most Christian Majesty".

It can scarcely be gainsaid, however, that, notwithstanding these mutual assurances there was a lack of complete confidence on both sides. It came about that, on the 13th of May, 1782, Congress had occa-sion to stage an elaborate reception for the French minister in order that he might present to the United States in Congress assembled a letter from his Most Christian Majesty announcing the birth of a dau-phin. "It was deemed politic at this crisis", Madison wrote to Randolph (May 14), "to display every proper evidence of affectionate attachment to our Ally"; and so they did, in solemn ceremonial, in the exchange of official greetings, and in every appropriate felicitation. "The prince who is just born", proclaimed the minister, "will one day be the friend and ally of the United States. He will, in his turn, support them with all his power, and while in his dominions he shall be the father and protector of his people, he will be here the supporter of your children, and the guarantee of their freedom." The members of Congress, probably less concerned about the infant dauphin than they were for the newly born additions to their own herds and flocks, yet, personifying as they did the sovereignty of the United States, must authorize their spokesman, the President, to assure the minister of their brother monarch, the King of France, that they had learned "with the most lively satisfaction" that it had pleased the Divine Giver of all good gifts to bless their august ally with an heir to the throne, and to add their earnest prayer "that he may with it inherit the virtues which have acquired to his Majesty so much glory, and to his dominions so much prosperity, and which will be the means of cementing and strengthening the union so happily established between the two nations". And more of like kind, closing with an assurance of "the affectionate attachment which every rank of people within these states manifest to your sovereign, and of their inviolable fidelity to the principles of the alliance". If some members of that august assembly, while these words were being pronounced in their behalf, listened with tongue in cheek, it was no more than other monarchs had done before and would do again.

In the closing days of July, 1782, came word that the United Provinces had recognized the independence of the United States. This, declared Arthur Lee, may be considered the epoch of our emancipation; by which he meant emancipation from the domination of France. In fact, said Madison (July 23), the news from Holland had "much emboldened the enemies of France". Lee, who was the leader of the antigallican party, definitely indicated a purpose to try to exclude both Franklin and Jay from the negotiations and "to withdraw the others from the direction of France". Accordingly on July 24 he offered a motion, which was seconded by Jackson of Massachusetts, "that the Commission of the 15th June, 1781, appointing Ministers Plenipotentiary to negotiate a Treaty of Peace with Great Britain, together with the instructions given to the said Commissioners be reconsidered".

There followed an almost ferocious struggle between the anti-gallicans and the friends of France, lasting full two months, during which Congress obtained occasional glimpses of the negotiations as they progressed, although they would of course learn of one stage only after they had passed into another. Intimations continued to appear from time to time that the war might be renewed, but upon the whole they aroused no serious forebodings. "We apprehend", wrote the North Carolina delegates (August 19), "that nothing but vigorous and persevering exertions on our part to convince the enemy of our ability to continue the *leaden* argument will compel them to make those offers of peace seriously which 'tis probable they are now making insidiously." The wrangle in Congress was brought to an end only when, on September 24, Luzerne laid before them an account of the progress of peace negotiations. In response Congress resolved *"unanimously"*, October 4, that it would "inviolably adhere" to the alliance with France, that it would "conclude neither a separate peace or truce with Great Britain", but that it would "prosecute the war with vigor, until, by the blessing of God on the united arms, a peace shall be happily accomplished, by which the full and absolute sovereignty and independence of these United States having been duly assured, their rights and interests, as well as those of their allies shall be effectually provided for and secured"; and, further, "that Congress will not enter into the discussion of any overtures for pacification, but in confidence and in concert with his Most Christian Majesty".

In mid-October, Congress learned that the British minister at Brussels, Alleyne Fitzherbert, had been commissioned to conclude a treaty of peace, but the satisfaction which this news might otherwise have given to an eager and anxious Congress was largely nullified by the fact that the stiff-necked king of Great Britain had refused to name the United States otherwise than in those vague and general terms, "any other Princes or States concerned". That intelligence was, however, already nearly three months old when it reached these shores, and much might have happened in the interval. Much indeed had happened, for in mid-December it was learned that, on the 21st of September, a commission had been issued to Richard Oswald authorizing him to treat with commissioners of the "Thirteen United States of America". On the 23d of December this intelligence was confirmed by official despatches; and members of Congress at once began to spread the glad tidings. "The Rubicon is therefore Past", Elias Boudinot wrote to a New Jersey friend (December 24). Others thought it might be too good to trust implicitly. Wrote Madison the same day: "It is no doubt on the whole a source of very soothing expectations, but if we view on the one side the instability and insidiousness of the British Cabinet, and, on the other the complication of interest and pretensions among the Allies, prudence calls upon us to temper our expectations with much distrust." Similarly Oliver Wolcott wrote: "Considering the Duplicity of the Enemy, The Volatility of their Councils, the Various Interests to be adjusted, the speedy settlement of peace is an Event that cannot be depended upon"; nevertheless, said he, the hope for peace was greater than at any former period.

Despite these hovering doubts, Christmas day, 1782, was probably the happiest that Congress had known since first it was a Congress.

Could it have known that already, on November 30, preliminary articles of peace had been signed, it would have been a day of genuine rejoicing. Peace at last, after seven toilsome and tormenting years! That comforting knowledge would not, however, be vouchsafed Congress until nearly three months later, and many days of agonizing perplexities and anxieties lay between. Peace with the outside world was drawing nigh perhaps; but what of that peace and tranquillity within their own borders for which they yearned and were so earnestly striving? Alas! all was not well in their own house. At that moment there was an ominous rumble as of threatening storm from the direction of the army. The United States of America had no doubt won its long struggle for independence, for place and title among the nations of the world, but it was not yet master in its own house.

CHAPTER XXVIII

THE ARMY GRUMBLES
CONGRESS STAMMERS . . . AND PROMISES

Although Congress had learned in April, 1782, that negotiations for peace were under way, so great were the uncertainties of the outcome that it was deemed essential to keep the army intact and be prepared for eventualities. But the army was an exceedingly expensive piece of governmental machinery, and Congress was so hard put to it to meet those expenses, that it naturally began to ponder whether, in view of the possibilities of peace, the army might not in some measure be reduced. In June, 1782, a committee was set to work on that problem, and, after nearly two months of consideration in committee and discussion in Congress, it was decided (August 7) to call upon the officers of the army for voluntary retirements in accordance with a prescribed program, the plan to go into effect on the first of January, 1783.

The plan was not, however, adopted without objection, particularly by the North Carolina delegates, who maintained that, in consequence of those resolves, "almost every Officer in the North Carolina Line would be deranged on the first of January". Convinced, however, that "A measure which the general good of the Army demanded, which had been recommended by the Commander-in-Chief and had been digested in Congress was not to be rashly opposed by a State", particularly one that had been so inattentive to the requisitions of Congress, the delegates (Williamson and Blount) refrained from registering their opposition at the time, preferring to wait for a later opportunity, to accomplish their wish, when they could "couch it under some colourable excuse". Two months later they moved for an amendment, in general terms, of the act of August 7, 1782, pointed to the probability that the enemy would continue in Charleston, and the consequent need of the North Carolina troops. When the secretary at war gave his approval of making an exception in the case of the North Carolina line, Congress readily adopted it (November 4, 1782).

The proposed reduction was, upon the whole, approved by General Washington at the time, but soon afterward, as he wrote the secretary at war (October 2, 1782), he began to fear the results of the measure "under the present circumstances". At that moment, he said, discontents prevailed "universally throughout the army"—he was speaking particularly of the officers—and he instanced their complaints of "the total want of Money, or the means of existing from one day to another, the heavy debts they have already incurred, the loss of Credit, the distress of their Families (i e such as are Maried) at home, and the prospect of poverty and misery before them." Then he went on to say:

When I see such a Number of Men goaded by a thousand stings of reflexion on the past, and of anticipation on the future, about to be turned into the World, soured by penury and what they call the ingratitude of the Public, involved in debts, without one farthing of Money to carry them home, after having spent the flower of their days and many of them their patrimonies in establishing the freedom and Independence of their Country, and suffered every thing that human Nature is capable of enduring on this side of death . . . I cannot avoid apprehending that a train of Evils will follow, of a very serious and distressing Nature.

In especial the officers were concerned over the resolutions of August 7, because of the proposed stoppage of promotions, the withholding of commissions from those justly entitled to them, the equivocal state in which compensation for their past services had been left, and the lack of any provision for their future payment.

In consequence of Washington's letter, Secretary Lincoln went to headquarters to confer with him, and on his return laid the case of the army before Congress (October 30). Some recommendations of the secretary for the modification of the act of August 7, in so far as to permit the retention of certain classes of officers in the service, were adopted, and the superintendent of finance was instructed (November 18-20) to report on the question of pay. Some pay for the army, the secretary at war declared, must be found, but where? And James Madison of the Congress groaned in response: "God knows!"

Thus far little had been done to quiet the discontents in the army.

One group in Congress had, in fact, repeatedly and strenuously endeavored to have the whole problem turned over to the states, but were unsuccessful. Neither the forward-looking men in Congress nor the army were ready to consent to a measure that would not only create thirteen armies instead of one, but strike a blow at the very vitals of the union. Unfortunately the hopes that had been builded on the adoption of the five-per-cent impost measure were just then brought to naught by Rhode Island's rejection of the measure.

Something of what Washington had feared soon began to manifest itself among the officers of the army. Weary of waiting for measures to be taken by Congress for the alleviation of their distresses, they decided to lay their case before Congress in a more direct manner than had hitherto been done. Washington gave a forewarning of this in a letter to Joseph Jones December 14, 1782. "The dissatisfactions of the Army", he wrote, "had arisen to a great and alarming height, and combinations among the Officers to resign, at given periods in a body, were beginning to take place when by some address and management their resolutions have been converted into the form in which they will now appear before Congress." The address was couched in respectful terms, he said, although he had once feared that matters would take a more unfavorable turn. On the 29th of December a deputation from the army, General Alexander McDougall and Colonels Matthias Ogden and John Brooks, arrived in Philadelphia, and on January 6, 1783, their memorial was laid before Congress and referred to a grand committee. Said the memorial:

. . . We have struggled with our difficulties, year after year, under the hopes that each would be the last; but we have been disappointed. We find our embarrassments thicken so fast, and have become so complex, that many of us are unable to go further. In this exigence we apply to Congress for relief as our head and sovereign. . . .

We complain that shadows have been offered to us while the substance has been gleaned by others. . . . The citizens murmur at the greatness of their taxes, and are astonished that no part reaches the army. The numerous demands, which are between the first collectors and the soldiers, swallow up the whole.

Our distresses are now brought to a point. We have borne all that men can bear—our property is expended—our private resources are at an end, and our friends are wearied out and disgusted with our incessant applications. We, therefore, most seriously and earnestly beg, that a supply of money may be forwarded to the army as soon as possible. The uneasiness of the soldiers, for want of pay, is great and dangerous; any further experiments on their patience may have fatal effects.

Such in part was the preamble to the memorial, which continued with the citation of specific grievances and the desired measures of redress. Chief among the demands were: an advance of some part of the pay due the army, a security for the residue, and a commutation of half-pay for life into full-pay for a certain number of years, or else a sum in gross; while other demands were for a settlement of sundry arrearages and deficiencies.

"The dilemma in which Congress are placed", Madison wrote to Governor Harrison, January 7, "pressed on one side by justice, humanity and the public good to fulfill engagements to which their funds are incompetent, and on the other left without even the resource of answering that every thing which could have been done had been done", was readily conceivable. To Edmund Randolph, the same day, he expressed the wish that "the disquietude excited by the prospect was the exclusive portion of those who impede the measures calculated for redressing complaints against the justice and gratitude of the public." And yet, he confided a few days later, what could a Virginia delegate say in reply to such complaints, when his own state was one of those that had failed to make the necessary contributions? He wished that the explanations given in the army's memorial "could with propriety be promulged throughout the United States. They would I am sure at least put to shame all those who have laboured to throw a fallacious gloss over our public affairs."

Hamilton, on the other hand, while he felt deep mortification that Congress was totally unable to comply with the just expectations of the army, was inclined to believe, so he wrote to Governor Clinton (January 12), that, if the affair were handled in a proper manner, it might be "turned to a good account". "Every day", he explained, "proves more and more the insufficiency of the confederation," and many of the most sensible men were acknowledging the wisdom of the measure lately recommended by the New York legislature, namely, the calling of a general convention to overhaul the entire system. Among those who took a similar view was Abner Nash of North Carolina. "The truth is", he wrote to James Iredell (January 18), "the fault is in the constitution of Congress; and if these distresses should happily point out a remedy, in the right place and way, we shall by and by say . . . all is for the best." But, he added, "things will soon be better or worse".

One evidence that they were likely to be worse before they were better had just been given by the superintendent of finance, to whom had been assigned, back in November, the problem of finding pay for the army. On January 9 he confidentially revealed to a committee that he had already overdrawn the known funds in Europe to the amount of three and a half million dollars and that further drafts on "contingent funds" were necessary to prevent a stop to the public service. Thereupon by unanimous vote (January 10) Congress authorized Morris to continue to draw bills of exchange on the loans directed to be made in Europe, "according to his discretion" and "as the public service may require", but not in excess of such authorized loans. And it was further resolved unanimously "That the whole of this matter be kept secret". "On this occasion", Madison recorded, "several members were struck with the impropriety of the late attempt to withdraw from France the trust confided to her over the terms of peace when we were under the necessity of giving so decisive a proof of our dependance upon her."

In the evening of January 13 the grand committee gave an audience to the deputies from the army, when General McDougall, so Madison recorded, "painted their sufferings and services, their successive hopes and disappointments throughout the whole war, in very high-colored expressions, and signified that if a disappointment were now repeated the most serious consequences were to be apprehended". McDougall further declared that the army "were verging to that state which we are told will make a wise man mad"; adding nevertheless that "the most intelligent and considerate part of the army were deeply affected at the debility and defects in the federal Government, and the unwillingness of the States to cement and invigorate it." In the event of its dissolution, McDougall went on to say, the benefits expected from the Revolution would be greatly impaired, and he predicted that contests would arise amongst the states, with the consequent embroilment of their respective officers. Colonel Brooks asserted that "the temper of the army was such that they did not reason or deliberate coolly on consequences and therefore a disappointment might throw them blindly into extremities"; while Colonel Ogden declared that, "if he was to be the messenger of disappointment to them", he did not wish to return to the army.

On January 25, having debated the report of the grand committee for three days, Congress adopted some resolutions that were about as far as possible from satisfying the demands of the army or mollifying their wrath. With regard to present pay, the superintendent of finance was directed, "conformable to the measures already taken for that purpose", to make payment "as soon as the state of public finances will permit". The phrase "conformable to the measures already taken", said Madison, was "meant to shew that the payment to the army did not originate in the Memorial". That face-saving phrase may have afforded unction to the committee and to Congress (there was really a modicum of truth in it), but it may well be doubted whether the curses of a single soldier were deflected by it. In the matter of arrearages Congress would request the states to settle with their respective lines up to August 1, 1780, and have the superintendent of finance take measures for the subsequent period.

When no money was available, Congress could always direct the superintendent of finance "to take measures". However much some members of Congress might deplore the one-man head of finance, few of them were averse to what some of their descendants have termed "passing the buck" to him. As to security for future payment, that, Congress declared, was an undoubted right of the troops, as well as of all other creditors, and Congress would make every effort in its power to obtain from the states "substantial funds, adequate to the object of funding the whole debt of the United States". The ways and means of accomplishing this purpose were presently to become a major subject of consideration.

Whether there should be some form of commutation of half-pay for life and just what, was a question that could not be so readily decided, and for the reason that Congress was much divided on the question and likewise not a little perplexed. The grand committee had reported in favor of leaving it to the option of the officers entitled to half-pay either to preserve their claim according to previous resolutions of Congress or to accept full pay for six years, payment to be made within one year after the conclusion of the war.

Here in the outset was a particularly difficult question. What is "a mean life" of the officers? Is it twelve years or ten years or somewhere between the two? The grand committee had consulted the actuaries and had been advised that the average life of the officers would be twelve years and had accordingly proposed whole-life payment for six years. When, however, a vote for that term had been negatived (January 25), up rose a member to propose that it be made six and a half. The result was some confusion. Better consult the actuaries again. The lesser committee to whom the matter was now referred appears rather to have done some figuring of its own and to have come to the conclusion that ten years of life were enough on the average to allow the officers. When again the question came under consideration (February 4), votes were taken on five and a half, five and a quarter, and five, but without a decision. In fact, attendance was so meager that no decision could be hoped for, whereupon Congress called upon the delinquent states (February 21) to send on their delegates immediately. "In this critical state of affairs", declared President Boudinot in his letter to the states, "all the wisdom of the States is required." Wisdom if possible, delegates at all events. Response was only meager, but on February 25 the debate on commutation was resumed. Thereupon the New England delegates, with the aid of one member from New Jersey and another from Virginia, endeavored to have the whole half-pay question, in so far as concerned the officers of state lines, referred to the respective states. It failed as had a similar proposition in the preceding November, and at length, on February 28, seven states voted for a commutation to five years' whole pay. But was a vote of a bare majority sufficient? By a nearly unanimous vote it was decided that such a proposition, under the Articles of Confederation, required the assent of nine states. For the time being therefore the whole question was left hanging in the air.

While the debate over the half-pay question had been dragging its weary way along, that other and more insistent problem stirred to agitation by the memorial of the officers, namely, how to find the wherewithal to fund the whole debt of the United States, had been brought under consideration by a motion of James Wilson, January 25. Wilson gently explained that one of his motives in making the motion was to prevent that resolve that Congress "would make every effort", etc., from becoming, like so many of that body's resolves, *"vox et preterea nihil"*. There was no gainsaying the fact that many and many a time the voice of Congress had been answered only by its own echo.

What to do about the whole debt was certainly an insistent problem, for not all the goads prodding Congress were wielded by the army. "The cloud of public creditors, including the army", groaned Hugh Williamson (February 17), "are gathering about us; the prospect thickens. Believe me, that I would rather take the field in the hardest military service I ever saw, than face the difficulties that await us in Congress within a few months." There were efforts both within Congress and without to bring about some sort of combination of all the creditors of the government, in the hope that this combined pressure would offer a better chance of success, and no less a person than Hamilton took a hand in the movement. In a letter to Washington, February 7, he asserted that "the great desideratum", "the object of all men of sense", was the establishment of general funds, and that "in this the influence of the army, properly directed, may cooperate". In a subsequent letter (March 17) he explained more fully his idea. The object at which he and other members of Congress aimed was that Congress should be prevailed on to adopt such a plan as would embrace the relief of all public creditors, including the army, and that "a mass of influence" should be exerted on each state in favor of the measures of Congress.

In its search for funds Congress was necessarily confined within very narrow limits, and those limits had already been raked time and time

again with a fine-toothed comb. Requisitions had become steadily less
dependable, and besides, dissatisfaction with the former method of
determining quotas had grown into an insistent demand for compliance with the provision of the eighth article of the Confederation,
which stipulated that expenses should be apportioned according to land
values. But that problem also had its complexities and perplexities, and
Congress wrestled with them for several weeks. "The only point on
which Congress are generally agreed," Madison wrote to Randolph
February 11, 1783, "is that something ought to be attempted; but what
that something ought to be is a theorem not solved alike by scarcely
any two members; and yet a solution of it seems to be made an indispensible preliminary to other essays for public relief." Meanwhile the
deputation from the army was "waiting the upshot of all these delays
and dilemmas".

The plan finally adopted, February 17, was that each state should
make a survey of its lands, buildings, number of inhabitants (distinguishing white from black), and transmit the returns to Congress by
March 1, 1784. Thereupon Congress would designate a grand committee (one from each state),

to take into their consideration the said returns, any nine of whom concur-
ring shall make a just and true estimate of the value of all lands in each of
the United States, granted to or surveyed for any person, and of the buildings and improvements thereon, and shall report such estimate to Congress,
to be subject only to their approbation or rejection.

That estimate, when approved, was to be the rule for apportionments
for a period not exceeding five years.

The plan "is not so good as we wished", Hugh Williamson wrote
to James Iredell (February 17), "but the best we could get. . . . I believe we failed in twenty different plans before we fixed on one."
Among those who voted against the plan was Alexander Hamilton,
who set forth his criticisms at length in a letter to Governor Clinton
(February 24). Besides numerous defects as a practicable measure,
Hamilton contended, the plan was founded on false principles and was
a compliance with the Confederation in appearance rather than in
reality. Notwithstanding his criticisms of the measure, Hamilton urged
that his state cheerfully comply with its requirements; for, he said,

"unless each state is governed by this principle there is an end of the union."

The background of all this discussion was of course the idea of requisitions; nonetheless there was an eagerness to explore other and possibly more promising fields, with the result that the discussion ranged over such taxes as a poll tax, a land tax, a house tax, a window tax, a tax on salt, an excise on imported wines, spirits, and coffee; with, of course, a renewed consideration of the general impost, notwithstanding the recent rejection of that measure by Rhode Island and the withdrawals and threatened withdrawals of acceptance by other states. All such propositions required the assent of nine states, and the arguments ran the gamut of legality, constitutionality, expediency, and what not; and most of the discussions, however circuitous, came around in the end to the impost.

One especially controversial question respecting an impost measure was, whether the collection and disposition of the funds should be by state or continental authority—a question that had previously been hammered on not a little. "Every engine is at work here", Arthur Lee wrote at the end of January, "to obtain permanent taxes and the appointment of Collectors by Congress, in the States. The terror of a mutinying Army is played off with considerable efficacy." The mere suggestion of an impost measure would naturally set a Rhode Island delegate to growling, and Jonathan Arnold sounded the characteristic note. The impost, he said, was extolled "as the infallible, grand political Catholicon". It was merely one more scheme to "throw a share of the power and strength of Government, now held by the States, into the hands of Congress".

As Congress attacked now one phase of the problem, now another, moved from commutation to general funds, then back again, it seemed to the army that Congress progressed, if progress it could be called, only in a circle, getting nowhere; and the news from the army that filtered back to Congress became more and more disturbing. "There is much reason to believe", Madison wrote to Randolph, February 13, couching his message in cipher, "that the cloud which has been some time lowering on the North River will not be dispelled by the rays of peace." In short, Congress was given to understand that an order for the discharge of the army before justice had been done them would hazard "dangerous convulsions".

On February 25, again covering his message in cipher, he wrote: "The discontents and designs of the army are every day taking a more solemn form. It is now whispered that they have not only resolved not to lay down their arms till justice shall be done them, but that to prevent surprise, a public declaration will be made to that effect." Madison's colleague, Joseph Jones, hoped that the army would "exercise awhile longer at least, that patient forbearance, which hath hitherto so honourably distinguished them". Persons acquainted with the deliberations of public bodies, he said, "especially of so mixed a Body as that of Congress", would make allowances for their slow determination.

There are good intentions in the Majority of Congress [Hamilton wrote to Washington, March 17]; but there is not sufficient wisdom or decision. There are dangerous prejudices in the particular states opposed to those measures which alone can give stability and prosperity to the Union. There is a fatal opposition to Continental views. Necessity alone can work a reform. But how apply it and how keep it within salutary bounds?

As first written, this latter sentence read: "But how is that necessity to be produced, how is it to be applied, and how kept within salutary bounds?" That is to say, might not something be done to stimulate the requisite necessity? Such at least would seem to have been the idea in Hamilton's mind. But he thought better of it and softened the suggestion. He did, however, drop the remark, "If no excesses take place I shall not be sorry that ill-humours have appeared. I shall not regret importunity, if temperate, from the army."

On March 15, General McDougall, the only member of the army deputation then remaining in Philadelphia, wrote to General Knox that, unless there should be a hopeful turn in affairs soon, he would confess the failure of his mission and return to the army.

During these several weeks in which Congress had been agonizing over the problem pertaining to the army and its other clamorous creditors, it was equally tormented over the uncertainties of peace. In mid-January had come a report that peace negotiations had broken up, but close upon the heels of that report came another that the negotiations were proceeding, with the goal in sight—a jumble of fact and inference drawn from the actualities of late October and early November. Followed soon information that seemed to carry definite implications of peace; then a report that the preliminaries of peace had actually been signed. "Extracts of letters" from here and there in the West Indies began to appear in the papers, some pointing one way, some the other. Rumors and shadows of rumors, coming from no one knew where, stirred a fleeting hope or a momentary disappointment, then faded into nothingness. Every scrap of news was dissected and analyzed and variously interpreted.

On February 13 came the king's speech to Parliament, in which it was plainly stated that provisional terms had been made with the "American Colonies", and among the gratifications that swelled the bosoms of Congress not the least was the delectable reflection, as one member expressed it, upon "the humble language in which the once haughty monarch of Britain had addressed his Parliament. Surely this was the herald of the dawn of peace". Still, who could know but that the wily British might yet play some trick on America? Until official confirmation should arrive Congress would be in a painful state of suspense. A characteristic note, even if not in quite characteristic language, was struck by doughty John Montgomery: "amirrica will be free . . ." he exulted; "poor torris must now hang thire heads. the day is now Come when the sun will Raise on amirrica never to set. I look forward with Pleasure to the happey days that our Children will see."

Even so the succession of puzzlements was not at an end. A letter from Secretary Townshend to the Lord Mayor of London, dated December 3, 1782, spoke of preliminary articles being signed between England and the United States on November 30, then added: "It now only remains to sign the same articles between Great Britain and France, to constitute a general peace." Immensely encouraging, if true —and true it did turn out to be—still, it was mysterious. Why these separate treaties? Why did not the ministers write and explain things? Then suddenly all these high hopes were dashed. Came a report, from some one in France this time, that the outcome of the negotiations might yet be not peace, but an obstinate continuation of the war. The silence of the ministers was ominous, the suspense tormenting. Philadelphia eagerly searched the papers of New York for news; British headquarters in New York, equally in the dark, scanned those of Philadelphia. "Here", wrote a member of Congress, March 11, "we wait with anxiety for the stage from Elizabethtown, and at New York, the shores are crowded, the evening they are to hear from Philadelphia." Wrote another the same day, "It is five months the 14th instant since we have received any dispatches from Europe, and all private accounts from any quarter are vague and not much depended on." It proved to be the dark hour before the dawn. On the morning of the 12th of March, 1783, arrived Captain Joshua Barney with despatches from the ministers and the provisional treaty between the United States and Great Britain signed on the 30th of November. Such in brief is the manner in which the good news was brought from Paris to Philadelphia.

If authentic news of the provisional treaty had been slow in reaching Congress, not so its dissemination by the members, who, immediately upon hearing it read, seized their pens to transmit the glad tidings to their governments and their friends. With the provisions of the treaty most members of Congress were well satisfied. "The terms granted to America", Madison recorded, "appeared to Congress on the whole extremly liberal." Said Gilman of New Hampshire, "The Articles respecting the Boundaries . . . and that respecting the right of Fishery, are Ample and I believe Equal to the most Sanguine Expectation"; while John Collins of Rhode Island declared that the terms were more favorable than he ever expected to obtain, and Richard Peters was of opinion that the treaty contained "everything we ought to wish".

Most of the members, however, viewed askance those provisions of the treaty in which it was agreed that Congress would "earnestly recommend" it to the states to revise their confiscation laws and would also endeavor to bring about a restoration of property to those Loyalists who had not taken up arms. Floyd said he did not like that article, yet he was clearly of opinion, as was nearly every one else who had seen the letters from our ministers, that these provisions were inserted in order that the king and his ministers might be able to say to the Tories, "that they had attended to their Interest as far as Lay in their power". If, however, Floyd continued, Congress should seriously make the recommendation, and if the states should seriously comply with it, "we should be Involved in very great Difficulties Indeed". Richard Peters likewise thought the provisions were inserted "to save British pride", but in any event, he was sure "the States will be left of Course to their own Way of thinking as to Compliance with this recommendation"; and so "the Chance for the Adherents to their gracious Sovereign is but a blue one". Other members declared that it looked to them like "sacrificing the dignity of Congress to the pride of the British King".

There was, however, one aspect of the treaty that did sorely disturb Congress. For it was revealed by the despatches that the American commissioners, in violation of their positive instructions "to make the most candid and confidential communications on all subjects" to the ministers of France and "to undertake nothing in the negotiations for peace or truce without their knowledge and concurrence"—instructions several times reiterated—had concealed from the French ministry their negotiations with the British authorities, until the treaty had been signed. It appeared that Jay had become suspicious of the designs of France, that Adams had heartily accorded with Jay, and that the two had finally prevailed upon Franklin to join them in separate and secret negotiations with the British envoy.

We are not here concerned with the justness of the suspicions or the rectitude of conduct on the part of the American commissioners, but only with the repercussions of that conduct upon Congress. Madison recorded that it "affected different members of Congress very differently"; differences that were brought out very pointedly in the course of the discussion that shortly followed. The attitude generally manifested at the outset, particularly among "the most judicious members", was one of disapproval. One view was that the American commissioners had been "in some measure ensnared by the dexterity of the British Minister". Moreover, a "separate", or secret, article respecting West Florida incorporated into the treaty was considered "most offensive", not only because it was "inconsistent with the spirit of the Alliance, and a dishonorable departure from the candor, rectitude, and plain dealing professed by Congress", but because it was believed to have been obtained by Great Britain "as a means of disuniting the United States and France". If and when this secret agreement should come to the knowledge of France, all confidence on the part of our ally would be at an end, and what course that power might in consequence pursue was a matter that might well give the United States serious concern. In short, it was the opinion of this considerable group that our commissioners had played into the hands of the enemy, who would of course take full advantage of the rift between the allies.

Whatever the conclusions, Congress necessarily found itself in a very delicate situation. "Some difficulties of importance", President Boudinot wrote to General Washington (March 17), not yet ready to reveal what they were, ". . . give us great uneasiness and add much to our perplexity." To another correspondent two days later, still withholding all particularization, he remarked, "I hope no American will ever have an Idea of deserting France upon any Terms what ever that are inconsistant with good Faith." In a letter to Edmund Randolph (March 18), using his presumably impenetrable cipher, Madison revealed in a few brief sentences the essential facts, then remarked:

The dilemma to which Congress are reduced is infinitely perplexing. If they abet the proceedings of their ministers, all confidence with France is at an end, which in the event of a renewal of the war must be dreadfull, as in that of peace it may be dishonorable. If they avow the conduct of their ministers by their usual frankness of communication, the most serious inconveniences also present themselves. The torment of this dilemma cannot be justly conveyed without a fuller recital of facts than is permitted. I wish you not to hazard even an interlined decypherment of those which I have deposited in your confidence.

What had taken place was of course not unknown to the French minister in Philadelphia; unless it be the separate article; and that, having been published through an inadvertance in a Philadelphia paper, soon became public knowledge. In fact, Luzerne had been instructed by Vergennes to remonstrate to Congress against the conduct of the American ministers, and he carried out these instructions in good diplomatic manner, admonishing the secretary for foreign affairs and several members of Congress besides, while to General Washington he pointed out the possibility of a renewal of the war and the necessity for taking measures accordingly. Naturally Luzerne did not fail to point to the fact that the American ministers had done this thing to their ally at the very moment when they were begging for aids. The fact that some part of the requested financial assistance, despite the serious strain on French finances, was sent by the same vessel that bore the despatches, was not therefore to be understood as indicative of a generous mood on Vergennes's part, but rather as a measure of precaution against a possible renewal of the conflict. Fortunately Franklin was subsequently successful in mollifying to some extent the ministerial displeasure.

In a letter to Congress, March 18, the secretary for foreign affairs, Robert R. Livingston, explained at some length the embarrassing, even dangerous, position in which the action of the ministers had placed Congress, and proposed three steps for easing the situation: the secretary to communicate the separate article to the French minister "in such a manner as would best tend to remove the unfavorable impressions on the court of France"; the ministers in France to be instructed to agree that the limit for West Florida proposed in the separate article be allowed to whatever power might be given possession of that colony by the treaty of peace; and Congress to declare that the preliminary articles would not take effect until peace had actually been signed between Great Britain and France.

Livingston's letter gave rise to debates extending over several days and developing no little warmth. Propositions were offered ranging from expressions of the "high sense" entertained by Congress of the services of their commissioners to demands that they be recalled and their action repudiated; but there were no decisions. A tense situation was relieved only by the arrival, March 23, of despatches announcing that a general peace had been concluded on the 20th of January. Announcing this news, John Francis Mercer began his letter: "At length mine eyes have seen my salvation"; and closed it, "Adieu, thank God".

One extraordinary fact about this affair is that, except for a brief note, March 24, respecting the general peace, which was learned through a letter from Lafayette, there is no record in the Journals of Congress of the proceedings relative to the provisional treaty, not even a mention of the debates that occupied most of the time from March 18 to 26, although some of the motions have been separately preserved. For a knowledge of those proceedings we are indebted mainly to the notes taken by James Madison. It was not until April 15 that Congress calmed down sufficiently to ratify the provisional treaty.

Because of its bearing on the crucial negotiations with the army then in progress, the peace treaty arrived at a most opportune time. On March 17, just when Congress was agitated by conflicting emotions respecting the treaty, the startling information was received from General Washington, dated March 12, that affairs in the army had come to a crisis. An anonymous, inflammatory address, designed to incite the army to take matters into its own hands, had been circulated through the army, then stationed at Newburgh, New York, and the outcome awaited a meeting of the officers set for March 15. The anonymous address, put into circulation on March 10, had called for a meeting of the officers on the 11th, and as soon as General Washington had learned of the proposed irregular meeting he proceeded to forestall it by issuing general orders for a meeting of the officers on the 15th. The anonymous author thereupon issued a second address. Together they are known as the Newburgh Addresses.

The authorship of the addresses is ascribed to Major John Armstrong, Jr., and he himself appears to have put forward, after a lapse of time, a claim to that authorship. Nevertheless it has been doubted whether he possessed that mastery of the language manifest in the admirable phrasing of the principal address and the skillful marshalling of the elements of appeal. A gift for sarcasm and invective Armstrong did possess, and, when presently he had failed in his great objective with the army and had dropped down to Philadelphia, he made liberal use of that gift, directing bitter denunciations against Congress, General Washington, and even against some of his fellow-officers, whom he charged with having had a share in thwarting his plans and purposes. Congress had proved itself "weak as water and impotent as old age", the states had shown themselves "obdurate and forgetful", and as for "the Illustrissimo of the age" (Washington), "Of all his illustrious foibles" the most ridiculous, in Armstrong's estimation, was "the affectation of Zeal in a cause he strove so anxiously to damn." These were some of his reflections uttered under the weight of humiliating failure. It is not of course to be supposed that Armstrong was alone in the promotion of the scheme, neither was the intrigue confined wholly to the army. The civil creditors of Congress appear also to have thrust a surreptitious hand into the affair, hoping thereby to obtain a share of the chestnuts when and if they should be roasted.

One aspect of the episode, as it stalked threateningly through the hall of Congress, should not be permitted to lapse into oblivion. In designating the committee to whom the despatches from the army should be assigned, those members of Congress who had long been laboring in behalf of remedial measures chose, so Madison reveals, "to saddle with this embarrassment the men who had opposed the measures necessary for satisfying the army". The five appointees were Gilman, Dyer, Clark, Rutledge, and Mercer, each of whom had opposed one or another of the measures. It has been asserted that James Madison was without a sense of humor; yet it is not beyond credence that this same James Madison, if not the principal, was at least *particeps criminis* in the perpetration, at a moment of the utmost seriousness, of this bit of grim humor. Else why should he have been chuckling over it, in the privacy of his study-chamber and alone with his diary?

There followed several days of feverish anxiety in Congress, but on March 22 it was learned that, through the consummate skill of the commander-in-chief, the blow designed by the Newburgh Addresses had been turned aside. Congress heaved a sigh of relief—and made haste to hold fast what had been won, by resolving to commute half-pay for life into whole-pay for five years, nine states voting *aye*. The only negative votes were Gilman and White of New Hampshire, Arnold of Rhode Island, and two of the three New Jersey delegates, Clark and Condict. The Massachusetts delegates, on the other hand, voted solidly in the affirmative; but they paid the penalty when the next election of delegates in their state came around.

The cup of joy was not, however, yet full; besides, it retained a tang of bitterness: Congress was still in labor with the measure designed to provide permanent funds, the army had not yet been paid, and there was every reason to believe that "events much more serious" would follow if these things were not done within a reasonable time.

Promises [the North Carolina delegates boldly declared, March 24], even those which are spacious, are found to be very light food. Our Army and all other public Creditors wish for something more substantial, for whatever has been fabled concerning the Chamelion, it is generally believed that no animal can live on the air. Money, or good securities are desired, we have neither.

"God only knows", said Madison, "how the plans in agitation for satisfying [the army's] just expectations will terminate; or what will be the issue in case they should be abortive."

Madison feared that the consummation of the great objective, the establishment of adequate and certain revenues, "call for more liberality and greater mutual confidence, than will be found in the American councils". "Unless", he wrote to Edmund Randolph (April 1), "some speedy and adequate provision be made beyond that of the Confederation, the most dismal alternative stares me in the face." Hamilton made much the same diagnosis. In a letter to Washington, April 9, he said:

There are two classes of men Sir in Congress of very different views— one attached to state the other to Continental politics. The last have been strenuous advocates for funding the public debt upon solid securities, the former have given every opposition in their power and have only been dragged into the measures which are now near being adopted by the clamours of the army and other public creditors.

At almost the same moment that Hamilton was writing, a letter went forth (April 7) from one in the opposite camp, Stephen Higginson of Massachusetts, who had, nevertheless, ventured to vote for the commutation measure of February 28. The letter was to Theophilus Parsons and ranged over a wide field, but touching the question acutely at issue, he said:

We are still hammering on a strange, though artful, plan of finance, in which are combined a heterogeneous mixture of imperceptible and visible, constitutional and unconstitutional taxes. It contains the impost, quotas, and cessions of Western lands, and no part of it is to be binding unless the whole is adopted by all the States. This connection and dependence of one part on another is designed to produce the adoption of the whole. The cessions are to serve as sweeteners to those who oppose the impost; the impost is intended to make the quotas more palatable to some States; and the receiving it in whole is made necessary to secure the adoption of the whole, by working on the fears of those States who wish to reject a part of it only. . . .

Congress [he went on to say] have not yet tried the strength of the Confederation, nor have they had a good opportunity to do it. If quotas are assigned to the several States . . . and a majority of the States should make provision for the discharge of their quotas, will they not find means to coerce those that are delinquent? Will not two or three frigates in time of peace be sufficient for the purpose?

This was on the assumption that only a minority of the states would be delinquent; but suppose it should be a majority? In that case, "a vote for coercion could not obtain, though Congress were possessed of the means". After all, Higginson concluded, there must be a disposition in a large majority of the states to act honestly, to accept their respective shares of the common burden, to adhere strictly to the principles of the Confederation, else the union will necessarily be dissolved.

The plan of finance that Higginson found so strange and so artful had been under consideration a full month, and a few days later (April 18), still retaining its essential elements, it was adopted. But the part that Higginson appears to have regarded as most artful and most objectionable, the clause reading, "That none of the preceding resolutions shall take effect until all of them shall be acceded to by every State", had been shifted, perhaps artfully, to a less objectionable position. Indeed that had been done before ever Higginson strode forth to denounce it. Madison records that in the original draft the clause was placed "last of all, so as to render the plan indivisible"; but in the first printed form, as well as in the act as adopted, that clause is made to apply only to the impost provisions.

As adopted, April 18, the resolution once more asks the states to invest Congress with a power to levy duties on imported goods, but the request in this instance differs from that of February 3, 1781, in that the imported goods are listed and the rates of duty specified, with an additional request for a duty of five per cent *ad valorem* on all other goods. It was further provided that the proceeds of these duties should be applied only to the discharge of the interest and principal of debts contracted on the faith of the United States and that their collection should be limited to a period of twenty-five years. The old controversy over the question whether collection should be by Congress or by the states was in a manner compromised by the provision that the collectors were in the first instance to be appointed by the states, but that when appointed they were to be amendable to and removable by Congress; and that, in the event a state failed to make such appointment within one month after due notice had been given, the appointment might be made by Congress.

To supplement the revenue from this source the states were requested to establish, for the same period of twenty-five years and for the same purpose, substantial and effectual revenues to the amount of one and a half million dollars annually in quotas as prescribed in the act, until the rule of the Confederation could be carried into practice. But, because both the rule and the method of applying it prescribed by Congress in an act of February 17 were unsatisfactory, Congress recommended an alteration in the eighth article of the Confederation so as to provide that the contributions of the states should be "in proportion to the whole number of white and other free citizens and inhabitants, of every age, sex and condition, including those bound to servitude for a term of years, and three fifths of all other persons not comprehended in the foregoing description, except Indians, not paying taxes". For this purpose a triennial census was to be taken. With regard to the western lands, the act went no further than to put forth one more recommendation to the claimant states to make cessions of their territorial claims in accordance with the resolutions of Congress of September 6 and October 10, 1780, including the revision of cessions that had not fully complied with those resolutions.

Like most measures of importance, that of April 18, 1783, was a compromise amongst conflicting elements. In a letter to Washington (May 6), Joseph Jones declared that it had been the most difficult and perplexing discussion that had engaged Congress for a long time. To reconcile the different interests of the states and make the system palatable to them "was a work not easily or speedily to be effected". Because of the prejudices and jealousies of states and individuals they had been obliged to take a middle course with regard both to the duration and to the appointment of collectors, or else hazard the loss of the measure. "As it stands", he remarked, "it will answer the purposes intended, if the States will grant their concurrence." And echo answered, *"if the states will grant their concurrence."*

It did not augur well for its acceptance that some of the states were right then repealing their acts of acceptance of the measure of February, 1781. If, however, the states would give heed to any appeal from Congress, surely they would have hearkened to that which accompanied the act (April 26). Drawn by James Madison, the address was a carefully reasoned explanation of the compelling influences underlying the enactment of the measure and of the purposes it was designed to accomplish. The address closes with this exhortation:

> The citizens of the United States are responsible for the greatest trust ever confided to a political society. If justice, good faith, honor, gratitude and all the other qualities which enoble the character of a nation, and fulfil the ends of government, be the fruits of our establishments, the cause of liberty will acquire a dignity and lustre which it has never yet enjoyed; and an example will be set which cannot but have the most favourable influence on the rights of mankind. If on the other side, our governments should be unfortunately blotted with the reverse of these cardinal and essential virtues, the great cause which we have engaged to vindicate will be dishonored and betrayed; the last and fairest experiment in favour of the rights of human nature will be turned against them, and their patrons and friends exposed to be insulted and silenced by the votaries of tyranny and usurpation.

A few days later (May 9) Congress instructed the President to inform the states "that it is the earnest desire of Congress that such of the legislatures as are neither sitting, nor about to sit in a short time, may be convened with all possible expedition".

While this plan for obtaining funds was being matured, Congress took some measures necessitated by the provisional treaty, among them the ratification of the treaty itself (April 15). Previously Congress had been informed by Sir Guy Carleton and Admiral Digby of the British proclamation of a cessation of arms, whereupon (April 11) Congress issued a proclamation of its own.

In view of all these assurances of peace the soldiers became eager for their discharge, although no more so than was Congress for the disbandment of the army. Washington had advised a committee of Congress that at least three month's pay would be necessary before disbandment; but whence was that money to come? Even the Rhode Island members acknowledged that Congress was thrown into "a very disagreeable dilemma". "Our Circumstances", Richard Peters wrote to Baron Steuben (April 23), "afford an odd Contrast to those we have heretofore experienced. The Difficulty which heretofore oppress'd us was how to raise an Army. The one which now embarrasses us is how to dissolve it." Then with a touch of irony, he added:

We have just under Consideration a Plan for establishing a Mint. All we want to put it into Execution is the *necessary Metal*. But this you will no Doubt think a trifling Impediment. Justice to our Creditors and Alacrity in paying our Taxes are the best Mines we can spring. But I fear we have not yet found the Vein in which these precious ores are lodged.

To add to the anxieties of Congress it was again rumored that the army would refuse to lay down its arms until paid; and it certainly did not lessen their difficulties that the man afterward reputed to have written the Newburgh Addresses, Major John Armstrong, Jr., was then in Philadelphia, continuing his efforts to incite the army to make decisive demands on Congress.

When Congress in its delemma turned to the superintendent of finance for counsel how to raise a sum of money sufficient for three months' pay to the army, estimated to require 750,000 dollars, Morris frankly said that he saw no means of acquiring such a sum except by a paper anticipation of the taxes, and that his own personal credit would have to be staked for the redemption of the obligations. At the end of January, Morris had given notice to Congress that unless effectual measures for establishing solid revenues should be taken by the end of May, he would resign the office of superintendent of finance, and the time of his expected retirement was now approaching, To carry through this "delicate and perilous undertaking" would therefore leave him, when he retired from office, answerable personally for about a half million dollars and dependent on the arrangements of those who should come after him. He was willing, he declared, to sacrifice much, to risk as much for his country as any man in America, but to risk his reputation as a man of integrity, to expose himself to absolute ruin, was more than he could undertake. If, however, Congress desired him to continue in office until his engagements could be completed, and if he could be assured of the firm support of Congress in fulfilling those engagements, he would undertake the necessary operations. Congress accordingly requested him to continue in the office and pledged him its support (April 28, May 2).

First of all, then, Congress must once more, "in the most earnest manner", call upon the states "to make every effort in their power to forward the collection of taxes"—phrases used so much that they were worn to a frazzle. In view however of the uncertainty of results, it were better to make another appeal to France for aid. Of course Congress had been quite definitely informed that France would make no more advances, but perhaps if his Majesty should be informed "that Congress will consider his compliance in this instance as a new and valuable proof of his friendship peculiarly interesting in the present conjuncture of the affairs of the United States" and that they would apply a part of the requisitions now subsisting upon the several states to the repayment of the loan—perhaps his Majesty would relent and add three millions to the six recently granted. It was so voted (May 2), and Morris took it upon himself to beseech both Franklin and Luzerne to lend their aid in obtaining the much needed money. To Franklin the superintendent of finance confided, "Nothing should induce me in my private character to make such applications for money as I am obliged to do in my public character."

Having thus, as well as seemed possible, bridged the financial chasm, Congress set about specific measures for discharging the army. Thereupon Daniel Carroll of Maryland urged "the expediency of caution"; for it was by no means certain that the war would not be renewed. Therefore, after several days of discussion, it was decided (May 26) that, instead of disbanding the army outright, the non-commissioned officers and soldiers who had enlisted to serve during the war, together with a proportionable number of commissioned officers, should be furloughed, with a promise that they should be discharged as soon as the definitive treaty of peace was concluded. Accordingly, despite the fact that there was delay in furnishing the notes to be given for the three months' pay, the furloughing proceeded rapidly, and soon many of the soldiers were returning to their homes, "with perfect good order", Washington reported (June 24), but "without the settlement of their Accounts or a farthing of money in their pockets". Six days after most of the soldiers had been furloughed the notes arrived in camp.

CHAPTER XXIX

CONGRESS GOES A-TRAVELLING
EMBRACES THE LONG-SOUGHT PEACE

The perplexing problem respecting the army settled at last, Congress might well heave another sigh of relief. If, however, there was aught of complacency within that chamber that served as the clearing house of national weal and woe, it was destined to be upset soon by two incidents, in themselves of only minor importance, but forerunners of a third occurrence that would make a wreck of complacency and ultimately have consequences for the government of the United States such as no one then could have foretold.

The first of these incidents was the transmission by General Washington (June 7, 1783) of a memorial to him from some officers—"a pathetic representation", Madison characterized it—lamenting that they were to end their toils and hardships by returning to inevitable distress, without any alleviation of their present wants. Congress could do no more than send the memorial and Washington's letter to the states (June 19), beseeching them to facilitate the punctual payment of the notes issued to the army on account of their pay.

The second incident, if not actually alarming, might well have been so. On June 13 the sergeants of one of the furloughed regiments, then in Philadelphia, sent to Congress what Madison termed "a very mutinous remonstrance", but to which Major Armstrong alluded as very spirited and "in language very intelligible". It was in effect a refusal of the furloughs and a demand for a satisfactory answer that same afternoon, accompanied by a threat that otherwise they would take their own measures with regard to the settlement of their accounts. Such a memorial naturally "excited much indignation" in Congress, where it was regarded as "of so insolent a nature as to forbid an answer". The memorial was turned over to the secretary at war, who, with the aid of General St. Clair, was able for the time being to soothe the discontents.

The third occurrence proved to be one that was not so easily turned into smooth channels. On Thursday, June 19, the very day on which Congress had given its unperturbed response to the first of the memorials mentioned, the executive council of Pennsylvania communicated to Congress a letter from Colonel Richard Butler of the third Pennsylvania regiment stationed at Lancaster, and another from William Henry, both letters dated at Lancaster, June 17, and directed to President Dickinson, conveying the information that about eighty men of that regiment, despite the fact that the necessary steps toward a settlement of their accounts were then in progress, had broken away from their officers and, under command of their sergeants, were on the way to Philadelphia, determined, as they asserted, "to obtain justice". Some of the men had even thrown out threats that they would rob the bank. Congress at once appointed a committee (Hamilton, Peters, and Ellsworth) to confer with the executive council and take such measures as they should find necessary. The council expressed to the committee its opinion that the Philadelphia militia would probably not be willing to take up arms unless provoked by some actual outrage, and that it would "hazard the authority of government" to attempt to prevent the troops from entering the city. Upon hearing the committee's report, several members were, to put it mildly, so peeved as to say that "if the City would not support Congress, it was high time to remove to some other place." As the mutinous troops had not yet put in their appearance, and as "matters seemed tolerably easy", Congress sent for General St. Clair to come to their aid, then adjourned. Next morning, however, the soldiers marched into the city and took possession of the barracks, where several hundred other troops were already quartered, but gave out that they had no other object than to obtain a settlement of their accounts. Thus assured that matters were still tolerably easy, Congress, according to custom, adjourned over till Monday.

By noon on Saturday new signs of brewing trouble appeared, whereupon President Boudinot called Congress together. Six states had assembled, when with fixed bayonets, the mutineers, joined by those previously at the barracks, to the number of four or five hundred, suddenly surrounded the State House, where the Pennsylvania Council as well as Congress was sitting. Presently the mutineers sent in a paper directed to President Dickinson and couched in language quite other than that of a humble petition. Their officers, they asserted, had "forsaken" them, and they demanded authority to appoint their own commissioned officers, with full powers to adopt such measures as they might judge most likely to procure them justice. "You will immediately issue such authority and deliver it to us", the address continued, "or otherwise we shall instantly let in those injured soldiers upon you, and abide by the consequences. You have only twenty minutes to deliberate upon this important matter."

Assuming that Congress was as much involved as Pennsylvania, if not more, and believing (as did Congress) that the threats were intended also for Congress, President Dickinson strode over to the Congress chamber and handed in the paper to that body, taking occasion to signify to Congress, as he had done to the committee, that the temper of the local militia could not be relied upon. Again indignation, rising to the point of wrath, boiled up in Congress. Hamilton thereupon proposed that General St. Clair, in concert with the Executive Council of Pennsylvania, "take order for terminating the mutiny". Read of South Carolina would temporize by having St. Clair endeavor to persuade the troops to withdraw by promising them that Congress would do them justice. But St. Clair had tried his influence with them only a little while before and had failed. Ralph Izard moved that Congress adjourn. To adopt a motion to adjourn was easy enough, but what about passing that cordon of soldiers, whose anger appeared to have been increased by the plentiful supply of liquor furnished them, so Madison records, by the rabble? "In this Situation", Madison reported, "Congress thought it most becoming their character to take no public notice of the insult, but to forbear any official act whatever."

And so, Congress sat quietly in its chamber, the soldiers maintained the siege without offering any violence (they did not even call time on the Pennsylvania Council at the expiration of the twenty minutes), while occasionally individuals among them uttered "offensive words" and "wantonly pointed their Muskets to the Windows of the Hall of Congress". Came three o'clock, the customary hour of adjournment, and Congress arose and passed out of the building through the ranks of the soldiers, who offered no more than "a mock obstruction". Their prisoners, the Congress, now at large, the soldiers presently retired to their barracks.

But Congress was far from being quiet in its mind. For lack of one member the afternoon session had been informal, but the members had unanimously directed President Boudinot to ask General Washington to send some of his best troops to their defense. Then, in the evening Congress was again assembled, when it was decided once more to test the spirit of the Pennsylvania government. In fact, so Madison recorded, the committee was instructed to "demand a categorical answer, whether they would make exertions to support government". In the event that the reply should be unsatisfactory, the president, on the advice of the committee, was authorized to summon the members to meet on the following Thursday at Trenton or Princeton. At the same time General Washington was expressly directed to detach a select force for the purpose of quelling the mutiny.

At four o'clock that afternoon, immediately upon the adjournment of Congress, President Boudinot had sent off a despatch to General Washington, and at eleven o'clock he sent another, transmitting the resolutions adopted that evening. On the 22d and again on the 23d of June the committee of Congress held conferences with the Executive Council of Pennsylvania, but the conference resulted, says Madison, in nothing "but a repetition of doubts concerning the disposition of the militia. . . . It was even doubted whether a repetition of the insult to Congress would be a sufficient provocation." Meanwhile, Madison relates, "Reports from the Barracks were in constant vibration"; and among the reports were intimations that the mutineers were meditating other and more violent measures. Accordingly, on Tuesday, June 24, President Boudinot issued a proclamation calling Congress to meet at Princeton on the 26th, "in order that further and more effectual measures may be taken for suppressing the present revolt, and maintaining the dignity and authority of the United States".

Whether it was the menace discovered in the president's proclamation, or the actual approach of the troops sent to overpower them, or just sober reflection, or a combination of all three incentives, the mutinying soldiers suddenly expressed repentance, laid down their arms, and impeached their officers, who, they declared, had betrayed them into the movement. At first, some of the troops from Lancaster, with whom the mutiny had begun, held back; whereupon their comrades gave them twenty-four hours to submit or be reduced by force.

Two of the officers, Captain Henry Carbery and Lieutenant John Sullivan, charged with having taken principal parts in the mutiny, fled and made their way across the Atlantic. Later they would recross the ocean, each to have another little part in the picture. Sullivan, just as he was leaving these shores, paid his uncomplimentary respects to Congress, adding that he possessed "the most perfect tranquility of mind, conscious of no unworthy action: all we regret", he asserted, "is failing in a noble attempt."

If many more agreed with Lieutenant Sullivan that the attempt was noble, they refrained from saying so. Washington aptly declared that the mutiny had had its beginnings, not with those who had "born the heat and burden of the War", not with soldiers who had "patiently endured hunger, nakedness, and cold", who had "suffered and bled without a murmur", but with "Recruits and Soldiers of a day", who had in reality "very few hardships to complain of".

None could have exceeded John Montgomery, himself a Pennsylvanian, in denunciation of the mutineers. Those fellows, he declared, had no right to complain, fellows who had received nine pounds bounty, a suit of clothes, and their arms, most of whom had been in service not more than five months and had never been in action—"the off-scourings and filth of the earth". Were those the men, he asked, to draw down the vengeance of the army and the public creditors on Congress? On the other hand, another Pennsylvanian, Major John Armstrong, who had taken part in an earlier projected mutiny and failed, although it was not yet generally known that he was the author of the Newburgh Addresses, was not ill-pleased over the humiliation of Congress. Writing to General Gates (June 26), he asserted that the mutiny had had one consequence that was "not unacceptable to many here". Declaimed he: "The grand Sanhedrin of the Nation, with all their solemnity and emptiness, have removed to Princeton, and left a state, where their wisdom has long been question'd, their virtue suspected, and their dignity a jest."

One member of Congress, Benjamin Hawkins of North Carolina, as he soberly observed the situation, wrote to his governor (June 24):

> In this State of things what can Congress do, without the means of paying those Debts they Constitutionally contracted for the safety of the United States, responsible for every thing, and unable to do any thing, hated by the public creditors, insulted by the Soldiery and unsupported by the citizens?

It was almost a matter of course that a quorum of members would not make their appearance at Princeton on June 26. Actually only one delegate was needed, and an additional one from either Delaware or South Carolina would have supplied the deficiency; but Rutledge of South Carolina had been involuntarily restrained in Philadelphia by what he supposed some people would call "a Touch of the Gout". The Rhode Island delegates, on the other hand, had chosen, so Oliver Ellsworth averred, to remain in Philadelphia "to shew their courage". On Monday, June 30, Congress was at length enabled to begin gathering up the tangled skeins of its affairs, and one of the first of these tangled skeins was a report from the committee deputed to confer with the Pennsylvania authorities. Naturally that report placed the Pennsylvania executive in anything but a favorable light. Naturally also the controversy was bound to continue through a good many months, with charges and counter charges, arguments offensive and defensive, with tempers waxing warm and voices rising high, with barrages of words that were barbed and bitter.

Notwithstanding the pleasantness and airiness of Princeton, attendance in Congress was exceedingly slack, much of the time no more than six states represented. It was not until July 29 that the requisite nine states were assembled for the ratification of the treaty with Sweden, which had come to hand before Congress departed Philadelphia. Meanwhile those who were in attendance had been aroused to a pitch of eagerness by news out of New York that the definitive treaty of peace had arrived. Expectantly they waited and waited through several dreary weeks, for not until September 12 was the "long silence" of the negotiators broken by the arrival of voluminous despatches, recounting the course of negotiations as late as July 27. These despatches necessarily gave rise to renewed discussions, but they were for the most part wasted effort, as the treaty had already been signed on September 3.

The interval of waiting was not, however, altogether unprofitably employed. On July 26, General Washington was invited to attend Congress in Princeton "as soon as may be convenient". The purpose, strangely enough, was not intimated in the invitation; but James McHenry, in a letter to Washington, supplied the reason thus: "The original resolve was that we should avail ourselves of your experience and advice in the formation of the peace establishment, but this was looped off in order to get Rhode Island to agree to the other. This State is opposed to a peace establishment." Congress was, in fact, resuming a business that had been initiated nearly four months before but had been interrupted by developments in the army. In the beginning of April a committee (Hamilton, Madison, Osgood, Wilson, and Ellsworth) had been appointed to report the proper arrangements to be taken in consequence of peace. As Madison explained it (Notes April 3-8), "The object was to provide a system for foreign affairs, for Indian affairs, for military and naval peace establishments; and also to carry into execution the regulation of weights and measures and other articles of the Confederation not attended to during the war."

It was a large order, and the committee first concentrated its attention on a military peace establishment. To this end Hamilton, in behalf of the committee, sought Washington's ideas on the subject, eliciting from him (April 16) a discussion of the problem in its general aspects, accompanied with a suggestion that the plan could be worked out more advantageously if Congress would send to headquarters a committee "with plenipotentiary powers". Then, on May 2, Washington sent to Hamilton his "Sentiments on a Peace Establishment". The committee prepared a report on the subject, drawn by Hamilton and bearing the date June 17, but the departure of Congress from Philadelphia appears to have prevented its being taken into consideration.

In response to the invitation, Washington came to Princeton, and on August 26 he was given an audience, when the president delivered a congratulatory address, and the general made an appropriate response. The committee with whom he was to confer was now, however, a new committee, appointed August 7, and of its personnel (Holten, Wilson, Carroll, Samuel Huntington, and Duane) Wilson only had been a member of the earlier committee. At the time of the appointment he was, in fact, the only member of the old committee in attendance, although Madison returned at the end of the month. On September 10 the committee reported some "Observations" of Washington on the report of June 17, but to what extent the subject was considered in Congress at that time the Journals do not reveal. On September 20, John Francis Mercer wrote, "We are pursuing the peace arrangement, but under many discouragements, which damp our ardor"; while Madison reported to Jefferson the same day that consideration of the question was "quickened by the presence of the Commander in Chief but without any prospect of a hasty issue." One question on which Congress was divided, he said, was "their Constitutional authority touching such an establishment in time of peace". That question had been raised by Howell on August 27, in a motion that Congress, in committee of the whole, should take into consideration "whether and what powers are vested in Congress by the confederation for making and supporting a peace establishment"; but the motion had been defeated.

The subject of the military peace arrangement does not appear to have been again taken into consideration in Congress until October 23, when the committee made a report, and a discussion of two days followed. (The report printed in the *Journals,* October 23, 1783, is not, however, the report then offered, but that of June 17.) The divided sentiments of Congress on the question seemed indeed incapable of composition, as a letter from the Virginia delegates (Lee and Mercer) to Governor Harrison, November 1, indicates. "Permanent measures on so important and delicate a subject", they wrote, "will no doubt be postpon'd untill our Constituents have time to deliberate and to express their sence on such plans as may be submitted to their consideration." When the subject was again taken up it had resolved itself mainly into the question what forces should be provided for garrisoning the western posts. As for those other items originally included in the agenda of the committee, some had died, some slept, some languished, others were still in embryo. Almost the only positive accomplishment had been some preliminary provisions (adopted October 15) for treaties with the Indians, mainly with a view to opening the way to settlement of the western country.

Efforts had been made to accomplish what might have seemed to be the very small task of choosing a secretary for foreign affairs; but without success. Robert R. Livingston had tendered his resignation in December, 1782, but had been prevailed on to continue in office through the winter, except for such times as it was necessary for him to attend to his duties as chancellor of New York. In June, 1783, he finally relinquished the office, chiefly because of an inadequacy of salary, whereupon the papers of the secretariat were turned over to the secretary of Congress, while the duties of the office chiefly devolved upon the President. June 11 was set for electing his successor, but the day came and went without an election.

A faction in Congress had long been critical of Livingston, and some of them appeared to prefer having no secretary, unless he could be one of their faction. On June 10, Stephen Higginson wrote that the event of Livingston's retirement was "a very agreeable one". "Who will succeed", he said, "or whether any Successor will soon be appointed is uncertain at present. I wish for one other removal and then I think Congress would be free of dangerous influences." The latter allusion was to Robert Morris, superintendent of finance. On the same day Madison wrote to Jefferson: "I am utterly at a loss to guess on whom the choice will ultimately fall. A[rthur] L[ee] will be started if the defect of a respectable competitor sh[oul]d be likely to force votes upon him." Major John Armstrong, who was not a member of Congress but appears to have known fairly well what went on in and around that assembly, wrote that many were in nomination. "Old Laurens", he said, "has been mentioned and is by far the most unexceptionable, but . . . he is not here." On September 20, Madison wrote to Jefferson, "The department of foreign Affairs both internal and external remains as it has long done. The election of a Sec[retar]y has been an order of the day for many months without a vote being taken." In fact, not until May, 1784, was a successor chosen, and then the choice fell upon

John Jay, who was then absent in Europe, and it was not until the beginning of 1785 that he assumed the office.

During these same tedious weeks at Princeton, Congress frequently, and not always mildly, was occupied with the problem of its abode, both temporary and permanent. It was not altogether a new subject of consideration, for, long before Congress had shaken off the dust of its shoes on the Philadelphia doorstep as a testimony against the city and the state whose protecting hand had been withheld in the hour of need, some members, believing that the city was corrupting the good morals of Congress, had been urging a removal, though whither, they could not quite decide. In the spring, however, Congress had received two offers of a permanent seat, one from New York, the other from Maryland. When the hurried removal did take place, it was the signal for other invitations, so that Congress was soon confronted with an embarrassment of riches in the numerous offers of more or less spacious dwelling-places.

From this time forth, until the "ten-mile-square" on the Potomac was finally fixed upon, the question of a little domain of its own, where none could molest or make it afraid, was seldom long absent from the thoughts and proceedings of the old Congress or of its successor. There was even a suggestion that, since Congress was bound to move somewhere in any case, it might do well to go west as far as Fort Pitt, grow up with the country, and thereby enhance the value of its vast western domain. The village of Princeton, though eager to have the national assembly abide with it permanently and zealous to provide all needed facilities, given time, was unable as yet to afford members of Congress accommodations suitable to their personal habits, or such other facilities as were requisite for carrying on the national business.

Naturally the prospect of losing Congress permanently was not comforting to Philadelphians. Chagrined over the predicament in which they found themselves, many of the citizens threw the blame on their council, while the council took refuge behind the militia officers, whose advice they had taken; but whosesoever the blame, Congress must be besought to return. There are "Prospects of Sugar Plumbs from the Citizens and Council", Richard Peters wrote to Thomas FitzSimons from his seat at Belmont, July 8 (he had not yet trailed over to Princeton). "But", he added, "the Devil has set his Mark on all this Business." "You wish Congress to return", John Montgomery wrote to Dr. Benjamin Rush the same day. "Will you proud Philadelphians Condessend to invite them to return or will you rather say they went without our Knowladge and they may return without an invetation?" For his part, he believed an invitation would have a "happey Effect". If the council and state would act a prudent and a wise part, if they would "Disscovere a Conceliating Dissposition", things would come to rights again, "mens tempers will Cool and thire fears Subside and Congrass will strut on the pavements of the grand metroplaiss and talk those woundefull things over and Congratulate Each other on the mervolous Esscape we made and the great Wisdom and prudence in Conducting affair[s] to a happey Esue."

In due time (possibly overdue time) came the sugar plums in the form of an address liberally signed by the citizens and believed to have been sweetened to the Congressional taste, bidding that august assembly come back to Philadelphia, where comfort, content, and even happiness awaited it. Nine-tenths of the members, Peters asserted (July 26), "have a secret Sigh after Philadelphia but some childish Reasons or those less innocent prevail with them", so that his hopes of a return grew less every day. There would be an answer to the invitation, and the answer "may be very sweet"; but he would be on his guard "lest the Bee be drowned in the Honey". It was "a Very Kind adreas", Montgomery wrote the same day; however, he thought Congress would remain in Princeton, at least until the hot season was over. "This is a pleasant ariee place and remarkably Healthy", he added, much in contrast with Philadelphia.

The Philadelphian bee meanwhile continued to make honey to set before Congress, although it did not at the same time forego the use of its sting. For instance, as late as September 30, Dr. Rush wrote to Montgomery, "The Congress is abused, laughed at and cursed in every company." The exchange of amenities was nevertheless all that could be asked for—as amenities; but, however deep and abounding may have been the sighs for the flesh pots and wine cellars and whatnot of Philadelphia, whether for childish reasons or for reasons of some degree of maturity, Congress could not quite be prevailed upon to return.

Among the various lures dangled before their eyes was an invitation from Germantown; but it was generally supposed that Germantown was only serving as Philadelphia's alternate, and there was not so much as a nibble at the bait. In the early days of October—the chilly weather may have had something to do with it—thought of returning to Philadelphia gained strength, and Peters took advantage of the mood to make one last, laborious effort. About the 10th of October he prepared for a frontal attack with a bombardment of whereases, extending to a thousand words or more, and closing with a motion that Congress be adjourned to meet at the State House in Philadelphia on the blank day of blank at blank o'clock in the forenoon. If the over-elongated preamble and the skeleton motion were actually fired, they proved to be duds, whereupon Peters withdrew from Congress in disgust, retired to his farm at Belmont, and declared that he would like to forget there ever was such a body as Congress. "For", said he, "I am much the happiest when I hear or think nothing of the erratic meteor which arose with so much splendor and I fear will set with no small disgrace."

By this time indeed the questions where Congress should have its temporary seat and how long, and where it should establish itself permanently, had become the principal pabulum of its ruminations. And the more Congress gave thought to the problem of a permanent abiding place the deeper became the conviction that the national government, whatever might be its form and whatever its power, should have a domain and a jurisdiction all its own. As the discussion progressed, however, the problem became more and more a tangle of geographical and political complexities. On the 7th of October, Congress came to a resolve to establish itself near the falls of the river Delaware. But this was by no means satisfactory to the southern states, therefore a few days later, when a slight change in representation had taken place, it was resolved that, inasmuch as "the alternate residence of Congress in two places will have the most salutary effects, by securing the confidence and affections of the states, and preserving the federal balance of power", a second residence should be established at the lower falls of the Potomac. It added to the complications that the maker of that motion was none other than Elbridge Gerry of Massachusetts; and it likewise stood to reason that the later decision, like the former, would stand only until its opponents should be able to overthrow it. At the same time it was further resolved that, until the permanent seats should be prepared, Congress would visit around among the neighbors, spending a half-year or may be a year at Annapolis, then betake itself to Trenton for a like period. "So that", President Boudinot wrote to Robert R. Livingston, "we are to be in future wandering Stars and to have our Aphelion and Perihelion."

Almost simultaneously with the decision to bid adieu to Princeton and go down to Annapolis for the winter Congress found itself, as the head of the nation, in an uncomfortable situation. Almost exactly a year before a treaty of amity and commerce with the States General of the Netherlands had been negotiated by John Adams, and in the close of January, 1783, the treaty had been ratified by Congress. In time of course a minister from that country would be presenting himself, and in April it was learned that Peter John van Berckel was the man. Next it was learned, late in August, that the minister was on his passage to America and might land any day. Congress was embarrassed over the problem of giving him a proper reception in the small town of Princeton. "We are crowded too much", Madison wrote, "either to be comfortable ourselves or to be able to carry on business with advantage." What was equally lamentable, "Mr. Jones and my self are in one room scarcely ten feet square and in one bed." With the Dutch minister expected at any moment, it was "the most awkward situation that can be imagined". No wonder these extremities of Congress were embraced as golden opportunities for the rival suitors for that assembly's favor. While Philadelphia sweetly beckoned Congress to return, Annapolis "courted their presence in the most flattering terms".

The minister did not appear so soon as expected, but on October 9, 1783, Congress was shocked out of all equanimity to learn that he had actually arrived in Philadelphia. "Congress are in a charming situation to receive him", Madison exploded (October 13); "in an obscure village undetermined where they will spend the Winter and without a Minister of F[oreign] A[ffairs]." The embarrassment was all the greater because, before Congress left Philadelphia, elaborate arrangements were begun for the minister's reception. "In pursuance of a commission from him", Madison had written from Philadelphia, September 30, "*six* elegant horses are provided for his coach, as was to have been one of the best houses in the most fashionable part of this City."

If Congress had its mortifications, Mynheer van Berckel likewise had his day of chagrin, when he arrived in Philadelphia and was not received in form. To Thomas FitzSimons he afterward confided "very politely" his mortifying surprise over his reception. When Mr. Adams arrived in Holland, he said, the States General had sent a person to receive him and had provided a proper place for his reception. Furthermore, to do honor to their first embassy to the United States, they had sent their minister with a respectable fleet.

After some days of chilly waiting, he wrote to President Boudinot (October 19) to announce his arrival and to ask for an audience that he might present his credentials. Unfortunately, despite the fact that between Philadelphia and Princeton there was a rapid transit service called "The Flying Machine", the minister's letter to President Boudinot had been unaccountably delayed. There was need for explanations, and, if the audience was to take place before the departure from Princeton, there was also need for haste. As for the ceremonial, that prepared for the reception of the first minister to the United States more than five years before and since used only for his successor, was drawn forth from its pigeon hole, furbished up and simplified, the president meantime smoothing as best he could the roughened way He put his own house at the minister's disposal, expressed the great satisfaction of Congress over the happy event of his coming, "big with the best consequences to both our nations", and sent him a copy of the ceremonial for his information. "We feel ourselves greatly mortified", he wrote, "that our present circumstances in a small Country village prevent us giving you a reception more agreeable to our wishes. But I hope these unavoidable deficiencies will be compensated by the sincerity of our Joy on this occasion."

In another respect Congress was somewhat handicapped for giving ceremonial receptions. There was no secretary for foreign affairs, on whom the chief function would normally devolve, the secretary at war was absent, and, though sent for, might not reach Princeton in time; accordingly the superintendent of finance, himself in Philadelphia, was called upon to serve as chief functionary, or conjointly with the secretary at war in the event of the latter's arrival. There was yet another problem: the minister's credentials were in Low Dutch, and there was not a soul in or about Congress who knew that language. Some one bethought himself of Frederick Frelinghuysen, a member elect from New Jersey but not then in attendance, whereupon a message was sent by express to Frelinghuysen requesting that he read the credentials to the assembled gathering. The audience was first set for Thursday, October 30, then, at the minister's request, was postponed to Friday.

This reception, like that to Luzerne, stirred no such ferment of excitation as the first, but the formalities—the risings, the bowings, the sittings—appear to have moved smoothly to their finish. The Low Dutch credentials were listened to politely but without comprehension; the address of the minister, which was in French, found a few ears attuned; but the response of the president, which was, as the law required, "in the language of the United States", all could understand. Said the Virginia delegates, reporting to their governor: "The reception and Ceremony were more conformable to present circumstances and embarrassments than to the Representatives of a great Nation. Still the characters who were in attendance, and the cordiality with which they were conducted may well compensate for Pomp splendor and Shew." Of the minister himself President Boudinot wrote (to John Adams November 1), "We are much pleased with this gentleman, and, as far as I can judge from present appearances, I may venture to predict that he will cement the union of the two Republics."

There was one occurrence that day that quickened the spirits of Congress more than the paying of the nation's formal respects to the Dutch minister. Just as the ceremonies were about to begin, Colonel Matthias Ogden, who had left Paris on September 10, arrived in Princeton, bringing authentic information that the definitive treaty between the United States and Great Britain had been signed on the 3d of September, and that the treaty itself, borne by John Thaxter, private secretary to John Adams, was already on its way to America. "This", wrote President Boudinot, "gave a large addition to the general Joy that was already great on the occasion of the day."

On Monday, November 3, 1783, the new Congress met, chose Thomas Mifflin of Pennsylvania president (although he was then absent), and on the 4th adjourned to meet at Annapolis, November 26. On the 22d, Thaxter arrived in Philadelphia and delivered the treaty to President Mifflin, who at once informed the several state executives by circular letter. It was pleasing to discover that the definitive differed but little from the provisional treaty, but it was disconcerting to learn that the ratifications were to be exchanged within the space of six months from the date of signature. Nearly half that time had already elapsed, therefore it was essential, the president said in his letter to the states, that the delegates be impressed with the necessity of attending Congress as soon as possible.

It might have seemed that no prodding would be needed to start members hastening to the seat of Congress to give their needed affirmation to this consummation of peace, an event toward which they had looked forward with anxious yearnings through two long years. But members were busy here and there with their personal affairs, and somehow many of them failed to be impressed with the urgency of ratification. On the 13th of December and not earlier representations from seven states, with one delegate from New Hampshire and one from South Carolina, assembled at the State House in Annapolis. On the 16th, Jefferson wrote to Edmund Randolph: "We have no certain prospect of nine states in Congress and cannot ratify the treaty with fewer, yet the ratifications are to be exchanged by the 3d of March." For a month and a day from the first assembling of seven states the attendance did not exceed that number and was often less.

While the meager group waited and pleaded with the absentees to hasten their coming, occurred an event impressive at the time and ever since memorable. On the 23d of December, 1783, in accordance with a prearranged program, General Washington was given an audience in Congress that he might resign his commission. On the preceding day Congress gave "an elegant public dinner" in honor of the general, at which the principal Maryland officials and citizens of Annapolis, about two hundred in all, were guests. "The entertainment", a committee subsequently reported, ". . . was exceedingly plentiful, and the provisions and liquors good in their kind." There were of course the customary thirteen toasts and the discharge of thirteen cannon. On the invitation of the governor the dinner was followed in the evening by a ball at the State House. The audience was likewise attended by the governor and council of Maryland, members of the two houses of assembly, and the principal gentlemen and ladies of Annapolis. Recorded one chronicler: "Congress were seated and covered, as Representatives of the sovereignty of the union, the spectators were uncovered and standing."

"The farewell of General Washington", David Howell recorded, "was a most solemn Scene. . . . And many testified their affectionate attachment to our illustrious Hero and their gratitude for his Services to his country by a most copious shedding of tears." James McHenry wrote that Washington deposited his commission and took his leave of Congress "in a very pathetic manner".

It was a solemn and affecting spectacle [he said]; such an one as history does not present. The spectators all wept, and there was hardly a member of Congress who did not drop tears. The General's hand which held the address shook as he read it. When he spoke of the officers who had composed his family, and recommended those who had continued in it to the present moment to the favorable notice of Congress he was obliged to support the paper with both hands. But when he commended the interests of his dearest country to almighty God, and those who had the superintendence of them to his holy keeping, his voice faultered and sunk, and the whole house felt his agitations.

Here, McHenry records, the general had to pause to recover himself; then, "in the most penetrating manner", he thus concluded his address: "Having now finished the work assigned me, I retire from the great theatre of action, and bidding an affectionate farewell to this august body, under whose orders I have so long acted, I here offer my commission, and take my leave of all the employments of public life."

The first act of Congress on the morning of December 23d was to resolve that letters be immediately despatched to the executives of the unrepresented states—New Hampshire, Connecticut, New York, New

Jersey, South Carolina, and Georgia—informing them "that the safety, honor and good faith of the United States require the immediate attendance of their delegates in Congress"; that, besides the ratification of the definitive treaty, "several other matters, of great national concern", were now pending before Congress that required the assent of at least nine states. New Hampshire had one delegate in attendance, and it would require six weeks to bring another; South Carolina also had one in attendance, although another, Richard Beresford, lay sick in Philadelphia; no delegates could be expected from New York at any time soon, for none had been elected; while information from Georgia was that no delegation was to be expected this winter. To aggravate the situation, one of the Delaware delegates, Eleazer McComb, was declaring that "the situation of his private affairs" would compel him to return home. The dependence for relief was therefore upon Connecticut and New Jersey, both if Delaware could not be held in line, one of them in any event; and to them accordingly went the most earnest entreaties to send on their delegations, "that the consequences to be expected from the Want of an immediate Representation of nine States may not be imputable to your State, which on every former Occasion has exerted itself with so much honor and Reputation".

The margin of time for ratifying and getting the ratification across the Atlantic was by now reduced to almost the minimum, therefore in view of the extreme uncertainty some members suggested that seven states were competent to the ratification, and the question was debated for several days. As late as January 5, Cadwalader Morris, a new member from Pennsylvania, was arguing, in a letter to William Bingham, that in his opinion seven states were perfectly competent. Even some of those who doubted the validity of a ratification by seven states insisted that it be done nevertheless and concealed from Great Britain. Jefferson led the argument against such a course on the ground that it was both invalid and unwise, and his cogent reasoning appears in the sequel to have tipped the scales. While, however, this question was still in agitation, there came a momentary hope of obtaining the nine states, but only by means of an extraordinary procedure. The hope rested on the coming of the New Jersey delegates. In that event, said Jefferson (January 1), "if Beresford will not come to Congress, Congress must go to him for this one act." In other words, Congress would go to Philadelphia and hold a session in Richard Beresford's sickroom, since by that means South Carolina could be represented. But the New Jersey delegation failed to appear betimes, and, because the seven-states group had become impatient, Jefferson proposed, as he expressed it, "to meet them on their own ground": Let the treaty be ratified by seven states and transmitted to the ministers, who should be instructed to obtain, if possible, an extension of time for the ratification; but, in the event that an extension could not be obtained, then to offer the treaty as ratified by seven states, with a pledge that a ratification by nine states would be transmitted as soon as that number could be assembled.

On the 5th of January it was ordered that a letter of that purport be written to the ministers; then Congress sat down to wait and to hope. On January 13 two delegates from Connecticut appeared, and one—one only—from New Jersey, John Beatty. Had he only brought a colleague the problem would have been solved. Fortunately it was solved the next day, when Beresford, now able to rise from his sick-bed, came to Congress and thereby saved Congress from going to him. Accordingly, immediately upon the assembling of Congress on the morning of January 14, 1784, the vote on ratification was taken, and, of the twenty-three members present and voting, there was not a dissenting voice.

It may be taken for granted that each and every of the twenty-three members of Congress, notwithstanding some of them had not theretofore manifested all commendable concern, now took a deep breath of relief. Yet their gratification was not unalloyed. The battle had been but half won, for over their heads still hung that threatening question whether the ratified treaty could be delivered by the dead-line of March 3. Those members of Congress who were deeply concerned for the outcome had for more than six weeks lived in a frenzy of exasperation lest the ratification be too late, and now they knew that it had only the remotest chance of escaping that fate.

It is well known [wrote Jefferson] that Great Britain wished to postpone the conclusion of the treaty. . . . It is not impossible then but she might hope for some favorable opportunity of changing the face of the treaty. If the ratifications are not there by the day she will have too much ground for objection to the validity of the treaty, and to ratify or not as she pleases.

Every effort therefore must be made to speed the treaty across the Atlantic, and every precaution taken to avoid mishap. Colonel Josiah Harmar, secretary to the president, was entrusted with the original ratification, and, since no vessel was sailing soon from Philadelphia, hurried to New York to catch a French packet about to sail thence; a duplicate was put into the hands of Robert Morris, as agent of marine, for transmission by any possible means; and, on second thought, Colonel David S. Franks was despatched with a triplicate, instructed to take passage on the first vessel sailing from any eastern port, excepting only those carrying either of the other instruments of ratification.

On the 2d of February, Morris informed Congress that he had not been able to despatch the duplicate. On the 13th it was learned that, though Harmar had sailed on the 21st of January, the packet had run aground and been obliged to return to port, and that neither he nor Franks was yet on his passage. In fact, it was almost exactly five weeks from the time they left Annapolis before either was able to begin the voyage. There was no longer any question that the ratification would fail the appointed exchange. "So much", commented Cadwalader Morris of the state of Pennsylvania and the city of Philadelphia, "for the politicians, who cunningly removed Congress to the Lee Ward." Jacob Read of South Carolina, on the other hand, comforted himself with the thought that "Nought but the Act of God" had prevented the ratification from getting to Europe in time, therefore he had faith that no ill would result to the union therefrom. Congress could but await the outcome, its hopes wrestling mightily the while with its fears.

As it turned out, Congress might just as well have spared itself all anxieties and every allocation of responsibility, for, though its messengers reached Paris a month late, the British ministers were not in the least disposed to higgle over the delay, and the ratifications were amicably exchanged on the 12th of May. That gratifying information would not come back across the Atlantic earlier than the end of July, but long before that time the tension had been relieved by word from Franklin that no difficulty was to be expected.

CHAPTER XXX

LOOSENING BONDS
THE COMMITTEE OF THE STATES

If the states and their delegates-elect to Congress had manifested an astonishing degree of indifference to the affairs of their union in that all-important matter of ratifying the definitive treaty, it was scarcely to be expected that concern for the union would straightway rise to new strength on the heels of that consummation. To the contrary, attendance began immediately to fall off and for a good many weeks grew steadily worse. On January 16, 1784, that is, two days after the ratification, Jefferson was writing to Governor Harrison of Virginia, and he listed six important subjects calling for determination by Congress, all of which involved such differences of opinion that determination would be difficult even with nine states in attendance. These subjects were: authorization of treaties of alliance and commerce with nations desiring them, the arrangement of the domestic administration, the establishment of arsenals within the states and of posts on the frontier, disposal of the western territory, treaties of peace and purchase with the Indians, and, last though not least, finances.

But even while he wrote, a number of members were preparing to decamp, and on the very next day only six states were in attendance. During the six weeks following the ratification of the treaty, on only sixteen days were as many as seven or eight states in attendance, on others, six, five, and even as low as three. Between the adjournment from Princeton and the first of March, a period of four months, on only three days, January 14, 15, and 16, were nine states represented. On February 16, Tilton of Delaware wrote to President Van Dyke of his mortification that his own state was to be "treated with another set of teazing resolutions" because of its delinquency. "But, sir", he wrote, "the situation of Congress is truly alarming; the most important business pending and not states enough to take it up; whilst those present are fatigued into resentment and almost despair, with loitering away their time, to little purpose, while waiting for others to come."

Some four days later it was proposed by several members that the delinquent states be informed that, unless representations sufficient to enable Congress to do the public business should speedily attend, those present would go home. The majority, however, Tilton wrote, "were unwilling to familiarize the idea of a dissolution of the federal government". And Jefferson, than whom no man was more anxious to prevent a dissolution, wrote to Madison the same day (February 20): "We have not sat above 3 days I believe in as many weeks. Admonition after admonition has been sent to the states, to no effect. we have sent one to-day. if it fails, it seems as well we should all retire."

Well, even though the national business must lag and loiter, that was no reason why life in Annapolis should be monotonous and dull, for there was no dearth of entertainment, at least for those gentlemen of the Congress who had an inclination for such things. "The polite Attention of the Gentlemen of the Town", wrote Dr. Samuel Dick, a member for New Jersey, "Engages all our leisure hours in Visits and Amusements. The Players Exhibit twice a week and there is a Brilliant Assembly or Ball once a fortnight to which We have Standing Cards of Invitation."

Even Thomas Jefferson, though his weather-eye seldom wandered for more than a moment from the national scene, did now and then cast a glance toward the frolicking; and once he was made to chuckle softly over a predicament into which his bachelor colleague, Arthur Lee, for whom he had no special fondness, had got himself. He was writing to Madison, and in their confidential cipher: "Lee, finding no faction among the men here, entered into that among the women, which rages to a very high degree. A ball being appointed by the one party on a certain night, he undertook to give one, and fixed it precisely on the same night. This of course has placed him in the midst of the mud." Evidently there was social as well as political mud-slinging in Annapolis. Some of the New Englanders, on the other hand, looked askance at all these gayeties. Said David Howell of Rhode Island:

Had my education in youth, or did my present taste admit of my participating in the amusements of this place such as plays, Balls, Concerts, routs, hops, Fandangoes and fox hunting, or I may add did my finances admit of mixing with the *bon-ton,* time might pass off agreeably; but four dollars a day . . . will not admit of seeing much Company, as you well know.

Elbridge Gerry likewise spoke of Annapolis as "not a place capable of administring much to my pleasure, or of promoting my Happiness". Quoth he:

The Inhabitants are almost universally disposed to enjoy themselves. Balls, Plays, dining and Tea parties, engross the time of the Ladies, Hunting, Fishing, gaming, Horseracing, etc. that of the Gentlemen. those of Congress who are wholly devoted to Pleasure, if there are any such, may indulge their Inclinations by being courteous and attentive to the Inhabitants; those who are for dispatching the publick Business, will never be interrupted by the Citizens of Annapolis, for the Idea of Business to them is neither agreeable nor reputable.

Whether resisting or succumbing to the lures of Annapolis, members of Congress found common ground in their complaint against the state of Maryland and the delegates thereof for leaving the state long unrepresented, and that, as Read of South Carolina grumbled, despite the fact that Congress was "actually Seated in the Capital of the State".

On the first day of March came Jonathan Blanchard of New Hampshire to join Abiel Foster, thereby giving representation to their state. Nine states at last, and Congress could go to work in earnest. Straightway the Virginia delegates laid before Congress a deed of cession from that state of her territory north and west of the Ohio. Thus one three-year-old dragging controversy was brought to a satisfactory conclusion, and, what was still better, it opened the way for measures that were to have the greatest significance. The cession made by Virginia in January, 1781, had contained conditions so unsatisfactory that, in October, 1782, Congress had declined to accept it. In September, 1783, after several months of discussion, Congress had specified the terms on which the cession from Virginia would be accepted, and in October the state had complied; although, in accordance with its policy of avoiding recognition of the validity of claims, Congress had declined to void certain private claims within the ceded territory or to guarantee to Virginia her remaining western territory. Even so, however, acceptance of the Virginia cession (March 1, 1784) narrowly escaped rejection at the hands of the higglers. The all-important fact was that the United States were now in possession of a princely domain of unoccupied lands, and it remained only to find the right solution for their disposition. True, possession of the territory ceded by Virginia was as yet to some degree qualified and complicated by claims of Connecticut and Massachusetts, to say nothing of Indian titles; but there was small doubt that in the near future these obstacles likewise would be cleared away.

The problem of the western territory had in fact two distinct phases, one how the lands should be disposed of, the other what manner of government should be set up for this domain; and both phases had been given much thought through the preceding years. Immediately upon the acceptance of the Virginia cession a committee, of which Jefferson was chairman, sometime before appointed (October 15, 1783, January 7, 1784) "to prepare a plan for the temporary government of the western territory", brought in their report (March 1, 1784). Prior to the appointment of this committee, on June 5, 1783, a resolution had been offered by Theodorick Bland, seconded by Alexander Hamilton, providing that the western territory be divided into a number of "districts", each of which, when it should contain 20,000 male inhabitants, should "become and ever after be and constitute a separate Independent free and Sovereign state, and be admitted into the Union as such with all privileges and immunities of those states which now compose the Union". The design at that time was primarily to make a provision for officers and soldiers of the army in lieu of commutation for half-pay and arrearages; and motions with a like aim had been made in October following. None of these motions crystallized into definite resolves, nevertheless they point toward the ultimate solution of the problem of territorial government.

The idea that the western territory should be carved into new states to be eventually admitted into the Union had in fact become accepted as a fixed feature of any government that might be set up for the western territory. Jefferson's report even designated the geographical boundaries of the proposed states, ten in number, and offered names for them: Sylvania, Michigania, Cherronesus, Assenisipia, Metropotamia, Illinoia, Saratoga, Washington, Polypotamia, Pelisipia. The names met with disapproval from unromantic members of Congress at the time, and it has since become a fixed habit in Territorial historiography to speak of the names as fanciful, or under similar implications of ridicule. Possibly it was an excess of sonorousness that became dissonance to so many ears. Perhaps it was because there were so many of them. Ultimately only five states were permitted to grow where, in contemplation, ten had been planted; and as for their names, "Let those acclaim their praise whose voices are attuned."

Upon a recommitment of the report a revised plan was brought in on March 22, with additions and also with eliminations, among the eliminations being the ten proposed states, names and all. One principle that Jefferson was particularly eager to have incorporated into the fundamental instrument of government for the western territory is stated in these words:

that after the year 1800 of the Christian era, there shall be neither slavery nor involuntary servitude in any of the said States, otherwise than in punishment for crimes, whereof the party shall have been duly convicted to have been personally guilty.

Still another proposal was that the governments of the new states should be "in republican forms", and should admit no person to be a citizen who held any hereditary title. Congress rejected both the proposed abolition of slavery and the exclusion of hereditary honors, although on very different grounds. The latter clause, Jefferson explained, was rejected, "not from an approbation of such honours, but because it was thought an improper place to encounter them." The proposition for the abolition of salvery in the territories failed in consequence of a peculiar situation. As the votes stand, six states were in favor of the proposition, three opposed, and two divided. The New England States, New York, and Pennsylvania voted aye, as did the one delegate of the New Jersey. Maryland and South Carolina were both in the negative, as was also Virginia, since of three members present Jefferson alone voted aye. North Carolina was divided. But for the illness of John Beatty, Jefferson explains, New Jersey would have given a seventh affirmative vote and carried the proposition; and he further adds that but for the illness of Monroe, Virginia's vote would have been divided. By such quirks of fate are the streams of human endeavor ofttimes directed or diverted.

On the 23d of April, 1784, the act as amended was adopted. Briefly, the act provided for the temporary government of any part of the territory upon the petition of the inhabitants or on the order of Congress, including as an initial step the adoption of the constitution and laws of any one of the original states. When such a territory shall have acquired 20,000 free inhabitants, authority would be given by Congress to call a convention of representatives to estabish a permanent constitution and government, under certain general restrictions and requirements. During the temporary government the territory was to have the privilege of keeping a delegate in Congress, with a right of debating but not of voting. When the number of inhabitants should become equal to that of the least numerous of the thirteen original states, "such State shall be admitted by its delegates into the Congress of the United States, on an equal footing with the said original states." These features, in their essential character, remained the core of the system finally adopted in 1787, with the re-incorporation, substantially as had been proposed by Jefferson, of the provision for abolishing slavery in the territories after 1800.

The other phase of the western problem, that of disposing of the lands, was likewise brought under the consideration of Congress early in March, although it was not until the last day of April that a committee, of which also Jefferson was chairman, offered a solution in the form of an "Ordinance for ascertaining the mode of locating and disposing of lands in the western territory". The ordinance was "read a first time" on May 7, and on May 28 was again taken into consideration, but with the result that only one state, North Carolina, out of nine represented, voted for its approval, although it won in addition two individual votes, Howell of Rhode Island and Mercer of Virginia. Howell was a member of the committee, as was also Williamson of North Carolina, and both had cooperated with Jefferson in framing the ordinance. On the other hand, Gerry of Massachusetts and Read of South Carolina, likewise members of the committee, voted in the negative. Jefferson had left Congress on May 3. There was yet conflict of minds, even confusion of ideas, on the subject, but it was mainly a question whether a New England or a southern system were best. It was almost exactly a year before ideas had sufficiently crystallized for the adoption of any system.

There were indeed reasons for delay other than immaturity of thought and differences of opinion. Indian titles remained to be cleared, and there were cessions yet to be made before the federal government could claim full possession of the desired territory. Measures for negotiating with the northern Indians had been concluded in March, and now, on the very day on which the land ordinance was rejected, a plan for negotiating with the southern Indians was adopted. As for satisfactory cessions from all the claimant states, they were destined to drag along more exasperatingly than the Indian treaties. Connecticut had three days before (May 25) laid before Congress an act of cession, but it was characterized by Williamson of North Carolina as "a curious act", while Hand of Pennsylvania wrote President Dickinson that it would "amuse" him. It was two years almost to a day before Congress was brought to accept the cession. Massachusetts, for her part, put in a claim (June 3, 1784) for lands within the reserved boundary of New York, and there must needs be a trial of the case. Accordingly, in December following, a court, in accordance with the provisions of the Confederation, was set up for the purpose. In mid-summer came a cession from North Carolina, but that state soon repented and withdrew the cession. More evangelistic work amongst the land-holding states would be necessary before this vital problem was to be finally solved.

The 28th of May, 1784, is memorable for yet another act of Congress having outstanding importance. This was a resolve to put the department of finance into commission; in other words, to substitute for the superintendent of finance a board of treasury composed of three commissioners. This was, on the one hand, a culmination of the attack on Morris that had long been brewing and, on the other, an outcome of one more tussle in Congress with the always troublesome finances. The movement against the financier was initiated in September, 1783, by Arthur Lee in a demand for an investigation into certain of Morris's acts as superintendent of finance. In this Lee was aided particularly by the Massachusetts delegates, Higginson and Osgood, and one result was an instruction from Massachusetts to her delegates in October to move for a new arrangement in the department of finance. "If two or three more States would give similar Instructions", Higginson wrote to Lee, "I should expect that Mr. F[inancie]r must give up the reins and retire."

Writing at great length to John Adams, December 7, 1783, Osgood attacked the "Systems of Intrigue and Influence" that began with the deplorable financial situation and had been aggravated by the creation of "great Officers of State". The sinister figures in this system were the French minister, the secretary for foreign affairs, who was characterized as "the eagle-eyed Politician of our great Ally" (Livingston had actually retired sometime before), and the superintendent of finance. The last, Osgood acknowledged, was a man of judgment and great decision, possessed of many excellent qualities for a financier, but these "do not comport so well with Republicanism, as Monarchy". A man of "inflexible Perseverance", he was nevertheless indifferent to popular confidence. "Ambitious of becoming the first Man in the United States, he was not so delicate in the Choice of Means, and Men for his Purpose, as is indispensably necessary in a free Government." Together the financier and the secretary were admirably adapted to become "the principal Engines of Intrigue", supported by "the good Ally of the United States", and supporting him in turn.

How blind was the obsession of the group represented by Osgood is indicated by his contention that the establishment of the system of executive departments was merely a maneuver of the minister of France for his own purposes. Others than Osgood then and afterward joined heartily in the prayer: "May Heaven finally extricate us from all foreign Intrigues"; others than he shuddered at the dark shadow of monarchy which they thought they perceived hovering over the United States, particularly exemplified in "the great officers of state"; but none other gave quite so free a rein to his fears and wild imaginings.

When, in March, 1784, Morris indicated a purpose to retire shortly, plans were at once set on foot to displace the one-man superintendent of finance with a board of three commissioners, and on May 28 the ordinance for the regulation of the department was adopted with but small opposition. On June 3, just when Congress was on the point of adjourning, Daniel of St. Thomas Jenifer, Oliver Ellsworth, and William Denning were chosen to constitute the board. All three eventually declined, and it was a good many months before the new board was actually functioning.

The fears generated by that other great office of state, the secretary for foreign affairs, had for the most part centered about the personality of the secretary, Robert R. Livingston, but they had persisted even after his retirement to such a degree that for a year it proved impossible to elect a successor. In the beginning of May, 1784, opposition to the election suddenly and in a rather remarkable manner melted away. Congress was informed that Mr. Jay was planning to return to America, whereupon he was immediately chosen secretary for foreign affairs. The opposition to the choice of Jay as one of the foreign ministers had been fierce and bitter on the part of the New England faction and their few southern adherents; but the part he had taken in breaking loose from the French leading-strings in the peace negotiations had given him immense popularity amongst that very group.

At the same time Congress brought to maturity a plan that had been taking shape since the ratification of the peace treaty, namely, for the negotiation of other treaties of alliance and commerce. In making these plans there was an insistence on the part of the southern members that the negotiators of these treaties be more evenly balanced between north and south, that "the commercial interest of the different parts of the union may be equally attended to" (Journals May 5), and an effort was made to choose two additional ministers to be joined to Franklin and Adams. The issue was, however, compromised by a decision to add one minister only, and the choice fell upon Jefferson (May 7). As a part of the plan Congress had adopted a few days earlier (April 30) a measure long sought for as essential not only to the furtherance and protection of American commerce but to national development as well. This was a recommendation to the states to vest Congress for a term of fifteen years with certain powers over foreign commerce.

It was just when Congress was planning to expand its foreign relations, that the minister of France made ready to take his leave. On the 6th of April, 1784, in language so sweetened with complimentary expressions that the bosoms of his bitterest critics must have swollen with self-gratification, Luzerne informed Congress that he purposed to return to France. Not to be outdone, Congress bade the minister adieu in like terms of approbation, affection, and good wishes. It was Luzerne's good fortune that, at the moment of his departure, he was the happy instrument of fulfilling a wish expressed by Congress before his coming, so long ago, in fact, that the present members of Congress probably knew nothing about it. There was good reason nevertheless for general gratification when Luzerene informed Congress that the request expressed on June 14, 1779, for portraits of the king and queen of France had at last been fulfilled. The portraits had arrived in Philadelphia, and the minister was safe-keeping them until Congress could receive them.

Alas! Congress had nowhere to put portraits of the king and queen or of anybody else. That assembly had indeed no place to put itself, except as one of its constituent states afforded it a place to sit, to ponder, to knit the brow, and stroke the chin. All Congress could do therefore was to request the minister that he continue to have the portraits kept safely "until proper places can be provided for them", and to express to their "Great, faithful and beloved Friend and Ally" the high degree of pleasure it had given them to receive the portraits and to promise that "these lively representations of our august and most beloved friends will be paced in our Council Chamber", where they could "never fail of exciting in the mind of every American an admiration of the distinguished virtues and accomplishments of the royal originals".

And let it here be recorded that Congress was so far faithful to that promise that, when presently it found itself a Council Chamber in New York, the portraits were transported thither and given their appropriate place in that chamber, where they remained to stir such memories and sentiments as they might, until the heir and assign of the Continental Congress took over the estate. Thence they were taken to the next abode of the Congress of the United States in Philadelphia, and finally to the permanent residence in Washington. But where they now are, if indeed they still exist, no man knoweth.

In this same period in which Congress was concerning itself, albeit with proper decorum, for the betterment of its foreign relations, that body was shaken internally by a near-revolution. One of the provisions of the Articles of Confederation was that "no person shall be capable of being a delegate for more than three years in any term of six years"; and on March 3, 1781, Congress had decided that, under a proper interpretation of this constitutional provision, the three-year term would date from the final ratification of the Articles. As March 1, 1784, marked the expiration of that three-year term, it behooved Congress to make an inventory of its present stock of members to determine whether there were any violations of that constitutional provision, whether any members were tarrying beyond their appointed terms.

A committee appointed to investigate reported (March 23) that Samuel Osgood of Massachusetts was incapable of sitting as a delegate after March 1, 1784. The verdict of the committee, though vigorously contested, was sustained, whereupon Mr. Osgood withdrew, vociferating the while (although with reservations) a "farewell all Connection with public life!"; he was "inexpressibly disgusted with it". The committee next pronounced the two Delaware delegates, Messrs. Tilton and Bedford, ineligible to sit after the first of February; which meant that they had given some six weeks of unentitled service. Both Tilton and Bedford had been slow in the coming, but neither hesitated on the going. Next to be gathered into the committee's net were the Rhode Island delegates, Messrs. Howell and Ellery. The verdict of the committee that the term of those delegates expired on the first Wednesday in May, 1784, fell short of being sustained by seven affirmative votes in Congress (May 15), since there was some question as to the exact expiration of the year for which they had been chosen; nevertheless their votes were challenged (May 18), and around that question a debate revolved (rather, raged) through several days. The Rhode Island gentlemen themselves had doubts respecting their right to sit longer, but that did not deter them from fighting tooth and toenail to retain their seats. Secretary Thomson recorded that the debates "were conducted with a good deal of warmth on both sides of the question"; Samuel Hardy asserted that the dispute had given rise to "more altercation" than he had ever seen, either in Congress or in any other place; while Monroe declared, "I never saw more indecent conduct in any assembly before." Howell himself wrote (May 22):

Some young men in Congress pursue the object of taking away our Seats in Congress as if it was of the first magnitude. . . . I have been in hot water for six or seven weeks. . . . I have received two written challenges to fight duels; one from Col. Mercer, of Virginia, the other from Col. Spaight, of N. Carolina. . . . I answered them that I meant to chastise any insults I might receive and laid their letters before Congress.

Before the case could be brought to decision it began to appear that, if the Rhode Island delegates should be ousted, Congress would practically be estopped from further business; accordingly the matter was dropped. Congress had resolved some three weeks earlier to adjourn on June 3d, and several important measures awaited final action. Said Samuel Hardy in a letter to Jefferson, May 21, "I begin seriously to apprehend we shall be forced to adjourn and confess to the World that the division of our Councils has prevented the adoption of those Measures which the interest of the Union so loudly call'd for at our hands."

From mid-summer of 1783, in fact, Congress had contemplated an adjournment whensoever peace should have been consummated, and no sooner had the definitive treaty of peace been ratified than the plan for adjournment rapidly crystallized into a definite purpose. Except for a brief adjournment in the summer of 1775, Congress had toiled at its tasks day in and day out almost without ceasing for nine long weary years. Those briefer periods of enforced travel when playing hide and seek with the British army, or, more recently, when fleeing the wrath of its own soldiers only to begin the career of a wanderer and a vagabond, could scarcely be classed as comforting relaxations. Most members felt that Congress would be better for a rest, and outside of Congress there was a growing conviction that the country might also benefit thereby. Some of the states had indeed accounts with Congress that they wished to have settled, to say nothing of sundry burdens great or small that they would fain gently shift to the shoulders of the Continent; but after that it appeared to matter very little to them whether Congress kept or not. Indeed a few of the states and more than a few of their statesmen seemed to be inclining to the belief that they would not need Congress any longer. Of the desirability of adjournment over the summer, just as soon as a few important measures could be consummated, there was scarcely a difference of opinion. Where opinion divided was over the question whether, so to speak, Congress should simply shut up shop and go off on its vacation, or should leave a caretaker in charge of the premises. To the minds of those who held to the latter opinion, there were flowers in the Congressional garden that, left untended, might wither; there were seeds in the ground that might perish.

It was for just such a situation that provision had been made in the Articles of Confederation for constituting a Committee of the States. Accordingly the discussion revolved about the question whether a Committee of the States should be left to hold base. A thought uppermost in the minds of some members, that of Jefferson in particular, was that a "visible head" of the federal government should be preserved, lest a complete disappearance of Congress for a few months should accustom the people to the absence of any federal head and thus pave the way all too easily for the dissolution of Congress and consequently to the ultimate collapse of the Union. It was chiefly through Jefferson's perseverance that the vital need of preserving a visible head of the federal government eventually won the support of a majority in Congress, with the result that when the resolve was taken on April 26 to adjourn on the 3d of June following, it was further resolved "that a committee of the states shall be appointed to sit in the recess of Congress". It was not, however, until May 29 that the powers of the committee were defined and its members appointed.

By the 3d of June, Congress had accomplished, after a fashion, most of its primary purposes, and some of second- and third-rate importance as well. The ordinance for the government of the western territory had been adopted, although its yoke-mate, the land ordinance, had failed of passage, while the ambitious peace establishment, upon which so much effort had been expended in the preceding year, had dwindled to a provision for a mere handful of troops for guarding the stores at

West Point and Fort Pitt, with a few hundred militia for garrisoning the western posts—whensoever the British might be prevailed on to surrender them.

On the other hand, Congress had done some things that were no part of its own agenda, but had been thrust upon it by persistent states, although to some of the latter projects that assembly had bravely, if not always complacently, turned a cold shoulder. New York, for instance, after remaining long without representation in Congress, had in the spring sent on two delegates, Charles DeWitt and Ephraim Paine, to obtain some urgent desiderata of their state. For one thing, would Congress, Messrs. DeWitt and Paine asked in almost peremptory tones, do its duty by New York in the matter of that state's chestnuts that had so long been burning in the Vermont fire? Well, Congress had already got its own mantle scorched in that fire and was in no mood to go a-raking in the hot embers for New York's over-cooked chestnuts.

New York also had some plans of her own for garrisoning those western posts that were assumed to be within her own boundary. The controversy between her and Massachusetts had not yet been adjusted, and she feared to have Massachusetts troops in possession of those strongholds, which seemed to be the plan in Congress, and the delegates even went so far as to tell Congress that New York would not permit it. On the other hand, there was a similar fear in Congress directed toward New York, particularly with regard to the posts at Oswego and Niagara. Altogether there was a tangle of Vermont, western garrisons, peace-time army, and state jealousies.

The New Yorkers failed in their efforts and were deeply chagrined thereby. "I believe Sir", DeWitt grumbled when reporting the failure to Governor Clinton, "a Plan is formed and perhaps wrought into System to take that Country from us." His colleague, Ephraim Paine, was even more vociferous and more sweeping in his criticisms of Congress. He had expected to find there "justice sit enthroned, supported by all the virtues"; instead he had found "caballing, selfishness, and injustice reign almost perpetually . . . tumult and disorder prevail, even to the degree of challenging in the house". And his grouch embraced not only the New Englanders, who had taken an active part in blocking the purposes of his state both with regard to the western posts and Vermont; he swept in the "Southern nabobs", who behaved "as though they viewed themselves a superior order of animals".

Other delegates also had their eager projects, which, it became evident, could not be accomplished within the time left, therefore they endeavored to obtain a postponement of the date of adjournment. Congress had, however, resolved to adjourn on the 3d of June, and the majority remained immovable. Chestnuts, chinquapins, or peanuts, whatever it might be that the states were roasting, if they must burn before the reassembling of Congress in the autumn, let them burn. And so, when the zero hour of midnight June 3d drew nigh, adjourn Congress did, albeit, as DeWitt reported to Governor Clinton, "in C—f—sion", meaning, in confusion. The date for the next meeting was set at October 30, and the place as Trenton.

On the following day, June 4, the Committee of the States met and organized; chose Samuel Hardy of Virginia as chairman; and themselves forthwith adjourned until June 26. The committee thus got off to a bad start. It was not until July 8 that a quorum of the committee had reassembled, and for a month thereafter it was an incessant struggle to hold the requisite nine members in leash. The committee's powers were necessarily limited, and it accordingly confined itself for the most part to routine functions. Of the four New England members only Dana of Massachusetts and Blanchard of New Hampshire were in attendance, both of whom had, in the first instance, opposed the formation of the committee, and were now not in the least averse to its dissolution. In fact, they manifested an eagerness to hasten its demise. First they endeavored to obtain an adjournment by vote, then, having failed in this, on the morning of the 11th of August they simply mounted their horses and rode off toward home. Later in the day Samuel Dick of New Jersey likewise took his departure. The committee was thereby effectually dissolved. Nevertheless, the six members who remained—Hardy of Virginia, Hand of Pennsylvania, Chase of Maryland, Spaight of North Carolina, Read of South Carolina, and Houstoun of Georgia—clung to their chairs or ambled about in the neighborhood for another ten days, vainly endeavoring to muster in substitutes; then they too disbanded, having first, however, requested the secretary of Congress to take measures for the safe-keeping of the records.

For some two months thereafter almost frantic efforts were made to reassemble the committee, but all to no avail. One of the incidents of that effort was that, in mid-September, John Francis Mercer, who had been besought by Chairman Hardy to come to his relief, journeyed from Virginia to Annapolis, thence to Philadelphia, in search of the committee, yet found never a vestige of it. Thereupon he blew off his surplus steam by writing to Jacob Read, then on a visit to Rhode Island, that, although the case appeared hopeless, "A desire that the State of Virginia might shew her respect for the Confoederal Government (if it is not a prostitution of the name of Government to apply it to such a vagabond, strolling, contemptible Crew as Congress) will induce me to spin out a Couple of weeks here." Read himself, before departing Annapolis, had indulged in a bit of grim humor by preparing an advertisement offering a reward ("Ten Pounds old Tenor or five pounds for either") for the apprehension of the two New England runaways, "Jonathan and Frank", who had deserted their employment "at the New Temporary Shop not far from the confluence of Severn River and Carroll's Creek in Farm No. 9". The lively descriptions of the persons of Jonathan and Frank (Blanchard and Dana) are evidently not wholly fanciful. For that other deserter Sam (Samuel Dick), "belonging to Farm No. 6", no reward was offered; for he was "very well intentioned and of a good Character", had been "seduced away by the persuasions of the others", and would doubtless return to the place of his employment "as soon as he recollects himself".

Chairman Hardy was especially concerned lest the break-up of the committee should "lessen the dignity of the foederal Government in the Eyes of our own Citizens as well as those of foreigners"; and Secretary Thomson voiced a similar apprehension.

Whatever little politicians may think [Thomson wrote (September 27)] time will evince that it is of no small consequence to save appearances with foreign nations, and not to suffer the federal government to become invisible. A government without a visible head must appear a strange phenomenon to European politicians and will I fear lead them to form no very favourable opinion of our stability, wisdom or Union.

By this time indeed it was no longer a question of resuscitating the committee. The crucial questions were: Could Congress itself be reanimated? Could the union be saved from dissolution?

Probably the two men most disturbed over the collapse of the committee of the states as the visible head of the nation were Thomson and Jefferson. On the 1st of October the faithful secretary wrote to Jefferson:

Though this invisibility of a federal head will have little effect on our affairs here, or on the minds of the citizens of the United States who can easily reconcile themselves to it and who will view it in no other light than the rising or dissolution of their several legislatures to which they have been accustomed, yet I am apprehensive it will have an ill aspect in the eyes of European Nations and give them unfavorable impressions, which will require all your address to remove.

Already, so Richard Dobbs Spaight, the North Carolina member of the committee, wrote to Governor Martin (October 16), the emissaries of the British court had spread throughout Europe "that the United States are only united in name and that a little time will show that we are incapable of governing ourselves". He doubted whether the New England members definitely purposed to break up the union, "but they press so extremely hard on the chain that unites us, that I imagine it will break before they are well aware of it." The philosophical secretary of Congress, in a letter to John Montgomery (August 22), endeavored to console himself with mirages and echoes, but wound up with an inevitable "Pish!"

Irascible Jacob Read, the South Carolina member of the committee, stomped about in Annapolis and Philadelphia for near a month, venting upon the runaways his choicest epithets, then went off to Rhode Island to visit his invalid mother, thence to Boston. In Boston he encountered one of the runaways, "Squinting Frank", who avoided speech with him. Elbridge Gerry likewise several times passed him by without speaking. Gerry was not one of the runaways, but he was regarded as in some measure an accomplice before the fact, and, besides, a chronic dealer in "troubled waters", as Spaight had affirmed. For Mr. Gerry was reserved Read's harshest epithet. These things did not by any means serve to cool Mr. Read's wrath or soften his speech. "I'll stick them in the Journals", he vowed; "a sett of good Stinging resolves" would make them squirm. Yet, even while he breathed denunciations of the culprits, he did not lose sight of the all-important issue: "I feel more for the Invisible State of the federal Government", he wrote, "than I can express at this time too when we know the Eyes of Europe are upon us."

Fretful John Francis Mercer, who had sweated his horse to no purpose in his effort to relieve Samuel Hardy and keep alive Virginia's regard for the Confederation, angrily declared, "If I do not find the ensuing Congress of a very different complexion from the last, and dispos'd to be very decisive, I will no longer myself degrade the Character of a human being by continuing an useless Cypher among others, who are become as contemptible to the world as they have long been to themselves." The only hope was that the states would no longer be "so regardless of reputation and interest, as to continue such a set of rascally Blockheads" in Congress. "Come to Trenton", he wrote to Read (September 23), "and if the present system won't do, some other ought."

Trenton would no doubt tell the tale, whether Congress was to survive, and with it the union, or whether both would be cast into the desolate gehenna without the ceremonial of a burial. By the time, however, that Congress began to assemble at Trenton tempers appear to have cooled, and sober reflection upon the consequences of a dissolution of the union slowly gained supremacy over the factional and personal squabbles to which the affair of the committee of the states had given rise. There was some talk at first of a Congressional investigation of the dispersion of the committee, but Monroe counseled, "had we not also better keep this affair out of sight and while we lament they could not in that instance be calm and temperate, prevail on them if possible to be so in future?"

CHAPTER XXXI

GRAPES FROM THORNS

CONGRESS AND THE LAND

"Trenton, Monday, November 1, 1784. Pursuant to the Articles of Confederation, the following gentlemen attended as delegates. . . ." Thereupon the names of seven delegates from five states are recorded: from Massachusetts, Mr. Samuel Holten; from Virginia, Mr. Richard Henry Lee, and Mr. James Monroe; from North Carolina, Mr. Hugh Williamson; from South Carolina, Mr. Charles Pinckney; from Georgia, Mr. William Houstoun and Mr. William Gibbons. On Tuesday, "the same gentlemen attended as yesterday; and from South Carolina, Mr. Jacob Read." And then there were eight.

Such is the beginning of the anxiously awaited story of the United States in Congress Assembled and the city of Trenton in New Jersey. Not an auspicious start for a young nation just come into its own; and, as day succeeded day with only one or two additional delegates strolling in, it began to seem as if this were the beginning of the end of the United States in Congress Assembled. Ten days of waiting, then the impatient delegates gathered there requested Secretary Thomson to sound the trumpet. On the 11th of November accordingly the secretary addressed a letter to the governors of those states that were delinquent in representation:

The States and Members present have waited with anxiety to this time in daily expectation of the arrival of Delegates from the other States, but finding themselves disappointed and being impressed with a deep sense of the many weighty and important matters which nearly concern the welfare and happiness of the Union and which demand the immediate attention of the United States in Congress Assembled they have desired me to give Your Excellency this information and to urge you in the strongest terms to send forward with all possible dispatch the Delegates appointed to represent your State in Congress.

613

The period of waiting was not, however, altogether wasted. It gave opportunity for serious reflection and for personal discussion, more amicable perhaps than a debate on the floor of Congress would have engendered. "Strange insensibility this, to public duty!" remarked one. This "total relaxation and inattention to the Confoederal Government", said another, ". . . must necessarily have an exceeding evil tendency both at home and abroad." In Europe, he added, the prevalent opinion is that we are "verging fast toward anarchy and confusion". Some people were even asking "whether we had any thing like a Government remaining among us". Wrote Richard Henry Lee (November 19): "But one delegate as yet from the eastward, whence formerly proceeded the most industrious attention to public business. I do not like this lentor, this strange lassitude in those who are appointed to transact public affairs." And Lee's colleague, John Francis Mercer, himself a late comer, declared (November 26) that there was "so great a relaxation in the Confoederal springs", he doubted whether the machine could be long kept in motion, "unless great and effectual repairs are made".

It was just this sorely perplexing question that chiefly engaged the anxious thoughts of the members then waiting in Trenton for the slow filling up of the quorum—waiting for the requisite players to appear before the play could begin. Could the Confoederal machine be repaired so that it would operate efficiently—even operate at all? Or, to change the Mercerian figure, was that assembly, once deemed august, stricken with a fatal disease for which the medico-political experts would find no specific? Was it destined to be discarded even as the symbol of the union that it had done so much to create? Or was there somewhere in the realm of political magic a formula by which this feeble, this decrepit, this moribund Congress might be endowed with new life, transmuted into a genuine sovereignty, capable of bringing unity of purpose and strength of endeavor to distracted and discordant states? There was indeed such a formula, and, remarkably enough, it had been glimpsed dimly during those informal discussions at Trenton. Writing to Madison, November 26, Richard Henry Lee revealed:

It is by many here suggested as a very necessary step for Congress to take —The calling upon the States to form a Convention for the sole purpose of revising the Confederation so far as to enable Congress to execute with more energy, effect, and vigor, the powers assigned it, than it appears by experience that they can do under the present state of things. It has been observed, why do not Congress recommend the necessary alterations to the States as is proposed in the Confederation? The friends to Convention answer—It has been already done in some instances, but in vain.

There had evidently been serious discussion of the question, nevertheless a month later Lee informed Madison that "the conversation concerning a Continental Convention has ceased for some time, so that perhaps it may not be revived again." Madison himself, although convinced that "the perpetuity and efficacy of the present system cannot be confided in", was not yet prepared to decide "in what mode and at what moment the experiment for supplying the defects ought to be made".

It was not until the afternoon of November 29 that seven states were represented, and one of the seven, be it observed, was Georgia, which had had no delegate on the floor of Congress for two full years. Houstoun and Gibbons had indeed presented themselves in June, 1784, between the adjournment of Congress and the meeting of the Committee of the States, and Houstoun had sat in that committee until its dissolution. And be it further observed that the two were prompt in their attendance on the first of November. The first business of Congress was to elect a president, and on November 30 the choice fell upon Richard Henry Lee, although only after a dozen ballots had been taken. With only seven states in attendance, major measures, such as required the assent of nine states, could not be undertaken; yet there was one piece of unfinished business, regarded by some as of prime importance, that might now be pushed to a conclusion. In accordance with his previous announcement, the superintendent of finance now offered his resignation, and thereupon Congress entered into an election to fill the places of Jenifer and Ellsworth, who had declined the honor of being commissioners of the board of treasury. While Congress was entangled in that election, unable to reach a decision, the third commissioner-elect, William Denning, likewise declined (December 6); whereupon a new election of the entire board became necessary.

There had usually been a great lack of unanimity respecting most matters pertaining to finance, so also in determining the personnel of this board sharp controversies arose, with the result that many months elapsed before the board was given its full complement of commissioners. It was one of the oddities of Congressional politics that Massachusetts in particular endeavored to place Arthur Lee on the board, whilst his fellow-Virginians sought to keep him off. The Virginia delegates, so Monroe revealed to Madison (December 18), "seem'd inclin'd to suffer Arthur Lee to retire from the publick service in the opinion it will be advantageous to the publick". Eventually the Virginia delegates yielded the point, but not until midsummer of 1785.

From the first meager gathering of members at Trenton the question of removal from that town had been a topic of outside conversation, for most of them seemed eager to cease their wanderings amongst the small towns, at least until such time as the two chosen seats might be made ready for their sitting, and settle down in some larger city where they could have the comforts of life. And of course there were only two such places anywhere near the middle of the country. "I am sorry to say", John Francis Mercer wrote November 14, "that, always more anxious about where we shall sit, than what we shall do, our chief dispute now is whether we shall spend the Winter in Philadelphia or N. York. The advocates for Philadelphia are more numerous and more zealous, so that I suppose we shall revisit the State House."

As yet no delegates from New York had appeared, and it was not without significance for the determination of the question that between the 2d and the 7th of December, four delegates from that state put in their attendance. One of them, John Jay, who had in the preceding May been chosen to the office of secretary for foreign affairs, immediately upon taking his seat (December 6) informed Congress that he would accept the office only upon condition that Congress would establish itself at some one place. Four days later (December 10) the question of removal was sprung, without designation of place, but the vote was postponed until the next day, when every member from Pennsylvania and all states southward voted in favor of removal, while every delegate to the northward voted against it. By states the vote stood five to three.

Ten days later the attendance of additional delegates offered the possibility of a different result. Accordingly on the 20th it was resolved to appropriate one hundred thousand dollars for the erection of public buildings for the accommodation of Congress and that it was expedient that such buildings be erected "at more than one place". Where Congress was to get the hundred thousand dollars no one ventured to suggest. As Jay had joined Howell of Rhode Island in promoting these resolutions, he was evidently seeking to prepare the way for his next proposition, offered in conjunction with Pinckney of South Carolina the next day, namely, that Congress determine on the place where it would sit "until proper accommodations in a foedereal town shall be erected". Pinckney and Jay also proposed that the resolutions respecting the alternate temporary residence in Trenton and Annapolis be repealed; but their motion did not prevail.

So far, there had been only skirmishing. The real battle came on the 23d, when an ordinance was proposed for carrying into execution the resolutions of the 20th. The ordinance would provide for the appointment of three commissioners to lay out a site for a federal town, not less than two nor exceeding three miles square on the banks of the Delaware, and to take measures for erecting suitable buildings for the residence of Congress; further, that, until those buildings should be ready for occupancy, Congress should adjourn on a blank date to meet at a blank place on a blank date. The Virginia delegates thereupon endeavored to have Georgetown on the Potomac substituted for the banks of the Delaware as the permanent place of residence; but not another delegate voted with them. The next problem was to fill the sundry blanks. For the place, New Jersey naturally wished to keep Congress at Trenton, wherein she was abetted by the delegates of Rhode Island and three of those of Massachusetts and New Hampshire. A vote on Philadelphia resulted in five ayes and four noes; and the advocates of that city could but bemoan the fact that Maryland and Delaware were both unrepresented, otherwise they would have won the victory. The Rhode Island delegates thereupon offered Newport in their state, doubtless without the least expectation of obtaining any votes for the proposition other than their own. And so it turned out to be.

A good many members of Congress, if they might have had their way, would in fact have been glad to accept less rather than more of Rhode Island. Richard Dobbs Spaight, for instance, wrote regretfully (December 28): "We have not yet got rid of those two dealers in *troubled* waters, Gerry and Howell. I am afraid they will prove an eternal plague to us." It remained only to take a vote on New York, and it was Howell of Rhode Island who made the motion for that city, and Spaight of North Carolina who seconded it, although the latter would much have preferred Philadelphia. As the motion was supported by every state representation except those of Pennsylvania and Georgia, the latter state being divided, New York was now fixed as the place. Fixing the dates gave rise to no difficulties, and it was accordingly promptly voted to adjourn from Trenton on December 24 (that is, the next day), to meet in New York on January 11, 1785.

Christmas Day, 1784, accordingly found Congress once more on its travels, or about to travel. A number of the delegates did not, in fact, even wait for the formal adjournment on the 24th, but immediately set out upon their northward journey, while others jaunted to Philadelphia for the holidays. A few tarried in Trenton, and among these was President Richard Henry Lee, who deemed it best to allow "a little time for fitting a President's House" in New York. There was, upon the whole, a hope, amounting almost to a conviction, that the removal to a more northerly seat would serve to reinvigorate the slackening interest in Congress on the part of some of the northern states, and thereby hold the Union together until some better system could be devised.

These hopes were not without fruition; for Congress began its new life in New York under favorable auspices. To be sure, the 11th of January, 1785, found only five states represented, yet within two days two more states had filled up their delegations, so that business could begin. Before the end of January, in fact, ten states were on the floor, and shortly afterward eleven. Encouraged, the members assembled were eager to be about their country's business.

Hitherto [wrote William Samuel Johnson of Connecticut, January 24] there appear on all sides, and in every Body here, good Dispositions to enter into the Consideration and Discussion of public Affairs with Diligence, Zeal, and Integrity, yet none of the *Ardua Regni,* such as Revenue, Western Territory etc. have hitherto been taken up, not from any direct Reluctance in any one to engage in them, but that on account of their extreme weight and difficulty, every one seems to hope by longer Reflection and Consideration of those very important Subjects to come to the discussion and Determination of them with yet greater Strength and Furniture of Mind.

One of the *"Ardua Regni"* here shrouded by the thoughtful Dr. Johnson under his "etc" he himself revealed two days later in a letter to Jonathan Sturges, seeking, with the aid of this colleague, then in Connecticut, to equip himself with the necessary furniture of mind. "One thing is in Contemp[latio]n here", Johnson wrote, "upon which I wish to know the sentiments of your Politicians in Connect't, that is to ask of the States to invest Congress with the Power of regulating their Trade as well with foreign Nations *as with each other."* Here were certainly three subjects that were to prove themselves *ardua regni;* while a fourth, as yet in the background, would presently thrust itself to the front, carrying the weal or woe of the union. This was the relations with Spain over the navigation of the Mississippi River.

Of necessity Congress applied itself first of all to the problem of its finances for the ensuing year; and, if any urge thereto had been needed, that urge was upon them in the forcible reminders recently received from their ministers abroad that interest was coming due on the European loans. Accordingly a grand committee was promptly appointed, with instructions "to report a requisition on the states for the supplies of the present year". This instruction was given on the 24th of January; the grand committee laid its report before Congress on the 31st of March; the requisition was finally adopted on the 27th of September!

During this period the attention of Congress was now and then of course drawn aside to other important matters, as, for instance, to the revision of the land ordinance and the sale of western lands; for after all, those western lands constituted the most hopeful source of revenue. And more than once it became necessary to pause in the arduous pursuit of revenue to engage in an equally arduous pursuit of delegates; for that bane of the life of the old Congress, insufficient representation, clung to it as an almost perpetual plague. Not a little of the delay, however, was caused by the usual disagreements among the delegations, and they must needs wear one another down before a compromise could be agreed upon.

One controversy was over the policy to be pursued respecting the admission of state claims and advances as credits toward a state's quota Other questions were, how much should be applied toward foreign debts, how much on domestic account, what proportion of the quotas should be paid in cash, and by means of what facilities and in what manner payments might be made on domestic indebtedness. "The public creditors press so hard", Samuel Holten wrote April 11, "there is not much pleasure in being a member of Congress, unless a man can bear duning very well."

Congress had, in fact, unintentionally invited clamor, controversy, and squabble, when, in sending forth the requisition of 1784, it had given a promise that new requisitions would not be made upon states that had paid their full quota, until all the other states had made up their deficiencies; with the further engagement that advances beyond the quotas then called for would be credited on the new requisition. Some states were accordingly presenting certain claims as advances to be credited on the requisition of 1785. That promise of the year before, Rufus King wrote (May 27), had become "the source of great embarrassment". The problem was further complicated by a promise that the old rule of apportionment, against which there had been much complaint, would be revised so as to make it conformable to justice on the basis of the best available evidence. It was "no mystery", said William Grayson (June 7), "why those who pay least should be most anxious for new requisitions"; for some states had done nothing toward complying with the requisition of 1784, and the something that others had done had been but inconsiderable. He made an exception of his own state of Virginia. (Other delegates were inclined to make like exceptions of their own states.)

For his part, Grayson had almost reached the conclusion that it was scarcely worth while to make requisitions at all; and actually there was a wealth of evidence to justify such a conclusion. Nothing, he asserted, could be more certain than "that requisitions will not support credit unless there are payments consequential thereon"; at the same time it was just as certain that "public credit ought to be supported by every nation who wishes to exist". He had presently resolved his doubts, however, as he explained to Madison (August 21): "I agree with you entirely as to the necessity of a requisition at any rate otherwise the public Creditors might be so clamorous, as to render the Governm[en]t in some degree odious."

Suspended at the end of April for lack of representation, consideration of the requisition had been resumed in June and was debated hotly at intervals for three months. On the 12th of September, Gerry wrote to Jefferson: "We have done very little in the present Congress. The Want of a full Representation has retarded all and prevented an Adoption of the most important foederal Measures. The Requisition labours exceedingly and I am apprehensive of an Adjournment without compleating it." Two weeks longer the labors continued with scarcely an abatement, but were at length brought to a consummation September 27, time to be planning for the year 1786.

Reduced to its simplest terms, the requisition called for the actual payment by the first of the following May of three-fourths of the unpaid dues under previous requisitions, and three million dollars in addition. As more than two-thirds the sum called for was to be applied to the payment of the interest on the domestic debt, the states were to be permitted to pay one-third in actual money and to discharge the other two-thirds by means of facilities. As to the rule of apportionment, since not all the states had yet complied with the recommendation of Congress of February 17, 1783, or that of April 18, of the same year, the quotas were adjusted agreeably to the best information in the possession of Congress.

As finally adopted, the measure was as a matter of course the result of numerous compromises, and dissatisfactions a plenty remained. McHenry of Maryland, for instance, wrote that it was "only calculated for one part of the union", that is, the states from Pennsylvania northward, "which are in possession of the great bulk of continental securities where they may be purchased at *eight* for *one*." Those states would be able to discharge their required two-thirds of their quotas "at a very easy rate", while the continental securities in possession of Maryland and her citizens would hardly exceed one-fourth of her quota. There was, however, said McHenry, one agreeable circumstance: By the rule governing the apportionments, "which was obtained after a great deal of squabbling", Maryland's quota had been considerably reduced. Grayson of Virginia was of like mind with McHenry that the plan was particularly favorable to the eastern and middle states. He had, however, given his assent "for the sake of peace". The vote on the measure is not recorded. That the eastern and middle states themselves counted the measure as a victory is borne out by the testimony of the Massachusetts delegates who reported (October 27) with gratification that by the new rule of apportionment, "the Result of a compromise", their state had obtained a substantial abatement of her quota.

Long before Congress had wrangled itself into a state of exhaustion and consequent acquiescence in any sort of requisition that a majority would accept, constructive measures had been taken for tapping a more promising source of the much desired revenues, the sale of western lands, a measure that had been allowed to lapse in the preceding spring. To a renewal of those efforts Washington had lately contributed an impetus with his forceful counsel. In the autumn of 1784 he had made a journey to the west and had become impressed with the necessity of speedy action on the part of Congress ere speculators and squatters had made impossible a rational system for the disposal of the lands. He expressed his views particularly to two members of Congress, Richard Henry Lee and Jacob Read, and Lee had replied (December 14, 1784) that Congress was only waiting to learn the results of the negotiations with the Indians.

Accordingly, on the 4th of March, 1785, when the reports from the Indian commissioners seemed sufficiently encouraging and while the grand committee was yet mulling over the terms of the requisition, the land ordinance that had failed of passage in May, 1784, was drawn forth from its pigeon-hole and "read a first time"—perhaps only for the purpose of starting discussion. At all events, when, on March 16, the ordinance was taken up for a second reading, it stirred a debate, with the result that a grand committee was instructed to prepare anew an ordinance for the purpose.

As previously stated, the chief conflict of ideas was as between a New England system of compact settlements or sale by townships, and a Southern system of indiscriminate or individual locations; although,

while the New Englanders generally pressed for their township system, the Southerners did not urge a system of indiscriminate locations
such as then prevailed in Virginia and North Carolina, but proposed
modifications of that practice. It was William Grayson, a Virginian,
who drafted the ordinance as first reported, yet it was evident enough
that New England ideas had materially influenced the form and substance of the measure as proposed. For instance, Rufus King, the
Massachusetts member of the committee, who had been corresponding
with Timothy Pickering on the subject and had received from Pickering some "ingenious communications", remarked to Pickering, when
sending him (April 15) a copy of the ordinance as then drawn, "You
will find thereby that your ideas have had weight with the committee
who reported this ordinance."

The committee presented its report April 12, and on April 14 the
ordinance was "read a first time". Thereupon began a tug-of-war over
its provisions, Rufus King leading the northern, and William Grayson
the southern cohorts respectively. In a letter to Washington, April 15,
Grayson summarized the main points of the controversy, closing his
summary with these remarks:

Some gentlemen looked upon it as a matter of revenue only and that it
was true policy to get the money with[ou]t parting with the inhabitants to
populate the Country, and thereby prevent the lands in the original states
from depreciating. Others (I think) were afraid of an interference with the
lands now at market in the individual States. part of the Eastern Gentlemen
wish to have the lands sold in such a manner as to suit their own people
who may chuse to emigrate, of which I believe there will be great numbers
particularly from Connecticut; But others are apprehensive of the consequences which may result from the new States taking their position in the
Confederacy. They perhaps wish that this event may be delayed as long as
possible.

Recurring to the subject some three weeks later, when prospects of
reaching an agreement appeared fairly good, Grayson remarked:
"There have appeared so many interfering interests, most of them
imaginary, so many ill founded jealousies and suspicions throughout
the whole, that I am only surpris'd the ordinance is not more excep-

tionable." But for the importunities of the public creditors and the reluctance to pay them by taxation, he was convinced that no ordinance could have been passed except one of such a character as "would in great degree have excluded the idea of actual settlements within any short length of time"; and he added, "This is not strange when we reflect that several of the States are averse to new votes from that part of the Continent."

One of the provisions incorporated into the first draft of the ordinance and only slightly altered in the final act, was that one section of every township should be reserved for the maintenance of public schools. As originally drawn, however, this provision was followed by another, which read: "and the section immediately adjoining the same to the northward, for the support of religion, the profits arising therefrom in both instances, to be applied for ever according to the will of the majority of male residents of full age within the same." That a proposition so contrary to the spirit of religious liberty should have crept into the measure is nothing short of astounding. Scarcely less remarkable, when a movement was undertaken to expunge it (April 23), seventeen members voted to retain the provision, only six to expunge it. Those six nays were: Ellery and Howell of Rhode Island, Melancton Smith of New York, James McHenry and John Henry of Maryland, and John Sitgreaves of North Carolina. By states, however, there were only five affirmative votes, and the provision was accordingly expunged. Commenting upon the matter in a letter to Monroe (May 29), Madison remarked: "How a regulation so unjust in itself, so foreign to the authority of Cong[res]s, so hurtful to the sale of the public land, and smelling so strongly of an antiquated Bigotry, could have received the countenance of a Com[mit]tee is truly matter of astonishment."

Meanwhile the debates stormed on day after day. There were controversies over the size of the townships, over the methods of sale, over the price; and the disputes, declared William Samuel Johnson (May 4), were "warm and unexpected". Complained Rufus King (April 26), "Virginia makes many difficulties." Retorted Richard Henry Lee (May 7), "The Ordinance . . . meets the assent of nine States and every Member of the Nine States, except one Man, who keeps the Ordinance from passing by the joint causes, as he alleges, of indisposition and dislike." The one man alluded to was King. Grayson wrote to Pickering, April 27, that there had been "as much said and wrote about it as would fill forty Volumes", and yet they were still far from a conclusion, "so difficult is it to form any system, which will suit our complex government". Both sides, he said, adhered stubbornly to their opinions, "so that here we stick, with[ou]t any movement either retrograde or progressive". The New Englanders, Grayson grumbled to Madison (May 1), "wish to sell the Continental land, rough as it runs"; and, with the dregs of his grouch still clogging his system a week after the ordinance had been finally adopted, he wrote (May 28): "The Eastern people who before the Revolution never had an idea of any quantity of Earth above a hundred acres, were for selling in large tracts of 30,000 acres while the Southern people who formerly could scarcely bring their imaginations down so low as to comprehend the meaning of a hundred acres of ground were for selling the whole territory in lots of a mile square." Wrote Howell of Rhode Isand (April 29), "The *Land-ordinance* . . . proves to be the most complicated and embarrassing Subject before Congress since peace has taken place."

At this stage it became necessary to pause until attendance, which had fallen to eight states, could be recruited. On the 4th of May nine states were again in attendance, and on the 5th the ordinance was given a second reading. When on the 6th Congress proceeded to the third reading, new efforts were made for amendments, although most members were already privately acknowledging that they had little hope of regaining lost ground. Neither side was quite ready to surrender, despite the fact that both sides recognized the danger of further delay. Followed another lull because of a lapse in attendance, another spurt (May 18) in behalf of amendments, then, on the 20th, all combattants laid down their arms, and the ordinance which is the foundation of our western land system was adopted.

The final vote is not recorded, but the New Hampshire delegates wrote to President Weare (May 29) that it was adopted "by the unanimous voice of all the States present". Some dissatisfaction was expressed even by eastern delegates, who nevertheless, upon the whole, counted it their victory. On the other hand, Spaight of North Carolina was particularly doleful in his prophecy. The plan, he asserted, would never answer the end proposed, and besides, so great were the numbers of people already going up into the land to possess it, that it would cost more than the lands were worth to dispossess them. Dr. Samuel Dick of New Jersey contented himself with hoping, that "It may Exhibit in the Execution Marks of Wisdom Proportioned to the Time and Expense it has and will cost."

The complete fruition of the land policy required the removal of two obstacles. The one, not indeed especially formidable for the inauguration of that policy, was the incomplete cessions of western lands by the claimant states. The other obstacle was the Indians and their claims. Negotiations for the latter purpose had sometime been going forward. A treaty had been negotiated at Fort Stanwix, October 22, 1784, another at Fort McIntosh on January 21, 1785, and on March 18 plans were made for a treaty to be held with the western Indians on June 20 following. The purpose of this latter treaty was partly for giving peace and security to the frontiers, but primarily for the purpose of obtaining a cession of lands. When presently obstacles arose and it became necessary to alter the plans and enlarge the powers of the commissioners, the latter were instructed (June 6, 15, 1785) "to avail themselves of the disposition of the Indians . . . to make such cession as extensive and liberal as possible".

With regard to cessions by claimant states, Virginia and New York had made satisfactory cessions of their claims upon that great northwest toward which eager eyes were peering, but the title was still encumbered by the claims of Massachusetts and Connecticut lying athwart that territory. Those claims appeared to others, to be sure, to be somewhat shadowy, but they were disturbing shadows nevertheless; and, as it turned out, shrewd Connecticut was able to convert her shadow into solid substance. That state had made its gesture of generous cession, although with a reservation that had anything but a flavor of generosity, with the result that, for the time being, Congress declined to accept it. Massachusetts, on the other hand, just when the land ordinance was under consideration, gracefully removed her shadow by a genuine deed of cession (April 19, 1785).

There remained the claims of North Carolina, South Carolina, and Georgia, but, as these claims lay in a different quarter, cessions of them were not so immediately imperative. Congress did not, however, fail to urge those states likewise to place large portions of their landholdings into the common fund for the general good. Some members even made expansive estimates of the amount of the public debt that might be extinguished by the sale of those lands, although Congress does not appear to have counted very confidently on doing any such flourishing land-office business in the south as in the west. North Carolina had, it is true, made a cession (June 2, 1784) of that part of her territory that subsequently became the state of Tennessee, but with conditions and reservations—one of the conditions being the acceptance of the cession by Congress within one year. It was not long, however, before the state of North Carolina became repentant and straightway repealed her act of cession (November 20, 1784).

By that time, in fact, the situation in the ceded territory had become exceedingly complicated and speedily became more so; for straightway upon the act of cession the inhabitants of that territory took steps to organize a separate state. Had not the ordinance of April, 1784, for the government of the western territory plainly advised them so to do? Long strides had already been taken toward erecting this new state, which was to receive the name of "The State of Franklin", when news of North Carolina's repeal of the cession act crossed the mountains. Thereupon those "Overmountain men", busily engaged in setting themselves up a government of their own, became exceeding wroth and refused to demolish the foundations they had laid, or even to pull down the scaffolding. Presently therefore the State of Franklin was beseeching Congress to be taken into the union as one of the family circle.

Congress was just then concluding its labors on the land ordinance, and the moment that ordinance had been adopted, consideration was given to the North Carolina case. To the plea of the State of Franklin for admission into the Union, Congress turned its deaf ear; nevertheless a strong effort was made in Congress to have the cession accepted, in spite of the fact it had been withdrawn. That effort was of no avail, and all that Congress would do was to recommend to the state of North Carolina that it once again hearken to "the principles of magnanimity and justice" that had first induced it to make the cession, by repealing its act of repeal and thereby "furnish a new proof of their liberality" in the execution of a deed to the territory formerly ceded to the United States. That new proof was eventually furnished, but not until the state had once more taken its seat on the anxious bench and repented of its repentance.

Meanwhile it had been deemed the part of wisdom to give heed to the Indians, south as well as west. As early as the 4th of March, 1785, a committee on Southern Indian affairs had brought in an elaborate report, whereupon Congress resolved to appoint three commissioners to negotiate with the Southern tribes. No sooner, however, had the three commissioners (Benjamin Hawkins of North Carolina, Daniel Carroll of Maryland, and William Peery of Delaware) been chosen than one of those squirts of jealousy and suspicion that so often curdled any sweetness generated in Congress was injected into the proceedings, with the result that the number of commissioners was raised to five, so as to include representatives of South Carolina and Virginia. Accordingly Andrew Pickens of the former state and Joseph Martin of the latter were added. What had brought about these additions, so Richard Dobbs Spaight explains, was a hint of suspicion "that under the Idea of making peace with the Indians we had some under hand designs, which might be fatal to their claim of an equal partition of unlocated western territory among the members of the Union", and for that reason the commission had been loaded with two middle-state men as against one Southerner. The Southerners therefore countered by loading on two more from their section.

The state of Georgia was, however, still without representation on the commission, and the attending member from that state, William Houstoun, was not a little peeved over the slight to his state. "As we were much connected with the So. Indians", he wrote to Governor Elbert (April 2, 1785), "I took the liberty to mention that I thought a Commissioner ought to be appointed from our State, but I was very severely replyed to for suggesting that the least countenance ought to be given to so unworthy a State, and one that had not taken a single foederal measure." In fact, Houstoun appears to have had more than one provocation.

The whole body of Congress [he declared] are become so clamorous against our State, that I Shudder for the consequences . . . it is very seriously talked of either to make a tryal of voting Georgia out of the Union or to fall upon some means of taking coercive measures against her . . . the most infamous motives are imputed to her.

Houstoun must have retorted with sufficient force to induce Congress to the conclusion that it might after all be well to offer the state of Georgia a gesture of appeasement; for, when Daniel Carroll presently declined the appointment, Lachlan McIntosh of Georgia was chosen in his stead (May 16). The business of treaty making did not, however, proceed very expeditiously, neither did the treaties when made solve all the difficulties; for complaints against some of their terms were soon descending upon Congress.

As for the delegate from Georgia, it is meet to observe that he had troubles of his own, the blame for which he could in nowise cast upon Congress. In this same letter of April 2d to Governor Elbert he sorrowfully stated that, from a disinterested zeal of serving his country ("God knows") and induced by "the warm persuasions of those who paid more attention to public Matters" than to his private interest, he had left "a comfortable place", in the midst of relations and friends, "to come to a strange land amongst Strangers", under a full confidence that his country would not make the ungrateful return of giving him up as a victim. Yet so it was. He would like very much to return home, but he had exhausted every shilling of his own, had been compelled to borrow from time to time, and at the moment he was so exceedingly pressed and so much involved that it was impossible for him to think of moving till he could receive a pecuniary relief sufficient to extricate him; meanwhile he was perplexed in finding means for his support. "Surely", he wailed, "no Christian people could treat me so unworthily."

Houstoun evidently found some means of keeping soul and body together, for he clung to his post until November, 1786. Probably two colleagues, Abraham Baldwin and John Habersham, who came to Congress at the end of May, 1785, brought him relief in some form. No doubt he had previously derived such comfort as might be from the discovery that other delegates frequently found themselves in a like predicament; that he was not the only member of that august assembly who every now and then found it necessary to get even his washing done on credit.

At the very moment when interest in the sale of western lands was intense, Congress was strangely apathetic toward the problem of providing a government for their western people, whether for the settlers then moving in upon the new lands and the greater throngs expected, or for the inhabitants already there. In April, 1784, the general features of a plan of government had indeed been adopted, but beyond adopting the ordinance nothing had been done. In framing that ordinance the eyes of Congress would seem to have been upon the people who were to come, forgetful of the older residents whom Congrsss had inherited. For, with the acquisition of the Northwest territory, the United States had acquired some old French communities; and, while these had fallen nominally under the jurisdiction of Congress, they had long been left to their own devices.

After enduring for several years an unsettled state of affairs a group of citizens of those old settlements laid before Congress, December 9, 1784, a memorial setting forth the great inconvenience to which they were subject from a want of order and good government, and this memorial was followed by a petition from a rival faction, presented to Congress, February 9, 1785, although bearing an earlier date than that presented in the preceding December. A committee was appointed to take these memorials into consideration, and on February 15 they reported in favor of appointing commissioners with authority to adjust the difficulties in those communities, "until more effectual arrangements can be made for extending to them a more regular establishment of security and good order". Congress accepted the committee's report in so far as to resolve "That one or more commissioners be appointed to repair to the Kaskaskies and Illinois settlements," but hesitated over the question of authority to be conferred on the commissioners and appointed another committee to report on that phase of the matter.

On the first of March one commissioner, William Stephens Smith, was appointed, but on the same day he was given an appointment as secretary to John Adams and accepted the latter office. On March 14 the second committee on the Kaskaskias and Illinois petitions reported a tentative form of government for those communities under a commissioner and secretary, but no action was taken on the report beyond assigning a day for its consideration.

Congress was, in fact, by this time becoming so deeply engrossed in the problems of the land ordinance and the requisition it could not be drawn away to matters that seemed so much less consequential. The strangest part of the proceeding is that the whole business pertaining to the Kaskaskia and Illinois people was allowed to lapse for more than a year, with scarcely a sidelong glance. On December 28, 1785, Secretary Thomson did call the attention of Congress to this important item of unfinished business, but it was not until March 27, 1786, that Congress once more took up the problem of a government for the western territory. Thereafter for nearly four months Congress occupied itself at intervals with an endeavor to revise the ordinance of 1784. By that time, however, it was becoming a serious question whether Congress itself would be able much longer to endure as a government.

One evidence there is, nevertheless, that government of the western territory had not, through all these months been entirely absent from at least some of the minds in Congress. On the 16th of March, 1785, that is, two days after the presentation of the proposed plan of government in response to the Kaskaskian petition, and on the day that Congress referred the old land ordinance to a new committee for revision. Rufus King offered a motion for the exclusion of slavery from any new states that might be formed of the western territory, a motion that he appears to have been induced to make by a suggestion of Timothy Pickering.

The language of the motion was not, however, original with King. The principal part of the motion is in almost the exact language of the proposition that Jefferson sought to have incorporated into the ordinance of 1784. The limiting clause of Jefferson's proposition, "after the year 1800 of the Christian era", was omitted in King's motion, but the committee who reported upon the motion (April 6) restored the omitted clause and added a provision for the recovery of fugitive slaves. That report was assigned for consideration on April 14, but it does not appear to have been taken up again. In a letter to Madison,

May 1, William Grayson wrote: "Mr. King of Massachusetts has a resolution ready drawn which he reserves till the Ordinance [*i. e.,* the land ordinance] is passed for preventing slavery in the new State. I expect Seven States may be found liberal enough to adopt it." Nevertheless the provision is not again heard of until the new ordinance for the government of the Northwest Territory was on the eve of its passage, in July, 1787. Thus far the only fruit of Jefferson's ordinance of 1784 was the abortive State of Franklin.

CHAPTER XXXII

FIGS FROM THISTLES
CONGRESS AND THE SEA

Not land hunger alone was stalking the country and pounding on the door of Congress in the summer of 1785; hunger for commerce was scarcely less voracious or less clamorous. Long thwarted by the war, no sooner had that restraining force been removed than both appetites surged up with renewed and even more ravenous intensity. At first it was mainly the rich and abundant lands of the west that stirred the imaginations, yearnings, and hopes of the American people; but soon the call of commerce began to be heard, at times even above that of the land. Upon the tympanums of the eastern members of Congress in particular the voice of commerce was sure to tap often and insistently. Together land and commerce were to become the two most potent factors in creating and shaping the destiny of the nation. Commerce was to draw the discordant states together into a firmer bond of union; the land, in ways as yet but dimly foreseen, would give character to the union in the long years to come.

Two problems in commerce, the one foreign, the other domestic, at this time confronted Congress with especial insistency. Ever since the peace the British restrictions on the trade of the states had been particularly annoying, and Congress had thus far found it impossible to overcome the difficulties that stood in the way of a commercial treaty with Great Britain. For that situation the failure of the states to carry out the provisions of the treaty with regard to pre-war debts was largely responsible; and because of its weakness Congress could do little about it. In a similar manner, though to a lesser degree, Congress found itself handicapped in making commercial treaties with other powers. In the domestic domain, at the same time, commercial conflicts had multiplied and become more and more acute. Each state was pursuing its own way, and the way of one usually ran counter to the ways of others. In so chaotic a situation most men of commerce became convinced that the only remedy was a power in Congress to regulate trade, not only with foreign nations, but also among the states. Said William Samuel Johnson (January 26, 1785), "The first is conceiv'd necessary in order to carry into effect the Treaties made and to be made with foreign Powers, the other to prevent Dissentions between State and State which might endanger the Union." And he added, significantly, "The Idea of many seems to be that the Comm[erc]e between S[tate] and S[tate] sho'd be absolutely free."

On April 30, 1784, Congress had asked the states for a power to regulate foreign trade in certain specific matters for a term of fifteen years, but several of the states had not complied with the recommendation, and furthermore it had become evident that a regulation of wider scope was needful. Upon the initiative of Monroe in December, 1784, an active movement for a fuller regulation began with the appointment, January 24, 1785, of a new committee, of which Monroe was chairman. The committee brought in a report, February 16, proposing an amendment to the ninth article of the Confederation, whereby the control of commerce should be invested in the United States. Congress went so far toward accepting the committee's proposal as to instruct it (March 11) to bring in a circular letter to accompany the proposition to the states. In its proposed circular letter, offered March 28, the committee argued cogently for the adoption of the amendment by the states, including this appeal: "If they wish to cement the Union by the Strongest ties of interest and affection, if they wish to promote its strength and grandeur founded upon that of each individual State, every consideration of local, as well as of foederal policy urge them to adopt the following recommendation."

The question was not, however, brought to a test of votes at that time, for the reason, as Monroe explained to Jefferson (April 12), that to press the measure at that time would pretty surely arouse prejudices and opposition, in the states as well as in Congress. Some two months later (June 16) Monroe observed to Jefferson: "The importance of the subject and the deep and radical change it will create in the bond of union together with the conviction that something must be done seems to create an aversion or rather a fear of acting on it." He added that the adoption of the measure would "certainly form the most permanent and powerful principle in the confideration", that it would "give the union an authority upon the States respectively which will last with it and patch it together in its present form longer than any principle it now contains will effect."

One of the consistent advocates of strengthening the hands of Congress was Jesse Root of Connecticut, and respecting this measure he wrote (May 28): "Congress must be invested with Competent powers to regulate Trade—to raise a revenue for national purposes and to govern the republic of States or we never Can perpetuate our union and free Constitution of Government." By July 13 the advocates of the amendment appear to have overcome their fears at least sufficiently to resume the discussion; and for two days it was debated in committee of the whole. There were three opinions, so Grayson wrote to Washington (July 25). One group favored the measure, provided eleven states instead of nine should exercise the power; a second group preferred a navigation act; while a third was opposed to any change whatsoever. The advocates of the amendment, said Monroe, argued that all the ends desired by the individual states would be more effectually secured by having the power to regulate commerce, whether externally or internally, in the hands of the union; while the chief emphasis of the opposition was upon the danger of concentrating power, since it might be turned to mischief. Declared Richard Henry Lee, the leader of the opposition, "The Spirit of Commerce is a spirit of avarice"—a favorite phrase of Lee—consequently the remedy, he maintained, would probably be worse than the disease, "bad as the last may be".

The eastern members, especially concerned for the restoration of commerce, meanwhile grew hesitant, partly, in Monroe's opinion (August 15), because of the real magnitude of the subject, partly from a belief that delay would strengthen the chances of the measure among the states. Time and the continued decline of commerce would probably have an educative influence. Accordingly the proposition was allowed to sleep. When, however, a year later (August, 1786), an effort was made in behalf of a genuine overhauling of the Confederation, nearly the same amendment was again proposed; but once more the house of cards collapsed. The fruit was not yet ripe, though it was ripening.

While the agitation of this question was in progress there arose a considerable flurry in the realm of commerce, some waves whereof were presently lapping on the doorsill of Congress, and, before the flurry had subsided, it had furnished one more impetus toward a federal convention. As there were no restrictions upon the importation of British goods into America, British merchants were gaining something like a monopoly of trade in the principal American cities, and what greatly added to the consequent discomfiture of American merchants was the further fact that their British competitors were gathering in most of the hard money of the country.

The Boston merchants at last rose in their wrath, drew up some vigorous resolutions designed to establish a thorough boycott of British goods, and sent a petition to their legislature and another to Congress. The latter petition besought the immediate interposition of Congress, with whatsoever powers it possessed. This was on the 11th of May, 1785, during the lull in the debate over the amendment to the ninth article of the Confederation, and Congress merely voted to let the petition lie until there had been further consideration of the proposition for the general regulation of trade then before that body. No doubt the Boston petition had its influence in stirring a renewal of the discussion in mid-July.

The Massachusetts people, on the other hand, were not at all disposed to stand still and wait for salvation. They pressed forward in search of it. Under the leadership of Governor Bowdoin the legislature passed an act (June 23, 1785) for the regulation of navigation and commerce, and besought the other states to do likewise. (New Hampshire did, in fact, follow immediately in the footsteps of Massachusetts.) The act was, however, designed as a temporary measure only, until such time as Congress might be vested "with a *well guarded* power to regulate the trade of the United States". Moreover, upon the governor's suggestion, the legislature went further and adopted resolutions (July 11) setting forth the inadequate powers of Congress under the Articles of Confederation and requesting Congress to recommend a convention of delegates from all the states "to revise the Confederation and report to Congress how far it may be necessary in their opinion to alter or enlarge the same in order to secure the primary objects of the Union." The state's delegates, Messrs. King, Gerry, and Holten, were instructed to lay these resolutions before Congress at an early day.

Those delegates chose, however, not to do so; and two months later, in a letter to Governor Bowdoin (September 3, 1785), they set forth at length their reasons for withholding the resolutions. In that letter the delegates indulge themselves in a multitude of doubts respecting the expediency or wisdom of endeavoring to enlarge the powers of Congress, commercial or other, at that time, especially through the instrumentality of a convention. Indeed they rose to a climax in their argument with an emphasis upon the danger of opening a door to aristocracy. Some part of this argument, put forth with deepest seriousness, is an appropriate exhibit in the history of a question soon to be so momentous for the life of the nation.

If an Alteration [wrote the Massachusetts delegates], either temporary or perpetual, of the commercial powers of Congress, is to be considered by a Convention, shall the latter be authorized to revise the Confederation *generally,* or only for express purposes?—the great object of the Revolution, was the Establishment of good Government, and each of the States, in forming their own, as well as the federal Constitution, have adopted republican principles. notwithstanding this, plans have been artfully laid, and vigorously pursued, which had they been successful, We think would inevitably have changed our republican Governments, into baleful Aristocracies. Those plans are frustrated, but the same Spirit remains in their abettors. . . . We are apprehensive and it is our Duty to declare it, that such a Measure would produce thro'out the Union, an Exertion of the Friends of an Aristocracy, to send Members who would promote a Change of Government . . . 'more power in Congress' has been the Cry from all quarters. . . . We are for increasing the power of Congress, as far as it will promote the Happiness of the people; but at the same Time are clearly of Opinion that every Measure should be avoided which would strengthen the Hands of the Enemies to a free Government.

The Massachusetts delegates did not merely view with alarm, they thought they beheld a horde of threatening dangers advancing in the train of this movement to enlarge the powers of the central government. At one danger in particular they pointed a monitory finger—the order of the Cincinnati. This hereditary patriotic society, organized by the officers of the army in May, 1783, had quickly brought down upon itself denunciation from many quarters; writers of large caliber and small had pitched into it tooth and toenail, and even some legislatures proceeded to disfranchise those who joined it. Of all those, however, who entered the lists for the slaughter of this dragon monster, none wielded a mightier pen than Aedanus Burke of South Carolina, who attacked the order in a pamphlet entitled, "Sound ye the Trumpet in Zion!" In Massachusetts especially, the fight on the Cincinnati attained the stage of a furor, and it is not to be wondered that the soul of Elbridge Gerry, the actual writer of the delegation letter, was sorely wrung. But that of which it is most behooving to take note is that the purpose of the Massachusetts delegates was all too effectively achieved, for the Massachusetts legislature was sufficiently persuaded by its arguments to rescind its resolutions; and thus was brought to an end a movement that might, had it not been repulsed, have led the way to constitutional reform at least a year earlier than was the case.

Meanwhile Congress was having trouble enough keeping its own body intact and its own constitutional soul functioning. In short, Congress time and time again found itself balked of progress toward the consummation of measures because of a dearth of representation. When in the closing days of January, 1785, after a period of weary waiting, Congress had gathered its requisite nine states and one more, there was a general expectancy that the essential business would be speedily completed and Congress might then adjourn for the remainder of the year. There was even thought of again leaving a Committee of the States to stand guard over the national interests, but a little reflection on what had happened to the Committee of the States in the summer of 1784 cast a damper on such a plan.

As early as March 9, 1785, Jacob Read wrote to Washington: "The great National Questions still remain untouched and will not be attempted till late in the Spring when it is hoped we may assemble the whole force of the Union and try if we can act as a Nation, which by the bye I very much doubt now the common tye of danger is removed."

At the end of August, when most of the great national questions, though not untouched, still required retouching, Read found occasion for even deeper lamentations, because not only was Congress "thin but the states seemed averse to doing anything to assert the dignity of the federal Government. To Madison he wrote (August 29),

We debate, make and hear long and often Spirited Speeches, but . . . the Welfare of the Union is trifled with . . . and if in a short time the States do not enable Congress to act with some Vigour and put the power of Compulsion into the hand of the Union I am free to Confess I think it almost time to give over the farce of what I cannot consider as an Efficient Government.

Only a short time before this Congress had so far lost its patience that it bristled up and resolved to speak frankly and boldly to its constituent states. Pressing appeals had theretofore been from time to time sent to the states delinquent in representation, sometimes with good results, quite as often with none; but on August 17 a plan was adopted that it was hoped would be more effective. The secretary was instructed to send monthly to the several legislatures a conspectus of the attendance for the month. This would carry names and dates; it would be a plain record of facts. With this first monthly record moreover went not so much an appeal as a rebuke:

Whereas from the want of a compleat representation the great interests of the Union have frequently been, and continue to be neglected and delayed; and the Confederation itself, or the administration thereof by Congress, may be considered as the cause of evils which solely result from an incompleat representation . . . it is incumbent on Congress to prevent opinions so derogatory to their honor, and so dangerous to the public welfare.

Elbridge Gerry, the author of this preamble, wished to have it carry this further admonition: "and tending so directly to a Change of our happy Form of Government, for others verging to Aristocracy or even to Despotism". The latter clause must, however, have been almost solely the dolorous voice of Gerry himself, for Congress ordered it deleted.

Whether or not it was the result of the circularized statement of representation and its accompanying admonition, the month of September brought an unexpected increase of attendance, so that on the 27th, Congress was enabled at last to decide on the requisition. After that it probably would have adjourned but for a recurrence of the fear that the disappearance of Congress might lead to a disintegration of the union. Individual members did, however, slink off home, with the result that attendance soon dwindled to seven states, sometimes less. Came the first Monday in November, the beginning of the new federal year, and only ten members were on hand. Not until November 23 was there a quorum of seven states, whereupon John Hancock, though absent, was elected president, and David Ramsay of South Carolina was chosen to serve as chairman until President Hancock should arrive. (It so happened that President Hancock never did serve under that election.) From that time until the end of December there were only ten days on which Congress was able to hold sessions, and through the month of January, 1786, no more than seven states were represented.

If the members in attendance had previously shown impatience, they now became exasperated. On the 30th of January it was resolved to press earnestly once more upon the delinquent states—Rhode Island, Delaware, Maryland, Virginia, North Carolina, and Georgia—to send on their delegates immediately. Accordingly, Chairman Ramsay took his pen in hand—being a doctor he may have wished that he might use a scalpel instead of a goosequill—and, first of all, made a few plain statements: during the three months of the federal year just elapsed only seven states had at any time been represented and in consequence no question except that for adjourning could be resolved without perfect unanimity; that important matters requiring the unanimous consent of nine states awaited action.

He then reminded the state executives "that even in private life where two persons agree to meet at a given time and place for the adjustment of their common concerns, the one who attends has a right to complain that he is not treated with common politeness by the other who breaks his appointment", and he further intimated that those who had been faithful to the engagement "might be justified in Resolving that as they had attended three months to no purpose they would in turn relinquish the public service, and leave the other states should they come on, to suffer a similar mortification". Finally he

offered this cogent observation: "The remissness of the States in keeping up a representation in Congress naturally tends to annihilate our
Confederation. That once dissolved our States would be of short duration. Anarchy, or intestine wars would follow till some future Caesar
seized our Liberties, or we would be the sport of European politics,
and perhaps parcelled out as appendages to their several Governments."

Chairman Ramsay's letter to the state executives is dated January 31,
1786. The next day, the coming of Henry Lee of Virginia completed
the representation of the eighth state, but the crippling deficiency remained. A few days later (February 11) Dr. Ramsay again took his
pen in hand, to write a private letter, this time to Dr. Benjamin Rush.
"There is a languor in the States", he wrote, "that forebodes ruin. The
present Congress for want of more States has not power to coin a
copper. In 1775 there was more patriotism in a village than there is
now in the 13 states." Wrote Nathan Dane the same day, "This inattention, this negligence and torpidity in some of the States will ruin
us, if suffered to continue." And to another correspondent he wrote
that the States must give more power to Congress or else must invent
some means of obliging their Delegates to attend, in order that Congress might exercise timely and to effect the powers that by the Confederation it did possess. Nearly a month later (March 6), when only
seven states were represented, Nathaniel Gorham declared that "as
unanimity is now necessary upon the most trivial questions, we feel
all the inconveniences of the liberum Veto of the Polish Diet."

Seven states might of course "mature" measures that required nine
votes, so as to be ready for the voting when and if the nine appeared—
for the voting, not necessarily for the adopting; for unanimity was all
but impossible to secure. The early months of the new year were accordingly consumed mainly in puttering at the minors and in efforts
to mature a few of the majors. During most of this time two additional
delegates, if they had come from the right states, would have given
Congress its requisite minimum of nine, for there were nearly always
two states with only one delegate each on the floor. In this respect the
adoption of the Confederation had really put Congress to a disadvantage; for under the old régime most of the states had eventually
permitted one delegate to give the state's voice.

The revenue problem was an annual affair, so far as concerned the enactment of a measure, but actually it had long been a perpetual headache. The requisition for 1785 had been brought to a conclusion only when the year had nearly passed, only when provisions for 1786 should have begun. Scarcely a breathing-spell was left until once again Congress found itself, like the Lady of Shalotte, enmeshed in the ancient curse. Requisitions had proved to be little else than a hollow hallo! with a mocking echo. One hope only remained—and that, in all conscience, was feeble enough—that the states would grant the request of April 18, 1783, for a right to levy imposts. On January 2, 1786, the secretary was called upon for a report respecting the responses to that request. Some of them had complied in full, some partially, two, namely New York and Georgia, not at all. With the request of April 30, 1784, for a limited power to regulate trade for a period of fifteen years there had been still fewer compliances. Just then the treasury board, reporting upon the French loans, warned Congress that a crisis was at hand, when the people of the United States must decide whether "for want of a timely exertion in Establishing a General Revenue and giving Strength to the Confederacy, they will hazard, not only the existence of the Union, but of those great and invaluable privileges, for which they have so arduously and honorably contended".

A committee, of which Monroe was chairman, went into solemn session on the subject, seeking to discover whether by any of the three means authorized by the Articles of Confederation—namely, requisitions, loans, bills of credit—the demands on Congress could be met. Payment of requisitions, the committee reported (February 3), had been disproportionate and inadequate; a loan was hardly feasible until Congress had at least paid the interest on what had already been borrowed; as for bills of credit, to say nothing of meeting current expenses and discharging the interest on the foreign debt, they would probably not serve even to pay off the domestic debt but would leave the creditors in a worse condition than before. There were of course the vacant lands, yet some time must elapse before any funds could be derived from that source. The committee must have bemoaned the absence of that generous ally to whom in the past, as a last resort, recourse could be had; yet it did not so much as mention to Congress asking France for another loan. One recourse alone was left: *prod* ("earnestly recommend" was the official language) New York and Georgia for a compliance with the recommendation of April, 1783. What a long, long time they had kept Congress waiting!

When Congress was particularly befuddled, in sore doubt what next to do, it was prone to pass a report of one committee on to another, in the hope that the new crew might generate some new ideas; and doubtless it was with the hope of obtaining new light, if light was to be found, that on February 9, various reports, motions, and documents were turned over to a new committee, under the chairmanship of Rufus King, but including Monroe, who had led the previous search. That committee likewise burrowed through the accumulation of materials and facts, but came out with nearly the same conclusions as its predecessor. What it mainly added was a solemn insistence that Congress could in nowise be held responsible "for those fatal Evils which will inevitably flow from a breach of Public faith . . . and a violation of those principles of Justice, which are the only solid Basis of the honor and prosperity of Nations."

There was still another committee that had been probing into a particular phase of the subject whose conclusions were of like kind. One and all these several groups had come forth from their committee chambers high-charged with pessimism. All were agreed that New York and Georgia in particular must be approached with supplications most forcible and fervent, and that those other states that had complied only partially with the recommendations of Congress should be besought to repent of their errors and do works meet for repentance. As for Georgia, before the end of March, Congress learned that the state had at last adopted the impost measure, but only after a vigorous campaign carried on through several months by Chief Justice George Walton, wherein the grand juries of numerous counties had solemnly presented "as a great and dangerous grievance the refusal of this state to grant powers to Congress to levy an impost". So far, then, as the impost measure was concerned, New York was left as the only non-complying state. So at least, if there should be no retrograde action.

At almost the exact moment, however, when Congress was putting forth its earnest pleas to the hitherto delinquent states, there fell one of the most stunning blows that body had at any time received. "Our foederal distresses gather fast to a point", Henry Lee wrote to Washington March 2, 1785: "New Jersey has refused the requisition, and will grant not a shilling, till New York accedes to the impost." Alarmed over the reported action of New Jersey, Congress despatched a special messenger to Trenton for an attested copy of the act. The messenger having returned on the night of March 5, the matter was on the next day referred to a committee. What had taken place was that the assembly, that is, the lower house of the legislature, had, "in a moody fit", as Grayson expressed it, adopted a resolution (February 20) that they would not comply with the requisition of September, 1785, or with any other requisition, until sundry grievances had been righted, among them the action of New York with regard to the impost.

New York was, in fact, taking advantage of the fortunate situation of her port to do a thriving impost business of her own, and the tax fell heavily upon New Jersey on the one side and Connecticut on the other. While it was the ill-usage at the hands of New York that had occasioned the outburst, other grievances that New Jersey had long kept smothered now broke out with violence. New Jersey had entered the Confederation, so it was averred, under highly disadvantageous terms, but had confidently expected that the unequal principles on which the compact had been founded would have been remedied. Now, however, they found that this was not to be done.

While the resolution of the lower house was not "an express act of the Legislature", Congress considered it nevertheless to be not only "in a high degree reprehensible", but actually tantamount to a declaration of independence. Nathaniel Gorham probably voiced the general fear when he wrote to James Warren (March 6) that nothing but the restraining hand of Congress, "weak as that is", prevented New Jersey and Connecticut "from entering the lists with N. York and bloodshed would very quickly be the consiquence." However New Jersey might suffer from having to pay taxes to New York, Gorham declared, "her refusal to comply with the requisition is unjustifiable", and unless she should rescind her resolution, it would mean "the end of all federal Government".

Congress could scarcely have been shocked at a failure to comply with one of its requisitions; it was full compliance rather that was apt to give that body surprise. At this very moment, for instance, Massachusetts was hanging back on compliance with this same requisition of 1785, and Nathan Dane was pleading in almost every letter that his state should not reject the requisition. What so startled Congress in the New Jersey case was the open and defiant refusal, with its threat of dangerous consequences. On March 7, Congress resolved to send a committee to plead with the New Jersey legislature to rescind its action, choosing Charles Pinckney of South Carolina, Nathaniel Gorham of Massachusetts, and William Grayson of Virginia for the mission.

Of what was said by these three gentlemen in the audience before the assembly (March 13) the speech by Pinckney has been preserved in full, while of those of Gorham and Grayson only the briefest summaries have survived. Pinckney's forceful array of arguments could scarcely have failed to be in a high degree convincing. Taking up, for instance, New Jersey's complaint that she had entered the Confederation under "unequal principles", Pinckney pointed out that it was the large states rather than the small that had made the greatest sacrifices for the sake of confederating. Only necessity, he declared, had compelled the larger states to confederate on terms that allowed the smaller states an equal voice with themselves in the national councils. "Had the system been formed in a time of peace—when no danger pressed . . . can it be thought", he asked, "that any union would have been formed upon principles so unequal and oppressive as the present?"

Let us suppose for a moment [he continued] the present confederation dissolved, and an assembly of the states convened for the purpose of adopting a system calculated to render the general government firm and energetic —is it not to be reasonably expected, that the large states would contend and insist upon a greater influence than they at present possess? Would they again consent to unite upon principles which should allow states not contributing a twelfth part of their quotas to public expences, an equal vote with themselves? It is not even to be hoped.

While Pinckney did not fail to emphasize the dangerous consequences both to the union and to the states individually of the course New Jersey was pursuing, he offered this significant counsel:

[New Jersey] ought immediately to instruct her delegates in congress, to urge the calling of a general convention of the states, for the purpose of revising and amending the federal system. In this constitutional application, she will meet with all the attention and support she can wish. I have long been of opinion, that it was the only true and radical remedy for our public defects; and shall with pleasure assent to, and support, any measure of that kind, which may be introduced, while I continue a member of that body.

The speeches of Gorham and Grayson, so declared a New Jersey newspaper, proved, "by a variety of arguments" and "in a very able and pointed manner", the impolicy of New Jersey's refusing the requisition. The French chargé, Otto, in some manner obtained what purported to be an extract of Grayson's speech, and transmitted it to Vergennes.

What is your object [Grayson exclaimed, characteristically loosing his indignation] in hastening the dissolution of a confederation that has cost us so dear? . . . do you suppose that in a new system of government you would be allowed the importance that you have had hitherto? Do you think that Virginia, South Carolina, Pennsylvania, and Massachusetts would be willing to stand on an equal footing with the handful of citizens which inhabit your state? . . . in a new confederation you will be put in your proper place.

Declared Otto, "These vigorous words produced a good effect. The assembly of New Jersey has just repealed its resolutions."

To the immense relief of Congress, the New Jersey assembly four days later rescinded the obnoxious resolution. Much, however, of the satisfaction afforded by New Jersey's recantation was soon afterward spoiled by the action of New York. In the early days of May, Congress learned that New York had nominally granted the impost, but had hedged the grant about with restrictions that made the State's act virtually a rejection rather than a compliance.

The New Jersey episode appears nevertheless to have been instrumental in stirring in or about Congress once more discussion of a general convention, and Pinckney awaited only an opportune time to move that Congress go into committee of the whole on "the state of public affairs". As yet the chronic deficiency of representation continued to such an exasperating degree that Grayson wrote March 22,

1786: "It seems as if many of the States had forgot the relation in which they stood to the Union as well as to foreign powers." The coming of one delegate two days later completed the representation of nine states, but the departure of another shortly afterward broke the chain—and Congress turnéd once more to its piddling and marking of time.

Through the month of April little was done, unless it be that members occupied their time studying a long report of the board of treasury on the establishment of a mint. Rufus King gave expression to the general disgust by proposing, so he asserted in a letter to Gerry, April 30, a resolution that, unless the delinquent states should send forward their delegates within a reasonable time, "Congress would adjourn without Day". "Something of this kind", King wrote, "must be done —it is a mere farce to remain here as we have done since last October." The fact was, he asserted, that during those six months, for three days only had nine states been on the floor. "We are without money, or the prospect of it, in the federal Treasury", he continued, "and the states, many of them, care so little about the Union that they take no measures to keep a representation in Congress." There is no record of King's resolution, but a committee was appointed (April 17) "to report the power which Congress may rightfully exercise to compel the attendance of the members". The committee belatedly (June 12) offered the opinion that a member had no right to withdraw without the consent of Congress or of his state; but Congress baulked at registering approval of that opinion.

In the beginning of May came a remarkable and unexpected spurt in attendance, including delegates from the long absent states of Delaware, North Carolina, and Georgia. Pinckney thereupon brought forward (May 3) his proposal that Congress go into committee of the whole on the state of the nation; and he and others must have made very persuasive pleas, for Dr. David Ramsay wrote to Dr. Rush that night that he had sat in the chair of Congress from eleven o'clock to half past three listening to "some of the best reasoning and most elegant speaking" he had ever heard in his life.

A few days later (May 12) Dr. Ramsay vacated the chair and departed Congress, his time as delegate having expired. Thereupon Nathaniel Gorham of Massachusetts was elected chairman (May 15). John Hancock was still nominally president, although he had not attended since his election in the preceding November. At length, on June 5, Congress received Hancock's resignation and thereupon chose Nathaniel Gorham as president (June 6).

It was not until June 26, nearly two months after Pinckney's proposal, that Congress finally resolved itself into a committee of the whole on the state of the nation, and then without immediate results; so that, on July 2, Charles Pettit was compelled to lament, "The State of the Nation is yet as loose as ever." Nevertheless, in that short month of May, 1786, during which there was a good attendance, Congress had made haste to legislate, while legislate it might, and had made encouraging progress. One piece of business that had only been waiting for such a time was the Connecticut cession. Curiously enough, there was presented in this instance a reversal of the usual state of affairs when cessions of western lands were the gristle on which Congress was gnawing. Congress had of old been wont to plead with the states for cessions, whilst the states would hang back reluctant. In this case, however, the eagerness was chiefly on the part of the state, and it was Congress that manifested an inclination to shy away from the proposition.

The lands ceded by Connecticut lay west of Pennsylvania and within the region already ceded by Virginia, and if the cession had meant no more than a surrender of claims the case would have been quite a simple one. But in making the cession Connecticut reserved a tract, since known as the Connecticut Reserve, or Western Reserve, and it was over this reservation that a controversy was waged in Congress through most of the month of May. How the trick was actually turned in favor of accepting the cession is revealed, in part, by Charles Pettit in a letter to Jeremiah Wadsworth, May 27, the next day after the acceptance.

Pettit explains that the delegates of the two states most concerned, Pennsylvania and Connecticut, entered into a sort of gentleman's agreement, the essence of which was that Connecticut would not countenance claims of the state or of her companies within Pennsylvania, while Pennsylvania would not question the implied right of Connecticut to the tract reserved. Pettit appears, however, to have been careful not to explain too minutely, even to members of Congress, the terms of the agreement. "These Things being understood rather than expressed", said he, "may be differently conceived by different Minds. . . . In Compromises of this kind it is found dangerous to go too minutely into Explanations." Nevertheless, he remarked, "These Objects were not unperceived by Congress and their Desire of promoting Peace and Harmony induced them to acquiesce in the Views of the two States." So indeed it did seem for the moment that peace and harmony between those two states had been promoted, even though there was plenty of growling elsewhere; as, for one instance, when William Grayson declared (May 28) that the Connecticut cession was "nothing but a State juggle contrived by old Roger Sherman to get a side wind confirmation to a thing they had no right to".

However all these things may have been, if ink had been used in the making of the gentleman's agreement between the Connecticut delegates and Pettit of Pennsylvania, the ink would scarcely have been dry when the Wyoming region, the main objective of the agreement so far as Pettit was concerned, became the scene of renewed disturbances, one phase of which was the appearance upon the scene of Ethan Allen of Vermont fame, with a boast, so it was reported, "that he had formed one new State, and with one hundred Green Mountain Boys, and two hundred Rifle men he could make that a new State in defiance of Pennsylvania." In due time the United States would pay good round penalties for the Connecticut bargain.

As it affected Congress, one of the penalties was not delayed; for the Connecticut delegates, having known full well what they wanted and having obtained it, forthwith wended their way back across Byram's River. (Mitchell did tarry a day or two, but Johnson departed immediately.) Thereupon the Rev. James Manning, delegate from Rhode Island, wrote to the governor (May 26, 1786), "I think it my duty to inform you that this honourable body is not a little alarmed at the present Crisis"; and he pointed to the empty treasury, the pressure on all sides for money, requisitions not complied with, trade almost prostrate, and numerous other ills. "This is our deplorable Situation", he continued, "and Congress obliged this day to adjourn for want of a sufficient Number of States to proceed in the necessary and most important business of the Confederacy. In a word, Sir, all the old members here look serious, and are alarmed for the safety of the Confederacy."

From William Grayson came a more specific grumble. Alluding to the departure of the Connecticut gentlemen he remarked (May 28): "It is a practice with many States in the Union to come forward and be very assiduous till they have carried some State jobb and then decamp with precipitation leaving the public business to shift for itself." Charles Pettit touched upon two other unfortunate consequences of the uncertain and irregular attendance. For one thing, the few who attended with constancy became wearied, soured, despondent, because they found themselves unable to pursue and plan with effect; for another thing, "The Comers and Goers . . . do not continue long enough to get the Information necessary to form a competent Judgment of the Business before them." "Is it possible", he queried, "that a great political System, however wisely formed, can be preserved and well conducted in this Manner? And yet we seem to be as supinely inattentive to our own Dangerous Situation as a flock of Sheep in their way to a Slaughter Pen." The Reverend Mr. Manning was convinced that only "the Interposition of Heaven" would extricate us from our difficulties; and he was about to lose faith in that interposition. "His former unmerited favour to this guilty Land", he wrote (May 17), "encourages me to hope for it, though it should almost be against hope."

For the moment, however, Delegate Manning was seeking personal aid from a less exalted source. On the 7th of June he wrote that he had been "reduced to the very last guinea and a trifle of Change . . . ; My lodging, washing, Barber's, Hatter's, Taylors Bills etc. not paid." At the mercy of his creditors, he could neither stay nor go. "Our affairs", he lamented, "are come very much to a point; and if the States continue to neglect keeping up their Delegation in Congress, the federal Government must *ipso facto* dissolve." He had besought his colleague, Nathan Miller, to apply to the legislature for money to support the delegation and to hasten with it to Congress; but all that Miller could obtain was a very small quantity of depreciated paper. To Manning he wrote (May 27), "I think I find a Disposition in many of our new faces in the Legislature to not send any Members to Congress, but they are small men, they Have Heads and so has board Nailes."

The season of relatively good attendance in May was taken advantage of for the promotion of another piece of much needed Congressional action. In the autumn Monroe had made a journey into the western region and he had returned fully impressed, he asserted, "with a conviction of the impolicy of our measures respecting it". In the light of subsequent history some of his convictions would appear to have been the result of short rather than long vision; nevertheless, convictions, even if erroneous, were better than indifference.

One of Monroe's conclusions was that those districts would "perhaps never contain a sufficient number of Inhabitants to entitle them to membership in the confideracy". Moreover, he was "clearly of opinion that to many of the most important objects of a federal government their interests, if not oppos'd will be but little connected with ours". He would therefore make the western government "subservient to our purposes", and at the same time "render them substantial service" by reducing the number of states. In pursuance of a motion by him a preliminary investigation of the subject was made by a grand committee, who offered a report (March 24, 1786) essentially in accordance with Monroe's ideas. To effect this change of plan it would be necessary to obtain a revision of the cessions of Virginia and Massachusetts and to repeal certain parts of the act of April 23, 1784, as well. Three days later (March 27) a committee of five (Monroe of Virginia, Johnson of Connecticut, King of Massachusetts, Kean and Pinckney of South Carolina) was appointed to report upon the forms of a temporary government for the western territory prior to the institution of government there under the ordinance of April 23, 1784.

The committee reported its plan on May 10, and May 18 was assigned for its consideration, but it does not appear to have been actually debated in Congress until July 7, when it was resolved to request Virginia so to revise her cession as to permit the erection in the district of not more than five nor less than three states, "as the situation of that country and future circumstances may require". Writing to Jefferson, May 11, concerning the proposed plan, Monroe said: "It is in effect to be a colonial gov[ernme]nt similar to that wh[ich] prevailed in these States previous to the revolution, with this remarkable and important difference that when such districts shall contain the number of the least numerous of the 'thirteen original States for the time being' they shall be admitted into the confederacy." In pointing to this particular provision Monroe could scarcely have supposed that he was telling Jefferson something new, for that provision was a direct inheritance from Jefferson's ordinance of 1784. He does, however, go on to say that the most important principles of that act were to be preserved.

The plan of May 10, 1786, provided for the appointment of a governor and a council of five members, all chosen for blank terms, revokable by Congress; a secretary to the governor and council; and a court of five members, whose commissions should continue during good behavior. The governor was required to take the advice of the council, but was at liberty to pursue it or not, as his own judgment should direct. In case of disagreement, however, the advice of the council and the reasons for the governor's dissent must be recorded in the latter's presence. Further, it was provided that, until the admission into the Congress of the United States, "the laws of [blank]" should be established in the district, subject, however, to the alteration of the general assembly when it should have been organized.

Between July 10 and 13 certain revisions of the plan of May 10 were effected, particularly in filling sundry gaps left blank and the omission of the governor's council. The term of the governor was fixed at three years, that of the secretary at two years, the number of "free male inhabitants of full age" requisite for taking the initial steps toward the formation of a general assembly was placed at 500, the term of a representative at one year. The general assembly, now somewhat more specifically defined, was to consist of the governor, a legislative council of five members appointed by Congress, "to continue in Office during pleasure", and a house of representatives, who should have complete legislative authority in the district.

In this interval of two months Monroe had become somewhat disturbed over developments, even to the extent of mistrusting his own former convictions and the plan largely founded on them. Writing to Jefferson July 16 he remarked: "The investigation of the subject has open'd the eyes of a part of the Union so as to enable them to view the subject in a different light from what they have heretofore done." He had observed particularly a disposition on the part of some members to increase the number of inhabitants required for admission to the Confederation. It was proposed to fix that requirement at one-thirteenth part of the free inhabitants of the United States. "This with some other restrictions they wish to impose on them," Monroe went on to say, "evinces plainly the policy of these men to be to keep them out of the confederacy altogether." It was a dangerous policy and calculated to throw them into the hands of Great Britain. If such a proposal should be pressed, the Virginia delegation would insist on leaving it upon the ground of the act of April 23, 1784, and would deny the right of the United States to make such a restriction.

There is little record of what took place at this time beyond the fact that the revision of July 13, 1786, was referred to a new committee, with a partial change of personnel. The new committee offered its report on September 19, but proposed no essential alteration in the general form of the government. It did however include the controverted requirement for admission to the union as a number of free inhabitants equal to "the one thirteenth part of the Citizens of the Original States" in place of a number equal to that of the least numerous of the states. The governor's council remained eliminated. The subject was made the order of the day for September 21, was debated September 29 and October 4, but was not again taken up until April 26, 1787, when was begun the final chapter in this long-laboring project. The problem of evolving a government for the western territory was, in fact, becoming much entangled in another western problem, that pertaining to the navigation of the Mississippi River.

CHAPTER XXXIII

BLOOD TRANSFUSION
THE ANNAPOLIS CONVENTION

The question pertaining to the navigation of the Mississippi River was by no means new. In one form or another, almost from the beginning of the war, the problem had confronted Congress, now threatening, now quiescent. In late 1780 and early 1781 some extraordinary measures were requisite to put the problem under a temporary restraint, effective for the time being; but the peace settlement of 1783 had failed to smooth down all the bristles, and in the close of 1784 the drowsing dog was again beginning to growl and threatening to break his leash.

In the early summer of 1785 a Spanish minister, Don Diego de Gardoqui, styling himself Encargado de Negocios, had arrived in the United States, had duly had his audience before Congress, and Secretary Jay had been commissioned to negotiate with him. Jay's instructions, adopted August 24, 1785, contained a requirement

particularly to stipulate the right of the United States to their territotial bounds, and the free Navigation of the Mississippi, from the source to the Ocean, as established in their treaties with Great Britain; and that he neither conclude nor sign any treaty, compact or convention, with the said Encargado de Negocios, until he hath previously communicated it to Congress, and received their approbation.

In a letter dated May 29, 1786, laid before Congress May 31, Jay stated that he was experiencing certain difficulties in his negotiations with Gardoqui and requested the appointment of a committee "with power to instruct and direct me on every point and subject relative to the proposed treaty with Spain". "It was immediately perceived", Monroe wrote to Madison, "that the object was to relieve him from the instruction respecting the Mississippi and to get a committee to cover the measure." A bomb tossed into the hall of Congress and about to explode would scarcely have produced greater consternation. Monroe himself, however, seems not to have been taken quite by surprise. Back in December, so he wrote to Governor Henry (August 12), Jay had discussed the matter with him with a certain degree of freedom, confiding that he was then discussing with Gardoqui whether the United States might not forego the use of the Mississippi for twenty-five or thirty years. "I soon found in short", Monroe wrote, "that Mr. Jay was desirous of occluding the Mississippi and of making what he termed advantageous terms in the treaty of commerce the means of effecting it."

This, then, was the nub of the controversy that was waged through the summer of 1786, and even then was by no means concluded, a contest that in fact presently threatened the break-up of the Confederation. In the main it was a contest between the easterners, on the one hand, concerned mainly for seaborne commerce, and the southerners, on the other, who believed that the free navigation of the Mississippi was vital to the development of the west. One Virginia member of Congress, Henry Lee, took essentially the same view as the easterners, as did also another Virginian who was not a member of Congress, namely George Washington. "Your reasoning on the navigation of the Mississippi", Lee wrote to Washington (July 3, 1786), "is perfectly conformable to the prevalent doctrine on that subject in Congress." For his part, Lee was entirely willing to yield the navigation of the Mississippi for a term of years for the sake of the great advantages to be gained through "a free liberal system of trade with Spain". Besides, he argued (August 7), in "the debilitated condition of the foederal government", it was "unwise to wish the offence of any part of the empire, unless to attain great good."

The main argument employed in support of Jay's proposition was that Spain would under no circumstances grant to the United States the right of free navigation of the Mississippi, therefore in agreeing to the occlusion of the river we should be yielding only what we could not use. In the minds of the eastern members there was indeed another reason, although it was for the most part kept in the background. They were concerned lest the development of the west be at the expense of the east, a fear that had cropped out on numerous occasions before and was only brought again to the surface by the Mississippi question. Rufus King, for instance, in a letter to Elbridge Gerry June 4, 1786, declared that he could discover no principle that would attach the settlers west of the mountains to a union that would in many points be inconvenient to them. "In true policy", he asked, "ought the U.S. to be very assiduous to encourage their Citizens to become Settlers of the country beyond the Apalachian?" In short, if there should be an uninterrupted use of the Mississippi at this time, he would consider "every emigrant to that country from the Atlantic States, as forever lost to the Confederacy". Recurring to the subject three months later King wrote:

Nature has severed the two countries by a vast and extensive chain of mountains, interest and convenience will keep them separate, and the feeble policy of our disjointed Government will not be able to unite them. For these reasons I have ever been opposed to encouragements of western emigrants. The States situated on the Atlantic are not sufficiently populous, and loosing our men, is loosing our greatest Source of Wealth.

This frank statement, be it understood, was not made in Congress, but in a very private letter; nevertheless enough had been revealed during the debates on the Spanish question and on the plan of government for the western territory to convince Monroe that he had penetrated the motives of the eastern gentlemen. Their object, he wrote to Governor Henry (August 12), "is to break up so far as this will do it, the settlements on the western waters, prevent any in future, and thereby keep the States southward as they now are. . . . To throw the weight of population eastward and keep it there, to appreciate the vacant lands of New York and Massachusetts." Indeed Timothy Bloodworth of North Carolina averred (August 28) that the eastern delegates "Openly declare on the floor of Congress, their desire if possible to prevent emigration".

Monroe was strongly inclined to believe that the main objective of the easterners was really the dismemberment of the union and that their maneuvers in the Mississippi affair were, in part at least, designed to aid in the accomplishment of that purpose. "In conversations at which I have been present", he wrote to Governor Henry (August 12), "the Eastern people talk of a dismemberment so as to include Pen[nsyl-vani]a . . . and sometimes all the states south to the Potomack." He had, in fact, learned that committees of easterners, including New Yorkers, had met in New York City to discuss the subject of "a dismemberment of the States east of the Hudson from the Union and the erection of them into a separate gov[ernmen]t." How far they had gone in their discussion he did not know, but, so he wrote to Madison September 3, they had been sounding prominent personages on the subject.

Clear evidence that such a movement was in contemplation is furnished by a letter of Theodore Sedgwick to Caleb Strong, August 6, 1786:

It well becomes the eastern and middle States, who are in interest one [Sedgwick wrote], seriously to consider what advantages result to them from their connection with the Southern States. They can give us nothing, as an equivalent for the protection which they derive from us but a participation in their commerce . . . an attempt to perpetuate our connection with them, which at last too will be found ineffectual, will sacrifice everything to a mere chimera. Even the appearance of a union cannot in the way we now are long be preserved. It becomes us seriously to contemplate a substitute; for if we do not controul events we shall be miserably controuled by them. No other substitute can be devised than that of contracting the limits of the confederacy to such as are natural and reasonable, and within those limits instead of a nominal to institute a real, and an efficient government.

At all events, Monroe was convinced, the situation was serious and required to be carefully guarded. "A dismemberment should be avoided by all the states", he declared (August 12), "and the conduct of wise and temperate men should have in view to prevent it." In any case, "It should be so managed (if it takes place), either that it should be formed into three divisions, or if into two, that Pen[nsylvani]a if not Jersey should be included in ours." He had some fears (September 3) that Pennsylvania might "have a contrary affection". If that should appear to be the case, it must be removed if possible. "A knowledge that she was on our side wo'd blow this whole intrigue in the air. To bring this ab[ou]t therefore is an important object of the Southern interest. If a dismemberment takes place that State must not be added to the eastern scale. It were as well to use force to prevent it as to defend ourselves afterward."

During the month of August the debate on the Spanish question had raged in a manner little short of ferocity. Congress had declined to appoint such a committee as Jay requested, a committee with powers to advise and direct the secretary in his negotiations; but it had appointed a committee to confer with him and report back to Congress. That committee had held back its report for two months, then Jay was called before Congress to explain his difficulties, which he did at length (August 3). Of the principal debate, which took place in mid-August, some records have fortunately survived. There are extensive notes of debates kept by Secretary Thomson, a long speech by Charles Pinckney, a briefer one by William Samuel Johnson, and, in addition, some cryptic but for the most part comprehensible notes by the latter. Monroe's letters are likewise informing. If any members of Congress on the one side or the other were drawn into the opposite camp by all this persuasive oratory, the records fail to reveal it; not then at all events. In the latter days of the discussion one or two members did break ranks and wabble for a brief space, but at the final test they were one and all to be found firmly planted on their own side of the line.

One effort of the southerners, which did not however succeed, was to take the negotiations entirely out of Jay's hands and transfer them to Madrid. The final test was on a motion of the Massachusetts delegates to repeal the ultimata in Jay's instructions. This motion had been carried in committee of the whole, and on August 29 it was carried by the same vote in Congress, every member from New Hampshire to Pennsylvania voting for the repeal, every member from Maryland to Georgia voting against it; that is, seven ayes to five noes, for Delaware had not a single delegate on the floor.

The southerners maintained that, inasmuch as nine states had assented to the instruction, seven states had not a right to alter that instruction so as to make it a new one; and further, what, in the view of some of the Southerners, gave to the case its most serious aspect, if the action in this instance should be accepted as valid, the precedent would be fraught with extreme danger to the union. "If seven states can carry on a treaty", Timothy Bloodworth wrote to Governor Caswell September 4, ". . . it follows of course that the Confederated compact is no more than a rope of sand, and if a more efficient Government is not obtained a dissolution of the Union must take place." In a way Jay and his adherents had won the first battle, but would they, could they, advance from a base so precarious? Monroe was convinced that they had gone too far to retreat. "They must either carry the measure", he declared, "or be disgraced . . . and sooner than suffer this they will labour to break the Union." But a lull fell over the battlefield. For a long time neither side moved.

The summer of 1786 had not, however, been wholly taken up with the project of a government for the western territory and the Spanish question. That other essential in the settlement of the problem of the west, namely, the negotiation of treaties with the Indians, had gone forward with results that, upon the whole, were satisfactory. Numerous treaties with the western and southern Indians had been negotiated in the spring, and during the summer Congress had worked out a general organization of its Indian affairs, laying down an ordinance for that purpose (August 7). Considerable time had also been devoted to the financial problem. When, on May 12, it appeared that New York had not complied with the impost measure in a manner satisfactory to Congress, that sorely bedeviled body turned once more in sorrow and humiliation to the discredited device of requisitions. On June 27 the board of treasury, apparently on its own initiative, laid before Congress a plan for the requisition for the current year.

The treasury board's report, which specifies as necessary a sum "in actual specie", is largely a summary of what had been done, was doing, or had not been done by the several states—mainly the latter; and the board frankly stated at the outset, "If it be asked what expectations there are that the several States will raise by the ordinary mode of Requisition, the sums required by the proposed Report, the Answer obviously is, That no reasonable hope of this nature can possibly exist." And in conclusion the board registered its conviction "that nothing but an immediate and general Adoption of the Measures recommended by the Resolves of Congress of the 18th April, 1783, can rescue us from Bankruptcy, or preserve the Union of the several States from Dissolution."

With both general conclusions all Congress seemed agreed. On August 2d the requisition, essentially as proposed by the treasury board, was adopted, although not without controversy over some of the details, and the board was instructed to prepare an address to the states on the subject. Some news of all this came to Stephen Mix Mitchell, then at home in Connecticut, whereupon that gentleman sat him down and penned a few lines to his colleague, William Samuel Johnson (August 9):

We hear you have again made out a Requisition upon the States and are preparing an Address to accompany it. I conjecture, your hopes must far exceed your Faith, or your faith would remove mountains. Pray speak plain Language to the states, paint your Situation and your feelings without Disguise, and let them know you are or soon will be, the most contemptible political Body which ever conven'd.

A month later (September 14) Mitchell wrote: "Your Address to the States will (I fear) prove like Water spilled upon the Ground and have no Influence to awake us from our Stupor. We must not only hear, but feel before we Stirr."

Mitchell might just as well have curbed his pessimism over the waste of even strong Congressional language on the dry ground of the states; for the address never reached them. The cream of the address was first skimmed off, then the residue all sloshed out on the floor of Congress. The board of treasury did prepare an address (August 31), and it was an impressive presentation of the case, if any address could impress the states, launching out, as it did, with a preamble reminiscent of the Declaration of Independence, and faring forth with much of that plain speaking for which Mitchell had pleaded. First, however, it was taken in hand (September 7) by a committee, headed by that same William Samuel Johnson to whom Mitchell had made his plea; and that committee evidently decided that there was room not only for an increase of plain speaking but also for an enlargement of factual particularity.

The proposed alterations (October 6) may have been merely symptomatic of a rivalry of rhetoricians. The record is darkened. What the record does, however, reveal is that Congress was dissatisfied with the address and demanded a further endeavor. On the 9th another effort was made to meet the demand, by desiccating the address of most of its pungent juices. One passage there was, nevertheless, that was as incisive as any one could have desired. Perhaps that was the trouble; it was too incisive. At all events, it placed Congress in an unaccustomed rôle. Hearken to that assembly's voice:

But whatever may be the fate of those measures on which you have a right to deliberate and determine, *We, the United States in Congress Assembled by Virtue of the powers Vested in us by the Confederation* do call on you as members of the Confederacy to pay into the general Treasury at the time stipulated your respective Quotas of the present requisition for the support of the general Government.

The next page of the record is quite as dark as the preceding. On the 17th of October the proposed address once more confronted the assembled Congress, yet alas! that brave appeal to the states had dwindled to to no more than a sadly emaciated ghost of its former robustness. There was neither speculation in its eyes nor resonance in its voice. No wonder, then, that, when the vote was taken whether it should be sent forward to the states, the secretary forebore to make any record whatsoever in the Journal; he merely made a notation on the report itself: "Oct. 17, 1786. Question taken and lost." The whole business of the requisition had begun with a note of despondency, and what more fitting than that it end in a gesture of despair?

After all, however, Congress had evidently not been wholly overcome by despair, for on the preceding day (October 16) a committee had been appointed to draft an ordinance for carrying into effect the impost system of April 18, 1783, just as if that system still had within it the breath of life. It was a new committee, though not indeed a new subject. On July 27 a resolution had been adopted providing for the appointment of such a committee, the committee had been appointed, and on August 9 had reported some resolutions, but not an ordinance. The main problem was to prevail on New York to pass an act acceding to the system according to the terms laid down by Congress, and upon Pennsylvania and Delaware to repeal the clauses in their respective acts "restraining the operation of their grants of the impost, until all the states shall have granted to Congress the supplementary funds".

The act of New York, instead of vesting in Congress the power to levy the duties, had reserved the power of levying and collecting to itself. Congress had appealed to Governor Clinton to reconvene the legislature for the purpose of prevailing upon that body to reconsider its act, but Clinton had declined, alleging a constitutional bar to such action on his part. Thereupon Congress reiterated its request (August 23), and more earnestly and more emphatically. Whereupon the legislature, as not a few members of Congress had expected, did but applaud the governor's action. Charged Stephen Mix Mitchell of Connecticut (January 24, 1787), the legislature of New York had "step'd as twere out of their way to give Congress a Slap in the face". And so that was the end of that chapter.

It had been confidently hoped that, if Pennsylvania could be prevailed on to comply, New York would scarcely dare to stand out alone. Accordingly, on August 15, it was resolved to send a committee to intercede with the Pennsylvania legislature, and on the 14th, King and Monroe were designated for the purpose. Without hope at any time of accomplishing the end in view, Monroe sought to evade the mission, but finally yielded and went. On September 13, he and King had their audience, when Monroe made, so he afterward declared, the best plea he could. King later confessed that, in his first attempt, he became confused and made a complete failure, but subsequently, having rallied his nerves, he went through his discourse "without trepidation and to my own satisfaction".

The committee of Congress had, in fact, invaded a hostile atmosphere. Said one writer in a Philadelphia paper (September 14):

If half the pains were taken to compel the delinquent states to pay into the treasury their quotas called for . . . that are now using to urge this state to comply with the unreasonable request which was made to the house at their last session, and unanimously rejected, the Congress would be more respectable in the discharge of their duty.

Another writer, however, took a different view of the matter. Mr. King, it was reported, had given "so lively, so pathetic, and just account of the state of this country, and urged the requisition of Congress with so much sound reasoning", that it was generally expected the assembly would adopt the measure proposed by the committee. "Nothing can save America", this writer went on to say, "but a union in Congress ... In an union of the states, the strength of the whole may always be directed against rebellions, or usurpations of each state. United we stand, divided we fall—and let all the people say amen." The Pennsylvania assembly did not, however, at that time yield to the appeal of Messrs. King and Monroe, but deferred the matter to the consideration of the next assembly.

Notwithstanding rebuffs received and rebuffs expected, Congress had not forfeited all hope. Just when the debate over the question of making one more futile requisition was under way, Congress was considering the question of undertaking a thorough-going revision of the Confederation in the orthodox manner. The movement inaugurated by Pinckney, May 3, in his motion to go into the committee of the whole on the state of the nation, appears to have looked toward a convention as the best instrument by which the needed reorganization might best be brought about; but there were yet in Congress a good many minds unreconciled to that plan. Accordingly the outcome of the discussion of the subject, June 26, was the appointment, July 3, of a grand committee "to report such amendments to the Confederation and a draft of such resolutions as it may be necessary to recommend to the several states for the purpose of obtaining from them such powers as will render the federal government adequate to the ends for which it was instituted." On the 7th of August the grand committee proposed seven additional articles to the Confederation, drawn mainly, it would appear, by Charles Pinckney.

The first of these amendments (Article 14) would vest Congress with the exclusive power of regulating commerce, both foreign and domestic, of laying duties on imports and exports, and of making regulations for their collection, such as were consistent with the respective state constitutions. The revenue was, however, to accrue to the use of the state in which it was payable. The second amendment (Article 15), which applied to requisitions, provided that Congress should fix the proper period within which the states should pass the necessary acts of compliance, and, in the event of neglect on the part of any state, the state should be assessed, in the case of a money quota, an additional charge of ten per cent of her quota, and, in the case of land forces, twelve per cent on the average expense of such quota. The third amendment (Article 16) was a rather complicated provision whereby, in the event a state had for ten months neglected to comply with a requisition, Congress might intervene, appporton the sums to counties and towns to be collected by the collectors of the last state tax. In the event of the refusal of these officers to act, Congress might appoint other collectors and have power to enforce the collections. Finally any opposition on the part of a state or of its citizens to such collection would be considered as "an open Violation of the federal compact".

Article 17 provided that a state would be allowed interest for advances and charged for arrears. Article 18 provided that in the establishment of a new system of finance the assent of eleven states was required, and in the same proportion if the number of states should be increased beyond thirteen. Article 19 would vest Congress with the sole and exclusive power of defining and punishing treason, etc., and with power to institute a federal court of seven judges, appointed from different parts of the Union, to which appeal was allowed from state courts in cases involving foreign powers, the law of nations, or federal questions generally. Article 20 was designed to enforce attendance on the part of members of Congress, but it consisted mainly of injunctions upon the states. A recalcitrant member might indeed be "proceeded against as Congress shall direct", but punishment was limited to disqualification any longer to be a member of Congress or to hold any office of trust or profit under the United States or any individual state.

Taken as a whole, these proposed amendments were the most ambitious effort made at any time to revise the Articles of Confederation, yet they were little more than an ineffectual groping after the remedy for the ills that did so mightily beset the Congress of the United States. A date (August 14) was set for their consideration, but Congress by then had become so deeply involved in the Spanish problem that nothing else could be thought of; and by the time Congress had worn itself to a frazzle reaching only an impasse on that question, it appears to have been the consensus of opinion that the project for amending the Confederation might as well be dropped. Said Timothy Bloodworth, September 4, "The additional powers to the confederation . . . now

appear out of View." Probably a chief reason for dropping the undertaking was the glimpse of new light from the direction of Annapolis.

The Annapolis Convention derives its origin directly from an effort
on the part of Virginia and Maryland to adjust their own problems
relating to the commerce of the Potomac, while indirectly it was an
outgrowth of the movement for a general regulation of trade by Congress. At a convention of commissioners of those two states at Alex-
andria and Mount Vernon in March, 1785, the questions at issue between those two states were satisfactorily adjusted; then, in order to a
fuller consummation of the purposes of the agreement, Maryland invited the accession of Delaware and Pennsylvania.

In the autumn of 1785, when this proposition came before the Virginia legislature, Madison embraced the opportunity to promote the
larger plan of a convention of commissioners from all the states "for the
purpose of digesting and reporting the requisite augmentation of the
power of Congress over trade". On January 21, 1786, just as the session
of the legislature was closing, the measure providing for the convention
was adopted. Subsequently Annapolis was chosen as the place for the
meeting, and the first Monday in September as the time. "It was
thought prudent", Madison explained to Jefferson (March 18), "to
avoid the neighborhood of Congress, and the large commercial towns,
in order to disarm the adversaries to the object, of insinuations of influence from either of these quarters." Yet the place was one of the
least of the elements that gave rise to anxiety. "Considering", Madison
wrote, "that the States must first agree to the proposition for sending
deputies, that these must agree in a plan to be sent back to the States,
and that these again must agree unanimously in a ratification of it", he
almost despaired of success.

Undoubtedly Madison entertained a hope, even though it was not a
very vigorous hope, that in some manner the Annapolis Convention
would not merely lead to more satisfactory commercial arrangements
among the states, but would open the door for such a thorough-going
revision of the instrument of government as would save the union
from dissolution. "The question whether it be possible and worth while
to preserve the Union of the States", he wrote to Monroe, April 9,
"must be speedily decided some way or other. Those who are indiffer-

ent to its preservation would do well to look forward to the consequences of its extinction. The prospect to my eye is a gloomy one indeed." Even as late as August 12, when the time for the convention to assemble was close at hand, he still had but a faint hope of its success.

It seems rather a remarkable state of affairs that Madison should have deemed it politically unwise to intimate, except to close personal friends, that his wishes in promoting the Annapolis Convention extended farther than a commercial reform; yet he was convinced that even in the Virginia legislature such an intimation would probably have defeated the whole plan, and the manner in which a good many statesmen looked askance at the proposal, suspicious particularly of its possible implications for the reform of the government, point clearly the wisdom of Madison's caution.

In Congress the proposed convention did not by any means meet with universal approval. Rufus King was at first not unfavorably disposed toward the convention. Writing to John Adams May 5, 1786, he expressed the hope "that wisdom will govern their deliberations, and that their result will produce an union of opinions on the subject of commercial regulations through all the states". Yet a month later he had doubts whether the convention would accomplish much toward effecting "those measures essentially necessary for the prosperity and safety of the States".

By that time the eastern members were questioning not only the ultimate purposes of the convention, but also its commercial purposes. King was of opinion (June 11) that the majority of Southern planters were opposed to general commercial regulations, favoring particular regulations by the states. His colleague, Theodore Sedgwick, strangely enough conceived the notion that the motives behind the calling of the convention were the precise opposite of those which actually animated Madison. "No reasonable expectations of advantage", Sedgwick wrote to Caleb Strong (August 6), "can be formed from the commercial convention. The first proposers designed none. The measure was originally brought forward with an intention of defeating the enlargement of the powers of Congress. Of this I have the most decisive evidence." That Madison had kept his own counsel, so far as the eastern members of Congress were concerned, is evidenced by a remark of

King in a letter to Jonathan Jackson, September 3. "Mr. Madison", said King, ". . . does not discover or propose any other plan than that of investing congress with full powers for the regulation of commerce foreign and domestic." Even that power, King thought, would "run deep into the authorities of the individual States".

Of the Virginia delegates in Congress, Grayson was not at all hopeful of good results from the Annapolis convention. "I am of opinion", he wrote to Madison, May 28, "our affairs are not arrived at such a crisis as to ensure success to a reformation on proper principles; a partial reformation will be fatal; things had better remain as they are than not to probe them to the bottom." He was inclined therefore to the opinion that it would not be "for the advantage of the Union that the Convention at Annapolis produce anything decisive". Since, however, the state of Virginia had gone thus far, it might be better for her to "go farther and propose to the other States to augment the powers of the delegates to comprehend all the grievances of the Union, and to combine the commercial arrangements with them, and make them dependant on each other". It was just this, however, that Madison had convinced himself it was impolitic to do.

Monroe, on the other hand, at first but mildly favorable to the plan, soon grew enthusiastic. On August 16, for instance, he wrote to President John Sullivan of New Hampshire: "I have looked forward to that convention as the source of infinite blessings to this country." Then, as the time for the assembling of the convention was approaching, he wrote to Madison, "I consider the convention of Annapolis as a most important era in our affairs."

So far as the immediate object of the convention was concerned, that proved to be a flash; for only a handful of delegates appeared—those of New York, New Jersey, Pennsylvania, Delaware, and Virginia. The eagerness, however, of those who did come that the opportunity should not be lost for furthering, if possible, the larger purpose that some of them had envisioned, was such that they resolved to embrace it. Of the five states that had sent delegates thither it was New Jersey, but recently raked over the coals for an act that seemed to threaten the breakup of the Union, that looked most earnestly to the Annapolis Convention for guidance toward a better future. For the delegates of that state were empowered to take into their purview "other important matters" that might be necessary to "the common interest and permanent harmony of the several states", suggesting that they report such an act on the subject as, when ratified by the states, "would enable the United States in Congress assembled effectually to provide for the exigencies of the union".

Accordingly the convention came to a resolution (September 14) to embody in their report to their several legislatures an expression of their "earnest and unanimous wish that speedy measures may be taken to effect a general meeting of the States in a future Convention", for such purposes "as the situation of public affairs may be found to require". Specifically they offered the suggestion that their own states

use their endeavours to procure the concurrence of the other States, in the appointment of Commissioners to meet at Philadelphia on the second Monday in May next, to take into consideration the situation of the United States, to devise such other provisions as shall appear to them necessary to render the constitution of the Federal Government adequate to the exigencies of the Union; and to report such an Act for that purpose to the United States in Congress assembled, as when agreed to by them, and afterwards confirmed by the Legislatures of every State, will effectually provide for the same.

From "motives of respect" the commissioners sent a copy of their "observations and sentiments" to the Congress of the United States. On the 20th of September, 1786, the report was laid before Congress. It was signed by John Dickinson, chairman of the Convention, but it is known to have been drafted by Alexander Hamilton.

At last the great question that had been mulled over from time to time these ten years past was placed squarely before Congress, to accept or reject; and he would have been a bold prophet who would at that moment have undertaken to foretell what the action of that body would be.

CHAPTER XXXIV

WATCHMAN, WHAT OF THE NIGHT?
THE FEDERAL CONVENTION

The reception of the Annapolis report by Congress was far from encouraging to the advocates of a Federal Convention. Indeed criticism of the recommendation had begun before ever that report was laid before Congress. Rufus King, for instance, who had been a critic of the Annapolis Convention from the beginning, had not yet left Philadelphia after his appearance before the Pennsylvania legislature, when the New York delegates to the Annapolis Convention passed through that city on their homeward journey, and a talk with them does not appear to have softened his mood toward the Annapolis proposal. To Governor Bowdoin he wrote (September 17, 1786): "Foreign nations had been notified of this convention, the friends to a good federal government through these states looked to it with anxiety and Hope; the History of it will not be more agreeable to the former, than it must be seriously painful to the latter." Then, on the 2d of October, twelve days after the report had been laid before Congress, he wrote to John Adams that the Annapolis Convention had "terminated without credit or prospect of having done much good". Whether the states would accede to the proposition of a federal convention was, he thought, uncertain. Furthermore, "Congress, I think, will not interfere in such a manner as to patronize the project. I am fully convinced that your opinion is a just and political one, that Congress can do all a convention can, and certainly with more safety to original principles." On the same day Monroe, who was about to move that the report be referred to a committee, wrote to Madison: "I am persuaded the Eastern States will not grant an unlimited commission, but wo'd accede to it if its objects were defind."

On the 11th of October, 1786, the Annapolis report was finally re-referred to a grand committee, which in this instance consisted of only ten members, for the reason that New Hampshire, Delaware, and North Carolina had no delegates in attendance. There is no record of this proceeding in the Journals, but Henry Lee has left some account of it in a letter (October 20) to St. George Tucker, one of the Virginia members of the Annapolis Convention.

With difficulty [wrote Lee] the friends to the system adopted by the convention induced Congress to commit your report, altho' all were truly sensible of the respect manifested by the convention to this body, and all zealous to accomplish the objects proposed by the authors of the commercial convention. Indeed their conviction of the inadequacy of the present federal government render them particularly zealous to amend and strengthen it. But different opinions prevail as to the mode; some think with the Annapolis meeting, others consider Congress not only the constitutional but the most eligible body to originate and propose necessary amendments to the confederation, and others prefer State conventions for the express purpose, and a congress of deputys, appointed by these conventions with plenipotentiary powers.

At the moment when this action was taken in Congress, Rufus King was in Boston reporting to the Massachusetts House of Representatives on various subjects before Congress, and he took occasion to express briefly his views of the Annapolis recommendation. His argument was that the Confederation was the act of the people, that no part of it could be altered but by the consent of Congress and confirmation by the state legislatures, and that therefore Congress ought to make the examination first; because, he argued, "if it was done by a convention, no Legislature could have a right to confirm it". If, on the other hand, it should be done agreeably to the Confederation, no such difficulty would exist. "Besides", he added, "if Congress should not agree upon a report of a convention, the most fatal consequences might follow."

About a month later King's colleague, Nathan Dane, appeared before the same body and voiced essentially the same views, although he hedged himself round about with a variety of queries. "It does not fully appear", he remarked, "whether they [the Annapolis Convention] had it in contemplation to do away the present system, and to adopt another on different principles, and with different features, or to preserve the principles and great outlines of the present, and to make some alterations in it, to give it more strength and energy." If the former was intended, was the public mind prepared for it? If the latter, would it not be best first to consider the measures already proposed for amending the Confederation?

The Annapolis recommendation closely coincided with certain disturbances in Massachusetts, known as the Shays Rebellion, of which it is needful to take note because of their influence in behalf of national unity and national strength. It is not within the scope of this narrative to probe into the causes or the nature of those discontents, except to observe briefly their consequences for the movement in behalf of a more efficient national government. While some of the discontents had a rational foundation, the irrational, as in all such upstirrings of the populace, overshadowed the rational. There were, for instance, loud complaints against taxes, but mainly by people who never paid a farthing of tax. Hard-pressed debtors, who constituted a large element in the uprising, had a better case; and, if they found themselves in a debtors' prison, their provocation to revolt is quite understandable. Nor is it at all incomprehensible that they should direct their attacks upon the lawyers, the judges, the courts, who had put them there. Thence it was an easy transition to a demand for the abolition of all debts and to a revolt against existing government generally.

Upon the whole it appears to have been a revolt of the have-nots against the haves, incited by the age-old envy of the shiftless toward the successful. In another aspect, and one of probably deeper significance, the revolt was a natural result of that unrestrained preachment of the rights of man, which the Revolution had offered in great abundance— the flowering and flourishing of that sinister offspring of liberty, which is license. And, as always under such conditions, demagogues sprang up to reap what harvest they might. Henry Lee was doubtless right when he wrote to Washington (September 8), that at the bottom of the movement were the "intriguing exertions" of a class "whose desperate fortunes are remediable only by the ruin of society", and that their schemes portended the dissolution of order and good government.

Naturally Congress became deeply concerned and sent the secretary at war, General Knox, to the region of disturbance to investigate and particularly to take measures for the protection of the arsenal at Springfield. Knox's reports served but to deepen anxieties. October 18 he admonished Congress: "The dreadful consequences which may be expected from wicked and ambitious men, possessing the command of a force to overturn, not only the forms, but the principles of the present constitutions, require the wisest councils and most vigorous measures on the part of Government." Having heard Knox's "melancholy information", Henry Lee wrote to Washington: "We are all in dire apprehension that a beginning of anarchy with all its calamitys has approached, and have no means to stop the dreadful work." He besought Washington to use his "unbounded influence" to bring the seditious "back to peace and reconciliation". The gist of Washington's reply was: *"Influence is no government."*

It was the unanimous decision of Congress that whatever means and power it might be able to command must be put forth to crush the insurrection, and it was accordingly resolved to raise a special body of troops for the purpose. Acutely aware at the same time that the interposition of the Union was an exceedingly delicate business and carried an element of danger, Congress chose to conceal the purpose of these troops behind the screen of reported "hostile intentions of the Indians in the Western country". Nor was the fear of openly avowing its purpose to go to the aid of Massachusetts the only fear that disturbed Congress. The reputation of Congress for keeping its promises to pay its soldiers had not in these latter years been of the best; therefore it was deemed wise to make provision for a special fund from which to pay this extraordinary body of troops. A loan of five hundred thousand dollars was accordingly authorized for the purpose. In its secret Journals (October 21) Congres not only recorded its "fullest confidence" in "the most liberal exertions of the money holders in the State of Massachusetts and the other States" for filling the loan, but it likewise recorded there the fears that actuated it in adopting this unusual course. Such were "the present embarrassments of the federal finance" that, but for this confidence, "Congress would not hazard the perilous step of putting arms into the hands of men whose fidelity must in some degree depend on the faithful payment of their wages."

The Massachusetts disturbances had, then, done far more than set that state to quaking with anxiety; they had deepened conviction everywhere that a more efficient national government was essential; and one consequence of this deepening conviction was soon manifesting itself in the Massachusetts delegation in Congress. For some time the attitude of Massachusetts toward the union of the thirteen states had been one of lukewarmness, if not of indifference. Now, however, when the state found herself betwixt the Devil and Daniel Shays, her eyes were opened, and she began to perceive in that union a virtue and a value for herself that latterly she had been prone to question. "The Massachusetts delegation", William Grayson wrote to Monroe (November 22), "have been much more friendly I have understood since the late insurrection in their State: they look upon the foederal assistance as a matter of the greatest importance, of course they wish for a continuance of the Confederation." So much at least had been gained. But there, on the preservation of the Confederation, with possible amendments, those delegates took their stubborn stand and long refused to budge.

Congress was no doubt disposed in any case to take its own time in considering the proposed federal convention, but even if the members present had been warmly inclined toward the proposition, the consideration of it would of necessity for a good many weeks have been limited to outdoor conversations; for, from November 3 to January 16, there was no Congress. On January 17, 1787, seven states were at last assembled, but they were retained for that one day only, and not again until February 2 did seven states appear. On that January 17, Congress endeavored to organize by choosing a president, but all to no avail. "There seem'd a Division of Sentiment", wrote Stephen Mix Mitchell of Connecticut. His colleague, Dr. Johnson, received two votes, "which was as many as any Gentleman could boast". William Blount of North Carolina likewise recorded that "not more than two states could agree in any one man."

Blount himself had fixed his eye upon the presidency, and as early as January 7 had written to his brother: "If it did not appear to me quite certain that a *Certain Friend* of yours will be president I would certainly return home as soon as I could." Three days later he wrote: "You know I determined when I left home if I was not President that I would return shortly." Then, on the 12th, he wrote to Governor Caswell: "The Object of my coming here so far as it respected myself appears quite in my power when a Congress is formed." Blount was over confident. On January 14, William Pierce of Georgia expressed the opinion that the choice would probably fall on his colleague, George Walton, if Walton were only there. "But as it is," he remarked, "a Mr. Blount from North Carolina is talked of." Blount's confident hopes took their flight when (January 17) the balloting began. To Governor Caswell he wrote (January 28): "I really am unable to unravel the Mystery of this Business nor can I form any Opinion who will be the man." Touching his own failure to obtain the election he said: "The ostensible Objection raised by the Yankees against a Delegate from No[rth] Carolina being put in the Chair is that that State is about to make some antifederal appropriation of her Tobacco." Strongly federal himself, Blount was inclined to agree with his adversaries that the North Carolina act had been "very antifederal". Nor was he less displeased because New York had just sent to Congress a delegation of whom four out of five were "antifederal peasants".

On February 2, when Congress had again obtained the requisite seven states, Arthur St. Clair of Pennslyvania was chosen president. Whether he had then any serious rivals is not revealed. It proved difficult to maintain a quorum, but on February 12, Congress was enabled to turn its attention once more to the question of the proposed federal convention, when it reconstituted the committee on the subject by appointing new members in the places of those who were absent—which was one among several indications that the Congressional mind was on the point of making itself up.

One inducement was doubtless the fact that Virginia had passed an act for appointing delegates to the convention, and on February 3 a letter from Governor Edmund Randolph (dated December 1, 1786) enclosing the act was laid before Congress. Without doubt, however, Congress had long known of the action of Virginia; for, on December 18, Edward Carrington wrote to Madison: "The business of a convention is well brought forward by Virginia, and I hope their act will be generally adopted. The dereliction of Massachusetts is, however, to be apprehended." What particularly gave rise to his apprehensions was the advice given to their legislature by Messrs. King and Dane not to accede to the recommendation of the Annapolis Convention, with the further suggestion that amendments to the Confederation ought to originate with Congress and be agreed to by the states, inasmuch as taking "a secondary position in the business . . . would derogate from the dignity and weight of that body".

That King at least had undergone some change of heart during these intervening months, even though he was not yet ready to profess conversion, is evidenced by a remark in a letter to Gerry, January 7. "If Massachusetts should send deputies", he wrote, "for God's sake be careful who are the men; the times are becoming critical; a movement of this nature ought to be carefully observed by every member of the Community." Evidence was, in fact, beginning to seep down into the region of Congress that Massachusetts was reconsidering its all too ready acceptance of the advice of King and Dane to disregard the Annapolis recommendation. As early as November 12, 1786, Stephen Higginson had written to General Knox:

The present moment is very favorable to the forming further and necessary Arrangements, for increasing the dignity and energy of Government . . . the public mind is now in a fit State, and will shortly I think be more so, to come forward with a System competent to the great purpose of all Civil Arrangements, that of promoting and securing the happiness of Society.

What had been done, Higginson maintained, "must be used as a Stock upon which the best Fruits are to be ingrafted". On February 7, 1787, Higginson ventured a thrust at his state's delegates for the part they had taken. "The State", he wrote General Knox, "entered into the measure of appointing a general Convention the last year with much readiness, but the Sentiments delivered to the two houses by Mr. King and Mr. Dane, have produced a great change in the disposition of the members. Those Gentlemen, I fancy, have now different Ideas of the matter."

He was right, for, on February 11, King wrote to Gerry:

For a number of reasons, although my sentiments are the same as to the legality of this measure, I think we ought not to oppose, but to coincide with this project. . . . Events are hurrying to a crisis; prudent and sagacious men should be ready to seize the most favorable circumstances to establish a more permanent and vigorous government.

Just one week later he was still farther on the road to that conversion that would presently place him in the ranks of the vigorous advocates of a convention as the best means of reform. He was again writing to Gerry, and he remarked:

I will not venture a conjecture relative to the policy of the measure in Mass[achusetts]: the thing is so problematical, that I confess I am at some loss. I am rather inclined to the measure from an idea of prudence, or for the purpose of watching, than from an expectation that much Good will flow from it.

The stage which the fermentation had reached in Congress is indicated by a letter of Madison to Edmund Randolph the same day (February 18):

A great disagreement of opinion exists as to the expediency of a recommendation from Cong[res]s to the backward States in favor of the meeting. It would seem as if some of the States disliked it because it is an extra-constitutional measure, and that their dislike would be removed or lessened by a sanction from Cong[res]s to it. On the other hand it is suggested that some would dislike it the more if Cong[res]s should appear to interest themselves in it.

Similarly he wrote to Washington, February 21: "Cong[res]s have been much divided and embarrassed on the question whether their taking an interest in the measure would impede or promote it." The backward states, he said, had scruples against acceding to it without constitutional sanction, while other states, it was feared, would interpret Congressional interference "as proceeding from the same views which have hitherto excited their jealousies", that is, that Congress would thereby betray "an ambitious wish to get power into their hands by any plan whatever that might present itself."

If the process of fermentation had thus far seemed slow, its speed was increasing. Doubt after doubt, as they rose to the surface, had been skimmed off, and if the residuum was not yet clear, it was rapidly clearing. The action of Virginia had resolved some hesitancies, and now, on February 20, New York took a step that resolved others. This was an instruction to the delegates of that state to move for the recommendation of a convention. It was on the same day that the grand committee on the Annapolis recommendation brought in its report, which was made the order of the day for February 21.

That report, although it was approved by only a majority of one in the committee, coincided with the Annapolis recommendation in proposing the assembling of a convention in Philadelphia in May for the purpose of devising "such farther provisions" as shall render the federal government "adequate to the exigencies of the Union". When the committee report was taken up for consideration, the New York delegates, in obedience to their instructions, offered a motion, in lieu of the committee's proposal, that a convention be assembled "for the purpose of revising the Articles of Confederation . . . and reporting to the United States in Congress assembled and to the States respectively such alterations and amendments" as they should judge "proper and necessary to render them adequate to the preservation and support of the Union". On the face of this motion, its aim was to hold the convention to amendments to the Confederation, which should be proposed by Congress to the states in the constitutional manner; but Madison indicates the existence of a suspicion that the real object was "to obtain a new convention under the sanction of Congress rather than to accede to the one on foot". It was even suspected that the aim might be to divide the states and thereby frustrate the whole purpose. The idea of creating two or more separate confederacies, as has already been pointed out, had in fact for some time been brewing, but on that day for the first time, Madison recorded, had any expression of the idea found its way into the newspapers. It was on that day also and probably for the first time, openly avowed in Congress, the proponent being William Bingham of Pennsylvania, on the ground that the great extent and various interests of the country were incompatible with a single government.

Despite the objections to the New York proposition, with its possible implications, some members of Congress, Madison in particular, were of opinion that it were better that Congress take a hand in the movement on the initiative of a state rather than "spontaneously". The proposition was nevertheless rejected, whereupon the Massachusetts members, King and Dane, came forward with a very similar proposition, but one that drew the restrictions on the convention a little tighter; and it was their proposition that, after some small emendation, was accepted. The essential part of the Massachusetts proposition was that a convention of delegates be held at Philadelphia in May

for the sole and express purpose of revising the Articles of Confederation and reporting to Congress and the several legislatures such alterations and provisions therein as shall when agreed to in Congress and confirmed by the States render the federal Constitution adequate to the exigencies of Government and the preservation of the Union.

In the sequel much of the argument would turn on the phrase, "for the sole and express purpose of revising the Articles of Confederation".

In modern political parlance probably both New York and Massachusetts would be charged with clambering for "the band wagon". They were in fact so charged at the time, although in the more dignified eighteenth-century vernacular. Madison understood that the Massachusetts delegates, of whom Dane in particular remained "at bottom unfriendly to the plan of a convention," had been prompted to their course by intimations from home. At all events, it was on the very next day (February 22) that the Massachusetts legislature took the decisive step of approving the plan of a convention—an instance, no doubt, of a coming event casting its shadow before, a shadow so unmistakable that the Massachusetts delegates had not failed to perceive it. Doubtless also they were not unaware of the fact that they were under some suspicion of "leaning towards some antirepublican establishment", and that the trend of opinion was hostile not only to any anti-republican innovations but to a dissolution of the Confederation.

Surprisingly enough, many members of Congress, so Madison records, considered the resolution adopted as "a deadly blow to the existing Confederation" and William Samuel Johnson of Connecticut "particularly declared himself to that effect". The majority, however, appear to have been "pleased with it as the harbinger of a better Confederation". The situation was thus characterized by William Irvine of Pennsylvania (March 6):

It was with some difficulty Congress carried the recommendation for a Convention. the Eastern Delegates were all much against the measure, indeed I think they never would have come into it, but that they saw it would be carried without them. then they Joined, which has made it a piece of patch work, but this was thought better than to keep the smallest appearance of opposition to public view.

It was well no doubt that, in launching the plan for a new government, the sails were trimmed to the breezes that blew from the wind-caves of popular sentiment. The first important task was to get the ship under way. It would be time enough to change the sails or shift the rudder when the wind altered its course. In due time the convention itself would decide whether to obey the injunction of Congress to the letter or to steer the course pointed by the compass of its own wisdom.

During this same period of anxiety respecting the future of the government, once again that pestiferous problem, the question of the free navigation of the Mississippi River, raised its threatening head. In mid-March, Madison had written to Jefferson, "The Spanish project sleeps", although he himself was far from finding comfort in the prospect of its awakening. Only a month later he was declaring, "The business with Spain is becoming extremely delicate, and the information from the Western settlements truly alarming."

The fact was that stories of seizures and confiscations on the Mississippi had stirred the West into fury, with the result that Congress was necessarily thrown into a dilemma of embarrassment. Secretary Jay was instructed (April 4) to lay before Congress the state of his negotiations with Gardoqui, the encargado de negocios of Spain, which he did on April 11. That report revealed that Jay had gone so far as to adjust with Gardoqui a treaty whereby the use of the Mississippi by Americans was to be suspended during the life of the treaty. Perplexed over the situation, the opponents of the treaty, led by Madison, sought to have the negotiations transferred to Madrid and put into the hands of Jefferson. To this proposition Jay was adverse and succeeded in winning a majority of Congress to his view. That, so Madison immediately reported to Jefferson (April 23), created "a very ticklish situation".

At this point two developments had the effect of inducing once more a period of quiescence, if not of slumber. One of these developments was the assurance that New Jersey and Rhode Island, if not also Pennsylvania, would come over to the Southern side; although at the same time it appeared that this gain might be offset by the loss of Maryland and possibly of South Carolina. The other development was that the spirit of revolt in the West induced a degree of caution in Gardoqui himself. Besides, the approaching meeting of the federal convention seemed to emphasize the wisdom of waiting. Accordingly, not until Congress was on the point of fading out was the question again actively stirred, and then only to assert (September 16, 1788) that "the free navigation of the river Mississippi is a clear and essential right of the United States", and to resolve that the subject "be referred to the federal government which is to assemble in March next".

It is not without significance that, at the moment when the federal convention was about to assemble for the purpose of seeking a formula for the cure of those ills from which the present Confederation suffered, and with the hope of erecting a system of government that would endow the union of the states with new life and vigor, Congress, for its own part, once again took up the long neglected task of providing an adequate system of government for those territories and peoples that were under its own dominion, though not of the Union. That was a task that now, since its acquisition of that dominion, devolved upon Congress and Congress alone. If Congress could justly complain that the states had failed to endow it with requisite powers, with equal justice might the communities under the dominion of Congress complain that the lord of their domain had, through a good many years, neglected to provide them with any system of government whatsoever.

To be sure, a system of government for their behoof had been adopted with all due formalities, but thus far it had remained only a collection of words on sheets of paper, had not been translated into action. Complaints against this inaction had now and again induced Congress to bestir itself briefly with revisions of the plan, but never to the extent of undertaking an application of it; and once again it was such complaints, otherwise termed memorials, from the western inhabitants that furnished the chief impulse to renewed consideration of the problem by Congress. Indeed not a little of the remaining active life of Congress was concerned with memorials from those same inhabitants.

Writing to Edmund Randolph, April 22, 1787, Madison spoke of the problem raised by these memorials as "infinitely embarrassing", while to Jefferson he wrote the next day (April 23, 1787, which chanced to be the third anniversary of Jefferson's ordinance for the government of the northwest territory): "The government of the settlements of the Illinois and Wabash is a subject very perplexing in itself; and rendered more so by our ignorance of many circumstances on which a right judgment depends. The inhabitants of those places claim protection against the savages, and some provision for both criminal and civil justice." More than that, some of them complained of being tormented by land-jobbers, who made collusive purchases through spurious titles, thereby multiplying litigation and defrauding the United States.

An additional impetus to resuming the endeavor to provide a government for the western region was furnished by recent reports of the surveyors and the consequent renewal of the old discussion whether the sales should be by townships, as advocated by the eastern states, or by means of "indiscriminate locations", as favored by most Southerners. Accordingly, on April 26, the ordinance reported September 19, 1786, and left as unfinished business October 4, was drawn forth, read a first time, and the following day assigned for a second reading. Actually, however, it did not receive its second reading until May 9, when the third reading was set for May 10. During these two days the ordinance appears to have been subjected to some emendations, but it did not receive its third reading. Instead it was postponed indefinitely and does not again make its appearance until two months later.

It was not indifference that checked the free flow of purpose toward the objective, not indifference toward the objective; for at that precise moment a new and quickening element had been injected into the project. There was reason enough for the delay, for during this whole period there was no Congress. After May 11, not again until July 4 were seven states in attendance, usually only three or four, sometimes only two, with an occasional lone delegate or two. Secretary Thomson, for his part, strove hard to toll wandering members back into the fold and did succeed in inducing some who were attending the convention in Philadelphia to return to New York for a time.

I think it of great importance to the honor and safety of the Confederacy [Thomson wrote to William Bingham, June 25] that Congress should be in session and the form at least of government kept up in the present situa-

tion of affairs. . . . You cannot imagine what an alarm the secession of the
Members from Congress at this crisis has spread through the eastern states.
Were I to hazard an Opinion it would be that the peace of the union and
the happy termination of the Measures of the Convention depend on the
Meeting and continuance of Congress and keeping up the form of govern-
ment until the New plan is ready for Adoption.

With seven states again answering the roll call, on the 9th of July the
ordinance was referred to a new committee, consisting of Edward
Carrington, Nathan Dane, Richard Henry Lee, John Kean, and
Melancton Smith. On July 11 this new committee reported "An Ordinance for the Government of the territory of the United States North
West of the river Ohio", which contained the essential features of government found in the preceding forms, but with important additions.
It was read a second time on July 12, and on July 13 it was read a third
time and adopted.

It deserves to be noted that Congress did not deem this measure one
that required the assent of nine States, else it would have fallen by the
wayside, since only eight states were in attendance. It needs also to be
observed that the ordinance was adopted by the unanimous vote of the
eight states present, represented by eighteen members, of whom Abraham Yates of New York alone voted in the negative. Indeed the yeas
and nays are recorded only because Mr. Yates so required in order that
he might register his emphatic *No.*

What had occurred in those early days of July to spur Congress into
such extraordinary activity in behalf of a measure over which it had
confusedly pondered and ineffectually piddled off and on for more than
three years? It was a proposition from a group of men, principally New
England Revolutionary soldiers, styling themselves the Ohio Company, offering to purchase immense tracts of western lands; and, more
effective still, the appearance on the scene of persuasive agents of that
company.

On the 9th of May, just when Congress was giving a second reading
to the revised ordinance for the government of the western territory, a
memorial of General Samuel Holden Parsons in behalf of the Ohio
Company was placed before them. The general, according to some
testimony, reinforced his written memorial with personal buttonholing

of members of Congress, but for some reason failed to overcome their indifference or obstinacy or scruples or whatnot. Thereupon the company secured the services of the Rev. Manasseh Cutler of Ipswich Village, Massachusetts, who speedily proved that whatever were the relative mights of pen and sword, the tongue of the preacher was more effective than both the tongue and the pen of the general. In short, the Rev. Mr. Cutler appears to have proved himself a past master of the art of lobbying, and in almost no time at all was stroking the bristles of all Congress—that is, of all except Abraham Yates of New York, and in his case, if Nathan Dane is to be believed, obstinacy merely sat stolidly on the stool of non-comprehension.

So thoroughly persuaded was Congress that, on July 10, while the committee was yet laboring on a revision of the ordinance, the committee to whom the Parsons memorial had been referred proposed that the treasury board be authorized and empowered to contract with any duly authorized agent of the Ohio Company for the purchase of the desired tract of land. Congress had long been dreaming dreams of the money to be obtained from those lands; now it was suddenly awakened to find those dreams come true. Real money, so it seemed, and lots of it was actually dangling before their eyes, and they convinced themselves, with good reason, that other like money-bearing trees would soon be springing up all about them. In this they were not disappointed, and Congress entered into such a harvest as that much belabored body had not known since the consummation of the peace. Some qualms respecting terms nevertheless remained—one respecting the precise boundaries of the tract, another respecting the price, others respecting the terms of payment. There was even a question whether, for political reasons, it might not be well to embosom another company, one rather more speculative in its purposes. All these hesitancies the Rev. Mr. Cutler was able to overcome, even though it be by the device now known as bluffing. Not however until October 27 was the contract of sale finally signed.

Altogether Congress seems to have worried much more over the terms of its land sales than over the terms of government for the people who occupied those lands. The revamping of the ordinance for the government of the western territory was accomplished in three or four days and was accepted with but little controversy. In the minds of the committee who made the revisions there appear to have been mainly three aims. One of these is pointed out by Richard Henry Lee in a letter to Washington, July 15, and again in a letter to his brother, July 25. In the latter he characterizes the aim as "the more perfect security of Peace and property among the rude people who will probably be the first settlers there". "The form of this government", he declared, ". . . is much more tonic than our democratic forms on the Atlantic are." In the letter to Washington he speaks of the settlers as "perhaps licentious" and therefore requiring "a strong toned government", as also of the need of clearly defining the rights of property.

Dane and Carrington appear to have been concerned more about the conditions required for the admission of new states. In the ordinance of April 23, 1784, the number of inhabitants necessary for admission was placed at that of the least numerous of the thirteen original states, a requirement retained in the ordinance proposed May 10, 1786. It was at that time, as Monroe indicated to Jefferson, that a disposition appears amongst some members to increase the number and fix it at one-thirteenth of the free inhabitants of the United States; accordingly that was the requirement embodied in the proposed ordinance of September 19, 1786, and also as printed May 9, 1787. In the report of July 11, 1787, this number was fixed at sixty thousand, a requirement retained in the definitive ordinance of July 13.

Dane thought the number too small; "but", he remarked, "having divided the whole Territory into three States, this number appears to me to be less important." Carrington was rather pleased, upon the whole, with the change, since it provided "a more easy passage" of the temporary government into permanent state governments. "Under the old arrangements", he remarked (to Jefferson October 23), "the country might upon the whole have become very populous, and yet be inadmissable to the rights of state government, which would have been disgusting to them and ultimately inconvenient for the Empire." The Virginia delegation wrote in similar terms to the governor (November 3), pointing out particularly that the proposed arrangement of the Territory into three States was, in their opinion, much better than that formerly made in conformity to the Virginia act of cession. "A Division of the Country into many Small States", they said, "would effectually disappoint the design of Virginia." An alteration of the terms of the Virginia act of cession in this regard was, in fact, necessary to the new plan, and a request for such a change had actually been made a year before (July 7, 1786).

A third feature of the new plan, one that especially drew the attention of Congress, although belatedly inserted, was the prohibition of slavery in the territory. That prohibition, it will be remembered, was in the ordinance as originally drawn by Jefferson in March, 1784, but, in the vote on the measure in April, the proposition was rejected by a narrow margin. A year later there was an effort, particularly by Rufus King, to restore the provision, with only a slight modification of Jefferson's language, and a further effort to insert a provision for the recovery of fugitive slaves; but once again those efforts came to naught. The committee of July 9, 1787, did not at first (the report of July 11) propose to insert the prohibition; and it was only at the last moment, so Nathan Dane records, that Congress was found to be favorable to the prohibition, whereupon it was inserted as the sixth of the articles of compact, and in language varying from Jefferson's proposition in no essential particular except in the omission of the clause "after the year 1800 of the Christian era" and in the inclusion of the clause respecting fugitive slaves. The fact that this provision was not in the form of the ordinance reported July 11, apparently with the approval of the Rev. Mr. Cutler, would seem to belie the contention often put forward that the Ohio Company had made that provision a *sine qua non* of their purchase and settlement.

In most of the discussions of the ordinance of July 13, 1787, it is extolled as essentially new in its fundamental provisions. It is not meet to undertake here a detailed comparison of the definitive ordinance with the numerous plans previously proposed, from Jefferson's first propositions in March, 1784, to that of May 9, 1787, but such a comparison will show that the definitive ordinance was, in nearly every fundamental feature, a development from previous proposals. There were elaborations, clarifications, emphases, all of real importance; still they were for the most part developments, not new conceptions. The administrative framework remained essentially the same as previously proposed. The feature of a governor's council had been eliminated exactly a year before, and the ordinance as read May 9, 1787, had reduced the number of judges from five to three. The idea of articles of compact, as well as much of their substance, was a direct inheritance from Jefferson's ordinance, although there were notable alterations in way of additions as well as of arrangement. The provision respecting the division of intestate estates had, in part at least, its origin in the report of September 19, 1786, in which are also found the provisions for allowing the benefits of the writ of habeas corpus and trial by jury. On the other hand, the ordinance of July 13, 1787, did incorporate a number of provisions for the protection of individual liberty, and in language not very different from similar provisions in the Constitution and the so-called Bill of Rights.

One provision, which first found place in the report of July 11 and was somewhat clarified in the definitive ordinance, deserves particular emphasis, namely, that the French and Canadian inhabitants of the Illinois country should have preserved to them "their laws and customs now in force among them relative to the descent and conveyance of property". This reservation was not, however, a new idea just then conceived. It was incorporated no doubt from a report (May 7) by a committee (Madison, Clark, and Dane), to whom had been referred (March 29) sundry papers relative to those settlements. It is, in fact, the chief animating idea of that report, which was drawn by Nathan Dane, a member also of the committee who made the report of July 11. It is indeed a curious state of affairs that this movement in Congress in behalf of a government for those inhabitants, culminating in the report of May 7, should have been running parallel to the ordinance but in a separate channel.

The plan of government having been settled, it was next in order to appoint the principal officers and set the government in motion. The territorial government did not offer a very juicy morsel of patronage, yet it had its enticements. Nathan Dane wrote (August 12) to his colleague Rufus King, who was down in Philadelphia attending the Convention, that, as there would probably be no settlements in the western country in the coming autumn, Congress would probably delay for some time the appointment of the officers. The eastern delegates, he said, had given up as much as could be expected of them for the sake of getting the government established, therefore it behooved them to establish eastern politics in the territory in so far as they could do so consistently.

Some slate-making had, in fact, been begun before ever the ordinance had been adopted. The Ohio Company had had it in mind that they might be able to get their own chief man, General Samuel Holden Parsons, put in as governor; but the Rev. Mr. Cutler found Congress rather cold to the suggestion, and he accordingly proposed General Arthur St. Clair, then president of Congress, for the office. Thereafter, he avers, his negotiations progressed with less difficulty. However this may have been, when at last Congress got around to the election, St. Clair was chosen governor and Winthrop Sargent as secretary (October 5). The latter appears to have been put forward for the office of secretary by Rufus King immediately upon the adoption of the ordinance. On October 16 the three judges were chosen, Samuel Holden Parsons, John Armstrong, jr., and James M. Varnum. In January following, Armstrong declined the judgeship, and John Cleves Symmes of New Jersey was elected in his stead (February 19). The Easterners had therefore succeeded in manning the territorial government, to the complete exclusion of the Southerners, and this apparently with little or no opposition from the Southern delegates. The salaries of all these officers had previously been determined (October 2).

Congress must of course fix the salaries of its officers, even though it might not have the wherewithal to pay them or any sure prospects of obtaining it; and it was only three days before this that doubts were added to its perplexities and perplexities to its doubts. As long ago as the 5th of February, 1787, that is, almost immediately upon finding itself enabled to do any business at all, Congress had instructed the board of treasury to prepare an estimate of the sums necessary for the service of the year 1787. That estimate was laid before Congress on April 2, and on May 3 was referred to a committee. On June 20, John Armstrong, jr., wrote that the requisition as well as the government of the western territory was "hanging in the Air"—and for the best of reasons; for, since May 11, there had been no Congress. On July 10, when a quorum had once more been gathered, a new committee was appointed

on the subject, and on July 14, the next day after the adoption of the
Northwest Ordinance, that committee offered its report. Thereupon
the board of treasury was instructed to prepare a requisition on the
states for the supplies necessary for the current year—more than half of
which had already gone over the dam—including one year's interest on
the foreign debt and such parts of the principal as may become due the
ensuing year, and also for one year's interest on the domestic debt.

It was not a difficult task to figure out those simple sums; the real
problem was to devise ways and means by which such sums might
be obtained. The wiseacres of the treasury had not yet solved the
puzzle when, on August 3, Congress found itself once more without
a quorum, which it did not recover until September 20. On that day
appeared the report of the Philadelphia convention, and that, to say
nothing of other business that had been piling up these past few weeks,
was more than a handful for Congress. It is perhaps significant that
on the following day the powers of the board of treasury, whose three-
year commission was about to expire, were continued until the 10th of
November, 1789. (Congress had not yet adjusted itself to the idea that
its own lease on life might well be terminated long before November,
1789.) On September 29 the treasury board made its report on the
requisition, a report which bestowed on the states an unusual quantum
and degree of caustic criticism for their delinquencies.

The board approached its task by begging leave to represent to Congress "with great Deference" that "it appears altogether impracticable,
in the present state of the Foederal Government to make the Interest,
or Honor of the Union coincide with what the several States appear
to judge for their convenience in this respect"; then it proceeded to
elaborate upon the shortcomings of the states in the matter of the
several former requisitions and upon the difficulties encountered by
the states as well as by Congress in the fulfillment of those requisitions,
and concluded by recommending that the states be called upon for
their respective quotas of the modest sum found necessary. As certain
difficulties had arisen hitherto in consequence of the acceptance of
indents or facilities in the payment of state quotas, the board recommended that payment be required in specie.

Now, to call upon the states to pay their entire quotas in specie was a hard saying, and few there were that would hear to it. Accordingly, when Congress had ripped rather fiercely into the treasury report, it came to a resolution (October 11) that, while specie was absolutely necessary for the sums required on the foreign debt, that part of the quotas designed for paying the interest on the domestic debt might be met by means of the so-called facilities. The ability of the states to make payment, it was argued in Congress, would thereby be increased. The argument turned on the question of ability, not of will. As a matter of fact, the whole argument was rather academic. Not a single state, as the treasury board reported, had complied with the requisition of 1786; as a good many of them had not done with previous requisitions. Probably nowhere was there real expectation that compliance with the requisition for 1787 would be any better.

How hopeless had become the whole business of requisitions is strikingly pointed out by Madison in a letter to Jefferson, December 20:

The States seem to be either wholly omitting to provide for the federal treasury; or to be withdrawing the scanty appropriations made to it. The latter course has been taken by Massachusetts, Virginia and Delaware. The Treasury Board seem to be in despair of maintaining the shadow of Government much longer. Without money, the offices must be shut up, and the handful of troops on the frontier disbanded.

A few days earlier (December 15) the North Carolina delegates had written their governor, "We may declare in one word that we are at the Eave of a Bankruptcy and a total dissolution of Government." Congress had been "reduced to the dreadful alternative of borrowing principal to pay interest", and even in that their efforts at home had been ineffectual. "Abroad where we were not known and where enthusiasm for liberty enrolled us among the most deserving of mankind, we were more Successful." That deception, they declared, "cannot be much longer kept up and unless something can be done before the close of the ensuing year we must cease to be a United Government. Our friends must give us up, and we shall become a laughing stock to our enemies." It is quite understandable that William Grayson should have been provoked (November 10) to refer to Congress as "that *caput mortuum of vitriol*". In sad truth, conditions would grow worse rather than better. On February 6, 1788, Samuel Alleyne Otis was writing to James Warren of the many circumstances that contribute to "debase the dignity" and "evince the most degrading poverty in the foederal Government", not the least of which was the fact that "even the small pittance necessary for the subsistence of the Presidents household, even in the most eligible stile, of republican neatness and simplicity" was attainable only from other inadequate appropriations.

It was therefore one of the major objectives of Congress through this fateful year, 1787, to save its own soul and to preserve its body from disintegration. The actuating motive was not, however, single. The motive of one group was to keep up the forms of government, to preserve a visible head of the union, until the federal convention should report its conclusions, whether it should be to perpetuate Congress as the head of the government but with a larger endowment of power, or to propose some other form with a new head. The motive of another group was to watch that convention at Philadelphia, lest it overstep its commission. The convention might propose to do away with Congress altogether. It might even endeavor to set up a monarchy! And how better could Congress keep its eye on the convention than by plumping itself down in the same city? There was even a notion that Congress might be able to help the convention along in its fearsome task. For instance, William Irvine wrote to James Wilson, March 6, 1787:

I am persuaded, Congress and the Convention sitting at the same time and place, might facilitate the business of the Convention. A free communication of Sentiments would be usefull to both these bodies, particularly as it might have a tendency to cause the Convention to propose such new articles of confederation, or alterations in the old, as Congress might probably approve, which would doubtless have weight with the several legislatures.

A movement in behalf of such a shifting of the sitting-place of Congress had in fact begun before a decision had been taken to put a qualified stamp of approval on the convention, and it naturally had the aid of many members who wished a removal for other reasons, such, for instance, as resentment toward New York on the part of New Jersey and Rhode Island. On the other hand, some members seemed to prefer that Congress should simply adjourn and cease to beat the futile air until the convention had taken whatever course it was destined to take. It is worth recording that the long-headed Madison definitely preferred that Congress steer clear of the convention.

To effect the adjournment to Philadelphia recruits would be necessary, and it was not until April 10 that the measure was definitely attempted; then the defection of one member spoiled the scheme. The members of the august Continental Congress were not unversed or unskilled in the art of plot and counterplot. During the night the Honorable Peleg Arnold of Rhode Island was, figuratively speaking, spirited into the camp of the opposition, although not unaccompanied by a fear on the part of his abductors that he might escape and yet give his vote for the adjournment. Exactly one month later the effort for a removal was renewed, but again failed, this time because Schureman of New Jersey deemed it of greater importance that he personally should catch the ferryboat for a visit to his homefolks than that Congress should betake itself bodily to Philadelphia. The result of all these maneuvers was just to furnish one more of the numerous factors destined, during the early days of the new government, to converge at a historic dinner table, whereat Hamilton and Jefferson are said to have entered into a gentleman's agreement respecting the location of the capital and the assumption of the state debts.

If it had been adjournment only that was aimed at, that end was almost as effectually attained by the lapse in attendance. As one turns the pages of the *Journals* the eye is caught by the great gaps blown as it were out of the record; and, as one reads the grumbles of those members who continued to hang around City Hall, mainly twiddling their thumbs, one can not help but marvel that they did not one and all pack their saddle-bags and silently steal away to their homes. Nothing but the hope of better things inspired by the convention sitting at Philadelphia did in fact keep them from so doing.

There was naturally an eagerness in Congress to draw aside, if possible, the veil that screened what was going on in the convention. "The Convention, as a Beacon", Edward Carrington wrote to Jefferson (June 9), "is rousing the attention of the Empire." But, wrote William Blount (June 11), "The Members of the Convention observe such inviolable Secrecy that it is altogether unknown out of doors what they are doing." So also Henry Lee (June 28): "The convention move with profound secrecy. . . . But it is certain that this august body is plying assiduously to their great work and possess the best dysposition to do what is good and right." Richard Henry Lee, pausing for a week in Philadelphia on his way to Congress, must have endeavored to get an inkling of what was going on behind those firmly closed doors; for he wrote to his brother, Francis Lightfoot Lee (July 14), "I found the Convention at Phila. very busy and very secret." Nevertheless he had picked up an intimation "that we shall hear of a Government not unlike the B[ritish] Constitution, that is, an Executive with 2 branches composing a federal Legislature and possessing adequate tone." There were evidently other tales out of school. Nathan Dane, for instance, wrote to Nathaniel Gorham (a member of the convention) that he was "very glad the Convention came fully into the determination of dividing the powers of Government". And the same Nathan Dane wrote a few days later (June 19) to Rufus King that, while he felt "a strong desire and curiosity to know how it proceeds", he thought "the public never ought to see anything but the final report of the Convention". He charged William Pierce of Georgia, who had recently come from the Convention to Congress, with having failed to understand "the true meaning, full and just extent of the order not to communicate etc." Whether or not Pierce had inadvertently dropped hints that found their way to Dane, William Blount found him uncommunicative. "I have not learned from him", Blount wrote (June 15), "what in particular is done. . . . I suppose he would not like to descend to particulars even to me who am a Member as I have not yet taken my seat."

Three days later Blount departed for Philadelphia to take his seat in the convention, but, at the solicitation of Secretary Thomson, returned to Congress not many days later, arriving in time to help enact the ordinance for the government of the western territory. On July 18, Blount received a letter from his friend William R. Davie, a member of the convention, informing him in very general terms that "since you left us We have progressed obliquely and retrograded directly so that we stand on the same Spot you left us." From his own observations while at the convention Blount had become alarmed over what appeared to be the trend of the convention, and now he ventured the prediction that before many years the Union would break up and each state be independent. After having written these things freely to his brother, he evidently concluded that he had violated the injunction of secrecy, and therefore left the letter unsigned. By the 20th of August, however, when Blount was once more in the convention, his fears seem to have vanished, for he wrote to Governor Caswell that "the Mode of Government that the Convention have in Contemplation . . . will be such a Form of Government as I believe will be readily adopted by the several States."

By this time, from pricking up its ears for every chance intimation concerning the proceedings of the convention, Congress had begun to look forward expectantly for the convention's report and was preening itself for the reception of that document, as yet deeply shrouded in mystery, on the nature of which rested the fate of the nation. Writing to Madison, August 11, Edward Carrington remarked that the convention was supposed to be "now in the state of parturition. This bantling", he added, "must receive the blessing of Congress this session, or, I fear, it will expire before the new one *will* assemble. . . . The peoples expectations are rising with the progress of this work, but will desert it, should it remain long with Congress."

If ever there had been need of a full Congress it was now. Accordingly, on August 13, President St. Clair sent forth an urgent call for members. Since the beginning of the federal year, the president pointed out, on three days only had as many as ten states been represented; on thirty days only had nine states had the requisite two members in attendance. One of the presidential functions had long been to try to rouse states to a redoubling of their diligence or to shame them for their delinquencies. It was now St. Clair's turn.

What Sir [he exclaimed in his address] must the Nations of the World think of us when they shall be informed that we have appointed an Assembly and invested it with the sole and exclusive power of Peace and War, and the management of all National concerns, and during the course of almost a whole year, it has not been capable, except for a few days, for want of a sufficient number of Members, to attend to these matters. . . . Besides Sir, the National Convention, which the people look up to for so much good, will soon rise, and it appears of great consequence that, when their report comes under consideration of Congress, it should be a full Congress, and the important Business which will be laid before them meet with no unnecessary delay.

The response was not as prompt as was desirable, but by September 20 nine states were in attendance, and within a few days eleven were on the floor. It was on September 20 that the Convention's report, comprising the proposed Constitution, two resolutions of the Convention, and a letter from its President, General Washington, was laid before Congress. "The budget was opened yesterday", Roger Alden, deputy secretary of Congress, wrote September 21, "and the important secret is now exposed to public view." On the same day William Bingham wrote to Thomas FitzSimons that the Constitution had been read in Congress on the 20th, and Wednesday, the 26th, fixed as the day for its consideration. He would have preferred earlier consideration and would endeavor to bring on the question immediately.

Within two days such a schism had taken place in the Virginia delegation that Edward Carrington urged Madison to hasten his return to Congress.

One of our Colleagues Mr. R. H. Lee [Carrington wrote, September 23] is forming propositions for essential alterations in the Constitution, which will, in effect, be to oppose it. Another, Mr. Grayson, dislikes it, and is, at best for giving it only a silent passage to the States. Mr. H. Lee joins me in opinion that it ought to be warmly recommended to ensure its adoption. A lukewarmness in Congress will be made a ground of opposition by the unfriendly in the States.

Carrington himself did not "implicitly accede in sentiment to every article", but felt that, until he could "withdraw from society", he must be content to "make some sacrifices to the general accommodation". The positions of Richard Henry Lee and William Grayson, he later (October 25) explained to William Short thus: "the disapprobation of Mr. R. H. L. and that of Mr. G. are founded on very opposite principles—the former thinks the Constitution too strong, the latter is of opinion that it is too weak."

Richard Henry Lee had, in fact, definitely paved the way for taking the part of a critic in Congress. He had been chosen as a delegate to the Convention but had declined on the ground, as he wrote to John Adams (September 5), that, "being a Member of Congress where the plan of Convention must be approved, there appeared an inconsistency for Members of the former to have session with the latter, and so pass judgment at New York upon their opinion at Philadelphia." Subsequently he found in Congress good reason for his scruples, for "the Members of Convention came to Congress in such numbers . . . that the Votes of 3 States were Convention Votes, 2 others divided by Conventioners, and Conventioners mingled with many other States."

Already the pros and cons were maneuvering for battle. Whatever the procceedings in Congress respecting the Constitution on September 26, the day set for its consideration, not a scratch of record thereof is found in the Journal for that day. Even the proceedings of the 27th stand erased, as though to consign these first skirmishes to oblivion. The first of these skirmishes was undertaken by Richard Henry Lee and Melancton Smith with a motion that the thirteenth article of the Confederation "limits the power of Congress to the amendment of the present confederacy of thirteen states, but does not extend it to the creation of a new confederacy of nine states." Nevertheless, "it is deemed respectful", says the motion, that the proposed plan be trans-· mitted "to the executive of every state in this Union to be laid before their respective legislatures." In short, Messrs. Lee and Smith would have the new plan decently interred in the first convenient cemetery.

Not content with so hasty a burial, Clark of New Jersey and Mitchell of Delaware offered a motion in like terms for the transmission of copies of the Constitution to the state executives to be submitted to their legislatures, but would add: "in order to be by them submitted to conventions of delegates to be chosen agreeably to the said resolutions of the Convention". To the eager friends of the Constitution, however, this was still too noncommittal. Accordingly, on a motion by Carrington and Bingham, the Clark and Mitchell motion was postponed to take into consideration a motion that Congress agree to the proposed Constitution, "and that it be recommended to the legislatures of the several states to cause conventions to be held as speedily as may be to the end that the same may be adopted, ratified, and confirmed." No vote on this motion is recorded. Besides, as previously stated, the proceedings of September 27 are erased in their entirety.

Still another motion was offered by Nathan Dane, who had been critical of the Annapolis proposal, and who was now unfriendly to the Constitution. Dane's motion was a prolix, lumbering propostion, setting forth that the resolution calling the Philadelphia convention had stipulated that it "should be held for the sole and express purpose of revising the Articles of Confederation, and reporting to Congress and the several legislatures", but that the convention had proposed a constitution which "appears to be intended as an entire system in itself, and not as any part of, or alteration in the Articles of Confederation"; therefore he proposed that, out of respect for their constituents and because of the importance of the subject, the report of the convention should, "with all convenient dispatch, be transmitted to the several States to be laid before the respective legislatures thereof". In effect, this was only the Lee and Smith proposition in a clumsier form. Precisely at what stage of the proceedings, or whether the motion was taken into consideration at all, is not recorded.

So far as Congress was concerned, these skirmishes quickly showed which side had the greater strength. On the following day (September 28) the Journal records briefly this proceeding:

Congress having received the report of the Convention lately assembled in Philadelphia
Resolved Unanimously that the said Report with the resolutions and letter accompanying the same be transmitted to the several legislatures in Order to be submitted to a convention of Delegates chosen in each state by the people thereof in conformity to the resolves of the Convention made and provided in that case.

That this resolution was obtained only after a contest and that it involves some elements of compromise is revealed by some of the participants in the struggle. Madison, for instance, in a letter to Washington, September 30, states: "I found on my arrival here that certain ideas unfavorable to the act of the Convention which had created difficulties in that body, had made their way into Congress. They were patronized chiefly by Mr. R. H. L[ee] and Mr. Dane of Mass[achuset]ts." In the course of his letter he summarizes the arguments pro and con on the propositions of Lee and Dane, then continues:

An attempt was made in the next place by R. H. L. to amend the act of the Convention before it should go forth from Congress. He proposed a bill of Rights [,] provision for juries in civil cases and several other things corresponding with the ideas of Col. M[ason]. He was supported by Mr. Me[lancton] Smith of this State.

These difficulties, he went on to say, "at one time threatened a serious division in Cong[res]s and popular alterations with the yeas and nays on the journals", but they were at length fortunately terminated by the adoption of the resolution quoted above. With regard to the mooted question of a direct approbation by Congress, he was of opinion that in some of the states the adversaries of the Constitution would make use of the ambiguous attitude of Congress, while in states like Virginia it would do no harm. "The circumstance of unanimity", he added, "must be favorable every where." What he failed to foresee was that to that very word "unanimously" Richard Henry Lee would point an accusing finger.

The situation is somewhat further clarified by a letter of Carrington. Writing to Jefferson sometime later (October 23) he explained that a great majority were in favor of giving the Constitution "a warm approbation", but that it was thought best by its friends "barely to recommend to the several Legislatures, the holding of Conventions for its consideration, rather than send it forth with even a single negative to an approbatory act." Lee and Grayson, for instance, so Carrington wrote to William Short (October 25), were actually against such an act, although they agreed to join in the bare recommendation of conventions for the consideration of the Constitution in the states. Lee himself wrote to George Mason (October 1): "This compromise was settled and they took the opportunity of inserting the word unanimously, which applies only to simple transmission, hoping to have it mistaken for an unanimous approbation of the thing. . . . It is certain that no approbation was given."

Of all the members of Congress who opposed the adoption of the Constitution or were critical of its provisions, Richard Henry Lee more than any other has set forth the grounds of that criticism. These grounds appear in a number of letters written by him in October, 1787, particularly to George Mason. In fact, the views of the two men so closely coincided that not infrequently Lee appears to be the mouthpiece of Mason. The gist of his views is fairly well stated in a letter to Washington, October 11, in which he says:

It is Sir, in consequence of long reflection upon the nature of Man and of government, that I am led to fear the danger that will ensue to Civil Liberty from the adoption of the new system in its present form. I am fully sensible of the propriety of change in the present plan of confederation, and although there may be difficulties, not inconsiderable, in procuring an adoption of such amendments to the Convention System as will give security to the just rights of human nature, and better secure from injury the discordant interests of different parts of this Union; yet I hope these difficulties are not insurmountable.

He concludes by suggesting as the best mode of procedure the calling of another convention.

Lee's objections to the Constitution were afterward, during the debates in the state conventions, elaborated into a series of articles under the title, *Letters of the Federal Farmer,* which became for the opposition a sort of textbook, as did the *Federalist* for the proponents of the Constitution. Because the opposition failed, the *Letters of the Federal Farmer* went into the discard and have there remained. Much profit might nevertheless be derived for this present day and time if those articles were drawn forth from their obscurity and reflectively read. Some of the dangers feared by Lee, and since much scoffed at this century and a half as imaginary, have lately risen from their long-time entombment to stir anxieties that can no longer be dismissed with a scoff. What also deserves to be remembered is that Lee's proposal of a bill of rights led the way to that invaluable addition to the Constitution.

As Richard Henry Lee's objection to the new government was, in general, that it was too strong, a consolidated rather than a federal government, so William Grayson was convinced that in many particulars it was given too little rather than too much power. Grayson's views are somewhat summarily set forth in a letter to William Short, November 10, 1787. He believed, for instance, that in order to preserve treaties with foreign powers the government should have a negative on state laws, "with several other incidental powers". On the other hand, the method of making treaties, that is, by the votes of two-thirds of the senators, would, in his opinion, lose the Mississippi forever. Representation in the Senate should, he thought, have been proportional, as in the House. In short, the system as a whole was "something like the legs of Nebuchadnezar's image ... formed by jumbling or compressing a number of ideas together." In a year or two the new government would probably be as contemptible as the present; yet it would probably "be crammed down our throats rough and smooth with all its imperfections". He was in agreement with Richard Henry Lee, and, as it proved, with popular sentiment generally, that one serious defect was the lack of a bill of rights.

The failure of North Carolina in the first instance to ratify the Constitution lends a particular interest to the views of that state's delegates in Congress at this early stage of the matter. The federalism of William Blount, member of the convention as well as of Congress, has already been indicated. Blount tarried in Congress just long enough to join in recommending the work of the convention to the states and was presently succeeded by James White, who wrote to him (October 25):

> I must own I had conceived an apprehension that all your labours would probably end in smoke; for what hope was there that so many jarring and biggotted sovereigns would descend from any of their fancied independencies for the common advantage? I hope however that the good *genius* of our young Empire will rise Superior.

Writing to Governor Caswell a few days later (November 13) White remarked upon some of the apprehensions of the opposition as wearing "too pusilanimous a complexion" and added, "Whatever may be our wish in theory, we find in practice, by our own example, that States in confederacy, like individuals in society, must part with some of their privileges for the preservation of the rest."

South Carolina delegates had been among the most ardent federalists. Charles Pinckney in particular had bent his energies as a member of Congress to promote an enlargement of the powers of Congress, or, failing that, to institute a better government through the instrumentality of a convention. As a member of the convention he had taken a notable part in the formation of the constitution that was now before the states for acceptance or rejection. It was to be expected therefore that the voice of South Carolina would lack nothing of the vibrant federalist tone. One such note came from David Ramsay, late a member of Congress and sometime its chairman. On November 10 he wrote to Dr. Benjamin Rush:

I am ready and willing to adopt the constitution without any alteration but still think objections might be obviated if the first State convention after accepting its present form would nevertheless express their approbation of some alterations being made on the condition that Congress and the other States concurred with them. I think this would cause no delay nor would it endanger the acceptance of the constitution. . . . The necessity of another convention would be obviated. I would not make these alterations conditions of acceptance: I would rather trust to the mode of alteration proposed in it than hazard or even delay the acceptance of the proposed plan. I think it ought to be a matter of joy to every good citizen that so excellent a form of government has passed the convention.

During the few days in which the Constitution was under consideration in Congress eleven states had been represented, with one delegate from Maryland—in all thirty-three members. Rhode Island, having declined to have any part in the federal convention and having furthermore, so it would seem, made up its sovereign mind to have no more to do with the irksome Union, had no delegates on the floor. Another time and other momentous decisions respecting the new government confronting Congress, Rhode Island would then perk up and come prancing to Congress as eager as if come to view the glories of its own handiwork. Considering the derelictions of most of the states, throughout the past year especially, the attendance during these critical days was something to be remarked upon.

The momentous question decided for the time being, it was scarcely to be expected that so good an attendance could long be maintained. By the middle of October only seven states were represented, although five others had lone delegates in attendance. Before the end of the month three of these seven had vanished, and on November 5, the beginning of the federal year, only five members answered the roll call—if there really was a roll call. Others did indeed drop in from day to day, one or two at a time, had their names duly recorded as attending, then wandered out on the street for such occupation or amusement as they might discover. Some of these had been members of that assembly in other days—in the times that tried men's souls; so no doubt they thought. But did they realize that these also were times to try men's souls? Not all of them. Some of them were new members, eager for the delectable privilege of seeing Congress in session and taking part in its proceedings. They had a long, irksome wait before their gratification. Two of these fledglings, destined to be granted a good many weeks in which to preen their political wings, were Samuel Alleyne Otis and George Thatcher of Massachusetts. On November 27, when Otis had already whiled away some two weeks of tedious waiting (all unaware that eight weeks more of like tedium were before him), he wrote to James Warren:

Your next probable question will be how go you on in Congress; To which I reply there is no Congress. Nor like to be before Xmas. . . . Indeed I think some states either from a zeal for New Government, Or indifferent about a larger Confederation upon any plan, voluntarily neglect sending on their Members—but this upon every principle is wrong. If the confederation ceases, puissant as any state may feel itself, I think its independence is at an end. If they prefer the Confederation upon the old, or rather present plan, they certainly ought to keep up their representation. And if they are zealous for the *new plan,* They ought to send their delegates to prepare the way, and I had like to have said make the paths straight before it. But I have no expectation of a speedy adoption of the *New System.*

And while the few on the ground waited for others to come forward that a Congress might be formed and proceed to business, a number of those yet lingering about their own firesides lingered on, waiting to hear that a Congress had been formed before they mounted their horses to journey thither. Dyre Kearny of Delaware, for instance, wrote to Secretary Thomson, December 1: "As tis neither my Wish nor intention to proceed to New York till there be either a Congress formed or a probability of Speedy One Upon the Arrival of our State, I have to request you would notify me when our Attendance may become necessary. A Line in immediate answer on this Subject, will much gratify me."

Madison had for some time been convinced that there was little likelihood of a quorum before spring. Writing to Jefferson, December 9, he remarked, "We have two or three States only yet met for Cong[res]s. As many more can be called in when their attendance will make a quorum. It continues to be problematical whether the interregnum will not be spun out through the winter." Furthermore, he was convinced that "if the present lax state of our General Government should continue, we shall not only lose certain capital advantages which might be drawn from it; but be in danger of being plunged into difficulties, which may have a very serious effect on our future fortunes." Meanwhile, he and others could but inform anxious inquirers respecting the doing of this, that, or the other, that "the authority of Congress has been out of existence for some time, and if we are to judge from the present aspect of things, will continue so for some time longer."

CHAPTER XXXV

PASSING THE TORCH
THE OLD GOVERNMENT SALUTES THE NEW

On January 21, 1788, and not earlier, laggard delegates in sufficient numbers had arrived to make a Congress: two each from the seven states of Massachusetts, New Jersey, Pennsylvania, Delaware, Maryland, Virginia, and South Carolina, with one delegate each from New Hampshire, Connecticut, North Carolina, and Georgia. Thereupon Secretary Thomson opened his Journal and wrote: "Congress assembled". Not indeed much of a Congress—exactly one-third the number that signed the Declaration of Independence—still, if they would only keep together and put their heads and hands to the task, they could do a lot of good, even though their day was far spent and the night of their Congress was at hand.

The credentials of the delegates having been read, Congress called it a day, leaving until the next morning the election of a President. This essential step in organization accomplished, Secretary Thomson deemed it his bounden duty to assume that the executives of the thirteen states were eagerly awaiting news of the opening of Congress and of the election of their President, and accordingly despatched a circular letter on the 23d to name the gentlemen in attendance and to add: "Yesterday Congress proceeded to the election of a President and made choice of His Excellency Cyrus Griffin." Thus, with her third President of the Continental Congress, Virginia had made a fair beginning toward that distinction subsequently achieved as the "Mother of Presidents".

Samuel Alleyne Otis of Massachusetts intimates that some doubt had actually arisen among the members whether it were really worth while to go to the trouble of electing a President, but that Congress had been prompted thereto largely by a sense of duty "at least to preserve the forms". At the same time he lets it be known that Congress was not by this act relieved of a sense of humiliation that the United States of America should be "viewed in a ridiculous light by her own Citizens, and a contemptible one by other Nations". Probably it was just this sense of humiliation and futility that induced Congress to contemplate an adjournment in the spring.

President Griffin, for his part, confided to Thomas FitzSimons (February 18): "I feel no addition of real satisfaction in being thus elevated, but truly and with sincerity I feel the reverse. . . . It is not in my power to do any essential services, but I will discharge my duty with honesty and to the best of my abilities." Touching the subject that was the center of every one's thoughts, he remarked, "The proposed Constitution now stands upon a firm basis". He was rejoiced to hear that two influential Virginians, Richard Henry Lee and John Page, were relinquishing their opposition; "but what to us is very extraordinary and unexpected", he added, "we are told that Mr. George Mason has declared himself so great an enemy to the constitution that he will heartily join Mr. Henry and others in promoting a Southern Confederacy—alas! how inconstant is the mind of man." Later, in voicing his own views, he characterized the Constitution as "beautiful in theory", yet "a Government of safety and Energy".

A month after the organization of Congress, Madison wrote to Jefferson (February 19): "Congress have done no business of consequence yet, nor is it probable that much more of any sort will precede the event of the great question before the public." Indeed, he added, the public was attentive to little else than the proposed federal Constitution. Still another month and Nathan Dane was writing (March 15): "We do but very little business. Indeed we have but very little to do. It does not appear to be the intentions of Congress to engage in any important business. An adjournment has been mentioned for a few months." The reasons offered against an adjournment, he said, were the old ones, chiefly the need of keeping up the forms of government.

In short, a contest was being waged between those who thought it wise to try to keep some sign of life in the old frame and those who were content to let the dead bury their dead. Lamented Paine Wingate of New Hampshire (March 29): "Nothing but the hope of a new, can,

I fear, keep the old Constitution from dissolution long. '*Sed nunquam in re Republica desperandum*'." (A former minister turned politician, Wingate had permitted his Latin to rust.) The new Constitution, he said, was the subject that engaged the general attention, yet the newspapers were so full of lies about it that one hardly knew what to believe. "Those who are well-wishers to their country", he remarked, "and best know the situation we are in, are the most sensible of the necessity of its adoption"; but at the same time, "there are powerful opposers to it, who avail themselves of some popular objections, and they are too successful with the less knowing part of the country."

While they argued in Congress whether to adjourn or not to adjourn, it began to appear that all efforts to keep the old Congress alive would be unavailing, that a dissolution was imminent, and that without any calling of the yeas and nays. On March 31 only six states reported; on April 2 only four; but the next three days found six again ready for business. "We are here in the old Style", Otis wrote April 6, ". . . yet it will not do to abdicate the Government." April 7 there were five states, April 8 four; then, under April 18, the secretary recorded: "During the course of this week only six states attended"; and under Saturday, April 26, "During the course of this week four states attended." And so on, through the month of April, four, five, or six states. "Here we remain", Nathan Dane wrote (April 20). "in an idle situation. . . six States and as many half States attend—the business of the union must be neglected, because one or two gentlemen, who are in the City, must attend to their private business." "To your demand to know what we are doing in Congress", Otis wrote to James Warren, April 26, "I answer—Nothing. To your enquiry what we have done? I answer—almost nothing. . . . The States have been in such a flutter about the New, that they have hardly paid attention to the old Government."

Hopeless as the case appeared, on May 2, Congress recovered its requisite seven states, so that, on May 5, President Griffin could write, "Once more we are going on with the business of Congress—but have finished nothing of consequence." "Congress have not been idle", Otis wrote, May 8, "altho they have been so interrupted by the appointment of its members to Convention, in one place and another that much less has been effected than could be wished." It was still however the general opinion, he declared, that, "during this uncertain and agitated year", it was better that Congress keep in session, even though nothing of importance should be accomplished, than to leave the states without any bond of union or even the semblance of a federal government. By this time, in fact, it had become all the more essential that Congress should remain in session, because the states, one after another, were reporting to Congress their adoption of the Constitution.

Besides, there was much that ought to be done, much that even seven states could do; and hopes for gathering nine were growing. Since the adoption of an ordinance for the purpose on May 7, 1787, progress had been made in the settlement of the accounts of the states. It was no easy problem at best, and just at that moment there was a good deal of grumbling against an account that Virginia had handed in for the conquest of the Northwest territory. Moreover, now that it appeared probable Congress would presently be giving place to a successor, it was deemed appropriate that the accounts of the late military departments be brought to some sort of close. Progress had been made in the settlement of those accounts also, and on May 8, 1788—nearly five years after the conclusion of peace—further resolutions were adopted with a view to speeding the completion of that task.

All this was looking toward the past. But there were other objectives confronting Congress that looked definitely toward the future; and one of them was the prospect of a cession of territory from the state of Georgia. South Carolina had, in 1787, ceded her claim to a strip of some twelve miles in width, running from her western boundary to the Mississippi, so that only Georgia and North Carolina (unless Connecticut should also be counted) were behind with their generosity. In October, 1787, Congress had once more appealed to those two delinquents—addressing the appeal to their "justice and magnanimity"—to surrender a portion of their territorial claims for the general benefit. Georgia hearkened, and on May 29 the delegates of that state informed Congress that they were ready to make the deed to the cession offered by their state. When, however, Congress came to look over the proposed cession (July 14, 15), it was found, so the South Carolina delegates wrote (August 16), "clogg'd with Conditions which were not thought proper to be acceded to by Congress". One of the conditions was a rather heavy payment for expenses incurred in defense of her territory; while another, which Congress found particularly unsatisfactory, related to the limited extent and to the boundaries of the cession. A third condition seemed rational enough, for the cession was to become effective when nine states should have acceded to the new government. Touching the first-mentioned condition, Paine Wingate opined, "If we should have a few more such presents, we should not know how to pay them." Said Abraham Baldwin of Georgia (April 20), respecting the cession by his state, "They have long only waited an issue of our present great national question, whither they might expect protection in return." Congress rejected the offer and besought the state for better terms.

Another territorial question aroused genuinely perplexing quandaries and acute anxieties. This pertained to that western part of Virginia that had come to be called Kentucky. For some four years that region had been agitating the question of erecting itself into an independent state, and had now and then petitioned Congress for admission into the union. At first Congress side-stepped the petitions, while Virginia sought to quiet the movement; but the latter had eventually found it discreet to yield, and accordingly (October, 1785, and October, 1786) made provision for the separation. Meanwhile the spirit of independence grew, and the threat of closing the Mississippi to Americans not only served greatly to intensify that spirit but otherwise to aggravate the case. It came about therefore that, on the last day of February, 1788, Kentucky once more applied to Congress for admission into the union. A motion was made by the Virginia delegates to accede to the request, but on the conditions laid down by their state in certain acts for the purpose, one of these conditions being that Kentucky should assume a proper proportion of Virginia's federal obligations.

It might seem that, with Kentucky so eager and Virginia so willing, the assent of Congress would have followed as a matter of course. But, strangely enough, the decision was not to hinge on the wish of Kentucky or the will of Virginia, but on other wills and wishes. Wrote Nicholas Gilman of New Hampshire (March 6): "This is not a time for the determination of so important a subject, but it is so strenuously urged and the people of that country are become so jealous and irritable as to require the most delicate management." Declared William Irvine of Pennsylvania: "Whichever way Congress may decide, it brings them into a dilemma. Some gentlemen are of opinion that no new State can be admitted under the present Confederation, others fear, that, if they should be rejected now, they will not come in when we wish them, instance Vermont." He had not a doubt, however, that Kentucky would be independent before the end of the year, whether Congress decided to admit it or not. One of the scruples, Madison pointed out (April 8), was "drawn from the peculiar State of our affairs, and from the defect of power under the existing Confederation"; but there were individuals, "who will throw obstacles in the way, till Vermont can be let in at the same time", while still others were willing to irritate Kentucky into an opposition to the new government. Wingate of New Hampshire hoped (April 23) that "some decent excuse" could be found for deferring the determination "without exciting the resentment of Kentucky". The decent excuse mainly put forward was the lack of power, but privately the emphasis was usually placed on the need of balancing Kentucky and Vermont.

As for stirring Kentucky into opposition to the new government, John Brown, the Virginia delegate, who was, in effect, the spokesman of Kentucky, acknowledged (May 12) that the district already entertained prejudices against the new constitution, although he himself was decidedly in favor of its adoption. His fears for the admission of Kentucky arose mainly from what he termed jealousy on the part of the eastern members, with whom, so he wrote Madison, June 7, Hamilton was cooperating, chiefly because of the bearing that the admission of Kentucky might have on the adoption of the Constitution. A refusal to admit Kentucky, Brown contended, was fraught with consequences "ruinous to that promising Country; or to the importance and dignity of the United States; and perhaps to both." All those possible consequences were, in fact, to be apprehended from the foreign intrigue then so rife throughout the west, and particularly in Kentucky.

On May 30, James R. Reid of Pennsylvania wrote to William Irvine: "This day is big with the fate of *Kentucky and the world*. I will write you next monday or as soon as we finish the [land] Ordinance and *liberate* Kentucky." The debate, then in progress, was continued on

Monday, June 2, when Congress came to a decision, "That in their opinion it is expedient that the district of Kentucky be erected into an independent state", with the further decision that a committee of one from each state be appointed "to prepare and report an act for acceding to the independence of the said district of Kentucky and for receiving the same into the Union as a member thereof, in a mode conformable to the Articles of Confederation".

To the outward view the way for Kentucky's admission to the Union would seem to have been cleared of every obstruction. But John Brown seems to have been able to peer beneath the surface of things, and he was not comforted by what he perceived. That resolution, he wrote to Madison (June 7), "contains all that has been done upon that Subject and I fear all that will be done." The confirmation of his pessimistic view was not long delayed. By June 25 he had learned that the committee had come to the conclusion "that there is no power vested in Congress for that purpose and that nothing further can be done under the present application than to report an Additional Article granting such powers to be referred to the different States for their ratification." On July 2 the committee asked to be discharged, and thereupon Brown and Carrington moved that the compact between the state of Virginia and the district of Kentucky be ratified. On the following day that motion was postponed, and a motion by Dane of Massachusetts and Tucker of South Carolina was substituted, deferring the question for determination by the new government. Such a motion could then be made with no doubts and perhaps with few qualms; for on July 2, Congress had learned that a ninth state, New Hampshire, had ratified the Constitution.

John Brown was rejoiced that the new government had come through the ordeal successfully, but he was disconsolate over the future of Kentucky. It was very problematical, he said (August 10), whether that district would apply for admission into the new confederacy, particularly since its citizens were generally opposed to the new Constitution, "apprehending much inconvenience and danger from the Judicial System and fearing that the Powers vested in the General Government may enable [it] to carry into effect the proposed Treaty with Spain relative to the navigation of the Mississippi." Indeed it seemed to him that that "ill advised attempt" had laid the foundation for the dismemberment of the American empire, by destroying the confidence of the western people in the justice of the union and driving them to despair of obtaining their right except by their own exertions. It was but little more than a month later (September 16) that the opponents of the proposed treaty with Spain found themselves enabled to put an effectual stop to Jay's negotiations and to pass the problem on to the new government. Before that time, however, John Brown had taken his departure for Kentucky, where alas! he would find trouble enough brewed and a-brewing.

Strange to tell, despite the almost total disappearance of Congress during April, 1788, the early days of May saw the beginning of a flood-tide of members flowing over the doorsill of the Congress chamber. By the 2d of June there were actually eleven states in attendance, only Connecticut and Maryland being absent. And not less strangely, Rhode Island had ceased for a brief space of time to pout and sulk and had duly despatched thither her requisite two members, in the persons of Peleg Arnold and Jonathan Hazard. Some Members, like Hugh Williamson of North Carolina, did not place a high estimate of worth on this new and unlooked for acquisition, nevertheless it was presently discovered that, even if to some their votes gave annoyance, in the opinion of others those same votes could be put to good use.

On June 5 this Rhode Island delegation wrote to Governor John Collins that, while they were unable to give him a particular account of the business before Congress, they could inform him that "There is several matters of importance under Consideration, one of which is the Dividing of the State of Virginia and thereby making a Fourteenth State by the Name of Kentucky." They would refrain from making any comment respecting the expediency of the measure, but solicited His Excellency's consideration of the subject. Another matter of importance, although not before Congress, was the necessity that the state make further provision for the support of its delegates, "in such a manner as to be least Injurious to the State, and be productive of the the greatest advantage to us".

On July 1, Connecticut completed her representation, as did Maryland in the first week of July. Had it not been for temporary deficiencies in other delegations Congress might on July 7 have counted for the first time in years the presence of all thirteen states; but it was not until July 11 that this marvelous consummation was attained. "We have this Day", Peleg Arnold wrote that notable July 11, "Thirteen States on the Floor of Congress which has not been until the present case Since the year 1776." "We have had Thirteen States frequently upon the floor", Samuel A. Otis wrote July 17, "and", he proudly added, "have been very industrious." On the last day of the month Paine Wingate wrote that thirty-eight members were in attendance, "the fullest Congress that has been since the present Confederation". Then, on August 18, he wrote that there were "40 members from 13 States a greater number it is said than has been for 12 years past." The statement that all thirteen states had not hitherto been represented since 1776 would seem to be erroneous; for three several members asserted in April, 1777, that every state had at that time a representation in Congress.

And to what was this extraordinary industry of this unusual array of talent applied? For one thing, the western territory called for the attention of Congress in several particulars—instructions to the governor, revision of the land ordinance, Indian affairs, etc.; for another thing, there were new problems in the settlement of accounts, to say nothing of claims and memorials of one sort or another. Ever since the close of the war claims arising out of the conflict had been coming into Congress or before commissioners appointed for their adjustment; but now that the old Congress appeared to be on the verge of its demise, these claims poured in in more copious stream. These are but a few of the items of business that claimed the attention of Congress in a period when its chief concern might well, it would seem, have been to provide for its own obsequies. And probably never before in its history had it been able to carry on its affairs with so little difficulty. For a good many weeks not once was heard the old lament for the requisite seven states, or even for the nine.

It was of course the new government, for whose coming the states were peering into the future—with hope or with dread—that had stirred this extraordinary interest in the union for which several of them had long manifested but little concern. The states must needs each have its watchers at the bedside as the old Congress gasped its last gasps, must needs hear the reading of the will of the deceased. The members of Congress had of course listened with the utmost eagerness for news from the state conventions. In the evening of July 1 the delegates of New Hampshire received the news that their state, the ninth, had ratified the Constitution, and the next morning laid that momentous communication before Congress. Close upon its heels that same day came the announcement that Virginia had also given an affirmative answer. For better or for worse, the new government had been accepted.

As was necessary, straightway Congress appointed a committee to report an act for putting the new Constitution into operation. Reporting on July 8, the committee proposed that the first Wednesday in December be the day for appointing electors in the several states, the first Wednesday in January for the electors to assemble and vote for a President, and the first Wednesday in February for commencing proceedings under the Constitution. The place for commencing proceedings was left blank, and with good reason. There would probably be a hot contest over that feature of the arrangement. The "plan for setting this new machine in motion", Madison wrote July 16, would "not be hurried to a conclusion", for New York, then furnishing Congress with a sitting-place, might not become a member of the union. The time, wrote Otis (July 17), would probably be agreed upon within a few days; but "The *place* will be a bone of Contention". The Southern people, he declared, were opposed to New York in any case; besides, "the Yorkers hang back in such manner am rather of opinion it will not be here".

With regard to the times for these three several processes, while there were some differences of opinion, there were no serious controversies, and by August 6 it had been agreed that the several stages be advanced one month; that is, to the first Wednesdays of January, February, and March, respectively; these later dates being preferred by most of the Southerners, particularly the South Carolinians. The place, however, as Otis had predicted, became a bone of contention, and the struggle, accompanied by not a little angry growling, went on through several weeks, sometimes with one pack in possession of the bone, sometimes another. "Those who wish to make N. York the place of meeting", Madison wrote July 21, "studiously promote delay. Others who are not swayed by this consideration do not urge despatch." In short, nobody seemed to be in any hurry to settle the question.

One motive for delay that was not without virtue is explained by Wingate. "Congress", he wrote (July 26), "have omitted making the necessary arrangement for putting the new Government into effect, out of delicacy to the situation of New York, whose decision upon the proposed constitution has been expected dayly for some time." News had, however, just come that New York had, on that very day, ratified. North Carolina had also given rise to anxieties, and, before she had made up her mind, she was destined to arouse more than mere worries. At the moment the state appeared to be hesitating, while her delegates in Congress, Hugh Williamson and John Swann, anxiously waited, hoping for the best but bracing themselves nevertheless for the news that their state had refused to come into the new system. "We are, Sir, in the most painful Suspence for Carolina", John Swann wrote to James Iredell as early as July 7. "I confess I shou'd be most sensibly mortified were Carolina to reject the Constitution . . . and doubly so when I reflect that in such a determination they would have the *Countenance of Rhode Island alone.*" Still hoping, the North Carolina delegates obtained the gracious consent of members of Congress that the determination of the time for putting the new government into operation would be put off as long as practicable.

On the 23d of July, three days before the state of New York had come to a decision whether it would or would not take shelter under the "new roof", the city of New York produced a celebration of the adoption of the Constitution by ten states. "The Yorkers", wrote Samuel A. Otis (July 17), "are determined however to have their frolic." Personally he was inclined to think that there was a "danger of running into excess in regard to processions". He thought the movements of the new government "should be mild discreat and attended with great circumspection". After he had viewed the parade there can be little doubt that his opinion was strengthened.

The celebration was certainly not mild, neither was it in all particulars attended with great circumspection; and one editor at least must have come to the conclusion that he had been far from discreet in his description of the event. For, in consequence, an angry mob descended upon his establishment, and, apparently failing to catch the printer himself, vented its wrath upon his equipment. Sharply indicative of the character of the contest that was raging over the adoption of the Constitution, that printer's provocative remarks deserve reproduction here:

YESTERDAY THE GRAND PROCESSION, *"in honor of the Constitution of the United States"*, paraded to and fro, and walked up and down, in this city, to the novel entertainment of all classes of people. The procession made a very pompous appearance, and was conducted in a regular and decent manner. . . .

It was really laughable to see the variety of phizzes on this occasion. The poar[*sic*] *antis* generally minded their own business at home; others, who were spectators at an *awful* distance, looked as sour as the Devil. As for the *feds,* they rejoiced in different degrees—there was the ha, ha, ha! and the he, he, he! . . .

We are informed, that the honorable the Congress and gentlemen of the clergy, declined *walking* at the procession, on account of this not being a *ratifying* state: they however accepted a seat at the table. . . .

A part of all which—and more besides—appears to have been true. Two members at least not only refrained from walking in the procession, but also declined sitting at the festal board. Said Williamson of North Carolina (July 26): "Congress were invited to dine with the company, some thousands, under a particular pavillion in the fields. The other States attended, but the North Carolina delegates stayed at home. We conceived it was a respect we owed the State, not to celebrate an event in our public characters, which the State we represent has not hitherto sanctioned by her approbation." Since the ratification by New York, so the North Carolina delegates reported (July 27), "The Inhabitants of this City . . . have hardly been moderate in their expressions of joy."

Although Congress was "extremely desirous to fix the Time and Place where and when Proceedings shall commence under the new Government", the North Carolina delegates further reported, "Hitherto they have been restrained, partly as we conceive, from a Regard to the feelings of our State". There was little restraint, however, in the contest over "the place", which raged on, fast at times, furious always. Wrote Paine Wingate, July 29: "There are great struggles between Philadelphia and New York, which shall be the place of Congress. I think the former most likely to prevail, but this is only a mere conjecture." Philadelphia had tried on July 28 and failed—"by a single voice from Delaware", Madison wrote, explaining further that this one delegate (it was Nathaniel Mitchell), "wishing to have a question on Wilmington previous to a final determination, divided that State and negatived the motion". New York then entered the lists; Lancaster was put forward in opposition, but failed. Baltimore was then offered (August 4), and, "to the surprize of every one", Madison records, carried the necessary seven states—Pennsylvania to Georgia. "It was not difficult to foresee", wrote Madison, "that such a vote could not stand." Accordingly there was an attempt the next day on the part of the eastern states to procure a reconsideration of the vote, with an offer (August 6) of Philadelphia in place of Baltimore. For the moment the hopes of the Pennsylvanians rose—but only for a moment. When it came to a vote, the South Carolinians unexpectedly plumped against Philadelphia and for New York; "so violent", asserted William Bingham, "are their Antipathies" to Philadelphia. They had voted in favor of Baltimore, but intimated that they had come to the conclusion that Baltimore was "only a circuitous Route to Philadelphia".

A part of the eastern maneuver involved the use of the Rhode Island delegates, who had for a time kept themselves in seclusion. Indeed they were about to take their departure, when, on August 4, they came out of their shell just to help their eastern friends out of a difficult situation, and remained in the open for the space of three days. Since they had been instrumental in defeating the vote for Philadelphia in favor of New York, Bingham was chagrined and reproachful. The Rhode Islanders, he declared, had been "seduced" into lending a hand to put in motion a government highly inimical to their views, and "The Indecency of such Conduct struck even their own Partisans with Astonishment." This, however, was the extent of their errancy. They refused to go the whole length by joining in a final vote to set up the new government, and thereupon took their departure. A further effort in behalf of New York was made August 13, and when that also failed, all hands rested until August 26, although out of doors the dispute between Philadelphia and New York went merrily (or violently) on.

And while the question hung thus suspended, came news that North Carolina had failed to ratify the Constitution. Chagrined and disgusted, Hugh Williamson wrote to James Iredell (August 23):

It appears that North Carolina has at length thrown herself out of the Union, but she happily is not alone; the large, upright and respectable State of Rhode Island is her associate. This circumstance, however, does not, I hope, render it necessary that the delegates from North Carolina should profess a particular affection for the delegates from Rhode Island.

The opinions he proceeded to express of Messrs. Arnold and Hazard were certainly not couched in terms of either affection or esteem, and if his expressions had come to the knowledge of those gentlemen, they would scarce have taken pride therein.

What however was of especial importance was the delicate situation in which the North Carolina delegates now found themselves. After the Rhode Island delegates had "voted on several questions respecting the organization of the new government, in order to fix it in New York, a corner of the Union", Williamson went on to explain, and when the final question was about to be taken on the ordinance, they induced a motion to be made "that nothing which the delegates from Rhode Island or North Carolina had done, or might do in voting on the subject, should be construed as in any measure affecting the rights of their constituents." Up bounced the North Carolina delegates to move "that the word North Carolina be struck out of the vote of *absolution*". The delegates of North Carolina asked for no absolution, they declared, and, what was more, they had no wish "to have North Carolina associated in any vote with Rhode Island". For their part, they proposed to refrain from giving their votes on the final arrangements, unless North Carolina should confederate; "for we would not be guilty of parricide, by throwing our State out of the Union." The motion was thereupon withdrawn, "and the Rhode Island gentlemen missed the promised pleasure of doing wrong, and on the next morning they returned home." These two events, the departure of Rhode Island and the refusal of North Carolina to participate further in the measure, Madison wrote to Jefferson that same day (August 23), "threatens a disagreeable issue to the business, there being now an apparent impossibility of obtaining seven states for any one place". "What and when the issue is to be", he wrote to Washington the next day, "is really more than I can foresee."

The lull in proceedings relative to the Constitution offered a good opportunity for taking into consideration the annual problem of a requisition for the needs of the current year. The board of treasury had furnished the estimates as long ago as July 9, and the committee to whom the treasury report had been referred had brought in its own report—a very elaborate statement—on August 4. On August 13 the requisition was taken into consideration, and August 20 it was brought to a vote. For once there was but little controversy over its terms. Of the twelve states present only Delaware and Maryland, joined by Thatcher of Massachusetts, voted in the negative. There were indeed some grumblings over the quotas, but the grumblers were summarily squelched. On August 13, North Carolina had endeavored to have some 7,000 dollars taken from that state's quota and assessed to South Carolina, while Delaware had similarly sought to have some 5,000 dollars assigned to its quota saddled on Georgia. Kearny of Delaware did indeed remain obdurate to the end, voting *no* on every question.

This was of course the last requisition that Congress would ever make upon the states, and it does not escape observation that, in the language of the resolution, the states were "required to pay". It is not quite the first instance of the use of the word *required,* instead of the wonted "requested" or "recommended"; but it seems to argue that, in the time of its acknowledged powerlessness, Congress was resolved to speak with all the greater boldness.

On the 26th of August efforts to fix upon New York as the place of meeting were renewed, and on the same day the Delaware delegates once more sprang their proposition in favor of Wilmington. All these efforts having failed, the Easterners began to stall for time, until, perchance, the Rhode Island delegates should return, weighted with instructions authorizing them to vote on the question at issue. The Southern delegates had likewise been indulging in some maneuvering, for their dearest aim was the ultimate establishment of the government on the Potomac.

The only chance the Potomac has [Madison had written to Washington, August 11] is to get things in such a train that a coalition may take place between the Southern and Eastern States on the subject, and still more that the final seat may be undecided for two or three years, within which period the Western and S. Western population will enter more into the estimate. Wherever Congress may be, the choice if speedily made will not be sufficiently influenced by that consideration. In this point of view I am of opinion Baltimore would have been unfriendly to the true object. It would have retained Congress but a moment, so many States being North of it, and dissatisfied with it, and would have produced a coalition among those States to a precipitate election of the permanent seat and an intermediate removal to a more northern position.

Further light is thrown on this phase of the matter by Henry Lee in a letter to Washington, September 13. "The southern gentlemen", Lee wrote, "did not accord in the place of temporary residence, from a discordance in sentiment, of its effect on the establishment of the permanent seat of gov[ernmen]t." Lee had, in fact, parted at times from his colleagues and joined the eastern coterie.

On September 2 the eastern group endeavored to have the place of meeting left undesignated for the present; then, on September 3, the Marylanders proposed Annapolis. These propositions having failed, the question was once more left hanging in the air. By September 12, however, the Southern group had decided to yield to the majority for New York, "rather than hazard the consequences of a longer suspension". First came a motion by Henry Lee of Virginia and Nicholas Gilman of New Hampshire proposing "the present seat of Congress" as the place for commencing proceedings under the Constitution; whereupon Carrington and Madison offered an amendment which, as Madison characterized it, "tendered a blank for any place the majority would choose between the North River and the Potomac". The latter motion having been rejected, the motion to adopt the ordinance with the present seat of Congress as the place was about to be put to vote, when the state of Delaware, exercising its rights in the premises, obtained a postponement until the following day. On September 13 the ordinance was accordingly adopted, with New York as the place and the first Wednesdays of January, February, and March, respectively, as the times for the three several stages of inaugurating the new government.

The opponents of New York as the place, so Madison wrote to Washington (September 14) had, in fact, been reduced to the dilemma of yielding or else "strangling the Government in its birth". For his own part, he had for some time been convinced of the necessity of yielding and of the impropriety of further delay, although some others had not viewed the matter in the same light. Maryland and Delaware had remained "absolutely inflexible". One of the consequences that he foresaw was that the question would be entailed on the new government, "which will have enough of other causes of agitation in its councils". But what especially gave him concern was an evident policy to keep Congress in New York until a permanent seat should be chosen, and then to fix the permanent seat at farthest not beyond the Susquehanna. New Jersey in particular aimed and hoped eventually to establish the government at Trenton.

Hugh Williamson acknowledged (to James Iredell Sept. 22) that his patience and temper had both been sorely tried by the question, "and the more so, perhaps", he added, "because for some time past I have not considered it proper to vote on the subject." His colleague, John Swann, who appears to have accepted the situation more philosophically, wrote to Iredell (September 21):

Congress have at length finished the preparations necessary to give the New Government Effect after a great deal of debating and perhaps some warmth . . . This Question, Sir had the power to collect all the delegations from the different parts of the Union, so that there has not been a fuller Congress since the declaration of Independence. However this business being settled, Congress, I fear, like all other Bodies about to expire, will scarcely have a Witness to its dissolution.

John Swann proved to be a good prophet. Already, three days before he had penned his prophetic utterance, the dissolution of Congress had well begun, and within less than three weeks it had ceased to function as an organized body, although some of the watchers at the bedside, including Secretary Thomson as chief physician, continued to nurse a hope for its restoration. After the 17th of September, Congress was seldom able to muster the requisite seven states, and on the 10th of October it mustered them for the last time. A good many members required at most but a slight additional impulse to induce them to break the fragile leash that held them to the spot, and at the beginning of October that additional impulse was supplied.

The City of New York, delighted over the privilege of clasping the new government to its bosom and eager to induce a reciprocal feeling, proceeded to new-model City Hall for its reception. "The workmen made such a continual noise", George Thatcher wrote to Nathan Dane (October 2), "that it was impossible to hear one another speek." Accordingly Congress, what was left of it, on that day (which was a Thursday) adjourned until the following Monday, then to meet in the rooms occupied by Secretary Jay. "I should not wonder", Thatcher continued, "if by the middle of next week Congress were to adjourn without delay. Many are uneasy and are for going home."

Just to prove, it may be, that it was not yet out of breath and still had power to function, on this same October 2d, when the din of the carpenter's hammer and the screech of his saw drowned the voices of those members who would fain make speeches, Congress completed its consideration of an extensive report on the proceedings of the war department that had been first presented on July 21. The committee closed its report with the expression of a confident opinion, based on a careful examination into the conduct of the department, "that the arrangement of the business is Judicious and that the duties of the Office are executed with ability and punctuality which reflect great honor on the Secretary at War"; further, that the secretary had reduced the expenses of his department "by various oeconomical arrangements and reforms".

Two days earlier a similar report on the department of finance had been given final consideration. The committee had particularly examined the receipts and expenditures of the treasury from November 1, 1784, the date when the superintendent of finance closed his accounts. In this instance the committee was "constrained to observe, that there are many strong marks of a want of Responsibility or attention in the former transactions respecting the public treasures." There were numerous deficiencies and irregularities, large sums paid out to individuals who "neglect to account"; other considerable sums "paid out of the Treasury of which no appropriation is to be found on the public Journal of Congress", several of them remaining unaccounted for. Again, there were those "large sums of Money received in France." The committee had been desirous to discover in what manner they had been accounted for; "but the subject of this enquiry seems to be involved in darkness."

These two reports were the most outstanding accomplishments of that general objective that Congress had set for itself in the beginning of July, as soon as it had received notice that it would presently be called upon to vacate the premises, namely, to put its house in order. On the 14th of August a committee on the department of foreign affairs had made a report, chiefly upon the manner in which the department was housed—two rooms, one for the secretary himself, the other for his deputy and clerks—the character of the records found there, the manner in which they were kept, and even to such a detail as this: "The Office is constantly open from 9 in the Morning to 6 O'Clock in the Evening; and either his Deputy or one of the Clerks remains in the Office while the others are absent at Dinner." Upon the whole, the committee found "neatness, method and perspicuity throughout the Department". Apparently Congress never got around to voting approval of the report; still, it did not matter.

In these latter and somewhat leisurely days Congress also undertook a survey of its oldest institution, the post office. From the beginning Congress had endeavored to do a good part by the post office, adopting from time to time ordinances for its regulation; and during the last three or four years especially had eyed that department every now and then with good intentions. During the years 1785 and 1786 the committee on the post office had several times been reconstituted, often with instructions to prepare a new ordinance for the regulation of the department, and on June 15, 1786, such an ordinance was actually reported. Not, however, until February 14, 1787, was it "read a first time", with February 21 assigned for a second reading. It was not done, however, and for some unexplained reason—perhaps for no sufficient reason—it lay neglected for more than a year. On March 27, 1788, it was turned over to a new committee—and that appears to have been the last of the ordinance. In these intervals nevertheless there had been numerous enactments respecting mail contracts, the establishment of post roads, the rates of postage, etc.

On July 7, 1788, the committee on the post office was renewed, and that committee reported, August 27, the results of a survey of the business of the post office. The report is an instructive document, since it sets forth the manner in which the business was conducted, the receipts, the estimated costs of transportation, etc. But of that report likewise Congress never succeeded in concluding its consideration. On September 30 the committee was allowed to take back its report for revision, and on October 9 the absentees of the committee were replaced by new appointments. As it came to pass, Congress had but one more day of active life, so that no revision of the report was ever made.

The adjournment of Congress from the 2d to the 6th of October to allow the rooms of the secretary for foreign affairs to be prepared for their reception must have had a demoralizing effect on the members. Came Monday, October 6, and only six states assembled, with five individual delegates. Came Tuesday, and only three states assembled, with, again, five single delegates, although only in part identical with the five of the preceding day. But on Wednesday, Thursday, and Friday there were actually seven states in attendance. The conduct of Congress on Friday, October 10, the last day on which it transacted any official business, was not quite, as one might have expected, in the manner of that famous band who prefaced their last act with the pronouncement, "We who are about to die salute you!" It was rather as if they had no thought that the end was at hand. Those last official acts were two: one positive, the other negative; the one prescribing certain lines of conduct for the commissioners appointed under the ordinance of May 7, 1787, for the settlement of accounts between the United States and individual states, the other taking action on a motion of Abraham Clark of New Jersey and Hugh Williamson of North Carolina proposing that the secretary at war be directed to forbear issuing warrants for bounties of land to such of the officers of the late army as had neglected to account for moneys received by them as paymasters of regiments or for recruiting or other public services, until they had settled their accounts and had paid into the treasury the balances found to be due from them. When the vote was taken on the motion, only the states of the movers registered an affirmative, although individually the votes were twelve ayes, seven noes. "So the question was lost", the secretary recorded. And so also, for all purposes of national business, the United States in Congress Assembled was lost beyond recovery.

Not so, however, the will to survive. On Tuesday, October 14, so reads the record, "Two states attended, namely Massachusetts and New Jersey", with eight additional members. On the 15th, "Four states attended, namely Massachusetts, New Jersey, Virginia and South Carolina", with five additional members. On the 16th, "Two states attended, namely Massachusetts and South Carolina", with seven additional members. On Tuesday, October 21, the same two states, with six additional members. The secretary might as well throw down his pen—and he probably did. Later, however, he picked it up again and recorded: "From the day above mentioned to the first of Nov[embe]r there attended occasionally . . . .", and he listed thirteen members from ten different states.

It is of interest, and not without a touch of amusement, to observe that one of those who watched and waited for the resuscitation of Congress was none other than Peleg Arnold of Rhode Island; and it is an evidence of faith and hope, if not of charity toward the Union which his state had been so assiduous in snubbing, that he wrote to Governor Collins (October 20): "I am under the Necessity of Informing that my Situation renders it Expedient for the State to make further Provision for my support." That there would be more of that Congress of which he was an accredited member he appears to have had never a doubt. "Such Matters as are unfinish'd at the end of this Year", he wrote, "and others that concern the Union will be taken into Consideration by the Congress which are to assemble the first monday in Novr. next." It should in particular redound to the credit of Peleg Arnold that, whether or not he had a facile pen, he did for once at least wield a fearless and a bold one.

I submit [he wrote the governor] whether it is not Expedient for the State to take the Proposed Constitution under Consideration and make their objections to the particular parts that are incompatible to a good System of Government, and make known to the States in the Union on what terms the State would Join them. This is a Subject on which I have Contemplated for a Considerable Time and it appears of such Importance as to require United wisdom and mature Deliberation to inable the State to pursue Prudent Measures.

Peleg Arnold might be hopeful that Congress would resume business, but the more penetrating James Madison had no such hopes. "It is pretty certain", he wrote to Jefferson, October 17, "that there will not again be a quorum of either [nine or seven states] within the present year, and by no means certain that there will be one at all under the old Confederation."

Came the first Monday in November, the beginning of the new federal year, and the secretary duly entered in the Journal: "Pursuant to the Articles of the Confederation only two Gentlemen attended as delegates namely: Mr. Contee for Maryland and Mr. Williamson for North Carolina." Full four months more of life and the pursuit of the national business were duly allotted under the law to the Congress about to die, and Secretary Thomson was determined to do what in him lay to enable it to fill out the allotted span. He would at least see to it that the old Congress should not, if he could prevent it, be permitted to pass out until the day thereunto decreed. And so, as every now and then a member strolled into his office, he would haul out the Journal, write down the date, the name of the member, and the state whence he came. Thus on the last day of December, it was: "Mr. S. A. Otis from Massachusetts." On the first day of January, 1789, it was: "Mr. J. R. Reid from Pensylvania [and] Mr. R. Barnwell from South Carolina."

In the early days of January, 1789, the members who had been hanging around and drifting in and out conceived the delusive hope that Congress was about to assemble, choose itself a president, and proceed to business. Some of them indeed had urgent business that they were anxious to lay before the assembled Congress, business that in some cases was as chestnuts in the fire, in others as irons that they would fain heat in the Congressional furnace and have hammered into the desired shape on the Congressional anvil. And so, as one member after another trudged into town in the early days of the new year, hopes began to take the place of anxieties.

On the 12th of January, Samuel A. Otis was able to report that South Carolina, Virginia, Pennsylvania, and New Jersey had their quota of delegates at hand, while another delegate each from North Carolina and Massachusetts were confidently expected. Wrote Tench Coxe the next day, "A Quorum from seven will be here by the 20th, when a president will be chosen. Mr. Wadsworth has been mentioned to me." Two weeks later (January 27), however, he could report only five states—South Carolina, Virginia, Pennsylvania, New Jersey, and Massachusetts—as represented, with one delegate each from Rhode Island, North Carolina, and Georgia. He was writing to Madison and he offered the opinion that "the Appearance in Europe, and perhaps even here, of the old Congress being in full operation and tranquilly yielding the seats to the new would have a good effect." He would like to see John Adams made president, although Adams's absence, Coxe thought, would probably be an insuperable obstacle. On the 29th, John Dawson of Virginia wrote to Madison that there were now six states represented, including New York, while an additional delegate from Rhode Island was on the way and another North Carolina delegate close at hand. Near-by Connecticut was only waiting for the word. They were that near to having nine states, and, apparently, they might have had their seven at any time, if only they had signaled to Connecticut. Or they might have rounded up James White of North Carolina and Abraham Baldwin of Georgia, both of whom were said to be within easy call.

And thus the days slid by, with no "Congress assembled", while a goodly number of members wandered about the city, or journeyed back to their homes, apparently too indifferent, most of them, even to report their presence to Secretary Thomson, who, it is safe to assume, sat in his office, pen in hand, the book of the chronicles of Congress open on his desk, eager to record them one and all as attending, happy if perchance he might be privileged to write "Congress assembled". But it was not to be. From that day when seven states were thought to be almost within grasp a whole month passed and not a single state had seen fit to have itself recorded as attending. From the 19th of February to the 2d of March not even one lone delegate thrust his head inside the door of the secretary's office. On that notable 2d of March, however, two days before the time set for the new Congress to assemble, "Mr. Philip Pell from New York" attended. Peradventure Mr. Thomson had buttonholed Mr. Pell on the street and enticed him into his office for this express purpose—but it sufficed. The faithful secretary had fought the good fight to preserve the "visible head" of the Union; he had persevered to the end, he had won the victory. The spark of life had been kept in the body of the dying Congress until its heir and successor was crossing the threshold.

In an important sense it is not correct to assume that the old Congress was even now defunct. There remained Secretary Thomson himself as a connecting link between the old and the new; and there were other links besides. Most of the executive departments of the old Congress were passed over to the new government intact and continued to function for several months. The secretary himself, having served Congress faithfully throughout the whole of its life of fifteen years, fondly hoped that he would be given a suitable place in the new order. He soon discovered, however, that, along with much else of that old order, the place for which he was destined was the place called discard. It came about therefore that, on the 23d of July, 1789, Charles Thomson transmitted to President Washington his resignation of the office of secretary of Congress; on the 24th the President accepted the resignation; and on the 25th, in accordance with President Washington's directions, "the books, records and papers of the late Congress, the Great Seal of the Federal Union, and the Seal of the Admiralty" were delivered over to Roger Alden, deputy secretary of Congress, who had been designated by President Washington as custodian for the time being. It was then only that the Continental Congress really came to an end.

INDEX

implemental powers, 455–459, 475, 483–
487, 504–509, 603, 619, 634–636, 642,
663–665; and "administration", 463;
status and functions under Confederation, 502–504; review of Yorktown
march, 522; freedom of speech, Howell
case, 533, 534; impotence, 558; danger
of dissolution, 595, 596, 606, 607, 610,
612–614, 618, 631, 638–641, 647, 649,
650, 659, 665, 689, 690, 693, 704–706;
refusal of state projects, 608, 609; effect
of irregular attendance, 650; and results
of Federal Convention, 690; last full
attendance, 700, 711, 719; last days,
end, 719, 720, 722–726; hopes of reconvening, 724, 725; records, 726. *See
also* Addresses; Administration; Committee of the States; Confederation;
Continental army; Delegates; Finances;
Foreign relations; Independence; Indians; Meeting; President; Public lands;
Reconciliation; Rights; Secrecy; States;
Trade; Union

Convention troops, terms of capitulation,
suspension, 261, 262; embarkation forbidden, 262–266, 278; protest on detention, 353

Conway, Thomas, as foreign volunteer,
281; Gates, letter, exposure, 282, 283,
285; duel, 283, 297; Canadian project,
290, 294; disposal, resignation, 295–297;
and Cabal, 297; apology to Washington,
297

Conway Cabal, origin, criticism of Washington, 267–270; Washington on criticism, 270; failure of commissary, responsibility, 270–275, 277; Valley Forge or
winter campaign, 275–277; character
and reality, 279–281; Gates as focus,
281; new Board of War, 281; Conway's
letter, exposure, 282, 283, 285; delegates
and, 284–286; anonymous documents,
Rush, 286–288; Canadian project, 290–
295; reaction, disposal of Conway, 295–
297

Cooke, Gov., Nicholas, on independence,
166; letter to, 265

Cooper, Gray, reconciliation, 94

Cornell, Ezekiel, member, on need of
central power, 458; on dictatorship, 460;
on Greene's resignation, 463; on char-

acter of Congress, 467; continental impost, 476, 481, 530

Corporations, power of Congress, 515

Council, protest on colonial, 54; Franklin
plan, 217; in consideration of Confederation, 239, 252; new suggestion, 509

Counterfeiting, paper money, 384, 385

Courts, congressional, cases, 541, 545, 546,
601; proposed amendment for, 664

Cox, John, as official, 462

Coxe, Tench, member, on reconvening
Congress, 725

Craik, James, on Conway Cabal, 284

Credentials of delegates, 34–36, 65, 66

Crown Point, capture, 68

Cumberland County, Va., on independence, 167

Cushing, Thomas, member, on prayers, 38

Cushing, William, letter to, 173

Customs. *See* Duties; Navigation Acts

Cutler, Manasseh, Ohio Company and
Northwest Ordinance, 683, 685, 687

Dana, Francis, member, Convention troops,
265; cartel incident and rebuke of
Washington, 301, 303; half-pay, 311;
ratification of Confederation, 345; committee on reconciliation, 324; Russian
mission, 479; Committee of the States,
departure, 609–611. *See also* Committee
of conference

Dane, Nathan, member, on absentees, 641;
requisitions, 645; Federal Convention,
670, 674, 677, 678, 692; influence of
Shays Rebellion, 673; territorial government, 682, 684–686; on Yates, 683;
ratification, 696; on lassitude of Congress, 704; on lack of quorum, 705;
Kentucky, 709; letter to, 720

Dartmouth, William Legge, Earl of, letter
to, 125

Dauphin, celebration of birth, 547

Davie, William Richardson, on Federal
Convention, 692

Dawson, John, member, on hope of reconvening Congress, 725

Dayton, Elias, letter to, 188

Deane, Silas, member, prophecy on Congress, 24; on southern delegates, 29, 30;
on rumor of Boston bombardment, 39;
on Duché's prayer, 40, 67; on entertainments, 45; on business of Congress,

AMERICAN HISTORY TITLES
IN THE NORTON LIBRARY

Fawn Brodie *Thaddeus Stevens* N331

Robert E. Brown *Charles Beard and the Constitution* N296

Edmund Cody Burnett *The Continental Congress* N278

Dudley T. Cornish *The Sable Arm: Negro Troops in the Union Army, 1861-1865* N334

John Paton Davies, Jr. *Foreign and Other Affairs* N330

Dwight Lowell Dumond *Antislavery* N370

Herbert Feis *The Diplomacy of the Dollar* N333

Herbert Feis *The Spanish Story* N339

Herbert Feis *Three International Episodes: Seen from E. A.* N351

Dewey W. Grantham *The Democratic South* N299

Fletcher Green *Constitutional Development in the South Atlantic States, 1776-1860* N348

Holman Hamilton *Prologue to Conflict: The Crisis and Compromise of 1850* N345

Pendleton Herring *The Politics of Democracy* N306

Rufus Jones *The Quakers in the American Colonies* N356

George F. Kennan *Realities of American Foreign Policy* N320

Douglas Edward Leach *Flintlock and Tomahawk: New England in King Philip's War* N340

Alpheus T. Mason *The Supreme Court from Taft to Warren* N257

Burl Noggle *Teapot Dome* N297

Douglass C. North *The Economic Growth of the United States, 1790-1860* N346

Norman Pollack *The Populist Response to Industrial America* N295

John W. Spanier *The Truman-MacArthur Controversy and the Korean War* N279

Frederick B. Tolles *Meeting House and Counting House* N211

Arthur B. Tourtellot *Lexington and Concord* N194

Frederick Jackson Turner *The United States 1830-1850* N308

Arthur P. Whitaker *The United States and the Independence of Latin America* N271

C. Vann Woodward *The Battle for Leyte Gulf* N312

DATE DUE